Key to Road and Regional Maps

NEWFOUNDLAND (NF) Pg.187
TOBA (MB) g.181
48
QUÉBEC (PQ) Pg.184
ONTARIO (ON) Pg.182
PRINCE EDWARD ISLAND (PE) Pg.186
NEW BRUNSWICK (NB) Pg.186
NOVA SCOTIA (NS) Pg.186
28
MINNESOTA (MN) Pg.116
MAINE (ME) Pg.104
VERMONT (VT) Pg.186
NEW HAMPSHIRE (NH) Pg.127
46
ASSACHUSETTS (MA) Pg.110
RHODE ISLAND (RI) Pg.155
WISCONSIN (WI) Pg.174
42
NEW YORK (NY) Pg.132
44
NNECTICUT (CT) Pg.78
MICHIGAN (MI) Pg.112
IOWA (IA) Pg.96
30
PENNSYLVANIA (PA) Pg.150
NEW JERSEY (NJ) Pg.128
DELAWARE (DE) Pg.80
MARYLAND (MD) Pg.106
WASHINGTON (DC) Pg.172
ILLINOIS (IL) Pg.90
INDIANA (IN) Pg.94
OHIO (OH) Pg.142
WEST VIRGINIA (WV) Pg.173
VIRGINIA (VA) Pg.168
40
MISSOURI (MO) Pg.120
32
KENTUCKY (KY) Pg.100
NORTH CAROLINA (NC) Pg.138
TENNESSEE (TN) Pg.158
OMA (OK) .146
ARKANSAS (AR) Pg.66
SOUTH CAROLINA (SC) Pg.156
ALABAMA (AL) Pg.60
34
GEORGIA (GA) Pg.86
MISSISSIPPI (MS) Pg.118
38
36
LOUISIANA (LA) Pg.102
FLORIDA (FL) Pg.82
18
55
PUERTO RICO (PR) Pg.190
VIRGIN ISLANDS (VI) Pg.190

The Money $aver's TRAVEL ATLAS

Reader's Digest

Table of Contents

Bass Harbor Head Lighthouse, Mount Desert Island, Maine

Guide to Money Saving

We've developed this money-saving atlas to help you plan and enjoy an efficient and budget-wise vacation. You'll find detailed, easy-to-navigate maps; listings of popular attractions, festivals, and events—free and for a fee—and tips on how to plan your trip, when to go, what to take, where to find discounts, and how to save on food, lodging, and attractions.

If you turn to the Regional Guides section of this book, you'll see that we have begun the planning process for you. We have added helpful icons (**$, R**) to each entry. These icons are quick references for you to use while deciding what attractions you will like to visit when traveling. The following is an explanation of each icon:

$ = fees
This icon is placed in any entry that has any type of fee.

R = reservations required
This icon is placed in any entry where reservations are required.

START PLANNING With a Phone Call or on the Internet

- Contact tourist information sources (See Tourism and Travel Information, page 229), such as national parks, state tourism offices, and city convention and visitor centers, for information about your destinations
- Ask about sights, weather, costs, and seasonal crowds
- Ask for a map and a calendar of events
- Use toll-free numbers to request information (you can call 800-555-1212 to find the toll-free number for a specific attraction)
- Begin gathering information at least two to six months in advance

The more lead time you give yourself to explore all available options before you leave home, the better you will be able to take advantage of money-saving early-booking discounts and will have the best chance of reserving rooms in the hotels and motels of your choice. (In the most popular national parks, lodging is often booked up to a year in advance.)

Seek out information at your local library where you can scan back issues of travel magazines and the Sunday travel sections of newspapers for ideas and tips.

Create an Itinerary

An itinerary is a great way to plan and set your travel budget. Before you leave, sit down with all your travel companions and work out an itinerary that outlines where you plan to be each day and what you would like to see there. Use a highlighter to mark your primary sights on a detailed road map. Then add up the mileage between sites to get an idea of how long you'll be driving each day and how much you'll need to budget for fuel. Plan to arrive early for the most popular sightseeing stops—you'll get the best vantage points and the most for your money. Or call the site the day before and ask if earlier hours are in effect than the posted ones.

Tips for RV Travelers

Travel by recreational vehicle (RV) is an economical way to tour the country, offering savings on dining and lodging, comfort, convenience, and independence. Visit www.rvamerica.com for useful advice on your trip.

Want to Avoid Crowds?

By choosing less well-known sites, you may avoid long lines, heavy traffic, and parking dilemmas. You may also save money since less popular sites may charge less. State and city tourism centers can provide information on less-visited areas in the vicinity of their major area attractions (See Tourism and Travel Information, page 229). National forests (see chart below) often offer an uncrowded, equally scenic alternative to major national parks and are ideal for enjoying outdoor activities, complete with less expensive lodging and camping facilities.

Traveling Off-Season

Most major tourist attractions have high (peak), low (off-peak, off-season), and shoulder seasons (immediately before and after the peak season). July and August are the peak tourism times in most national parks. If possible, plan your visit for a time when the crowds are thinnest.

To avoid the biggest crowds, skip the summer months, spring school breaks, and holiday weekends. Besides fewer people, off-season travel has another advantage: resorts that are open year-round offer substantially lower rates. The only drawback is that some sights and facilities may not be open.

The following is a listing of some national forest alternatives:

National Park	Nearby National Forest
Glacier	Flathead
Grand Canyon	Kaibab
Grand Teton	Bridger Teton
Great Smoky Mountains	Nantahala and Pisgah
Rocky Mountain	Arapaho and Roosevelt
Yellowstone	Gallatin
Yosemite	Toiyabe

Traveling with a Disability

The Americans with Disabilities Act has made travel much more accessible for the disabled. Now all new public establishments must conform to requirements. Before making reservations, call ahead to hotels, restaurants, and sightseeing destinations to find out what access and equipment are available. You can also contact the Society for Accessible Travel & Hospitality (SATH), 347 Fifth Avenue, Suite 610, New York, NY 11701; 212/447-7284, or visit them online at www.sath.org.

Packing

- Stick to the basic clothes you will need to see you through the activites you have planned and the weather you expect to encounter.
- Choose hand-washable, wrinkle-resistant separates that can be mixed and matched to create different outfits and will also save costly trips to the laundromat or dry cleaners.
- Pack cotton-polyester blends. They'll wrinkle less and dry faster than lightweight cotton.
- Bring broken-in shoes that you know don't cause blisters.

LOOK FOR TRAVEL BARGAINS

You can save money by doing some comparison shopping in advance of your trip. You can get the most for your vacation dollars by knowing what to ask when booking a hotel room or choosing a tour, and by taking advantage of programs and organizations that can help you streamline expenses. Never jump at the first discount offered; keep looking.

When looking for lodging, for example, first ask for the lowest rate available. Then ask if there are any package rates. Finally, ask if further discounts apply for any of your memberships or credit cards, and what restrictions apply.

Make Use of Memberships

Travel discounts may be available to you through a wide range of organizations, clubs, and programs, including:

- AARP and other senior organizations
- Youth and student organizations
- Half-price hotel clubs and frequent-guest programs
- Travel clubs
- Credit cards
- Museum and club memberships
- Professional association memberships

Join a Travel Club

Travel clubs offer access to sizable discounts on transportation, lodging, dining, and certain attractions. The cost of membership will be money well spent in terms of the savings you will ultimately reap if you take mulitple trips.

Many clubs offer such benefits as two-for-one dining and discounts on car rental and entertainment.

Try a Discount Booking Service

Discounts of up to 65% off the list rates in hundreds of hotels in major cities are available through a booking service called Hotel Reservations Network. No membership is required to take advantage of this program. Call 800-96-HOTEL to ask for a specific hotel or for hotel suggestions. You can also log on to www.hotels.com for details.

Look for Senior Discounts

Seniors are often entitled to a wide range of discounts on hotel rates, restaurants, museums, theaters, transit, concerts, and more. Since many establishments do not openly advertise senior discounts, always ask before you pay. The following is a list of some of the discounts offered to seniors:

- AARP, the National Council of Senior Citizens, offers travel discounts and other related services for people 50 and older.
- The National Park Service's free Golden Age Passport, available to people 62 and older, gives free entry to all sights in the National Park System, and 50% off park fees for camping and using other facilities.
- Many states offer seniors a variety of discounts, such as free access to state parks, museums, and public transportation, and discounts on lodging and restaurants. Contact the state's tourism office (See Tourism and Travel Information, page 229) for more information.

Mount Shuksan, Washington

Discounts for the Disabled

Many establishments and attractions offer discounted rates for disabled travelers, but—as in the case of senior discounts—they may not be widely advertised. Again, ask about eligibility when making reservations or before paying.

The National Park Service's Golden Access Passport, available to permanently disabled persons, offers free entry to all national parks and a 50% discount on all facility fees. Call or write any national park for further information.

Get the Best Room Rate

Use the following steps to get the best rate at the hotel or motel of your choice:

- Call the hotel's direct number—not the chain's central reservations 800 number—to get the lowest rate.
- Ask for any special rates or packages in effect for the dates you plan to visit.
- Inquire about any seasonal specials and discounts for your club memberships.

DON'T FORGET THE OBVIOUS

Make a copy of the following checklists to use while you pack. They will serve as reminders and may spare you the annoyance of having to pay on-the-road prices to replace essentials you left sitting at home.

Documents & Essentials
- Cash, traveler's checks, check book
- Credit cards and other membership cards
- Driver's licenses, car registration
- Address book with vital telephone numbers
- Tickets, vouchers, travel itinerary
- Car, house, and luggage keys
- Watch

Carry an emergency medical record index card for each traveler in your group. Be sure to add the following information:
- Personal information
- Doctor's information
- Medical conditions/allergies
- Blood type
- Prescription medications
- Medical insurance company's information
- Emergency contact

Medical Kit
- Prescription medication
- Medical-alert tag if you have a serious medical condition
- Aspirin, aspirin substitute
- Antidiarrhea medication
- Laxative
- Adhesive bandages, gauze pads, adhesive tape
- Elastic bandage
- Antibiotic ointment
- Insect repellent
- Sunscreen
- Hydrocortisone cream
- Muscle-ache ointment
- Motion-sickness remedy
- Cold remedies, dosage spoon
- Decongestant/antacid
- Thermometer
- Scissors/tweezers
- Cotton balls
- Eyedropper
- Premoistened towelettes
- First-aid booklet

Personal Care & Sundries
- Personal grooming and medicinal products that may not be readily available
- Eyeglasses, sunglasses, contact lenses, and copy of prescription
- Antibacterial soap
- Toothbrush, toothpaste
- Mouthwash
- Deodorant
- Feminine hygiene products
- Shampoo, conditioner
- Comb, brush, hair accessories
- Portable hair dryer
- Hand/body lotion, lip balm
- Cosmetics, perfume
- Shower cap
- Small mirror
- Shaving kit
- Swabs, tissues
- Travel iron
- Travel sewing kit
- Travel alarm

- Some cities offer discounts of up to 50% for same-day theater and dance performance tickets at special ticket centers.

Hotels
- Save money by finding a nearby restaurant, laundromat, hairdresser, and dry cleaner since in-house services are expensive.
- Instead of calling from your room, use your telephone calling card at a public phone. Hotels charge a premium for telephone calls.
- Avoid eating at hotels where food is often overpriced. Hotel room service is also expensive, with an extra charge usually added to the restaurant's already inflated prices.
- The in-room minibar is also outrageously expensive. Bring in your own snacks.

When Traveling by Car
- Have the car checked thoroughly a week or two before you leave. Make sure the air-conditioning and heater are in working order.
- Carry spare keys, a driver's license for each driver, insurance and registration cards, and your road-service membership card. Pack emergency tools and supplies in the trunk (see checklist). Don't forget to pack for extreme climates. For cold climates, take warm, heavy gloves; a sleeping bag; ice scraper and brush; deicer; folding shovel, sand or cat litter; traction mat; and candles or matches. For warm climates, pack extra water, a sun hat, and windshield and window shades.

- Ask for the corporate rate, which is usually 10%-15% off the rack rate.
- Ask for specific dollar costs—not percentage of discounts, which can be misleading. Be aware that advance bookings often get discounts of up to 30%-65%.
- Ask the reservations clerk if children under a certain age can stay for free in the same room with their parents. (Some hotels offer a second room at half price to families.)
- Check rates at hotels outside major cities; they are often substantially lower.
- If you do stay in a city, visit on weekends, when rates are usually lower. Resort sites, on the other hand, generally cost less on weekdays.
- Rates at seasonal vacation centers are lower off-season.

Bargain Hunting on the Road
Don't relax your bargain-hunting efforts once you leave home. With a bit of forethought, you can significantly reduce your daily expenditures on such items as entertainment, transportation, food, and other services.

Look for Dining Bargains When Traveling
- Ask about senior discounts and children's menus when making reservations or before ordering.
- Take advantage of the early-bird specials offered at many restaurants. This can be particularly rewarding at high-priced eateries, where you can enjoy the same fare at a substantial savings.
- You can eat at lower prices at an otherwise expensive restaurant by having lunch there instead of dinner.
- Get two meals for the price of one in a wide selection of restaurants—an added bonus offered through half-price hotel clubs.

Sites and Entertainment
- Check local newspapers and the local tourist center for information on free concerts, festivals, street fairs, lectures, and walking tours. Also note that museums, zoos, and other attractions often have a free-admission day during the week. Always inquire as to what discounts are available before you pay admission.

IF YOUR CAR BREAKS DOWN
- If possible, drive far enough to pull off on a well-lit, well-traveled shoulder. Even if you have a flat tire, drive until you reach a safe area before you change it.
- Turn off the ignition and turn on the hazard flashers.
- Put flares behind the car to alert other drivers.
- Raise the hood and place a "Call Police" sign in the window or tie a white cloth to the car radio antenna. If someone offers to help, roll down your window just enough to ask him or her to call the police.
- Stay inside the car with the doors locked until a police car or towing service arrives. If the car is in the roadway, stand well away from it.
- Lean on the horn if you find yourself in a threatening situation.

CAR EMERGENCY CHECKLIST
Before leaving on your trip, check to make sure you have these important items in your trunk.
- A spare tire in good condition and properly inflated
- Car jack, lug wrench, and small board to place under jack
- Jumper cables
- A kit of essential tools (pliers, standard and Phillips screwdrivers, adjustable wrenches, utility knife, duct tape)
- Work gloves
- Unopened containers of motor oil, antifreeze, brake fluid (do not carry gasoline, which is flammable)
- 1 to 2 gallons of water in plastic jugs
- Can of aerosol tire-inflator/sealant
- Emergency flares
- Blanket
- Spare belts, fuses, hoses, wiper blades, spark plugs
- White cloth to act as an emergency flag in case of breakdown
- A "Help" or "Call Police" sign
- A small fire extinguisher
- A squeeze-type siphon
- A flashlight
- A first-aid kit

To Keep Food Fresh While Traveling:
- Pack foods that have been well refrigerated, and try to carry only the edibles and drinks you will need for one to two days.
- Fill a plastic milk jug with water, leaving a little room for expansion, and freeze overnight. Use it as an ice pack, then as cool drinking water.
- Keep your cooler in the passenger section of the car, not in the trunk.

South Manitou Island Lighthouse, Michigan

SAVING MONEY AT THEME PARKS
Theme parks are one of the most popular attractions for travelers. You can have your fun there without breaking your budget with some of these tips:
- Pack a lunch and some snacks in a cooler. Instead of spending money on expensive park meals, go out to the parking lot and have a car-side picnic.
- If you decide to eat in the park, share a meal with a fellow traveler.
- Call your credit card company before you leave on your trip to see if your card offers any discounts.
- Check with your company's human resources department to see if they offer discount tickets to their employees.
- Call the property where you will be staying on your trip and ask if they offer any discounted tickets.
- Contact the state's tourism office and ask if they offer any discounts or coupons.
- If you plan on spending multiple days at the park(s), purchase a multi-day ticket—this usually gives you a sizable discount.
- Call the park directly and speak with a clerk in customer service. (See Amusement & Theme Parks, page 256) Ask the clerk to send you a brochure, a calendar of events for the park, and a park schedule. You can also ask if they will have any special promotions occurring during your visit.
- Arrive ahead of time and you may get in sooner than planned. Or call the site the day before you arrive and ask if earlier hours are in effect.
- Stay at a hotel off of park grounds. They are considerably less expensive. Look for one that has shuttle service to the park.
- Visit the parks during off season and save 30%-40% on lodging expenses.
- Avoid buying gas near the park—prices can be up to 30¢ more than at other gas stations down the road.

How To Use This Book

The Money Saver's Travel Atlas has been designed to help you research, plan, and enjoy your vacation by car without spending more than you budgeted. The atlas is a complete trip-planning kit that provides all the basic information you need—plus money-saving tips on accommodations, restaurants, attractions, and other out-of-pocket vacation costs.

The Money Saver's Travel Atlas covers all the fundamentals: road maps, information on what to do in each state, guides to national parks; and routes for scenic drives that will take your breath away.

Because car travelers often explore more than one state at a time, **The Money Saver's Travel Atlas** describes America region by region, highlighting both unique and popular attractions in each of 24 geographical areas from the Far West to Northern New England. The regions include all 50 states, all 10 Canadian provinces, as well as Mexico, Puerto Rico, and the U.S. Virgin Islands.

The information provided below and on the next page will help you use the atlas. Each of the book's chapters has its own color code, which is used throughout the volume for easy cross-referencing. For example, start by looking at the Southern Rockies pages from the Regional Guide chapter (shown below). The hand-drawn topographical map is a great starting place. The page numbers on the boxed areas lead you to detailed descriptions about the singled-out national parks and scenic drives. The yellow tabs on the left side of the page refer you to state maps in the Road Maps chapter. The red tabs lead you to pages in the Index, where extensive listings of place names help you find unfamiliar destinations on the road maps quickly. A Points of Interest index starts on page 251, which can help you quickly locate the sites you want to see.

Regional Guides Pages 8-55
The Regional Guides provide valuable overviews of what festivals, activities, landmarks, attractions, and scenic landscapes each of the 24 regions is famous for. A detailed topographical map shows you each region's mountain ranges, plains, river valleys, and deserts.

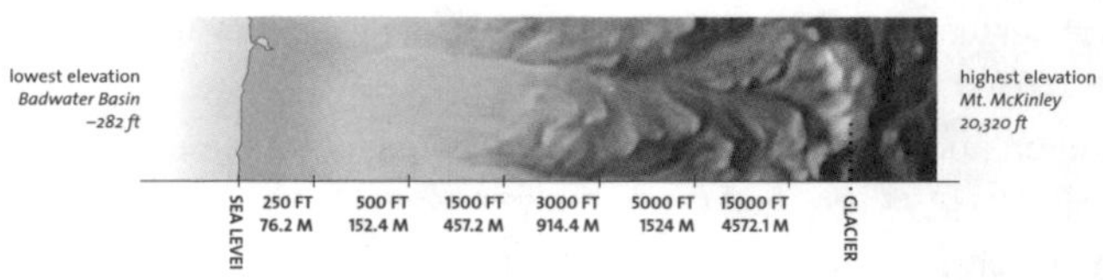

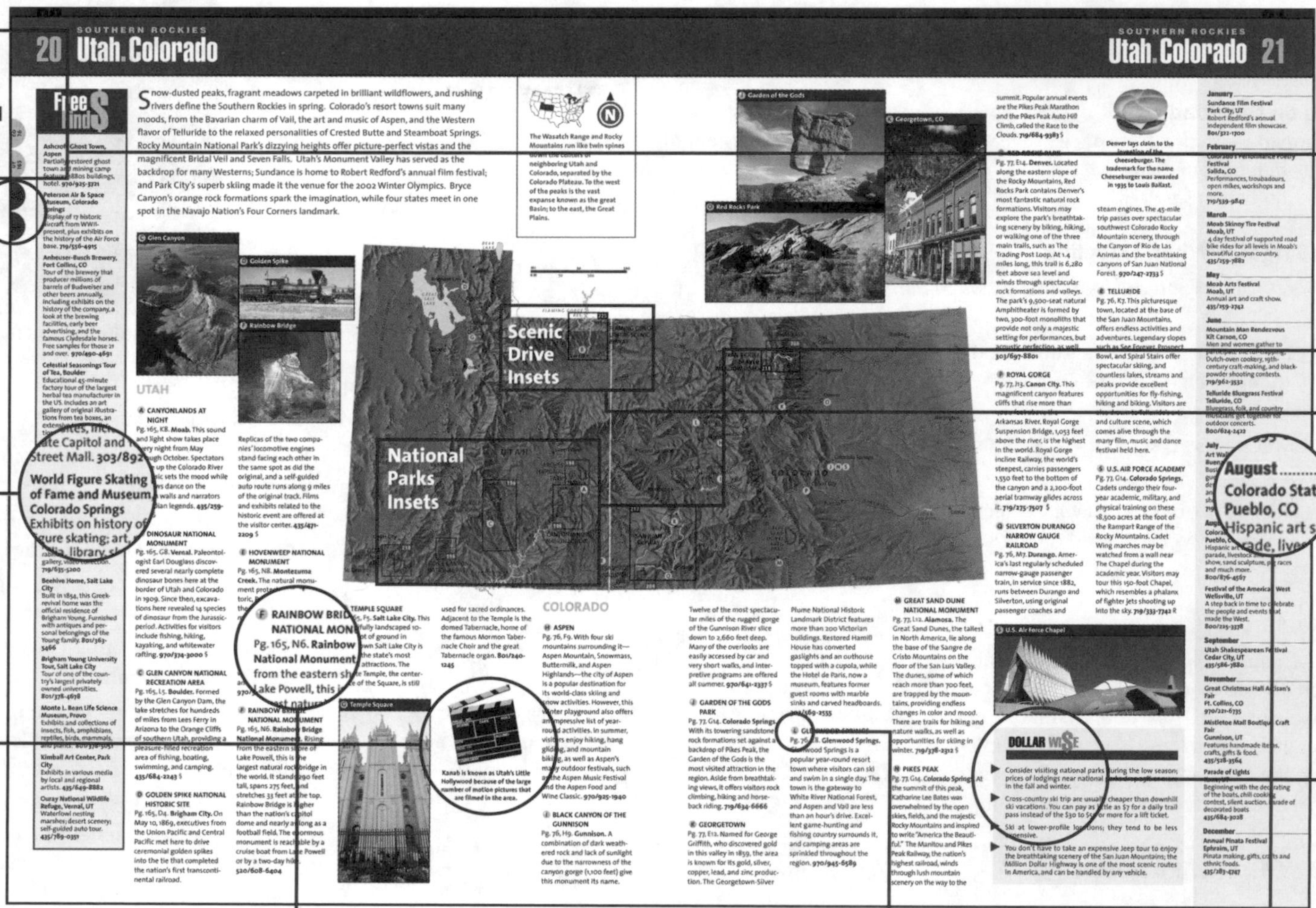

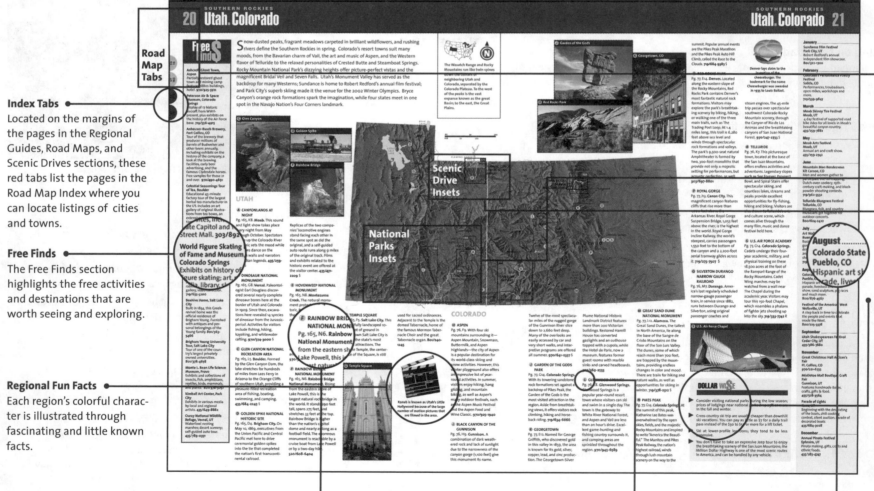

Index Tabs
Located on the margins of the pages in the Regional Guides, Road Maps, and Scenic Drives sections, these red tabs list the pages in the Road Map Index where you can locate listings of cities and towns.

Free Finds
The Free Finds section highlights the free activities and destinations that are worth seeing and exploring.

Regional Fun Facts
Each region's colorful character is illustrated through fascinating and little known facts.

Dollar Wise
This section provides you with smart ideas for big savings. It includes tips on easy ways to save money and where to find the discounts and deals.

Top Landmarks & Attractions
This section functions as a quick reference to each state's most distinctive landmarks and attractions. Descriptions offer travelers a glimpse of what makes each state unique. Listings include recreational and cultural activities that are available—for example, museums, state parks, historic sites, and national monuments.

Landmark & Attraction Map Coordinates
The coordinates listed in red for each landmark help you to easily locate the attraction on the indicated map in the Road Map chapter; simply use the map grid quadrant as marked along the margins of each road map to locate the correct coordinate.

Calendar of Festivals & Events
This quick reference calendar will help you plan your trip around events that interest you. Listings include major sports attractions, art festivals, local festivities, state fairs, theater seasons, and more. Since dates are subject to change, call ahead to verify.

Road Maps Pages 56-191

Road maps are organized as follows: all 50 states are in alphabetical order and the Canadian provinces are west to east. Road maps for Mexico, Puerto Rico, and the U.S. Virgin Islands are also included.

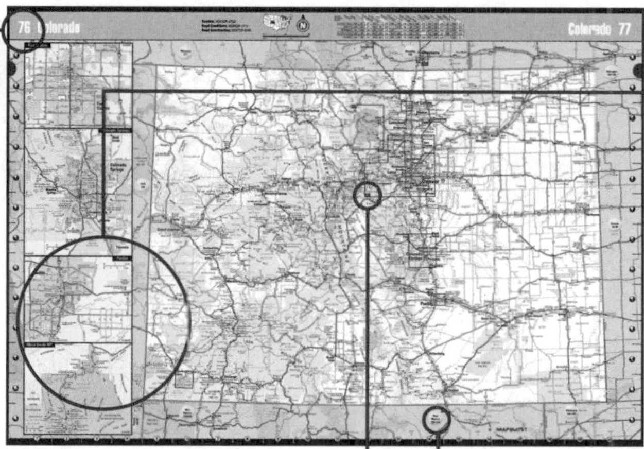

Road Map Tabs
Each state in the atlas has red tabs that list the pages in the Index where you'll be able to locate cities and towns.

Large-Scale City & Downtown Maps
These highly detailed maps help you to navigate around new or unfamiliar cities.

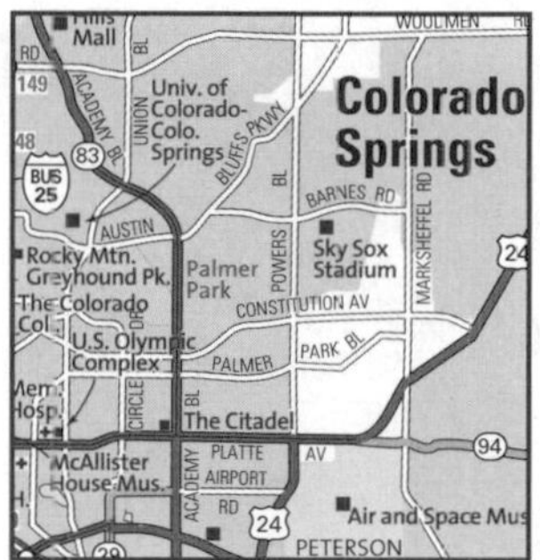

Inset Map Boxes
Greater metropolitan regions, city downtowns, national parks, and major recreational areas are highlighted with red boxes. If a detail map does not appear on the same page as its home map, a page number in white type refers you to the correct page.

Multi-Map Navigation
These yellow tabs indicate adjacent states and their page numbers.

National Parks Pages 192-213

This chapter features a collection of profiles highlighting 34 top national parks in the United States, and two parks from Canada. Each profile explains the history of the park and describes the park's natural highlights and scenic attractions. Descriptions of specific hikes and activities are also included for the outdoor enthusiasts.

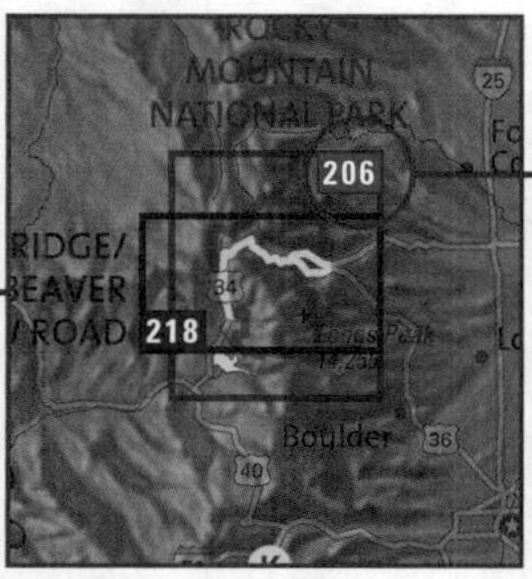

National Park Insets
Located on the regional maps, the inset boxes outline the parks which are featured in the National Parks chapter. The page number listed inside the box refers you to the correct National Parks page.

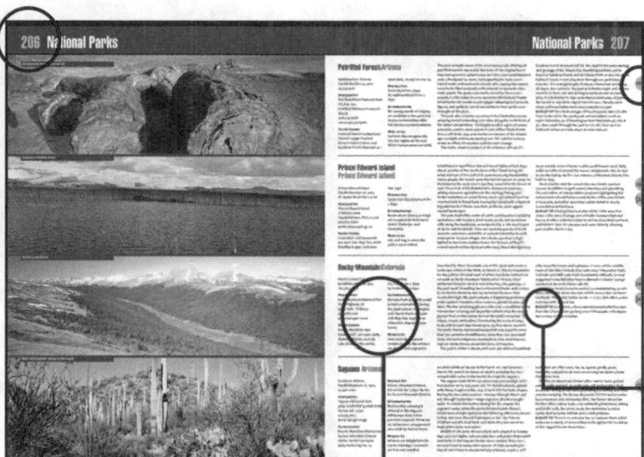

Cross-Reference Tabs to Park Maps
Each park lists at least one yellow road map tab to direct you to the state in which the park appears. A second tab references the page on which an individual park detail map appears.

Handy Visitor Information
This is a quick reference section that includes the location of the visitor center, entrance fees, accommodations, and tips on when to go.

Budget Tips
Highlighted in red and located at the end of each national park entry, these are quick tips on how to get the most for your money during your visit. They include such tips as what park passes to purchase, the best time of year to visit, free campgrounds, and available informative programs.

Scenic Drives Pages 214-227

This section features 36 of America's most scenic, off-the-beaten-path highways and byways. Detailed route descriptions take you on an unforgettable journey past beautiful landscapes and natural wonders.

Scenic Drive Insets
Inset boxes highlight the scenic routes in each region. Page numbers direct you to where in the Scenic Drives chapter to locate a trip itinerary and a detail map.

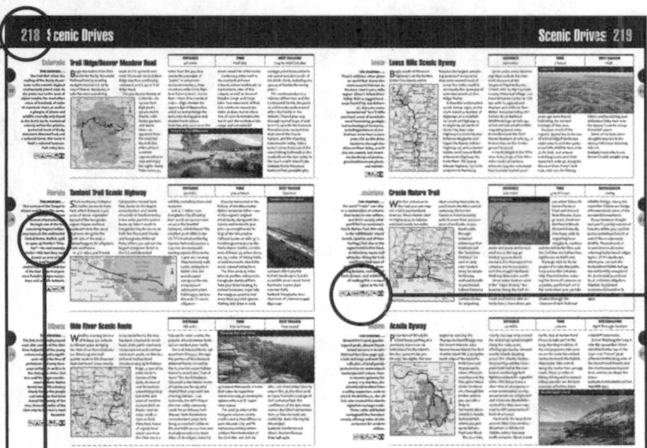

Scenic Drive Icons
These are quick reference icons to what activities are available along each drive. The icons include: biking, camping, boating, fishing, picnicking, swimming, and wildlife viewing.

Road Tips
"For Starters" describes the type of terrain (mountainous, plains, marshlands, etc.) you will encounter during each scenic drive. Road condition advisories are listed, as well as the advantages of traveling during specific times of the year.

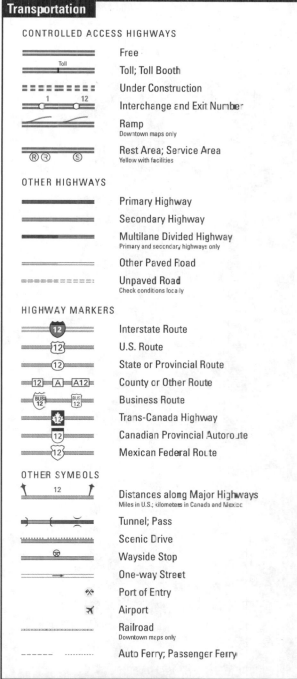

Transportation

CONTROLLED ACCESS HIGHWAYS

- Free
- Toll; Toll Booth
- Under Construction
- Interchange and Exit Number
- Ramp (Downtown maps only)
- Rest Area; Service Area (Yellow with facilities)

OTHER HIGHWAYS

- Primary Highway
- Secondary Highway
- Multilane Divided Highway (Primary and secondary highways only)
- Other Paved Road
- Unpaved Road (Check conditions locally)

HIGHWAY MARKERS

- Interstate Route
- U.S. Route
- State or Provincial Route
- County or Other Route
- Business Route
- Trans-Canada Highway
- Canadian Provincial Autoroute
- Mexican Federal Route

OTHER SYMBOLS

- Distances along Major Highways (Miles in U.S.; kilometers in Canada and Mexico)
- Tunnel; Pass
- Scenic Drive
- Wayside Stop
- One-way Street
- Port of Entry
- Airport
- Railroad (Downtown maps only)
- Auto Ferry; Passenger Ferry

Recreation and Features of Interest

- National Park
- National Forest; National Grassland
- Other Large Park or Recreation Area
- Small State Park with and without Camping
- Public Campsite
- Trail
- Point of Interest
- Visitor Information Center
- Public Golf Course; Private Golf Course (Professional tournament location)
- Hospital (City maps only)
- Ski Area

Cities and Towns

- National Capital; State or Provincial Capital
- County Seat (State maps only)
- Cities, Towns, and Populated Places (Type size indicates relative importance)
- Urban Area (State and province maps only)
- Large Incorporated Cities

Other Map Features

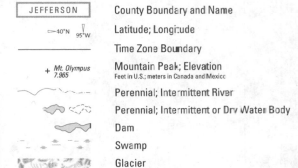

- JEFFERSON — County Boundary and Name
- 40°N 95°W — Latitude; Longitude
- Time Zone Boundary
- Mt. Olympus 7,965 — Mountain Peak; Elevation (Feet in U.S.; meters in Canada and Mexico)
- Perennial; Intermittent River
- Perennial; Intermittent or Dry Water Body
- Dam
- Swamp
- Glacier

8 Regional Guides

Moab Valley with Colorado River and La Sal Mountains, Utah

AK 62
AK 272

Free $ Finds

Fraternal Order of Alaska State Troopers Museum, Anchorage
Exhibits on Alaska's police force, both past and present. **907/279-5050**

Alaska Bird Observatory, Fairbanks
Information about birds and bird watching; staff-guided bird walks; workshops. **907/451-7059**

Alaska Heritage Library and Museum, Anchorage
Displays of a variety of Native Alaskan artifacts, including paintings, dolls, and rare books. **907/265-2834**

Elmendorf Air Force Base Wildlife Museum, Anchorage
Self-guided museum with hands-on displays, and mounted grizzlies, polar bears, birds, and moose. **907/552-2282**

St. Nicholas Orthodox Church, Juneau
Russian Orthodox church constructed in 1894; tours available. **907/780-6320**

Mendenhall Glacier, Juneau
Located at the head of Glacier Spur Road, this is the easiest glacier to get to in Alaska. Visitor center includes a theater and an exhibit gallery. **907/586-6640**

Admiralty Island National Monument, Juneau
Hike, fish, camp, or view wildlife at this national monument with breath-taking vistas. **907/586-8800**

Alaska Chilkat Bald Eagle Preserve, Haines
Year-round home for 200-400 bald eagles. **907/766-2292**

Alaskaland Park, Fairbanks
Numerous free attractions include museums, a theater, an art gallery, a native village, and a reconstructed gold town. **907/459-1087**

Tongass Historical Museum, Ketchikan
Admission to this one-room museum with revolving exhibits is free in the winter. **907/225-5600**

Corrington Museum of Natural History, Skagway
Eclectic exhibits tell Alaska's history in 32 pieces of ivory scrimshaw **907/983-2580**

The breathtaking beauty of million-year old glaciers, the rugged landscape and exotic wildlife make Alaska a paradise for nature lovers. Its national forests and parks are America's largest, and the abundant coastal waters provide some of the best salmon and halibut fishing in the world. Veteran rock and ice climbers routinely assault Mount McKinley, the highest peak in North America at 20,320 feet, and the truly intrepid compete in the annual Iditarod sled dog race. Surprisingly cosmopolitan and comfortable, Anchorage is home to about half the state's population and offers first-class restaurants, nightclubs, and entertainment.

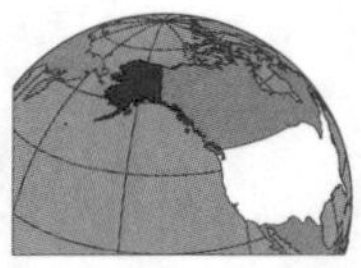

The great Yukon River cuts the Alaskan interior almost in half, carving tremendous valleys along the way, as it makes its 1,265-mile journey from the state border to the Bering Sea. The mazelike convergence of land and water in the famed Inside Passage of the panhandle was sculpted into its present form by thousands of years of glacial ice scoring its way toward the sea, and eventually melting.

Ⓒ Alaska State Museum

Ⓓ The Alaska Zoo

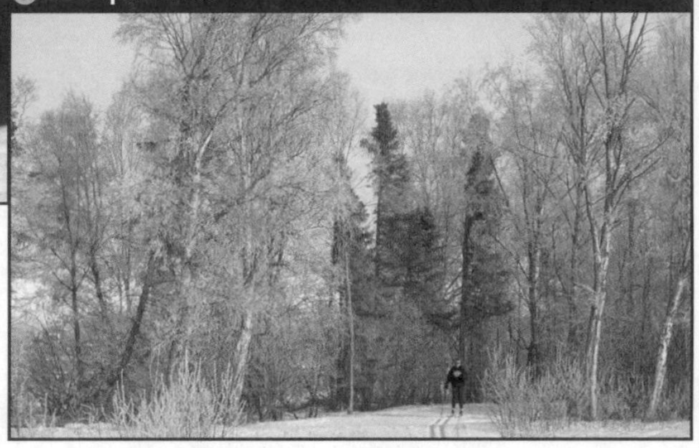

Ⓕ Earthquake Park

Ⓐ ALASKA BOTANICAL GARDEN

Pg. 62, F6. **Anchorage.** Encompassing 110 acres of land once used by the Athabascan Indians, the gardens contain over 480 varieties of cultured plants. Visitors may learn about flora in Alaska by exploring the themed gardens, which include two perennial gardens, a rock garden, and an herb garden. The Lowenfels Family Nature Trail, once used by military tanks during WWII maneuvers, features most of the trees native to the area, as well as its wildlife. **907/770-3692**

Ⓑ ALASKA HIGHWAY

Pg. 62, D7. **Fairbanks.** This 1,522 mile long road from Dawson Creek, British Columbia, to Fairbanks, Alaska was constructed shortly after the attack on Pearl Harbor, when a need for an inland route to Alaska was vital. Highlights along the way include Muncho Lake, Liard Hot springs, Kluane Lake, and the Trans-Alaska Pipeline Crossing. **907/452-1105**

Ⓒ ALASKA STATE MUSEUM

Pg. 62, G10. **Juneau.** Permanent collections and traveling exhibits highlight Alaska's native peoples, its natural history, the Alaska-Yukon gold rushes, and the American Period of Alaska's history. Artwork and artifacts include photographs, murals, kayak models, a life-sized eagle tree, and tiny thimble baskets. A children's room features a one-third scale model of the stern of the ship Discovery, used by Capt. George Vancouver during his famous explorations of Alaska, dress-up clothes, and historic exhibits. **907/465-2901** $

Ⓓ THE ALASKA ZOO

Pg. 62, F6. **Anchorage.** With annual attendance over 200,000, the zoo is one of the most visited places in the state. It exhibits 38 species of arctic and sub-arctic wildlife on 25 acres of land. Some exotic animals, such as elephants, camels and llamas are housed here, but most are native Alaskan species, such as black bears, polar bears, mink, moose, red foxes, and wolverines. **907/346-3242** $

Ⓔ CLAM GULCH STATE RECREATIONAL AREA

Pg. 62, F6. **Soldotna.** This area is famous for the hundreds of thousands of razor clams harvested annually from the sandy beaches adjacent to the State Recreation Area. Clam Gulch is located on steep bluffs overlooking Cook Inlet, with sweeping views of the Aleutian Mountains and their three tallest peaks: Mount Iliamna, Mount Redoubt and Mount Spurr. **907/262-5581** $

Ⓕ EARTHQUAKE PARK

Pg. 62, F6. **Anchorage.** The Good Friday earthquake in 1964 was the biggest ever in North America, registering 9.2 on the Richter scale, killing 131 people, and leveling a number of area neighborhoods. An interpretive display shows the effect of this event, and explains the area's geology, flora and fauna. **907/276-4118**

Ⓖ GIRDWOOD

Pg. 62, F6. **Anchorage.** Forty miles south of Anchorage Alaska, nestled among the Turnagain Arm and spectacular Mt. Alyeska, Girdwood has evolved from a gold mining town into Alaska's only year-round resort community. Driving from Anchorage, visitors may see dall sheep, moose, numerous eagles, or Beluga Whales in the Turnagain arm. Girdwood features many B&B's, restaurants, shops and boutiques, and offers many opportunities for Alaska adventures, including kayaking, rafting, hiking, and fishing. **907/929-2200**

Ⓗ GLACIER BAY

Pg. 62, G10. **Gustavus.** Just 200 years ago, this area was covered in ice. Today, tidewater glaciers, wildlife viewing, and rain forests are abundant and more than 200 species of birds, as well as salmon, whales, seals, and black bears make it their home. Activities include fishing, hiking trails, kayaking, and boat rides from visitor center. **907/697-2230**

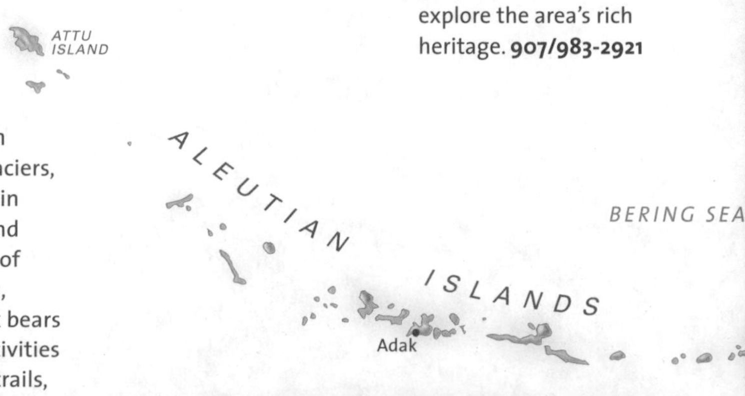

Ⓘ INDEPENDENCE MINE STATE HISTORICAL PARK

Pg. 62, F7. **Wasilla.** This park was just one of the places in Alaska where adventurers flocked to seek out their fortunes. A self-guided historical trail leads visitors through the abandoned mine camp. Heavy snowfall in the winter provides opportunities for cross country and alpine skiing, as well as snowboarding. **907/745-2827** $

Ⓙ KATMAI NATIONAL PARK AND PRESERVE

Pg. 62, G5. **King Salmon.** Katmai is known for its volcanoes (all 14 are considered active, but not currently erupting), brown bears, and rugged wilderness. Popular activities here include fishing, kayaking, climbing, boating, camping, and snow skiing. **907/271-3751**

Ⓚ KLONDIKE GOLD RUSH NATIONAL HISTORIC PARK

Pg. 62, F10. **Skagway.** Many historic structures and artifacts from the gold rush of 1897-98 are preserved here to interpret the history of stampeders and the many hardships they faced. Hikers and backpackers can follow the footsteps of these gold rushers along the 33-mile-long Chilkoot Trail, one of the most popular routes used during the gold rush. For the less adventurous, there are many area museums and guided tours that let visitors explore the area's rich heritage. **907/983-2921**

Ⓗ Glacier Bay National Park and Preserve

Ⓚ Klondike Gold Rush National Historic Park

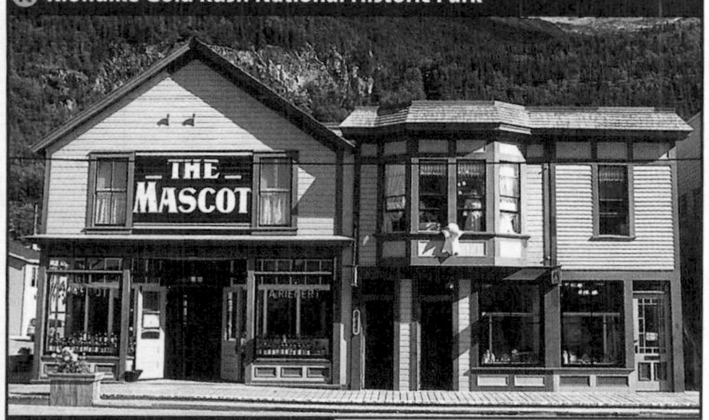

Ⓜ Last Chance Mine

Ⓛ KODIAK ISLAND
Pg. 62, G6. **Kodiak.** Not the frozen wilderness that is usually associated with Alaska, Kodiak Island is known as the state's Emerald Isle because of its green snow-tipped mountains and tree-lined fjords. Located off the coast of Alaska, it is one of the largest commercial fishing ports in the nation, and famous for its Kodiak brown bears. Activities here include fishing, kayaking, hiking, biking, and wildlife viewing. **907/486-4782**

Alaska has almost twice as many caribou as people

Ⓜ THE LAST CHANCE MINING MUSEUM
Pg. 62, G10. **Juneau.** Listed on the National Register of Historic Places and Alaska Gold Rush Properties, the museum is housed in a historic compressor building associated with the former Alaska Juneau Gold Mining Company which operated in Juneau from 1912 until 1944. It explores the history of the region's mining industry with exhibits of industrial artifacts associated with hard rock gold mining. **907/346-3242** $

Ⓝ MISTY FJORDS NATIONAL MONUMENT
Pg. 62, H11. **Ketchikan.** This area at the southern border of Tongass National Forest derives its name from the almost constant precipitation occurring in the region; the area receives almost fourteen feet of precipitation annually, giving rise to the many lakes, streams, and waterfalls. Despite this rainy climate, kayaking and camping are popular with adventurers. **907/225-7535**

Ⓞ THE PRATT MUSEUM
Pg. 62, F6. **Homer.** The only natural history museum on the Kenai Peninsula, the collection has exhibits on art, natural history, native cultures, homesteading, fishing and marine ecology. Also shown are Alaska birds and mammals, including complete skeletons of a Bering Sea beaked whale, Beluga whale and Steller's sea lion; a tide-pool tank featuring live Kachemak Bay sea creatures; and the historic Harrington Homestead cabin. **907/235-8635** $

Ⓟ TOTEM BIGHT STATE HISTORICAL PARK
Pg. 62, H11. **Ketchikan.** In 1938 the U.S. Forest Service began a program aimed at salvaging and reconstructing magnificent examples of Tlingit, Haida, and Tsimshian symbolic carvings.Today, it is the largest collection of totem poles in the world. **907/247-8574** $

Ⓠ WRANGELL-ST. ELIAS NATIONAL PARK AND PRESERVE
Pg. 62, F7. **Copper Center.** Just a day's drive east of Anchorage, this park is often called the "mountain kingdom of North America." It comprises the Wrangell, St. Elias and Chugach mountain ranges, the continent's largest assemblage of glaciers, and its greatest collection of peaks above 16,000 feet. Hiking and climbing are for experienced sportsmen. **907/822-7216** $

Ⓝ Misty Fjords

Ⓠ Wrangell-St. Elias National Park

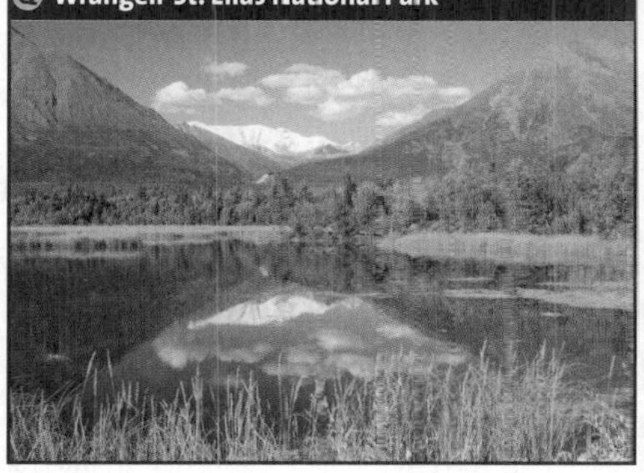

DOLLAR WI$E

- Stay in B&B accommodations; they are generally less expensive than a standard hotel room, and the complimentary breakfast will cut down on food costs.
- You can save as much as 25% traveling before and after the summer peak season, when hotel and guided activity prices drop.
- If renting a car, shop early over the Internet; you can book a car during the low season for less, even if you will be using it in the high season.
- Fill the tank before you return your rental car; rental companies charge to refill the tank, and do so at prices of up to 50% more than the local gas station.
- The Alaska Pass provides discounted one-price travel on trains, buses, and boats throughout Alaska, British Columbia, and the Yukon.

January
Polar Bear Jump-Off Festival
Seward, AK
Costumed jumpers take the plunge into icy Resurrection Bay. Parade, goofy golf, slippery salmon toss and more.
907/224-5688

February
Willow Winter Festival
Willow, AK
907/495-6633

March
Buckwheat Ski Classic
Skagway, AK
A cross-country ski race along White Pass mountain. Amateurs and professionals alike will find this course matches their abilities.
907/983-2544

Iditarod
Famous dog sled race from Ankorage to Nome.
Anchorage, AK
907/376-5155

Windfest
Skagway, AK
A community celebration of the anticipation of spring. Activities include Toilet Seat Toss, Dessert Bake-off, Ugly Animal Competition, and Fire Department Water Extravaganza
907/983-2544

April
Alaska Folk Festival
Juneau, AK
907/463-3316

Whalefest
Kodiak, AK
Whale watchers celebrate the return of migrating whales.
907/486-3737

June
Alaska State Museum Summer Exhibit
Juneau, AK
Contemporary Northwest Coast Native art is featured in this juried exhibition.
907/465-2901

Midnight Sun Festival
Fairbanks, AK
Summer solstice celebration. Music, food, and family activities.
907/452-8671

Top of the World Music Festival
Anchorage, AK
World-beat sounds of salsa, reggae, merengue, folk music, bluegrass, country, jazz, and soul.
907/277-7469

August
Alaska State Fair
Palmer, AK
907/745-4827

Kodiak State Fair and Rodeo
Kodiak, AK
907/487-4438

September
Bathtub Race
Nome, AK
Bathtubs mounted on wheels race down Front St. at high noon.
907/443-2798

October
Oktoberfest
Kodiak, AK
Traditional German feast and music.
907/486-2000

November
Juneau Public Market
Juneau, AK
A community holiday event that includes arts and crafts, imports, photography, wearable art, and much more.
907/586-1166

WA 170
OR 148

Free Finds$

Hoyt Arboretum, Portland
Displays of more than 700 kind of woods and one of the nation's largest collections of needle-bearing trees; self-guided trails with Vietnam Veterans Living Memorial. **503/228-8733**

Bonneville Dam, Portland
Attend a 30- 60-minute interpretive presentation. See a navigation lock, fish hatchery and fish ladder. **541/374-8820**

Oregon Zoo, Portland
Second Tuesday of each month free (after 1 pm). Features 1,029 specimens representing 200 species of birds, mammals, reptiles, amphibians and invertebrates. **503/226-1561**

Astoria Column, Astoria
A 125-ft tower commemorates the first settlement; observation deck at top. **503/325-7275**

Pendleton Woolen Mills, Pendleton
Guided tours of woolen manufacturing; carding, spinning, rewinding, and weaving processes. **541/276-6911**

Honeywod Winery, Salem
Tour of Oregon's oldest producing winery with tasting. **503/362-4111**

Seattle Art Museum, Seattle
Free first Thursday of each month. Collection of Asian art and Chinese jades; modern art; ethnic art. **206/654-3255**

Washington Park Arboretum, Seattle
Over 200 acres containing more than 5,000 species of trees and shrubs from all parts of world **206/543-8800**

Washington Apple Commission Visitors Center, Yakima
Offers an in-depth look at the state's largest agricultural industry. **509/662-3090**

Boehm's Chocolate Factory, Issaquah
The candy-making process and the Edelweiss Chalet, filled with artifacts, paintings, and statues, can be toured. **425/392-6652**

Wyvern Cellars, Spokane
Tour and tasting of Gold Medal wines. **509/455-7835**

Of Sea and Shore Museum, Port Gamble
One of the largest shell collections in the country. **360/297-2426**

Preston Estate Vineyards, Pasco
Self-guided tour of tasting room, oak aging casks, storage tanks, and bottling line. **509/545-1990**

The spirit of the pioneers is alive and well in the scenic Pacific Northwest, whether retracing the steps of the legendary Lewis and Clark expedition or keeping up with the latest offerings from Microsoft. Defined by its famously rainy weather, this region pulses with the energetic beat of artistic innovation, from the urbane and culture-conscious Portland, framed by the spectacular snow-capped Mount Hood, to the sophisticated, yet relaxed spirit of Seattle, with its inviting coffeehouses, bookstores and clubs. Oregon's 400 miles of dramatic windswept beaches bewitch the traveler and are matched only by Washington's unspoiled wilderness of ancient rain forests. Majestic Mount Rainier and Snoqualmie Falls dazzle visitors, while the unique San Juan Islands are home to majestic orca whales.

The Cascade Range cuts across both Washington and Oregon, acting as a barrier for coastal weather systems and keeping things wet and mild in the west and more arid in the east. The mighty Columbia River flows along the Washington-Oregon border.

E Oregon's Central Coast

A Astoria

G Rogue River

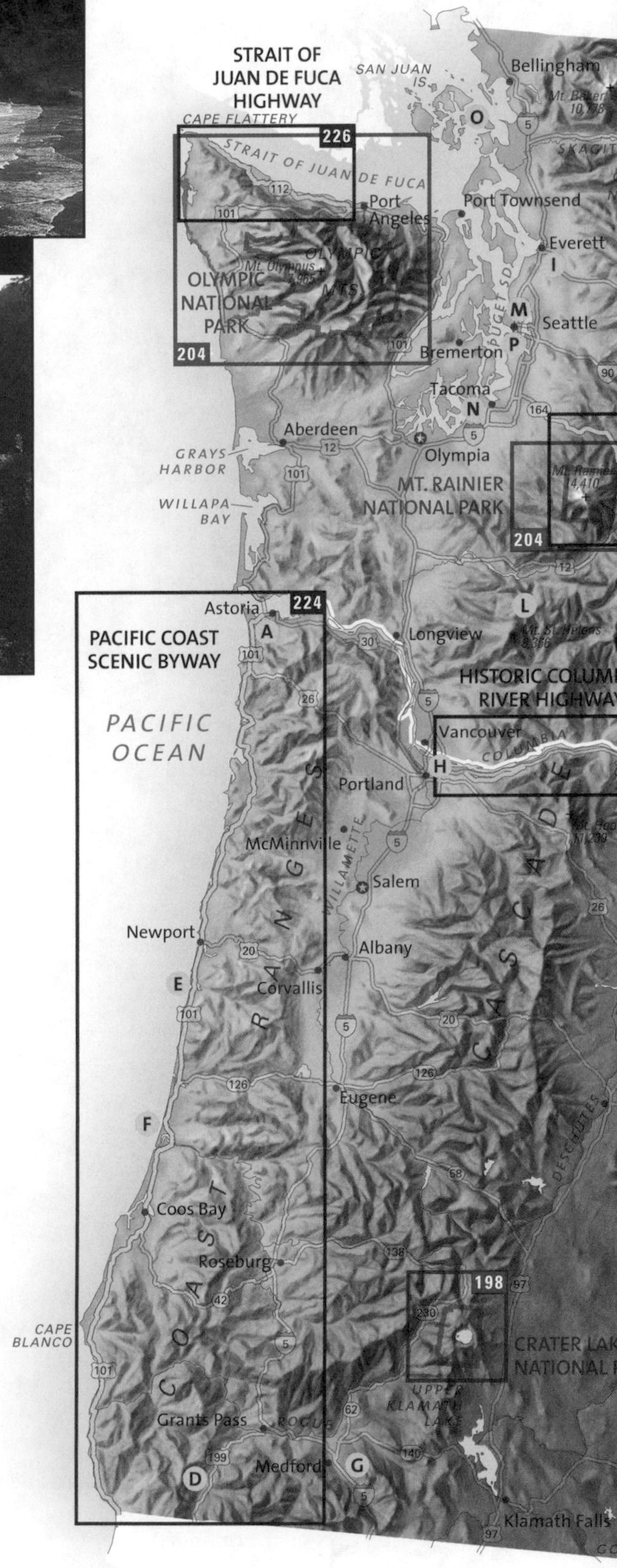

OREGON

A ASTORIA
Pg. 148, A3. The oldest American settlement west of the Rockies, Astoria sits at the mouth of the Columbia River. During the 1880s, sea captains and rich industrialists built homes overlooking the river which you can still see. The 125-foot Astoria column offers a great view of the Pacific Ocean, the Columbia River, Saddle Mountain, and the Clatsop Plain. The Columbia River Maritime Museum has a fine display of model ships. Today, these Victorian structures make visitors feel as if they have been transported to another time as they stroll through Astoria's revitalized 1920s-era downtown. **503/325-6311**

B HELL'S CANYON NATIONAL RECREATION AREA
Pg. 149, C16. **Imnaha.** Created by the Snake River, at the Idaho/Oregon border, Hell's Canyon is the deepest gorge in North America. The recreation area includes parts of the Nez Perce and Payette national forests in Idaho and the Wallowa-Whitman National Forest in Oregon. Activities include float trips, jet boat tours; auto tours, backpacking, and horseback riding. **541/426-4978**

C JOHN DAY FOSSIL BEDS NATIONAL MONUMENT
Pg. 149, E11. **Kimberly.** Within the volcanic deposits of a river basin, this huge collection of well-preserved plant and animal fossils spanning 40-million years is world renowned. Visitors learn about the fossils through ranger-led hikes and presentations on geology and paleontology. Other activities include camping, fishing, and wildlife viewing. **541/987-2336**

D OREGON CAVES NATIONAL MONUMENT
Pg. 148, M2. **Cave Junction.** This area was discovered in 1874, when hunter Elijah Davidson's dog followed a bear into the cave. Inside, the cave has many chambers—Paradise Lost, Joaquin Miller's Chapel, and Ghost Room. Visitors can join a cave tour, or hike one of the many loop trails. **541/592-2100 $**

E OREGON'S CENTRAL COAST
Pg. 148, E2. **Newport.** Oregon's Central Coast boasts dramatic scenery, along with mild temperatures, vast sandy beaches and rugged clifflines. It is a popular destination for biking, hiking, golfing, fishing, swimming, windsurfing, clam digging, crabbing, surfing and scuba diving. **541/265-2064**

F OREGON DUNES NATIONAL RECREATION AREA
Pg. 148, J1. **North Bend.** Large coastal sand dunes, forests, and wetlands comprise this 32,000-acre area in Siuslaw National Forest. The Dunes area holds one of the largest bodies of sand outside of the Sahara—two miles wide and 40 miles long. Popular activities here are beach combing, fishing, boating, hiking, horseback riding, and camping. **541/271-3611 $**

G ROGUE RIVER NATIONAL FOREST
Pg. 148, M4. **Medford.** The 632,045-acre forest has extensive stands of Douglas fir, ponderosa, and sugar pine. Activities here include swimming, hiking, backpacking, and—in winter—cross country skiing. **541/776-3600**

H WASHINGTON PARK
Pg. 148, C4. **Portland.** This 129-acre gardener's delight above the city encompasses the International Rose Test Garden with 8,000 bushes of more than 400 varieties, a Shakespeare Garden, the Hoyt Arboretum, and Japanese Gardens. **503/823-2223**

H Washington Park

More than half of all apples grown in the United States for fresh eating come from orchards in Washington state.

I Boeing Everett Facility

J Grand Coulee Dam

L Mount Saint Helens

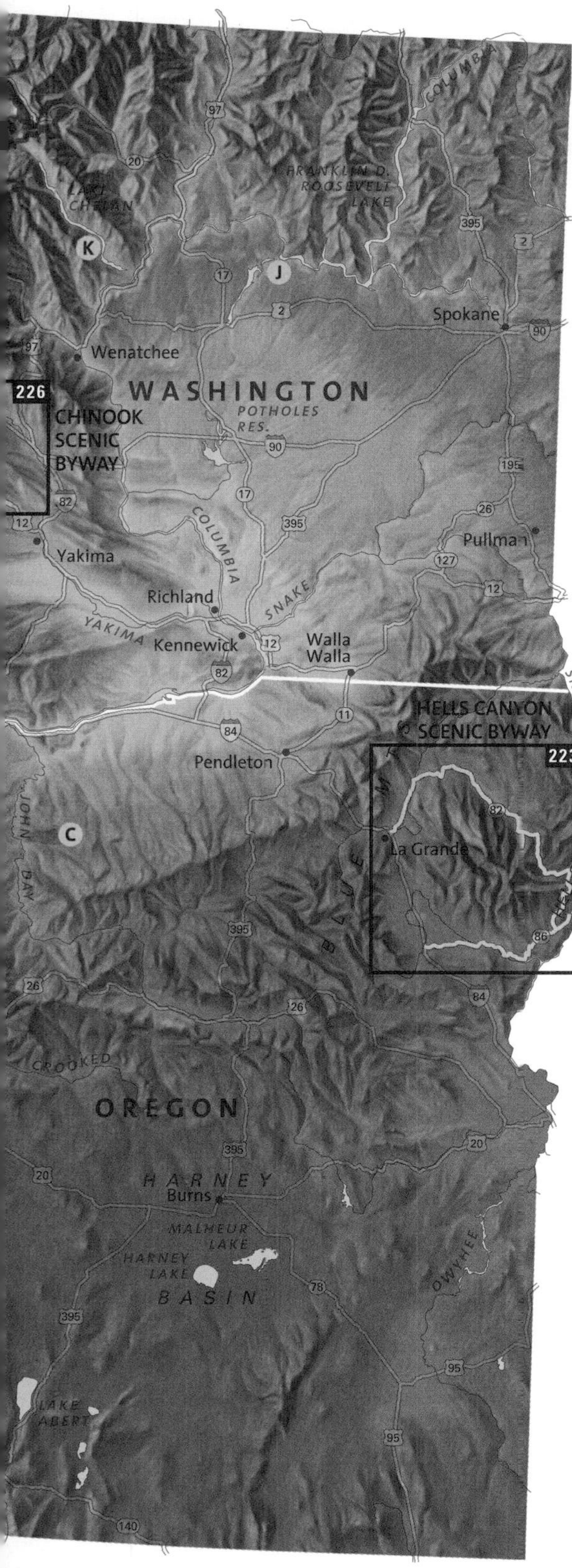

MI 50 100
KM 50 100

WASHINGTON

I BOEING EVERETT FACILITY
Pg. 170, D9. **Everett.** Housing assembly for Boeing wide-body aircraft, this complex is recognized by the Guinness Book of World Records as the largest building in the world by volume. It has grown to enclose 472 million cubic feet of space, and covers 98.3 acres. On the Boeing flight line, visitors can see airplanes in various stages of manufacture. **800/494-1476** $

J GRAND COULEE DAM
Pg. 171, E16. **Grand Coulee.** One of the largest concrete structures in the world, the dam towers as high as Niagara Falls and is 5,223-ft-long. Its power plants contain some of the world's largest hydro-electric generators. **509/633-3074**

K LAKE CHELAN
Pg. 171, E14. **Chelan.** This fjordlike lake, the largest and deepest in the state, stretches northwest for approximately 55 miles through the Cascade mountains to the community of Stehekin in the North Cascades National Park. In some areas, it is nearly 1,500 ft deep. Along the lake are two state parks, offering swimming, fishing, boating and camping. **800/452-5687**

L MOUNT SAINT HELENS
Pg. 170, K7. **Castle Rock.** In March of 1980, Mount St. Helens blew, ending 123 years of inactivity. Less than two months later, another even more massive eruption transformed this beautiful snow-capped mountain and the surrounding forest into an eerie, desolate landscape. Mount Saint Helens provides a rare, natural laboratory in which scientists and visitors alike can study the effects of a volcanic eruption. **360/247-3900** $

M PIKE PLACE MARKET
Pg. 170, F8. **Seattle.** This nine-acre historic district is the oldest continuously operating farmer's market in the country. Buy anything from artichokes to zithers from the more than 100 farmers and fishermen, 150 craftspeople, and 300 commercial vendors. More than 50 street performers entertain and there are many restaurants if you need to take a break. **206/682-7453**

N POINT DEFIANCE PARK
Pg. 170, G8. **Tacoma.** This 700-acre park, flanked by the waters of Puget Sound, contains a wealth of gardens, the city zoo and aquarium ($), and a number of recreational and historic sites, including a logging museum and a reconstruction of an 1833 British fort. The park includes hiking trails that lead to sheltered beaches. **253/305-1000**

O SAN JUAN ISLANDS
Pg. 170, C7. **Friday Harbor.** This tranquil wooded archipelago near the Strait of Juan de Fuca is accessible by ferry from Anacortes. Over 500 miles of roads swing through virgin woodlands and along lovely shorelines. In Friday Harbor there is a whale museum ($) and on San Juan Island a park commemorating a border dispute with Great Britain. **360/378-2240**

P Seattle Center

P SEATTLE CENTER
Pg. 170, F8. **Seattle.** The Center's ample site holds the 605-ft Space Needle, which gives visitors a spectacular view; the Fun Forest Amusement Park; a Monorail; and the Pacific Science Center, which has more than 200 hands-on exhibits, an IMAX Theater, live science demonstrations, planetarium shows, laser light shows, and other special events. **206/684-7200** $

DOLLAR WI$E

- If traveling with children, find hotels where kids stay free.
- Consider rooms with kitchen facilities; you will reduce restaurant costs by preparing some meals for yourself.
- When visiting major cities, stay in hotels just outside the city limits; these are usually less expensive than those in downtown locations.
- Take advantage of The Seattle Super Saver program, which offers reduced rates — up to 50% — on hotels from November 15-March 31.
- Search out free camp sites in Oregon, such as national forests and city parks. Not only will you save money on hotels, you will be provided with peaceful, scenic settings and numerous recreational opportunities.
- Purchase a Seattle CityPass, which gets you into six famous attractions for nearly a 50% discount.

January
Bavarian Ice Fest
Leavenworth, WA
Snowshoe races, dogsled rides. Fireworks.
509/548-5807

February
Oregon Shakespeare Festival
Ashland, OR
Elizabethan Theater (outdoor); Angus Bowmer Theater (indoor); Black Swan Theater (indoor). Series of 12 classic and contemporary plays. Tues-Sun.
541/482-4331

March
Chocolate Fantasy
Yakima, WA
Chocolate manufacturers from across the nation showcase their wares.
509/575-6062

April
Holland Happening
Oak Harbor, WA
Tulip show, arts and crafts, Dutch buffet, and other festivities
360/675-3755

Washington State Apple Blossom Festival
Wenatchee, WA
Parades, carnival, arts and crafts, musical productions.
509/662-3616

May
Portland Rose Festival
Portland, OR
Held for more than 90 yrs, this festival includes three parades; band competition; rose show; championship auto racing; hot-air balloons; air show; carnival; Navy ships.
503/227-2681

June
Bach Festival
Eugene, OR
Numerous concerts by regional and international artists; master classes; family activities.
800/457-1486

Chamber Music Northwest
Portland, OR
Nationally acclaimed summer chamber music festival offers 25 concerts featuring 40-50 artists (Mon, Tues, Thurs-Sat). Catered picnic preceding each concert.
503/294-6400

July
Salem Art Fair and Festival
Salem, OR
Arts and crafts booths and demonstrations, children's art activities and parade, ethnic folk arts, performing arts, street painting, 5K run, food; tours of historic Bush House.
503/581-2228

August
Oregon State Fair
Salem, OR
Horse racing, wine competition and tasting, agricultural exhibits, horse show, livestock, food, carnival, entertainment.
503/947-3247

December
Holiday Parade of Christmas Ships
Portland, OR
Along Willamette and Columbia rivers. More than 50 boats cruise the two rivers in a holiday display.
503/225-5555

NV 126
CA 68
NV 241
CA 232

Free Finds

Hollywood Forever Cemetery, Hollywood
Crypts of Tyrone Power, Cecil B. De Mile, Rudolph Valentino, Douglas Fairbanks, Sr., Nelson Eddy and Norma Talmadge, as well as other famous stars, statesmen, and industrialists. **323/469-1181**

California Science Center, Los Angeles
Hands-on exhibits on science, mathematics, economics, the urban environment, energy, and health. **323/724-3623**

Municipal Rose Garden, San Jose
Approximately 5,000 rose plants on six acres, peak blooming in late Apr-May. **408/277-5422**

CBS Television City, Los Angeles
West Coast studios of CBS Television and source of many of its network telecasts. Write for free tickets well in advance, or pick up at Information Window (first-come, first-served basis). **323/575-2458**

Stanford University, Stanford
Founded by Senator and Mrs. Leland Stanford in memory of their only son, it has become one of the great universities of the world. Free campus tours daily. **650/723-2300**

Buena Vista Winery, Sonoma
Cellars built in 1857. Historical panels, tasting room, art gallery, picnic area. **707/938-1266**

Exploratorium, San Francisco
Free first Wednesday of the month. Hands-on museum dedicated to providing insights into scientific and natural phenomena. **415/397-5673**

Buccaneer Bay at Treasure Island, Las Vegas
This eight-minute pirate battle in front of the Treasure Island hotel takes place daily every 90 minutes from 4 pm-11:30 pm. **702/894-7111**

Holy Cow! Casino, Café & Brewery tour, Las Vegas
Guided tours of the microbrewery. **702/732-2697**

MGM Lion Habitat, Las Vegas
Houses up to five lions, and is a multilevel habitat that features four waterfalls, overhangs, a pond and Acacia trees. **702/891-7777**

Mystic Falls Park, Las Vegas
Located in the center of Sam's Town Hall and Casino, this faux park is filled with small streams and places to sit or walk. In the evenings, the "Sunset Stampede" takes place — a dancing water, laser and light show. **702/456-7777**

Whether you prefer the glamour of Hollywood, the beauty of the Sierra Madre, the wine tasting in Napa and Sonoma, the desert sanctuary of Palm Springs, or the legendary Big Sur coastline, California is a must-see. Towering sequoias stand silent sentinel in the 1,200 square miles of Yosemite. To the south, there are historic Spanish missions and a chance to meet Mickey at Orange County's Disneyland. Nevada's vivacious spirit is evident in the ultimate playgrounds of glittering Las Vegas and Reno, with their world-class entertainment, exceptional dining, and thrilling casinos. Lake Tahoe's crystal-clear water, the ghost towns of Virginia City and Eureka, the nearly fluorescent Red Rock Canyon, and the majestic Cathedral Gorge provide a pleasing alternative to life in the fast lane.

Nevada sits in the sparsely populated Great Basin, an arid, elevated land with no drainage to seas; its chief drainage center is the Great Salt Lake in Utah. A spine of mountains, the Sierra Nevada, defines most of the California-Nevada border. Beyond this majestic range, home to Yosemite, Kings Canyon and Sequoia National Parks, lies the richly fertile soil of California's Central Valley, where the Sacramento and San Joaquin Rivers wend to a delta emptying into the San Francisco Bay.

CALIFORNIA

B Golden Gate

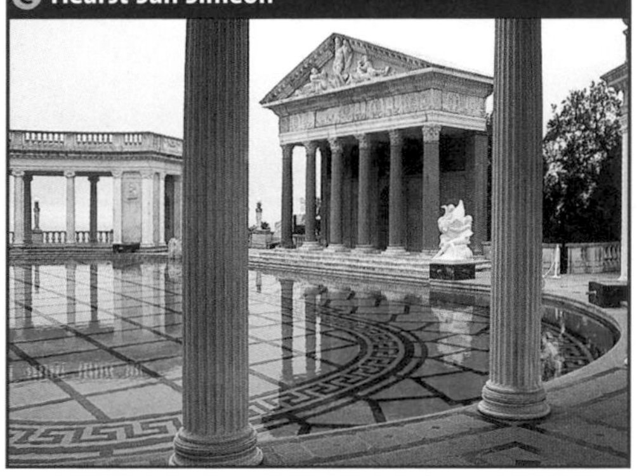

C Hearst San Simeon

A BALBOA PARK
Pg. 71, Y18. **San Diego.** Situated on 1,200 acres, Balboa Park is the center of San Diego and America's largest urban cultural park. Within its borders are over 85 cultural and recreational organizations, including the Timken Museum of Art , The San Diego Museum of Art, the Old Globe Theatre, the San Diego Aerospace Museum, the San Diego Natural History Museum, the Japanese Friendship Garden, and the San Diego Zoo, which houses more than 3,200 rare and exotic animals. **619/239-0512** $ for many attractions

B GOLDEN GATE NATIONAL RECREATION AREA
Pg. 68, L6. **San Francisco.** Within the recreation area is most of the shoreline of San Francisco, the countryside extending 20 miles north into Marin County and a 1,047-acre parcel of San Mateo County to the south. The Golden Gate Bridge connects the two segments of the park. The most popular visitor areas are the former penitentiary on Alcatraz Island, the historic Cliff House, Fort Point National Historic Site, Muir Woods National Monument, and Fort Mason Center (a restored fort under the Golden Gate Bridge). **415/556-0560**

C HEARST SAN SIMEON STATE HISTORICAL MONUMENT
Pg. 70, R9. **San Simeon.** This grand scale pleasure palace was built by William Randolph Hearst, the wealthy owner of a media conglomerate. Now open to the public, the estate includes a 115-room castle, three luxurious "guest houses," the outdoor Neptune Pool with a colonnade leading to an ancient Roman temple façade, an array of marble statuary, an indoor pool, and magnificent gardens with fountains and well-trimmed walkways. **805/927-2020** $

D LASSEN VOLCANIC NATIONAL PARK
Pg. 68, E8. **Mineral.** This 165-square-mile park was formed by volcanic activity and still holds quiescent Lassen Peak, a volcano last active in 1921. The park—in the southernmost part of the Cascade Range—contains glacial lakes, virgin forests, mountain meadows, and snow-fed streams, as well as thermal mud pots and fumaroles. Popular activities within the park include boating, camping, fishing, snowshoeing and snowmobiling. **530/595-4444** $

E MONTEREY
Pg. 70, P8. Once a whaling center, fishery and cannery, Monterey is now a popular vacation spot, with its world-class golf courses, a unique variety of shops and galleries, preserved adobe structures in Monterey State Historic Park, and the Monterey Bay Aquarium ($), which features sea otters and sharks. **831/649-1770**

F MUIR WOODS NATIONAL FOREST
Pg. 68, L6. **Mill Valley.** This was the first area in the National Park system to preserve an old growth stand of redwoods, the world's tallest species of tree. Every effort has been made to preserve this area as it was when the first European settlers saw it in 1850. The forest's beautiful surroundings can be enjoyed through hikes, nature walks, and ranger-led interpretive programs. **415/388-2595** $

G POINT REYES NATIONAL SEASHORE
Pg. 68, K5. **Inverness.** Shipwrecks and explorers, including Sir Francis Drake, who is believed to have landed here, mark the history of this area. Earthquake Trail leads along the San Andreas Fault to a place where a rift in the earth was made in 1906. Recreational opportunities include kayaking, biking, hiking, and camping. **415/669-1534**

H WALK OF FAME
Pg. 71, V16. **Los Angeles.** The world's most famous sidewalk has more than 2,000 stars embedded in its charcoal and coral-colored terrazzo that runs along Hollywood's main business district. The walk honors show business celebrities who receive a star based upon their career achievements as well as their charitable and civic contributions. **323/469-8311**

I WINE COUNTRY (SONOMA/NAPA)
Pg. 68, K7. **Napa.** This wine-rich region, just north of San Francisco, features beautiful vineyards, magnificent ocean vistas, and breathtaking mountain views. While visitors love touring the wineries, they also can enjoy excellent hiking, biking, horseback riding, fishing, hot-air ballooning, and dining. **707/996-1090**

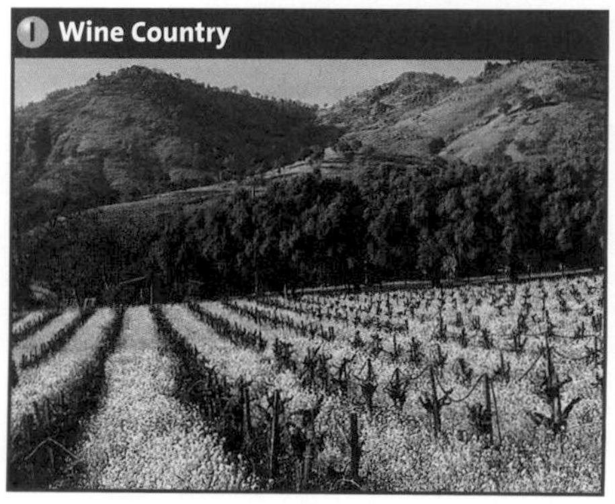

I Wine Country

L Hoover Dam

O Red Rock Canyon

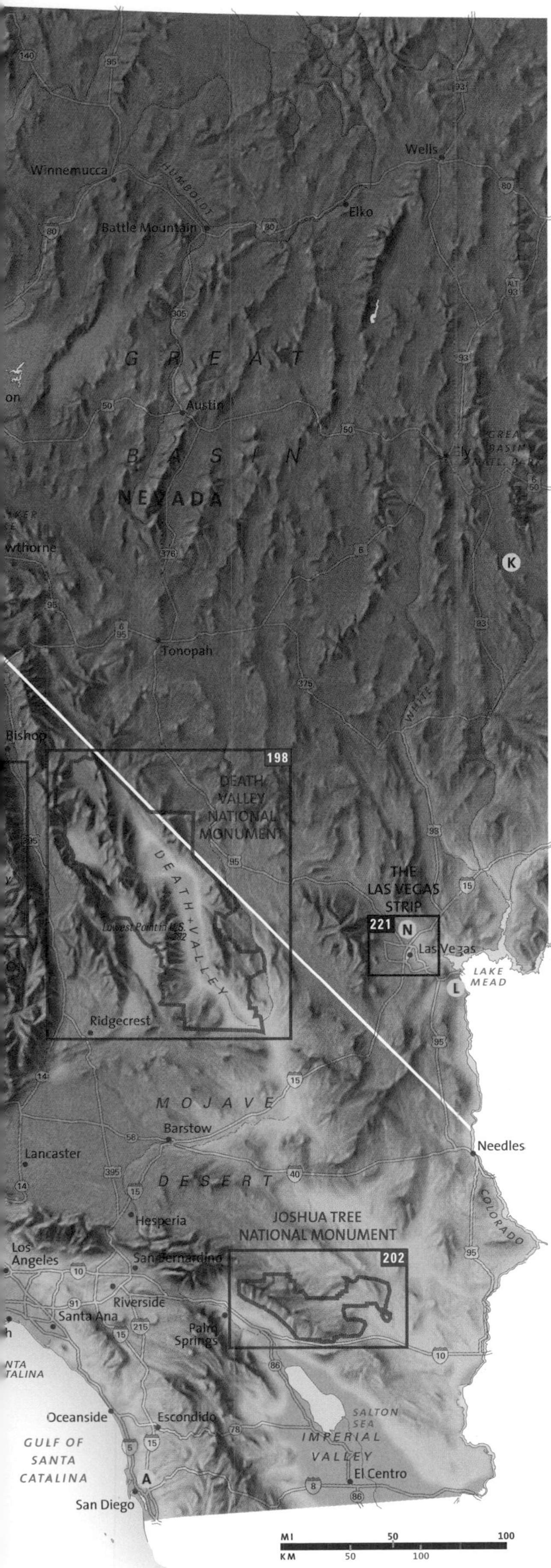

NEVADA

J CARSON CITY
Pg. 126, F3. The State Capitol, Carson City became the social center for nearby settlements and shared Wild West notoriety in the silver stampede days of the last century. Gold prospectors hit the largest silver find in the hills just east of Carson City. Today, visitors come to enjoy the area's many golf courses, ski runs, casinos, and the city's historic downtown shopping district. **775/687-7410**

K GREAT BASIN NATIONAL PARK
Pg. 126, F10. **Baker.** Established as a national park only in 1986, Great Basin includes Lehman Caves, Wheeler Peak, the state's only glacier, and Lexington Arch, a natural limestone arch more than six stories tall. The park consists of 77,092 acres of diverse scenic, ecologic, and geologic attractions from desert flats to alpine heights. **775/234-7331**

L LAKE MEAD/HOOVER DAM
Pg. 126, M9. **Boulder City.** Lake Mead, impounded by Hoover Dam, is by volume the largest man-made reservoir in the world. Hoover Dam, considered a major engineering achievement, supplies nearly 1.5 million kilowatts of power to Arizona, Nevada, and southern California. Many tours are offered, including SUV, off-road, and air tours, as well as cruises and river rafting opportunities. **702/293-8421 $**

M LAKE TAHOE
Pg. 126, F2. Lake Tahoe is one of the most magnificent mountain lakes in the world, with an area of about 200 square miles, an altitude of approximately 6,230 feet, and a maximum depth of more than 1,600 feet. Mostly in California, partly in Nevada, it is circled by paved highways edged with campgrounds, lodges, motels, and resorts. The lake, with some fine beaches, is surrounded by forests of ponderosa, Jeffery and sugar pine, white fir, juniper, cedar, aspen, dogwood, and cottonwood, as well as a splendid assortment of wildflowers. **530/544-5050 $**

N PYRAMID LAKE
Pg. 126, D2. **Flanigan.** Surrounded by rainbow-tinted, eroded hills, this is a remnant of prehistoric Lake Lahontan, which once covered 8,400 square miles in western Nevada and northeastern California. The largest natural lake in the state, Pyramid is about 30 miles long and from 7 to 9 miles wide, with deep-blue sparkling waters. Camping, boating, and fishing at Pyramid Lake are considered by many to be the best in the state. **775/476-0500 $**

O RED ROCK CANYON NATIONAL CONSERVATION AREA
Pg. 126, L3. **Las Vegas.** Red Rock Canyon offers a spectacular view of the natural wonders of the Mohave Desert. The area's awe-inspiring red- and white-colored sandstone formations and petrified sand dunes provide visitors with opportunities for hiking, camping, and rock climbing. A 13-mile loop drive offers interesting sightseeing, vistas and overlooks. **702/363-1922 $**

P RENO
Pg. 126, E2. Reno, renowned as a gambling and vacation center, also has several museums — the Nevada Museum of Art and the Nevada Historical Society — as well as the Fleischmann Planetarium and displays at the Mackay School of Mines. **775/329-2787**

DOLLAR WI$E

- Buy a Muni Passport for unlimited rides on San Francisco cable cars, streetcars and buses; it is also good for discounts on some area attractions.
- Consider Las Vegas hotel packages; they typically include meals, drinks, and show tickets for a reasonable price.
- If gambling in Las Vegas, set a daily budget and be realistic about how much you can afford to lose.
- Skip the "fantasy" hotels in Las Vegas; non-themed, less-hyped properties on The Strip can have rooms for as low as $50 per night.
- Join the "Slot Club" of any Las Vegas hotel/casino that you visit, and get comps for free meals or rooms for any gambling you indulge in.
- Las Vegas' Strip is famous for food bargains, especially late at night. Get a New York steak at Binion's Horseshoe for less than $5, starting at 11 pm.
- Get from San Francisco's Union Square to Fisherman's Wharf for $2 on the famous cable cars.
- Don't spend a lot of money taking a harbour tour in San Diego. Instead, take the inexpensive public ferry that sails frequently from the Seaport Village area of downtown. It will take you across to Coronado Island and afford wonderful views of the city sky line.

January

Cowboy Poetry Gathering
Elko, NV
Working cowpersons participate in storytelling verse. Demonstrations; music.
775/738-7135

Tournament of Roses
Pasadena, CA
Spectacular floral parade attracts more than a million people. Special tournament events during preceding wk.
626/449-4100

February

Chinese New Year
San Francisco, CA
Largest and most colorful celebration of this occasion held in US. Week-long activities include Golden Dragon Parade, lion dancing, carnival, cultural exhibits.
415/982-3000

March

Whale Festival
Fort Bragg, CA
Whale-watching cruises and walks; whale run; beerfest; chowder tasting.
707/961-6300

May

Fallon Air Show
Fallon, NV
Military exhibition flying, civilian aerobatics, aircraft displays; Blue Angels Demonstration Team. Ground events and static displays of vintage and modern aircrafts.
775/426-2880

Laughlin Riverdays
Laughlin, NV
Rodeo, bull-riding, off-road racing, golf tournament.
702/298-2214

July

Carmel Bach Festival
Carmel, CA
Concerts, recitals, lectures, special events.
831/624-2046

August

California State Fair
Sacramento, CA
Includes traditional state fair activities; exhibits, livestock, carnival food, entertainment on ten stages. Thoroughbred racing and one-mi monorail.
916/263-FAIR

Great Gatsby Festival
Lake Tahoe, CA
Event at Tallac Historic Site re-creating the 1920s, with vintage clothing, music, cars, and children's games.
530/541-5227

Nevada State Fair
Reno, NV
775/688-5767

September

Carson Valley Fine Arts & Crafts Street Celebration
Gardnerville, NV
Street celebration with hundreds of crafters, treasures, entertainment, and food.
775/782-8144

October

Invensys Classic
Las Vegas, NV
PGA tournament with more than $4.5 million in prize money.
702/256-0111

November

Calico Fine Arts Festival
Barstow, CA
Calico Ghost Town. Native American dance and works of art by many of the West's foremost artists displayed along Main St
760/254-2122

NM 130
AZ 64

Free Finds

Parker Dam & Power Plant, Parker
One of the deepest dams in the world. **760/663-3712**

Cerreta Candy Company, Glendale, AZ
30-minute guided tour of family-owned candy factory. Monday-Friday from June-August. **623/930-1000**

Center for Creative Photography, Tucson
Houses one of the world's-best collections. The more than 50,000 photographs include the Ansel Adams bequest, as well as the works of more than one thousand other photographers. **520/621-7968**

Phoenix Art Museum
Permanent and traveling exhibits; Western, contemporary, decorative arts, European galleries; Thorne miniature rooms; Arizona Costume Institute; Asian art; sculpture court. **602/257-1880**

Arizona Hall of Fame Museum, Phoenix
Changing exhibits focus on people who have made significant contributions to Arizona. **602/255-2110**

Navajo Nation Zoological and Botanical Park, Window Rock, AZ
Features a representative collection of animals and plants of historical or cultural importance to the Navajo people. **520/871-6573**

Bradburg Science Museum, Los Alamos, NM
Displays artifacts relating to the history of the laboratory and the atomic bomb. **505/667-4444**

Smokey Bear Museum, Ruidoso
Features 1950s memorabilia of famed fire-fighting bear found in the nearby Capitan Mountains. **505/354-2298**

Telephone Pioneer Museum, Albuquerque
Displays trace the development of the telephone from 1876-present. More than 100 types of telephones; switchboards, early equipment, pioneer telephone directories. **505/842-2937**

International UFO Museum & Research Center, Roswell, NM
Museum includes exhibits on various aspects of UFO phenomena and a video view room. **505/625-9495**

Georgia O'Keefe Museum, Santa Fe
Free Fridays 5-8 pm. Houses world's largest permanent collection of O'Keeffe's work. **505/995-0785**

Incredibly enough, the world-famous Grand Canyon, nearly 280 miles in length, is only one of Arizona's many scenic wonders. The Red Rocks of Sedona, the Navajo cliff dwellings, and the Coconina and Coronado National Forests are also spectacular and spellbinding. Sophisticated Phoenix and Scottsdale attract pleasure and culture seekers, while old mining towns conjure up images of the Wild West. From the Rocky Mountains to the Chihuahuan Desert, New Mexico has something for everyone. Visitors explore the unique Carlsbad Caverns, follow the Santa Fe Trail, ski the slopes of Taos, and can visit Roswell for some "UFO-spotting." The peaks of the Sandia Mountains are visible from cosmopolitan Albuquerque, and Santa Fe captures the heart and soul of the Southwest.

The Sonoran Desert reaches up from Mexico to cover most of southern Arizona, and the Chihuahuan Desert blankets much of southern New Mexico. The northern sections of the Southwest are dominated by the 5,000-foot high Colorado Plateau and its deep canyons, including one of the world's greatest natural wonders, the Grand Canyon.

(A) Canyon De Chelly

(C) London Bridge

(F) Sedona

ARIZONA

(A) CANYON DE CHELLY NATIONAL MONUMENT
Pg. 64, C12. **Chinle.** The smooth red sandstone walls of this canyon extend straight up as high as 1,000 feet from the nearly flat sand, where the Navajos still live and farm. Prehistoric Native Americans built apartment-like pueblos in these walls. Visitors may explore these ruins through one of the many auto or hiking trails, or by taking a horseback ride through the canyon. **520/674-5500** $

(B) CASA GRANDE RUINS NATIONAL MONUMENT
Pg. 65, L7. **Casa Grande.** The structure was built as an irrigation canal during the 14th century by the Hohokam people, who lived in the Salt and Gila river valleys. Among the ruins left behind is the Casa Grande, or "Big House." This four-story building is the only one of its type and size in southern Arizona. It is now protected by a huge modern steel roof structure. **520/723-3172** $

(C) LONDON BRIDGE
Pg. 64, G2. **Lake Havasu City.** By 1962, the 131-year-old London Bridge could no longer handle the traffic across the Thames. The British government put the bridge up for sale, and Robert McCulloch, Founder of Lake Havasu City, and Chairman of McCulloch Oil Corporation, submitted the winning bid of $2,460,000. The bridge was dismantled and shipped to its present site, where reconstruction began in 1968. It was dedicated in 1971. **502/855-0880**

(D) MONTEZUMA CASTLE
Pg. 64, G7. **Cottonwood.** This five-story, 20-room structure was built by Native Americans more than 800 years ago and is one of the most remarkable cliff dwellings in the United States. Perched under a protective cliff, the dwelling is 70 feet straight up from the base. Visitors are not permitted to enter the castle, but a self-guided trail offers a good view of the structure and of other ruins in the immediate area. **520/567-3322** $

(E) ORGAN PIPE CACTUS NATIONAL MONUMENT
Pg. 65, N5. **Ajo.** This 516-square-mile Sonoran desert area on the Mexican border features an extraordinary collection of plants. The organ pipe cactus grows as high as 20 feet and has 30 or more slender stems, which resemble organ pipes. Nearly 30 species of cactus grow in this unspoiled desert. **520/387-6849** $

(F) SEDONA
Pg. 64, F8. Known worldwide for the beauty of the red rocks surrounding the town, Sedona has grown from a pioneer settlement into a favorite film location. This is a resort area with great hiking, fishing, and biking that can be enjoyed all year. The town is known for its fine art galleries and the Chapel of the Holy Cross. **520/282-7722**

(G) TOMBSTONE
Pg. 65, P11. **Tombstone.** Silver prospectors founded Tombstone in the 1870s. It is most famous for the 1881 shoot-out at the O.K. Corral between the Earp brothers and "Doc" Holliday on one side and the Clanton and McLowry brothers on the other. Now a health and winter resort, it is also a museum of Arizona frontier life. **888/457-3929**

(H) TUCSON MUSEUM OF ART
Pg. 65, N9. **Tucson.** The extensive permanent collection includes pre-Columbian, Western, and contemporary American art. The grounds are also home to the Mexican Heritage Museum in an 1850's adobe house, La Casa Cordova, and the mission revival J. Knox Corbett House. **520/624-2333** $

Among all the states, Arizona has the largest percentage of its land set aside and designated as Indian lands.

M El Maplais

R White Sands

P Albuquerque

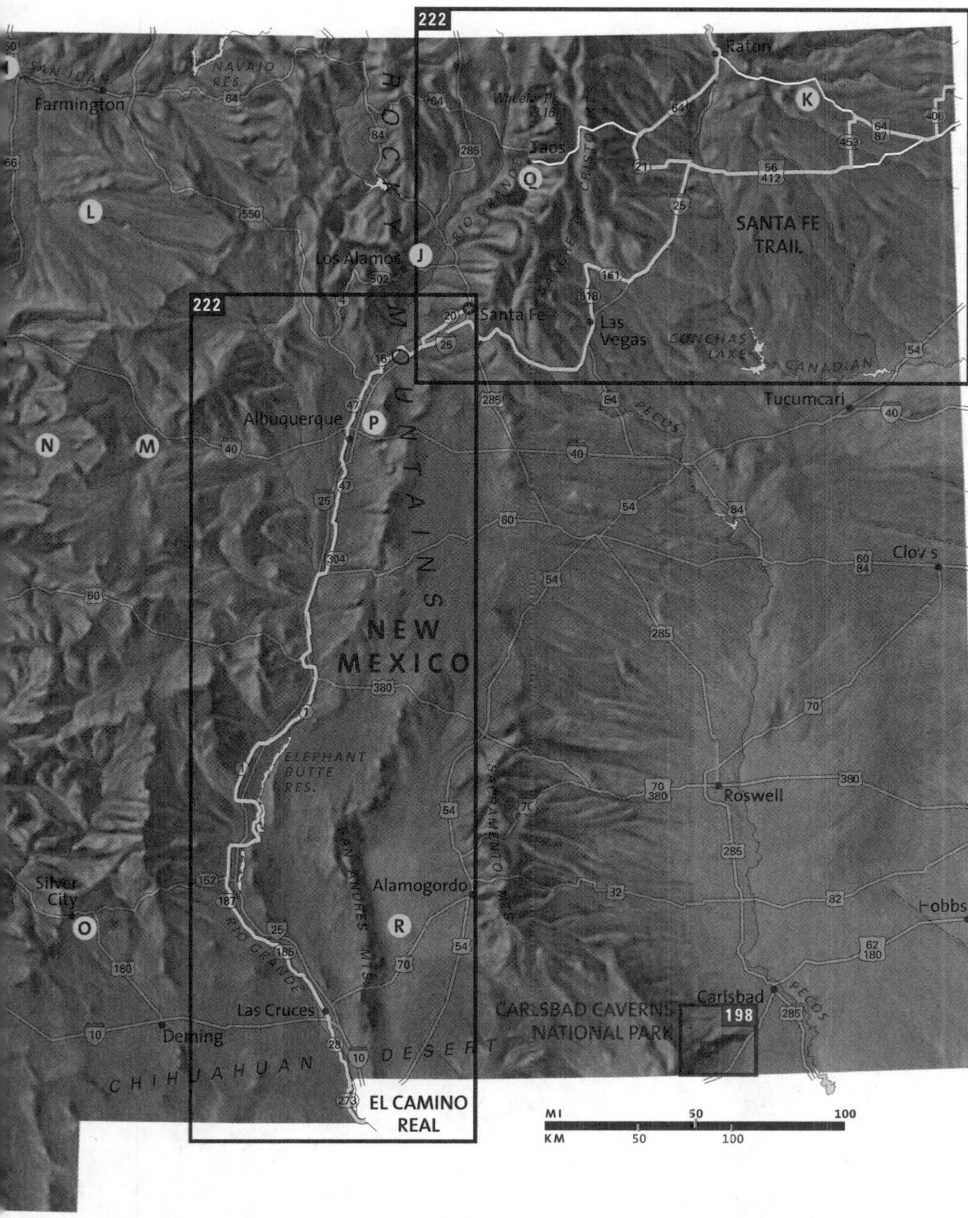

NEW MEXICO

J AZTEC RUINS NATIONAL MONUMENT

Pg. 130, B4. **Aztec.** One of the largest Anasazi towns ever found, this one was occupied between A.D. 1100–1300. Misnamed by early settlers, who assumed the dwellings were Aztec, the partially excavated ruins and restored kiva, or ceremonial room, can be seen on a self-guided tour. **505/334-6174** $

J BANDELIER NATIONAL MONUMENT

Pg. 130, D7. **Los Alamos.** A major portion of this 32,000-acre area set among spectacular mountains, mesas and canyons, is designated wilderness. Anasazi Indians lived here from A.D. 1200-1500. In Frijoles Canyon, you will see their dwellings carved out of the soft volcanic turf and pictographs and petroglyphs. Hiking trails are rugged but lead to great vistas. **505/672-0343** $

K CAPULIN VOLCANO

Pg. 130, B11. **Capulin.** This dormant volcano last erupted approximately 10,000 years ago. Its strikingly symmetrical cinder cone rises more than 1,500 feet from the ground. Visitors can spiral up the mountain on a paved road to the volcano's rim where—on clear days—they can see four states. **505/278-2201** $

L CHACO CULTURE NATIONAL HISTORIC PARK.

Pg. 130, C4. **Nageezi.** From A.D. 900 to 1150, Chaco Canyon was a major center of Anasazi culture. Researchers speculate that Chaco Canyon was once the center of a vast, complex, and interdependent civilization in the American Southwest. The site includes eight major towns, a visitor center, and a campground. **505/786-7014** $

M EL MALPAIS NATIONAL MONUMENT AND NATIONAL CONSERVATION AREA

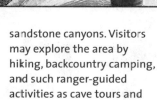

Pg. 130, F4. These two areas encompass 376,000 acres of volcanic formations and sandstone canyons. Visitors may explore the area by hiking, backcountry camping, and such ranger-guided activities as cave tours and nature walks. **505/783-4774**

N EL MORRO NATIONAL MONUMENT

Pg. 130, F4. Here, on the ancient trail taken by the Conquistadors from Santa Fe to Zuni, is the towering cliff that served as the guest book of New Mexico. First are Anasazi petroglyphs. Then Don Juan de Oñate carved his name in 1605; others followed. Camping, hiking and bird watching are popular activities now. **505/783-4226** $

O GILA CLIFF DWELLINGS NATIONAL MONUMENT

Pg. 131, L3. **Silver City.** The site has the ruins of 42 rooms in six caves, high on a cliff face. The dwellings were occupied by the Mogollon Indians about A.D. 1300. A one-mile trail leads up a canyon to the ruins. **505/536-9461** $

P OLD TOWN

Pg. 130, F6. **Albuquerque.** Old Town, the site of the city's original 1706 settlement, is a visible record of a Spanish colonial past. Old Town features specialty shops, galleries, restaurants, and artwork, many in historic buildings. The Albuquerque Museum, which focuses on the city's Spanish heritage, and the New Mexico Museum of Natural History, which has life-size dinosaurs, are nearby. **505/842-9918**

Q TAOS

Pg. 130, C8. Many artists and craftspeople live and work amid Taos' stimulating mixture of peoples and cultures: Native American, Spanish-American, and Anglo-American. Visitors can see evidence of all three in the city's architecture and museums ($), such as the Kit Carson Home and the Ernest Bulmenschein Home. **505/758-3873**

R WHITE SANDS NATIONAL MONUMENT

Pg. 131, L7. **Alamogordo.** These dazzling white dunes are a challenge to plants and animals. The lizards and mice, for example, are white to blend in. Dunes shaped by the wind can rise to 60 feet—the largest gypsum dune field in the world. The geology is explained at the visitor center. There are hiking and driving trails as well as picnic areas. **505/672-2599** $

DOLLAR WI$E

- Get the most gas mileage out of your car by making sure it is properly tuned-up, and keeping your tires properly inflated.
- Stick around your hotel for a day or two and take advantage of any amenities offered, such as a swimming pool or exercise facilities; not only will you save money, it will give you a chance to unwind.
- Save on lodging costs in the Grand Canyon by staying in the park's gateway village of Tusayan, or in outlying cities such as Flagstaff or Cameron.
- Those with RVs can camp for free on government land in Quartzite, AZ, the center of one of the largest flea markets in the country.
- Native American artisans gather every morning and sit shoulder-to-shoulder under the long, covered portal fronting the Palace of the Governors in Santa Fe. It's a wonderful place to shop for silver and turquoise jewelry and enjoy the Plaza, built in 1610. It's one of the oldest landmarks in the U.S. and there's no admission charge.

January

Fiesta Bowl
Tempe, AZ
Classic college football game.
480/350-0900

Native American Festival
Litchfield Park, AZ
Approx 100 Native American craft vendors. Native American dancing and other authentic entertainment both days.
623/932-2260

February

Old West Gun Show
Deming, NM
Western art facts, jewelry; military equipment, guns, ammunition.
800/848-4955

March

Indian Fair and Market
Phoenix, AZ
Native American artisans, demonstrations, dances, native foods.
602/252-8840

May

Spring Arts Festival
Taos, NM
Three-wk festival of visual, performing, and literary arts.
800/732-8267

Zuni Artists' Exhibition
Flagstaff, AZ
The Museum of Northern Arizona.
928/774-5213

June

New Mexico Arts & Crafts Fair
Albuquerque, NM
Exhibits and demonstrations by craftsworkers representing Spanish, Native American, and other North American cultures.
800/284-2282

July

Flagstaff Festival of the Arts
Flagstaff, AZ
Symphonic/pops concerts, chamber music; theater; dance; art exhibits; poetry; film classics.
520/774-7750

UFO Encounters Festival
Roswell, NM
UFO Expo trade show, alien chase, alien parade, costume contest, guest speeches.
505/625-9495

August

San Juan County Fair
Farmington, NM
Parade; rodeo; fiddlers' contest; chili cook-off; exhibits.
800/448-1240

September

Santa Fe Fiesta
Santa Fe, NM
This ancient folk festival, dating back to 1712, features historical pageantry, religious observances, arts and crafts shows, street dancing. Celebrates the reconquest of Santa Fe by Don Diego de Vargas in 1692.
505/988-7575

October

Arizona State Fair
Phoenix, AZ
602/252-6771

Aspenfest
Ruidoso, NM
Including motorcycle convention, official state chili cook-off, arts and crafts.
800/253-2255

Tucson: Meet Yourself
Tucson, AZ
Commemorates Tucson's heritage with a torchlight pageant, Native American dances, and fiesta.
520/806-9004

Legendary, larger-than-life Texas is unlike any other state in the union. From Dallas' Fair Park to the 400 miles of the Gulf of Mexico shoreline, the Lone Star State wrangles the hearts of its visitors. Significant creature comforts are available in urbane Dallas, Fort Worth, and Houston, and a cowboy welcome awaits visitors in Abilene, Laredo, and Austin. In Oklahoma, tourism is one of the largest industries, but it was oil that made it a rich state—first during the Big Boom around Oklahoma City in the 1920s and 1930s, and later in western Oklahoma in the 1980s. Today, visitors from around the country come here to view fine art at Tulsa's Philbrook Museum and enjoy the outdoors at Chickasaw National Recreation Area in Sulphur. A former commercial district, Bricktown, in Oklahoma City, is now a fashionable dining and entertainment area.

A vast plateau, the High Plains of the Texas Panhandle and western Oklahoma are the southern extreme of the Great Plains. Many major rivers traverse these states: The Red River forms much of the Oklahoma-Texas border as it drains into the Mississippi; and the Rio Grande, one of the longest and most historic rivers in North America, forms about 1,250-miles of the U.S.-Mexico border.

Free $ Finds

Dallas Museum of Art
Includes pre-Columbian, 18th- and 19th-century, and contemporary American art; African and Asian art; European painting and sculpture. **214/922-1200**

Imperial Holly Corporation, Houston
Guided tours of all processes of sugar cane refining. **281/491-9181**

Edison Plaza Museum, Beaumont, TX
Largest collection of Thomas A. Edison artifacts west of the Mississippi and the only electric industry museum in the South. **409/839-3089**

Wilson Historic District Walking Tour, Dallas
Scenic guided tour of one of Dallas' oldest neighborhoods. Tours begin at the Wilson Carriage House. **214/746-6600**

The Alamo, San Antonio
Defended to the death by Texas heroes in the 1836 battle. The former church (now the shrine) and the Long Barracks Museum (formerly the Convento) are all that remain of the original mission buildings. **210/225-1391**

Sam Houston Memorial Museum Complex, Huntsville, TX
Eight-structure complex surrounding a 15-acre park. Exhibits with artifacts pertaining to the Republic of Texas and relating to Houston and his family. **936/294-1832**

Nellie Johnstone Oil Well, Bartlesville, OK
Replica of the original rig, the first commercial oil well in the state. Located on an 83-acre park with a low water dam on the Caney River.

Martin Park Nature Center, Oklahoma City
More than 180 species of birds and local wildlife on 140 acres. **405/755-0676**

Gene Autry Oklahoma Museum, Gene Autry
Collection of Old West memorabilia, with an emphasis on famed Western movie star Gene Autry. **580/294-3047**

Oklahoma Jazz Hall of Fame, Tulsa
Devoted to gospel, jazz, and blues musicians with Oklahoma ties. Includes audio, video, and photographic material about featured artists, as well as a Hall of Fame into which musicians are inducted each June. **918/596-1001**

Sequoyah's Cabin, Sallisaw, OK
Historic one-room log cabin built by Sequoyah, famous Cherokee who created an 86-character alphabet for the Cherokee language. **918/775-2413**

Pawnee Bill Ranch Site, Pawnee, OK
House of Pawnee Bill, completed in 1910; 14 rooms with original furnishings. **918/762-2513**

Ⓐ Austin

Ⓑ Fair Park

Ⓒ Fort Worth Stockyards

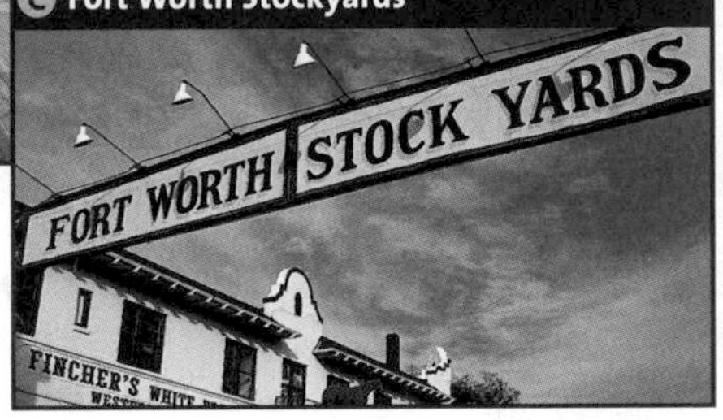

TEXAS

Ⓐ AUSTIN
Pg. 162, N17. Capitol of Texas, Austin has sites such as the Elisabet Ney Museum, Ziker Botanical Garden, the O. Henry Home and Museum, and the Greek revival governor's mansion. The city has its own symphony, ballet, and opera as well as the cornerstone campus of the University of Texas with the Lyndon B Johnson Library and Museum, and the Henry Ransom Humanities Research Center with more than 300 paintings and ancient sculptures. **512/478-0098**

Ⓑ FAIR PARK
Pg. 162, H17. **Dallas.** Art deco buildings constructed in 1936 for the Texas Centennial distinguish this 277-acre entertainment park that includes the Cotton Bowl Stadium, the African-American Museum, the Science Place ($), the Dallas Aquarium ($), and Music Hall. It is also home to the annual Texas state fair, one of the world's largest expositions, held in the fall. **214/670-8400**

Ⓒ FORT WORTH STOCKYARDS NATIONAL HISTORIC DISTRICT
Pg. 162, H17. **Fort Worth.** Renovated buildings house Western-style retail shops, nightclubs, and restaurants. Favorite stops include the Stockyards Museum, Billy Bob's Texas, a family fun center with live entertainment; and Old Trail Driver's Park. A restored 1896 Tarantula excursion steam train will take you to the stockyards from nearby Grapevine and back. **817/624-4741** $

Ⓓ GUADALUPE MOUNTAINS NATIONAL PARK
Pg. 161, K4. **Pine Springs.** Standing like an island in the desert, these mountains—a favorite with hikers—hold a 250 million-year-old fossilized reef and Guadalupe Peak, the highest point in Texas. The park has deep canyons, desert lowlands, unusual flora and fauna, and more than 80 miles of hiking trails. **915/828-3251**

Ⓔ PADRE ISLAND NATIONAL SEASHORE
Pg. 163, T17. **Corpus Christi.** Stretching 113 miles along the Gulf Shore from Corpus Christi to a point near Port Isabel, Padre Island is rarely more than three miles wide. The National Seashore—70 miles of undeveloped sandy beach and dunes—offers swimming, surf fishing, camping, picnicking, and, especially, bird watching: more than 350 species of birds inhabit the island or are seasonal visitors. **512/937-2621**

Ⓕ SPACE CENTER HOUSTON
Pg. 163, P21. **Houston.** Visitors can take a guided tram excursion through the Johnson Space Center facilities, including Rocket Park, Missioin Control Center, the vacuum chamber, astronaut training areas, and an exhibit of early space craft and space suits. **281/244-2100** $

Ⓖ STRAND HISTORIC DISTRICT
Pg. 163, Q22. **Galveston.** The Strand, once known as the "Wall Street of the Southwest," contains more than 50 restored 19th-century commercial structures interspersed with apartments, restaurants, shops, and galleries. A visitor center gives information for self-guided tours. **409/766-7068**

Ⓗ SUNDANCE SQUARE ENTERTAINMENT DISTRICT
Pg. 162, H17. **Fort Worth.** This lively entertainment district in the heart of downtown has something for everyone. There are a number of boutiques, theatres, restaurants and galleries for visitors to enjoy, as well as performances by well-known celebrities at Bass Hall. **817/339-7777**

Ⓘ TEXAS STATE AQUARIUM
Pg. 163, T17. **Corpus Christi.** Ten major indoor and outdoor exhibit areas focus on marine plant and animal life indigenous to the Gulf of Mexico. The aquarium holds more than 250 species of sea life in approximately 350,000 gallons of saltwater. **361/881-1200** $

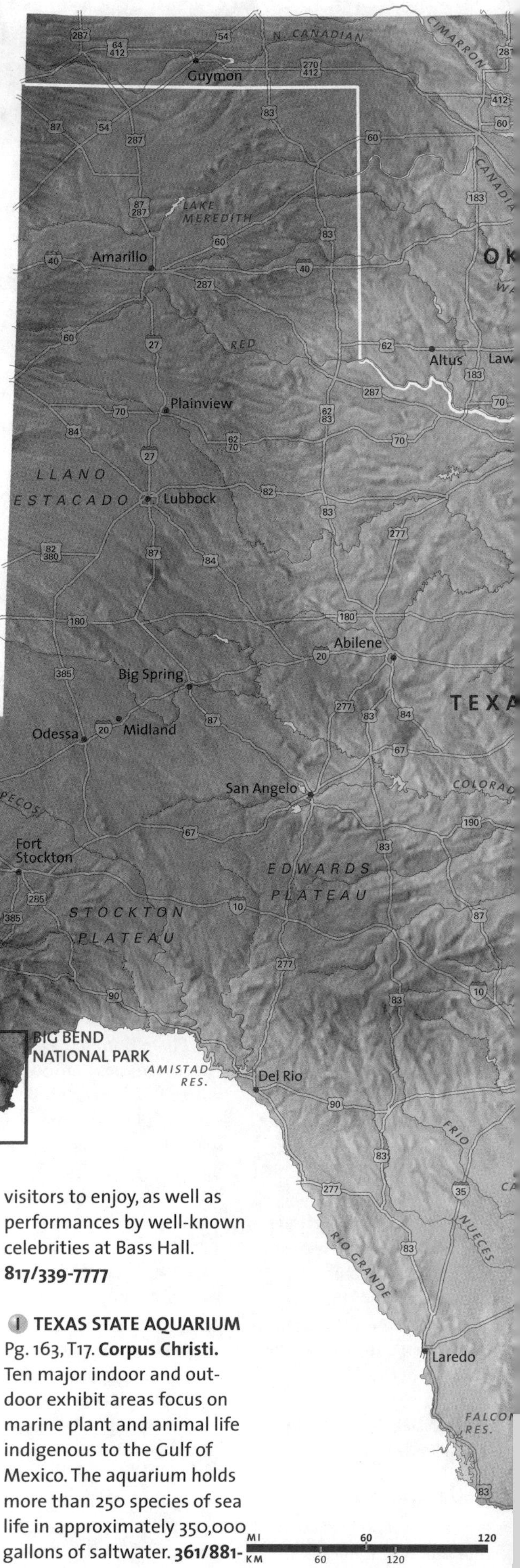

J Cherokee Heritage Center

K Chickasaw National Recreation Area

M Cowboy Hall of Fame

O Philbrook Museum of Art

Oklahoma has produced more astronauts than any other state.

OKLAHOMA

J CHEROKEE HERITAGE CENTER

Pg. 147, D18. **Tahlequah.** Dedicated to the preservation and promotion of Cherokee history and culture, the center includes a 1,500-seat outdoor amphitheater where the drama, *Trail of Tears*, is presented, a 1650 Tsa-La-Gi ancient village, Adams Corner Rural Village and Farm, and the Cherokee National Museum. **918/456-6007** $

K CHICKASAW NATIONAL RECREATION AREA

Pg. 147, H14. **Sulphur.** Outdoor lovers will find campgrounds and picnic areas, as well as water sports and fishing for catfish, largemouth bass, sunfish, crappie, and walleyed pike. There are natural history exhibits at Travertine Nature Center. **580/622-3165** $

L GILCREASE MUSEUM

Pg. 147, D16. **Tulsa.** Founded by Thomas Gilcrease, an oil man of Creek descent, the museum exhibits works by Frederic Remington, Thomas Moran, Charles Russell, George Catlin as well as Winslow Homer, John Singer Sargent, and John James Audubon. Native American artifacts range from 12,000 years ago to the present. The library houses some 90,000 items, including many rare books and the earliest known letter sent to Europe from the New World. The museum also has beautiful grounds with historic theme gardens. **918/596-2700** $

M NATIONAL COWBOY HALL OF FAME AND WESTERN HERITAGE CENTER

Pg. 147, F13. **Oklahoma City.** This complex celebrates America's Western heritage with a recreated turn-of-the-century western street, and three major halls of fame: the American Cowboy Gallery, the American Rodeo Gallery, and the Western Entertainment Gallery. **405/478-2250** $

N OMNIPLEX

Pg. 147, F13. **Oklahoma City.** Several museums share this site: The International Photography Hall of Fame and Museum, featuring one of the world's largest photographic murals; the Kirkpatrick Science and Air Space Museum; and the Red Earth Indian Center, with exhibits and programs encouraging appreciation of Native American cultures. **405/602-6664** $

O PHILBROOK MUSEUM OF ART

Pg. 147, D16. **Tulsa.** The permanent collection includes Italian Renaissance, 19th-century English, American, and Native American paintings; Native American baskets and pottery; Chinese jades and decorative arts; Southeast Asian tradeware; and African sculpture. The museum is housed in an Italian Renaissance-style villa on 23 acres of formal and informal sculpture gardens. **918/749-7941** $

P WOOLAROC

Pg. 147, B16. **Bartlesville.** This nature preserve and museum covers 3,600 acres and is home to herds of American bison, longhorn cattle, Scottish Highland cattle, elk, deer, and other native wildlife. At the museum are paintings by Charles Russell, Frederic Remington, and other great Western artists, exhibits on the development of America, and artifacts of several Native American tribes, pioneers, and cowboys. **918/336-0307** $

DOLLAR WI$E

- Use Houston's 37 free trolleys to get around; they link office buildings to major attractions, including shopping and theater.
- Visit the Tulsa Zoo on Mother's Day or Father's Day, when admission is half-price for everyone.
- An enjoyable, no-cost way to see central San Antonio is to park and take the pleasant River Walk, with its park-like setting and outdoor cafes. It's close to the famous Alamo, as well.
- Visit www.traveltex.com for money-saving coupons on lodgings and attractions throughout the state.
- The Texas Association of Campground Owners offers a free booklet describing commercial campgrounds, which includes a "Texas Saver Card" for discounts of 10% or 15% at many facilities.

January

International Finals Rodeo
Oklahoma City
International Pro Rodeo Association's top 15 cowboys and cowgirls compete in seven events to determine world championships.
405/948-6700

April

Azalea Festival
Muskogee
Parade, art shows, garden tours, entertainment.
888/687-6137

Festival of the Arts
Oklahoma City, OK
International foods, entertainment, children's learning and play area; craft market; artists display their work.
405/270-4848

Fiesta San Antonio
San Antonio, TX
Celebrating Texas heroes since 1891 with three major parades (one on the San Antonio River), sports, and food. More than 150 events held throughout city.
210/227-5191

May

Magnolia Festival
Durant, OK
Crafts, rides, art show, entertainment.
580/924-0848

June

Boerne Berges Fest
San Antonio, TX
German Festival of the Hills; continuous German and country and western entertainment, arts and crafts, horse races, pig races, parade, 10K walk, special events.
830/249-8000

Red Earth
Oklahoma City
Native American heritage and culture featuring dancers and artists from most North American tribes. Dance competition, arts festival.
405/427-5228

July

Independence Day Celebration & Fireworks Extravaganza
South Padre Island, TX
956/761-3000

August

Tulsa Powwow
Tulsa, OK
918/744-1113

September

Southwest Festival of the Arts
Weatherford, OK
Crafts, performing arts, concerts.
580/772-7744

State Fair of Oklahoma
Oklahoma City
405/948-6700

State Fair of Texas
Dallas, TX
214/565-9931

October

Tulsa State Fair
Tulsa, OK
918/744-1113

November

Fiestas Navidenas
San Antonio, TX
Christmas festival; bands; Mexican folk dances; Christmas foods.
210/207-8600

December

Harbor Lights Celebration
Corpus Christi, TX
Lighting of boats in marina. Lighting of 70-ft tree of lights. Children's parade. Gingerbread and holiday tree village.
361/985-1555

CO 76
UT 165
CO 233
UT 247

Free Finds $

Ashcroft Ghost Town, Aspen
Partially restored ghost town and mining camp features 1880s buildings, hotel. **970/925-3721**

Peterson Air & Space Museum, Colorado Springs
Display of 17 historic aircraft from WWII-present, plus exhibits on the history of the Air Force base. **719/556-4915**

Anheuser-Busch Brewery, Fort Collins, CO
Tour of the brewery that producer millions of barrels of Budweiser and other beers annually, including exhibits on the history of the company, a look at the brewing facilities, early beer advertising, and the famous Clydesdale horses. Free samples for those 21 and over. **970/490-4691**

Celestial Seasonings Tour of Tea, Boulder
Educational 45-minute factory tour of the largest herbal tea manufacturer in the US. Includes an art gallery of original illustrations from tea boxes, an extensive teapot collection, and an open tea bar offering samples of 47 different tea blends. **303/581-1202**

Downtown Denver Walking Tour, Denver
A guided stroll among the city's sites, including the State Capitol and 16th Street Mall. **303/892-1112**

World Figure Skating Hall of Fame and Museum, Colorado Springs
Exhibits on history of figure skating; art, memorabilia, library, skate gallery, video collection. **719/635-5200**

Beehive Home, Salt Lake City
Built in 1854, this Greek-revival home was the official residence of Brigham Young. Furnished with antiques and personal belongings of the Young family. **801/363-5466**

Brigham Young University Tour, Salt Lake City
Tour of one of the country's largest privately owned universities. **801/378-4678**

Monte L. Bean Life Science Museum, Provo, UT
Exhibits and collections of insects, fish, amphibians, reptiles, birds, mammals, and plants. **801/378-5051**

Kimball Art Center, Park City, UT
Exhibits in various media by local and regional artists. **435/649-8882**

Ouray National Wildlife Refuge, Vernal, UT
Waterfowl nesting marshes; desert scenery; self-guided auto tour. **435/789-0351**

Snow-dusted peaks, fragrant meadows carpeted in brilliant wildflowers, and rushing rivers define the Southern Rockies in spring. Colorado's resort towns suit many moods, from the Bavarian charm of Vail, the art and music of Aspen, and the Western flavor of Telluride to the relaxed personalities of Crested Butte and Steamboat Springs. Rocky Mountain National Park's dizzying heights offer picture-perfect vistas and the magnificent Bridal Veil and Seven Falls. Utah's Monument Valley has served as the backdrop for many Westerns; Sundance is home to Robert Redford's annual film festival; and Park City's superb skiing made it the venue for the 2002 Winter Olympics. Bryce Canyon's orange rock formations spark the imagination, while four states meet in one spot in the Navajo Nation's Four Corners landmark.

The Wasatch Range and Rocky Mountains run like twin spines down the centers of neighboring Utah and Colorado, separated by the Colorado Plateau. To the west of the peaks is the vast expanse known as the great Basin; to the east, the Great Plains.

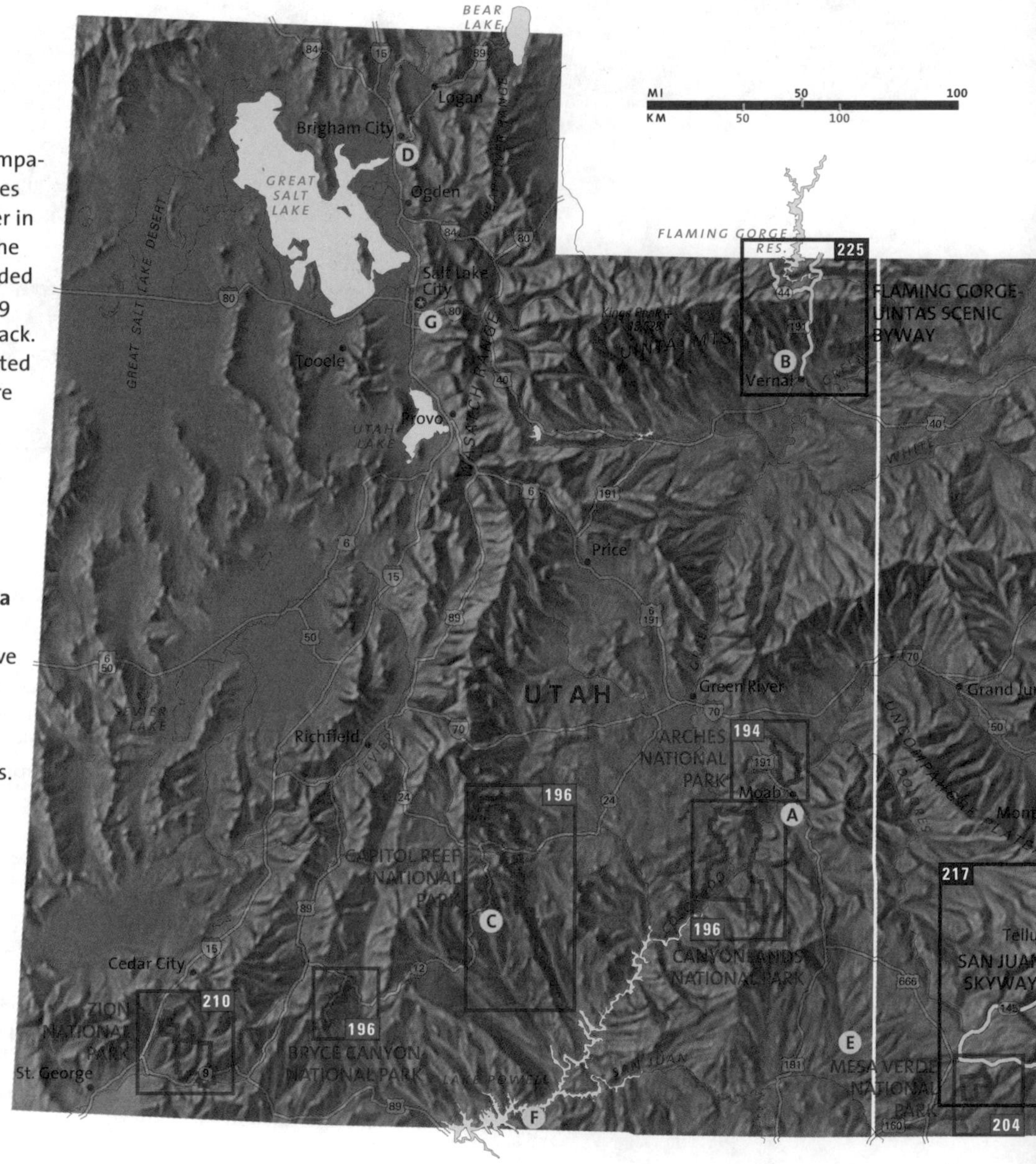

UTAH

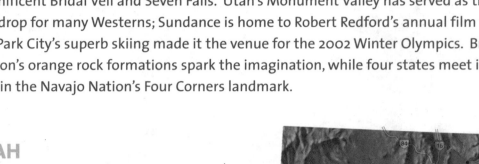

Ⓐ CANYONLANDS AT NIGHT
Pg. 165, K8. **Moab.** This sound and light show takes place every night from May through October. Spectators cruise up the Colorado River as music sets the mood while shadows dance on the canyon walls and narrators tell Indian legends. **435/259-8825** $

Ⓑ DINOSAUR NATIONAL MONUMENT
Pg. 165, G8. **Vernal.** Paleontologist Earl Douglass discovered several nearly complete dinosaur bones here at the border of Utah and Colorado in 1909. Since then, excavations here revealed 14 species of dinosaur from the Jurassic-period. Activities for visitors include fishing, hiking, kayaking, and whitewater rafting. **970/374-3000** $

Ⓒ GLEN CANYON NATIONAL RECREATION AREA
Pg. 165, L5. **Boulder.** Formed by the Glen Canyon Dam, the lake stretches for hundreds of miles from Lees Ferry in Arizona to the Orange Cliffs of southern Utah, providing a pleasure-filled recreation area of fishing, boating, swimming, and camping. **435/684-2243** $

Ⓓ GOLDEN SPIKE NATIONAL HISTORIC SITE
Pg. 165, D4. **Brigham City.** On May 10, 1869, executives from the Union Pacific and Central Pacific met here to drive ceremonial golden spikes into the tie that completed the nation's first transcontinental railroad. Replicas of the two companies' locomotive engines stand facing each other in the same spot as did the original, and a self-guided auto route runs along 9 miles of the original track. Films and exhibits related to the historic event are offered at the visitor center. **435/471-2209** $

Ⓔ HOVENWEEP NATIONAL MONUMENT
Pg. 165, N8. **Montezuma Creek.** The natural monument protects five prehistoric, Pueblo-era ruins, along the Utah-Colorado border of mesa tops and canyons. Multi-story towers perched on canyon rims and balanced on boulders attest to the skills of the builders. The Square Tower group offers a visitor center, campground, and interpretive trail. **970/562-4282** $

Ⓕ RAINBOW BRIDGE NATIONAL MONUMENT
Pg. 165, N6. **Rainbow Bridge National Monument.** Rising from the eastern shore of Lake Powell, this is the largest natural rock bridge in the world. It stands 290 feet tall, spans 275 feet, and stretches 33 feet at the top. Rainbow Bridge is higher than the nation's capitol dome and nearly as long as a football field. The enormous monument is reachable by a cruise boat from Lake Powell or by a two-day hike. **520/608-6404**

Ⓖ TEMPLE SQUARE
Pg. 165, F5. **Salt Lake City.** This beautifully landscaped 10-acre plot of ground in downtown Salt Lake City is one of the state's most visited attractions. The granite Temple, the centerpiece of the Square, is still used for sacred ordinances. Adjacent to the Temple is the domed Tabernacle, home of the famous Mormon Tabernacle Choir and the great Tabernacle organ. **801/240-1245**

Ⓒ Glen Canyon

Ⓓ Golden Spike

Ⓕ Rainbow Bridge

Ⓖ Temple Square

Kanab is known as Utah's Little Hollywood because of the large number of motion pictures that are filmed in the area.

COLORADO

Ⓗ ASPEN
Pg. 76, F9. With four ski mountains surrounding it—Aspen Mountain, Snowmass, Buttermilk, and Aspen Highlands—the city of Aspen is a popular destination for its world-class skiing and snow activities. However, this winter playground also offers an impressive list of year-round activities. In summer, visitors enjoy hiking, hang gliding, and mountain biking, as well as Aspen's many outdoor festivals, such as the Aspen Music Festival and the Aspen Food and Wine Classic. **970/925-1940**

Ⓘ BLACK CANYON OF THE GUNNISON
Pg. 76, H9. **Gunnison.** A combination of dark weathered rock and lack of sunlight due to the narrowness of the canyon gorge (1,100 feet) give

Denver lays claim to the invention of the cheeseburger. The trademark for the name Cheeseburger was awarded in 1935 to Louis Ballast.

this monument its name. Twelve of the most spectacular miles of the rugged gorge of the Gunnison River slice down to 2,660 feet deep. Many of the overlooks are easily accessed by car and very short walks, and interpretive programs are offered all summer. **970/641-2337** $

guest rooms with marble sinks and carved headboards. **303/569-2555**

L GLENWOOD SPRINGS
Pg. 76, E8. Glenwood Springs is a popular year-round resort town where visitors can ski and swim in a single day. The town is the gateway to White River National Forest, and Aspen and Vail are less than an hour's drive. Excellent game-hunting and fishing country surrounds it, and camping areas are sprinkled throughout the region. **970/945-6589**

M GREAT SAND DUNE NATIONAL MONUMENT
Pg. 77, L12. **Alamosa.** The Great Sand Dunes, the tallest in North America, lie along the base of the Sangre de Cristo Mountains on the floor of the San Luis Valley. The dunes, some of which reach more than 700 feet, are trapped by the mountains, providing endless changes in color and mood. There are trails for hiking and nature walks, as well as opportunities for skiing in winter. **719/378-2312** $

J Garden of the Gods

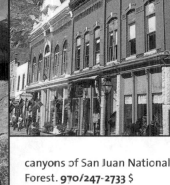

K Georgetown, CO

O Red Rocks Park

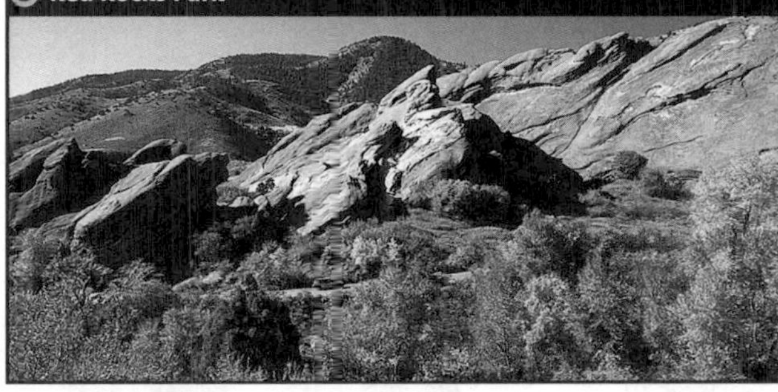

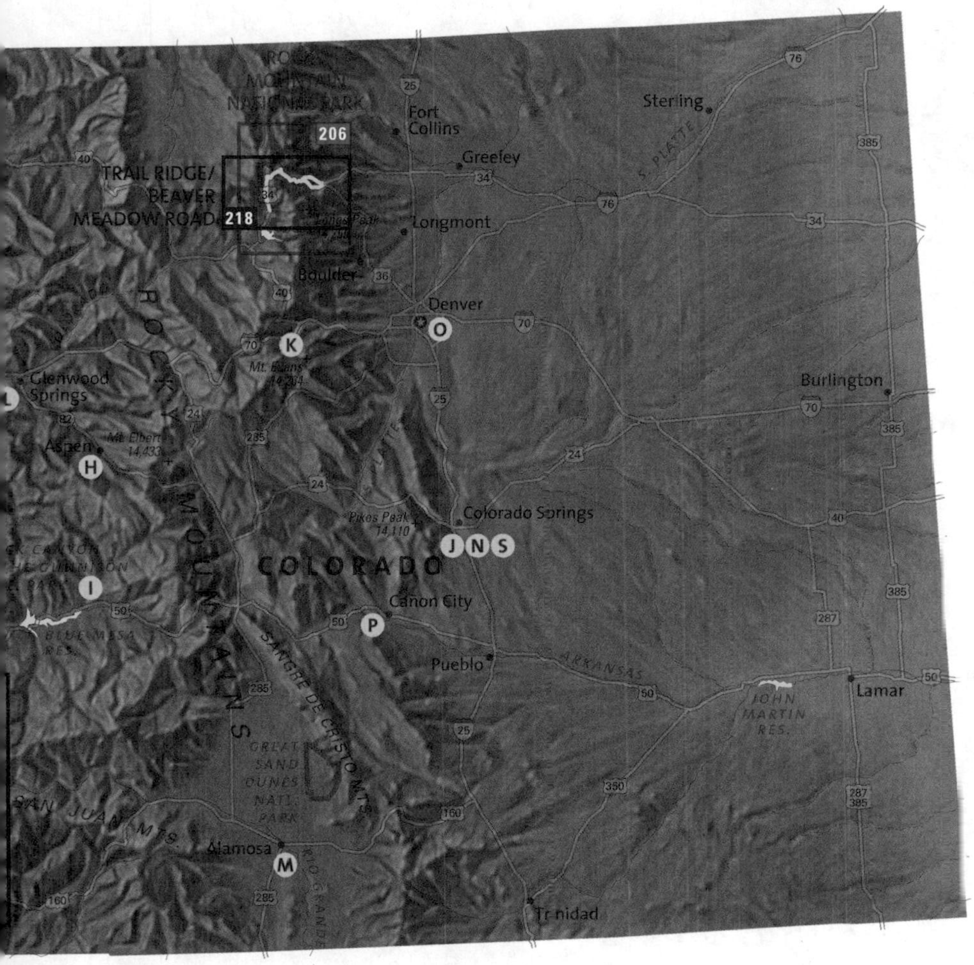

J GARDEN OF THE GODS PARK
Pg. 77, G14. **Colorado Springs.** With its towering sandstone rock formations set against a backdrop of Pikes Peak, the Garden of the Gods is the most visited attraction in the region. Aside from breathtaking views, it offers visitors rock climbing, hiking and horseback riding. **719/634-6666**

K GEORGETOWN
Pg. 77, E12. Named for George Griffith, who discovered gold in this valley in 1859, the area is known for its gold, silver, copper, lead, and zinc production. The Georgetown-Silver Plume National Historic Landmark District features more than 200 Victorian buildings. Restored Hamill House has converted gaslights and an outhouse topped with a cupola, while the Hotel de Paris, now a museum, features former

N PIKES PEAK
Pg. 77, G14. **Colorado Springs.** At the summit of this peak, Katharine Lee Bates was overwhelmed by the open skies, fields, and the majestic Rocky Mountains and inspired to write "America the Beautiful." The Manitou and Pikes Peak Railway, the nation's highest railroad, winds through lush mountain scenery on the way to the summit. Popular annual events are the Pikes Peak Marathon and the Pikes Peak Auto Hill Climb, called the Race to the Clouds. **719/684-9383** $

O RED ROCKS PARK
Pg. 77, E14. **Denver.** Located along the eastern slope of the Rocky Mountains, Red Rocks Park contains Denver's most fantastic natural rock formations. Visitors may explore the park's breathtaking scenery by biking, hiking or walking one of the three main trails, such as The Trading Post Loop. At 1.4 miles long, this trail is 6,280 feet above sea level and winds through spectacular rock formations and valleys. The park's 9,500-seat natural Amphitheater is formed by two, 300-foot monoliths that provide not only a majestic setting for performances, but acoustic perfection, as well. **303/697-8801**

P ROYAL GORGE
Pg. 77, J13. **Canon City.** This magnificent canyon features cliffs that rise more than 1,000 feet above the Arkansas River. Royal Gorge Suspension Bridge, 1,053 feet above the river, is the highest in the world. Royal Gorge Incline Railway, the world's steepest, carries passengers 1,550 feet to the bottom of the canyon and a 2,200-foot aerial tramway glides across it. **719/275-7507** $

Q SILVERTON DURANGO NARROW GAUGE RAILROAD
Pg. 76, M7. **Durango.** America's last regularly scheduled narrow-gauge passenger train, in service since 1882, runs between Durango and Silverton, using original passenger coaches and steam engines. The 45-mile trip passes over spectacular southwest Colorado Rocky Mountain scenery, through the Canyon of Rio de Las Animas and the breathtaking canyons of San Juan National Forest. **970/247-2733** $

R TELLURIDE
Pg. 76, K7. This picturesque town, located at the base of the San Juan Mountains, offers endless activities and adventures. Legendary slopes such as See Forever, Prospect Bowl, and Spiral Stairs offer spectacular skiing, and countless lakes, streams and peaks provide excellent opportunities for fly-fishing, hiking and biking. Visitors are also drawn to Telluride's arts and culture scene, which comes alive through the many film, music and dance festival held here.

S U.S. AIR FORCE ACADEMY
Pg. 77, G14. **Colorado Springs.** Cadets undergo their four-year academic, military, and physical training on these 18,500 acres at the foot of the Rampart Range of the Rocky Mountains. Cadet Wing marches may be watched from a wall near The Chapel during the academic year. Visitors may tour this 150-foot Chapel, which resembles a phalanx of fighter jets shooting up into the sky. **719/333-7742** R

S U.S. Air Force Chapel

DOLLAR WI$E

- Consider visiting national parks during the low season; prices of lodgings near national parks drop 25% or more in the fall and winter.
- Cross-country ski trip are usually cheaper than downhill ski vacations. You can pay as little as $7 for a daily trail pass instead of the $30 to $50 or more for a lift ticket.
- Ski at lower-profile locations; they tend to be less expensive.
- You don't have to take an expensive Jeep tour to enjoy the breathtaking scenery of the San Juan Mountains; the Million Dollar Highway is one of the most scenic routes in America, and can be handled by any vehicle.

January

Sundance Film Festival
Park City, UT
Robert Redford's annual independent film showcase.
801/322-1700

February

Colorado's Performance Poetry Festival
Salida, CO
Performances, troubadours, open mikes, workshops and more.
719/539-9847

March

Moab Skinny Tire Festival
Moab, UT
4 day festival of supported road bike rides for all levels in Moab's beautiful canyon country.
435/259-7882

May

Moab Arts Festival
Moab, UT
Annual art and craft show.
435/259-2742

June

Mountain Man Rendezvous
Kit Carson, CO
Men and women gather to participate in fur-trapping, Dutch-oven cookery, 19th-century craft-making, and black-powder shooting contests.
719/962-3532

Telluride Bluegrass Festival
Telluride, CO
Bluegrass, folk, and country musicians get together for outdoor concerts.
800/624-2422

July

Art Walk
Buena Vista, CO
Businesses feature local and guest artists. Open houses, demonstrations, entertainment and refreshments. Includes quilt show at the community center.
719/395-6612

August

Colorado State Fair
Pueblo, CO
Hispanic art show, a Fiesta parade, livestock and horse show, sand sculpture, pig races and much more.
800/876-4567

Festival of the American West
Wellsville, UT
A step back in time to celebrate the people and events that made the West.
800/225-3378

September

Utah Shakespearean Festival
Cedar City, UT
435/586-7880

November

Great Christmas Hall Artisan's Fair
Ft. Collins, CO
970/221-6735

Mistletoe Mall Boutique Craft Fair
Gunnison, UT
Features handmade items, crafts, gifts & food.
435/528-3564

Parade of Lights
Kane, UT
Beginning with the decorating of the boats, chili cooking contest, silent auction. Parade of decorated boats
435/684-3028

December

Annual Pinata Festival
Ephraim, UT
Pinata making, gifts, crafts and ethnic foods.
435/283-4747

WY 176
MT 122
ID 89
WY 248
MT 240
ID 234

Free Finds $

Teton Flood Museum, Rexburg, ID
Artifacts, photographs, and films document the 1976 flood caused by the collapse of the Teton Dam, which left 11 people dead and $1 billion in damage. **208/359-3063**

Idaho Museum of Natural History, Pocatello, ID
Features exhibits on Idaho fossils, especially large mammals of the Ice Age; Native American basketry and beadwork. **208/282-3168**

Luna House Museum, Lewiston, ID
On site of first hotel in town. **208/743-2535**

State Capitol, Boise
Neo-classical design, faced with Boise sandstone. Murals on fourth floor symbolically tell state's past, present, and future. **208/334-5174**

Frontier Town, Helena
Rustic pioneer village shaped with solid rock and built with giant logs. **406/442-4560**

Hungry Horse Dam and Power Plant, Columbia Falls, MT
One of the world's largest concrete dams (564 ft) is set in a wooded canyon near Glacier National Park. The 2,115-ft-long crest is crossed by a 30-ft-wide roadway. The reservoir is approximately 34 miles long and 3 1/2 miles at its widest point. Self-guided tours, pictorial and interactive displays; video. **406/387-5241**

Malstrom Air Force Base, Great Falls, MT
Home of the 43rd Air Refueling Wing and center of one of the largest intercontinental ballistic missile complexes in the world. Museum featuring historical military displays. Tours by appt. **406/731-4046**

Interagency Aerial Fire Control Center, West Yellowstone, MT
A US Forest Service facility. Guided tour by smoke-jumpers who explain firefighting techniques. **406/646-7691**

Buffalo Bill Dam & Visitor Center, Cody, WY
A 350-ft dam, originally called the Shoshone Dam. The name was changed in 1946 to honor Buffalo Bill, who helped raise money for its construction. The visitor center has a natural history museum, dam overlook, and gift shop. **307/527-6076**

Nicolaysen Art Museum and Discovery Center, Casper, WY
Features a diverse range of work from renowned artists. Includes a hands-on art-making studio that offer 10-15 different stations at which people of all ages can use their creativity. **307/235-5247**

The Northern Rockies are synonymous with wild beauty and thrilling adventure. With Hell's Canyon, the deepest river gorge in the country, and Shoshone Falls, higher than the more famous Niagara Falls, Idaho is a place of many natural wonders. Idaho City recalls its mining legacy; the capital, Boise, is full of pioneer reminders; and Sun Valley's elegance and charm attracts visitors from around the world. Wyoming is home to many firsts: the first national monument, Devils Tower, and the first national park, Yellowstone. Fossil Butte has the largest deposit of freshwater fish fossils in the Western Hemisphere, while Cheyenne is recognized for its Western art collections. Montana's Big Sky Country shares enchanting vistas in its renowned Glacier National Park. Visitors can also relive the Battle at Little Bighorn or take a whitewater raft ride.

Two great landforms meet in this rugged country of sky-high mountains and open prairies: the Rocky Mountains and the Great Plains. From the long ridge of the Continental Divide, great rivers like the Snake, Columbia and Missouri start their journeys either west, toward the Pacific Ocean, or east, toward the Gulf of Mexico.

A Boise

D Lava Hot Springs

IDAHO

A BOISE
Pg. 89, K2. Established during gold rush days, Boise is the largest city and capitol of Idaho. Its pioneer and military past may be explored at the Idaho Historical Museum ($), and the Idaho Military Museum. During the summer, the 1890's-style puffer-belly open air Boise Tour Train ($) leaves from here for a lively look at the town. **308/344-7777**

B CITY OF ROCKS NATIONAL RESERVE
Pg. 89, N5. **Almo.** This 25-square-mile area of granite spires and sculptured rock formations resembles a city carved from stone. The walls are inscribed with messages and names of westward-bound settlers, and remnants of the California Trail are still visible. Among the recreational opportunities offered here are world- class technical rock climbing, as well as mountain biking, hiking, cross country skiing and snowshoeing. **208/824-5519**

C HELL'S CANYON NATIONAL RECREATION AREA
Pg. 89, F2. **Grangeville.** Spanning the Idaho/Oregon border, Hell's Canyon is a popular recreation area. The Snake River rushes nearly 8,000 feet below Seven Devils rim. Dams have created lakes in formerly inaccessible areas that now provide boating, fishing, waterskiing, whitewater rafting and jet boat tours. **541/426-4978**

C Hell's Canyon

D LAVA HOT SPRINGS
Pg. 89, M8. More than three million gallons of steaming hot water course each day through these mineral pools fed by 30 different springs. Visitors may soak their troubles away and relax in one of the mineral pools, or take a vigorous swim in the Olympic -size swimming pool. **208/776-5221** $

E SUN VALLEY
Pg. 89, K4. This sun-drenched, bowl-shaped valley is one of the most famous resort towns in the world. Sheltered by surrounding ranges, it attracts both winter and summer visitors and offers nearly every imaginable recreational opportunity. Powder snow lasts until late spring, and there is hunting, mountain biking, and superb fly-fishing. **208/622-4111**

F TARGHEE NATIONAL FOREST
Pg. 89, J8. **Ashton.** Wilderness areas Jedediah Smith (adjacent to Grand Teton National Park) and Winegar Hole (a grizzly bear habitat bordering Yellowstone National Park) sprawl over 1.8 million acres. The area offers trout fishing on Henry's Fork of the Snake River and Henry's Lake Reservoir, big game hunting, camping, picnicking, and winter sports. **208/524-7500**

Montana has the largest grizzly bear population in the 48 states.

MONTANA

G BIG HOLE NATIONAL BATTLEFIELD
Pg. 122, J5. **Wisdom.** Fleeing the U.S. Army from what are now the states of Idaho and Oregon, five "nontreaty" bands of Nez Perce were attacked here before dawn on August 9, 1877, by U.S. troops and citizen volunteers. More than 655 acres of the battlefield are preserved today as a memorial to those who died here. **406/689-3155** $

H GRANT- KOHRS RANCH NATIONAL HISTORIC SITE
Pg. 122, G6. **Deer Lodge.**

I Helena, MT

H Grant-Kohrs Ranch

Established by Canadian fur trader John Grant, and American cattle baron Conrad Kohrs, the site commemorates the cattle industry. Maintained as a working ranch, the park has 90 buildings, including a blacksmith shop and a granary. Visitors can tour the house, barns, and bunkhouse, as well. **406/846-2070**

I HELENA
Pg. 122, F7. Montana's capital and fourth largest city, Helena was the site of one of the state's largest gold rushes. In 1864, a party of discouraged prospectors decided to explore a gulch—now Helena's Main Street—as their "last chance." The Last Chance Tour Train ($) provides informative and entertaining tours of the city, and The Museum of Gold Collection at Norwest Bank features displays of gold dust and nuggets as large as 244 ounces. **406/442-4120**

J Little Bighorn Battlefield

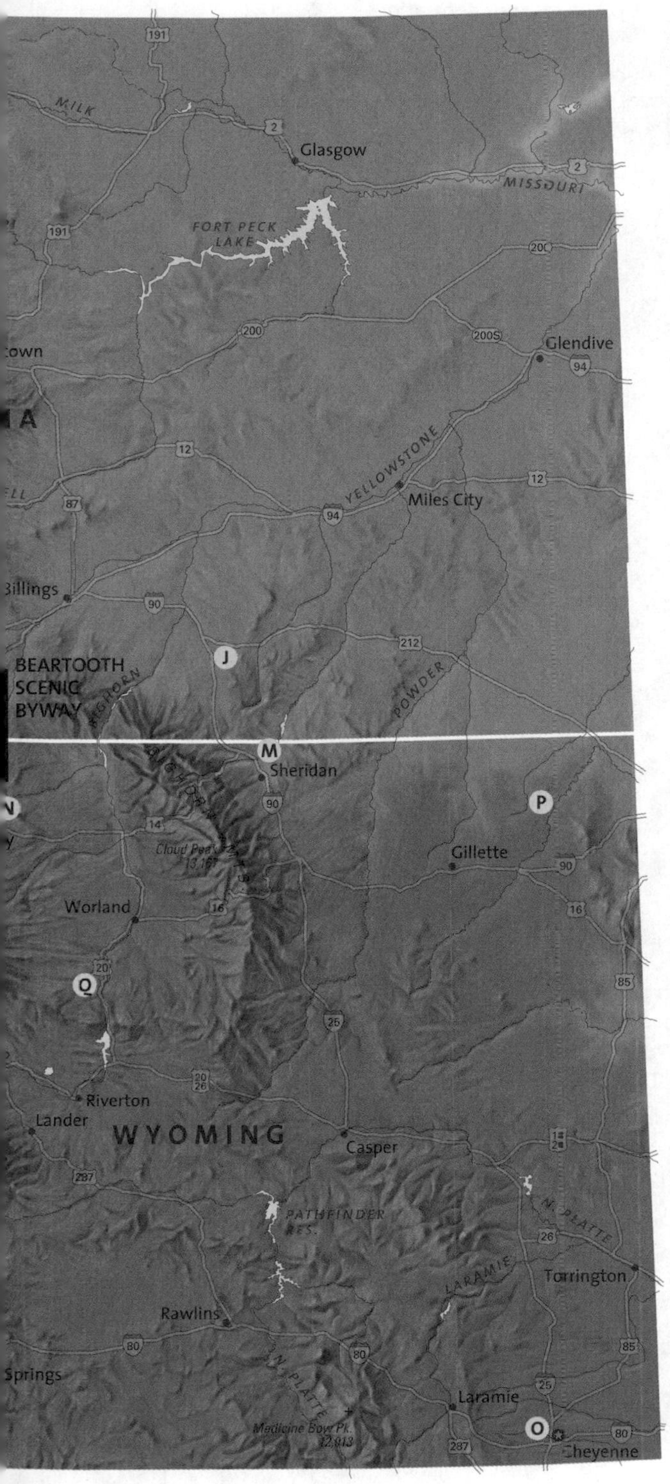

J LITTLE BIGHORN BATTLEFIELD NATIONAL MONUMENT
Pg. 123, J15. **Crow Agency.** The scene of Custer's "last stand," this monument memorializes one of the last armed clashes between the Northern Plains' tribes and the United States forces. Lieutenant Colonel George A. Custer and approximately 263 men of the U.S. Army Seventh Cavalry were killed in a battle against Lakota and Cheyenne warriors here in 1876. **406/638-2621** $

K MADISON RIVER CANYON EARTHQUAKE AREA
Pg. 122, L9. **West Yellowstone.** In a 1959 earthquake, a landslide piled up 400 feet of debris against the northern wall of Madison River Canyon, forming what is now called Earthquake Lake. Several overlooks give a view of the quake's aftermath, and the visitor center, which is built on the landslide area itself, provides exhibits related to the phenomenon. **406/646-7369**

L VIRGINIA CITY
Pg. 122, J7. The rough and tough days of the West are rekindled in this restored gold boomtown, once the capital of the territory. In 1946 a restoration program began, which has brought back much of the early mining-town atmosphere, including Victorian hotels, a music hall, and a narrow-gauge railroad line to Nevada City, another restored frontier town. **406/843-5377**

WYOMING

M BIGHORN NATIONAL FOREST
Pg. 176, A9. **Sheridan.** The Big Horn Mountains rise abruptly from the arid basins below to more than 13,000 feet. Fallen City, a jumble of huge rock blocks, can be seen, as well as Sibley Lake and Shell Canyon and Falls. Medicine Mountain is the site of the "medicine wheel," a mysterious circle of boulders, and Medicine Lodge State Archeological Site is known for its Indian petroglyphs and pictograms. **307/674-2600**

N BUFFALO BILL HISTORICAL CENTER
Pg. 176, B6. **Cody.** Five museums— the Buffalo Bill Museum, the Cody Firearms Museum, the Plains Indian Museum, the Whitney Gallery of Western Art, and the Draper Museum of Natural History—honor the cowboy entertainer for whom the town was named. The Historical Center offers seminars, symposia, and youth programs designed to help the public acquire a deeper understanding of the museum's permanent displays. **307/587-4771** $

O CHEYENNE
Pg. 176, H12. Named for an Algonquian tribe, Cheyenne is the state capital. Its museums—the Old West Museum ($), the Wyoming State Museum, and the Wyoming Transportation Museum—celebrate the Old West, and its Botanic Gardens are solar-heated. **307/778-3133**

P DEVILS TOWER NATIONAL MONUMENT
Pg. 176, B12. Located on 1,347 acres of parkland, five miles west of the Black Hills National Forest, this 865-foot landmark rises from the prairie like a giant tree stump. Sixty million years ago volcanic activity pushed molten rock toward the earth's surface and as it cooled, Devils Tower was formed. There are hiking and cross-country ski trails around the base. **307/467-5283** $

Q HOT SPRINGS STATE PARK
Pg. 176, C7. **Thermopolis.** The world's largest mineral hot springs pour out millions of gallons of water every 24 hours at 134°F into the Big Horn River. Mineral deposits have made dramatic terraces, which you can see from a scenic walkway. Visitors can relax in the indoor/outdoor mineral swimming pools and public bathhouse. **307/864-2176** $

R JACKSON
Pg. 176, C4. This town is the center for the mountain-rimmed, 600-square-mile valley of Jackson Hole. Mountain scenery, dude ranches, national parks, and big game —including deer, elk, and moose—surround it. The spectacular views and first-class ski slopes make it a popular ski resort. **307/733-3316**

P Devils Tower

M Bighorn National Forrest

DOLLAR WI$E

- If making multiple trips to national parks in one year, purchase a National Park Pass. For $50, you and a companion are admitted into all parks for one year.
- Take advantage of early-bird, late season and Internet lodging specials for Yellowstone National Park; you can save as much as 55%.
- Check Wyoming's travel and tourism web site, *www.wyomingtourism.org*, for special coupons and discounts on lodgings, restaurants, shops, and recreational activities.
- Enter a free world of quiet and solitude on one of Wyoming's scenic byways, such as the Bighorn Scenic Byway. The spectacular drive passes the geological formations Buffalo Tongue, the Fallen City and Steamboat Point before reaching Burgess Junction and 9,000-ft Granite Pass.

January
Montana Winter Fair
Bozeman, MT
406/585-1397

February
Wild West Winter Carnival
Riverton, WY
307/856-4801

Winter Carnival
McCall, ID
Parades, fireworks; ice sculptures, snowmobile and ski races, snowman-building contest, carriage and sleigh rides.
208/634-7631

June
Boise River Festival
Boise, ID
Night parade, contests, entertainment, fireworks.
208/338-8887

Little Bighorn Days
Hardin, MT
Custer's last stand reenactment. Military Ball, rodeo, street dance, bed races, children's games.
406/665-1672

July
Cheyenne Frontier Days
Cheyenne, WY
One of country's most famous rodeos; originated in 1897. Parades, carnivals; USAF *Thunderbirds* flying team; pancake breakfast; entertainment, square dancing nightly.
800/227-6336

Last Chance Stampede and Fair
Helena, MT
Rodeo.
406/442-1098

Lincoln County Fair
Shoshone, ID
208/886-2030

Montana State Fair
Great Falls, MT
Rodeo, livestock exhibits, horse racing, petting zoo, commercial exhibits, entertainment, carnival.
406/727-8900

August
Montana Fair
Billings, MT
406/256-2400

Western Idaho Fair
Boise, ID
Largest fair in state.
208/376-3247

Wyoming State Fair and Rodeo
Douglas, WY
Including rodeo events, horse shows, exhibits.
307/358-2398

September
Jackson Hole Fall Arts Festival
Jackson, WY
Three-week celebration of the arts featuring exhibits in more than 30 galleries, demonstrations, special activities. Also dance, theater, mountain film festival, Native American arts, and culinary arts.
307/733-3316

Paul Bunyan Days
Saint Maries, ID
Including parade, fireworks, logging events, water show, carnival.
208/245-3563

November
Currier & Ives Winter Festival
Thermopolis, WY
Town is decorated in 19th-century holiday style. Christmas choir, sleigh rides. Beard contest, cookie contest.
800/786-6772

North Dakota . South Dakota . Nebraska . Iowa

Free Finds

Dakota Westmoreland Coal Mine, Beulah, ND
Tour of all plant functions, including main control room, boilers, cooling tower, slag tanks, coal crushers. **701/873-2571**

Minot AFB, Minot, ND
Air Combat Command base for B-52 bombers, UH-1 helicopters, and Minuteman III missiles under 91st Space Wing. **701/723-6212**

Coal Creek Station, Underwood, ND
Tour of the largest lignite coal-fired plant in the country. **701/442-3211**

Double Ditch Indian Village, Bismarck, ND
State historic site contains the ruins of the Mandan Native American earth lodge village inhabited from 1675-1780; earth lodge and two surrounding fortifications are clearly discernible. **701/328-2666**

National Museum of Roller Skating, Lincoln, NE
Skates, costumes, and photographs documenting the sport from 1700 to the present; also archives dealing with world and national competitions since 1910. The only museum in the world devoted solely to roller skating. **402/483-7551**

Girls and Boys Town, Omaha, NE
Visit Father Flanagan's historic house and shrine, history museum, chapels, stamp center and gift shop. **402/498-1140**

Gerald Ford Birth Site, Omaha, NE
Model of original house, White House memorabilia; park, gardens, Betty Ford Memorial Rose Garden.

Storybook Island, Rapid City, IA
Fairyland park illustrating children's stories and rhymes; outdoor settings with music and animation. **605/342-6357**

Shrine to Music Museum, Vermillion, SD
More than 6,000 antique musical instruments from all over the world and from all periods. **605/677-5306**

Medical Museum, Iowa City, IA
Photographs, artifacts, and hands-on displays focusing on history of medicine and patient care in Iowa. **319/356-7106**

John Deere Waterloo Works, Waterloo, IA
Guided 1-1/2-hr tours of farm tractor facility. **319/292-7668**

Living Heritage Tree Museum, Storm Lake, IA
Seedlings and cuttings of more than 30 noteworthy trees, including the Charter Oak Tree and the NASA Seedling sent into space with Apollo 14.

Home to the Sioux and Chippewa Indians, North Dakota's rodeos, powwows, festivals, and country fairs delight travelers. The memorable Red River Valley and hauntingly beautiful Badlands, shared with South Dakota, are not to be missed. With its Black Hills National Forest, Jewel and Wind Caves, and Custer State Park, South Dakota attracts history buffs and outdoor enthusiasts. Mount Rushmore, the "shrine of democracy," is a must-see. In Nebraska, Lincoln's Morrill Hall houses one of the world's largest collections of fossils, while live animals are studied at Omaha's Doorly Zoo. Country music fans flock to the annual Comstock Festival. A true slice of Americana, Iowa's farmlands and small towns provide a warm welcome to visitors, and romantics can enjoy Madison County's famous bridges.

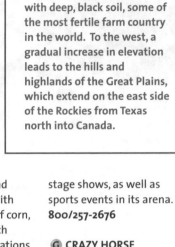

Iowa's relatively flat land of gently rolling prairies is filled with deep, black soil, some of the most fertile farm country in the world. To the west, a gradual increase in elevation leads to the hills and highlands of the Great Plains, which extend on the east side of the Rockies from Texas north into Canada.

E Fort Union

NORTH DAKOTA

A BONANZAVILLE
Pg. 141, F12. **West Fargo.** More than 45 buildings reconstruct the 19th-century farm era, including the Hemp Antique Vehicle Museum; the Plains Indian Museum; a train depot, model railroad, and 1884 locomotive; log cabins, pioneer farm homes, and a sod house; general stores, farm machinery buildings and operating farmsteads; and an old doll house. **701/282-2822** $

B CHÂTEAU DE MORES STATE HISTORIC SITE
Pg. 141, F2. **Medora.** An elegant 26-room house—with fine furniture, buffalo-skin robes, bear traps and French watercolors—is all that remains of the cattle empire of the Marquis de Mores. A wealthy Frenchman, he built up his cattle business and established the town, which he named for his American wife. Theodore Roosevelt came here in 1883 and won respect as part-owner of the Maltese Cross and Elkhorn ranches and as organizer and first president of the Little Missouri Stockmen's Association. **701/623-4910** $

C FORT ABERCROMBIE STATE HISTORIC SITE
Pg. 141, G12. **Abercrombie.** The first federal military post in the state has been rebuilt—only one original building remains—on authentic lines and includes blockhouses, guardhouses, and a stockade. Built on the west bank of the Red River, the fort regulated the fur trade, helped keep peace between the Chippewa and the Sioux, and served as a gateway through which wagon trains, stagecoaches, and army units moved west. A museum at the site interprets the history of the fort and the area.. **701/224-2666** $

D FORT ABRAHAM LINCOLN STATE PARK
Pg. 141, F6. **Mandan.** This is the post from which George Armstrong Custer and the Seventh Cavalry rode out on their ill-fated expedition against the Sioux at Little Big Horn. The Custer House, main commissary, and central barracks have been reconstructed and may be toured, as can a museum and a Mandan village that preceded the fort. **701/663-9571** $

E FORT UNION TRADING POST NATIONAL HISTORIC SITE
Pg. 141, C1. **Buford.** The American Fur Company built this fort in 1829 at the confluence of the Yellowstone and Missouri rivers. During the next three decades it was one of the most important trading depots on the western frontier. In 1867, the government bought the fort, dismantled it, and used the materials to build Fort Buford two miles away. Today excavated remains and reconstructed buildings let visitors sense its spirited past, guided by staff members dressed as trappers and traders. **701/572-9083**

North Dakota grows more sunflowers than any other state.

SOUTH DAKOTA

F CORN PALACE
Pg. 157, F10. **Mitchell.** Erected in 1892, early settlers displayed the fruits of their harvest on the building's exterior in order to prove the fertility of South Dakota soil. This huge structure, replete with domes, towers, and turrets, is gussied up with splashy murals made of corn, grains, and grasses. Each year, the exterior decorations are completely stripped down and new murals, designed by local artists, are created. The facility hosts stage shows, as well as sports events in its arena. **800/257-2676**

G CRAZY HORSE MEMORIAL
Pg. 157, E2. **Custer.** This large sculpture, still being carved from Thunderhead Mountain,

F Corn Palace

G Crazy Horse Memorial

was the life's work of the late Korczak Ziolokowski, who briefly assisted on Mount Rushmore. The work is being continued by the sculptor's wife and several of their children. It honors Crazy Horse, the Sioux chief who helped defeat Custer and the United States Seventh Cavalry, as well as all Native American tribes. **605/673-4681 $**

H DEADWOOD
Pg. 157, D2. This town is best known for gold and such characters as Calamity Jane, Preacher Smith, and Wild Bill Hickock, memorialized in the Adams and Deadwood Gulch Wax Museums ($). At the height of the 1876 gold rush, 25,000 people swarmed over the hillsides to dig gold. Tour the Broken Boot Gold Mine ($) and the Black Hills Mining Museum ($). **605/578-1876**

I MOUNT RUSHMORE NATIONAL MEMORIAL
Pg. 157, E2. **Rapid City.** The faces of four great American presidents—Washington, Jefferson, Lincoln, and Theodore Roosevelt—have been carved on a 5,675-foot mountain in the Black Hills. It was begun by sculptor Gutzon Borglum in 1927 and taken over and finished in 1941 by his son, Lincoln. The sculptor's studio, below the visitor center, contains a model of the work, several work-in-progress photographs, and an assortment of sculptors' tools. An exhibit hall features interactive displays through which visitors can discover more about the men and methods used to create this memorial. **605/574-2523**

IOWA

P AMANA COLONIES
Pg. 97, H15. **Amana.** Populated by the religious Amish community, the Amana Colonies produce smoked meats, woolen goods, bakery products, furniture, ovens, refrigerators and freezers, and air conditioners. The colonies were founded in the 1840s when members of the Inspirationists, a Lutheran separatist group, immigrated to the United States and bought 25,000 acres of prairie land in Iowa. **319/622-7622**

Q COVERED BRIDGES
Pg. 96, K9. **Winterset.** Five of Iowa's original 19 bridges remain today, all listed on the National Register of Historic Places. The bridges were covered by order of the County Board of Supervisors to help preserve the large flooring timbers, which were more expensive to replace than the lumber that had been used to fabricate the bridge sides and roof. Usually, the bridges were named for the resident who lived closest. **515/462-7785**

R Effigy Mounds

Q Covered Bridges

R EFFIGY MOUNDS NATIONAL MONUMENT
Pg. 97, C17. **Marquette.** Built in shapes of animals and other forms, the mounds were created by an indigenous civilization 2,500 years ago. The Great Bear Mound is the largest known bear effigy in the state, at 70 feet across the shoulders, 137 feet long, and 3 feet high. Visitors can take a walking tour of the area conducted by park rangers, who offer possible interpretations of the significance of the mounds. **563/873-3491 $**

S MISSISSIPPI RIVER MUSEUM
Pg. 97, E18. **Dubuque.** This complex of six Dubuque County Historical Society museums includes the National Rivers Hall of Fame, which celebrates the nation's river heroes; the Boatyard, with exhibits and replicas of small craft that sailed the Mississippi; and the Woodward Riverboat Museum, which dramatizes 300 years of Mississippi River history. **563/557-9545 $**

K Chimney Rock

L Fort Robinson

NEBRASKA

J BROWNVILLE
Pg. 125, L20. This restored riverboat town of the 1800s includes more than 30 buildings, including the Agricultural Museum, Carson House ($), Old Dental Office, and Nebraska's oldest repertory theater, the Village Theater ($). **402/274-3521**

K CHIMNEY ROCK NATIONAL HISTORIC SITE
Pg. 124, G2. **Bayard.** A landmark of the Oregon Trail, Chimney Rock rises almost 500 feet above the south bank of the North Platte River. Starting as a cone-shaped mound, it becomes a narrow, 150-foot column towering above the landscape. For westbound American pioneers, Chimney Rock marked the end of the prairies. The Visitor Center houses museum exhibits, a video presentation on the migration West, and a hands-on opportunity to "pack your own wagon." **308/586-2581 $**

L FORT ROBINSON STATE PARK
Pg. 124, E3. **Crawford.** This historic park served as an active military post from 1874 to 1948, and is the site where the Sioux chief Crazy Horse was killed in the 1870s. Visitors to the park will find approximately 22,000 acres of pine-covered hills and rocky buttes, where they may climb aboard the Tour Train, take an open-air jeep ride, or ride the Fort Robinson Express for a nature tour. **308/665-2660**

M OLD MARKET
Pg. 125, J19. **Omaha.** Once the city's produce marketplace at the turn of the century, this historic four-block section of town is now lined with art galleries, antique and specialty shops, restaurants and pubs. The district features some of the city's oldest commercial buildings, and the original cobblestone streets have been preserved. **402/444-4660**

N SCOTTS BLUFF NATIONAL MONUMENT
Pg. 124, G2. **Gering.** This 800-foot bluff in western Nebraska was a landmark to pioneers who traveled the California/Oregon Trail by wagon train. Historians often speak of this natural promontory in the North Platte Valley, which was originally named me-a-pa-te, "hill that is hard to go around," by the Plains Native Americans. Visitors can drive to the top of Scotts Bluff via the Summit Road for a spectacular view of the valley. **308/436-4340 $**

O STRATEGIC AIR & SPACE MUSEUM
Pg. 125, K18. **Ashland.** The museum houses a permanent collection of 33 aircraft and six missiles relating to the history of the Strategic Air Command and its importance in the preservation of world peace. Visitors to the museum can learn about math, science, engineering, aviation and space through traveling and permanent exhibits and educational programs. **402/944-3100 $**

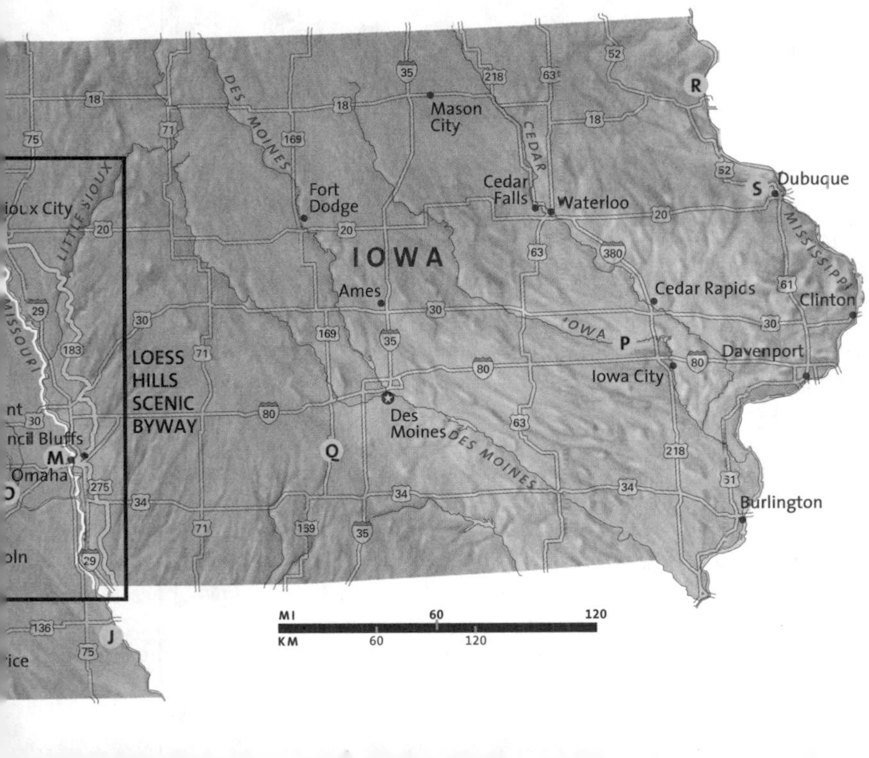

DOLLAR WI$E

- Call around to colleges to inquire about campus lodging. It is cheaper than a hotel, and is available at many colleges year-round.
- For $1, you can visit Nebraska's Ak-Sar-Ben Aquarium, as well as its terrarium, fish hatchery museum, and nearby geological display, and hike nearby trails.
- Book accommodations in advance to ensure availability, selection, and to guarantee the best rate.
- At Nebraska's Two Rivers State Recreation Area, a restored Union Pacific caboose can sleep up to six people—at a cost of only $55 a night.

May

Tulip Time Festival
Pella, IA
Citizens dress in Dutch costumes; scrubbing the streets is a colorful and traditional feature; Dutch dancers; stage performances, parades.
641/628-4311

United Tribes PowWow
Bismark, ND
One of the largest powwows in the nation, featuring Native American dancing and singing, food, games, crafts, and contests.
701/255-3285

June

Fort Seward Wagon Train
Jamestown, ND
A week-long wagon train experience. Participants dress and camp in the manner of the pioneers.
701/252-6844

Fort Sisseton Historical Festival
Sisseton, SD
Includes muzzleloading rendezvous, cavalry and infantry drills, square dancing, melodrama, frontier crafts and Dutch-oven cook-off.
605/448-5701

Iowa Arts Festival
Iowa City, IA
Celebration of the arts.
319/337-7944

Medora Musical
Medora, ND
Outdoor musical extravaganza; western songs, dance.
800/633-6721

My Waterloo Days Festival
Waterloo, IA
Citywide festival features air show, balloon rallies, parade, laser and fireworks show, music, renaissance fair, food.
319/233-8431

July

Chicken Show
Wayne, NE
Music contests, parade, omelet feed, chicken dinner feed, egg games, craft show, antique show and sale.
402/375-2240

August

Central States Fair
Rapid City, SD
Rodeo, carnival, horse and tractor pulls, auto races, demo derby.
605/355-3861

Iowa State Fair
Des Moines, IA
One of the oldest and largest in country; including farm machinery, fine arts, giant midway, grandstand stage and track events, free entertainment, exhibits and contests.
515/262-3111

L. Frank Baum Oz Festival
Aberdeen, SD
605/626-3310

Nebraska State Fair
Lincoln, NE
402/473-4109

September

Applejack Festival
Nebraska City, NE
Celebration of the apple harvest. Parade, antique and craft show, classic car show, football game.
402/873-3000

Corn Palace Festival
Mitchell, SD
605/996-5567

December

Christmas at Union Station
Omaha, NE
402/444-5071

AR 66
MO 120
KS 98
AR 232
MO 240
KS 236

Free $ Finds

South Arkansas Arboretum, El Dorado
Seventeen-acre arboretum featuring indigenous trees and plants. **870/862-8131**

Arkansas Entertainers Hall of Fame, Pine Bluff
Programs and displays trace the careers of featured Arkansas entertainers. Included are Johnny Cash, Glenn Campbell, Billy Bob Thornton, and Mary Steenburgen. **870/536-7600**

Wiederkehr Wine Cellars, Alma, AR
Guided wine-tasting tour (non-alcoholic beverage tasting for persons under 21); self-guided tour of vineyards; observation tower. **5001/468-9463**

Gann Museum, Benton, AR
This is the only known building made of bauxite; dug from a nearby farm, hand-sawed into blocks, and allowed to harden. Originally a medical office, it was built in 1893. **501/778-5513**

Delta Cultural Center, Helena, AR
Housed in 1912 Missouri Pacific rail depot, the center has exhibits on history of "the Delta." **870/338-4350**

Gallery of Also-Rans, Norton, KS
Photographs and biographies of unsuccessful presidential candidates. **785/877-25001**

Finnup Park and Lee Richardson Zoo, Garden City, KS
More than 300 mammals and birds can be found in the zoo. Picnic area, playgrounds; swimming pool. **316/276-1250**

Emporia Gazette Building, Emporia, KS
Houses William Allen White's widely-quoted newspaper; small one-room museum displays newspaper machinery used in White's time. **620/342-4800**

Overland Park Arboretum and Botanical Gardens, Overland Park, KS
Six hundred acres include three miles of hiking trails through gardens. Naturalized areas feature a Meadow Garden, Butterfly Garden, and Woodland Garden. **913/685-3604**

Anheuser-Busch, Inc., St. Louis
Guided 1 1/2 hour brewery tour. **314/577-2626**

Truman Farm Home, Grandview, MO
Truman lived in this two-story, white frame house in the decade preceding WWI; during these years, he farmed the surrounding 600 acres, and courted Bess Wallace. Interior features period furnishings, including original family pieces. Free guided tours May-Labor Day. **816/254-2720**

Land of the Pony Express, Buffalo Bill Cody, and Jesse James, this region time-travels visitors to the American frontier. From the annual Renaissance and Winfield Bluegrass Festivals to the sight of bison still roaming the rolling prairies, Kansas is a great vacation spot. Serene and unspoiled, the Tallgrass Prairie National Preserve, with its 19th-century ZBar/Spring Hill Ranch is especially popular. In Missouri, the toe-tapping rhythm of Branson, the hickory-smoked flavor of Kansas City, known as "The City of Fountains," and the cosmopolitan style of St. Louis, with its remarkable Gateway Arch provide visitors with many pleasures. Enjoy the peaks and lovely valleys of Arkansas' Ozark Mountains, or follow the path of trailblazers on the historic Katy and Santa Fe Trails.

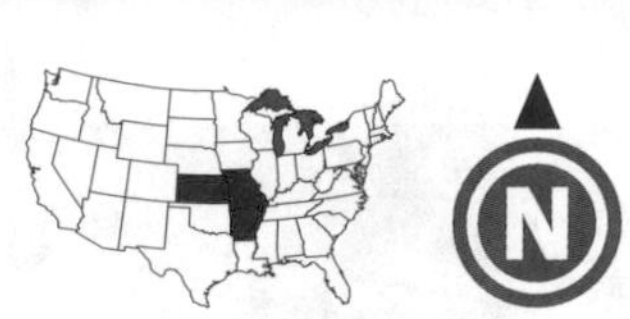

The Missouri and Mississippi Rivers flow across the central plains, draining much of the land that stretches between the Rocky and Appalachian Mountains. The two great rivers come together near St. Louis and flow south to the Gulf of Mexico.

A Eisenhower Center

B Fort Larned

E Potwin Place

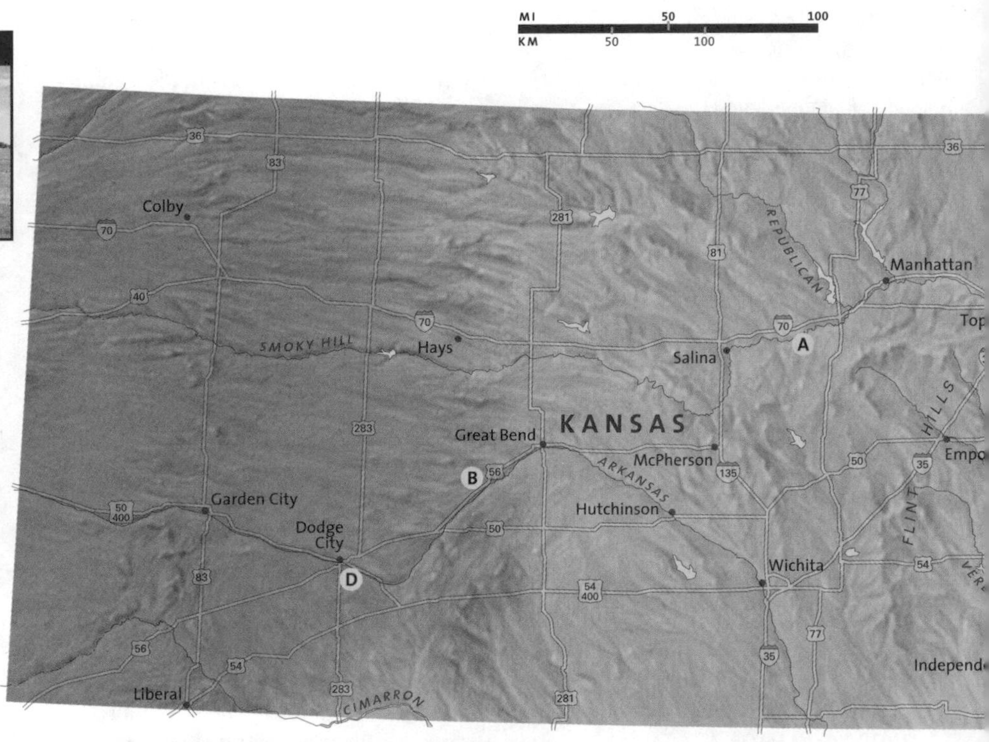

KANSAS

A EISENHOWER CENTER
Pg. 99, E14. **Abilene.** This five-building complex on 22 acres of land is located in the hometown of Dwight Eisenhower. It houses changing exhibits of mementos, souvenirs, and gifts received during Eisenhower's career. Murals in the house's lobby depict his life. Included in this complex is the Eisenhower Family Home, where the Eisenhowers lived from 1898 until 1946. **785/263-4751** $

B FORT LARNED NATIONAL HISTORICAL SITE
Pg. 98, G8. **Larned.** Considered one of the best-preserved frontier military posts along the Santa Fe Trail, this site boasts nine original buildings, including officers' quarters, enlisted men's barracks, blacksmith and carpenter shops, a post bakery, and a hospital. **316/285-6911** $

C FORT SCOTT NATIONAL HISTORIC SITE
Pg. 99, H18. **Fort Scott.** Established in 1842, the fort was the base for infantry and dragoons protecting the frontier. The buildings, including a post hospital, officers' quarters, powder magazine, dragoon stable, guardhouse, bakery, and post headquarters, have been restored. **316/223-0310** $

D HISTORIC FRONT STREET
Pg. 98, H6. **Dodge City.** Two blocks of this main thoroughfare have been rebuilt as though it were still 1870. Beeson Gallery displays items of historical significance from Dodge City and the old southwest, while Hardesty House, home of an early cattle baron, has been restored and furnished with exhibits of early banking. **316/225-8186**

E POTWIN PLACE
Pg. 99, D16. **Topeka.** Topeka's heritage lives on in this community of beautiful Victorian homes situated on brick streets with towering trees, and distinctive circular parks. As the city's most famous neighborhood, Potwin Place brings back the look of yesteryear. **785/234-1030**

MISSOURI

F BRANSON
Pg. 120, M6. Branson's evolution from a town of 1,200 people to "The Live Music Show Capital of the World" began shortly after the debut of its first show in 1959. Today, with more than 40 theaters and 50 shows, Branson is home to many nationally known country music stars who provide wholesome, family-oriented entertainment. These shows, along with its many other attractions, such as Silver Dollar City, have made Branson a popular destination for families. **417/334-4084**

G CROWN CENTER
Pg. 120, E3. **Kansas City.** This entertainment complex offers shopping, theaters, restaurants, and hotels around a landscaped central square. Crown Center is also home to the international headquarters of Hallmark Cards. Visitors can tour the Hallmark Visitors Center to learn the history of Hallmark Cards. For children, Hallmark's Kaleidoscope offers 55-minute sessions where they can explore their surroundings and expand their imaginations in a hands-on environment. **816/274-8444**

I Lake of the Ozarks

J Mark Twain Boyhood Home

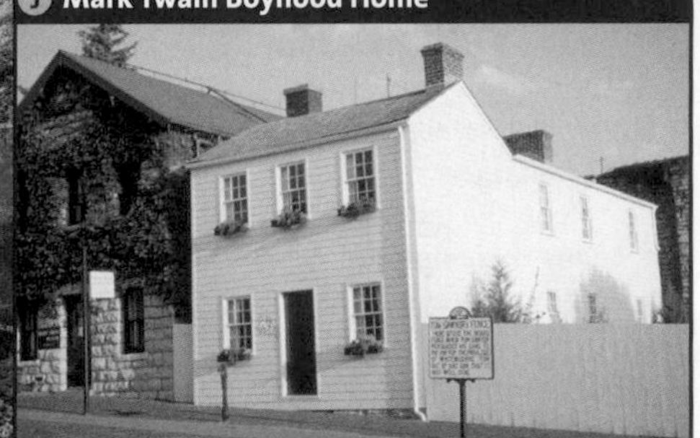

K St. Louis Riverfront

H GEORGE WASHINGTON CARVER NATIONAL MUSEUM
Pg. 120, L3. **Diamond.** This memorial commemorates George Washington Carver — an African-American teacher, humanitarian, botanist, agronomist, and pioneer conservationist. A 3/4-mile self-guided trail encompasses the birthplace site, the restored 1881 Moses Carver house, the family cemetery, and the woods and streams where Carver spent his boyhood. **417/325-4151**

I LAKE OF THE OZARKS STATE PARK
Pg. 120, H7. **Kaiser.** This more than 17,000-acre park, the largest in the state, has 89 miles of shoreline with two public swimming and boat launching areas. A large cave with streams of water that continuously pour from stalactites remains a popular attraction. The brilliantly colored Ozark Caverns can be toured, and, at nearby Ha Ha Tonka State Park, the ruins of a once-magnificent 60-room castle can be visited. **573/348-2694**

J MARK TWAIN MUSEUM AND BOYHOOD HOME
Pg. 120, C9. **Hannibal.** The two-story white frame house in which the Clemens family lived in the 1840s and 1850s has been restored and furnished with period pieces and relics. The museum houses the writer's memorabilia, including books, letters, photographs, and family items. **573/221-9010** $

K RIVERFRONT
Pg. 121, F12. **St. Louis** The Riverfront area features Eads Bridge, the first bridge to span the wide southern section of the Mississippi River. Other highlights include the Jefferson National Expansion Memorial and Eero Saarinen's Gateway Arch, a 630-foot stainless steel arch that symbolizes the starting point of the westward expansion of the United States. **314/421-1023**

M UNION STATION
Pg. 121, F12. **St. Louis.** This block-long stone chateau-style railroad station was the world's busiest passenger terminal from 1905 until the late 1940s. After the last train pulled out — on October 31, 1978 — the station and train shed were restored and redeveloped as a marketplace with more than 100 specialty shops and restaurants, nightclubs, and hotels. **314/421-6655**

R Quapaw Quarter

O Buffalo National River

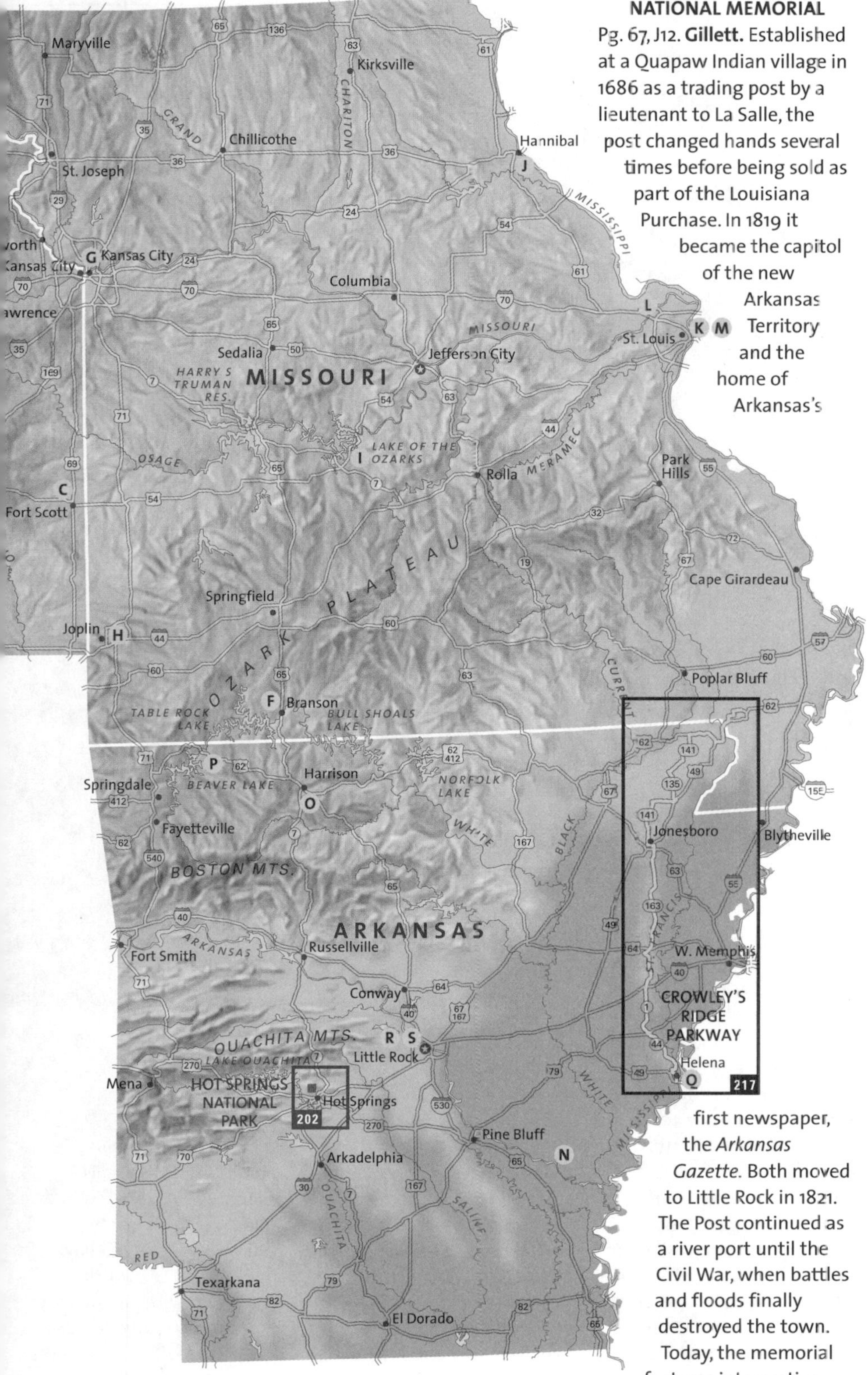

ARKANSAS

N ARKANSAS POST NATIONAL MEMORIAL
Pg. 67, J12. **Gillett.** Established at a Quapaw Indian village in 1686 as a trading post by a lieutenant to La Salle, the post changed hands several times before being sold as part of the Louisiana Purchase. In 1819 it became the capitol of the new Arkansas Territory and the home of Arkansas's first newspaper, the *Arkansas Gazette*. Both moved to Little Rock in 1821. The Post continued as a river port until the Civil War, when battles and floods finally destroyed the town. Today, the memorial features interpretive trails and a visitor center museum that interprets the history of the Post, Arkansas and its archeology. **501/548-2207**

O BUFFALO NATIONAL RIVER
Pg. 66, B7. **Harrison.** Some 135 miles of free-flowing river draw whitewater enthusiasts and campers in the spring. Hikes along the river offer views of springs, waterfalls, streams, and woods. Lost Valley is a two-mile loop trail that ends in a cave with a 35-foot waterfall inside. **870/741-5443**

P EUREKA SPRINGS
Pg 66, B6. This 19th century town was well-known for its waters' curative powers. Thousands of people with every possible affliction flocked to the city. The healing traditions continue today, as many spas soothe and pamper modern travelers. Other attractions include the New Holy Land re-creation ($), where visitors may stand in a full-scale replica of the Old Testament Tabernacle; a 10-foot section of the Berlin Wall; and the historic downtown area, which features blocks of Victorian architecture, as well as shops and art galleries. **501/253-8737**

Q MISSISSIPPI RIVER DELTA
Pg. 67, H14. **Helena.** This eastern part of Arkansas bordering the Mississippi River is home to a rich natural and cultural heritage. Tour the area by its scenic byways. The 200-mile stretch of Crowley's Ridge offers picturesque views of rolling hills, while the Great River Road follows the Mississippi River as it cuts through the delta lands. **870/338-8327**

R QUAPAW QUARTER HISTORIC NEIGHBORHOODS
Pg. 66, G9. **Little Rock.** Encompassing the original town of Little Rock and its early additions, this area contains three National Register historic districts and well over 150 buildings listed on the National Register of Historic Places. Named for Arkansas's native Quapaw Indians, the area includes sites and structures associated with the history of the capital city from the 1820s to the present. **501/376-4781**

S TOLTEC MOUNDS ARCHEOLOGICAL STATE PARK
Pg. 66, G9. **Little Rock.** This 182-acre park is the site of one of the largest prehistoric Native American settlements in the Lower Mississippi Valley, a large ceremonial and governmental complex inhabited from A.D. 600 to 1050. Mounds can be viewed on guided tours or from paved trails. Two mounds—at 49 and 41 feet high—are the tallest in Arkansas The visitor center has artifacts exhibits, and an archeological laboratory. **501/961-9442**

L ST. CHARLES HISTORIC DISTRICT
Pg. 121, F12. A nine-block historic area along south Main Street once launched the Lewis and Clark expedition to the Pacific Ocean. Today the neighborhood features a museum honoring the explorers and restored houses, antique shops, restaurants, and the First Missouri State Capitol State Historic Site. **636/946-7776** $

At one time it was against the law to serve ice cream on cherry pie in Kansas.

DOLLAR WI$E

- Travel at moderate speeds on the open road; higher speeds require more gasoline.
- You'll get more shows for your money in August in Branson, MO, when lots of theaters offer hefty discounts or two-tickets-for-the-price-of-one deals.
- A good stop-over on your cross country drive is The Ozark Folk Center in Arkansas. It is a one-of-a-kind state park with 20 craft and lifestyle demonstrations, as well as concerts and other festivities that are free. Reasonably-priced accommodations are available at the park's lodge.
- For $5, you can spend the day digging for diamonds at Crater of Diamonds State Park in Arkansas—and keep what you find.
- The "Rent-A-Camp" program, developed by the Kansas Department of Wildlife and Parks, provides inexperienced campers—or those without equipment—enough basic camping gear for four, for $15 per night.

April

Festival of the Two Rivers
Arkadelphia, AR
Arts and crafts, juried art show, contests, games, food.
870/246-5542

Jazz Festival
Wichita, KS
316/262-2351

May

Gypsy Caravan
St. Louis, MO
One of the largest flea markets in the midwest, with more than 600 vendors; arts and crafts, entertainment, concessions.
314/286-4452

Mississippi River Arts Festival
Hannibal, MO
573/221-6545

Wichita River Festival
Wichita, KS
Includes twilight pop concert and fireworks; antique bathtub races; hot air balloon launch; athletic events; entertainment.
316/267-2817

June

Mark Twain Outdoor Theater
Hannibal, MO
Performances based on the books of Mark Twain. Stage setting is a reconstruction of mid-1800s Hill St, where Twain lived.
573/221-2945

Midsummer's Day Festival
Lindsborg, KS
Swedish ethnic celebration. Folk dancing, arts and crafts.
785/227-3706

Wildwood Festival
Little Rock, AR
Series of musical programs, exhibits, and events centered on the performing arts.
501/821-7275

July

Kansas City Blues and Jazz Festival
Kansas City, MO
816/753-3378

Tom Sawyer Days
Hannibal, MO
National fence painting contest, frog jumping, entertainment.
573/221-2477

August

Great Arkansas PigOut Festival
Morrilton, AR
Softball, volleyball, bike rides, tennis, three-on-three basketball tournaments. Children's activities; hog calling, pig chase.
501/354-2393

September

Buster Keaton Festival
Iola, KS
620/365-4765

Great Forest Park Balloon Race
St. Louis, MO
Food, entertainment, parachute jumps, and other contests.
314/289-5300

Lawrence Indian Arts Show
Lawrence, KS
Juried exhibit featuring work by contemporary American Indian artists from across the US.
785/864-4245

October

Arkansas State Fair and Livestock Show
Little Rock, AR
Rodeo and other events.
501/372-8341

Maple Leaf Festival
Carthage, MO
Parade, marching band competition, arts and crafts, house tours.
417/358-2373

MI 112
WI 174
MN 116

Free Finds

Spam Museum, Austin, MN
Museum paying homage to SPAM Luncheon Meat, one of America's best-loved icons. **507/437-4563**

Minnesota Baseball Hall of Fame, Saint Cloud
Features great moments from amateur and professional baseball. **320/255-7272**

Minneapolis Grain Exchange, Minneapolis
Visit cash grain market and futures market. Tours Tues-Thurs; reservations required. **612/321-7101**

Karpeles Manuscript Library Museum, Duluth, MN
Holds original drafts of the US Bill of Rights, Emancipation Proclamation, Handel's Messiah, and others. **218/728-0630**

Honey of a Museum, Oconomowoc, WI
Bee Tree provides a close-up view of bee activities; pollination and beeswax exhibits; multimedia show about beekeeping yesterday, today and around the world; nature walk; honey tasting. **262/474-4411**

Miller Brewing Co., Milwaukee
One-hour guided tour with free samples. **414/931-2337**

High Cliff General Store Museum, Neenah-Menasha, WI
Museum depicts life in the area from 1850 to the early 1900s. **920/989-1106**

Quality Candy Shoppes/Buddy Squirrel of Wisconsin, Inc., Milwaukee
See Wisconsin's award winning chocolates being made. Tour with free samples. **414/483-4500**

Eastern Market, Detroit
Built originally on the site of an early hay and wood market, this and the Chene-Ferry Market. Today the Eastern Market encompasses produce and meat-packing houses, fish markets, and storefronts offering items ranging from spices to paper. **313/833-1560**

Soo Locks, Sault Ste. Marie, MI
The famous locks can be seen from both the upper and lower parks paralleling the locks. The upper park has three observation towers, a working lock model, photos, and a movie in its visitor building. **906/632-3311**

Meyer May House, Grand Rapids, MI
Frank Lloyd Wright house from the late prairie period. **616/246-4821**

Fenn Valley Vineyards and Wine Cellar, Saugatuck, MI
Self-guided tour overlooking wine cellar with wine tasting. **616/561-2396**

The heart of this region is the Great Lakes, but its soul can be found in the cultural richness and diversity of its cities, villages, and farms. Lake Michigan's scenic eastern shore is dotted with lighthouses and galleries, and Mackinac Island offers many natural and historic treasures. Ann Arbor's intellectual resources stimulate the mind, while Detroit's roaring engines and Motown beat stir the soul. Celebrate Oktoberfest Minnesota-style in the German town of New Ulm; roam Paul Bunyan's woods in Bemidji; visit Windom, where the Jeffers Petroglyphs date from 3,000 B.C.; or stay in the Twin Cities, the undisputed cultural capital of the region. Wisconsin's Sturgeon Bay proves that shipbuilding is an art, while Phillips is known for its off-beat concrete sculptures. Refurbished railroad cars run in Spooner, and there's always Milwaukee with its famous brew.

Forming a watery staircase that spans 750-miles, the Great Lakes drop 24-feet from Superior to Michigan and Huron. Another eight feet separates that pair from shallow Erie. Ontario, the smallest, lies 326-feet lower–a descent that includes the 167-foot plunge of the Niagara Falls.

B Grand Portage

E Pipestone National Monument

MINNESOTA

A FORT SNELLING STATE PARK
Pg. 117, Q8. **Minneapolis.** This 4,000-acre park at the confluence of the Minnesota and Mississippi rivers offers extensive swimming, fishing, boating, hiking and biking opportunities as well as cross-country ski trails that link the Minnehaha Park and the Minnesota Valley National Wildlife Refuge. **612/725-2389** $

B GRAND PORTAGE NATIONAL MONUMENT
Pg. 116, C11. **Grand Marais.** This monument marks the site of the "great carrying place," where 18th-century fur traders carried goods and pelts over an 8 1/2 –mile trail into the Canadian wilderness. This partially reconstructed summer headquarters of the North West Company includes a stockade, great hall, kitchen, and warehouse. **218/387-2788** $

C ITASCA STATE PARK
Pg. 116, J5. **Lake Itasca.** In the deep virgin woodlands covering most of the 32,000 acres of this park lies the headwaters of the Mississippi River at its Lake Itasca source, one of 100 lakes in the area. Wilderness Drive passes the 2,000-acre Wilderness Sanctuary, one of Minnesota's seven National Natural Landmarks, and swimming, fishing, boating, biking, hiking, snowmobiling, and cross-country skiing are among the recreational activities offered. **218/266-2114**

The Mall of America in Bloomington is the size of 78 football fields — 9.5 million square feet.

D NICOLLET MALL
Pg. 117, Q8. **Minneapolis.** Spacious walkways, bubbling fountains, shade trees, seasonal flowers, and a skyway system have helped make this beautifully designed shopping promenade world famous. It features a variety of retailers, restaurants, museums, and art galleries, as well as art shows and symphony orchestra performances. **612/332-3101**

E PIPESTONE NATIONAL MONUMENT
Pg. 117, T2. **Pipestone.** This monument protects remaining red pipestone quarried by Native Americans and carved into ceremonial pipes. Leaping Rock was used by Native Americans to test the strength of men attempting to leap from the top of ridge. Visitors may travel the 3/4-mile Circle Trail through native prairie to the pipestone quarries and Winnewissa Falls. **507/825-5464** $

F U.S. HOCKEY HALL OF FAME
Pg. 116, H10. **Eveleth.** The hall honors American athletes who have made outstanding contributions and achievements in the development of hockey. Visitors experience the thrilling game action and inspiring achievements of players, coaches, administrators, referees, and teams through authentic, informative and entertaining displays and memorabilia. **218/744-5167** $

WISCONSIN

G CIRCUS WORLD MUSEUM
Pg. 175, N7. **Baraboo.** There are 50 acres and eight buildings filled with circus lore at this original winter quarters of Ringling Brothers Circus. Visitors can see live circus acts, circus parades, steam calliope concerts, a P. T. Barnum sideshow, a wild animal menagerie, and a band organ. **608/356-8341** $

H DEVILS LAKE STATE PARK
Pg. 175, N7. **Baraboo.** These 11,050 acres, with spring-fed Devil's Lake, form Wisconsin's most beautiful state park. Remnants of an ancient mountain range surround the lake, about one-mile long in the midst of sheer cliffs of quartzite rising 500 feet above the water. Unusual rock formations may be found at the top of the bluffs. Visitors may mountain bike, hike, fish, or take a scenic drive around the park. **608/356-6618**

I DOOR COUNTY
Pg. 174, J12. **Sturgeon Bay.** Famous for its fish boils, foliage, and 250 miles of shoreline, Door County is a peninsula with Green Bay on the west and Lake Michigan on the east with picturesque villages, rolling woodlands, limestone bluffs, and beautiful vistas. Often referred to as the Cape Cod of the Midwest, Door County offers opportunities for fishing, sailing, beachcombing,

G Circus World Museum

I Door County

camping, hiking, biking, and horseback riding. **920/743-4456**

J EAA AIR ADVENTURE MUSEUM
Pg. 175, M10. **Oshkosh.** More than 90 aircraft are on display including antiques, classics, ultralights, home-built, aerobatic and rotary-winged planes as well as a special World War II collection. The museum houses extensive aviation art and photography; engines, propellers, and scale models. **920/426-4800** $

K GREEN BAY PACKER HALL OF FAME
Pg. 174, K11. **Green Bay.** Memories of both victory and defeat resonate throughout this museum, which features exhibits and multimedia presentations that highlight the history of the Packers from 1919 to the present day. Memorabilia found here include original game programs and jerseys from the legendary 1967 "Ice Bowl," and replica Super Bowl trophies won by the Packers. **888/442-7225** $

L HOUSE ON THE ROCK
Pg. 175, P7. **Spring Green.** This house was designed and built by artist Alexander J. Jordan on top of a chimney-like rock, 450 feet above the Wyoming Valley. Its 14 rooms contain waterfalls, pools, and trees growing through floors and ceilings. A collection of antiques, Asian art and automated music machines, as well as the world's largest carousel, can also be found here. **608/935-3639** $

M MILWAUKEE ART MUSEUM
Pg. 175, Q11. The museum features permanent collections of nearly 20,000 works from antiquity to the present, and include American decorative arts, German Expressionism, folk and Haitian art, and post-1960 American art. Among important artists represent here are Auguste Rodin, Edgar Degas, Georgia O'Keeffe, Jasper Johns, and Andy Warhol. **414/224-3200** $

MICHIGAN

N CRANBROOK EDUCATIONAL COMMUNITY
Pg. 113, S11. **Bloomfield Hills.** Spread on more than 300 acres, Cranbrook was the former estate of George Booth, publisher of the Detroit Evening News. Now an educational and cultural complex, its facilities include Cranbrook House and Gardens, a Tudor-style house built in 1908 and set in 40 acres of gardens; the Cranbrook Art Museum, which houses a collection of the finest contemporary art; and the Cranbrook Institute of Science, an extensive natural history museum with hands-on exhibits, a planetarium, and a nature center. **877/462-7262** $

O Wright home, Henry Ford Museum

Q Pictured Rocks National Lakeshore

P Grand Hotel, Mackinac Island

O HENRY FORD MUSEUM AND GREENFIELD VILLAGE
Pg. 113, T11. **Dearborn.** The museum and village, built by Henry Ford, stand as monuments to America's culture, resourcefulness, and technology. A collection of over one million artifacts, 26 million documents, and 78 historic structures depict the ever-changing world of transportation, manufacturing, home life, entertainment and technology. Artifacts on display include the car in which John F. Kennedy was assassinated, and one of Thomas Edison's early phonographs. **313/271-1620** $

P MACKINAC ISLAND
Pg. 112, F8. Mackinac Island, labeled the "Bermuda of the North," retains both a contemporary and historic atmosphere. Surrounded by Lake Huron's sparkling blue waters, the islanders limit transportation to horse and buggy, bicycle, or foot. It is a popular romantic weekend getaway, as well as a destination for families. Attractions here include Fort Mackinac—a National Historic Landmark ($), the Wings of Mackinac Butterfly Conservatory ($), and the Historic Downtown District ($). **906/847-3783**

Q PICTURED ROCKS NATIONAL LAKESHORE
Pg. 112, D3. **Munising.** This scenic stretch of shoreline begins at the western edge of Grand Marais and continues west to Munising. It is composed of multicolored sandstone cliffs eroded into arches and caves, followed by a 12-mile stretch of sand beaches and the Grand Sable Banks, topped by sand dunes. Swimming, fishing, rock climbing, cross-country skiing, and snowmobiling are among the activities here, and boating is permitted in inland lakes. **906/387-3700**

R R.E. OLDS TRANSPORTATION MUSEUM
Pg. 113, R8. **Lansing.** Named after Ransom Eli Olds, founder of the Olds Motor Vehicle Company, the museum houses Lansing-built vehicles. The collection includes buggies, bicycles, trucks and engines, the oldest Oldsmobile, and rare vehicles like REO, Star, and Viking. Also featured here are period clothing, a photographic display of Olds' Victorian home, and a "Wall of Wheels" from the Motor Wheel Corporation. **517/372-0422** $

S SLEEPING BEAR DUNES NATIONAL LAKESHORE
Pg. 112, J4. **Empire.** This area was named for an Ojibway legend about a mother bear that climbs to the top of a solitary bluff to watch for her bear cubs that fell behind her. Her "cubs" are thought of as the Manitou Islands, which lie a few miles offshore. The 7.6-mile Pierce Stocking Scenic Drive crosses the spectacular dunes, overlooks North Manitou and South Manitou islands, and passes picnic areas and hiking trails. **231/326-5134** $

T WINDMILL ISLAND
Pg. 113, R4. **Holland.** Windmill Island is nestled within the natural habitat of the Macatawa River, and depicts the sights and sounds of an authentic Netherlands village. In the spring, over 100,000 tulips bloom. In the summer, there is a beautiful array of annual plants and flowers. The 240-year-old windmill, "De Zwaan" (the swan), is the only operating imported Dutch windmill in the U.S, and is still used to grind flour. Guided tours of the island are offered ($), and "Tulip Time," held every May, draws visitors from around the country. **616/836-1490** $

DOLLAR WI$E

- Enjoy original performances at the Milwaukee Public Theatre, where many shows are free.
- Get half-price or 2-for-1 tickets for various performances through TC Tix, located at the Minneapolis Information and Visitor Center.
- Take a 75-minute tour of Minneapolis for only $5 aboard the River City Trolley.
- Picnic at Detroit's Belle Isle Park, and afterwards visit North America's largest continuously operating aquarium, Belle Isle Aquarium, for a $4 admission fee.

January

International Auto Show
Detroit, MI
248/643-0250

Winter Carnival
Houghton, MI
Snow sculptures and statues; dogsled and snowshoe racing, broomball, skiing, skating; skit contests; Queen Coronation and Snoball Dance.
906/487-2818

February

Polar Fest
Detroit Lakes, MN
Wkend filled with sports, entertainment, polar plunge.
218/817-9202

May

Tulip Time Festival
Holland, MI
A celebration of Dutch heritage: 1,800 klompen dancers, three parades, street scrubbing, Dutch markets, musical and professional entertainment, and millions of tulips.
800/822-2770

June

Bristol Renaissance Fair
Kenosha, WI
Re-creation of a 16th-century European marketplace featuring royal knights and swordsmen, master jousters, musicians, mimes, dancers, and hundreds of craftsmen and food peddlers.
800/52-FAIRE

Strawberry Festival
Cedarburg, WI
Strawberry foods, contests, craft fair, entertainment.
262/377-9620

July

Art Fair on the Square
Madison, WI
Exhibits by 500 artists and craftspersons; food, entertainment. Contact Madison Art Center.
608/257-0158

Sailing Races
Mackinac Island, MI
Port Huron to Mackinac and Chicago to Mackinac.
906/847-3783

Sommerfest
Minneapolis, MN
Summer concert series of Minnesota Orchestra with Viennese flavor; food booths.
612/371-5656

August

Michigan State Fair
Detroit, MI
313/366-3300

Minnesota State Fair
St. Paul, MN
Midway, thrill show, horse show, kids' days, all-star revue; more than one million visitors each year; 300 acres of attractions.
651/642-2200

Wisconsin State Fair
Milwaukee, WI
Entertainment, 12 stages, auto races, exhibits, contests, demonstrations, fireworks.
800/884-FAIR.

September

Sturgeon Bay Harvest Fest
Sturgeon Bay, WI
Art show, huge craft show, farmers market, food booths, music and entertainment.
800/301-6695

October

Apple Festival
Bayfield, WI
800/447-4094

Fall Festival of the Arts
Red Wing, MN
651/385-5934

OH 142
IN 94
IL 90
OH 234
IN 235
IL 235

Free Finds $

Museum of Broadcast Communications, Chicago
Collection of antique radios and televisions, archives of vintage and current radio and television series and events, Radio Hall of Fame. **312/629-6000**

Lincoln Park Zoo, Chicago
Houses more than 1,600 animals, including many exotic and endangered species. **312/742-2000**

Nauvoo Restoration, Inc. Visitor Center, Nauvoo, IL
Buildings and exhibits highlight Nauvoo history. **217/453-2237**

Birks Museum, Decatur, IL
Decorative arts museum with more than 1,000 pieces of china, crystal, and pottery. **217/424-6337**

Indiana World War Memorial Plaza, Indianapolis
A five-block area dedicated to Indianans who gave their lives in the two World Wars and the Korean and Vietnam conflicts. **317/232-7615**

Butler Winery, Bloomington, IN
Tour of wine cellar with tasting. **812/339-7233**

Fort Knox II, Vincennes, IN
Military post built and garrisoned by new American nation during early 1800s.

Sheldon Swope Art Museum, Terre Haute, IN
The museum's permanent collections range from ancient to contemporary art with a special section of 19th- and 20th-century American paintings and master prints. **812/238-1676**

United States Air Force Museum, Dayton, OH
One of the world's most comprehensive military aviation museums with more than 200 major historic aircraft and missiles; exhibits span period from Wright brothers to space age. **937/255-3284**

Boyd's Crystal Art Glass, Cambridge, OH
Tours of glass factory, showing evolution of glass from molten form to finished product. **740/439-2077**

German Village, Columbus, OH
Historic district restored as Old World village with shops, old homes, gardens. **614/221-8888**

Hoover Historical Center, Canton, OH
Hoover farmhouse restored to Victorian era; boyhood home of W.H. Hoover, founder of the Hoover Company. Includes one of the most extensive antique vacuum cleaner collections in the world. **330/499-0287**

You can enjoy both electric excitement and serenity in America's Heartland. Relive bygone days in Ohio's Amish and Mennonite communities. Visit the birthplaces of George Custer and Thomas Edison or stay in Cincinnati, where you can enjoy Kings Island and Coney Island Amusement Parks. From the speedway of the Indy 500 to the college basketball courts, the "Hoosier State" of Indiana is heaven for sports lovers. Be cool at Fairmont's James Dean Memorial Gallery or admire vintage military aircraft in Peru. Illinois is home to the nation's first highway, along with the exuberant Route 66 Hall of Fame in McLean. Stop by the boyhood homes of Abraham Lincoln in Springfield and Ronald Reagan in Pekin, but be sure not to miss Chicago's museums and the Magnificent Mile, one of the world's great shopping areas.

Heavily industrialized along their northern tier on Lake Erie and Lake Michigan, the Heartland states are nonetheless agricultural outriders of the rich prairie lands to the west. The Ohio River, long a highway of settlement and commerce between East and West, forms the region's southern border.

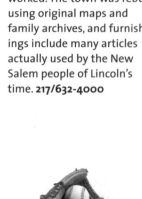

(A) Art Institute of Chicago

(D) Field Museum

(E) Frank Lloyd House

ILLINOIS

(A) THE ART INSTITUTE OF CHICAGO

Pg. 90, C12. World-renowned for its collections of American and European paintings and decorative arts and a range of sculpture, prints, and drawings, the Art Institute is a favorite for Chicagoans and tourists alike. Highlights include a stained-glass window by Marc Chagall, sixty-eight miniature rooms that illustrate home interiors through history, and the reconstructed Chicago Stock Exchange Trading Room. **312/443-3600** $

(B) CAHOKIA MOUNDS STATE HISTORICAL SITE

Pg. 91, Q5. This site preserves nearly 70 earthen ceremonial mounds of Cahokia, the only prehistoric city north of Mexico. Monks Mound, the great platform mound named for Trappist monks who lived nearby in the 1800s, is the largest prehistoric earthen construction in the New World. **617/346-5160**

(C) CHICAGO BOTANIC GARDEN

Pg. 90, B12. **Glencoe.** The 23 unique gardens—from Japanese, aquatic and herb gardens to roses, waterfalls and acres of native prairie—bring out thousands of nature lovers every year. The site comprises six miles of Lake Michigan shoreline, nine islands, a sensory garden for the visually impaired and a learning garden for the disabled. **874/835-5440** $ (parking)

(D) FIELD MUSEUM

Pg. 90, C12. **Chicago.** One of the largest natural history museums in the world, the Field Museum includes exhibits on world culture, history, animals, and gems. A must-see is a tour of the Egyptian tomb complex with its burial shaft, chamber, and mummies. An exhibit on the natural history and culture of the Pacific invites guests into a reconstructed Maori meeting house. **312/922-9410** $

(E) FRANK LLOYD WRIGHT HOME AND STUDIO

Pg. 90, C12. **Oak Park.** Wright built this house for himself in 1889, when he was 22 years old. Testing the ideas that would serve as the foundation of his Prairie Style, Wright remodeled the interiors of this home continuously and used what he learned to design many of the surrounding homes for clients. **708/848-1976** $ R

(F) GALENA

Pg. 90, A5. With 90 percent of its buildings listed on the National Register of Historic Places, Galena preserves a time long gone. Not just for history buffs, the town is also a favorite weekend destination for antique collectors and shoppers. **800/747-9377**

(G) LINCOLN'S NEW SALEM STATE HISTORIC SITE

Pg. 90, J6. **Petersburg.** A complete reconstruction of the village as it appeared when Abraham Lincoln lived there in the 1830s, New Salem boasts twelve timber houses, a school, ten workshops, and the Denton Offutt store, where Lincoln first worked. The town was rebuilt using original maps and family archives, and furnishings include many articles actually used by the New Salem people of Lincoln's time. **217/632-4000**

The first professional baseball game was played in Fort Wayne on May 4, 1871.

INDIANA

(H) AMISH ACRES

Pg. 94, C9. **Nappanee.** The only Amish farm listed on the National Register of Historic Places, Amish Acres offers a glimpse of the Amish lifestyle through guided tours of the farm, hay wagon rides, live musical theater in a traditional round barn, craft demonstrations and shops. The Amish Acres Arts & Crafts festival, held here annually, is widely renowned as one of America's best traditional crafts shows. **219/773-4188** $

(I) CHILDREN'S MUSEUM OF INDIANAPOLIS

Pg. 94, K8. A five-story building, the Children's Museum teaches kids — and adults — about science, social cultures, space, history, and exploration. Highlights include learning to tell time by a thirty-foot water clock, exploring a simulated limestone cave, and choosing the perfect mount for a ride on the museum's famous carousel. **317/924-5431** $

(J) COLUMBUS

Pg. 95, N9. This small Hoosier town put itself on the architectural map in the late 1930s by commissioning Eliel Saarinen to design a church. Since then

Q Cuyahoga Valley

T Pro Football Hall of Fame

U Rock and Roll Museum

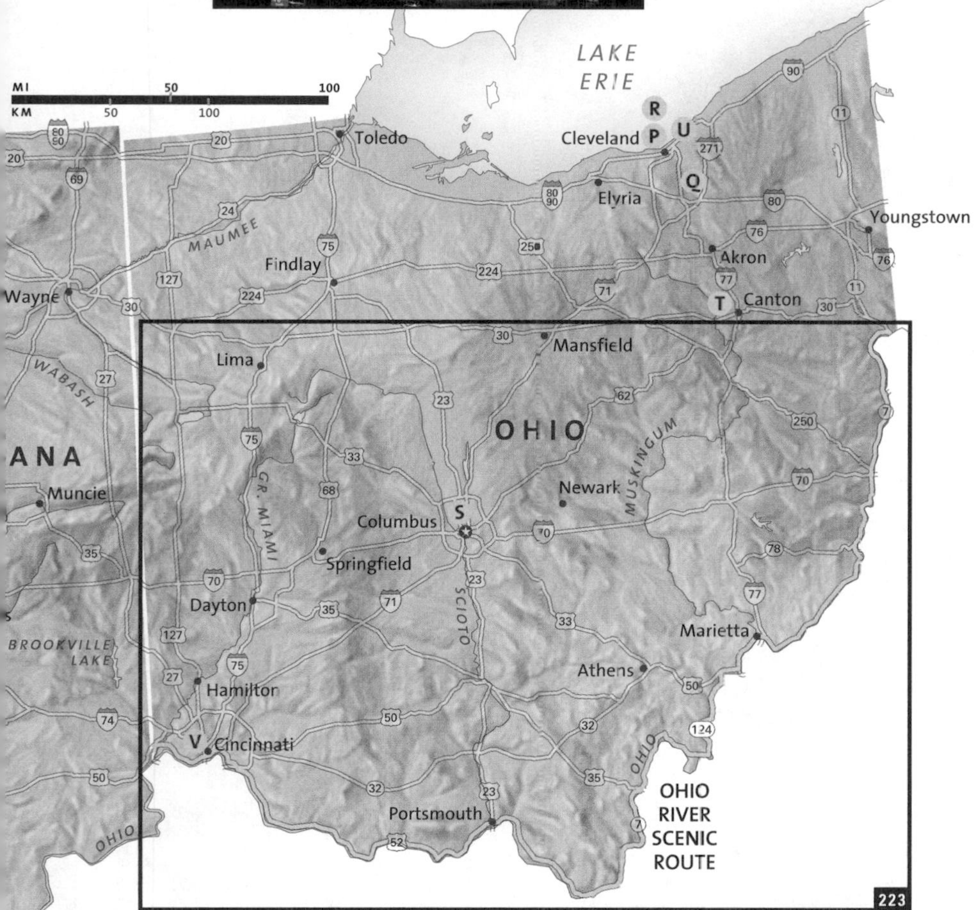

Columbus has added more than 50 public and private buildings designed by architectural giants, including John Carl Warnecke, Harry Weese and I.M. Pei. In addition to architectural walking tours, Columbus offers many museums— including the Atterbury-Bakalar Air Museum and the Bartholomew County Historical Society Museum. **812/378-2622**

K HISTORIC CREEK VILLAGE
Pg. 94, K4. **Rockville.** The good ol' days are alive and well in this re-created turn-of-the-century village and working farmstead. The village is home to a one-room schoolhouse, country store, blacksmith shop, livery, governor's house, and three covered bridges. **765/569-3430** $

L INDIANA DUNES NATIONAL LAKESHORE
Pg. 94, B5. **Porter.** The 15,000 acres comprising Indiana Dunes State Park feature miles of Lake Michigan beaches, towering sand dunes, bogs, marshes,

L Indiana Dunes

woodlands, and the various plants and animals peculiar to each. **219/926-7561** $

M INDIANAPOLIS MOTOR SPEEDWAY AND HALL OF FAME MUSEUM
Pg. 94, K8. The center of the racing world in the month of May, the speedway's 2-1/2 mile oval track is the home of the famous 500-mile race and a testing site of many modern automobile innovations. The Hall of Fame Museum exhibits antique and classic passenger cars, many built in Indiana. **317/484-6747** $

N NCAA HALL OF CHAMPIONS
Pg. 94, K8. **Indianapolis.** Indiana may be the basketball capital, but twenty-two

N NCAA Museum

men's and women's intercollegiate sports share the limelight here. The hall celebrates student athletes and their sports through photographs, video presentations, and displays, including one that plays well-known college fight songs. **800/735-6222** $

O WYANDOTTE CAVES
Pg. 95, T8. **Corydon.** Both novice and advanced spelunkers will find adventure in the seven miles of mapped passages. Cave tours feature the Garden of Helictites, a large collection of rare, twisted formations, Rothrock's Cathedral, a 105-foot underground mountain, and Pillar of the Constitution, a stalagmite approximately 71 feet in circumference. **812/738-2782** $

M Indy Speedway Museum

OHIO

P THE CLEVELAND MUSEUM OF ART
Pg. 143, E15. Considered to be one of the finest general art museums in the United States, the museum's collection of over 30,000 works represents nearly every culture and historical period, including those of the pre-Columbian Americas, Asia, and Europe. **216/421-7340**

Q CUYAHOGA VALLEY NATIONAL PARK
Pg. 143, G15. **Akron.** A beautiful and varied area on 33,000 acres, this park offers extensive recreational facilities, including a fully accessible twenty-mile trail on the towpath of the Ohio and Erie Canal. The park also features ranger-guided programs, scenic train rides, and opportunities for horseback riding, fishing, hiking, and cross-country skiing. **800/433-1986**

R NASA GLENN VISITOR CENTER
Pg. 143, E15. **Cleveland.** Space travel comes to Earth in exhibits that educate visitors on the history and future of space exploration. On display here are the Apollo Command Module used on Skylab 3, the space suit worn by Jim Lovell on Apollo 8. and a real Moon rock. The Solar System gallery provides an overview of planetary exploration. Outside, visitors are greeted by a full-scale replica of the Centaur rocket. **216/433-2001**

S OHIO'S PREHISTORIC NATIVE AMERICAN MOUNDS
Pg. 144, N9. **Columbus.** More than 10,000 Native American burial and ceremonial mounds remain in Ohio, including some built in complex shapes, such as the form of a bird or other animals. The famous effigy mound in Peebles, the Serpent Mound, was constructed in the shape of an uncoiling snake. **614/221-6623**

T PRO FOOTBALL HALL OF FAME
Pg. 143, H-6. **Canton.** This five-building museum, celebrating football, chronicles the sport from 1892 to the present. Visitors may visit GameDay Stadium, a total sensory experience that combines state-of-the-art sound, film and video to present "Football As You've Never Experienced It," the Pro Football Adventure Room, where mementos of today's star players and record holders are featured, and the NFL Films Theater, where a different NFL film is shown every hour. **330/456-8207** $

U ROCK AND ROLL HALL OF FAME AND MUSEUM
Pg. 143, E15. **Cleveland.** Cleveland rocks! The new home of rock and roll explores rock music's revolution and ongoing evolution. Exhibits on rhythm and blues, soul, country, folk, and blues music celebrate the greats and music's impact on culture. **216/781-7625** $

V UNION TERMINAL
Pg. 144, S3 **Cincinnati.** One of Cincinnati's treasures, this famous Art Deco landmark was built in the early 20th century as a solution to the city's chaotic railroad system, which consisted of seven lines operating out of five stations. Today, the terminal houses three museums—the Cincinnati History Museum ($), the Museum of Natural History and Science ($), and the Cinergy Children's Museum ($) — an OmniMax theater ($), and a working Amtrak terminal. **513/287-7000**

DOLLAR WI$E

- When sightseeing in Chicago, take advantage of the city's free trolley, which provides daily service to top cultural attractions and shopping destinations.
- Use Chicago's public transportation to get around the city. A Visitor Pass offers unlimited rides on CTA buses or trains for one price with a 1, 2, 3, or 5-day pass.
- Purchasing a CityPass gets you into six famous Chicago attractions for nearly a 50% discount.
- Look for Hot Tix locations throughout Chicago; this service offers half-price theater tickets for day-of shows. Weekend shows are often released Thursday evening.

February

Chicago Auto Show
Chicago
Hundreds of foreign and domestic cars are displayed.
312/744-3370

April

Madison In Bloom
Madison, IN
Visit several private courtyard gardens in the historic downtown during peak spring color.
812/265-2335

Tri-City JazzFest
Cleveland
216/987-4400

May

Indianapolis 500
Indianapolis, IN
317/484-6780

May Festival
Cincinnati
Oldest continuous choral festival in the nation; choral and operatic masterworks.
513/381-3300

June

Chicago Blues Festival
Chicago, IL
Three-day festival featuring concerts from blues artists worldwide.
312/744-3370

Greater Columbus Arts Festival
Columbus, OH
Exhibits, music, dancing.
800/345-4FUN

Taste of Chicago
Chicago
Selected Chicago restaurants offer sample-size specialties.
312/744-3370

July

Galena Arts Festival
Galena, IL
815/777-9341

Venetian Night
Chicago
Venetian aquatic parade, fireworks.
312/747-2474

August

Amish Acres Arts & Crafts Festival
Nappanee, IN
Paintings, ceramics, jewelry; entertainment, dancing, feasts.
800/800-4942

Illinois State Fair
Springfield, IL
217/782-6661

Indiana State Fair
Indianapolis
Grand circuit horse racing, livestock exhibitions, entertainment, and special agricultural exhibits.
317/927-7500

Ohio State Fair
Columbus, OH
800/OHO-EXPO

September

Cleveland National Air Show
Cleveland, OH
216/781-0747

Johnny Appleseed Festival
Fort Wayne, IN
Pioneer village, period crafts, contests, entertainment, Living History Hill, farmers market.
260/420-2020

October

Harvest Festival
Akron, OH
Celebrates end of the harvest season. Hands-on 19th-century rural activities include cider pressing, hayrides, crafts, musical entertainment, food.
800/589-9703

WV 173
KY 100
TN 158
WV 248
KY 237
TN 245

Nestled beneath the Great Smoky Mountains, Tennessee takes pride in its traditions. Graceland fascinates fans of The King; the Grand Ole Opry still plays to a packed house; Dollywood entertains the lighthearted; and the Appalachian Trail welcomes hikers and backpackers. In neighboring Kentucky, natural wonders include the world's largest cave at Mammoth, the spectacular Cumberland Falls and Cumberland Gap, and the ice age Breaks Park. Sportscar lovers can check out the Corvette Museum at Bowling Green, and race enthusiasts can wager on the horses at Churchill Downs. West Virginia attracts nature lovers who explore the Monongahela National Forest and Greenbrier River Trail. The thermal waters at Berkeley and White Sulphur Springs attract visitors from around the world. Civil War buffs revisit the past at Harpers Ferry.

Straddling the Appalachians, West Virginia's terrain is a tortuous series of ridges and hollows. Kentucky and Tennessee share the heights of the Allegheny Mountains in the east and then descend westward to fertile lowlands along the Mississippi Valley.

Free Finds

Jack Daniels Distillery, Lynchburg, TN
Nation's oldest registered distillery. One-hour and 20-minute guided tours include rustic grounds, limestone spring cave, old office. **931/759-4221**

Tennessee State Museum, Nashville, TN
Exhibits on life in Tennessee from early man through the early 1900s. **615/741-2692**

Sunsphere, Knoxville, TN
Built for the 1982 World's Fair, this 266-ft tower has an observation deck that provides views of downtown and the Smoky Mountains. **800/523-4227**

Casey Jones Village, Jackson, TN
Complex of turn-of-the-century shops and buildings centered around the life of one of America's most famous railroad heroes. **731/668-1222**

Morgan Row, Harrodsburg, KY
Probably the oldest standing row house west of the Alleghenies; once a stagecoach stop and tavern. Houses Harrodsburg Historical Society Museum. **606/734-5985**

Kentucky Military History Museum, Frankfort
Exhibits trace Kentucky's involvement in military conflicts through two centuries. **502/564-3265**

Old Mud Meeting House, Harrodsburg, KY
First Dutch Reformed Church west of the Alleghenies. **859/734-5985**

Toyota Motor Manufacturing, Kentucky, Inc., Georgetown
About 400,000 cars and 350,000 engines are made here annually. One-hour tour of the plant includes video presentation and tram ride through different levels of production. **502/868-3027**

Tours of Charles Town, WV
Historical walking tours; candlelit tours of Jefferson County Courthouse; carriage rides. **304/728-7713**

Middleton Doll Company, Parkersburg, WV
Tour of vinyl and porcelain doll factory. **614/423-1481**

State Capitol, Charleston, WV
One of America's most beautiful state capitols, the building was designed by Cass Gilbert in Italian Renaissance style. **304/558-3456**

West Virginia State Farm Museum, Point Pleasant
Contains more than 30 farm buildings depicting early rural life. **304/675-5737**

B Graceland

E Lookout Mountain

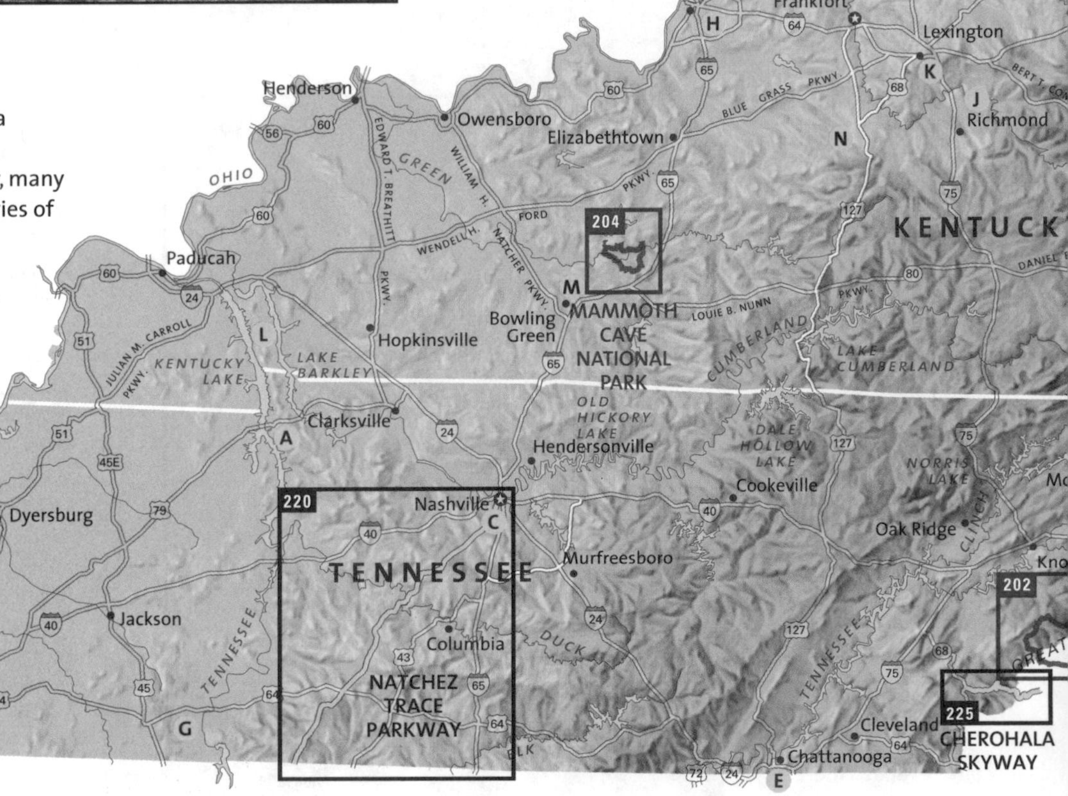

TENNESSEE

A FORT DONELSON NATIONAL BATTLEFIELD AND CEMETERY
Pg. 158, B8. **Dover.** "Unconditional and immediate surrender!" was the answer General Ulysses S. Grant gave when the Confederates proposed a truce at Fort Donelson. The decisive victory here opened up the heart of the Confederacy to Union troops. The fort walls, outer defenses, and river batteries remain as a testament to the battle. Visitors may tour the park by car, hike the park trails, and attend park programs and presentations. **931/232-5706**

B GRACELAND
Pg. 158, F2. **Memphis.** The former home of Elvis Presley is now the nation's next-to-most-visited home, second only to The White House. Guided tours of the elaborate mansion include his pool, TV and music rooms, trophy room, and his magnificent show costume collection. The tour ends in the garden, where his tomb is located. **901/332-3322** $

C THE HERMITAGE
Pg. 159, C11. **Nashville.** The Greek Revival-style residence of President Andrew Jackson is furnished almost entirely with original family pieces, many of which were associated with Jackson's military career and years in the White House. The 660-acre estate contains a garden with the graves of Jackson and his wife, Rachel. **615/889-2941** $

D JONESBOROUGH
Pg. 159, L14. The oldest town in Tennessee was the first capitol of the State of Franklin when the area separated from North Carolina in 1784. Today, many visitors enjoy its galleries of fine arts and crafts, antique shops, and specialty stores. Many festivals take place here, including the World Music Festival, Music on the Square, and the National Storytelling Festival. **423/461-8000**

E LOOKOUT MOUNTAIN
Pg. 159, G15. On clear days, the view from the top of this 2,120-foot peak includes Georgia, North Carolina, South Carolina, Alabama, as well as Tennessee. During the Civil War the "Battle above the Clouds" — named for the famous fog that descends halfway down the slope — was fought here. **423/756-8687**

F NATIONAL CIVIL RIGHTS MUSEUM
Pg. 158, F2. **Memphis.** Built on the site of the Lorraine Motel—the place of Martin Luther King Jr.'s assassination—this is the first museum in the nation to honor the American civil rights movement and the people behind it, from Nat Turner, Sojourner Truth and Dred Scott to King and Malcolm X. **901/521-9699** $

G SHILOH NATIONAL MILITARY PARK
Pg. 158, F6. **Savannah.** Bitter, bloody Shiloh was the first major Civil War battle in the West and one of the fiercest in history. In two days, nearly 24,000 men were killed, wounded, or missing. Among the men who fought this dreadful battle were John Wesley Powell, who lost an arm but later went down the Colorado River by boat and became head of the U.S. Geological Survey; James A. Garfield, 20th president of the United States; and Henry Morton Stanley, who later uttered the famous phrase, "Dr. Livingstone, I presume." The visitor center contains uniforms, firearms, and other artifacts found on the battlefield. **901/689-5696** $

G Shiloh Military Park

KENTUCKY

H CHURCHILL DOWNS
Pg. 100, G8. **Louisville.** Founded in 1875, this historic and world-famous thoroughbred race track is the home of the Kentucky Derby, "the most exciting two minutes in sports." Located here is The Kentucky Derby Museum, where a film, The Greatest Race, puts viewers in the middle of Derby Day action, and a "time machine" allows visitors to select footage of Derbys as far back as 1918. **502/636-4400** $

I CUMBERLAND GAP NATIONAL HISTORIC PARK
Pg. 101, N15. **Middlesboro.** Cumberland Gap, a natural passage through the mountain barrier that effectively sealed off the infant American coastal colonies, was the open door to western development. Nearly 22,300 acres of this dramatically beautiful countryside in Kentucky, Tennessee, and Virginia have been set aside as a national park. More than 50 miles of trails offer hikes of varying difficulty. **606/248-2817**

J FORT BOONESBOROUGH STATE PARK
Pg. 101, G14. **Winchester.** The site where Daniel Boone defended his fort against Native American sieges is now a living museum where costumed "pioneers" produce crafts to sell in the park's shops. The Kentucky River Museum celebrates the trailblazer, who helped explore Kentucky, opening it to settlers. **606/527-3131** $

K KENTUCKY HORSE PARK
Pg. 101, G13. **Lexington.** Situated on more than 1,000 acres of beautiful bluegrass, the park features the grave of thoroughbred champion Man O'War, the International Museum of the Horse, and a collection of hand-carved horse miniatures. **606/233-4303** $

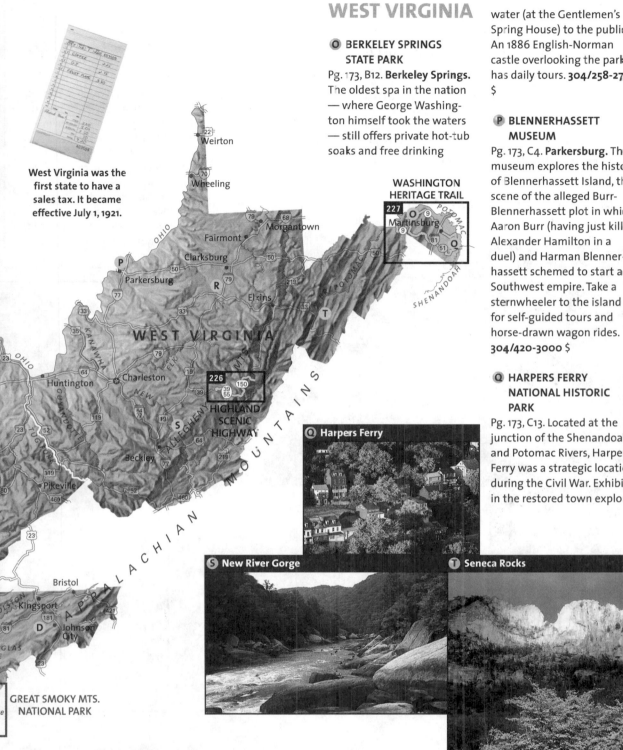

West Virginia was the first state to have a sales tax. It became effective July 1, 1921.

WEST VIRGINIA

O BERKELEY SPRINGS STATE PARK
Pg. 173, B12. **Berkeley Springs.** The oldest spa in the nation — where George Washington himself took the waters — still offers private hot-tub soaks and free drinking water (at the Gentlemen's Spring House) to the public. An 1886 English-Norman castle overlooking the park has daily tours. **304/258-2711** $

P BLENNERHASSETT MUSEUM
Pg. 173, C4. **Parkersburg.** The museum explores the history of Blennerhassett Island, the scene of the alleged Burr-Blennerhassett plot in which Aaron Burr (having just killed Alexander Hamilton in a duel) and Harman Blennerhassett schemed to start a Southwest empire. Take a sternwheeler to the island for self-guided tours and horse-drawn wagon rides. **304/420-3000** $

Q HARPERS FERRY NATIONAL HISTORIC PARK
Pg. 173, C13. Located at the junction of the Shenandoah and Potomac Rivers, Harpers Ferry was a strategic location during the Civil War. Exhibits in the restored town explore its pivotal role in the war, as well as ties to the water-power industry and Storer College, a school established for freed slaves after the war. **304/535-6298** $

R JACKSON'S MILL HISTORIC AREA
Pg. 173, D5. **Weston.** The boyhood home of "Stonewall" Jackson, the site includes Blaker's Mill, an operating water-powered gristmill, a blacksmith shop, and several cabins from the 18th and early 19th century. A museum illustrates the area's agriculture and home arts as practiced over one hundred years ago. **304/269-5100.** $

S NEW RIVER GORGE NATIONAL RIVER
Pg. 173, J5. **Hinton.** One of the oldest rivers on the continent, the New River — popular with whitewater rafters — rushes northward through a deep canyon. The bridge 876 feet overhead is the second highest in the nation (behind the Royal Gorge Bridge in Colorado). Get a good view from the Canyon Rim Visitors center on U.S. 19, 24 miles north of Beckley. **304/574-2115**

T SENECA ROCKS
Pg. 173, E9. A landmark for serious rock climbers, Seneca Rocks rises 900 feet above the tumbling North Fork River. For the less adventurous, a more moderate 1.3-mile self-guided interpretive trail ascends the north end of the Rocks, offering panoramic vistas of the surrounding area. **304/636-8400**

Q Harpers Ferry

S New River Gorge

T Seneca Rocks

H Churchill Downs

I Cumberland Gap

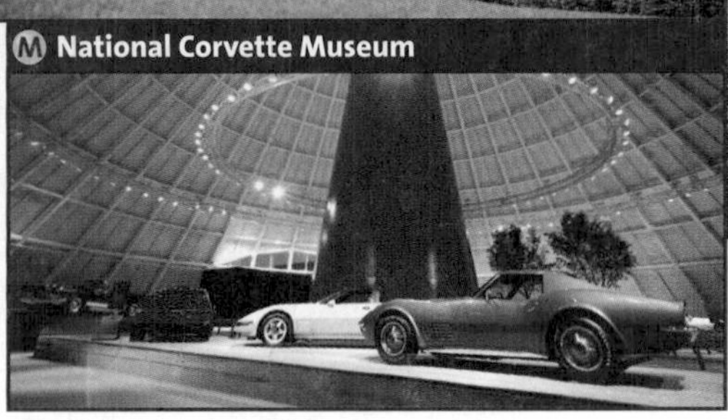

M National Corvette Museum

L LAND BETWEEN THE LAKES
Pg. 100, M2. **Cadiz.** The wooded peninsula running the 40 miles between Kentucky Lake and Lake Barkley in western Kentucky and Tennessee is one of the largest outdoor recreation areas in the country. Located here are the Elk and Bison Prairie ($), The Golden Pond Planetarium and Observatory ($), and the Woodlands Nature Station ($). **270/924-5897** $

M NATIONAL CORVETTE MUSEUM
Pg. 100, L6. **Bowling Green.** America's classic sports car since 1953, the Corvette has many fans, and this is their mecca. Hands-on educational exhibits and the chance to see more than 50 vintage models draw Corvette owners and enthusiasts from all over the world. **270/781-7973** $

N PERRYVILLE BATTLEFIELD STATE HISTORIC SITE
Pg. 101, J11. **Perryville.** This 300-acre park appears much as it did in 1862 when Confederate forces and Union troops clashed in one of the bloodiest battles of the Civil War. The Crawford House, used by the Confederacy as its headquarters, and Bottom House, the center of some of the heaviest fighting, still stand. The Perryville Battlefield Museum ($) features a Civil War display, a map with the layout of the battle, and actual battle artifacts. **859/332-8631**

DOLLAR WI$E

- Local artisans and craftmakers offer great deals and bargains at the Tennessee State Fairgrounds Flea Market Nashville, and admission is free.
- For a package price of $8, you can visit Memphis' Mississippi River Museum, take a guided River Walk tour and monorail ride at the Mud Island River Park. Or, you may stroll the park's River Walk, a miniature 5-block long replica of the lower Mississippi, at your leisure for no admission charge.
- Half-price tickets for performances at the Actor's Theater of Louisville are sold from 2-6 pm on the day of a particular performance, or one hour prior to an early matinee performance.
- Enjoy your picnic lunch set amid beautiful scenery at Lambert Vintage Wines in Weston, WV, and afterwards, take a tour of the winery and enjoy samples—all at no charge.
- Spend the day at Droop Mountain Battlefield Park—the site of West Virginia's last significant Civil War Battle—free of charge. Bring a picnic, visit its museum of Civil War artifacts, hike trails to scenic overlooks, and visit the lookout tower.
- "Music on the Row" offers free country music concerts on Nashville's Music Row every Wednesday evening from June until August. And you can visit the Grand Ole Opry Museum, the Roy Acuff Museum and the Minne Pearl Museum at no charge.

April

Dogwood Arts Festival
Knoxville, TN
Arts and crafts exhibits and shows, over 80 public and private gardens on display, musical entertainment; parades; sporting events.
865/637-4561

May

Beale Street Music Festival
Memphis, TN
International roster of musicians returns to Memphis for a musical family reunion.
901/278-0243

Kentucky Derby
Louisville, KY
Churchill Downs. The first jewel in the Triple Crown.
502/636-4400

Little River Days
Hopkinsville, KY
Road races, canoe races; arts and crafts, entertainment; children's events.
270/885-9096

Three Rivers Festival
Fairmont, WV
Entertainment, parade, Civil War reenactment, carnival, games.
304/363-2625

June

Festival of the Bluegrass
Lexington, KY
More than 20 top bands. Including special shows for children, crafts, workshops.
859/846-4995

Riverbend Festival
Chattanooga, TN
Music and sporting events, children's activities, fireworks display.
423/756-2211

July

Mountain State Art & Craft Fair
Ripley, WV
Features traditional crafts, art, folk music, and foods.
304/372-7860

August

Elvis Presley International Tribute Week
Memphis, TN
More than 30 events take place throughout the city in honor of Presley and his music.
901/332-3322

Kentucky State Fair
Louisville, KY
Livestock shows, championship horse show, home and fine arts exhibits, entertainment.
502/367-5002

West Virginia State Fair
Lewisburg, WV
304/645-1090

September

Corn Island Storytelling Festival
Louisville, KY
Recaptures bygone days of yarn spinning. Ghost stories in Long Run Park, storytelling cruises.
502/245-0643

Mason-Dixon Festival
Morgantown, WV
River parade, boat races, arts and crafts, concessions.
304/599-1104

October

Fall Color Cruise & Folk Festival
Chattanooga, TN
Riverboat trips, arts and crafts, entertainment.
706/275-8778

December

Old Tyme Christmas
Harpers Ferry, WV
Caroling, musical programs, children's programs, taffy pull, candlelight walk.
304/535-2627

Free $ Finds

Historic New Orleans Custom House, New Orleans
Used in part as an office by Major General Benjamin "Spoons" Butler during Union occupation, and in part as a prison for Confederate soldiers.

Heritage Museum and Village, Baton Rouge, LA
Turn-of-the-century Victorian house with period room and exhibits. Also rural village replicas include church, school, store, and town hall. **225/774-1776**

Stansel Rice Company, Gueydan, LA
Guided tours of family-owned mill at the oldest and largest gourmet popcorn and rice company. **337/536-6140**

Gadsden Museum of Fine Arts, Gadsden, AL
Features works by local, national, and international artists. **205/546-7365**

Biloxi Historical Walking Tour, Biloxi, MS
Visitor center offers self-guided walking tour that includes historical landmarks. **228/374-3105**

Cactus Plantation, Edwards, MS
World's only cactus plantation features over 3,500 varieties of exotic cacti, tropical foliage, and seasonal plants. **601/852-2705**

Historic Jefferson College, Natchez, MS
Site of the first state Constitutional Convention in 1817. **601/442-2901**

Three Notch Museum, Andalusia, AL
Located in 1899 Central of Georgia Depot. Railroad memorabilia, old photographs, handmade lace and linens, depression glass, hand-woven baskets, farm implements. **334/222-0674**

George Washington Carver Museum, Tuskegee, AL
The museum includes Dr. Carver's original laboratory, his extensive collection of native plants, minerals, needlework, paintings, drawings, personal belongings, and the array of products he developed. **334/727-320**

F. Scott and Zelda Fitzgerald Museum, Montgomery, AL
The author and his wife lived in this house from 1931-1932. Personal artifacts detail the couple's public and private lives. **334/264-4222**

From the outrageous celebrations of New Orleans' Mardi Gras to the serenity of Nottoway Plantation, Louisiana is a veritable jambalaya of options. Its bayous and swamps are home to alligators and exotic birds; Preservation Hall hosts nightly jazz performances; and the Kisatchie National Forest attracts backpackers and hikers. Mississippi's Gulf Island National Seashore stretches for 150 beautiful miles, and Gulfport and Natchez casinos really heat up the nights. In Biloxi, historic mansions have been carefully preserved and beg to be admired. Air and space fans will enjoy the NASA Marshall Space Flight Center in Huntsville, Alabama, and the Tuskegee Airmen National Historic Site at Moton Field. Birmingham's Five Points South offers exciting nightlife, while Mobile's sedate historic section displays a variety of architectural styles.

Alabama, with a heavily forested interior came later to plantation agriculture than its neighbors—but enjoyed in its old port of Mobile a magnificent location for shipbuilding and commerce. Mississippi and Louisiana are creatures of the Mississippi River, which endowed both the famously fertile Delta and the busy port of New Orleans.

Ⓐ Audubon Park

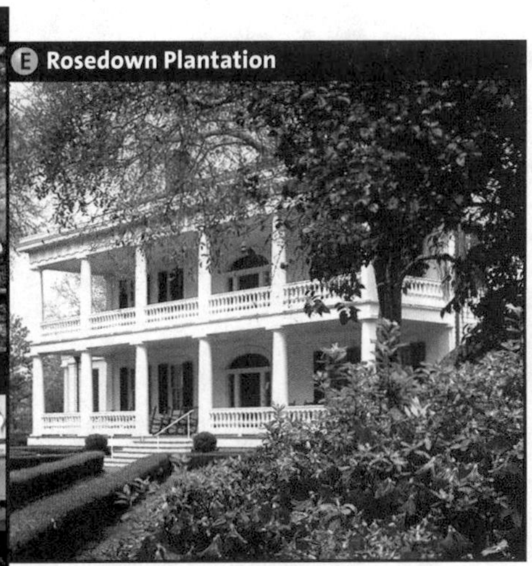

Ⓔ Rosedown Plantation

Ⓒ French Quarter

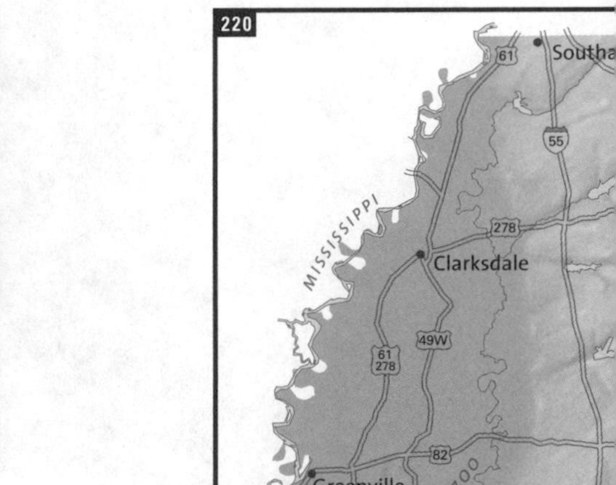

LOUISIANA

Ⓐ AUDUBON PARK AND ZOOLOGICAL GARDENS
Pg. 103, K15. **New Orleans.** This 400-acre park designed by the Olmstead brothers is nestled between St. Charles Avenue and the Mississippi River and surrounded by century-old oak trees. It features an 18-hole golf course, bicycle and jogging paths, and tennis courts. The zoo hosts more than 1,800 animals in naturalistic settings. **504/861-2537** $

Ⓑ DOWNTOWN RIVERFRONT
Pg. 103, J12. **Baton Rouge.** Visitors to Baton Rouge's riverfront entertainment district are never at a loss for things to do; the area is host to many lively festivals, and home to many restaurants and dance clubs. Also along the banks of the Mississippi are the Louisiana Arts and Science Museum ($), the Old State Capitol ($), and the U.S.S. Kidd ($), on which visitors may roam decks and explore interior compartments. **225/383-1825**

Ⓒ FRENCH QUARTER
Pg. 103, K15. **New Orleans.** Established in 1718 as a French military outpost, this is the city's oldest neighborhood. Known for its vibrant culture, the "Vieux Carré" offers live music, delectable dining, art, architecture, history, and supernatural culture. Highlights include Jackson Square, the French Market, Cathedral Garden, St. Louis Cathedral, The Old U.S. Mint ($), and Madame John's Legacy. **504/566-5011**

Ⓓ HISTORIC "CHARPENTIER"
Pg. 102, K7. **Lake Charles.** Named in honor of the carpenters who constructed the homes of downtown Lake Charles in the early 20th century, this 20-block historic district includes architectural styles ranging from Queen Anne, Eastlake, and "Carpenter's Gothic" (known locally as "Lake Charles style") to Western stick-style bungalows. Aside from touring the finest Victorian architecture in the state, visitors are afforded unique shopping and dining opportunities. **337/436-9588**

Ⓔ PLANTATION TOUR
Pg. 103, J12. **Baton Rouge.** Start this drive tour at Oakley, where John James Audubon painted 32 of his Birds of America; head to Rosedown Plantation and Gardens ($) in St. Francisville, a magnificently restored antebellum mansion with many original furnishings; and end at The Myrtles ($), known as one of "America's most haunted mansions." **225/383-1825**

Ⓕ SHADOWN-ON-THE-TECHE
Pg. 102, L10. **New Iberia.** This red brick and white-pillared Greek Revival house was built on the banks of the Bayou Teche by sugar planter David Weeks. Home to four generations of his family, it served as the center of an antebellum plantation system. **337/369-6446** $

MISSISSIPPI

Ⓖ ANTEBELLUM HOUSES
Pg. 118, G5. **Vicksburg.** These historic houses includes Anchuca, a restored Greek Revival mansion; Cedar Grove, shelled by Union gunboats in siege; Duff Green, used as a hospital during the Civil War; Martha Vick House, built by the daughter of the founder of Vicksburg; and the McRaven Home, the heaviest-shelled house during the Siege of Vicksburg. **601/636-9421** $

Ⓗ GULF ISLANDS NATIONAL SEASHORE
Pg. 118, M9. **Ocean Springs.** This area includes part of the mainland coast and four offshore islands, where wildlife sanctuaries can be found. Camping enthusiasts will be drawn to the beautiful sparkling beaches and coastal marshes. Films and exhibits at the headquarters examine the flora and fauna of the region, and nature trails follow the winding bayou. **850/934-2600** $

Ⓘ JOHN C. STENNIS SPACE CENTER
Pg. 118, M8. **Gulfport.** This Center hosts NASA and other agencies involved in oceanographic, environmental, and national defense programs. It was the test site of Saturn V, and the first and second stages for the Apollo manned lunar program (including Apollo 11 which landed the first men on moon). **228/688-2370**

Ⓙ NATCHEZ
Pg. 118, J3. Natchez embodies the enchantment of the Old South, a plantation atmosphere where everything seems beautiful and romantic. Greek Revival mansions,

Ⓝ Ave Maria Grotto

Ⓡ Russell Cave

Ⓢ Tuskegee Institute

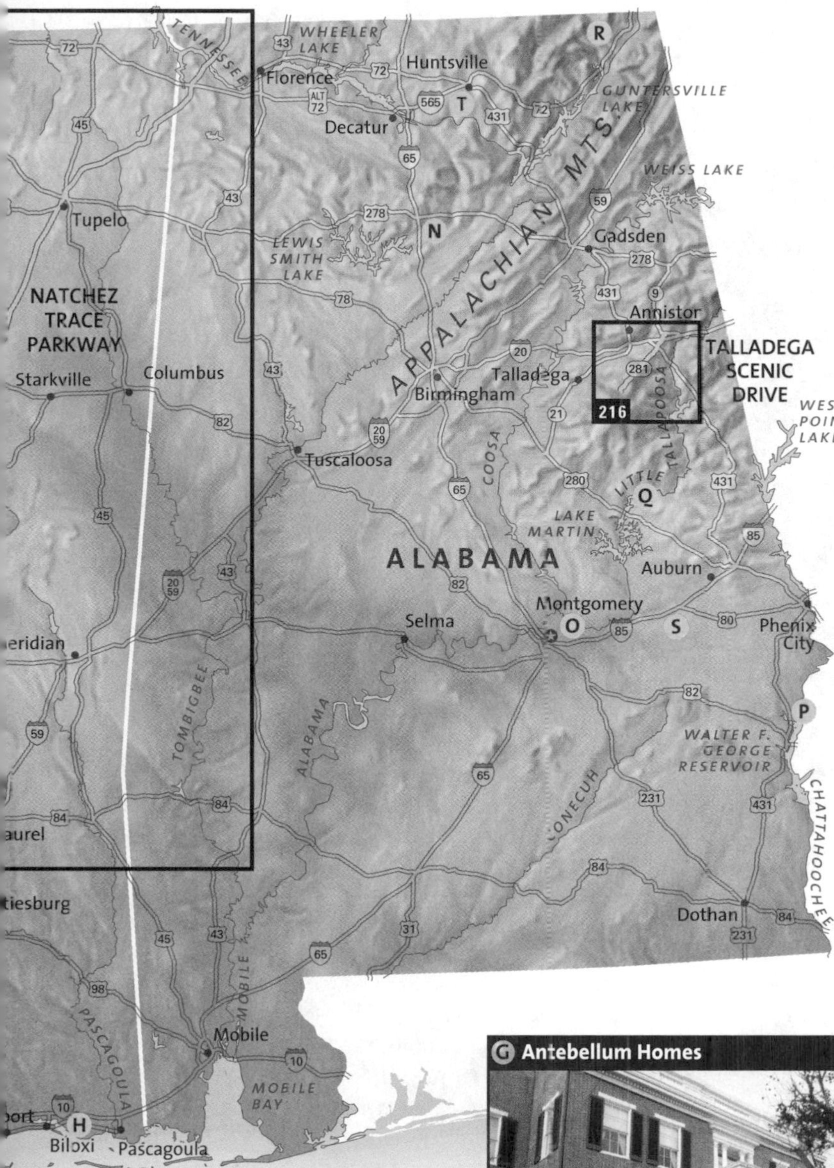

Ⓖ Antebellum Homes

Ⓙ Natchez

manicured gardens and lawns, tree-shaded streets, and southern hospitality can be found in this museum of the antebellum South. **601/446-6345**

Ⓚ ROSEMONT PLANTATION

Pg. 118, K4. **Woodville.** Jefferson Davis' boyhood home displays many family furnishings, including a spinning wheel that belonged to his mother, Jane. Shaded by magnolias and live oaks, the plantation grounds have been bordered by split-rail fences. Many of the rosebushes for which the plantation was named continue to bloom today. Five generations of the Davis family are buried here. **601/888-6809** $

Ⓛ ROSSWOOD PLANTATION

Pg. 118, H4. **Port Gibson.** This Greek Revival mansion designed by David Shroder, architect of the nearby Windsor plantation, features columned galleries, 10 fireplaces, 15-foot ceilings, a winding stairway, and a basement slave quarters. The first owner's diary survives and offers details of antebellum life on a cotton plantation. **800/533-5889** $

Ⓜ VICKSBURG NATIONAL MILITARY PARK & CEMETERY

Pg. 118, G5. This is the site of Union siege lines and the Confederate defense, bordering the eastern and northern sections of the city. A visitor center, museum and exhibits help tell the stories of this historic military site. **601/636-0583** $

ALABAMA

Ⓝ AVE MARIA GROTTO

Pg. 60, D6. **Cullman.** Benedictine monk Brother Joseph Zoettl spent 50 years building miniature replicas of famous churches, buildings, and shrines using cement, stone, bits of jewelry, and marble. Visitors will find renditions of Bethlehem, Nazareth, Jerusalem, the Basilica of St. Peter's, and the California missions. **256/734-4110** $

Ⓞ DEXTER AVENUE KING MEMORIAL BAPTIST CHURCH

Pg. 60, K8. **Montgomery.** The Reverend Dr. Martin Luther King, Jr. was a pastor here from 1954 -1960. From this church he directed the Montgomery bus boycott, which sparked the civil rights movement and propelled King into the national spotlight. See a mural and original painting entitled "The Beginning of a Dream." **334/263-3970**

Ⓟ EUFAULA NATIONAL WILDLIFE REFUGE

Pg. 61, M11. Partially located in Georgia and superimposed on the Walter F. George Reservoir, the refuge was established to provide a feeding and resting area for waterfowl migrating between the Tennessee Valley and the Gulf Coast. Ducks, geese, egrets, and herons are among the 281 species of birds found here. A seven-mile wildlife drive is popular with cyclists and motorists, and anglers find bass, crappie, catfish and bluegill. **334/687-4065**

Ⓠ HORSESHOE BEND NATIONAL MILITARY PARK

Pg. 60, H10. **Daviston.** In the early 1800s, General Andrew Jackson and a 3,300-man army attacked Chief Menawa and 1,000 Upper Creek or Red Stick warriors fortified in the "horseshoe" bend of the Tallapoosa River. The Upper and Lower Creeks were forced to give the U.S. nearly 20 million acres of what is now land in Alabama and Georgia. **205/234-7111**

Ⓡ RUSSELL CAVE NATIONAL MONUMENT

Pg. 60, A9. **Bridgeport.** This cave shelter is located on the edge of the Tennessee River Valley. Stone Age humans made their home here in a giant room 210 feet long, 107 feet wide and averaging 26 feet high. Excavation of refuse and debris deposited in the cave has dated the site to approx mately 7000 B.C. Hiking trails traverse the park's 310 acres, and the visitor center displays artifacts belonging to the cave dwellers. **256/495-2672**

Ⓢ TUSKEGEE INSTITUTE NATIONAL HISTORIC SITE

Pg. 60, K9. Many original buildings are located here on the campus of Tuskegee University, an industrial school for African-Americans founded by Booker T. Washington. Among the points of interest are The Oaks, which was once Washington's home, and the George Washington Carver Museum, displaying the horticulturalist's collections. **334/727-6390**

Ⓣ U.S. SPACE AND ROCKET CENTER

Pg. 60, B7. **Huntsville.** Along with one of the largest rocket collections in the world, the Center offers hands-on learning experiences, thrilling rides, and actual vehicles and artifacts from U.S. and Russian Space Programs. Visitors can get an astronaut's view of the Earth while watching a film on the 67-foot domed screen of the Spacedome IMAX Theater, walk under the world's only "Full Stack" shuttle in Shuttle Park, and sit inside an Apollo Command Module. **256/837-3400** $

DOLLAR WI$E

- Visit www.neworleanscoupons.com for discount coupons for attractions, hotels, and restaurants.
- Listen to some of the best New Orleans jazz at Preservation Hall for only $5.
- Don't buy souvenirs on Bourbon Street—head to the downriver end of the French Market for deals on such things as tee shirts and Mardi Gras masks.
- Making a stop in Natchez, MS? The city's web site, www.natchez.ms.us, offers coupons good for discounts on area attractions.

February

Mardi Gras
New Orleans
Carnival, perhaps the most famous celebration in the US, includes torchlight parades, dancing, balls, masquerades.
504/566-5011

March

Historic Selma Pilgrimage
Selma, AL
Daylight tours of historic houses; antique show.
800/457-3562

April

Azalea Dogwood Festival
Dothan, AL
Marked route through residential areas at peak of bloom.
334/794-6622

Arts in the Park
Meridian, MS
Concerts, plays, art shows, children's programs.
601/693-2787

New Orleans Jazz & Heritage Festival
New Orleans, LA
Outdoor weekend activities with Louisiana specialty foods, crafts, and 15 stages of simultaneous music.
504/522-4786

June

Melrose Plantation Arts & Crafts Festiva
Natchitoches, LA
Juried works of more than 100 artists and craftspeople.
318/379-0055

July

Faulkner Conference
Oxford, MS
Various programs celebrate the author's accomplishments.
662/232-7282

August

Sunflower River Blues and Gospel Festival
Clarksdale, MS
Weekend of outdoor concerts—blues on Fri, Sat, gospel on Sat—with local barbecue and other Southern specialties.
601/359-3297

September

Red River Revel Arts Festival
Shreveport, LA
Fine arts, crafts, pottery, jewelry; music, performing arts, creative writing, poetry, ethnic foods.
318/424-4000

Seafood Festival
Biloxi, MS
Arts and crafts show, entertainment, seafood booths, contests.
601/359-3297

October

Alabama State Fair
Birmingham, AL
205/786-8100

Louisiana State Fair
Shreveport, LA
Entertainment, agriculture and livestock competition.
318/635-1361

Mississippi State Fair
Jackson, MS
Agricultural and industrial exhibits and contests, midway, entertainment.
601/961-4000

December

Blue-Gray Football Classic
Montgomery, AL
334/242-4413

Christmas Festival of Lights
Natchitoches, LA
More than 140,000 lights are turned on to welcome the Christmas season.
318/352-8072

FL 82
FL 234

Free Finds

Depot Museum, Lake Wales
Built as a passenger station by the Atlantic Coast Line Railroad in 1928, this pink stucco structure now houses memorabilia of early Lake Wales. **863/678-4209**

Goodyear Blimp Visitor Center, Pompano Beach
Base for the airship Stars and Stripes. Visitors are not offered rides, but may view the blimp on the ground. **954/946-8300**

Florida Adventure Museum, Punta Gorda
Natural history displays; fossils, mounted exhibits of lions, leopards, and bears. **941/639-3777**

Old Town, Kissimmee
Replica turn-of-the-century Florida village with brick-lined streets; specialty shops and restaurants, general store, and antique hand-carved wooden carousel. **407/396-4888**

The Pier, St. Petersburg
A five-story inverted pyramid located at the end of this 1/4-mile pier contains an observation deck with a view of the city, restaurants, shops, an aquarium, and miniature golf. **727/821-6164**

Air Force Armament Museum, Fort Walton Beach
Exhibits include historical aircraft and weapons. **850/882-4062**

Whetstone Chocolate Factory, St. Augustine
Self-guided tour with free sample. Includes a 15-minute video and a walk through the factory where chocolates are made. **904/825-1700**

Mission of Nombre de Dios, St. Augustine
A 208-ft stainless-steel cross marks the site of the founding of St. Augustine, September 8, 1565. Also here is the Shrine of Our Lady of La Leche. **904/824-3045**

Mounts Botanical Garden, West Palm Beach
Oldest and largest public botanical garden in Palm Beach County. Over 13 acres of tropical and subtropical plants, including herb, palm, cactus, tropical fruit collections, and more. **561/233-1749**

Southbank Riverwalk, Jacksonville
A 1.2-mile stretch of shops, hotels, restaurants and theaters that run along the St. John's River. Provides beautiful vistas of downtown. The focal point is Friendship Fountain, a series of seven sprayers that shoot water 120 feet into the sky. **800/733-2668**

Anheuser-Busch Brewery, Jacksonville
Tours of the brewery conclude in a Hospitality Room for beer tasting. **904/751-8117**

Although Florida is clearly the ultimate beach destination, the Sunshine State is wonderfully diverse. The fascinating, age-old Everglades includes 1.5 million miles of subtropical flora and fauna, and St. Augustine, the oldest city in America, bears its age proudly. In stark contrast, the Kennedy Space Center keeps its eye on the future. Families are entertained at Walt Disney World, Sea World, and Busch Gardens, and racecar enthusiasts pilgrimage annually to Daytona Beach. With its eye-catching art deco architecture, trendy nightclubs, and infectious Latin rhythm, Miami sizzles both day and night. Genteel Boca Raton and Palm Beach are noteworthy for their high-end lifestyles. Offer a toast to the Florida Keys while drinking in the sensational sunset, or walk in the steps of pirates at Dry Tortugas National Park.

Beneath the surface of the northern part of Florida, fissures and cracks in the limestone bedrock have left a landscape dotted with hundreds of freshwater springs and thousands of sinkholes. Near Gainesville, at Devils Millhopper State Geological Site, a sinkhole 120-feet deep and some 600-feet wide testifies to the porous nature of the state's underbelly. To the south, a giant ecosystem includes tropical forests, the Everglades, and coral reefs off the keys.

Ⓑ Art Deco District, Miami

Ⓒ Castillo De San Marcos National Monument

Ⓓ Cypress Gardens

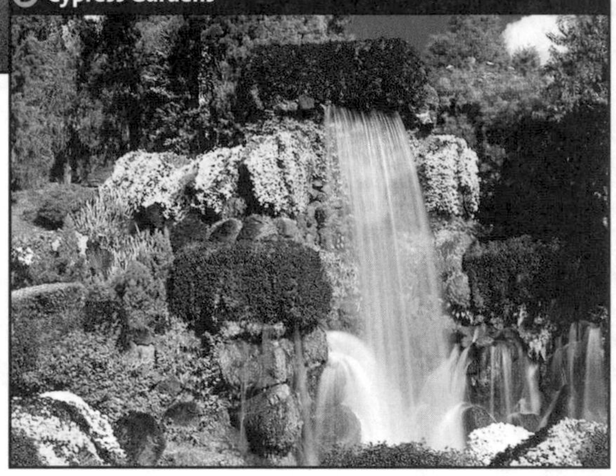

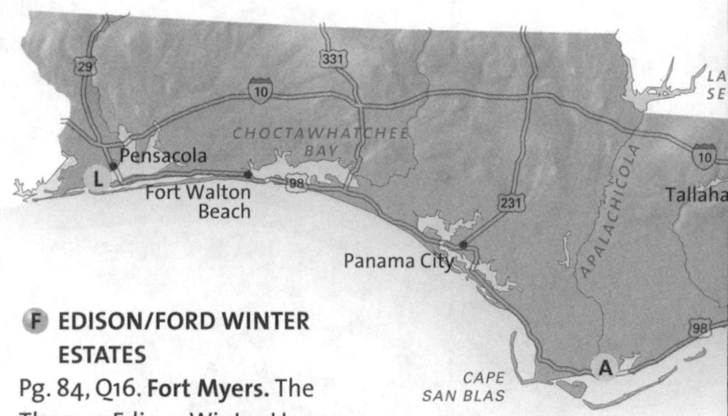

FLORIDA

Ⓐ APALACHICOLA
Pg. 82, G8. Once known as West Point, the town took the name Apalachicola (Native American for "people on the other side") soon after it was incorporated. Though at one time it was a leading cotton-shipping port, the town now turns to the sea for its major crop; nearly 90 percent of Florida's oysters are harvested from nearby St. George Sound. Visitors can take a scenic walking tour of the Apalachicola Historic District, which features many fine homes and buildings dating back to the 1830s, or visit the Apalachicola Maritime Museum, which highlights the maritime history of the area. **850/653-9419**

Ⓑ ART DECO DISTRICT
Pg. 81, L9. **Miami.** This one-of-a-kind National Historic District is a square mile of art deco, streamline moderne, and Spanish Mediterranean Revival architecture. Former art deco apartment buildings, ballrooms, and warehouses have been restored to pastel-and-neon luminosity and sometimes serve as canvases for murals, trompe l'oeil images, and elaborate graffiti created by local artists. **305/672-2014**

Gatorade was named for the University of Florida Gators; the drink was first developed there for the football team.

Ⓒ CASTILLO DE SAN MARCOS NATIONAL MONUMENT
Pg. 83, F17. **St. Augustine.** This massive masonry structure, constructed between 1672 and 1695, was built to be a lasting replacement for a succession of nine wooden fortifications. Castillo de San Marcos was never conquered. It withstood a 50-day siege when St. Augustine was captured by the South Carolinians in 1702, and another siege of 38 days in 1740. Ranger programs are offered year-round, and there are museum exhibits within the walls of the Castillo. **904/829-6506** $

Ⓓ CYPRESS GARDENS
Pg. 83, L16. **Winter Haven.** Towering cypress trees shelter more than 8,000 varieties of exotic plants and flowers at one of the world's most famous botanical gardens. The 223-acre theme park includes shows, museums, and a children's amusement ride and game area; as well as an elaborate model railroad and more than a dozen shops in a replica of an antebellum town. **863/324-2111** $

Ⓔ DRY TORTUGAS NATIONAL PARK
Pg. 84, V16. **Key West.** Covering approximately 64,000 acres of land and water, this national park includes not only the remains of the largest 19th-century American coastal fort, Fort Jefferson, but also the cluster of seven islands known as the Dry Tortugas. These islands provide a peaceful vantage point for viewing coral reefs and nesting seabirds. Other attractions include swimming, shorkeling, picnic sites, camping, and a visitor center. **305/294-7009**

Ⓔ Dry Tortugas

Ⓕ EDISON/FORD WINTER ESTATES
Pg. 84, Q16. **Fort Myers.** The Thomas Edison Winter House and Botanical Gardens comprise a 14-acre estate built by Edison in 1885. Guided tours of the estate include the inventor's furnished house, a botanical garden consisting of some 6,000 species, and the laboratory and workshops where he researched domestic plant sources for rubber. The automaker Henry Ford, Edison's friend, wintered at the home next door. Visitors can tour his restored house, furnished in the style of the 1920's, and see antique cars. The grounds are planted with citrus trees and tropical plants. **239/334-7419** $

Ⓖ FERNANDINA BEACH
Pg. 83, E17. The 50-block historic district here contains numerous Victorian mansions, as well as the Palace Saloon, decorated with a mural and fine antiques, and once the haunt of the Rockefellers; the Florida House Inn, where Ulysses Grant slept; and many shops and cafes. **904/277-0717**

Ⓗ FORT MATANZAS NATIONAL MONUMENT
Pg. 83, F17. **St. Augustine.** This reservation extends over an area of 298 acres that includes the southern tip of Anastasia Island and Rattlesnake Island, where the fort itself is located. The fort is considered a fine representative of a vanished style of military architecture. Fishing is permitted along the shoreline of Matanzas River. **904/471-0116**

Ⓘ GAMBLE PLANTATION STATE HISTORIC SITES
Pg. 81, F4. **Ellenton.** This Confederate memorial features the only surviving antebellum house in south Florida. Major Robert Gamble ran a 3,500-acre sugar plantation and refinery here with 190 slaves. Tours of this fortress-like mansion are offered and the visitor can relax in the beautifully landscaped garden. **941/723-4536** $

Ⓙ KENNEDY SPACE CENTER
Pg. 83, K19. **Titusville.** All US manned space missions since 1968 have been launched here. On July 16. 1969, Apollo 11 astronauts left Earth to land on the moon. Visitors can experience a dramatic re-creation of the first manned Apollo launch, get a bird's-eye view of today's space adventures at a 60-foot observation tower, and walk through full-scale mock-ups of space

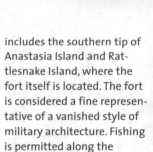

Ⓖ Fernandina Beach

Ⓙ Kennedy Space Canter

Ⓝ Salvador Dali Museum

station modules at the International Space Station Center. **321/867-5000** $

Ⓚ KEY WEST
Pg. 84, V16. This southern-most city in the continental United States, on the final inhabited island in the string of Florida Keys, is enjoying its busiest days since 1890, when it was the largest city in Florida. Key West is noted for its 19th-century colorfully painted houses, first introduced to the island by Bahamian settlers. It is also a city of Cuban foods and dialects that have been assimilated into the culture since the time of the big cigar industry, almost a century ago. **305/294-2587**

Ⓛ NATIONAL MUSEUM OF NAVAL AVIATION
Pg. 82, E3. **Pensacola.** One of the largest of its kind, this museum has more than 140 historically significant aircraft on display, including the A-1 Triad, the U S. Navy's first biplane; the NC-4 Flying Boat, the first plane to cross the Atlantic; a vintage 1930s Marine Corps fighter; four A-4 Skyhawks (Blue Angels) suspended in a diamond formation; and full-size, modern-day jets. The museum traces the history of naval aviation from the dawn of flight to space exploration. **850/452-3604**

Ⓜ RINGLING MUSEUM OF ART
Pg. 84, N14. **Sarasota.** The 66-acre estate of John Ringling is a cultural complex, left to the people of Florida upon Ringling's death in 1936. Recognized as the state art museum of Florida, it includes 21 galleries of internationally recognized European and American art. In addition, the estate encompasses Cà d'Zan, the restored 32-room Ringling mansion and the Circus Museum, which exhibits the colorful history of the circus. The landscaped grounds overlooking Sarasota Bay include a sculpture courtyard and a rose garden. **941/355-5101** $

Ⓝ SALVADOR DALI MUSEUM
Pg. 81, D3. **St. Petersburg.** The museum houses the world's largest collection of original works by Spanish artist Salvador Dali. With 95 oil paintings, over 100 watercolors and drawings, 1,300 graphics, photographs, sculptures, and objects d'art, and an extensive archival library, visitors can follow Dali's career from his early Impressionist and Cubist styles through his transition to Surrealism. **727/823-3767** $

Ⓞ SANIBEL AND CAPTIVA ISLANDS
Pg. 84, Q15. Connected to the mainland by a causeway, these resort islands are renowned for their beaches. Visitors enjoy boating, snorkeling and SCUBA diving, as well as golf, tennis and bicycling. The J.N. "Ding" Darling National Wildlife Refuge ($) is home to alligators, armadillos, and more than 200 species of birds, and provides opportunities for hiking and canoeing. Sanibel Island, considered one of the best shelling sites in the Western Hemisphere, is home to the Bailey-Matthews Shell Museum ($), the only institution in the U.S. devoted entirely to the shells of the world. **941/472-1080**

Ⓟ SPANISH QUARTER
Pg. 83, F17. **St. Augustine.** This village has been carefully preserved to maintain the atmosphere of 18th-century St. Augustine. Employees allow visitors a close-up glimpse of how St. Augustine operated in the 1740s: Their clothing is spun, woven and sewn on-site; food for their meals is grown in the Spanish Quarter gardens; and structures are built by hand, using tools of the period. **904/825-6830** $

Ⓠ VIZCAYA MUSEUM AND GARDENS
Pg. 81, M8. **Miami.** This elaborate 70-room Italian Renaissance–style villa—once home to industrialist James Deering—houses an extraordinary collection of European furnishings and art objects from the 15th through the 19th centuries. All 34 rooms of the villa are open to the public, and visitors may stroll the 10-acre formal gardens, which feature water displays and sculptures, on a moonlight garden tour. **305/250-9133** $

Ⓡ YBOR CITY
Pg. 83, L14. **Tampa.** With its Spanish restaurants, coffeehouses, and cigar factories, this area retains some of the atmosphere of the original Cuban settlement. Spanish is spoken as much as English. The entertainment district of Ybor City, with more than 60 restaurants, bars and nightclubs, draws up to 30,000 people on weekend nights. **813/223-1111**

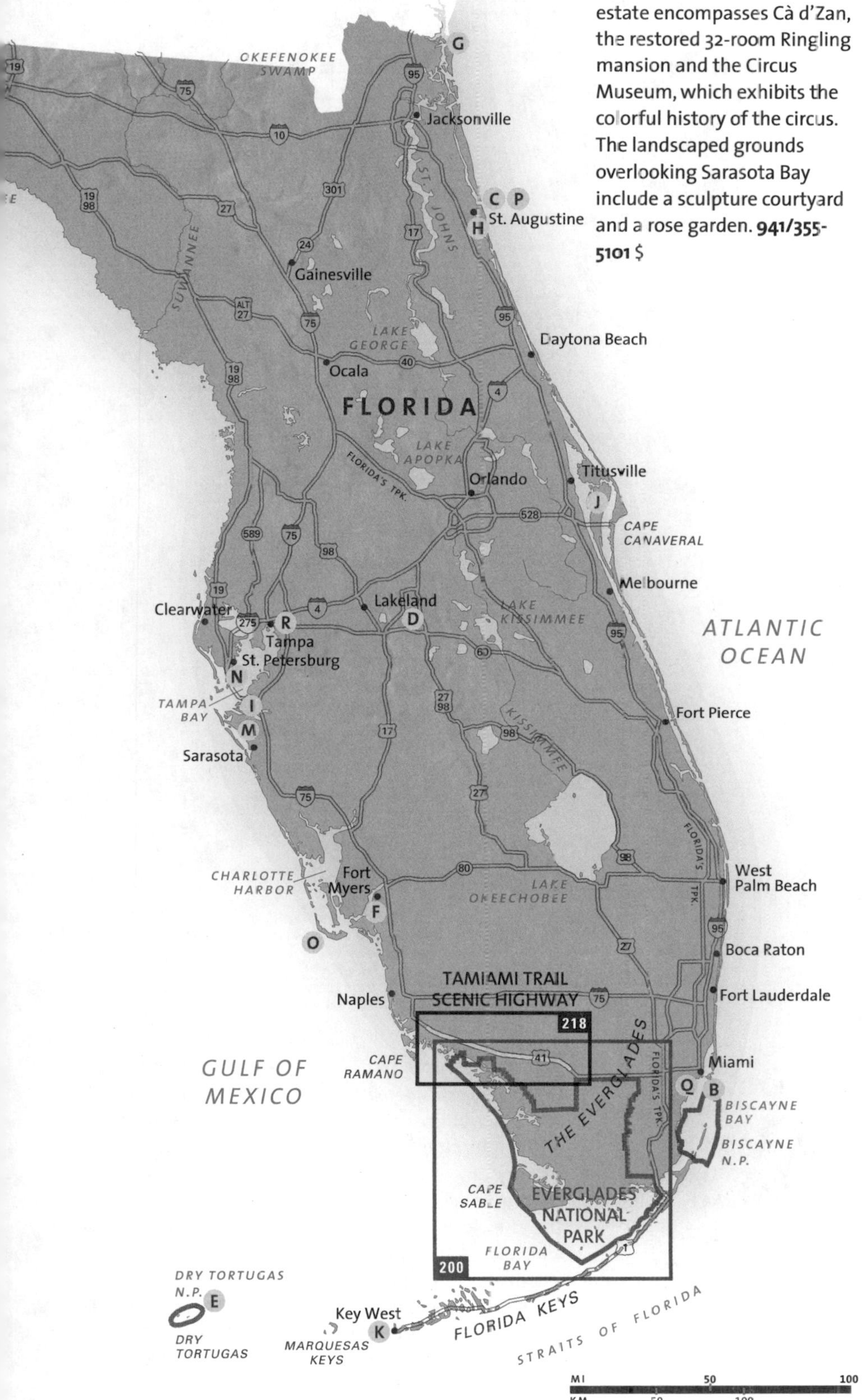

DOLLAR WI$E

- Purchase discounted attraction tickets for the Orlando area through the Orlando/Orange County Convention & Visitors Bureau.
- Not only are restaurants on Ocean Drive in Miami crowded with tourists, they are also expensive. Dining in a restaurant just west of Ocean Drive can save money.
- You can obtain discounts on admission to Universal Studios Florida by visiting their "fan club" at www.universalstudios.com/fanclub.
- A concentration of budget lodgings can be found in Ft. Lauderdale in a corridor formed by Las Olas Boulevard and Highway AIA; depending on the season, they can start anywhere from $33 to $65 per night, and are close to the beach, as well as dining and night life.
- If you want to stay in Disney World, consider booking several months in advance and planning your trip around the available dates at the value-based Disney resorts. Being flexible and planning in advance can get you an official Disney room for less than $100 a night.

January

Art Deco Weekend
Miami Beach
Vintage cars, music, tours, and entertainment.
813/969-6011

Florida Citrus Bowl
Orlando
407/849-2500

Orange Bowl
Miami
305/371-4600

South Florida Fair & Exposition
West Palm Beach
Livestock shows, entertainment, midway.
561/793-0333

February

Coconut Grove Arts Festival
Miami
Over 300 artists display their works. Entertainment, international foods.
305/447-0401

Doral Ryder Open PGA Golf Tournament
Miami
Held on the famed "Blue Monster" course of the Doral Resort & Country Club.
305/477-4653

Edison Festival of Light
Fort Myers
Tribute to Thomas Edison; including athletic contests, dances, sailing regattas, entertainment and a Parade of Light.
941/334-2999

Florida State Fair
Tampa
813/621-7821

March

Sanibel Shell Fair
Sanibel and Captiva Islands
Shell collectors display their wares in specimen shell and live shell exhibits; contests and prizes.
941/472-2155

April

Bloomin' Arts Festival
Bartow
Juried art show, flower show quilt show, entertainment.
813/969-6011

Sharks Tooth Festival
Venice
Music, seafood, shark tooth scramble.
941/488-2236

May

Southern Shakespeare Festival
Tallahassee
Professional open-air Shakespearean theatre; crafts, sword fights, a living chess match.
850/513-3087

June

Sarasota Music Festival
Sarasota
Guest artists perform with festival chamber orchestra at the Sarasota Opera House.
941/953-4252

July

Blue Angels Air Show
Pensacola
850/452-2583

Hemingway Days Festival
Key West
305/294-2587

October

Jazz Holiday
Clearwater
One of the Southeast's largest free jazz festivals.
727/461-5200

December

Gator Bowl
Jacksonville
904/798-1700

NC 138
SC 156
GA 86

Free $ Finds

Museum of Contemporary Art of Georgia, Atlanta
Showcases the works of artists around Georgia. Features over 250 paintings, sculptures, photographs, prints, digital and installation works by 110 artists. **404/881-1109**

Rock Eagle Effigy, Eatonton, GA
This eight-ft-high mound of milky white quartz is shaped like a great prone bird, wings spread, head turned eastward. Estimated to be more than 5,000 years old. It may be viewed from an observation tower. **706/485-2831**

Factors Walk, Savannah, GA
This row of business houses "on the Bay" is accessible by a network of iron bridgeways over cobblestone ramps.

Jimmy Carter National Historic Site, Americus, GA
Visitor center is located in Plains High School, where Jimmy and Rosalynn Carter attended grammar and high school. Campaign memorabilia; cassette auto driving tour of Plains available. **229/824-4104**

The Citadel, Charleston, SC
On Fridays, the public is invited to a precision-drill parade on the quadrangle at 3:45pm. For history of The Citadel, visit The Citadel Archives Museum. **843/953-6846**

World of Energy, Clemson, SC
Three-dimensional displays on the "Story of Energy," with exhibits on hydro, coal, and nuclear production of electricity. **864/885-4600**

Congaree Swamp National Monument, Columbia, SC
Old-growth, bottomland hardwood forest, approximately 22,200 acres. Trees and waters teem with wildlife. **803/776-4396**

Greenville County Museum, Greenville, SC
Permanent collection of American art, featuring historical and contemporary works. Changing exhibits include painting, sculpture, and photography. **864/271-7570**

World's Largest Chest of Drawers, High Point, NC
Building designed to look like a 19th-century dresser; symbolizes city's position as a furniture center. **336/883-2016**

Sarah P. Duke Gardens, Durham, NC
55 acres of landscaped gardens, pine forest. **919/684-3698**

Reed Gold Mine, Charlotte, NC
Exhibits of gold and historical mining equipment, and an orientation film highlighting the first gold discovery. **704/721-4653**

The starting point of the Appalachian Trail, Georgia's other natural attractions include the 438,000-acre Okefenokee Swamp, the Chattahoochee-Oconee National Forests, and the subtropical Golden Isles. Savannah's historic restoration has romantic appeal but Atlanta is the region's industrial and financial giant. Long and narrow, the barrier islands of North Carolina's Outer Banks provide perfect beach getaways. The incredible Biltmore Estate in Asheville, the college communities of Chapel Hill, Durham, and Raleigh and the Moravian settlement at Winston-Salem all contribute to the tourist appeal of the Tarheel State. South Carolina is famous for historic homes, low-country cooking, and high culture. Take a step back in time in lovely Charleston, a cosmopolitan port city with historic houses, churches, and gardens. Golf enthusiasts will appreciate Myrtle Beach's links.

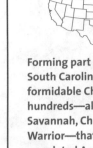

Forming part of the border between South Carolina and Georgia, the formidable Chattooga River is one of hundreds—along with the Altamaha, Savannah, Chattahoochee and Black Warrior—that originate in the sparsely populated Appalachian Mountains and gather force crossing the Piedmont, a broad swath of foothills that descend to the lowlands. Rich with fecund salt marshes on its shores, the southeast's coastal plain offered early settlers fertile plantation lands and secure harbors sheltered by barrier islands.

Ⓐ Chickamauga

Ⓑ Martin Luther King Jr. National Historic Site

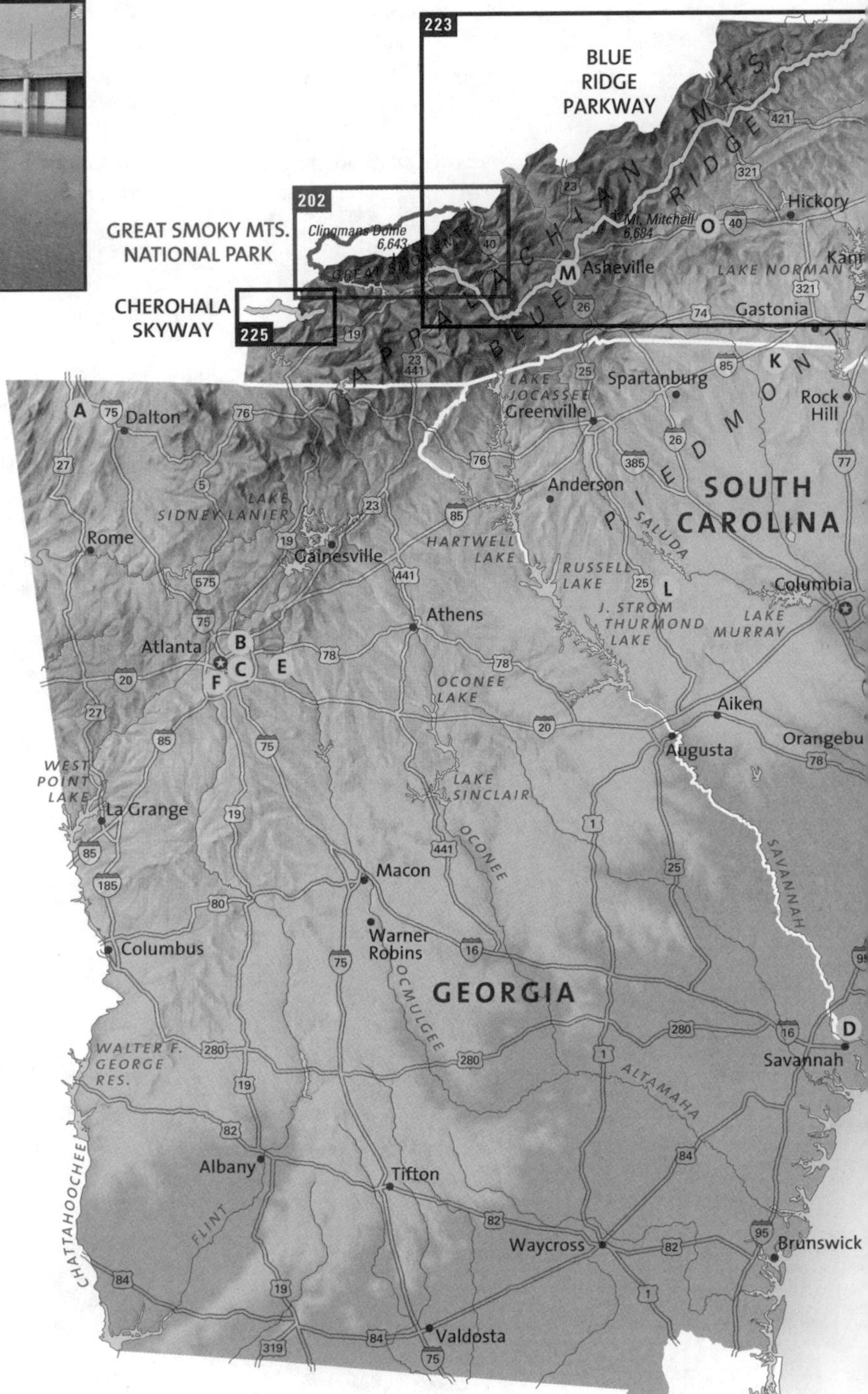

GEORGIA

Ⓐ CHICKAMAUGA AND CHATTANOOGA NATIONAL MILITARY PARK
Pg. 86, B2. **Chickamauga.** The oldest and largest national military park in the nation was the site of one of the fiercest Civil War battles. The park features a 7-mile self-guiding auto tour, monuments, historical tablets, hiking trails and horse trails. The visitor center contains exhibits and a 26-minute multi-media program, the Battle of Chickamauga. **706/866-9241** $

Ⓑ MARTIN LUTHER KING JR. NATIONAL HISTORIC SITE
Pg. 86, F4. **Atlanta.** The childhood home of King and the Ebenezer Baptist Church, where three generations of the King family pastured, now create a memorial to the famed leader of the civil rights movement and winner of the Nobel Peace Prize. **404/331-5190**

Ⓒ THE HIGH MUSEUM OF ART
Pg. 85, L9. **Atlanta.** With a permanent collection of significant 19th and 20th century American art, five centuries of European painting and sculpture, as well as an extensive collection of African art, The High Museum is regarded as Atlanta's leading art museum. The building itself, designed by noted architect Richard Meier, has received many design awards since its opening in 1983, including a citation from the American Institute of Architects as one of the "10 best works of American architecture of the 1980s." **404/733-4444** $

Ⓓ SAVANNAH HISTORY MUSEUM
Pg. 87, L12. This is the only museum in Savannah that is dedicated to the history of the entire coastal community. Located in the passenger station of the Central Railroad, its many exhibits reflect Savannah's history from 1733 to the present. **912/238-1779** $

Ⓔ STONE MOUNTAIN PARK
Pg. 86, E4. **Stone Mountain.** This 3,200-acre park surrounds the world's largest granite monolith. A monument to the Confederacy, the carving on the mountain's face depicts General Robert E. Lee, Lt. General Thomas "Stonewall" Jackson, and Confederate President Jefferson Davis. To get a breathtaking view of the carving, take a ride on the Skylift's Swiss cable cars. **770/498-5600** $

Ⓕ UNDERGROUND ATLANTA
Pg. 86, F4. A trip to Atlanta would not be complete without a visit to this 6-block, 12-acre, 3-level entertainment district. Underground Atlanta features an array of shops, street performers and artists, over 20 restaurants and nightclubs, and more. It also hosts Atlanta's largest gathering of people (up to 350,000) during the New Year's Eve Peach Drop Celebration. **404/523-2311**

Georgia is the nation's largest producer of peanuts, pecans, and peaches.

SOUTH CAROLINA

Ⓖ CHARLESTON
Pg. 156, H9. Considered one of the most historic and enchanting cities in the country, Charleston features historic homes, shrines, old churches, lovely gardens, and winding streets that exude charm and dignity. Visitors are never at a loss for ways to occupy their time: the city is surrounded by arts and culture with the Gibbs Museum of Art ($) and the Charleston Stage ($); many recreational activities from golf and tennis to fishing and jet skiing; and historic forts, houses, and plantations, such as Middleton Place, and the internationally famous gardens of the Magnolia Plantation($). **800/774-0006**

Ⓗ FORT SUMTER NATIONAL MONUMENT
Pg. 156, H9. **Charleston.** Site of the first engagement of the Civil War (a Confederate

Babe Ruth hit his first professional home run in Fayetteville, SC on March 7th, 1914.

Ⓜ Biltmore

Ⓝ Cape Hatteras

Ⓢ Wright Brothers

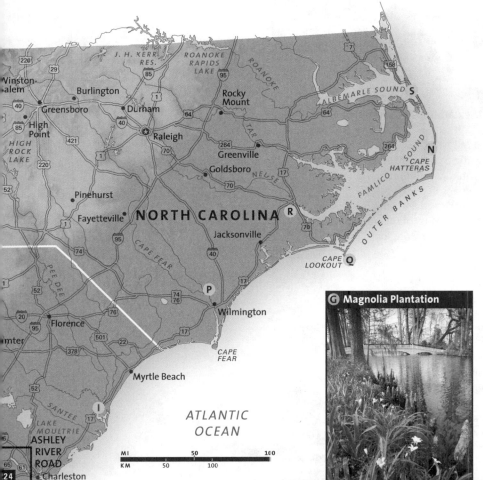

Ⓖ Magnolia Plantation

Ⓗ Fort Sumter

Ⓙ Hilton Head Island

victory), the national monument includes Fort Sumter, located three miles southeast of Charleston at the harbor entrance, and Fort Moultrie, one mile east on Sullivan's Island. **843/883-3123**

Ⓘ **"THE GRAND STRAND"**
Pg. 156, F11. **Georgetown.** Stretching for sixty miles of beach from the North Carolina border south to Georgetown, the Grand Strand is one of the most popular tourist destinations in the country. Main attractions are Little River, Surfside Beach, Garden City, and Pawleys Island. **843/626-7444**

Ⓙ **HILTON HEAD ISLAND**
Pg. 156, K8. This year-round resort island is bordered by one of the few remaining unpolluted marine estuaries on the East Coast and is the largest sea island between New Jersey and Florida. The island offers golf courses, tennis courts, swimming, miles of bicycle paths, horseback riding, and deep-sea, sound, and dockside fishing. **843/785-3673**

Ⓚ **KINGS MOUNTAIN NATIONAL MILITARY PARK**
Pg. 156, A6. **Bethany.** This site commemorates a pivotal and significant victory by American Patriots over American Loyalists during the southern campaign of the Revolutionary War. Near the center of the ridge. There is a 1-1/2-mile self-guiding trail that loops around the park, as well as over 16 miles of hiking and horse trails. **803/222-3209**

Ⓛ **NINETY SIX NATIONAL HISTORIC SITE**
Pg. 156, D4. **Greenwood.** This is the site of old Ninety Six, an early village in the South Carolina backcountry. This was the site of the South's first land battle of the American Revolution in 1775; earthworks of the British-built Star Fort remain, along with reconstructed fortifications. **864/543-4068**

NORTH CAROLINA

Ⓜ **BILTMORE ESTATE**
Pg. 138, L6. **Asheville.** Built in the 1890's as the private home of George Washington Vanderbilt, this is one of America's largest private residences. The 250-room French château has hand-carved limestone on the exterior; inside are hand-tooled Spanish leather walls in the breakfast room, 72-foot-high ceilings in the banquet hall, and priceless antiques. The 8,000-acre estate features 75 acres of formal gardens. Self-guided tours take 3 to 4 hours and include restored barns, stables, a carriage house, and a winery. **828/255-1700** $

Ⓝ **CAPE HATTERAS NATIONAL SEASHORE**
Pg. 139, E20. This thin broken strand of islands stretches for 75 miles along the Outer Banks, threaded between the windy, pounding Atlantic and shallow Pamlico Sound. Spring and fall offer what many consider to be the best fishing on the East Coast.

Ⓞ **HISTORIC OLD SALEM**
Pg. 138, E2. This 18th century trade and cultural center built by Moravians (from a province of the Czech Republic) is now a living museum of the religious settlement. Although most buildings are open to the public, a ticket is required to enter the historic tour buildings, or the museums in the Frank L. Horton Museum Center. **336/721-7300**

Ⓟ **MOORES CREEK NATIONAL BATTLEFIELD**
Pg. 139, J13. **Currie.** This site commemorates the decisive February 27, 1776, victory by 1,000 Patriots over 1,600 Loyalists that defeated British hopes of an early invasion through the South. **910/283-5591**

Ⓠ **OUTER BANKS**
Pg. 139, J17. **Cape Lookout.** The Outer Banks are a chain of narrow, sandy islands stretching 175 miles from Cape Lockout to Back Bay, Virginia. Parts of the chain are thirty miles from the mainland. A drive along the coast offers scenic views of both the islands and their many lighthouses.

Ⓡ **TYRON PALACE HISTORIC SITES AND GARDENS**
Pg. 139, G16. **New Bern.** Built between 1767-1770 by the Royal Governor, William Tryon, this "most beautiful building in the colonial Americas" burned by accident in 1798 and lay in ruins until it was rebuilt between 1952-1959. It served as the colonial and first state capitol. **800/767-1560** $

Ⓢ **WRIGHT BROTHERS NATIONAL MEMORIAL**
Pg. 139, C19. **Colington.** This is the actual field where the Wrights' first powered flight took place on December 17, 1903. The living quarters and hangar buildings used by the Wrights during their experiments have been reconstructed. Adjacent to the camp buildings are granite markers which designate the lengths of the four successful powered flights. The visitor center houses a replica of the history-making plane, the Wright Flyer that defied belief as well as gravity. **252/441-7430** $

DOLLAR WI$E

- When visiting Hilton Head Island, consider renting a condo or town house during your stay; not only are they less expensive than a hotel, you can save money by preparing some of your own meals.
- Call chambers of commerce or look on the Internet for money-saving coupons for area attractions and lodging.
- Be aware of extra charges, such as those for a kid's program, before booking a resort.
- See Atlanta's cultural and historical sites for $5 through guided walking tours offered by the Atlanta Preservation Center.

March

Festival of Houses & Gardens
Charleston, SC
Many of the city's finest private residences (ca. 1710-1850) and gardens are open to visitors. Afternoon and candlelight tours; reservations recommended.
843/723-1623

Savannah Tour of Homes and Gardens
Day and candlelight tours of more than 30 private houses and gardens.
912/234-8054

April

Atlanta Dogwood Festival
Atlanta, GA
404/329-0501

Dogwood Festival
Fayetteville, NC
910/323-1934

Night In Old Savannah
Savannah, GA
Foods of more than 25 countries; entertainment includes jazz, country, and rhythm and blues.
912/651-3673.

North Carolina Azalea Festival
Wilmington, NC
Tours, horse show, celebrity entertainers, parade, street fair.
910/794-4650

June

American Dance Festival
Durham, NC
Six wks of performances by the finest major and emerging modern dance companies from the US and abroad.
919/684-4444

Spoleto Festival
Charleston, SC
Internationally acclaimed counterpart to the arts festival in Spoleto, Italy, featuring opera, ballet, visual arts, theater, jazz, symphonic and choral performances, and much more
843/722-2764

Sun Fun Festival
Myrtle Beach, SC
More than 60 seaside entertainment events, including parades.
843/347-4604

Theater of the Stars
Atlanta, GA
Six Broadway musicals with professional casts.
404/252-8960

August

Georgia Mountain Fair
Hiawassee, GA
Arts and crafts, produce, flowers, minerals, Native American relics; board splitting, soap and hominy making, quilting.
706/896-4191

September

Bull Durham Blues Festival
Durham, NC
919/683-1709

Hilton Head Island Celebrity Golf Tournament
Hilton Head Island, SC
843/842-7711

October

Beaufort Shrimp Festival
Beaufort, SC
Bridge Run, shrimp recipe tastings, frogmore stew contest, Bless'en de Fleet.
843/524-3163

Georgia State Fair
Macon, GA
912/746-7184

North Carolina State Fair
Raleigh, NC
919/733-2145

South Carolina State Fair
Columbia, SC
803/799-3387

DE 80 · MD 106 · DC 172 · VA 168 · DE 234 · MD 238 · DC 234 · VA 247

From Mount Vernon to Monticello, from Arlington Cemetery to Alexandria, from Jamestown to Williamsburg, Virginia has a rich history. Natural wonders include the 23-story Natural Bridge and the 750-square-mile Dismal Swamp. In Washington, D.C. history unfolds daily within the Capitol and the White House. The Mall museums are required viewing, as are the Washington, Lincoln, and Jefferson Memorials. U.S. Naval cadets pass in formation at Annapolis in Maryland, while the fishing boats of St. Michael provide a scenic backdrop for a magical waterworld. The Baltimore Aquarium draws rave reviews, and Ocean City is a favorite for beach lovers. Proud of being the first state, Delaware's many attractions include Rehoboth Beach, the Winterthur estate, cosmopolitan Wilmington, and outlet shopping at Lewes.

The fertile Delmarva Peninsula, which contains the entire state of Delaware, as well as parts of Maryland and Virginia, lies east of the Chesapeake Bay, a flooded estuary of the Susquehanna River. West of the nation's capital, which sits on the banks of the Potomac River, the Maryland and Virginia hinterlands climb from tidewater to the mountains of the Appalachian range.

Free Finds

George Washington Masonic National Memorial, Alexandria, VA
American Freemasons' memorial to their most prominent member, this 333-ft-high structure houses a large collection of objects that belonged to George Washington, which were collected by his family or the masonic lodge where he served as the first master. **703/683-2007**

Maymont Park, Richmond, VA
100-acre park with Dooley mansion, which houses an art collection and decorative arts exhibits. Also here are formal Japanese and Italian gardens, an arboretum, a nature center with wildlife habitat for native species, an aviary, a children's farm, and a working carriage collection. **804/358-7166**

Historic Hilton Village, Newport News, VA
Listed on the National Register of Historic Places, this village was built between 1918-1920 to provide wartime housing for workers at Newport News Shipbuilding. The architecturally significant neighborhood features 500 English cottage-style homes and antique and specialty shops.

University of Virginia, Charlottesville, VA
Walking tour of university founded and designed by Thomas Jefferson. **804/924-1019**

National Gallery of Art, Washington, D.C.
Highlights include the only Leonardo da Vinci painting in the western hemisphere, Ginevra de' Benci; a collection of Italian paintings and sculpture; major French Impressionists; and numerous Rembrandts. **202/737-4215**

National Archives, Washington, D.C.
Original copies of the Declaration of Independence, Bill of Rights, Constitution; a 1297 version of the Magna Carta and other historic documents, maps, and photographs. **202/501-5205**

Vietnam Veterans Memorial, Washington, D.C.
The memorial's polished black granite walls are inscribed with the names of the 58,175 US citizens who died in or remain missing from the Vietnam War. **202/634-1568**

Thomas Jefferson Memorial, Washington, D.C.
Honors the third President of the United States and author of the Declaration of Independence and Bill of Rights. **202/426-2598**

Washington Monument, Baltimore, MD
First major monument to honor George Washington. Museum in base; view city from top. **410/396-1049**

VIRGINIA

Ⓐ ARLINGTON NATIONAL CEMETERY
Pg. 167, D9. The national cemetery has the Tomb of the Unknown Soldier and the graves of John and Robert Kennedy, as well as 250,000 others who served their country. Arlington House was built by George Washington's adopted son and was once the residence of Robert E. Lee. It displays original furnishings and is open to the public. **703/979-0690**

Ⓑ COLONIAL NATIONAL HISTORIC PARK
Pg. 169, L16. **Jamestown.** Retrace the steps of colonial settlers and American patriots while discovering the sites of the first permanent English settlement at Jamestown and the last battle of the American Revolution at Yorktown — literally the beginning and end of English colonial America. The Colonial Parkway, a 23-mile memorial roadway, connects the two sites. **757/898-3400** $

Ⓒ MANASSAS NATIONAL BATTLEFIELD PARK
Pg. 167, D4. **Manassas.** This 5,000-acre park was the scene of two major Civil War battles. More than 26,000 men were killed or wounded here in struggles for control of a strategically important railroad junction. The park offers Civil War exhibits, a 13-minute slide program, and a 5-minute battlefield map program. Guided tours and other programs are scheduled on a regular basis during the summer season and on the weekends during the remainder of the year (weather permitting). Self-guided walking and driving tours are also available. **703/361-1339** $

Ⓐ Arlington National Cemetery

Ⓓ Monticello

Ⓓ MONTICELLO
Pg. 167, C3. **Charlottesville.** Located on a mountaintop, Thomas Jefferson's estate was designed and built over 40 years. Most of the interior furnishings are original. **434/984-9822** $

Ⓔ MOUNT VERNON
Pg. 169, D15. **Alexandria.** President George Washington built this estate on land he inherited with his wife, Martha. After he retired from public life, he practiced pioneering farming methods here and left an indelible stamp of his personality and tastes. **703/780-2000** $

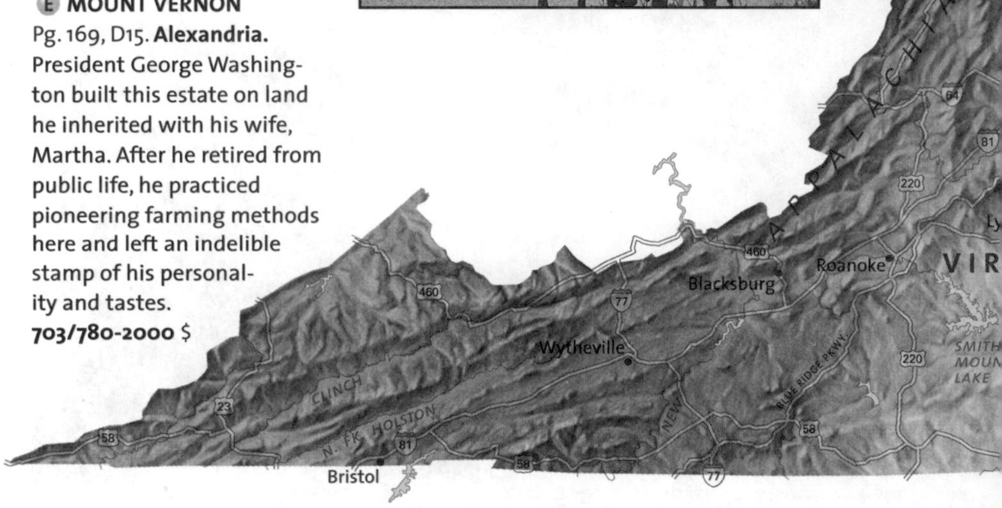

WASHINGTON, D.C.

Ⓕ THE CAPITOL
Pg. 172, D5. The Capitol is where Congress —the legislative branch of the government—meets. George Washington laid the cornerstone in 1793 and part of the originally planned building opened in 1800. Statuary Hall, built originally as the House chamber, contains an impressive collection of statues contributed by the states. The Capitol is open to the public for guided tours only. **202/225-6827**

Ⓖ GEORGETOWN
Pg. 172, D5. A neighborhood within the city's northwest quadrant, Georgetown is actually older than Washington. In Colonial days it was a busy commercial center. Today Georgetown is an area of fine 18th-and 19th-century residences, fashionable shops, and restaurants.

Ⓗ NATIONAL AIR AND SPACE MUSEUM
Pg. 172, D5. Some of the famous aircraft displayed at this popular museum include the Wright Flyer, the Spirit of St. Louis, and an X-15. Exhibits on space include rockets; aerospace computers; capsules from the Mercury, Gemini, and Apollo missions; and a special moon rock display. There is also a five-story IMAX movie screen and a planetarium. **202/357-1387**

Ⓘ SMITHSONIAN INSTITUTE
Pg. 172, D5. This is the world's largest museum complex and research organization. Its immense collection contains over 142 million objects, including The Hope Diamond, the world's largest deep blue diamond; the flag that inspired Francis Scott Key to write our national anthem; and the top hat Abraham Lincoln wore to Ford's Theatre when he was assassinated. The complex is composed of sixteen museums and galleries, as well as the National Zoo. Most of the museums are located on the National Mall and cover art, science, history, and culture. **202/357-2700**

Ⓙ WASHINGTON MONUMENT
Pg. 172, D5. The obelisk, the tallest masonry structure in the world at 555 feet, was dedicated in 1885 to the memory of the first U.S. president. It stands near the center of a cross formed by four of America's most famous buildings: the U.S. Capitol, the Lincoln Memorial, the White House, and the Jefferson Memorial. Visitors take a 70-second elevator ride to the 500-foot level for a bird's-eye view of the city. Within the monument are commemorative stones, exhibits, and a small book shop. **202/426-6839**

Ⓕ U.S. Capitol

Ⓙ Washington Monument

Ⓚ THE WHITE HOUSE
Pg. 172, D5. The President's house was begun under the supervision of George Washington, and has been lived in by every president since John Adams. Sections of the house have been reconstructed and redecorated by succeeding administrations. The visitor center houses exhibits on many aspects of the White House, including its architecture, furnishings, first families, social events, and relations with the press and world leaders. **202/456-7041**

MARYLAND

L ANNAPOLIS
Pg. 107, N12. The capital of Maryland, gracious and dignified in the Colonial tradition, Annapolis has had a rich history. Planned and laid out as the provincial capital in 1695, it was the first peacetime capital of the United States. Town life centers on sport and commercial water-oriented activities, state government, and the U.S. Naval Academy. **410/268-8687**

M ANTIETAM NATIONAL BATTLEFIELD
Pg. 106, B9. **Hagerstown.** Approximately 350 iron tablets, monuments, and battlefield maps describe the events of the bloodiest Civil War battle that took place here on September 17, 1862. More than 23,000 men were killed or wounded as Union forces blocked the first Confederate invasion of the north, and the battle led to Lincoln's issuance of the Emancipation Proclamation. The best way to view the battlefield is to take the self-guided driving tour. The tour road is 8 miles long with 11 stops. **301/432-5124** $

N ASSATEAGUE ISLAND NATIONAL SEASHORE
Pg. 107, L20. **Ocean City.** Assateague, with 37 miles of secluded white sandy beaches, is known for its population of ponies (numbering approximately 200), descendants of shipwrecked horses who swam to safety hundreds of years ago. The herd will mingle with visitors, but should not be fed—a handout is illegal and can lead to aggressive behavior by an otherwise gentle animal. **410/641-1441** $

O CIVIL WAR SITES OF FREDERICK
Pg. 106, D10. Frederick is a well-preserved city of elegant 18th- and 19th-century structures including the National Museum of Civil War Medicine, the Barbara Fritchie House & Museum, and a small office in Courthouse Square where Francis Scott Key practiced law. **301/663-8687** $

P FT. MCHENRY NATIONAL MONUMENT AND HISTORIC SHRINE
Pg. 107, D13. **Baltimore.** Built in 1803, the fort was used in every American conflict through World War II. A 25-hour bombardment of the fort by the British during the War of 1812 provided the inspiration for Francis Scott Key to write "The Star Spangled Banner." Historical exhibits are contained in the restored powder magazine, guardroom, officers' quarters, and barracks. Presentations include performances by the Ft. McHenry Guard and reenactments of garrison life. **410/962-4299** $

Q NATIONAL AQUARIUM
Pg. 107, D13. **Baltimore.** Here visitors will find an Atlantic coral reef, shark tank, specimens of 500 different types of mammals, fish, birds, reptiles, amphibians, invertebrates, and plants. **410/576-3800** $

R Bombay Hook National Wildlife Refuge

U Winterhur Museum

DELAWARE

R BOMBAY HOOK NATIONAL WILDLIFE REFUGE
Pg. 80, F4. **Smyrna.** This is the annual fall and spring resting and feeding spot for migratory waterfowl, including a variety of ducks, snow geese, Canada geese, bald eagles, and shorebirds. The refuge has nature trails, observation towers, and a 12-mile auto-tour route which can be enhanced with an interpretive cassette tape rental. The Visitor Center features displays and information. **302/653-6872** $

S BRANDYWINE VALLEY
Pg. 80, B3. **Wilmington.** This region offers visitors many ways to enjoy their stay. Its museums and historic mansions reflect the art, culture, and history of the area, and its many gardens—in full bloom in spring and summer—offer peaceful surroundings for a leisurely stroll. Wineries, shopping, and dining surround the area. **302/652-4088**

T FT. DELAWARE STATE PARK
Pg. 80, D2. **Delaware City.** Located on Pea Patch Island, this state park is home to a coastal defense fort built in 1859, which was also used as a prison for Confederate prisoners of war, housing as many as 12,500 prisoners at one point. Hourly ferries transport visitors to the island, where authentically-clad historic interpreters are guides on a journey back in time. **302/834-7941** $

U WINTERTHUR MUSEUM, GARDEN & LIBRARY
Pg. 80, B3. **Wilmington.** An extensive collection of American decorative arts from 1640-1860 is displayed in two Henry Francis du Pont buildings. The museum is surrounded by natural landscaping. **302/888-4600** $

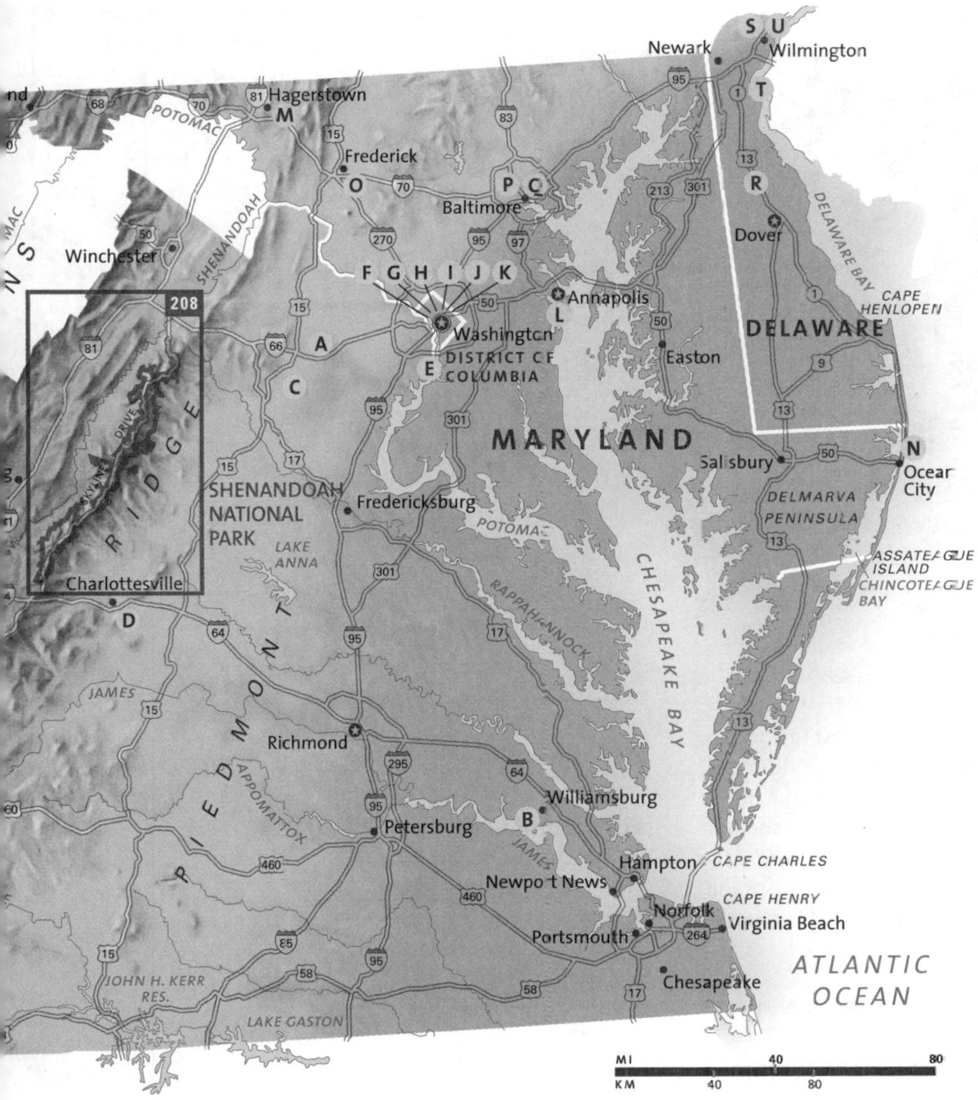

DOLLAR WI$E

- Save the hassle of navigating Washington, D.C. by car; the city's Metro is one of the best around, and an all-day pass is $5.
- For lunch or a snack, the cafeterias at many Washington museums and galleries offer inexpensive and varied menus.
- The best hotel rates in Washington, D.C. are offered on weekends—30% to 50% lower than during the week.
- There are lots of good hotel room buys in Washington in December, January, July, and August—and any time congress recesses.
- See Virginia for $3. The Doorways to Old Virginia tour takes you along the cobblestone streets and vintage buildings of Old Alexandria, led by a guide in 18th-century costume.
- You can walk anywhere in Colonial Williamsburg, taking in the "street theater" of 18th-century costumed interpreters engaging passers-by in conversation about the "stamp act" and other "current" events, without paying the admission fee. You can return the next day and purchase a one-day admission, which allows you to enter the buildings and attend events—and you'll save about $25 per person on your visit.
- The hotels at Colonial Williamsburg can be expensive. Consider one of the small guest houses near the historic district—they run about $50 per couple per night for a room with a private bath.

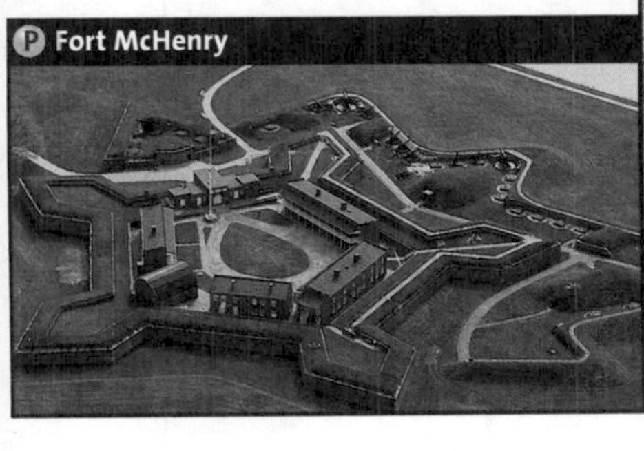
P Fort McHenry

M Antietam

January
Winter whale-watching boat trips
Virginia Beach, VA
757/437-4882

April
Easter Egg Roll
Washington, D.C.
White House Lawn.
202/456-2200

Georgetown Garden Tour
Washington, D.C.
Fourteen or more different gardens open to the public Proceeds go to Georgetown Children's House. Self-guided tours.
202/333-6896

Virginia Waterfront International Arts Festival
Norfolk, VA
Eighteen days of music, dance, visual arts and theater performances.
757/664-6492

May
Festival in the Park
Roanoke, VA
Art exhibits, crafts, sports, food, parade, entertainment.
757/625-1445

Mid-Atlantic Maritime Festival
St. Michael's, MD
Nautical celebration with fly-fishing demonstration, skipjack races, boat building contest
410/745-2916

Old Dover Days
Dover, DE
Tours of historic houses and gardens not usually open to the public.
800/233-KENT

June
Festival of American Folklife
Washington, D.C.
The Mall. Folklife traditions from America and abroad. Sponsored by the Smithsonian Institution and National Park Service.
202/357-2700

Harbor Expo
Baltimore, MD
Boat parades, seafood festival; entertainment; events.
888/225-8466

July
Artscape
Baltimore, MD
Salute to the arts and culture.
410/396-4575

Delaware State Fair
Dover, DE
302/398-3269

July 4 Celebration
Washington, D.C.
Washington Monument and Capitol west steps. Music, celebrations; extensive fireworks.
202/426-6841

Victorian Ice Cream Festival
Wilmington, DE
302/761-4340

Virginia Scottish Games
Alexandria, VA
Athletic competition. Highland dance and music, antique cars, displays, food.
703/838-4200

August
Boardwalk Arts Festival
Bethany Beach, DE
302/539-2100

September
Maryland Seafood Festival
Annapolis, MD
410/268-7682

New Market Days
Frederick, MD
Nostalgic revival off a 19th-century village.
301/831-6755 **Virginia State Fair**
Richmond, VA
804/228-3200

Free Finds $

Edgar Allan Poe National Historic Site, Philadelphia
Where Poe lived before his move to New York in 1844. Exhibits, slide show, tours, and special programs. **215/597-8780**

U.S. Mint, Philadelphia
Produces coins of all denominations. Gallery affords visitors an elevated view of the coinage operations. **215/408-0114**

The Frick Art and Historical Center, Pittsburgh, PA
Museum complex built on grounds of estate once belonging to industrialist Henry Clay Frick; gardens, carriage house, greenhouse, and café. Restored children's playhouse serves as a visitor's center. **412/371-0600**

Hershey's Chocolate World, Hershey, PA
Tour simulates steps of chocolate production from cacao bean plantations through chocolate making in Hershey. **717/534-4900**

Staten Island Ferry, New York City
Famous ferry to St. George, Staten Island, offers passengers a close look at both the Statue of Liberty and Ellis Island, as well as to the lower Manhattan skyline. **718/815-2628**

Brooklyn Bridge, New York City
The first bridge across the East River from Manhattan to Brooklyn, it was a remarkable engineering feat when opened in 1883. An easy walk.

Empire State Plaza, Albany, NY
A 98-acre, 11-building complex providing office space for state government, cultural, and convention facilities. On 42nd floor is the Tower Building observation deck. **518/474-2418**

American Museum of Firefighting, Hudson, NY
Antique fire-fighting equipment includes 1725 Newsham fire engine; memorabilia, art gallery. **518/828-7695**

Stephen Crane House, Asbury Park, NJ
Early home of the author of *The Red Badge of Courage*; photos, drawings, and artifacts. **732/988-2260**

Walt Whitman House State Historic Site, Camden, NJ
The last residence of the poet and the only house he ever owned; he lived here from 1884 until his death. Original furnishings, books, and mementos. **856/964-5383**

Edison Memorial Tower, Edison, NJ
A 131-ft tower topped by a 13-ft-high electric light bulb stands on the spot where the first incandescent bulb was made. Museum contains some of Edison's inventions. **732/248-7298**

Reliving history in Pennsylvania is unavoidable at Valley Forge, Philadelphia's Liberty Bell, and Gettysburg. Amish communities populate Lancaster, and the Poconos are a craft lovers' mecca. In the west, the Carnegie Museum educates and inspires visitors to Pittsburgh. In New York, visitors delight in limitless options. They can hobnob in the Hamptons, sightsee in the Hudson River valley, review the cadets at West Point, explore Fire Island, check out home run statistics in Cooperstown, or simply get romantic at Niagara Falls. New York City, naturally, remains the jewel in the crown, with its endless number of museums, its famous Broadway shows, and the world's largest cultural complex, Lincoln Center. New Jersey, whose coastline includes Victorian Cape May, Sandy Hook, and Atlantic City, is a beach lover's fantasy. With 1,000 miles of marshland, the Pine Barrens are a wildlife oasis, and farther north, the Delaware Water Gap offers river recreation.

With its source in the Adirondack Mountains, the Hudson River empties into the Atlantic at New York Bay. The region's other great rivers are the Delaware and the Susquehanna, which drain New York, New Jersey and Pennsylvania along their respective routes to the Delaware and Chesapeake Bays. In northeastern Pennsylvania, rugged folds of Appalachians bear rich seams of anthracite coal, historically important but today commercially slight.

B Delaware Water Gap

F Independence Hall

D Fallingwater

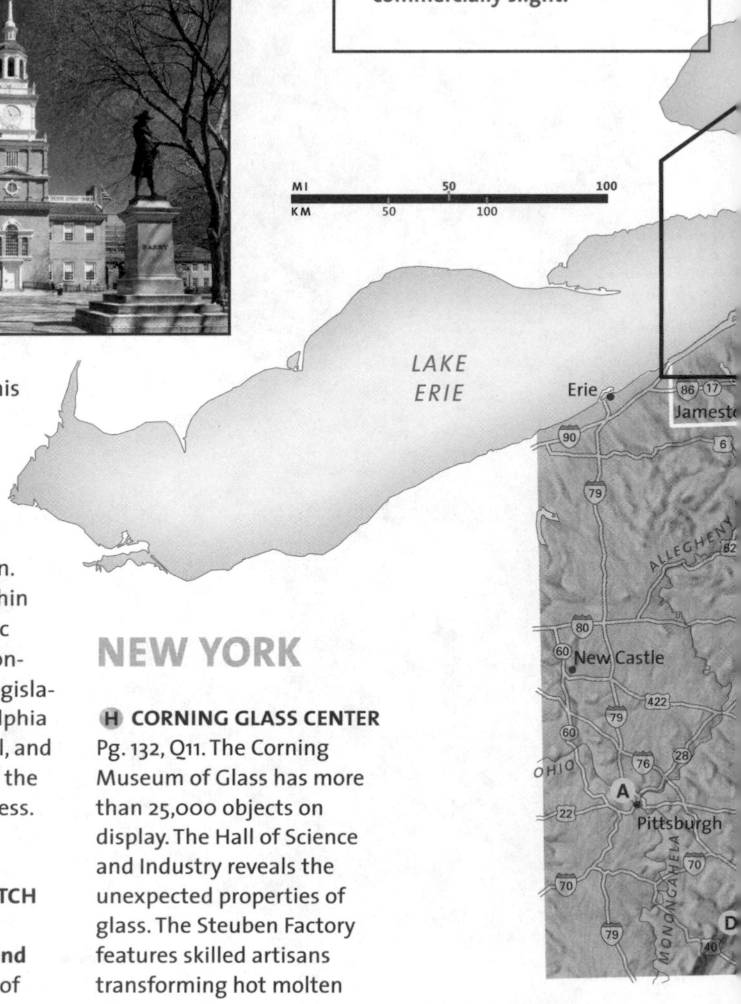

PENNSYLVANIA

A THE CARNEGIE MUSEUMS
Pg. 151, N3. **Pittsburgh.** In 1895, Pittsburgh industrialist Andrew Carnegie donated this cultural complex to help people improve their lives through educational and cultural experiences. His vision is now embodied in a collective of four distinctive museums — Carnegie Museum of Art, Carnegie Museum of Natural History, Carnegie Science Center, and The Andy Warhol Museum — that serve more than 1.67 million people each year. **412/622-3360** $

B DELAWARE WATER GAP NATIONAL RECREATION AREA
Pg. 152. K23. **East Stroudsburg.** The numerous activities in this recreation area include canoeing, boating, hunting, fishing and camping. Trails and overlooks offer scenic views. Following the Kittatinny Mountains, the trail remains relatively level. A 1-1/2 mile, sometimes steep side trail leads to the beautiful Buttermilk Falls. **908/496-4458**

C FAIRMONT PARK
Pg. 153, R23. **Philadelphia.** One of the nation's largest urban parks, this covers 8,700 acres beginning at the Philadelphia Museum of Art. It is also home to the America's first zoo, a Japanese Exhibition House featuring a garden, pond, and bridge; and preserved and furnished colonial houses in varying architectural styles. **215/685-0000**

D FALLINGWATER
Pg. 151, R5. **Connellsville.** Designed by Frank Lloyd Wright in 1936, Falling Water is cantilevered on three levels over a waterfall. The interior features Wright-designed furniture, textiles, and lighting, as well as sculpture by modern masters. The extensive grounds are heavily wooded and planted with rhododendron. **724/329-8501** $ R

E GETTYSBURG NATIONAL MILITARY PARK
Pg. 153, S15. **Gettysburg.** In the summer of 1863, Union and Confederate forces fought here in a terrible, blood-soaked battle. Exhibits in the visitor center and a circular painting in the Cyclorama Center portray the encounter. The hallowed battlefield, immortalized by Lincoln's Gettysburg Address, is toured via more than 35 miles of roads through 5,900 acres. **717/334-1124**

F INDEPENDENCE NATIONAL HISTORIC PARK
Pg. 153, R23. **Philadelphia.** Appearing very much as it did in the 18th century, Independence Hall is this park's main attraction. Blemished by its famous crack, the Liberty Bell is displayed across the street in a glass pavilion. Other historic sites within "America's most historic square mile" include Congress Hall, where the legislature met when Philadelphia was the nation's capital, and Carpenters' Hall, site of the first Continental Congress. **215/597-8974**

G PENNSYLVANIA DUTCH COUNTRY
Pg. 153, Q18. **Lancaster and environs.** Descendants of German immigrants, ranging from the Amish to the Brethren, live here in close to turn-of-the-century style. Visit covered bridges, one-room schoolhouses, and Amish homes. Activities include restaurants and markets offering Pennsylvania Dutch cooking, horse and buggy rides, tours of the area, miniature golf, steam locomotive rides, and an abundance of local museums and historical sites dating back to the 1700s. **717/299-8901**

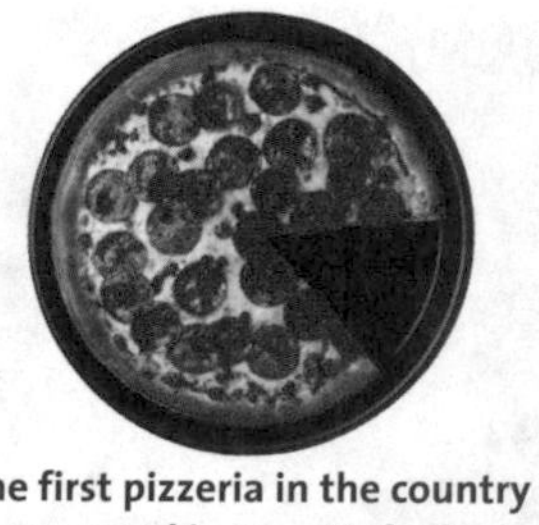

The first pizzeria in the country was opened in New York City in 1895 by Gennaro Lombardi.

NEW YORK

H CORNING GLASS CENTER
Pg. 132, Q11. The Corning Museum of Glass has more than 25,000 objects on display. The Hall of Science and Industry reveals the unexpected properties of glass. The Steuben Factory features skilled artisans transforming hot molten glass into fine crystal. **607/974-8173** $

I FIRE ISLAND NATIONAL SEASHORE
Pg. 135, X26. Beautiful ocean shores, a maritime forest, and the estate of William Floyd are just a few of the sites on this island paralleling the southern shore of Long Island. Five areas are open to the public: Otis Pike Wilderness, Sailors Haven, Sunken Forest, Watch Hill, and Fire Island Lighthouse. There are two bridges that lead to the island—the Robert Moses Causeway on the western end, and the William Floyd Parkway on the eastern end. **516/399-2030**

J FORT TICONDEROGA
Pg. 133, F23. **Ticonderoga.** This reconstructed fort was a strategic stronghold in the Revolutionary War. The fort was built by the French, taken by the British, then captured during the Revolution by Ethan Allen and the Green Mountain Boys before being recaptured by the British. A museum displays muskets, uniforms, and period memorabilia. **518/585-2821** $

J Ft. Ticonderoga

K HIGH FALLS IN THE BROWNS RACE HISTORIC DISTRICT
Pg. 132, K9. **Rochester.** One of Rochester's earliest industrial districts has been renovated to preserve the area where flourmills and manufacturers once operated and Eastman Kodak and Gleason Works originated. Today the district houses businesses in reno-

vated historic buildings. A short walking tour features a panoramic view of the Genesee River 96-foot waterfall and spectacular gorge. **716/325-2030**

L METROPOLITAN MUSEUM OF ART
Pg. 134, X22. **New York City.** More than two million objects from a 5,000-year-time span make this the most comprehensive collection in America. Art from Egypt, Greece, Italy, the Near and Far East, Africa, the Pacific Islands, pre-Columbian and Native America, Europe, and America is represented in addition to a rooftop sculpture garden. **212/535-7710 $**

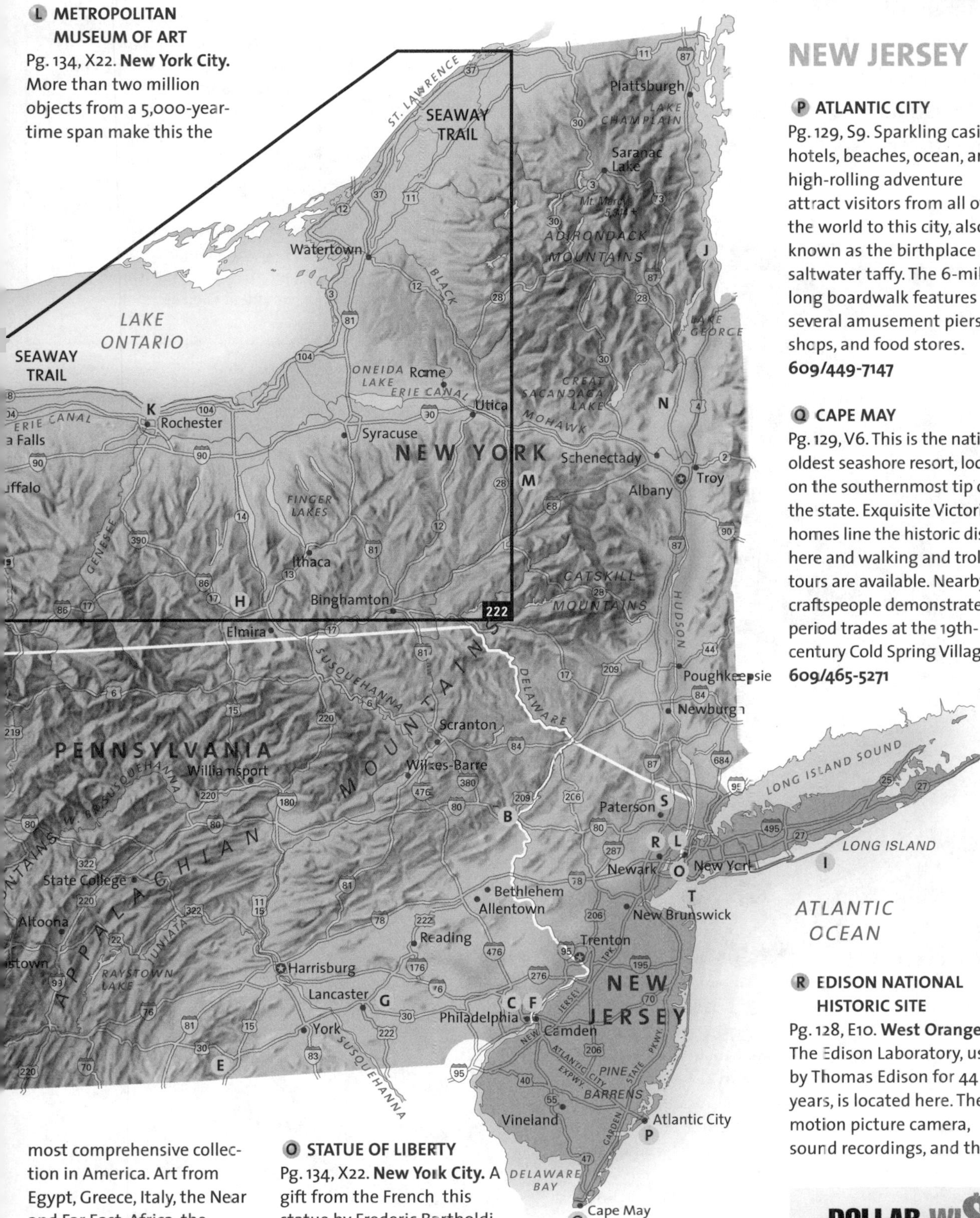

M NATIONAL BASEBALL HALL OF FAME MUSEUM
Pg. 133, M18. **Cooperstown.** This nationally known museum celebrates the game of baseball and its players. The museum features displays on baseball's greatest moments, the World Series, All-Star Games, ballparks, and a complete history of the game. **607/547-7200 $**

N SARATOGA SPRINGS
Pg. 133, K22. Saratoga Springs is a rural, yet cosmopolitan, resort city. Much of the town's Victorian architecture has been restored. Springs, geysers, and mineral baths first made the town famous. Now thoroughbred racing and the summer Saratoga Performing Arts Center bring visitors. **518/584-3255**

O STATUE OF LIBERTY
Pg. 134, X22. **New York City.** A gift from the French this statue by Frederic Bartholdi is 152 feet high. Made of 3/32 inch-thick copper on a framework designed by Gustav Eiffel, there are 354 steps to the crown. The Statue is located near Ellis Island, the gateway through which more than 12 million immigrants passed between 1892 and 1954. Here, the Ellis Island Immigration Museum retraces the immigrants' journey through this gateway with audio/visual displays and exhibits. **212/363-3200 $**

O Statue of Liberty

M Baseball Hall of fame

P Atlantic City

Q Cape May

NEW JERSEY

P ATLANTIC CITY
Pg. 129, S9. Sparkling casino-hotels, beaches, ocean, and high-rolling adventure attract visitors from all over the world to this city, also known as the birthplace of saltwater taffy. The 6-mile-long boardwalk features several amusement piers, shops, and food stores. **609/449-7147**

Q CAPE MAY
Pg. 129, V6. This is the nation's oldest seashore resort, located on the southernmost tip of the state. Exquisite Victorian homes line the historic district here and walking and trolley tours are available. Nearby craftspeople demonstrate period trades at the 19th-century Cold Spring Village. **609/465-5271**

R EDISON NATIONAL HISTORIC SITE
Pg. 128, E10. **West Orange.** The Edison Laboratory, used by Thomas Edison for 44 years, is located here. The motion picture camera, sound recordings, and the nickel-iron alkaline electric storage battery came out of this laboratory. In all, Edison and his workers completed more than half of his 1,093 patents at this laboratory. **973/736-5050**

S GREAT FALLS HISTORIC DISTRICT
Pg. 128, D10. **Paterson.** This 118-acre industrial landmark is home to the largest and best example of early American manufacturing mills. It contains waterpower remnants, including a three-tiered water raceway system, the second largest waterfall by volume east of the Mississippi, and a park and picnic area. **973/279-9587**

T SANDY HOOK NATIONAL RECREATION AREA
Pg. 128, H11. **Highlands.** A barrier peninsula features the oldest (1764) operating lighthouse in the United States and the U.S. Army Proving Ground. Fort Hancock is the last of several forts erected on Sandy Hook to protect the shipping channels into New York harbor. Sandy Hook is a popular destination for bicyclists and hikers. **732/872-5970**

DOLLAR WI$E

- Stay uptown or downtown when in Manhattan; Midtown hotels in the Theater District are generally more expensive.
- For one reasonable price, you can purchase a New York Pass, which allows you entry into 40 of New York's most exciting attractions, as well as unlimited rides on subways and buses. Visit www.citypass.com for more information.
- Check with the New York City Convention and Visitors Bureau for promotional hotel packages, which may include Broadway shows, sightseeing excursions, and shopping discounts.
- Use New York's TKTS for discounts on same-day tickets to Broadway and off-Broadway shows. Locations include Times Square and South Street Seaport.
- Purchase a Philadelphia CityPass, which gets you admission into five well-known attractions at a 50% discount. Visit www.citypass.com for information.
- Staying on a working farm in Pennsylvania Dutch Country—which can start around $40 per night—not only saves money on hotels, but provides a close-up look of Amish culture.
- An easy and inexpensive way to see the sights in Philadelphia is to take the PHLASH, a group of shuttle buses that continually circle the city. For $4 a day, you can get on and off the bus as often as you like.

February

Chinese New Year
New York City
Parade with lions, dragons, costumes, firecrackers.
800/225-5697

Chocolate Lovers' Extravaganza
Hershey, PA
Chef-taught classes, decorating instructions, and more.
800/533-3131

April

Philadelphia Open House
Philadelphia, PA
House and garden tours; selection of over 150 homes, gardens, historic sites.
215/928-1188

Tulip Festival
Cape May, NJ
609/884-5508

May

Folk Festival
Pittsburgh, PA
888/849-4753

Washington Square Art Show
New York, NY
Outdoor art show.
800/225-5697

June

New York Shakespeare Festival & Shakespeare in the Park
New York City
At the 2,000-seat outdoor Delacorte Theater in Central Park.
212/539-8750

Sea & Sky Festival
Cape May, NJ
Sample Cape May's variety of seafood while colorful kites and blues music fill the air.
609/884-5508

July

Central Pennsylvania Festival of the Arts
State College, PA
814/237-3682

Jazz Fest
Asbury Park, NJ
732/502-5728

August

Great Allentown Fair
Allentown, PA
610/435-SHOW

Middlesex County Fair
New Brunswick, NJ
732/356-7400

New York State Fair
Syracuse, NY
315/487-7711

September

Lakeside Festival
Lake George Village, NY
Juried craft show; boat show with demo rides; food, music, fireworks.
518/668-5771

Wings 'n Water Festival
Stone Harbor, NJ
609/368-1211

October

Apple Harvest Festival
Gettysburg, PA
800/379-7448

Atlantic City Marathon
Atlantic City, NJ
609/601-1RUN

November

NYC Marathon
New York City
212/860-4455

December

First Night
Albany, NY
Celebration of the arts and fireworks to welcome the new year.
518/434-2032

MA 110
RI 155
CT 78
MA 229
RI 245
CT 233

Free Finds $

Fish Family Farm Creamery and Dairy Farm, Bolton, CT
One of four dairy farms in the state that milk cows, pasteurize, and bottle their own milk. Self-guided tours anytime. Make ice cream on premises. **860/646-9745**

Caprilands Herb Farm, Storrs, CT
More than 30 different theme gardens using herbs, spices, and wild grasses.

Hickory Hill Orchards, Cheshire, CT
Free hayrides to pick-your-own apples, peaches, pears and pumpkins. Includes pie garden, gourmet store, pony rides, and a picnic area. **203/272-3824**

Barker Character, Comic, and Cartoon Museum, Cheshire, CT
Comic strip, cartoon, and advertising character memorabilia. Includes Cartoon Theatre, storybook stage, children's playhouse, California Raisin and Gumby museum. **203/699-3822**

Rhode Island State House, Providence
Contains a Gilbert Stuart full-length portrait of George Washington, the original parchment charter granted to Rhode Island by Charles II in 1663, and the world's fourth largest self-supported marble dome. **401/222-2357**

Walking Tour of Historic Apponaug Village, Warwick, RI
More than 30 structures of historic and/or architectural interest are noted on walking tour brochure, available through Department of Economic Development, Warwick City Hall.

Cliff Walk, Newport, RI
Scenic walk overlooking Atlantic Ocean adjoins many Newport "cottages."

Vincent House, Martha's Vineyard
Oldest known house on the island, built in 1672. Carefully restored to allow visitors to see how buildings were constructed 300 years ago. **508/627-4440**

Cape Cod Potato Chips Factory Tour, Hyannis
From a glass-enclosed corridor, watch chip makers at work as they transform potatoes into America's favorite snack. Free sample bag. **508/775-3358**

Simply put, Connecticut's countryside is picture-perfect. Stroll Litchfield's green fields and valleys, or visit Mystic Seaport. Submarine aficionados can happily immerse themselves in Groton, while budding paleontologists can create footprint casts at Dinosaur State Park. Neighboring Rhode Island's varied topography includes rugged hills and rolling countryside. Relive the elegant Gilded Age in Newport, or sail Narragansett Bay. Block Island is a popular summer destination, and Jamestown boasts a historic 18th-century lighthouse. Massachusetts is a truly delightful combination of old and new. Enjoy Faneuil Hall and Old North Church in Boston while relishing the city's modern amenities. Cape Cod's pristine coastline is complemented by quaint towns, and the emerald bluffs of Martha's Vineyard and Nantucket rival those of Ireland, while remaining distinctly Yankee.

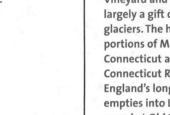

Their coastlines raggedly cut like pieces of a jigsaw puzzle by Narragansett, Buzzards and Cape Cod Bays, Massachusetts and Rhode Island favored early maritime ventures. Cape Cod itself, along with Martha's Vineyard and Nantucket, is largely a gift of Ice Age glaciers. The hilly central portions of Massachusetts and Connecticut are drained by the Connecticut River, New England's longest, which empties into Long Island sound at Old Saybrook.

Ⓑ Dinosaur State Park

Ⓔ Mystic Seaport

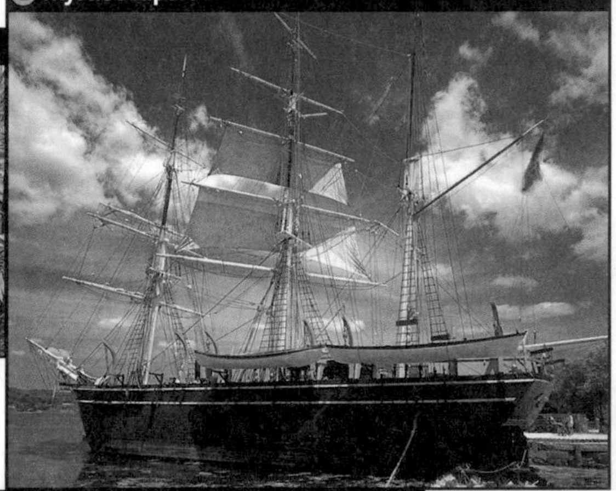

Ⓓ Lichfield

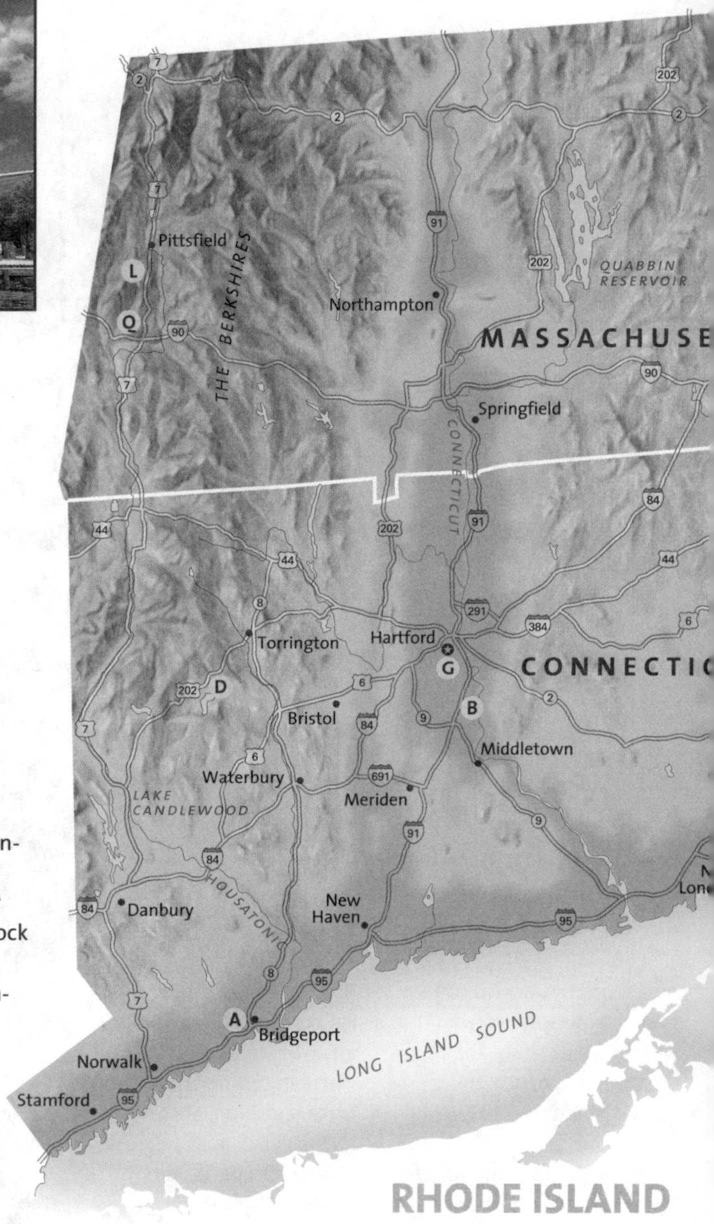

CONNECTICUT

Ⓐ **BARNUM MUSEUM**
Pg. 78, J6. **Bridgeport.** This museum houses memorabilia from P. T. Barnum's life and circus career, including artifacts relating to his famous discoveries, General Tom Thumb and Jenny Lind. Exhibits include a scale model of a three-ring circus and displays of Victorian Bridgeport. **203/331-1104** $

Ⓑ **DINOSAUR STATE PARK**
Pg. 78, D10. **Rocky Hill.** During excavation for a new building in 1966, a stone slab bearing the three-toed tracks of dinosaurs, which roamed the area 200 million years ago, was discovered. Construction was halted, and a 65-acre area was designated a state park. Under the park's geodesic dome, visitors can view 500 of these dinosaur tracks, as well as life-size Jurassic and Triassic dioramas. **860/529-8423** $

Ⓒ **HISTORIC SHIP U.S.S. NAUTILUS AND SUBMARINE FORCE LIBRARY AND MUSEUM**
Pg. 79, H14. **Groton.** The world's first nuclear-powered submarine, *U.S.S. Nautilus*, is permanently housed here. The museum exhibits depict the history of the U.S. Submarine Force and features working periscopes, an authentic submarine control room, and four minisubs. The museum also includes interactive exhibits which emphasize the contributions made by the Submarine Force and its industry partners to the winning of the Cold War. **860/694-3174**

Ⓓ **LITCHFIELD**
Pg. 78, D6. Litchfield, on a plateau above the Naugatuck Valley, has the feel of an 18th-century town. Because the railroads laid their main lines below in the valley, industry largely bypassed it. The Reverend Henry Ward Beecher and his sister, Harriet Beecher Stowe, author of *Uncle Tom's Cabin*, grew up in Litchfield. Tapping Reeve established the first law school in the country, the Litchfield Law School, here in the late 18th century. **860/567-4506**

Ⓔ **MYSTIC SEAPORT**
Pg. 79, H15. **Mystic.** This 17-acre complex is the nation's largest maritime museum, dedicated to the preservation of 19th-century maritime history. Visitors may board the 1841 wooden whaleboat *Charles W. Morgan*, square-rigged ship *Joseph Conrad*, or fishing schooner *L. A. Dunton*. **860/572-5315** $

Ⓕ **ROSELAND COTTAGE**
Pg. 79, B15. **Putnam.** Influential abolitionist publisher Henry C. Bowen's summer home, located on Woodstock Hill, is one of the most important surviving examples of a Gothic-revival "cottage." With its bright pink exterior and picturesque profile, it stands in contrast to the otherwise colonial character of this New England village. The cottage contains period furnishings. **860/928-4074** $

Ⓖ **WADSWORTH ATHENEUM MUSEUM OF ART**
Pg. 78, D10. **Hartford.** The museum has more than 40,000 works of art spanning 5,000 years. One of the nation's oldest continuously operating public art museums, its collections include 15th- to 20th-century paintings, American furniture, sculpture, porcelains, English and American silver, and the Amistad Collection of African American art. **860/278-2670** $

Connecticut is home to the oldest U.S. newspaper still being published: *The Hartford Courant*, established in 1764

RHODE ISLAND

Ⓗ **BLOCK ISLAND**
Pg. 155, N4. Called Rhode Island's "air-conditioned" summer resort, Block Island covers 21 square miles. Lying 12 miles out to sea from Point Judith, it received its nickname because it is 10 to 15 degrees cooler than the mainland in summer and consistently milder in winter. It has become a favorite "nature retreat" for people seeking to escape fast-paced city living. **401/466-2982**

Ⓘ **GREEN ANIMALS TOPIARY GARDENS**
Pg. 155, H7. **Portsmouth.** Planted in 1880 with California privet, golden boxwood,

Harvard University, the nation's oldest college, was chartered in Cambridge in 1636

Ⓜ Cape Cod

Ⓞ New England Aquarium

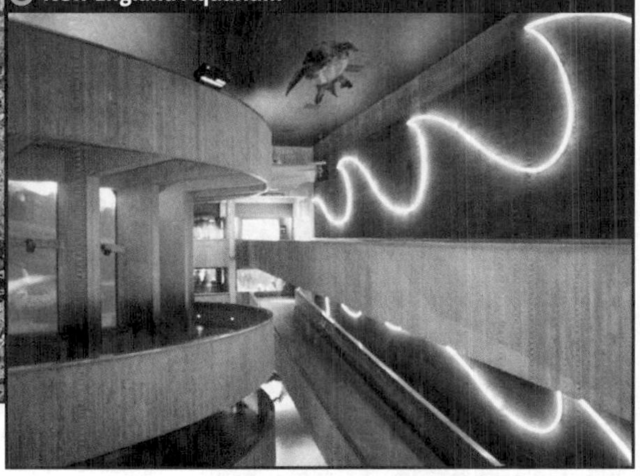

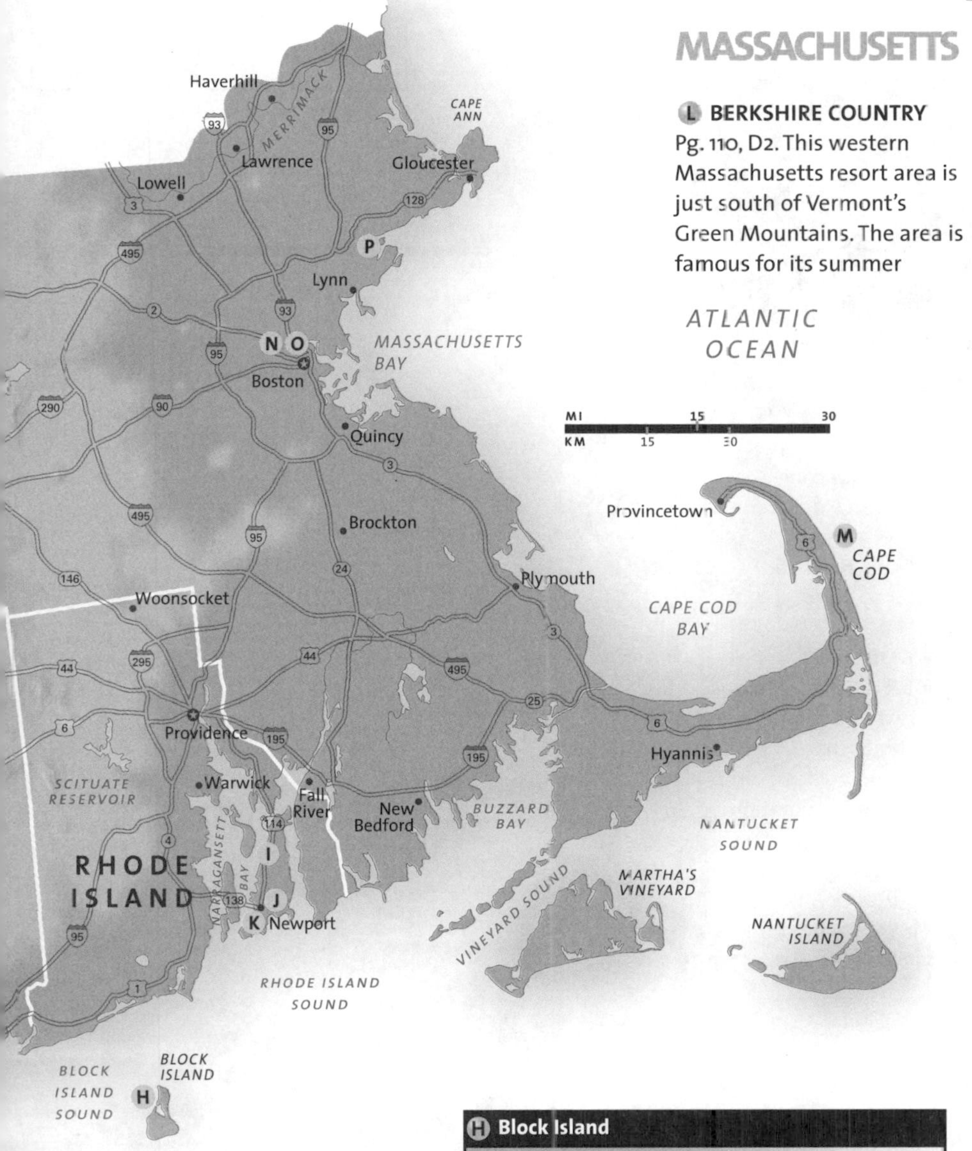

Ⓗ Block Island

and American boxwood, the gardens are sculpted into animal forms, geometric figures, and ornamental designs. The 7-acre grounds also feature a rose garden and formal flower beds. The main house features Victorian toys. **401/847-6543 $**

Ⓙ Historic Mansions

Ⓙ HISTORIC MANSIONS AND HOUSES

Pg. 155, J6. **Newport.** Highlights include Astor's Beechwood, the Italianate summer residence of Mrs. Caroline Astor; the Breakers, a 70-room Northern Italian palazzo and the largest of all of the Newport mansions; and Hammersmith Farm, the unofficial summer White House during the Kennedy administration. **401/849-8048 $**

Ⓚ TRINITY CHURCH

Pg. 155, J6. **Newport.** Built in 1726—and still in use today—this was the first parish in the state. George Washington and philosopher George Berkeley worshipped here, and Queen ElizabethII and the Archbishop of Canterbury visited in 1976. The interior features Tiffany windows, an organ that was played by Handel, and the only three-tiered wineglass pulpit in America. **401/846-0660 $**

MASSACHUSETTS

Ⓛ BERKSHIRE COUNTRY

Pg. 110, D2. This western Massachusetts resort area is just south of Vermont's Green Mountains. The area is famous for its summer cultural life from the Tanglewood Music Center to Jacob's Pillow Dance Festival and the Willamstown Theater. Its fall leaf show—one of the best in the US—fills every hotel and motel room months ahead. **413/443-9186**

Ⓜ CAPE COD

Pg. 111, K18. The popularity of the automobile changed Cape Cod from a group of isolated fishing villages, big estates, and cranberry bogs into one of the world's prime resort areas. Visitors to Cape Cod are never at a loss for things to do: golfing, boating, bicycling, and shopping in one of the many antique and specialty shops are just some of the recreational opportunities available. **508/362-3225**

Ⓝ FANEUIL HALL MARKETPLACE

Pg. 111, E14. **Boston.** Bostonian Peter Faneuil bequeathed this two-story, bronze-domed building to the city in 1742 as a public meeting hall and marketplace. Called the "Cradle of Liberty" because it was the scene of mass meetings during the pre-Revolutionary period, the building (along with two other restored structures) today houses a bustling marketplace of more than 100 specialty shops, 20 restaurants and pubs, and a variety of pushcarts and food stalls. **617/523-1300**

Ⓞ NEW ENGLAND AQUARIUM

Pg. 111, E14. **Boston.** The aquarium houses one of the largest cylindrical saltwater tanks in the world, stocked with hundreds of specimens of marine life. Permanent exhibits include marine mammals, birds, and reptiles. Other displays feature marine life in American rivers, including exotic animals from the Amazon Basin area: electric eels; turtles; and a 4,000-gallon replica of an Amazon rain forest. **617/973-5200 $**

Ⓟ SALEM MARITIME NATIONAL HISTORIC SITE

Pg. 111, D15. **Salem.** This nine-acre area is the only remaining intact waterfront from America's age of sail almost 200 years ago. The site has twelve historic structures along the waterfront, as well as a visitor center in downtown Salem. **978/740-1660**

Ⓠ TANGLEWOOD

Pg. 110, E2. **Lenox.** Nathaniel Hawthorne lived and wrote here and planned Tanglewood Tales. Many of the 526 acres, developed into a gentleman's estate by William Aspinwall Tappan, are in formal gardens. Tanglewood is well-known today as the summer home of the Boston Symphony Orchestra and the Tanglewood Music Center, the symphony's training academy for young musicians. **413/637-1600**

DOLLAR WI$E

- Get same-day concert or theater tickets half-price through BosTix (locations throughout the city).
- The Boston CityPass provides admission to six popular attractions at nearly a 50% discount.
- For a refreshing change of scenery from the beaches of Cape Cod, visit the Skunknett River Wildlife Sanctuary. For under $5, you can escape the summer heat by walking on its scenic, tree-covered trails.
- Visit The Freedom Trail in Boston, a three-mile marked trail connecting 16 historical landmarks. The National Park Service rangers offer free guided tours. Sites like the Old North Church and the Paul Revere House charge nominal admission fees. **617/536-4100**

February

Mid-winter New England Surfing Championship
Narragansett, RI
401/789-1954

Newport Winter Festival
Newport, RI
Ten days of more than 200 cultural and recreational events.
401/849-8048

April

Boston Marathon
Boston
617/236-1652

Connecticut Storytelling Festival
New London, CT
860/439-2764

Daffodil Festival
Nantucket Island, MA
508/228-1700

May

Gaspee Days
Warwick, RI
Celebration of the capture and burning of British revenue schooner *Gaspee* by Rhode Island patriots.
401/781-1772

Lobsterfest
Mystic, CT
860/572-5315

June

International Festival of Arts and Ideas
New Haven, CT
888/278-4332

Newport Music Festival
Newport, RI
401/847-7090

Spring Festival of Historic Houses
Providence, RI
401/831-7440

July

Harborfest
Boston
Concerts, chowder fest, children's activities, Boston Pops Orchestra, fireworks.
617/227-1528

Hot-Air Balloon Festival
Kingston, RI
401/783-1770

Lowell Folk Festival
Lowell, MA
Concerts, crafts, and demonstrations, ethnic food, street parade.
978/970-5000

Mark Twain Days
Hartford, CT
Celebration of Twain's legacy and Hartford's cultural heritage with more than 100 events.
860/247-0998

September

Durham Fair
Middletown, CT
860/349-9495

The "Big E"
Springfield, MA
Largest fair in the Northeast.
413/737-2443

October

Apple Harvest Festival
Meriden, CT
860/628-8036

Haunted Happenings
Salem, MA
Psychic festival, historical exhibits, haunted house.
978/744-0013

December

Stockbrige Main Street at Christmas
Stockbridge, MA
413/298-5200

ME 104
NH 127
VT 166
ME 237
NH 241
VT 247

Free Finds

Cold Hollow Cider Mill, Waterbury Center, VT
Watch cider making and enjoy free samples of cider, fudge, and other specialty foods. **802/244-8771**

Rock of Ages Granite Quarry, Graniteville, VT
Narrated tours of the world's largest granite quarry. **802/476-3119**

Ethan Allen Park, Burlington
Part of Ethan Allen's farm. **802/863-3489**

Candle Mill Village, Arlington, VT
Three buildings, including a gristmill built in 1764 by Remember Baker of the Green Mountain Boys; many music boxes, candles, cookbook, and teddy bear displays. **802/375-6068**

New England Ski Museum, Franconia, NH
Details history of skiing in the east; exhibits feature skis and bindings, clothing, art, and photographs. **603/823-7177**

Christie's Maple Farm, Lancaster, NH
See how maple syrup is made, and try free samples at the Taste Testing Bar. **603/788-4118**

Hampshire Pewter, Wolfeboro, NH
Guided factory tour, where the fine art of hand casting pewter is practiced. **800/639-7704**

Webster Cottage, Hanover, NH
Residence of Daniel Webster during his last year as a Dartmouth College student; Colonial and Shaker furniture, Webster memorabilia. **603/643-6529**

Maine State Museum, Augusta
Exhibits of Maine's natural environment, pre-history, social history and manufacturing heritage. **207/287-2301**

Nervous Nellie's Jams and Jellies, Deer Isle, ME
Visitors may visit the jelly kitchen to see how jam is made, May-October. **800/777-6845**

John Paul Jones State Memorial, Kittery, ME
Memorial to the sailors and soldiers of Maine. **207/384-5160**

Rackliffe Pottery, Blue Hill, ME
Family manufactures wheel-thrown dinnerware from native red-firing clay. Open workshop. **207/374-2297**

Vermont's Green Mountains attract downhill and cross-country skiers and snowboarders, all of whom are challenged by countless trails. Hiking, biking, fishing, antiquing, and simply admiring the spectacular fall foliage are but a few of the many alternatives. New Hampshire's rugged and beautiful White Mountains delight rock, ice, and mountain climbers; the seacoast and lake regions lure water sports enthusiasts; and the picturesque farms and villages of the Monadnock Region offer a serene stroll through New England's history. Offering more than 3,500 miles of coastline, Maine entices would-be seafarers with historic lighthouses, windjammer cruises, and world-famous lobster dinners. Visit Acadia National Park for its spectacular sunrises or travel to Baxter State Park, home to lofty Mount Katahdin.

Maine's rockbound coast, dotted with hundreds of islands, gives way to immense forests drained by powerful rivers. Farther west, the lofty peaks of New Hampshire's White Mountains and the gentler Green Mountains of Vermont stand sentinel over rolling farmlands. Northern New England borders New York State along scenic Lake Champlain, 125-miles long and up to 12-miles wide.

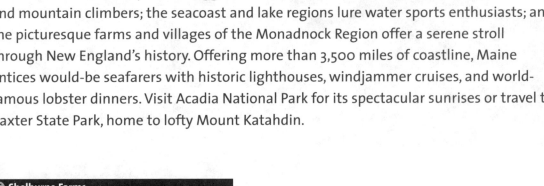

E Shelburne Farms

G Woodstock

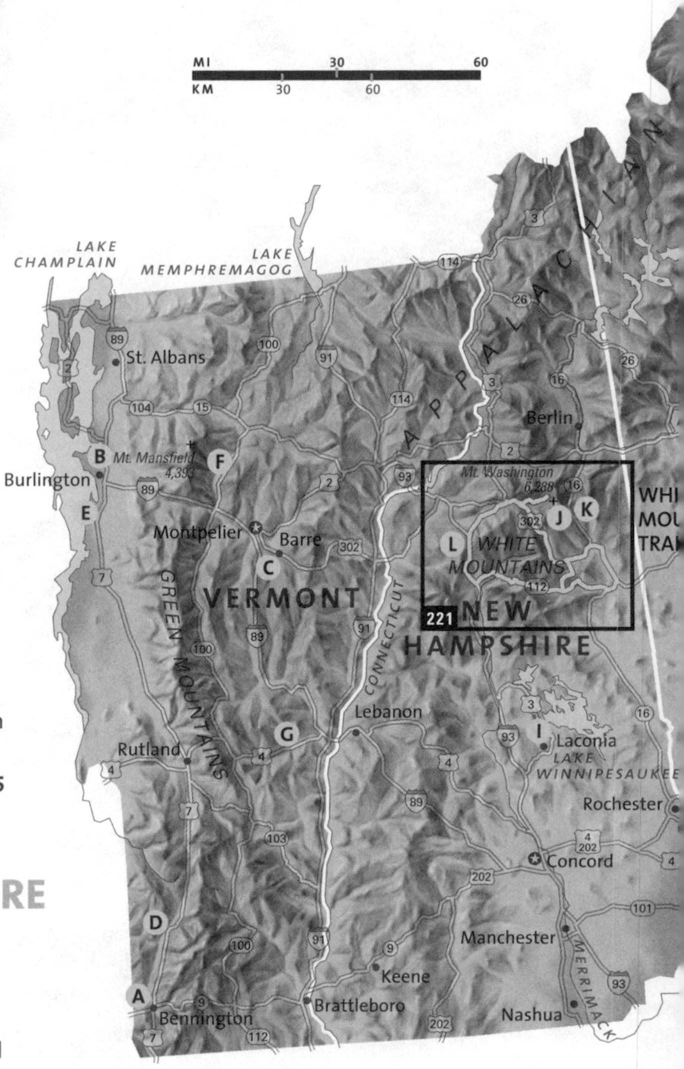

VERMONT

A BENNINGTON
Pg. 166, L3. Headquarters for Ethan Allen's Green Mountain Boys (known to New Yorkers as the "Bennington Mob"), Bennington boasts a Victorian and turn-of-the-century downtown; Colonial houses, church, and commons in Old Bennington; three covered bridges in North Bennington; the Bennington Museum; and a number of historical landmarks including the Old First Church and Robert Frost gravesite. **802/447-3311**

B CHURCH STREET MARKETPLACE
Pg. 166, D3. **Burlington.** This is one of the most popular tourist attractions in Vermont. More than 100 shops, restaurants, galleries, and cafes line the four traffic-free art deco and 19th-century blocks of this bustling marketplace. Events and festivals make it a wonderful year-round attraction. **802/863-1648**

C GRANITE SCULPTURES
Pg. 166, E6. **Barre.** Known as the "Granite Capitol of the World," Barre's sculptures include a figure of poet Robert Burns and "Youth Triumphant," a soldier's and sailor's memorial erected on Armistice Day in 1924. Hope Cemetery features headstones that rival the world's finest granite carvings. **802/454-8311**

D NORMAN ROCKWELL EXHIBITION
Pg. 166, K3. **Arlington.** A historic 1875 church in the illustrator's home town displays hundreds of magazine covers, illustrations, advertisements, calendars, and other printed works. Several of Rockwell's former models that posed for his paintings work at the exhibition and are available to answer questions. **802/375-6423** $

E SHELBURNE FARMS
Pg. 166, D3. **Shelburne.** The former mansion of Dr. Seward Webb and his wife, Lila Vanderbilt, is the centerpiece of this beautiful estate on the shores of Lake Champlain. The museum has old farm equipment, examples of fine needlework, early Vermont furniture and tools, old railroad equipment, and other historic artifacts. **802/985-8686** $

F STOWE
Pg. 166, D5. Stowe, a year-round resort area, is home to Mount Mansfield, Vermont's highest peak, where winter visitors ski, snowboard, and snowshoe. Summer guests enjoy outdoor concerts, hiking, biking, golf, tennis, and other attractions, including a Ben & Jerry's ice cream tour. **802/253-7321**

G WOODSTOCK
Pg. 166, H5. Determined preservationists have saved the antique charm of Woodstock, handing down property through generations and replacing a condemned iron bridge across the Ottauquechee River at Union Street with a covered wooden bridge. **802/457-3555**

The first U.S. public library is founded in Peterborough, NH.

NEW HAMPSHIRE

H FORT STARK STATE HISTORIC SITE
Pg. 127, B6. **New Castle.** A former portion of the coastal defense system dating back to 1746, the site reveals many of the changes in military technology from the Revolutionary War through WW II. A walking trail crosses the ten-acre fort site. **603/ 433-8583**

I LACONIA
Pg. 127, J7. Laconia has 19 miles of lakefront shoreline on four different lakes with five public beaches and 150 acres of parks and recreation facilities. It is the commercial center of an area known as the Lakes Region. **603/524-5531**

J MOUNT WASHINGTON
Pg. 127, G8. **North Conway.** At 6,288 feet, Mount Washington towers over the other peaks of the White Mountains and is the highest point in the northeastern United States. The mountain claims the world's first cog railway. The view from the top is the "second greatest show on earth" according to P.T. Barnum.

K NORTH CONWAY
Pg. 127, G8. This is the heart of the famous Mount Washington Valley. Several local ski areas make this town a popular destination for winter-sports enthusiasts. However, North Conway is a wonderful four-season destination. From mid-April to December, the Conway Scenic Railroad offers rides with striking views of Mount Washington. There are also several theme attractions, golf courses, horseback riding, and bicycling trails.**603/356-5701**

K Conway Scenic Railroad

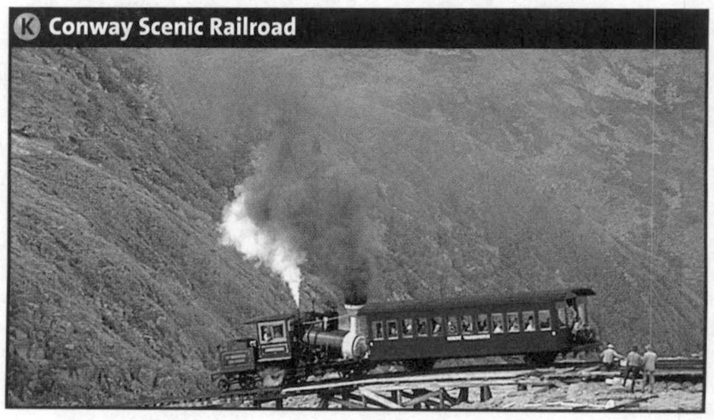

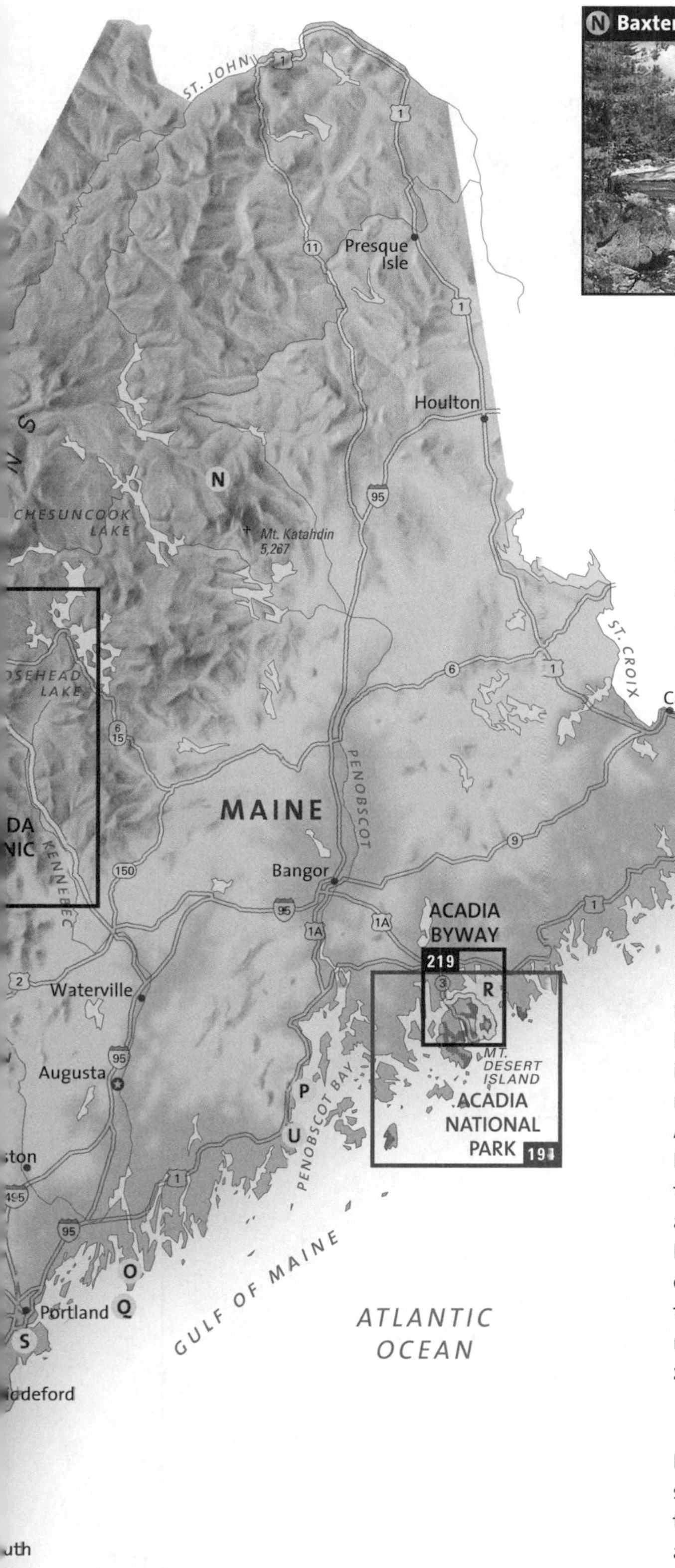

Ⓝ Baxter State Park

Ⓞ Boothbay Harbor

Ⓣ Shaker Muesum

MAINE

Ⓝ BAXTER STATE PARK
Pg. 104, J8. **Millinocket.** As a legislator and later as governor, Percival P. Baxter urged creation of a wilderness park around Mount Katahdin, Maine's highest peak. Rebuffed, Baxter bought the land with his own money and deeded it to the state of Maine, a 201,018-acre park "to be forever left in its natural, wild state." **207/723-5140** $

Ⓞ BOOTHBAY HARBOR
Pg. 105, S5. This protected harbor, a haven for boatmen is the scene of well-attended regattas each summer. The Annual Windjammer Days Festival is a popular attraction, as are excursion boats and fishing. The nearby Boothbay Railway Village recreates an old village and features antique vehicles and rides aboard a steam train. **207/633-2353**

Ⓟ CAMDEN
Pg. 105, Q7. Camden's unique setting—where the mountains meet the sea—makes it a popular four-season resort area. Recreational activities include boat cruises and rentals, swimming, fishing, camping, hiking, and picnicking, as well as winter activities. The Pulitzer-winning poet Edna St. Vincent Millay grew up in Camden. **207/236-4404**

Ⓠ MONHEGAN ISLAND
Pg. 105, S6. Known for its rugged beauty and delicious lobsters, this small island retains an unspoiled quality. With no automobiles allowed, visitors come here by boat to enjoy the quintessential Maine scenery—high headlands, rocky shores, and evergreen forests. There are many nature trails to choose from, and visitors can often observe harbor seals during half tide on the island's northern end.

Ⓡ OCEANARIUM
Pg. 105, P9. **Bar Harbor.** An extension of the Mount Desert Oceanarium in Southwest Harbor features salt-marsh walks and a viewing tower; a lobster hatchery, where young lobsters are hatched from eggs then returned to the ocean; and a lobster museum with hands-on exhibits. **207/288-5005** $

Ⓢ PORTLAND
Pg. 105, S3. Maine's largest city is on Casco Bay, dotted with islands popular with summer visitors. The Portland Museum of Art includes works by European masters and 18th-century decorative and fine arts as well as Winslow Homer and Andrew Wyeth paintings. The architecture and cobblestone streets of the Old Port Exchange evoke the city's seafaring days. The 1807 Portland Observatory offers fine views. **207/772-5800**

Ⓣ SHAKER MUSEUM
Pg. 105, R3. **New Gloucester.** The last active Shaker community opens six of its structures to the public, displaying Shaker furniture, folk and decorative arts, textiles, tin and woodenware, and early American tools and farm implements. Guided tours include the meetinghouse, built in 1794, Boys' Shop, Sisters' Shop, and the Spin House. **207/926-4597** $

Ⓤ WINDJAMMERS
Pg. 105, R7. **Rockland.** These large, old-time schooners sail out for three to six days following the route through Penobscot Bay into Blue Hill and Frenchman's Bay, stopping at small villages and islands along the way. Each ship carries an average of 30

Ⓛ Old Man of the Mountains

Ⓛ OLD MAN OF THE MOUNTAINS, FRANCONIA NOTCH STATE PARK
Pg. 127, F6. **Easton.** This craggy likeness of a man's face is a natural rock profile, an icon for the state's official emblem formed from five layers of granite. Also known as the "Great Stone Face," the Old Man is forty feet high and has been reinforced to prevent erosion. **603/823-5563**

Ⓜ PORTSMOUTH HISTORIC HOMES
Pg. 127, L10. A walking tour of six historic residences, dating from 1716 to 1807, includes the Governor John Langdon House; the John Paul Jones House, where the famous naval commander twice boarded; the Warner House, one of New England's finest Georgian houses; and the Jackson House, the oldest house in New Hampshire. **603/436-1118** $

Ⓜ Portsmouth

DOLLAR WI$E

- You don't have to visit the Rockies to experience awesome, above-the-treeline views. Take the exciting cog railway to the top of Mt. Washington in the Presidential Range of Northern New Hampshire. If your vehicle is up to it, you can drive to the top as a cheaper option. Or, hike to the top on the Appalachian Trail for no fee.
- For a day of inexpensive fun, head to Yankee Kingdom Orchard in Vermont. You can tour its greenhouse, nursery and gardens, visit the petting zoo, picnic in the orchard, and enjoy beautiful views of the mountains and Lake Champlain while taking a hayride—all for no admission price.
- If it's Friday, view the extensive collection of fine art at The Portland Museum of Art from 5-9 pm, when admission is free.
- An easy and inexpensive way to see Portland, Maine, is by taking one of the many walking tours through its distinct neighborhoods. Maps are available at the Visitor Information Center.

February
Kennebunk Winter Carnival
Kennebunk, ME
Snow sculpture contests, snow palace moonwalk, magic show, ice-skating party, chili and chowder contests, children's events.
207/985-6890

Winter Carnival
Brattleboro, VT
802/254-4565

April
Maple Sugar Festival
St. Albans, VT
A number of producers welcome visitors who join sugarhouse parties for sugar-on-snow, sour pickles, and raised doughnuts.
802/524-5800

May
Lilac Time Festival
Franconia, NH
Celebration of the state flower and observance of Memorial Day.
603/436-3988

Maine State Parade
Lewiston, ME
207/783-2249

June
Market Square Days
Portsmouth, NH
Summer celebration with 10K road race, street fair, entertainment.
603/436-3988

Mountain Bike World Cup Race
West Dover, VT
800/245-7669

Portsmouth Jazz Festival
Portsmouth, NH
603/436-3988

Windjammer Days
Boothbay Harbor, ME
Old schooners that formerly sailed the trade routes and now cruise the Maine coast sail en masse into the harbor.
207/633-2353

July
Festival de Joie
Lewiston, ME
Celebration of Lewiston and Auburn's Franco-American heritage.
207/783-2249

Festival on the Green
Middlebury, VT
Classical, modern, and traditional dance; chamber and folk music; theater and comedy presentations.
802/388-0216

August
Lakes Region Fine Arts and Crafts Festival
Meredith, NH
603/279-6121

Maine Lobster Festival
Rockland, ME
207/596-0376

September
Riverfest
Manchester, NH
Outdoor festival with family entertainment, concerts, arts and crafts, food booths, fireworks.
603/623-2623

Vermont State Fair
Rutland, VT
802/775-5200

October
Vermont Apple Festival and Craft Show
Springfield, VT
802/885-2779

December
Christmas by the Sea
Camden, ME
207/236-4404

PE 186
NF 187
NS 186
NB 186
PQ 184
ON 182
PE 250
NF 249
NS 249
NB 249
PQ 250
ON 249

Free Finds $

Ontario Parliament Buildings, Toronto
Guided tours of the Legislative Building and walking tour of grounds.
416/325-7500

Stone Consolidated, Kenora, ON
Paper manufacturing process is followed from debarking of logs to the finished product.
807/467-3000

Museum of Canadian Scouting, Ottawa
Depicts the history of Canadian Scouting; exhibits on the life of Lord R.S.S. Baden-Powell, founder of the Boy Scouts.
613/224-5131

Montréal Museum of Fine Arts, Montréal
Canada's oldest art museum; wide variety of displays, ranging from Egyptian statues to 20th-century abstracts.
514/285-1600

Chocolate Shop and Museum, Quebec City
See how chocolate is made, learn its history, and taste handmade chocolate and homemade ice cream.
418/524-2122

Notre Dame du Cap, Trois Rivieres, QC
Small stone church and large octagonal basilica renowned for its stained-glass windows. Important pilgrimage site. **819/374-2441**

Notre Dame Basilica, Montréal
In 1672, a church described as "one of the most beautiful churches in North America" was erected on the present Notre-Dame site. When this became inadequate for the growing parish, a new church designed by New Yorker James O'Donnell was built. It was completed in 1829.

Province House, Halifax, NS
Guided tour of oldest provincial Parliament building in Canada.
902/424-8967

Cape Forchu Lighthouse, Yarmouth, NS
Entrance to Bay of Fundy and Yarmouth Harbour. Route travels along rocky coastline and through colorful fishing villages.
800/565-0000

York Redoubt National Historic Site, Halifax, NS
A 200-year-old fortification on a high bluff overlooking the harbor entrance. Features muzzle-loading guns, a photo display, and picnic facilities. **902/426-5050**

Aitken Bicentennial Exhibition Centre, St. John, NB
Promotes the arts and sciences through touring and local exhibitions; includes ScienceScape, a permanent hands-on children's science gallery.
506/633-4870

Ontario is defined by its economic epicenter, Toronto, whose skyline is dominated by the celebrated CN Tower and whose flourishing cultural scene includes world-class opera, ballet, and museums. Moving eastward, Quebec's French-Canadian flair is evident from the villages of the Laurentian Mountains to Montreal, where sidewalk cafés and shops are distinctly Parisian. Quebec City, overlooking the St. Lawrence River, maintains an Old World charm, while starkly beautiful Newfoundland introduces visitors to icebergs and fjords. Visitors can relax on the pastel sands of Prince Edward's beaches and cool off in its cerulean waters. Known as the Loyalist Province, New Brunswick is home to the famous reversing falls of St. John and the unique Bay of Fundy, and Nova Scotia's coastal highways offer a panorama of breathtaking vistas.

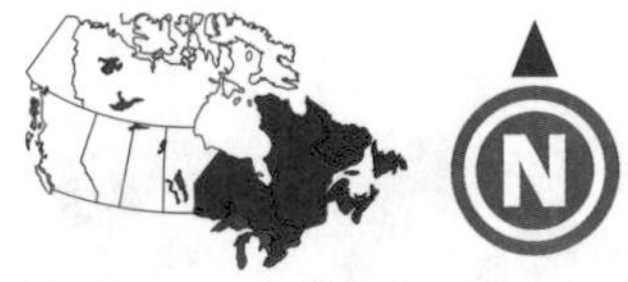

Craggy Newfoundland and mainland Labrador are no strangers to offshore icebergs and Atlantic gales. Nova Scotia enjoys one of the world's finest natural harbors, at Halifax; its interior—and that of New Brunswick—is heavily forested, while Prince Edward Island is mostly cleared for farming. The St. Lawrence River drains much of Ontario and Québec, carrying the waters of the Great Lakes to the sea.

C Niagara Falls

E Toronto

ONTARIO

A MARINE MUSEUM OF THE GREAT LAKES

Pg. 183, G16. **Kingston.** Ships have been built in Kingston since 1678. This museum explores the tales, adventures, and enterprise of "inland seas" history. Highlights include a shipbuilding gallery and an 1889 engine room with dry dock engines and pumps. **613/542-2261** $

B NATIONAL GALLERY OF CANADA

Pg. 183, D17. **Ottawa.** Permanent exhibits include European paintings from the 14th century to the present; Canadian art from the 17th century to the present; contemporary and decorative arts, prints, drawings, photos, and Inuit art; and video and film. The reconstructed 19th-century Rideau convent chapel with a neo-Gothic fan-vaulted ceiling is the only known example of its kind in North America. **613/990-1985**

C NIAGARA-ON-THE-LAKE

Pg. 183, K11. The beautiful old homes lining the tree-shaded streets testify to the prosperity of this area, once a busy shipping, shipbuilding, and commercial center. The town's attractions now include theater, historic sites, beautiful gardens, and Queen Street, with its shops, hotels, and restaurants. Delightful in any season, this is one of the best-preserved and prettiest remnants of the Georgian era. **905/468-4263**

D ST. LAWRENCE ISLANDS NATIONAL PARK

Pg. 183, F17. **Mallorytown.** Established in 1904, this park lies on a 50-mile stretch of the St. Lawrence River between Kingston and Brockville. It consists of 21 island areas and a mainland headquarters at Mallorytown Landing. The park offers boat-launching facilities, beaches, natural and historic interpretive programs, island camping, picnicking, hiking, and boating. **613/923-5261** $

E TORONTO

Pg. 183, J11. Toronto is a cosmopolitan city. Once predominantly British, the population is now multicultural. A major theater center with many professional playhouses, including the Royal Alexandra Theatre, Toronto is also a banking center, with several architecturally significant banks. There are many attractions throughout the city including Casa Loma, Centreville Amusement Park, CN Tower, the Ontario Science Centre, and the Toronto Zoo. **416/203-2500**

There are no snakes, skunks, deer, porcupines or groundhogs on the island of Newfoundland. Chipmunks were introduced to Newfoundland from Nova Scotia in 1962 and 1964.

QUÉBEC

F LA CITADELLE

Pg. 185, H17. **Québec City.** Forming the eastern flank of the fortifications of Québec, La Citadelle was begun in 1820. Vestiges of the French regime, such as the Cap Diamant Redoubt (1693) and a powder magazine (1750), can still be seen. During the summer, the Royal 22e Régiment performs the Changing of the Guard. La Citadelle is an active military garrison and can only be visited on guided tours of 55 minutes, which are offered in French or English. **418/648-5175** $

G GASPÉ PENINSULA

Pg. 185, E20. **Rivière-du-Loup.** Jutting out into the Gulf St. Lawrence, the Gaspé Peninsula is a region of varying landforms, including mountains, plateaus, beaches, and cliffs. It is blessed with abundant and rare wildlife, such as black bears, moose, and red fox, and some unique flora, including 12-foot-high, centuries-old fir trees. With the exception of a few side trips, the entire Gaspé Peninsula Auto Tour follows Highway 132. Until this highway was developed, access to most of the peninsula was only by boat, accounting for much of the area's unspoiled character. **418/788-5676**

G Gaspe Peninsula

H NATIONAL BATTLEFIELDS PARK

Pg. 185, H17. **Québec City.** Also

called the Plains of Abraham (or "the Plains" by locals), the park was the site of a 1759 battle between the armies of Wolfe and Montcalm that changed the course of North American history. Events are held here throughout the year, and the Edwin Bélanger Bandstand presents a number of free shows every summer. The Plains also offers a 10-km jogging trail, a 15-km cross-country trail, walking paths, a playing field with permanent football and soccer fields, and a baseball diamond. **418/648-4071** $

NEW BRUNSWICK

J CARLTON MARTELLO TOWER HISTORIC PARK

Pg. 186, K6. **St. John.** These circular coastal forts, built for the War of 1812, also were used in World War II as fire command posts for harbor defenses. In addition to a restored powder magazine of the 1840s and a barrack room from about 1865, highlights include a panoramic view of the city, harbor, and surrounding landscape. **506/636-4011** $

L Fundy National Park

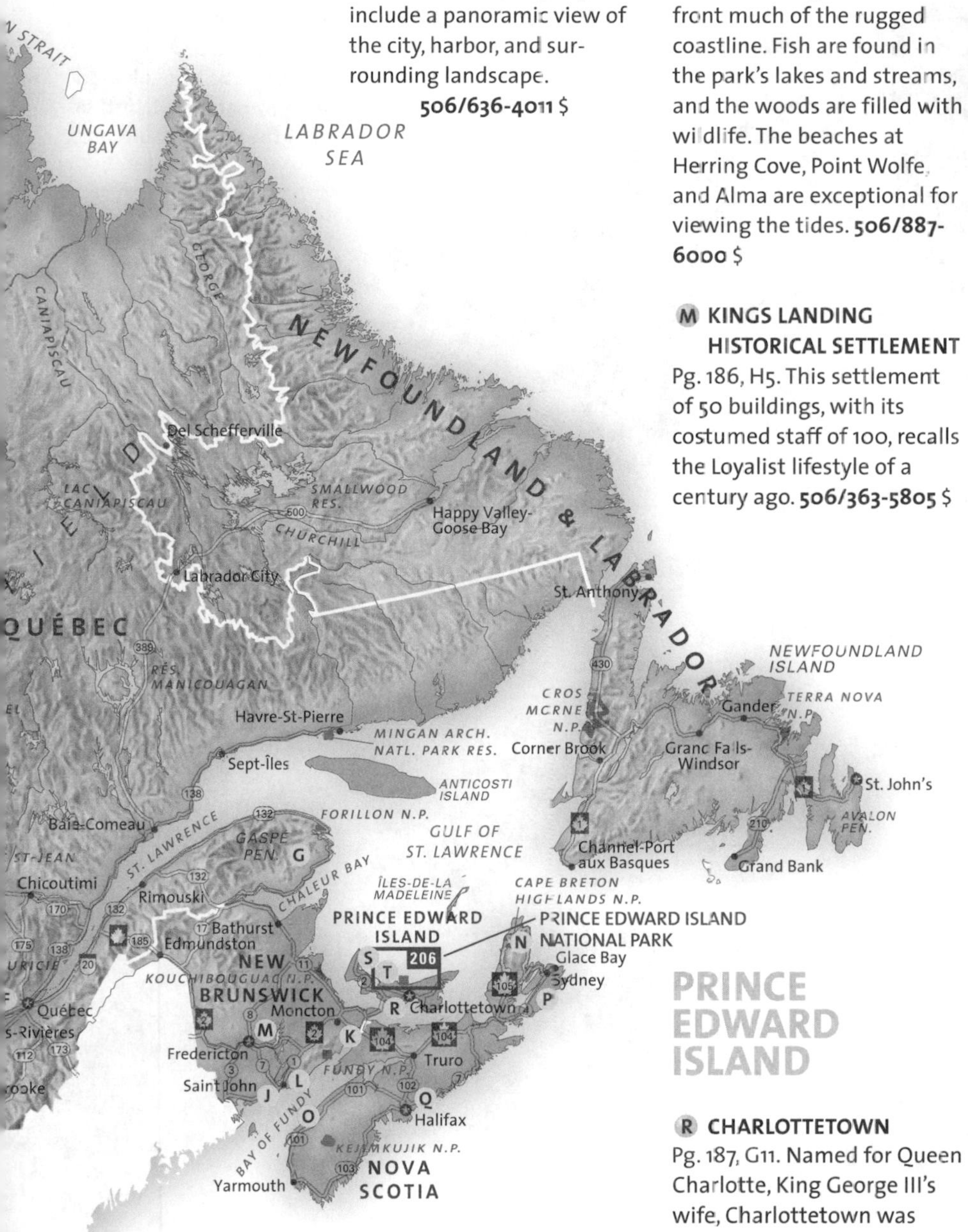

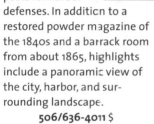

I OLD MONTRÉAL

Pg. 185, L12. **Montréal.** The city of Montréal evolved from the small settlement of Ville-Marie founded by de Maisonneuve in 1642. The largest concentration of 19th-century buildings in North America is found here. The area roughly forms a 100-acre quadrangle that corresponds approximately to the area enclosed within the original fortifications. Points of interest include the Place d'Armes, the square that is the heart of the city, the Notre Dame Basilica, and the Château Ramezay, the oldest private museum of history in Quebec. **514/873-2015**

K FORT BEAUSEJOUR NATIONAL HISTORIC SITE

Pg. 186, H9. **Aulac.** Built by the French between 1751 and 1755, during their long struggle with England for possession of Acadia, the fort also withstood an attack during the American Revolutionary War and was manned by a small garrison during the War of 1812. Visitors can view displays on the history and culture of the Isthmus of Chignecto, as well as outdoor paintings showing the garrison as it existed in the 18th century. **506/536-0720** $

L FUNDY NATIONAL PARK

Pg. 186, J8. **Alma.** On the coast between St. John and Moncton, the 80 square miles of forested hills and valleys are crisscrossed by miles of hiking trails. Cliffs front much of the rugged coastline. Fish are found in the park's lakes and streams, and the woods are filled with wildlife. The beaches at Herring Cove, Point Wolfe, and Alma are exceptional for viewing the tides. **506/887-6000** $

M KINGS LANDING HISTORICAL SETTLEMENT

Pg. 186, H5. This settlement of 50 buildings, with its costumed staff of 100, recalls the Loyalist lifestyle of a century ago. **506/363-5805** $

PRINCE EDWARD ISLAND

R CHARLOTTETOWN

Pg. 187, G11. Named for Queen Charlotte, King George III's wife, Charlottetown was chosen in 1765 as the capital of Colonial St. John's Island, as it was then known. The name was changed to Prince Edward Island in 1799. Known as the birthplace of Canada because the conference that led to confederation was held there in 1864, the city has many attractions located within easy reach such as Province House, the birthplace of the Canadian nation, and the Confederation Centre of the Arts, Canada's National Memorial to the Fathers of Confederation. Charlottetown is encircled by a scenic natural harbor, with boating, swimming, and other water sports, and a variety of seafood readily available. **902/368-4444**

S GREEN GABLES

Pg. 186, G10. **Cavendish.** Each year hundreds of thousands of visitors from around the world visit the site that inspired Lucy Maud Montgomery to create her beloved tale of a red-haired orphan, Anne of Green Gables. The house, grounds, and farm outbuildings portray the Victorian setting described in the novel. **902/672-6350** $

S Green Gables

T WOODLEIGH REPLICAS AND GARDENS

Pg. 186, G10. **Kensington.** This extensive outdoor display of large-scale models of famous castles and buildings includes the Tower of London, Dunvegan Castle, and Anne Hathaway Cottage. Several models are furnished and are large enough to enter. **902/836-3401** $

NOVA SCOTIA

N CAPE BRETON HIGHLANDS NATIONAL PARK

Pg. 187, F15. **Ingonish Beach.** In the northern part of Cape Breton Island, this park is bounded on the west by the Gulf of St. Lawrence and on the east by the Atlantic Ocean. The famous Cabot Trail, a modern 184-mile paved highway loop beginning at Baddeck, runs through the park and boasts spectacular vistas, especially between Ingonish and Cheticamp. **902/224-2306** $

O FORT ANNE NATIONAL HISTORIC SITE

Pg. 186, L7. **Annapolis Royal.** Fort Anne was built between 1702 and 1708 in one of the central areas of conflict between the English and French for control of North America. Of the original site, only the 18th-century earthworks and a gunpowder magazine remain. On the grounds is Canada's oldest English graveyard, dating from 1720. **902/532-2397**

P FORTRESS OF LOUISBOURG NATIONAL HISTORIC SITE

Pg. 187, H16. **Louisbourg.** This park includes a fortress erected by the French between 1720 and 1745 to defend their possessions in North America. It was once one of the busiest harbors in the New World and an important trading center. Highlights include the governor's apartment, the soldiers' barracks, the chapel, various guardhouses, and the king's storehouse. **902/733-2280** $

Q HALIFAX CITADEL NATIONAL HISTORIC PARK

Pg. 186, L10. **Halifax.** This star-shaped hilltop fort, built between 1828 and 1856 on the site of previous fortifications, offers an excellent view of the city and harbor. Visitors can see restored signal masts, a library, barrack rooms, a defense casemate, and a garrison cell. **902/426-5080** $

O Ft. Anne

DOLLAR WI$E

- Get the best exchange rate in Canada by using an ATM with a bank card.
- Plan your visit to coincide with one of the many festivals that take place all across Canada; you will experience a part of Canadian culture and have some cheaper fun.
- If visiting Nova Scotia, experience the amazing tidal bores of the Bay of Fundy. The tidal range of over 40 feet can be seen at no cost, if you have the time to park and watch for a few hours.
- Visit the Art Gallery of Nova Scotia on Tuesdays, when the admission fee is "pay what you wish."
- For the price of a drink, you can enjoy a panoramic view of Quebec City at L'Astral, the revolving restaurant atop Loews le Concorde Hotel.

January

Ontario Winter Carnival Bon Soo
Sault Ste. Marie, ON
Features more than 100 events: fireworks, fiddle contest, winter sports, and more.
705/759-3000

February

The Days of Wine and Roses
Niagara-on-the-Lake, ON
905/468-4263

June

Changing of the Guard
Ottawa, ON
613/239-5000

Charlottetown Festival
Charlottetown, PE
Original Canadian musicals, including *Anne of Green Gables*.
902/628-1864

International Caravan
Toronto, ON
Fifty pavilions scattered throughout the city present ethnic food, dancing, crafts.
416/977-0466

Trois-Rivieres International Vocal Arts Festival
Trois-Rivieres, QC
A celebration of song.
819/372-4635

July

Canada Day
Ottawa, ON
Celebration of Canada's birthday with many varied events including sailing regattas, music and dance, art demonstrations, children's entertainment, fireworks.
613/239-5000

Festival of Lights
Charlottetown, PE
Buskers, children's concerts, Waterfront Magic, children's midway. Fireworks display on Canada Day.
902/629-1864

Highland Games
Antigonish, NS
Scottish festival; pipe bands, Highland dancing, massed pipe band tattoo.
902/863-4921

Just for Laughs
Montreal, QC
International comedy festival.
514/845-2322

August

Expo Quebec
Quebec City, QC
Agricultural, commercial, and industrial fair: shows, games.
418/691-7110

Western Nova Scotia Exhibition
Yarmouth, NS
Animal judging, equestrian events, agricultural displays, crafts, midway.
902/742-8222

World Film Festival
Montreal, QC
514/848-3883

September

Harvest Jazz and Blues Festival
Fredericton, NB
888/622-5837

Toronto International Film Festival
Toronto, ON
C416/967-7371

October

Canadian International
Toronto, ON
One of Canada's most important horse races.
416/675-7223

November

Winter Festival of Lights
Niagara Falls, ON
800/563-2557

MB 181
SK 180
AB 178
BC 178
MB 249
SK 250
AB 248
BC 249

Framed by the Rocky Mountains, Alberta's resorts at Banff, Jasper, and Kananaskis attract jet-setters and thrill-seekers. Lake Louise, with turquoise water reflecting snowcapped mountains, is magnificent, and visitors often stampede to nearby Calgary for cowboy attractions. Beautiful Winnipeg in Manitoba is a flourishing cultural center. Lake Manitoba is extremely popular with water sports enthusiasts. Nestled between the Pacific and the Rockies, British Columbia is wonderfully diverse. From the 19th-century architecture of Victoria to the Thompson-Okanagan vineyards, choosing a favorite spot is impossible. Saskatoon, the "City of Bridges", is one of the loveliest in Saskatchewan, and capital city, Regina, is home to the enormous Wascana Centre Park. Hikers and nature lovers can enjoy Prince Albert National Park in the north.

The Prairie Provinces include Manitoba, Saskatchewan and Alberta. Near-level Manitoba has many lakes and rivers-including Lake Winnipeg (larger than Lake Ontario)—most of which drain into Hudson Bay. The Canadian Rockies rise from the prairies in southwestern Alberta, reaching to the north and west through Canada's most mountainous province, British Columbia, and into the Yukon Territory and Alaska. Components of the Rockies, such as the Monashee, Cariboo, and Selkirk Mountains in British Columbia are roughly paralleled, further west, by the Coast Mountains.

Free Finds $

Museum of Anthropology at the University of British Columbia, Vancouver
Free Tuesday evenings 5-7 pm; free guided tours daily. **604/822-3825**

Penticton Museum, Penticton, BC
Collection of Salish artifacts; taxidermy, ghost town, and pioneer exhibits. **250/492-6025**

Dominion Astrophysical Observatory, Victoria, BC
Public viewing through 72-in (185-cm) telescope. Features tours and display galleries.

Nanaimo Art Gallery and Exhibition, Nanaimo, BC
Gallery with changing exhibits of art, science, and history. **250/755-8790**

Devonian Gardens, Calgary, AB
Approximately 2 1/2 acres (1 1/2 hectares) of indoor vegetation in the heart of the city, playground, reflecting pool, waterfalls, fountains.

Edmonton Art Gallery, Edmonton, AB
Free admission Thursday after 4 pm; houses over 4,000 historical and contemporary paintings, sculptures, prints, installation works and photographs **780/422-6223**

Energeum, Calgary, AB
Public visitor center that involves guests in the story of Alberta's energy resources. Hands-on exhibits cover geology, exploration, conservation, and more. **403/297-4293**

Medicine Hat Museum and Art Gallery, Medicine Hat, AB
Displays depict the history of the Canadian West, featuring pioneer items, local fossils, relics, and Native artifacts. **403/527-6266**

Regina Plains Museum, Regina, SK
Exhibits on the culture and history of the Plains Indians, and the development of the city of Regina. **306/780-9434**

Vanguard Centennial Library Museum, Vanguard, SK
Museum depicts history of the community from homesteading days to the present. **306/582-2244**

Saskatchewan Baseball Hall of Fame and Museum, Battlefords
Contains over 2,000 artifacts and 5,000 pictures along with other items of archival nature pertaining to baseball in Saskatchewan. **306/445-8485**

Assiniboine Park, Winnipeg, MB
A 376-acre park featuring colorful English and formal gardens, conservatory with floral displays, and zoo. **204/986-3989**

A Butchart Gardens

C Chinatown

B Capilano Bridge

BRITISH COLUMBIA

A BUTCHART GARDENS

Pg. 178, N7. **Victoria.** These 55 acres offer spectacular views from the many paths of the four main areas. The gardens originated in the 1900s when the Butchart family carted topsoil into their depleted limestone quarry, creating the Sunken Garden. A Rose Garden, Japanese Garden, and Italian Garden were later added. Today, the gardens display more than one million plants throughout the year. During the summer, musical entertainment and fireworks displays are featured, and the gardens are illuminated with a beautiful display of lights. **250/652-5256** $

B CAPILANO SUSPENSION BRIDGE AND PARK

Pg. 178, A3. **North Vancouver.** More than 200 feet over the Capilano River, a 450-foot-long gently swaying footbridge spans the canyon. The surrounding park contains gardens, walking trails, trout ponds, a living forest exhibit, totem poles, and a large trading post. **604/985-7474** $

C CHINATOWN

Pg. 178, B3. **Vancouver.** This downtown area is the nucleus of the third-largest Chinese community in North America (only San Francisco's and New York's are larger). At the heart lies the Dr. Sun Yat-Sen Classical Chinese Garden, and the Chinese Market where visitors can try 100-year-old duck eggs and traditional cures made from herbs and powdered bone. **604/683-2000**

D GASTOWN

Pg. 178, B3. **Vancouver.** The original heart of Vancouver, Gastown is named for "Gassy Jack" Deighton, who opened a saloon here in 1867. With cobble-stoned streets, courtyards, an antique steam clock, and Victorian architecture set against a back drop of snow-capped mountains, Gastown embraces its past while catering to modern visitors with antique shops, boutiques and galleries, restaurants, and nightlife. **604/683-2000**

E PENTICTON

Pg. 179, M11. Farmers in Penticton, situated between the beautiful Okanagan and Skaha lakes on an alluvial plain, grow peaches and other fruits—earning the area the nickname "the land of peaches and beaches." On the lakefront promenade, visitors may rent watercraft at a marina, visit an art gallery, join in a game of beach volleyball, or people-watch. Lakeshore Drive is lined with hotels and restaurants. **250/492-4103**

ALBERTA

F DINOSAUR PROVINCIAL PARK

Pg. 179, K18. **Patricia.** Discoveries of fossils at the heart of Alberta's badlands earned the park's designation. The area contains some of the most important fossil discoveries ever made from the period dating about seventy-five million years ago, in particular about thirty-five species of dinosaur. More than 300 complete skeletons have been recovered for display in museums worldwide. Join park interpreters for one of the many programs offered, including a bus tour of the park, a bone bed hike, a fossil safari hike, or a lab talk. **403/378-4342** $

G ELK ISLAND NATIONAL PARK

Pg. 179, F17. **Ft. Saskatchewan.** Forests, meadowlands, quiet lakes, and beaver ponds form an island in a sea of developed land. The park is a sanctuary for a herd of protected elk and other species, including moose, deer, trumpeter swans, beaver, coyote, and more than two hundred species of birds. Activities include camping, hiking, golf, and cross-country skiing. **780/922-5790** $

H JASPER NATIONAL PARK

Pg. 179, G12. **Jasper.** The largest park in the Canadian Rockies, Jasper National Park is one of the country's most scenic. Take the tramway up the Whistlers, the most accessible summit in the area or spend time among the park's many square miles of waterfalls, lakes, canyons, and glaciers. 780/852-617 $

I LAKE LOUISE

Pg. 179, J14. Located in the heart of the Canadian Rockies, Lake Louise is one of the finest year-round resort towns in this area. International royalty, Hollywood stars, and heads of state have been known to come here to

SASKATCHEWAN

K CUMBERLAND HOUSE PROVINCIAL HISTORIC SITE
Pg. 180, D10. This site was home to the first inland Hudson Bay Company fur trading post and the oldest village in the province. Today, parts of the *Northcote*, a steamboat used by the fur trade, are preserved here, along with remnants of the stone-walled powder house. **306/888-5810 $**

L FORT BATTLEFORD NATIONAL HISTORIC SITE
Pg. 180, F4. **Battleford.** The site commemorates the North West Rebellion of 1885 (an uprising of descendants of early fur traders against the North West Mounted Police of the young Dominion of Canada). Museums and galleries describe the events, and costumed guides delineate the daily life of the early Mounties. **306/937-2621 $**

M GEM LAKES
Pg. 180, D8. **Narrow Hills Provincial Park.** So pretty that they were named for jewels, the Gem Lakes (Jade, Diamond, Opal, Sapphire, and Pearl), are a spectacular sight. The depth of the water, the sandy bottom, and the surrounding forest give the lakes the ability to reflect sparkling blues and magnificent greens. The lakes are small, but surprisingly deep (100 feet in some cases) and attractive to SCUBA divers. The hills surrounding them have hiking trails. **306/426-2622**

M Gem Lakes

N HOLY TRINITY ANGLICAN CHURCH HISTORIC SITE
Pg. 180, K8. **Regina.** Built between 1854 and 1860, this church is the oldest building in Saskatchewan. It was constructed from hardwood logs cut by Native Canadians; its stained glass, hinges, and locks were shipped from England and are still intact. Located on the opposite shoreline of the Churchill River from the community of Stanley Mission, local residents ferry visitors to the site. **306/425-4234**

World's largest herd of free roaming bison is located in Wood Buffalo National Park

MANITOBA

O ASSINIBOINE PARK AND ZOO
Pg. 181, F18. **Winnipeg.** Spread out over 378 acres along the Assiniboine River, the park features colorful English and formal gardens, the Leo Mol Sculpture Garden, a conservatory with floral displays, a duck pond, and a miniature train. In summer, picnic areas and cycling and walking trails are popular. In the winter, cross-country skiing, tobogganing and skating on the Duck Pond can be enjoyed. The zoo has the second largest animal collection in Canada, with three dozen endangered species on display, including the polar bear, snow leopard, and Siberian tiger. **204/986-3989**

P THE FORKS NATIONAL HISTORIC SITE
Pg. 181, E19. **Winnipeg.** Situated on ten acres at the confluence of the Red and Assiniboine rivers, the Forks has a riverside promenade, historical exhibits, and evening musical performances. **204/983-2007**

Q SEVEN OAKS HOUSE MUSEUM
Pg. 181, E19. **Winnipeg.** One of the oldest surviving residences in Manitoba, the house was named for trees that once stood on the estate. Privately occupied until the 1950s, the house was the site of a battle between the servants of the Hudson's Bay Company, the Selkirk Settlers and representatives of the rival North West Company in 1816. **204/339-7429 $**

R TURTLE MOUNTAIN PROVINCIAL PARK
Pg. 181, N13. **Boissevain.** Turtle Mountain is one of Manitoba's smaller provincial parks, with 47,000 acres of forested hills, ponds, and lakes. Its lakes provide a good environment for western painted turtle, beaver, muskrat, and mink. Swimming, hiking trails, fishing, and boating draw nature lovers, while snowmobile and cross-country skiing trails entice winter weather enthusiasts. **204/534-7204 $**

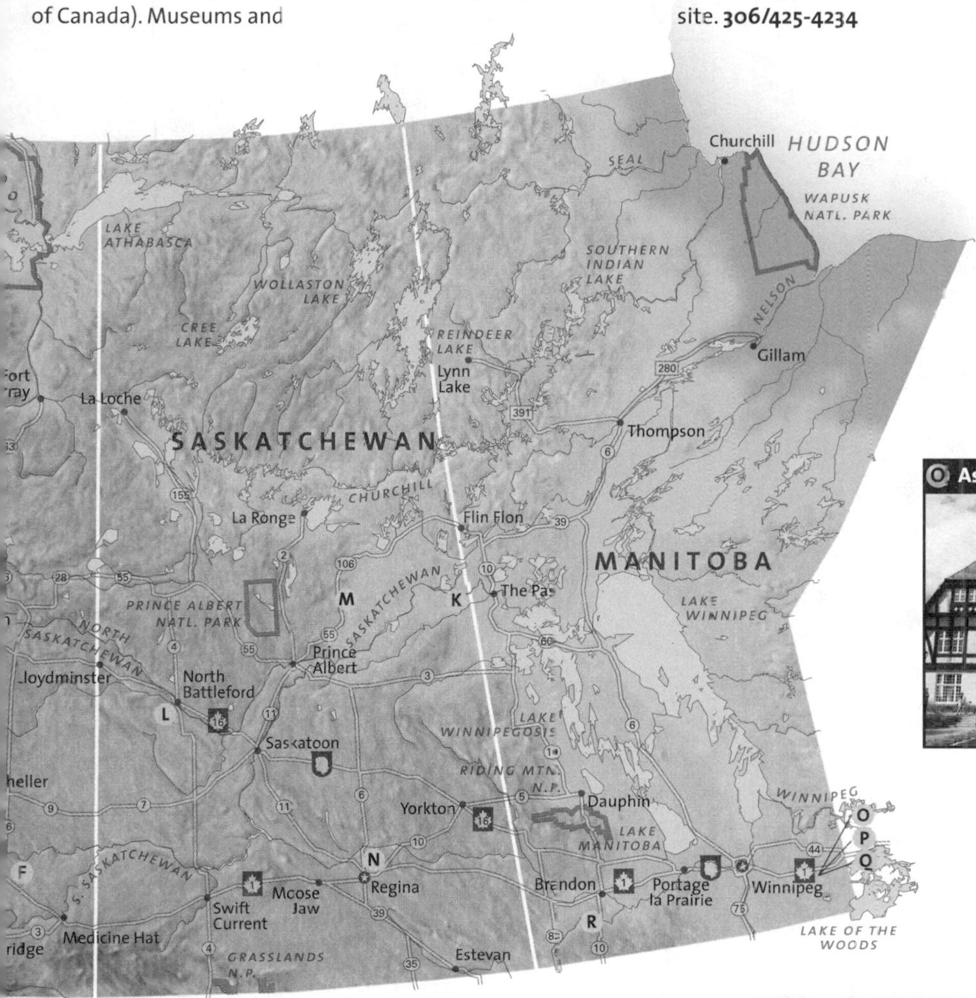

O Assimibone Park

Q Seven Oaks House Museum

relax and enjoy its old world charm. The Rockies provide miles of trails for hiking, walking, and horseback riding, natural beauty for the photographer, and a world-class ski area with infinite and varied terrain. The village has fine restaurants, accommodations, and shopping. **403/522-3833**

J ROYAL TYRRELL MUSEUM OF PALEONTOLOGY
Pg. 179, J17. **Drumheller.** This site houses the world's largest display of dinosaurs—more than 35 complete skeletons in all—and a "Paleoconservatory" displaying more than 100 species of tropical and subtropical plants that once thrived in this region. Visitors are invited to learn about the projects and passions of the museum's scientists, watch technicians as they work to discover new clues to the past, and tour the Discoveries Hall to see some of the museum's prize specimens. **403/823-7707 $**

F Dinosaur Provincial Park

H Jasper National Park

DOLLAR WI$E

- Avoid making phone calls, changing money, or sending out laundry from your hotel; hefty fees are added to these transactions. Instead, change money at a bank, use a public phone, and visit a laundromat.
- Save receipts from purchases; visitors to Canada can get a rebate on federal and some provincial sales taxes.
- For a $5 admisson charge, you can take a step back into 1930 and explore the coal mining history of Alberta's Drumheller Valley—The Atlas Coal Mine National Historic Site lets you tour the only wooden tipple mine left in Canada, visit restored mine offices, and climb aboard antique mining machines.
- Take a break from your travels and enjoy the beautiful and natural scenery at Wakamow Valley, a series of parks offering various recreation facilities. For no cost, you can picnic, walk paved trails, or play ball at the baseball diamond.

January

Polar Bear Swim
Nanaimo, BC
Prizes for all participants; free ice cream, bananas, and suntan lotion.
250/756-5200

Saskatoon Farm Toy and Collectibles Show
Saskatoon, SK
306/237-4747

February

Calgary Winter Festival
Calgary, AB
403/543-5480

Festival du Voyageur
Winnipeg, MB
Winter festival celebrating the French-Canadian voyageur and the fur trade era.
204/237-7692

Midwinter Breakout
Penticton, BC
250/493-4055

Mushers Rendezvous
Preeceville, SK
World class dog-sled races.
306/547-2810

March

Royal Manitoba Winter Fair
Brandon, MB
204/726-3500

April

Northwest Trade Fair
Meadow Lake, SK
306/236-6355

May

Park Art
Moose Jaw, SK
Annual sale of arts and crafts.
306/692-4471

June

Banff Festival of the Arts
Banff, AB
800/413-8368

Jazz City Festival
Edmonton, AB
780/432-7166

Red River Exhibition
Winnipeg, MB
204/888-6990

Spruce Meadows
Calgary, AB
Only internationally sanctioned outdoor horse jumping show held in North America.
403/974-4200

July

Edmonton's Klondike Days
Edmonton, AB
Entertainment, exhibits, midway, parade; events.
780/471-7210

International Bathtub Race
Vancouver, BC
Thirty-four-mi (55-km) race from Nanaimo to Vancouver.
800/663-7337

August

Folklorama
Winnipeg, MB
Multicultural festival.
204/982-6210

Pacific National Exhibition Annual Fair
Vancouver, BC
Second-largest fair in Canada.
604/253-2311

November

The Enchanted Forest
Saskatoon, SK
Over 450 large-size lighted images, over a 2km drive.
306/668-8171

Manitoba Fall Fair
Brandon, MB
204/726-3500

MEX 188
MEX 230

Free Finds

Palacio Nacional, Mexico City
Initiated by Cortés on the site of Montezuma's home and remodeled by the viceroys. Houses two museums dealing with 19th-century president Benito Juárez and the Mexican Congress. **5542-6466**

Casa de la Cultura, Acapulco
Cultural complex with archeological museum, art gallery, and an exhibit of Mexican and international crafts. **74/84-40-04**

Parque Chankanaab, Cozumel
Natural preserve with archeological park, botanical garden, dolphin aquarium, and wildlife sanctuary. Free admission after 5 pm.

Museo Regonal de Guadalajara, Guadalajara
Contains artifacts and memorabilia tracing the history of western Mexico from prehistoric times through the Spanish conquest; arts and crafts exhibits. Tuesdays free. **3/614-9957**

Museo Arqueologico, Zihuatanejo
View pre-Hispanic murals, maps and archeological pieces describing the Aztec, Olmec, and Tarascan cultures. **7/553-2552**

Centro Platero de Zacatecas, Guadalupe
School where young silversmiths learn the art of metalworking. **4/923-1007**

Convento de Guadalupe/Museo Virreinal de Guad, Guadalupe
Free admission on Sunday. Tour of Franciscan monastery where missionaries were educated; part of the building is still in use today as a college of instruction in the Franciscan order. **4/923-2089**

Centro Cultural Ignacio Ramírez , San Miguel
Houses art exhibits and classrooms for drawing, painting, sculpture, lithography, textiles, ceramics, dramatic arts, ballet, regional dance, piano, and guitar. Includes a work by world-famous muralist David Alfaro Siqueiros along with some of his memorabilia. **4/152-0289**

La Parroquia, San Miguel
Church that has become the emblem of San Miguel.

Catedral de la Asunción de María, Cuernacava
Construction on this church was begun in 1529 and completed in 1552. A Franciscan monastery is still here today, and open to the public.

The Anthropology Museum, La Paz
Exhibits on the geological history of Baja, fossils, and colonial history. **1/122-0162**

Mexico's exciting rhythm, ancient ruins, sapphire seas, and white-sand beaches attract visitors. Mexico City, once the capital of the Aztecs, is the oldest and highest city in North America. Carved out of the jungle on the Yucatán Peninsula, Cancun is a sybaritic paradise, while further south lie the ruins of an ancient Mayan civilization. Acapulco, a former hideaway for movie stars, retains its essence of 1950's Hollywood; Guadalajara is the traditional Mexico of mariachi bands and sombreros; and many villages share a legacy as silver mining areas. Once sleepy fishing villages, Zihuatanejo and nearby Ixtapa are now top resorts. Los Cabos, at the southern tip of the Baja Peninsula, is known for its thrilling sportfishing and luxurious hotels.

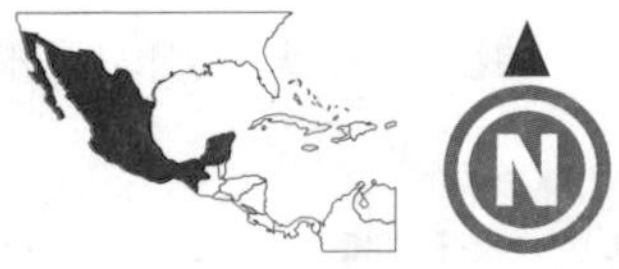

Like a glass slipper, with Baja as its heel, Mexico links the U.S. and Central America. Bordered by the Pacific Ocean, the Gulf of Mexico and the Caribbean Sea, Mexico is dominated by two rugged north-south mountain ranges, the Sierra Madre Occidental and the Sierra Madre Oriental, which overlook arid coastal plains to the east and west, and the Sonoran and Chihuahuan desert regions in the north. A mild temperate central plateau reaches to Mexico City, beyond which the mountains achieve their greatest heights (18,855-feet) in the Cordillera Neo-Volcánica. To the east, the tropical rain forests of southern Chiapas give way to thorny forest in the upper Yucatán Peninsula.

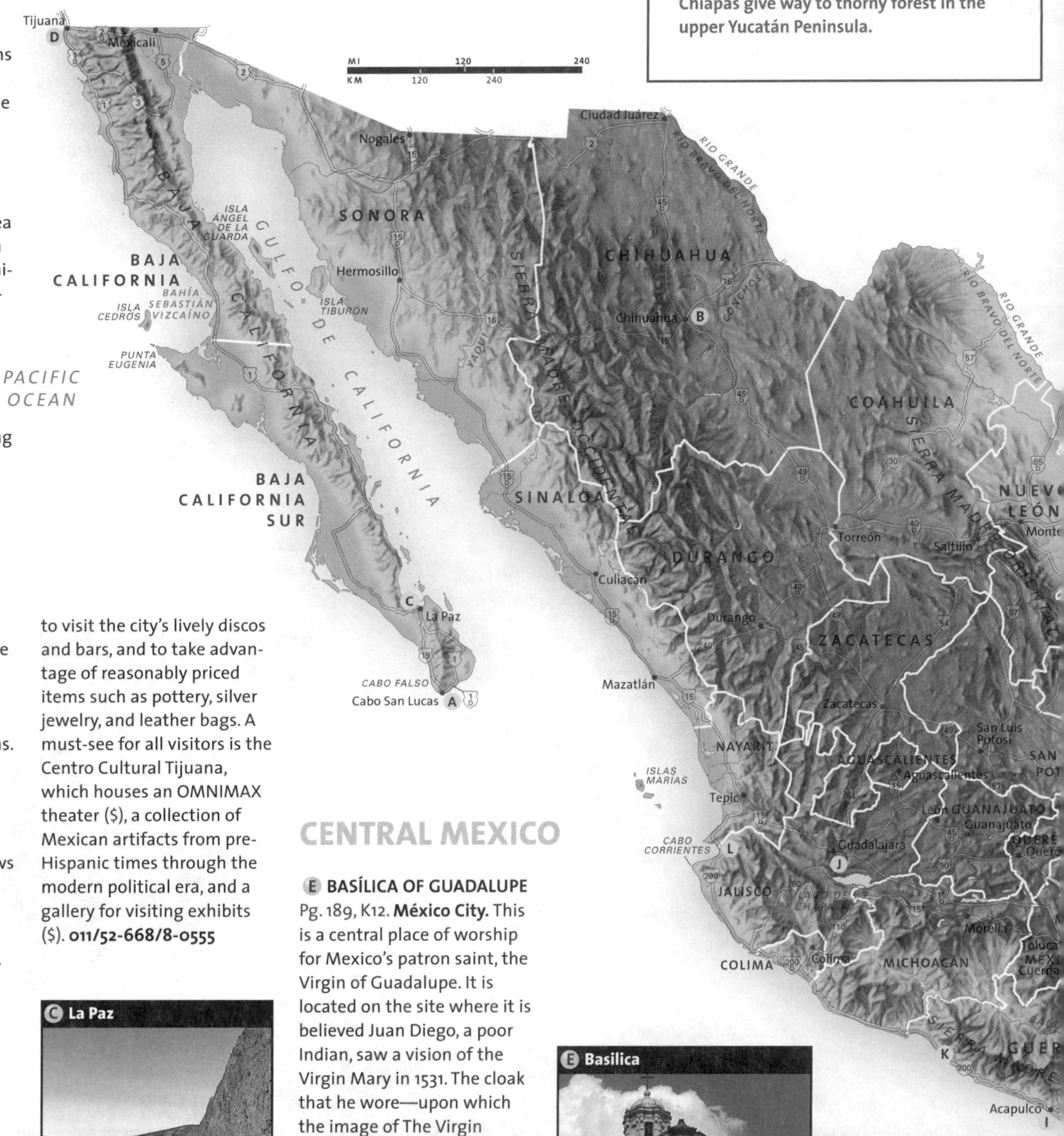

BAJA AND THE NORTH

Ⓐ LOS CABOS
Pg. 188, H5. **Cabo San Lucas.** Comprised of the twin towns of Cabo San Lucas and San Jose del Cabo, Los Cabos (The Cape) is located at the southern tip of the Baja Peninsula. The cities are connected by an 18-mile highway that follows the Sea of Cortez and is dotted with resorts, residential communities, golf courses, and swimming and snorkeling areas. **1/142-0446**

Ⓑ COPPER CANYON
Pg. 188, D8. **Chihuahua City.** This network of breathtaking canyons covers 20,000 square miles in Mexico's largest state (four times larger than the Grand Canyon.) Visitors can take a 17-hour train ride to the canyon from Los Mochis to Chihuahua City, reaching to heights of 7,000 miles above sea level, passing through upland ranches, temperate-zone orchards, lakes, and unexplored mountain chains. **3/668-1600** $

Ⓒ LA PAZ
Pg. 188, G5. Located on the Tropic of Cancer, La Paz draws sport fishing, diving, and water enthusiasts to its sunny beaches, as well as hikers and mountain bikers. Its name, which means "peace," is reflected in its easy-going, relaxed atmosphere, and its shopping is considered the best on the peninsula. **1/122-5939**

Ⓓ TIJUANA
Pg. 188, A1. Due to its proximity to Southern California, visitors can make a day trip to visit the city's lively discos and bars, and to take advantage of reasonably priced items such as pottery, silver jewelry, and leather bags. A must-see for all visitors is the Centro Cultural Tijuana, which houses an OMNIMAX theater ($), a collection of Mexican artifacts from pre-Hispanic times through the modern political era, and a gallery for visiting exhibits ($). **011/52-668/8-0555**

Ⓒ La Paz

Ⓐ Los Cabos

CENTRAL MEXICO

Ⓔ BASÍLICA OF GUADALUPE
Pg. 189, K12. **México City.** This is a central place of worship for Mexico's patron saint, the Virgin of Guadalupe. It is located on the site where it is believed Juan Diego, a poor Indian, saw a vision of the Virgin Mary in 1531. The cloak that he wore—upon which the image of The Virgin miraculously appeared—hangs above the altar. The Basílica Museum ($), houses a display of religious art. **5/557-6022**

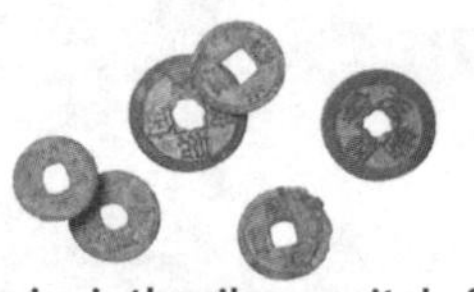

Mexico is the silver capitol of the world. Many craftsmen use this metal to create jewelry. Each finished piece is marked with a symbol to verify that it was made from silver

Ⓔ Basilica

Ⓖ Templo Mayor

Ⓕ PLAZA DE SANTO DOMINGO
Pg. 189, K12. **México City.** This plaza features street vendors, fountains, and arcades, and is home to a sculpture of Josefa Ortiz de Dominguez, a supporter of Mexico's independence, as well as the Palace of the Inquisition. It is best known for the scribes who compose and type

J Guadalajara

I Acapulco

PACIFIC COAST

I ACAPULCO
Pg. 189, M12. With its tropical beaches, jungles and lagoons, and perfect year-round climate, Acapulco is a popular spot for relaxation and fun. Just about every watersport is available here, including scuba diving, water skiing, deep sea fishing, sailing, wind surfing, and jet skiing. Visitors will also enjoy its night-clubs, bars and discotheques, many of which are open until sunrise. **7/484-4583**

J GUADALAJARA
Pg. 188, J9. Although this city—Mexico's second largest—has been dubbed "The Silicon Valley of Mexico," it retains much of its traditions and history. As the homeland of mariachi music, the Mexican hat dance, and tequila, Guadalajara is often thought of as the most Mexican of cities. These traditions, along with its mild climate, great shopping and restaurants, make it a favorite destination for vacationers. **3/668-1600**

K IXTAPA
Pg. 188, L10. Part of the Mexican Riviera, Ixtapa is located within a pristine setting of natural beauty. It is also known as a glitzy resort with luxurious hotels on sandy beaches. Playa la Ropa, a short distance away, features many water sports, as well as many charming, open-air restaurants. **7/553-1967**

L PUERTA VALLARTA
Pg. 188, J8. Once a quaint fishing village, Puerta Vallarta has emerged as one of the best-known beach resorts on Mexico's central Pacific coast. The beaches are lined with hotels and restaurants, and cruise ships pull into port daily. Visitors snorkel, whale watch, mountain bike, or simply walk along the city's main waterfront street, the malecón. **3/223-2500**

OAXACA AND THE MEXICAN CARIBBEAN

M CANCÚN
Pg. 189, J20. Cancún offers everything vacationers are looking for—breathtaking natural beauty, white-sand beaches, high-quality accommodations, and abundant shopping, dining, and nightlife. Its lagoon, enclosed by the L-shape of the island, makes it ideal for sailing and water-skiing, snorkeling, and scuba diving. **9/884-8073**

N CHICHÉN-ITZÁ
Pg. 189, J19. **Pisté.** This is the site of ancient Mayan ruins and is regarded as one of the most impressive archeological areas in the modern world. The Pyramid of Kukulcan, The Castle, the Platform of Skulls, and The Nunnary are located here. **5/203-1103** $

O COZUMEL
Pg. 189, J20. The largest island of the Mexican Caribbean, Cozumel is near the Palancar Reef, proclaimed by Jacques Cousteau as one of the best places for diving in the world. Non-divers enjoy Cozumel for its nature parks, beaches, and historic sites such as the Mayan ruins of El Cedrel and Castillo Real. **9/872-7563**

P MONTE ALBAN
Pg. 189, M14. **Oaxaca.** This site was first occupied between 800 and 400 B.C. by the Zapotecs, and was one of the first cities in Mesoamerica. It is located atop limestone-sandstone hills, approximately 400 miles above the floor of the Valley of Oaxaca. Its principal constructions, including the Great Plaza, Ball Court, System II, and The Palace are open to visitors. **9/516-0123** $

The pyramids, which the Mayan Indians built, are quite a mystery to historians.The only other place in the world where pyramids are found is in Egypt, half way across the world from Mexico.

Q MUYIL
Pg. 189, J19. This archeological site, located 15 miles south of Tuliem on Highway 307, served as a port between Coba and the Maya centers in Belize and Guatemala, and has been continuously inhabited since about 200 B.C. Today, the main ruins are a small group of buildings, the most notable being the 56-foot-tall Castillo pyramid at the center of a large plaza. **5/203-1103** $

R PUERTO MORELOS
Pg. 189, J20. Just 20 miles south of Cancun, Puerto Morelos greatly contrasts with the glamorous resort. This small coastal town, with calm waters and peaceful surroundings, has more guesthouses and bed and breakfast facilities than hotels. It is an ideal spot for simply lying on the beach and enjoying the beauty of Mexico.

O Cozumel

N Chichen-itzá

letters for clients unable to do so for themselves. Nearby, visit the Latin-American Tower ($), a 47-story building with an observation deck offering fabulous views of the whole city. **5/525-9380**

G TEMPLO MAYOR AND MUSEO DEL TEMPLO MAYOR
Pg. 189, K12. **México City.** The Templo Mayor is located in the historic center of Mexico City, and on the site where numerous archeological excavations have taken place. The museum contains tools, jewelry, sculptures, reliefs, and thousands of other artifacts recovered from the Templo Mayor project from 1978 to the present. Also here is a large stone wheel of the moon goddess Coyolxauhqui. The Aztecs believed she ruled the night, but died at the dawning of every day, slain and dismembered by her brother, the sun god. **5/542-0606** $

H TEOTIHUACÁN
Pg. 189, K12. **México City.** The inhabitants of this area mysteriously disappeared without a trace around 700 A.D., but left behind magnificent pyramids and palaces covering 12 square miles. Among its main constructions are The Pyramid of the Sun and the Moon, The Citadel, and The Temple of Quetzalcoatl. **5/203-1103** $

DOLLAR WI$E

- Look for a multi-course meal, known as comida corrida or menu del dia, which is served from 1-4 pm almost everywhere in Mexico, and the most inexpensive way to get a full dinner.
- Prices may drop 20% to 50% during the low season, which begins the day after Easter and continues to mid-December.
- Rental car discounts are often available when renting for one week or longer, and when made in advance from the United States.
- For a $1 admission, you can watch high divers perform at La Quebrada in Acapulco. From a spotlit ledge on the cliffs, divers (holding torches for the final performance) plunge into the roaring surf 130 feet below—after praying at a small shrine nearby.
- In Crucecita, a free trolley takes visitors on a short tour of the town.
- Vist museums on Sunday, when admission to most is usually free.

January

Fiesta de Enero
Chiapa de Corzo
A series of colorful festivals including parading dancers and musical celebrations.
961-24535

February

Carnaval
Nationwide
Carnaval takes place the 3 days preceding Ash Wednesday and the beginning of Lent. It is celebrated with special gusto in the cities of Tepoztlán, Huejotzingo, Chamula, Veracruz, Cozumel, and Mazatlán. In some places, such as Veracruz, Mazatlán, and Cozumel, the celebration resembles New Orleans' Mardi Gras, with a festive atmosphere and parades.
800/446-3942

April

San Marcos National Fair
Aguascalientes
Mexico's largest fair begins the third week in April and lasts 22 days. Visitors come for nationally famous bullfights and rodeos as well as ranchera music and mariachis.
800/446-3942

May

Cinco de Mayo
Nationwide
The anniversary of Mexico's victory over France in 1862 is celebrated with parades and music.
800/446-3942

June

La Fiesta de los Locos
San Miguel de Allende
Young and old alike dress in grotesque costumes and parade around the center of town. Keep an eye out for practical jokes.
4/152-6565

July

Feria Nacional
Durango
Celebration of the town's founding.
18-112139

October

Fiestas de Octubre
Guadalajara
3/660-3186

Festival Internacional Cervantino
Guanajuato
Dedicated to the author of Don Quixote, this is one of the largest arts festivals in the country.
5-5147635

November

Days of the Dead: Los Días de los Muertos
Nationwide
People head out to the cemetery for all-night vigils and sing and pray for the souls of the dearly departed.
800/446-3942

December

Las Posadas
Mexico City
Mary and Joseph's journey is reenacted. The candlelight processions lead to nativity scenes around the Alameda.
5/250-8555

Night of the Radishes
Oaxaca
Sculptures are built out of radishes (the most prized vegetable cultivated during the colonial period), flowers, and dried corn husks. They are then put on display and on December 24th each church organizes a procession to the sculptures.
9/51-60123

VI 190
PR 190
HI 88
PR 251
HI 234

Free Finds

Kodak Hula Show, Honolulu, Oahu
Free, authentic hula show (Tues-Thurs 10 am). **808/533-3181**

Kauai Coffee Company, Eleele, Kauai
Lean how coffee is grown, harvested, processed and graded; samples of estate coffee. **808/335-5497**

Maui Arts and Cultural Center, Kahului
Visual and performing arts complex with free exhibits. **808/242-2787**

Tedeschi Vineyards, Ulupalakua, Maui
Tour of grounds and winery operation; tasting room. **808/878-6058**

Whale Center of the Pacific, Ka'anapali, Maui
Two museums with exhibits and educational displays on Lahaina's whaling history, and the biology and physiology of whales. **808/661-9918**

Ahuena Heiau, Kaulua-Kona, Big Island
Ancient temple that was the court of King Kamehameha I. **808/329-2911**

Hawaiian Ethnic Art Museum, Haleiwa, Oahu
Indigenous art; Maui Loa rock image collection. **808/638-7841**

Volcano Winery, Volcano, Big Island
Tour of the only commercial winery on The Big Island. Includes free tastings. **808/967-7772**

Kukaniloko Birthstones State Monument, Oahu
A complex of approximately 180 stones—ancient Hawaiian royalty came here for the birth of their children. The stones are said to be a powerful place, and some have petroglyphs

Holo Holo Ku Heiau, Kauai
The oldest place of worship on Kauai—where human sacrifices were made.

The Kuilau Ridge Trail, Kauai
This 5-mile trail drops 2,000 feet into Waimea Canyon, and offers the shortest route to the canyon floor. Features a large swimming hole at the bottom.

Lava Tree State Monument, Hilo
Short self guided tour around tree molds made when lava swept through this forested area and left behind lava molds of the tree trunks **808/974-6200**

Soaring volcanic peaks, gorgeous beaches, and tropical flora and fauna make the Hawaiian Islands a place of astounding beauty. Oahu's fun-loving nature is best expressed on Honolulu's golden beaches, while the USS Arizona Memorial serves as a solemn tribute to World War II veterans at Pearl Harbor. Kaua'i, is known as the "garden isle" thanks to its lush mountains and cool rain forests. A former pineapple plantation, Lana'i is the most secluded and intimate of the islands, and is now home to five-star resorts. Watch the sunrise from Maui's majestic Haleakala Crater, a dormant volcano, or ride the waves with humpback whales. The Big Island is steeped in traditional Polynesian culture, while the sleepy Moloka'i offers a different take on Hawaii.

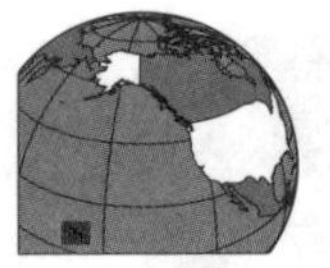

The Hawaiian Islands are crests of volcanic mountains built by magma welling up from beneath the ocean floor over millions of years. Measured from their bases at the bottom of the Pacific, these mountains are the tallest in the world. The youngest of the Hawaiian Islands is also the largest: The Big Island of Hawaii is almost twice the size of the others combined and is still growing, thanks to its two active volcanoes, Kilauea and Mauna Loa. Also on Hawaii is the chains' highest point, at 13,796-feet, dormant Mauna Kea. Southeast of Hawaii, a new island, called Loihi, is slowly growing toward the surface.

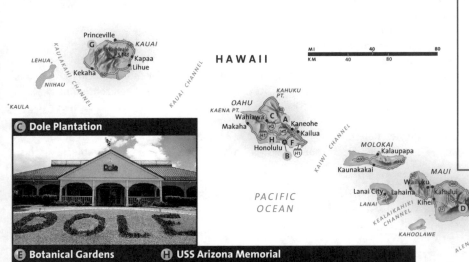

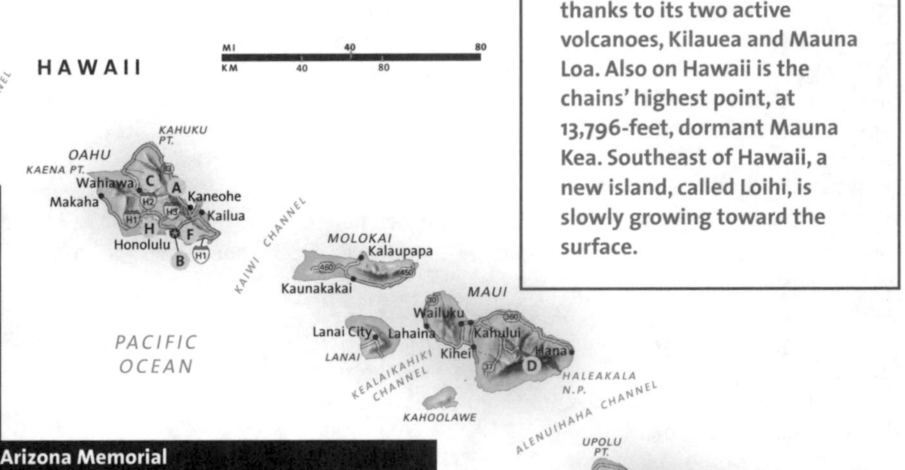
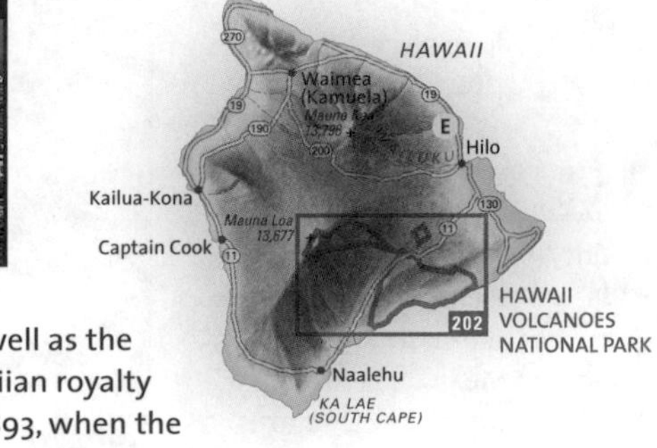

Ⓒ Dole Plantation

Ⓔ Botanical Gardens

Ⓗ USS Arizona Memorial

Ⓐ AHUPU'A 'O KAHANA STATE PARK (FORMERLY KAHANA VALLEY STATE PARK)
Pg. 88, F5. **Kahana (Oahu).** This scenic 5,200-acre wildland has become an archaeological dig. Archaeologists have found extensive remnants of Hawaiian culture, including religious temples, fishing shrines, stone-walled enclosures, and agricultural terraces. Presently, most are inaccessible to the public. However, visitors can still take advantage of canoeing, picnicking in a coconut grove, hiking through dense rain forest, and viewing the park's archaeological sites. **808/237-7766**

Ⓑ DIAMOND HEAD CRATER
Pg. 88, H5. **Honolulu (Oahu).** Extinct for 150,000 years, this volcano was an important lookout point for enemy activity during World War II. Evidence of the command post is still present along the 1³/₄-mile Diamond Head Trail ($), a popular trail for hikers. Visitors may ascend 560 feet of Diamond Head for a spectacular, 360-degree view of the island. **808/923-1811**

Ⓒ DOLE PLANTATION
Pg. 88, F3. **Wahiawa (Oahu).** The plantation is home of the Pineapple Garden Maze ($), named the world's largest maze in the 2001 Guinness World Records. Visitors learn the history of the pineapple and the Dole Company through informal displays and presentations. **808/621-8408**

Ⓓ HALEAKALA NATIONAL PARK
Pg. 88, E9. **Kula (Maui).** This 28,655-acre park was established to preserve the Haleakala Crater. Later additions gave protection to the fragile ecosystems of the Kipaulu Valley. Visitors flock here to see the amazing sunrises and sunsets, plus magnificent views. **808/572-4400** $

Ⓔ HAWAII TROPICAL BOTANICAL GARDEN
Pg. 88, L9. **Papaikou (Hawaii).** Located in a 40-acre valley considered to be one of the most beautiful areas in all of Hawaii, the gardens feature more than 2,000 species of tropical plants, representing more than 125 families and 750 genera. **808/964-5233** $

Ⓕ IOLANI PALACE STATE MONUMENT
Pg. 88, H5. **Honolulu (Oahu).** This magnificent building served as Hawaii's capitol until 1969, as well as the home of Hawaiian royalty from 1882 to 1893, when the monarchy was overthrown. It is now restored to its former opulence. **808/522-0824**

Ⓖ NA PALI COAST
Pg. 88, A3. **Haena (Kauai).** This 15-mile landmark features 4,000-foot cliffs. Na Pali's coastal wilderness provides excellent opportunities for hiking, backpacking, camping, swimming, and snorkeling. Its stunning vistas have been the backdrop for a number of films, including *Jurassic Park* and *King Kong*. **808/245-3971**

Ⓗ USS ARIZONA MEMORIAL
Pg. 88, H4. **Honolulu (Oahu).** This memorial is the final resting place of many of the 1,177 crewmen killed on December 7, 1941, when the battleship *USS Arizona* was bombed by Japanese naval forces. The interpretive program features a talk, followed by a documentary on the attack. Afterwards, visitors board a Navy shuttle boat for a trip to the memorial, which spans the hull of the sunken ship, and contains the ship's bell, as well as a shrine room with the names of the dead carved in stone. **808/422-2771**

DOLLAR WI$E

- Make a checklist of travel essentials and purchase them before you leave; don't get stuck buying expensive sunscreen at the beach, or over-priced film at the airport.
- If traveling to Oahu, save money on a rental car by using their public transportation system, known as The Bus, which stops at just about every tourist attraction.
- Tantalus and Round Top Drive is the perfect place to spend a few hours. The views of Diamond Head, downtown, Honolulu and Punchbowl Crater are fantastic. At sunset, the views of the city's lights are spectacular.
- Buy your souvenirs at flea markets or swap meets rather than expensive hotel or museum gift shops.
- Hawaii's State Parks offer modern housekeeping cabins that sleep four for $50 a night.

January

Honolulu Street Market
Honolulu, Oahu
808/221-6042

February

NFL Pro Bowl
Honolulu, Oahu
808/486-9300

Waimea Town Celebration
Waimea, Kauai
Celebrates Waimea's Hawaiian and multiethnic history.
808/245-3971

March

Haiku Ho'olaulea and Flower Festival
Lahaina, Maui
808/573-8618

Ocean Arts Festival
Maui
Celebration of the annual migration of the humpback whales. Art, entertainment, games, and activities.
888/310-1117

April

Bankoh Ki-ho'alu Kona Style Hawaiian Slack-Key Guitar Festival
Kona, Big Island
Hawaii's folk music performed by the best musicians in Hawaii.
808/239-4336

May

Lei Day
On all islands
Parades, entertainment, contests, and exchanging of leis.
866/888-6284

World Fire-Knife Dance Championships and Samoan Festival
Laie, Oahu
808/293-3333

June

King Kamehameha Celebration
On all islands
It's a state holiday with a floral parade, hoolaulea (party), and much more.
808/586-0333

Taste of Honolulu
Honolulu, Oahu
808/536-1015

July

Hawaii International Jazz Festival
Honolulu, Oahu
808/941-9974

Makawao Parade and Rodeo
Makawao, Maui
808/244-3530

August

Hawaii State Fair
Honolulu, Oahu
808/531-3531

September

Aloha Festivals
On all islands
Parades and other events celebrate Hawaiian culture.
800/852-7690

October

Hamakua Music Festival
Hamakua, Big Island
808/775-3378

November

Annual Kona Coffee Cultural Festival
Kailua-Kona, Big Island
Celebrates the coffee harvest.
808/326-7820

December

Festival of Lights
On all islands
808/547-4397

The emerald cliffs, turquoise waters, and wondrous beaches of the Caribbean are paradise's calling card. Rappel along waterfalls in Puerto Rico's lush El Yunque rain forest; sample the rum at the Barcardi distillery; track the constellations at Arecibo Observatory; or go spelunking in the Rio Camuy Caverns. The Phosphorescent Bay in Vieques and the dazzling nightclubs of the walled city of Old San Juan light up the night. The Virgin Islands are the quintessential West Indies destination. Explore the ruins of 18th-century plantations and snorkel in Buck Island Reef on St. Croix, or relax on St. John, where two-thirds of the island is a national park. Bluebeard and Captain Kidd stashed booty on St. Thomas, where luxury resorts have transformed their former haunts.

Volcanoes launched Puerto Rico and the Virgin Islands from the ocean floor. Today, their steep and rugged terrain typifies that of Caribbean islands formed in volcanic tumult. An east-west mountain chain sharply divides the northern and southern portions of Puerto Rico, with the north receiving considerably greater amounts of rainfall.

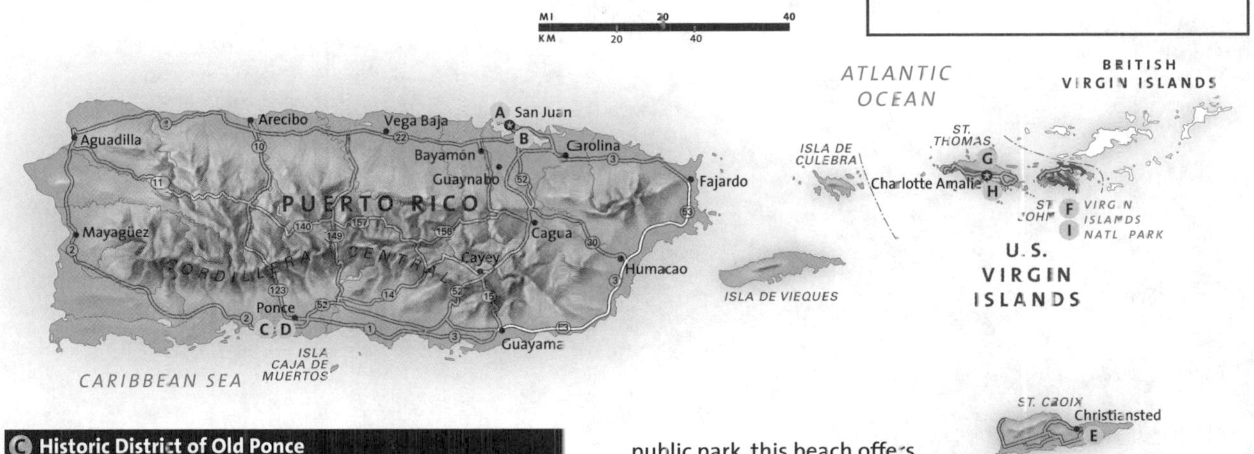

Free Finds

Jardin Botanico, Rio Piedras, PR
75-acre forest with over 200 species of tropical and subtropical vegetation; walking trail; orchid garden; palm garden. **787/767-1710**

Museum of Puerto Rico Music, Ponce, PR
Showcases the development of Puerto Rican music. Features memorabilia of composers and performers. **787/848-7016**

Bacardi Rum Distillery, Catano, PR
Tour covering both the rum distillery & the history behind Bacardi. **787/788-1500**

Cathedral of Our Lady of Guadalupe, Ponce, PR
After fires and earthquakes destroyed this chapel built in 1660, it was rebuilt in 1931. It is an important place for prayer for many residents of Ponce. **787/842-0134**

Parque de Bombas, Ponce, PR
Designated as Puerto Rico's first permanent headquarters for a volunteer fire-fighting brigade. **787/284-4141**

Alcaldía (City Hall), San Juan, PR
Constructed in stages from 1604 to 1789. Located here are a tourist information bureau and a small exhibit gallery. **787/724-7171**

Bordeaux Mountain, St. John
This is St. John's highest peak (1,277 feet). Picture point offers spectacular views.

Government House, St. John
Home of the governor; first floor open to the public. **340/774-0001**

Estate Mount Washington Plantation, St. Croix
Self-guided tour of 13 acres of the island's best-preserved sugar plantation (the on-site private residence is closed to the public). **340/772-1026**

Ft. Frederick, St. Croix
Site where 8,000 slaves marched in 1848 to demand their freedom; historical exhibits; art gallery. **340/772-2021**

Fort Christian, St. Thomas
Danish built fort named after Christian V; now a local history museum. **340/776-4566**

99 Steps, St. Thomas
These famous steps leading to the summit of Government Hill were erected in the early 1700s. From here, you can see the 18th-century Crown House.

C Historic District of Old Ponce

PUERTO RICO

A CASTILLO SAN FELIPE DEL MORRO

Pg. 190, A4. **San Juan.** A fort built in 1540 to protect against sea invasion, "El Morro" guards the bay from a rocky promontory on the northwestern tip of the old city. Visitors taking the staircase to the Santa Barbara Bastión are provided with stunning views of the Atlantic. **787/729-6777** $

B HISTORIC DISTRICT OF OLD SAN JUAN

Pg. 190, A4. More than four hundred Spanish colonial-style buildings have been restored within the 17th century walls of El Viejo San Juan. The old city's narrow streets are paved with cobblestones, leading past romantic courtyards and charming, overhanging balconies, as well as open-air cafes, shops, restaurants, and bars. **800/875-4765**

C HISTORIC DISTRICT OF PONCE

Pg. 190, C2. Founded in 1692, Puerto Rico's second-largest city is Ponce or "La Perla del Sur" (Pearl of the South), located 90 minutes from San Juan. Second only to Old San Juan in terms of historic significance, the central district of Ponce is a blend of Ponce Creole and art deco buildings, dating mainly from the 1890s to the 1930s. **787/721-2400**

D MUSEO DE ARTE DE PONCE

Pg. 190, C2. This museum has the finest collection of European and Latin American art in the Caribbean. Displaying contemporary work by Puerto Ricans as well as an array of old masters, the structure is itself a piece of art, designed by Edward Durell Stone. **787/848-0505** $

U.S. VIRGIN ISLANDS

E CHRISTIANSTED

Pg. 190, E6. **St. Croix.** The pastel-painted city on the north side of St. Croix, has been called the prettiest town in the Caribbean. **888/468-6878**

F CRUZ BAY

Pg. 190, D7. **St. John.** Situated on a picturesque harbor at the west end of the island is the charming town of Cruz Bay, formerly an outpost for a detachment of Danish soldiers from St. Thomas. **340/776-6450**

G MAGENS BAY

Pg. 190, D6. **St. Thomas.** Deeded to the island as a public park, this beach offers all the comforts a beach-comber might want—covered picnic tables, showers, dressing rooms, a boutique, a snack bar, a pizzeria, full-service bar, and snorkeling. **519/631-1981**

H PARADISE POINT TRAMWAY

Pg. 190, D6. **St. Thomas.** A tram ride to Paradise Point — 700 feet above sea level — leads to one of the best views of the Caribbean. A prime vantage point situated on Flag Hill, Paradise Point overlooks the town of Charlotte Amalie, the harbor, and the cruise ships on the open sea. **340/774-9809** $

I TRUNK BAY

Pg. 190, D7. **St. John.** By far the most popular beach among visitors, this is the site of the renowned underwater snorkel trail: fifteen underwater plaques that identify the corals and fish that inhabit these waters. **340/776-6450**

G Magens Bay

DOLLAR WI$E

- Head to the Caribbean during "summer" season—which lasts from mid-April to mid-December—when you can save up to 30% on hotels and air travel.
- Spend a relaxing day at San Juan's Parque Luis Munoz Marin for $1. This scenic, 90-acre tree-shaded park features gardens, lakes, playgrounds, and picnic areas. An aerial gondola, which connects the park to the parking area, provides a 6½-minute tour of the grounds.
- An inexpensive alternative to taxis in Puerto Rico are Linéas, which are private taxis shared with three to five other passengers. They are not only affordable, but a great way to meet other people.
- At Emancipation Square Visitor Center in St. Thomas, you can pick up a booklet, St. Thomas This Week, which has maps of St. Thomas and St. John as well as up-to-date touring information and current event listings.

January

San Sebastian Street Festival
Old San Juan, Puerto Rico
787/721-1476

Three Kings Day
Island-wide, Puerto Rico
On this traditional gift-giving day, there are festivals with lively music, dancing, parades, puppet shows, and more.
787/721-2400

February

Coffee Harvest Festival
Maricao, Puerto Rico
Folk music, a parade of floats, typical foods, crafts, and demonstrations of coffee preparation.
787/838-2290

March

Carnival Ponceno
Ponce, Puerto Rico
The island's Carnival celebrations feature float parades, dancing, and street parties.
787/284-4141

Emancipation Day
Island-wide, Puerto Rico
787/721-2400

April

St. Thomas Carnival
St. Thomas
This annual celebration is the most spectacular carnival in the Virgin Islands. "Mocko Jumbies", people dressed as spirits, parade through the streets on stilts nearly 20 feet high. Steel and fungi bands, "jump-ups", and parades bring the event to life.
340/774-8784

Sugar Harvest Festival
San German, Puerto Rico
Festival marks the end of the island's sugar harvest, with live music, crafts, and typical foods.
787/721-2400

June

Casals Festival
San Juan, Puerto Rico
The Caribbean's most celebrated cultural event at San Juan's Performing Arts Center includes a glittering array of international guest conductors, orchestras, and soloists.
787/721-7727

San Juan Bautista Day
Island-wide, Puerto Rico
787/721-2400

July

Carnival of St. John
St. John
284/494-3134

Loiza Carnival
Loiza, Puerto Rico
Festival and religious ceremony honors Loiza's patron saint, John (Santiago) the Apostle.
787/876-3570

September

International Billfish Tournament
Island-wide, Puerto Rico
This is one of the premier game-fishing tournaments.
787/721-2400

November

Festival of Puerto Rican Music
San Juan, Puerto Rico
787/721-5274

December

Christmas in St. Croix
St. Croix
This major event launches the beginning of a 12-day celebration. It ends on January 6th with the Feast of Kings.
340/773-0495

Barcadi Artisans' Fair
San Juan, Puerto Rico
787/788-1500

Blue Ridge Parkway, North Carolina

CANADIAN CITIES

MEXICAN CITIES

PUERTO RICAN CITY

NATIONAL PARKS & RECREATION AREAS

*Also has downtown city map.

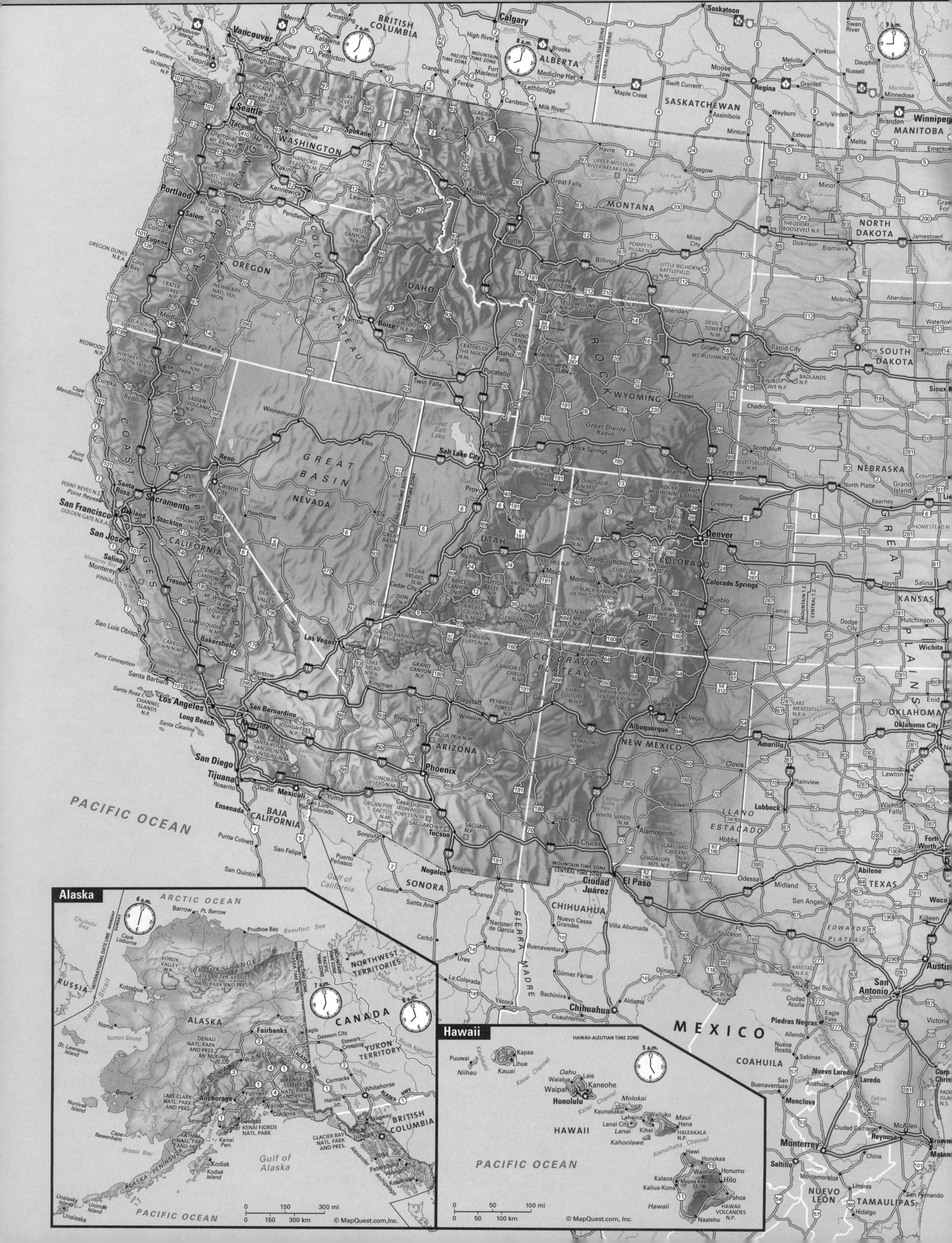

MI 125 250
KM 125 250
BRITISH COLUMBIA
ALBERTA
SASKATCHEWAN
MANITOBA
Vancouver
Victoria
Calgary
Saskatoon
Regina
Winnipeg
Seattle
Tacoma
Olympia
Spokane
WASHINGTON
Portland
Salem
Eugene
OREGON
IDAHO
Boise
MONTANA
Helena
Missoula
Great Falls
Billings
Bismarck
NORTH DAKOTA
SOUTH DAKOTA
Pierre
Rapid City
WYOMING
Cheyenne
Casper
NEBRASKA
North Platte
Denver
COLORADO
Colorado Springs
Pueblo
KANSAS
Wichita
OKLAHOMA
Oklahoma City
TEXAS
Amarillo
Lubbock
El Paso
Abilene
San Antonio
NEW MEXICO
Albuquerque
Santa Fe
ARIZONA
Phoenix
Tucson
Flagstaff
UTAH
Salt Lake City
NEVADA
Reno
Carson City
Las Vegas
GREAT BASIN
CALIFORNIA
Sacramento
San Francisco
San Jose
Fresno
Bakersfield
Los Angeles
San Diego
Tijuana
Mexicali
BAJA CALIFORNIA
SONORA
CHIHUAHUA
Ciudad Juárez
Chihuahua
COAHUILA
NUEVO LEÓN
Monterrey
TAMAULIPAS
MEXICO
PACIFIC OCEAN
ROCKY MOUNTAINS
COLORADO PLATEAU
COLUMBIA PLATEAU
CASCADE RANGE
COAST RANGES
SIERRA NEVADA
SIERRA MADRE
GREAT PLAINS
LLANO ESTACADO
EDWARDS PLATEAU
PACIFIC TIME ZONE
MOUNTAIN TIME ZONE
CENTRAL TIME ZONE
7 a.m.
8 a.m.
9 a.m.
Alaska
ARCTIC OCEAN
Barrow
Prudhoe Bay
Beaufort Sea
Chukchi Sea
RUSSIA
INTERNATIONAL DATE LINE
BROOKS RANGE
ALASKA
Fairbanks
Anchorage
Juneau
Nome
Kodiak
ALASKA RANGE
ALASKA PENINSULA
Gulf of Alaska
NORTHWEST TERRITORIES
YUKON TERRITORY
CANADA
Whitehorse
BRITISH COLUMBIA
PACIFIC OCEAN
6 a.m.
7 a.m.
8 a.m.
0 150 300 mi
0 150 300 km
© MapQuest.com, Inc.
Hawaii
HAWAII-ALEUTIAN TIME ZONE
5 a.m.
Kauai
Niihau
Oahu
Honolulu
Molokai
Lanai
Maui
Kahoolawe
Hawaii
Hilo
Kailua-Kona
Mauna Kea 13,796
HAWAII
PACIFIC OCEAN
0 50 100 mi
0 50 100 km
© MapQuest.com, Inc.

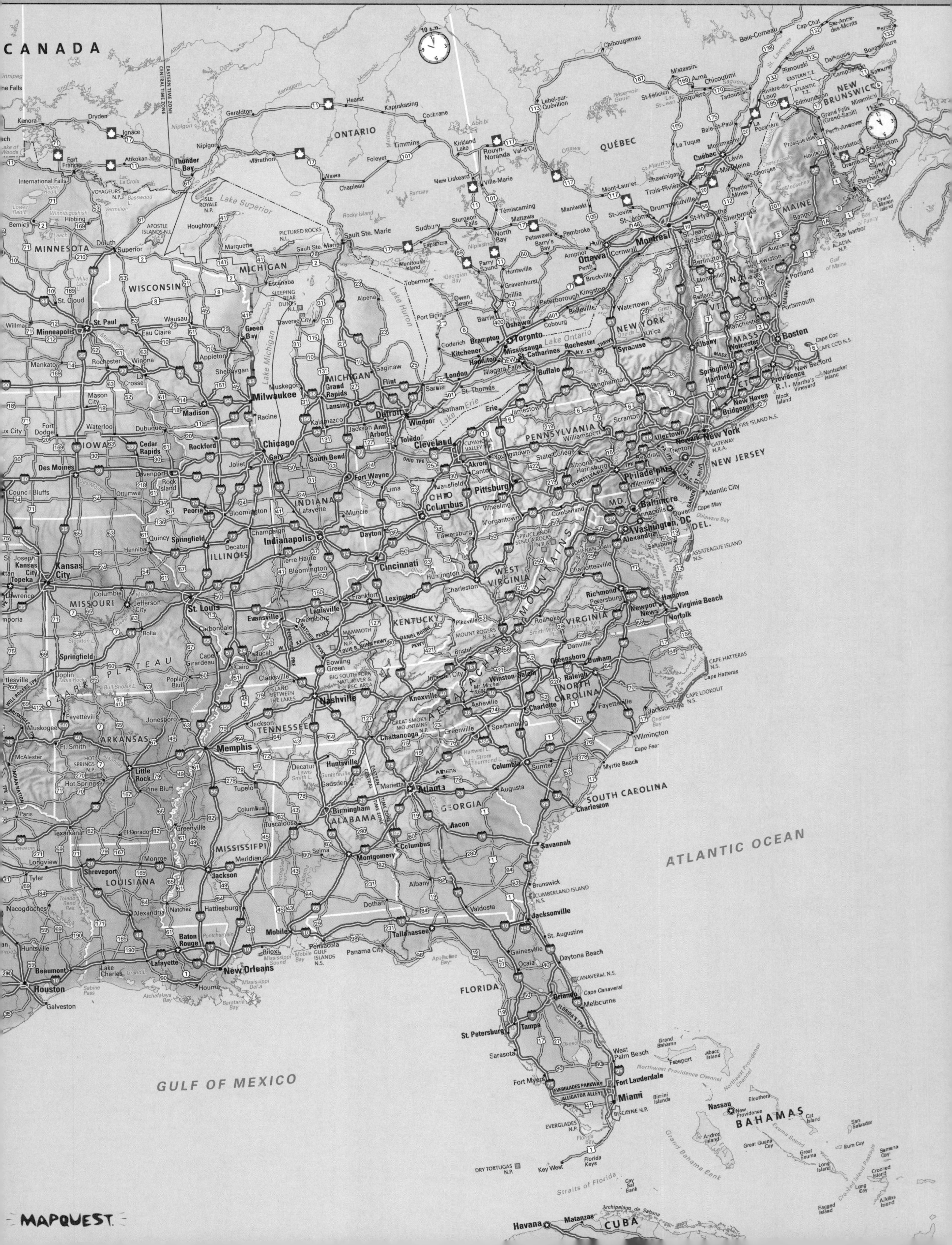
CANADA
ONTARIO
QUÉBEC
NEW BRUNSWICK
MINNESOTA
WISCONSIN
MICHIGAN
IOWA
ILLINOIS
INDIANA
OHIO
PENNSYLVANIA
NEW YORK
VT.
N.H.
MAINE
MASS
R.I.
CT
NEW JERSEY
MD.
DEL.
WEST VIRGINIA
VIRGINIA
KENTUCKY
TENNESSEE
NORTH CAROLINA
SOUTH CAROLINA
GEORGIA
ALABAMA
MISSISSIPPI
LOUISIANA
ARKANSAS
MISSOURI
FLORIDA
BAHAMAS
CUBA
OZARK PLATEAU
APPALACHIAN MOUNTAINS
Lake Superior
Lake Michigan
Lake Huron
Lake Erie
Lake Ontario
ATLANTIC OCEAN
GULF OF MEXICO
Straits of Florida
EASTERN TIME ZONE
CENTRAL TIME ZONE
Chicago
Detroit
Toronto
Montréal
Ottawa
Boston
New York
Philadelphia
Baltimore
Washington, DC
Pittsburgh
Cleveland
Columbus
Cincinnati
Indianapolis
Milwaukee
Minneapolis
St. Paul
Kansas City
St. Louis
Louisville
Nashville
Memphis
Atlanta
Birmingham
Charlotte
Jacksonville
Orlando
Tampa
Miami
New Orleans
Houston
Havana
Nassau
MAPQUEST

Tourism: 800/252-2262
Road Conditions: 888/411-7623

DRIVING DISTANCES IN MILES	ANNISTON	AUBURN	BIRMINGHAM	CHATTANOOGA, TN	COLUMBUS, GA	DECATUR	DEMOPOLIS	DOTHAN	FLORENCE	GADSDEN	HAMILTON	HUNTSVILLE	MERIDIAN, MS	MOBILE	MONTGOMERY	OPP	SELMA	TUSCALOOSA
BIRMINGHAM	66	141		149	167	83	120	191	121	63	92	101	149	258	88	166	94	61
DOTHAN	207	125	191	311	97	273	198		310	251	282	291	246	199	103	66	147	237
HUNTSVILLE	100	241	101	109	266	25	215	291	65	74	104		245	357	187	265	194	156
MOBILE	279	227	258	403	252	340	144	199	377	317	286	357	132		173	146	194	205
MONTGOMERY	106	54	88	234	79	170	100	103	207	148	179	187	153	173		81	51	134

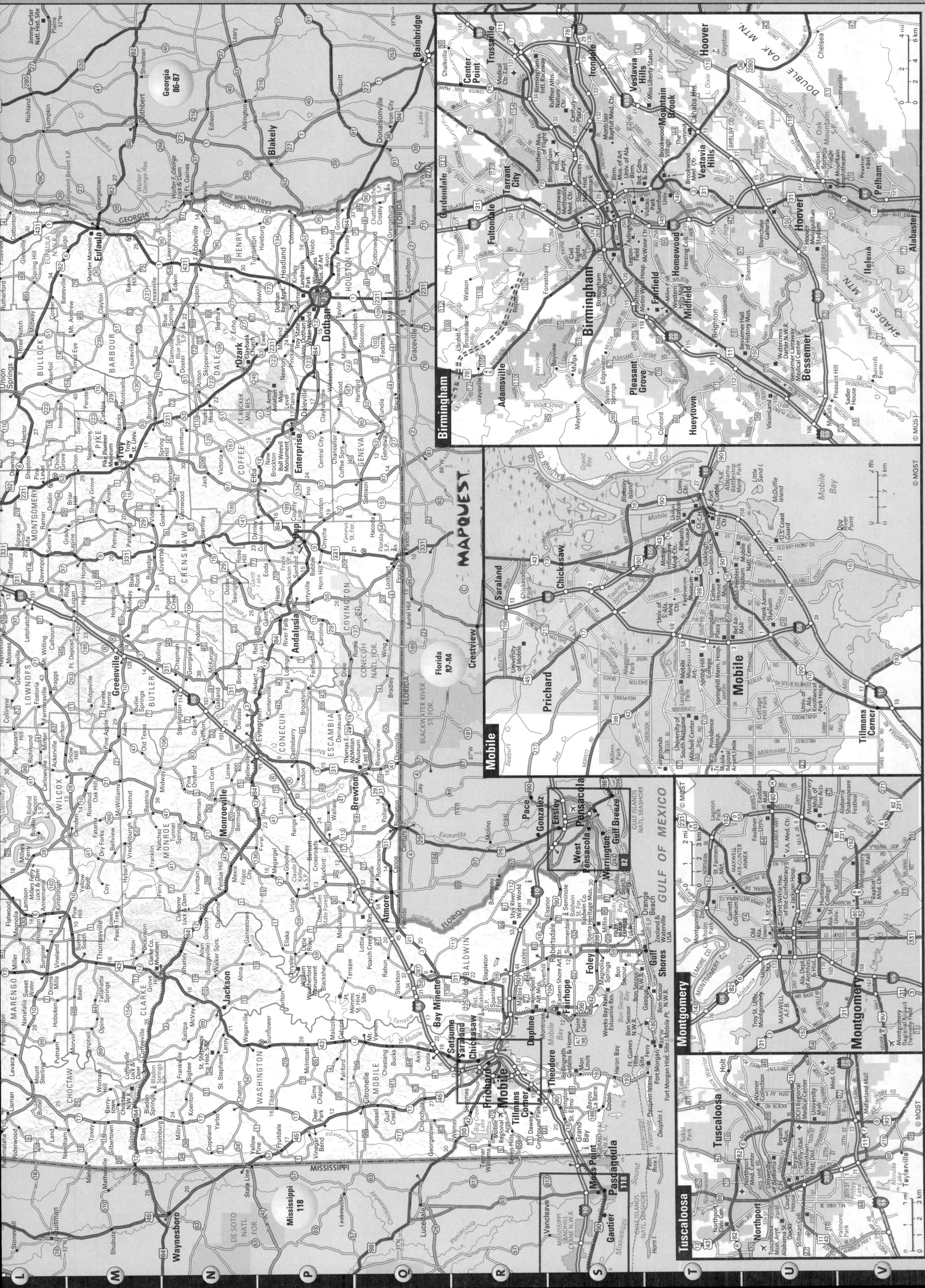

Tourism: 907/465-2017
Road Conditions: 907/273-6037

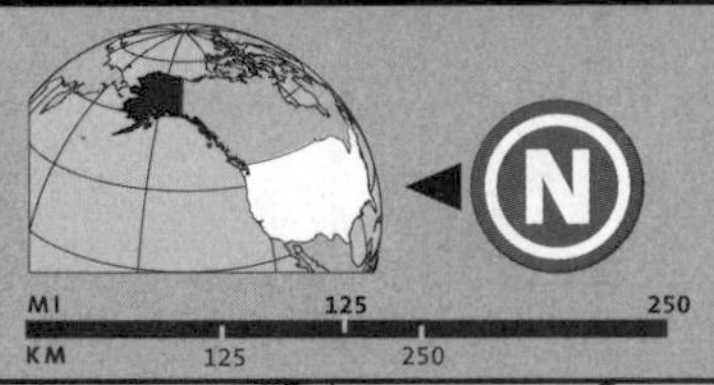

DRIVING DISTANCES IN MILES	ANCHORAGE	FAIRBANKS	GLENNALLEN	HAINES	HOMER	JUNEAU	KENAI	KETCHIKAN	SEWARD	SKAGWAY	TOK	VALDEZ
ANCHORAGE		378	184	760	225	841*	161	1608*	129	807	323	301
FAIRBANKS	378		249	645	603	726*	539	1493*	507	691	207	366
HOMER	225	603	408	985		1066*	87	1833*	172	1031	547	525
SKAGWAY	807	691	623	27	1031	101*	968	954*	935		484	740
TOK	323	207	139	438	547	518*	484	1258*	451	484		256

* DISTANCE INCLU
FERRY TRA

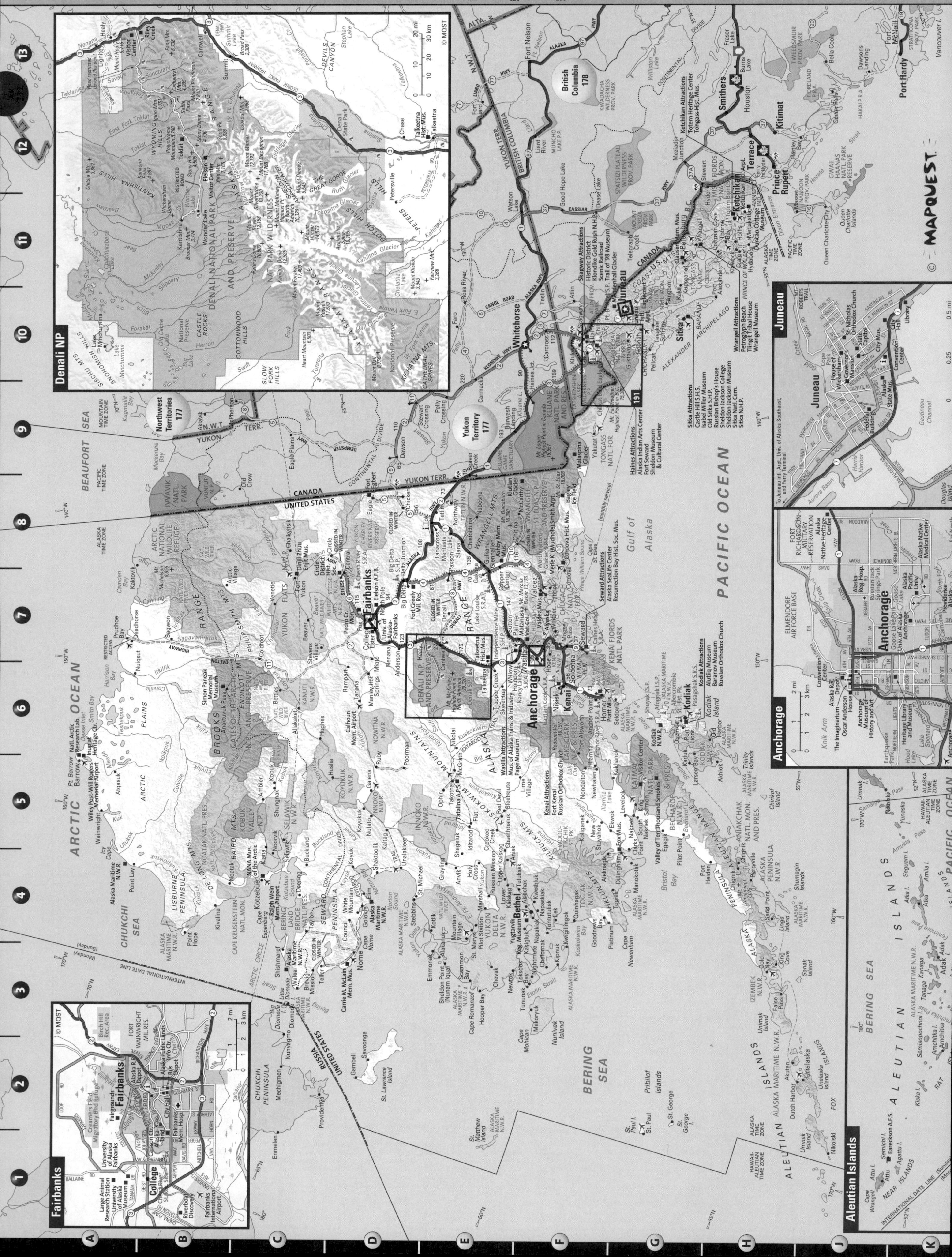

Phoenix
Morristown
Circle City
Wittmann
Lake Pleasant Reg. Park
New Waddell Dam
Pioneer Arizona Living Hist. Museum
Ben Avery Rec. Area
Cave Creek
Carefree
Cave Creek Rec. Area
Apache Pk. 3,219
Continental Mtn. 4,521
Desert Mountain
TONTO NATL. FOREST
Bartlett Res.
Bartlett Dam
Sunflower
Maverick Mtn. 4,644
Herder Mtn. 3,693
Rio Verde
Peoria
Thunderbird Park
Waterworld Safari
Adobe Dam Co. Rec. Area
Rawhide
Scottsdale
Fleischer Museum
TPC of Scottsdale
Westworld
Taliesin West
McDowell Mountain Reg. Park
FORT MCDOWELL IND. RES.
Fountain Hills
The Fountain
Ft. McDowell Casino
Out of Africa Wildlife Park
Stewart Mtn. 2,998
Stewart Mtn. Dam
Webb Mem. Hosp.
Sun City West
Sundome
Challenger Learning Center
West Valley Art Mus.
Arrowhead Towne Center
Mayo Clinic Hosp.
Surprise
Sun City
Boswell Mem. Hosp.
Peoria Stadium
Thunderbird Samaritan Medical Center
Phoenix
Moon Valley
Paradise Valley Hosp.
Paradise Valley Mall
Scottsdale Airport
White Tank Mountain Reg. Park
Waddell
Youngtown
El Mirage
Sahuaro Ranch
Arizona St. Univ. West
Metrocenter
North Mtn. Rec. Area
Lincoln Health Net.
Paradise Valley
Scottsdale Healthcare-Shea
Manistee Town Ctr.
Squaw Peak Rec. Area
McCormick Railroad Park
Casino AZ-Indian Bend
SALT RIVER INDIAN RESERVATION
Wildlife World Zoo
LUKE A.F.B.
Old Towne & Cadin Court
Grand Canyon Univ.
Glendale
Arizona Biltmore
Biltmore Fashion Park
Scottsdale Fashion Sq.
Scottsdale Pavilions
Granite Reef Dam
Usery Mtn. Rec. Area
Buckeye (part)
Litchfield Park
Maryvale Hosp. Med. Ctr.
Maryvale Mall
Maryvale Baseball Pk.
St. Joseph's Hosp.
V.A. Med. Ctr.
Scottsdale Center for the Arts
Papago Mall
Desert Sky Mall
Cricket Pavilion
Columbia Med. Ctr.
Scottsdale Stadium
Avondale
Tolleson
Cashion
State Capitol
Perryville
Santa Maria
Phoenix Sky Harbor Intl. Airport
Phoenix Zoo & Desert Botanical Garden
Ariz. Hist. Soc. Mus.
Big Surf
Mesa Southwest Museum
Arizona Temple
Mesa
Champlin Fighter Museum
Apache Junction
Goldfield
Lost Dutchman S.P.
Valley Lutheran Hospital
Superstition Springs Ctr.
Apache Greyhound Park
BUCKEYE VALLEY
Goodyear
Old Town Tempe
Sun Devil Stadium
Mesa Lutheran Hospital
Fiesta Mall
Golfland/SunSplash
Tempe Diablo Stadium
The Petersen House
Arizona Mills
Arizona State Univ.
Tempe
Desert Samaritan Medical Center
Buckeye
Liberty
Casey Abbot Rec. Area
Phoenix International Raceway
Maricopa Village
Laveen
Guadalupe
Mystery Castle
Dobbins Lookout
SOUTH MOUNTAIN
South Mountain Park
AHWATUKEE FOOTHILLS
Gilbert
East Valley Mall
Palo Verde
Estrella Mountain Reg. Park
GILA RIVER INDIAN RES.
Buckeye Hills Rec. Area
BUCKEYE HILLS
RAINBOW VALLEY
SIERRA ESTRELLA
Gila River Ved Quiva Casino
Komatke
Chandler
Chandler Regional Hospital
Arizona St. Univ. East
Higley
Whirlwind Gila River Wild Horse Casino
Firebird Intl. Raceway
Queen Creek
Santa Cruz
Sun Lakes
MARICOPA CO.
PINAL CO.
Chandler Heights
Goldmine Mtn. 2,403
Santan Mts. Reg. Park
SANTAN MTS.
Montezuma Pk. 4,354
Casa Blanca
Bapchule
Gila River Arts & Crafts Center
Olberg
Sacaton
GILA RIVER INDIAN RES.
Maricopa
Harrah's Ak-Chin Casino
Ak Chin
MARICOPA (AK-CHIN) INDIAN RESERVATION
PALO VERDE MTS.
SACATON MTS.
Casa Grande Ruins National Monument
Coolidge
Casa Grande
© MQST
Downtown Phoenix
Encanto Park
Arizona State Fairgrounds
Heard Museum
Monterey Park
Coronado Park
Phoenix Art Mus.
Ariz. Vet. Mem. Col.
Margaret T. Hance Park
Good Samaritan Reg. Med. Ctr.
Edison Park
St. Luke's Med. Ctr.
Univ. Park
Herberger Theater Ctr.
Arizona Center
Phoenix Mus. of Hist.
Ariz. Mining & Mineral Mus.
Ariz. Hall of Fame Museum
U.S. Ct. Hse.
City Hall
Civic Plaza
Heritage Square
Verde Park
Ariz. Sci. Ctr.
Ariz. Capitol
Bolin Mem. Park
Court House
Bank One Ballpark
Eastlake Park
America West Arena
Union Station
Bus Terminal
To Phoenix Sky Harbor Intl. Airport
Central Park
Alkire Park
Harmon Park
Phoenix Mem. Health System
Coffelt-Lamoreaux Park
Barrios Unidos Park

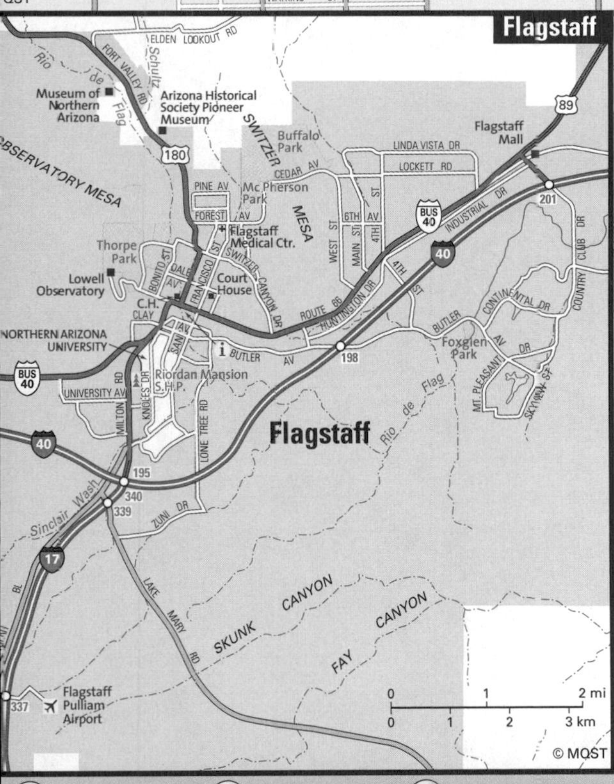
Flagstaff
Museum of Northern Arizona
Arizona Historical Society Pioneer Museum
Flagstaff Mall
Buffalo Park
Mc Pherson Park
Flagstaff Medical Ctr.
Thorpe Park
Lowell Observatory
Court House
NORTHERN ARIZONA UNIVERSITY
Riordan Mansion
Foxglen Park
OBSERVATORY MESA
SWITZER MESA
SKUNK CANYON
FAY CANYON
Flagstaff Pulliam Airport
© MQST

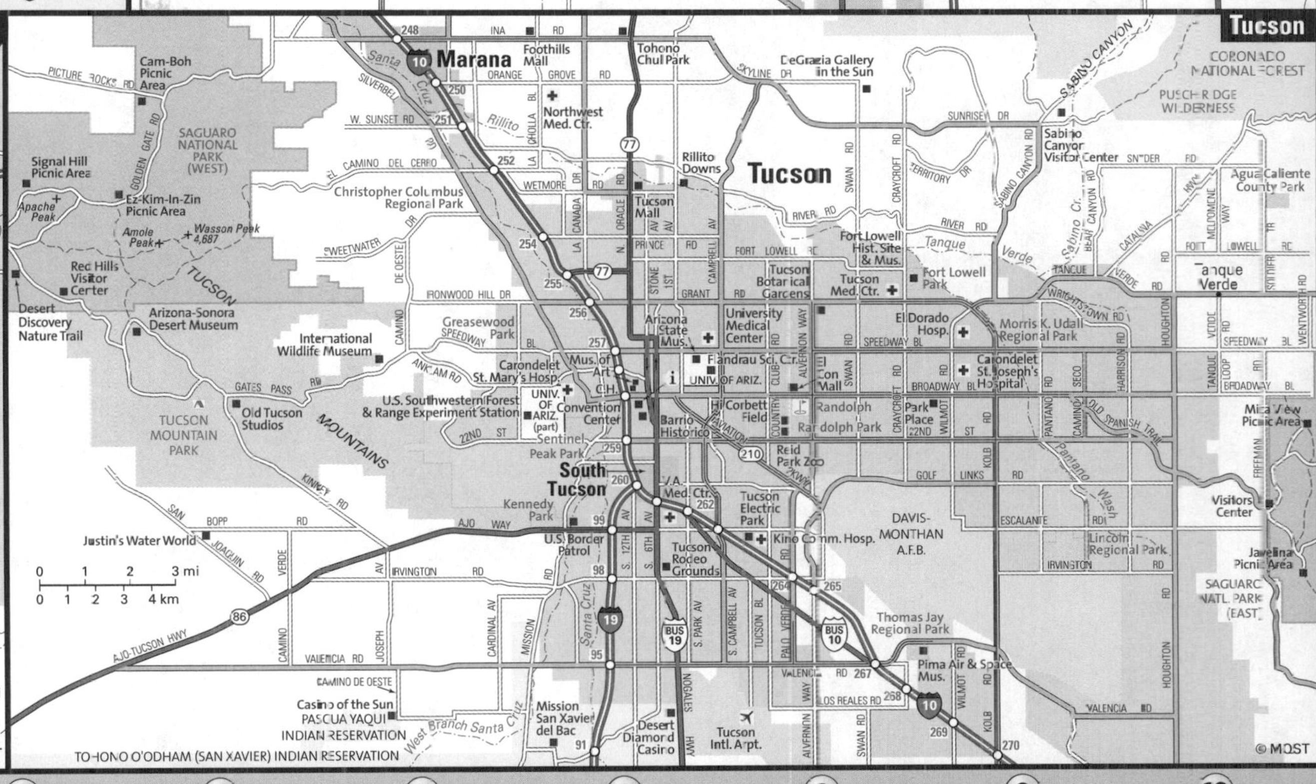
Tucson
Marana
Foothills Mall
Tohono Chul Park
DeGrazia Gallery in the Sun
CORONADO NATIONAL FOREST
PUSCH RIDGE WILDERNESS
Cam-Boh Picnic Area
SAGUARO NATIONAL PARK (WEST)
Northwest Med. Ctr.
Sabino Canyon Visitor Center
Agua Caliente County Park
Signal Hill Picnic Area
Ez-Kim-In-Zin Picnic Area
Christopher Columbus Regional Park
Rillito Downs
Tucson
Tucson Mall
Wasson Peak 4,687
Fort Lowell Hist. Site & Mus.
Fort Lowell Park
Rec Hills Visitor Center
Tucson Botanical Gardens
Tucson Med. Ctr.
Tanque Verde
Desert Discovery Nature Trail
Arizona-Sonora Desert Museum
University Medical Center
Arizona State Mus.
El Dorado Hosp.
Morris K. Udall Regional Park
International Wildlife Museum
Greasewood Park
Flandrau Sci. Ctr.
Carondelet St. Joseph's Hospital
Carondelet St. Mary's Hosp.
UNIV. OF ARIZ.
Mus. of Art
U.S. Southwestern Forest & Range Experiment Station
Old Tucson Studios
TUCSON MOUNTAIN PARK
Convention Center
Barrio Historico
Corbett Field
Randolph Park
Park Place Mall
Reid Park Zoo
Mica View Picnic Area
South Tucson
Peak Park
V.A. Med. Ctr.
Tucson Electric Park
DAVIS-MONTHAN A.F.B.
Visitors Center
Kennedy Park
Kino Comm. Hosp.
Justin's Water World
U.S. Border Patrol
Tucson Rodeo Grounds
Lincoln Regional Park
Javelina Picnic Area
SAGUARO NATL. PARK (EAST)
Thomas Jay Regional Park
Pima Air & Space Mus.
Casino of the Sun
PASCUA YAQUI INDIAN RESERVATION
Mission San Xavier del Bac
Desert Diamond Casino
Tucson Intl. Arpt.
TOHONO O'ODHAM (SAN XAVIER) INDIAN RESERVATION
© MQST

Tourism: 602/364-3700
Road Conditions: 602/651-2400 ext. 7623
Road Construction: 888/411-7623

MI 0 25 50
KM 0 25 50

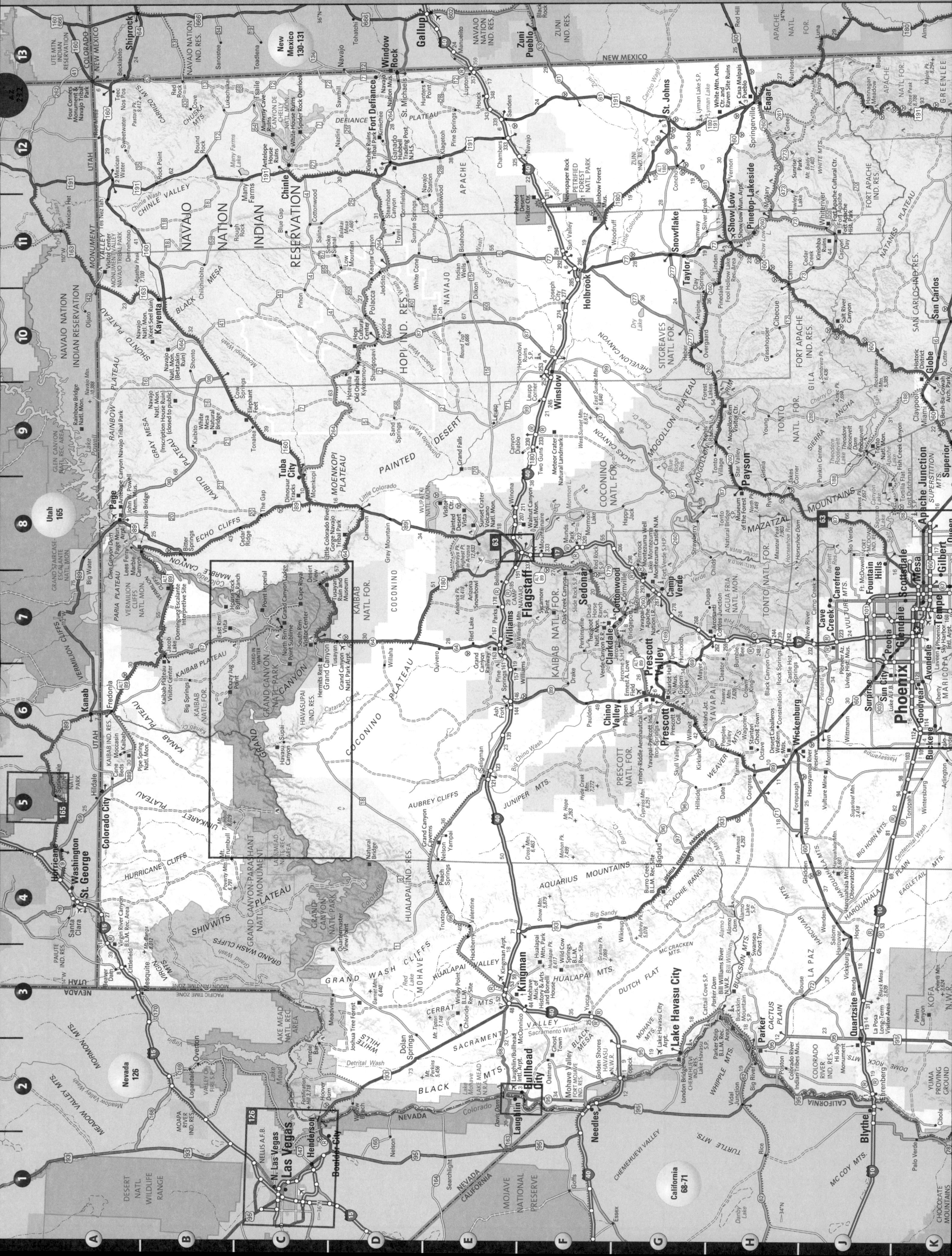

DRIVING DISTANCES IN MILES

	BULLHEAD CITY	CASA GRANDE	CHINLE	DOUGLAS	FLAGSTAFF	GRAND CANYON	HOLBROOK	KINGMAN	LAKE HAVASU CITY	NOGALES	PAGE	PHOENIX	PRESCOTT	SAFFORD	SHOW LOW	TUCSON	WICKENBURG	YUMA
FLAGSTAFF	180	188	216	374		89	93	148	209	318	135	137	89	271	140	255	147	320
KINGMAN	34	235	364	421	148	175	240		60	365	281	184	150	353	288	302	134	215
PHOENIX	217	50	353	237	137	226	230	184	193	181	272		96	169	178	118	51	183
TUCSON	335	68	366	120	255	345	240	302	311	65	390	118	214	128	193		169	241
YUMA	222	179	536	360	320	409	413	215	155	304	455	183	213	368	352	241	170	

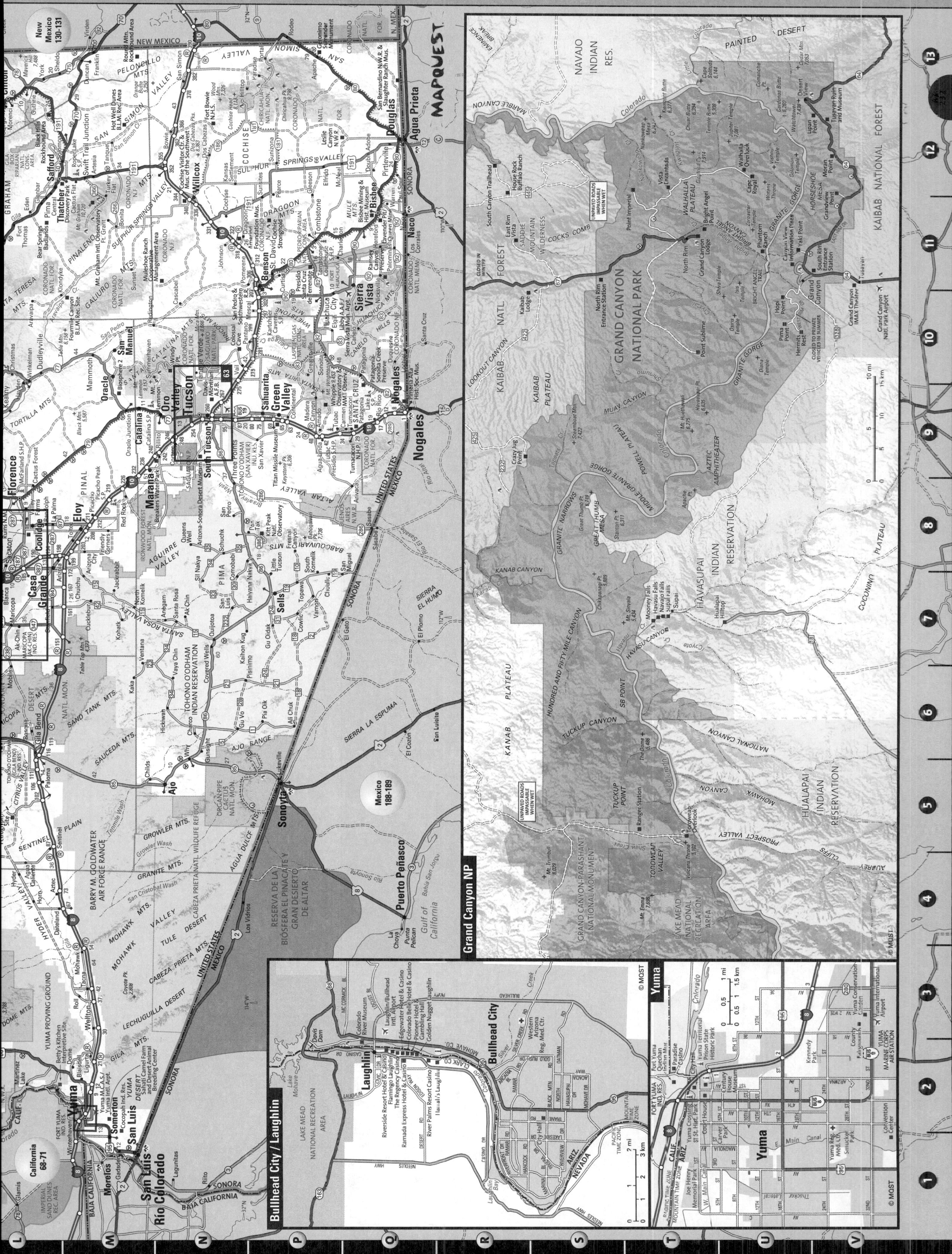

Tourism: 800/628-8725
Road Conditions: 501/569-2374
Road Construction: 501/569-2227

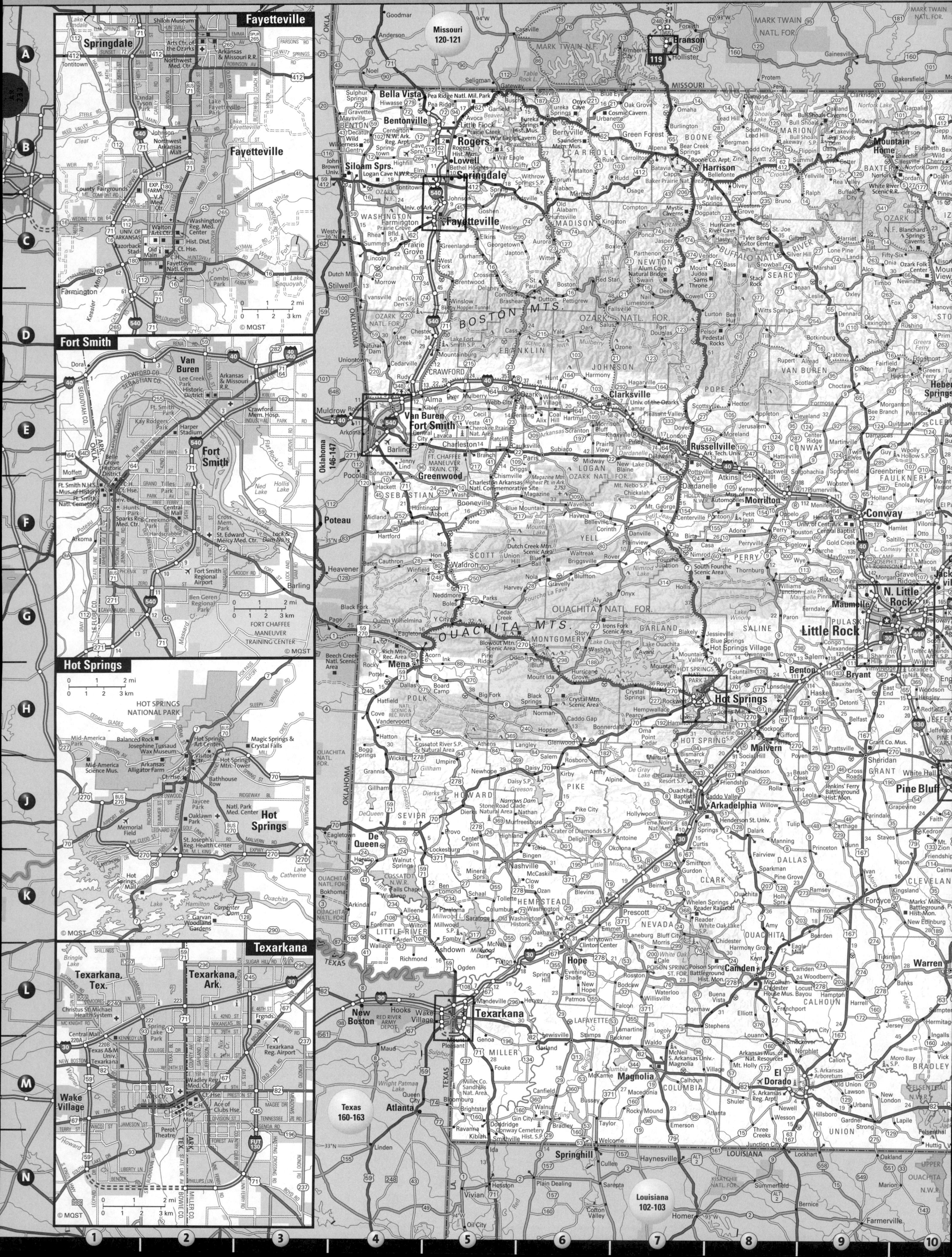

DRIVING DISTANCES IN MILES	BLYTHEVILLE	CAMDEN	CONWAY	DUMAS	EL DORADO	FAYETTEVILLE	FORT SMITH	HARRISON	HELENA	HOT SPRINGS	JONESBORO	LITTLE ROCK	MEMPHIS, TN	MENA	NEWPORT	PINE BLUFF	RUSSELLVILLE	TEXARKANA
FORT SMITH	353	201	134	255	232	64		141	280	126	266	165	298	81	220	210	87	180
JONESBORO	53	236	133	185	253	287	266	178	111	200		135	70	276	45	180	182	288
LITTLE ROCK	195	101	31	90	118	186	165	136	122	65	135		140	141	89	45	81	153
PINE BLUFF	213	76	76	45	93	231	210	181	106	76	180	45	157	151	134		126	163
TEXARKANA	347	90	176	208	88	244	180	281	273	117	288	153	291	99	241	163	180	

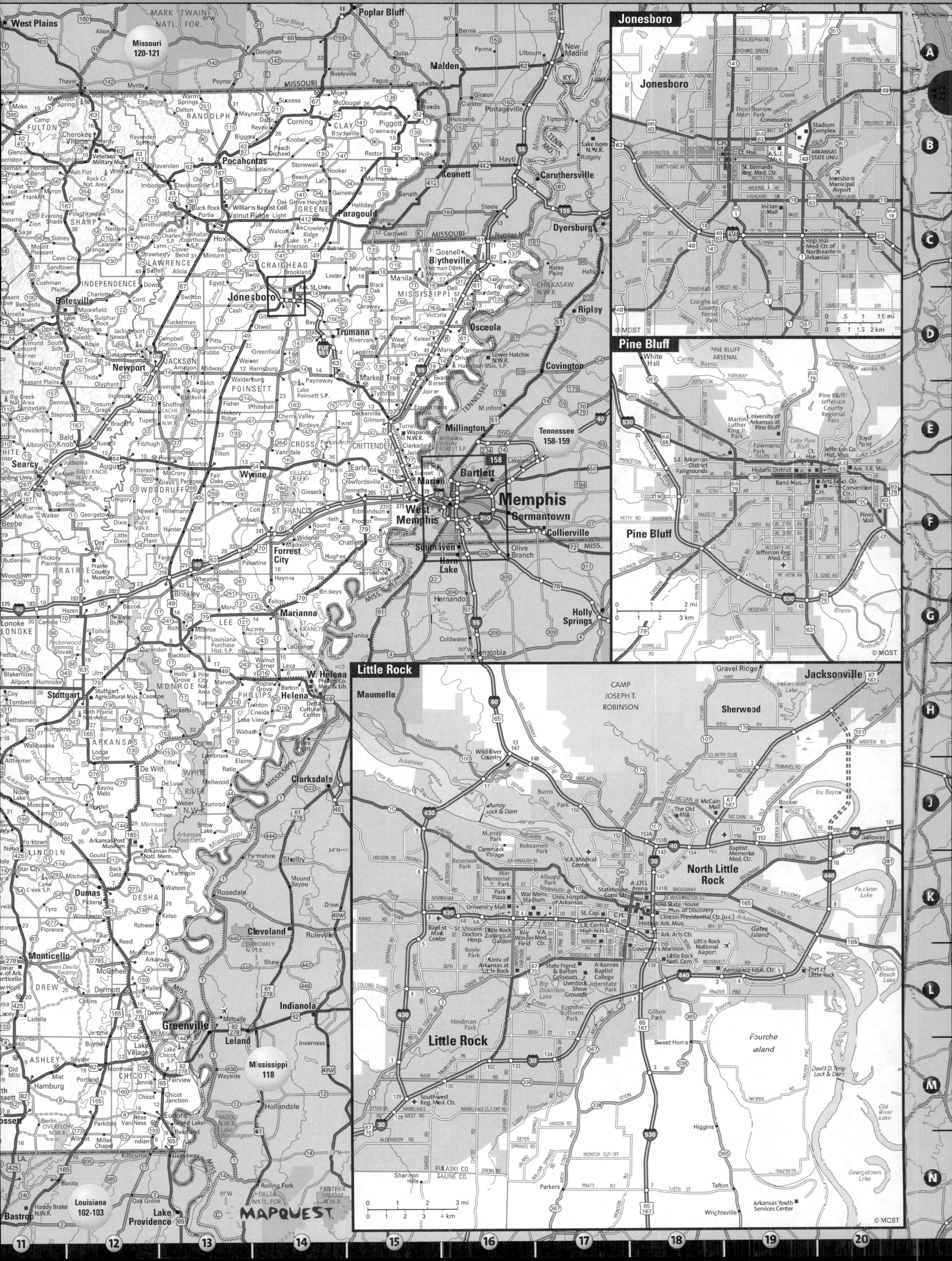

California

Tourism: 800/862-2543
Road Conditions: 916/445-7623

TRAVEL NOTE: Beginning January 2002, California started numbering freeway exits using a mileage-based numbering system. Full implementation is expected to take three years. For more details, including a complete listing of California's exit numbers, go to *www.dot.ca.gov/hq/traffops/signtech/calnexus/index.htm.*

DRIVING DISTANCES IN MILES

	BISHOP	CHICO	EUREKA	FRESNO	MERCED	MONTEREY	NAPA	OAKLAND	REDDING	SACRAMENTO	SAN FRANCISCO	SAN JOSE	SANTA ROSA	SOUTH LAKE TAHOE	STOCKTON	SUSANVILLE	UKIAH	YOSEMITE VILLAGE
EUREKA	537	186		444	385	380	235	262	133	278	263	306	208	379	336	247	148	436
REDDING	426	74	133	344	284	323	193	213		166	222	250	228	266	214	114	193	336
SACRAMENTO	260	88	278	178	118	188	58	78	166		87	115	93	100	48	183	153	170
SAN FRANCISCO	283	182	263	190	131	114	47	9	222	87		43	56	185	82	277	116	183
SOUTH LAKE TAHOE	179	165	379	267	208	286	156	176	266	100	185	213	191		142	146	251	180

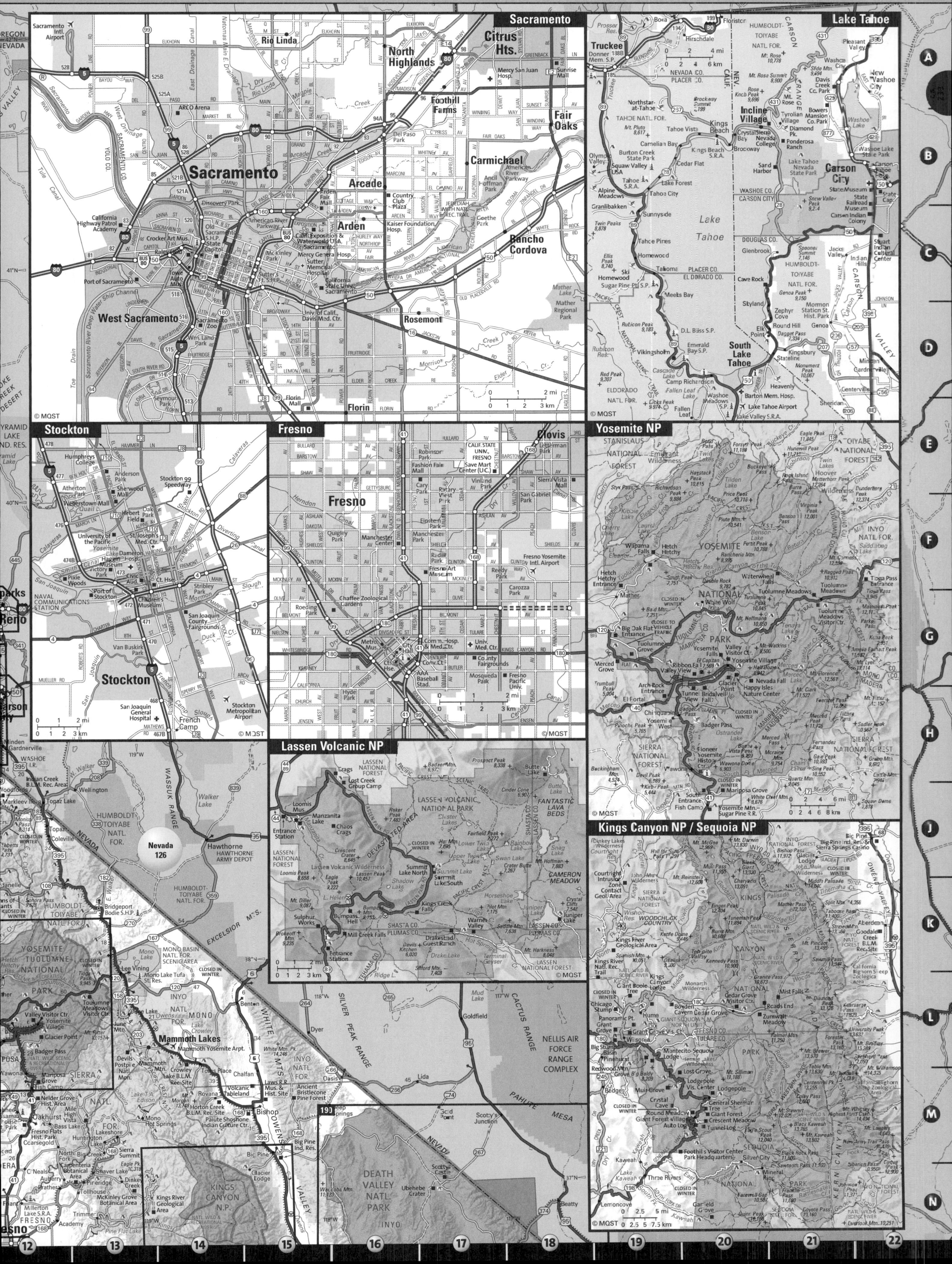

Tourism: 800/862-2543
Road Conditions: 916/445-7623

DRIVING DISTANCES IN MILES	BAKERSFIELD	BARSTOW	BISHOP	EL CENTRO	FRESNO	LAS VEGAS, NV	LOS ANGELES	MERCED	MONTEREY	PALM SPRINGS	SAN BERNARDINO	SAN DIEGO	SAN FRANCISCO	SAN JOSE	SAN LUIS OBISPO	SANTA BARBARA	VISALIA	YOSEMITE VILLAGE
FRESNO	111	246	219	451		399	219	59	158	324	277	342	190	153	134	258	43	90
LOS ANGELES	111	118	270	234	219	274		278	327	110	62	124	385	342	190	97	183	308
MONTEREY	229	365	315	559	158	517	327	122		432	385	450	114	74	149	242	204	20
SAN DIEGO	234	181	366	117	342	337	124	401	450	143	111		508	465	314	221	306	43
SAN FRANCISCO	287	423	283	617	190	575	385	131	114	490	443	508		43	234	327	233	18

MI 5 10
KM 5 10 15

TRAVEL NOTE: Beginning January 2002, California started numbering freeway exits using a mileage-based numbering system. Full implementation is expected to take three years. For more details, including a complete listing of California's exit numbers, go to *www.dot.ca.gov/hq/traffops/signtech/calnexus/index.htm.*

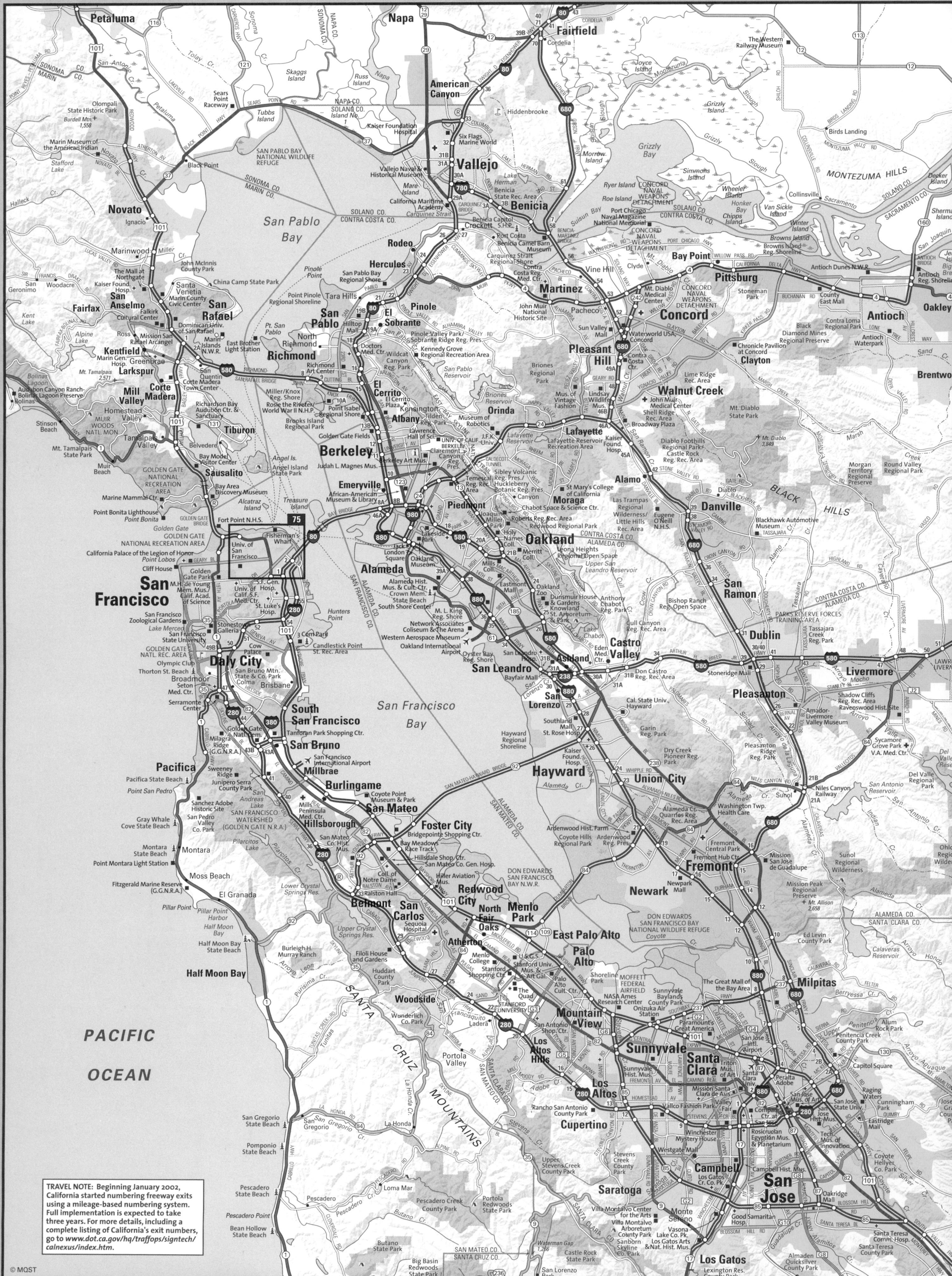
MI 5 10
KM 5 10 15
Petaluma
Napa
Fairfield
American Canyon
Vallejo
Benicia
Novato
San Pablo Bay
Pittsburg
Concord
Martinez
Antioch
Oakley
Brentwood
San Rafael
San Anselmo
Fairfax
Kentfield
Larkspur
Mill Valley
Corte Madera
Tiburon
Sausalito
Richmond
San Pablo
El Sobrante
Pinole
Hercules
Rodeo
El Cerrito
Albany
Berkeley
Emeryville
Piedmont
Oakland
Alameda
Orinda
Lafayette
Walnut Creek
Pleasant Hill
Clayton
Moraga
Alamo
Danville
San Ramon
Dublin
Pleasanton
Livermore
Castro Valley
San Leandro
San Lorenzo
Hayward
Union City
Fremont
Newark
Milpitas
San Francisco
Daly City
South San Francisco
San Bruno
Millbrae
Burlingame
San Mateo
Foster City
Hillsborough
Belmont
San Carlos
Redwood City
Menlo Park
Atherton
East Palo Alto
Palo Alto
Mountain View
Sunnyvale
Santa Clara
Los Altos
Los Altos Hills
Cupertino
Campbell
Saratoga
San Jose
Los Gatos
Monte Sereno
Pacifica
Montara
Moss Beach
El Granada
Half Moon Bay
San Francisco Bay
PACIFIC
OCEAN
SANTA CRUZ MOUNTAINS
BLACK HILLS
MONTEZUMA HILLS
TRAVEL NOTE: Beginning January 2002, California started numbering freeway exits using a mileage-based numbering system. Full implementation is expected to take three years. For more details, including a complete listing of California's exit numbers, go to www.dot.ca.gov/hq/traffops/signtech/calnexus/index.htm.
© MQST

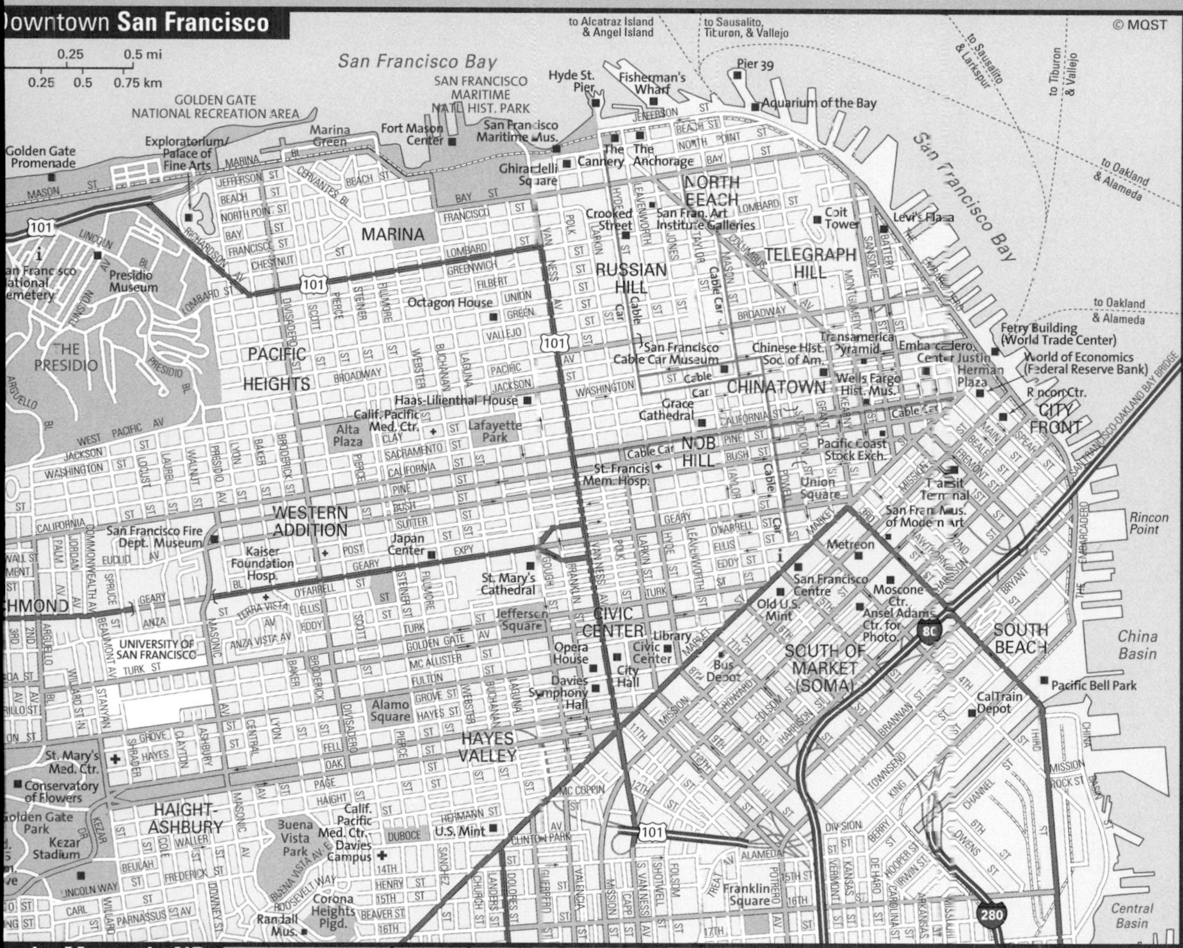
Downtown San Francisco
© MOST
San Francisco Bay
Golden Gate National Recreation Area
San Francisco Maritime Natl. Hist. Park
Fisherman's Wharf
Pier 39
Aquarium of the Bay
Exploratorium/Palace of Fine Arts
Marina Green
Fort Mason Center
Ghirardelli Square
The Cannery
The Anchorage
Marina
North Beach
Russian Hill
Telegraph Hill
Coit Tower
Levi's Plaza
The Presidio
Presidio Museum
Octagon House
Pacific Heights
Chinatown
Transamerica Pyramid
Ferry Building (World Trade Center)
World of Economics (Federal Reserve Bank)
Embarcadero Center
Justin Herman Plaza
Rincon Ctr.
City Front
Nob Hill
Grace Cathedral
San Francisco Cable Car Museum
Haas-Lilienthal House
Lafayette Park
Alta Plaza
Calif. Pacific Med. Ctr.
St. Francis Mem. Hosp.
Pacific Coast Stock Exch.
Union Square
Transit Terminal
San Francisco Mus. of Modern Art
Western Addition
San Francisco Fire Dept. Museum
Kaiser Foundation Hosp.
Japan Center
St. Mary's Cathedral
Metreon
San Francisco Centre
Moscone Center
Old U.S. Mint
Ansel Adams Ctr. for Photo.
Jefferson Square
Civic Center
Opera House
Davies Symphony Hall
City Hall
Library
Civic Center
South of Market (SOMA)
Bus Depot
South Beach
Rincon Point
China Basin
Pacific Bell Park
CalTrain Depot
University of San Francisco
Alamo Square
Hayes Valley
St. Mary's Med. Ctr.
Conservatory of Flowers
Golden Gate Park
Kezar Stadium
Haight-Ashbury
Buena Vista Park
Calif. Pacific Med. Ctr. Davies Campus
U.S. Mint
Corona Heights Plgd.
Randall Mus.
Franklin Square
Central Basin
to Alcatraz Island & Angel Island
to Sausalito, Tiburon, & Vallejo
to Sausalito & Larkspur
to Tiburon & Vallejo
to Oakland & Alameda

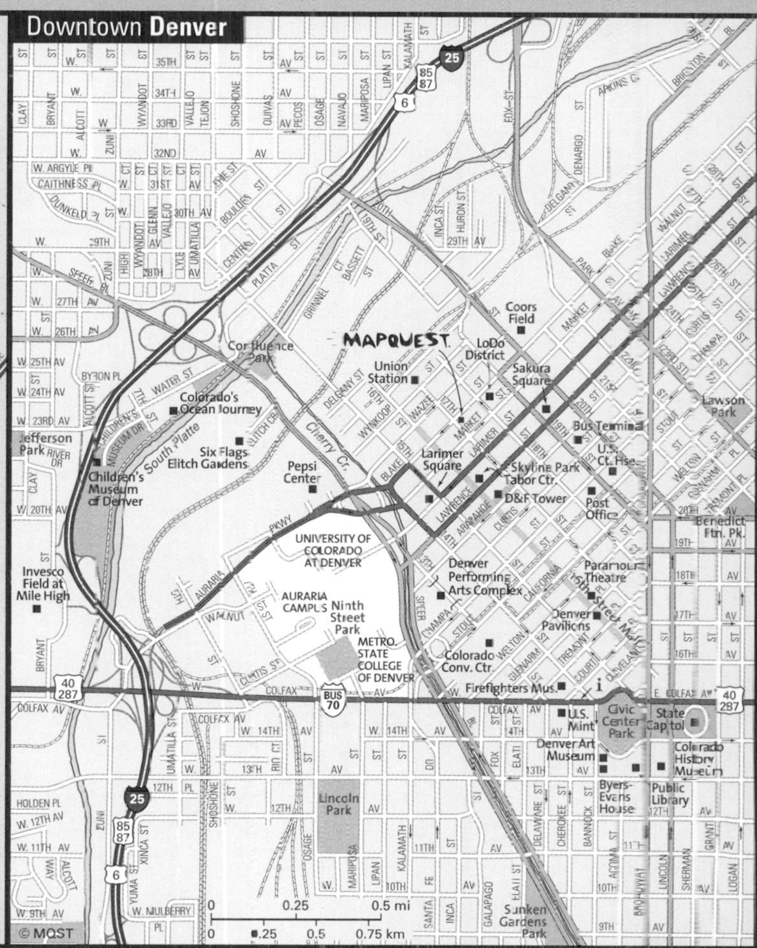
Downtown Denver
MAPQUEST
Coors Field
LoDo District
Union Station
Sakura Square
Confluence Park
Colorado's Ocean Journey
Six Flags Elitch Gardens
Pepsi Center
Children's Museum of Denver
Jefferson Park
Larimer Square
Skyline Park
Tabor Ctr.
D&F Tower
Bus Terminal
U.S. Cl. Hse.
Post Office
Lawson Park
Benedict Fntn. Pk.
University of Colorado at Denver
Auraria Campus
Ninth Street Park
Metro. State College of Denver
Denver Performing Arts Complex
Paramount Theatre
Denver Pavilions
Colorado Conv. Ctr.
Invesco Field at Mile High
Firefighters Mus.
Civic Center Park
State Capitol
U.S. Mint
Denver Art Museum
Colorado History Museum
Byers-Evans House
Public Library
Lincoln Park
Sunken Gardens Park
Colfax Av
Speer Blvd
Cherry Cr.
South Platte River
0 0.25 0.5 mi
0 .25 0.5 0.75 km
© MOST

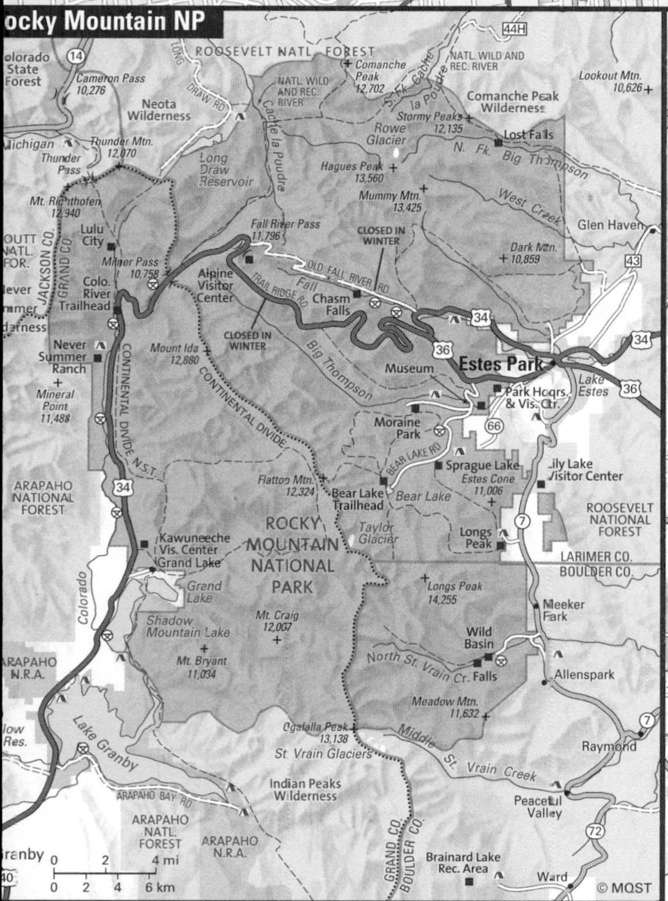
Rocky Mountain NP
Roosevelt Natl. Forest
Comanche Peak Wilderness
Neota Wilderness
Cameron Pass 10,276
Long Draw Reservoir
Hagues Peak 13,560
Mummy Mtn. 13,425
Lost Falls
Glen Haven
Fall River Pass 11,796
Alpine Visitor Center
Milner Pass 10,758
Colo. River Trailhead
Chasm Falls
Estes Park
Park Hdqrs. & Vis. Ctr.
Lake Estes
Moraine Park
Sprague Lake
Bear Lake
Bear Lake Trailhead
Flattop Mtn. 12,324
Taylor Glacier
Longs Peak 14,255
Lily Lake Visitor Center
Rocky Mountain National Park
Kawuneeche Vis. Center
Grand Lake
Shadow Mountain Lake
Mt. Craig 12,007
Mt. Bryant 11,034
Wild Basin Falls
Meeker Park
Allenspark
Meadow Mtn. 11,632
Ouzel Falls
St. Vrain Glaciers
Indian Peaks Wilderness
Lake Granby
Arapaho Natl. Forest
Arapaho N.R.A.
Continental Divide N.S.T.
Raymond
Peaceful Valley
Brainard Lake Rec. Area
Ward
Larimer Co.
Boulder Co.
Grand Co.
Boulder Co.
0 2 4 mi
0 2 4 6 km
© MOST

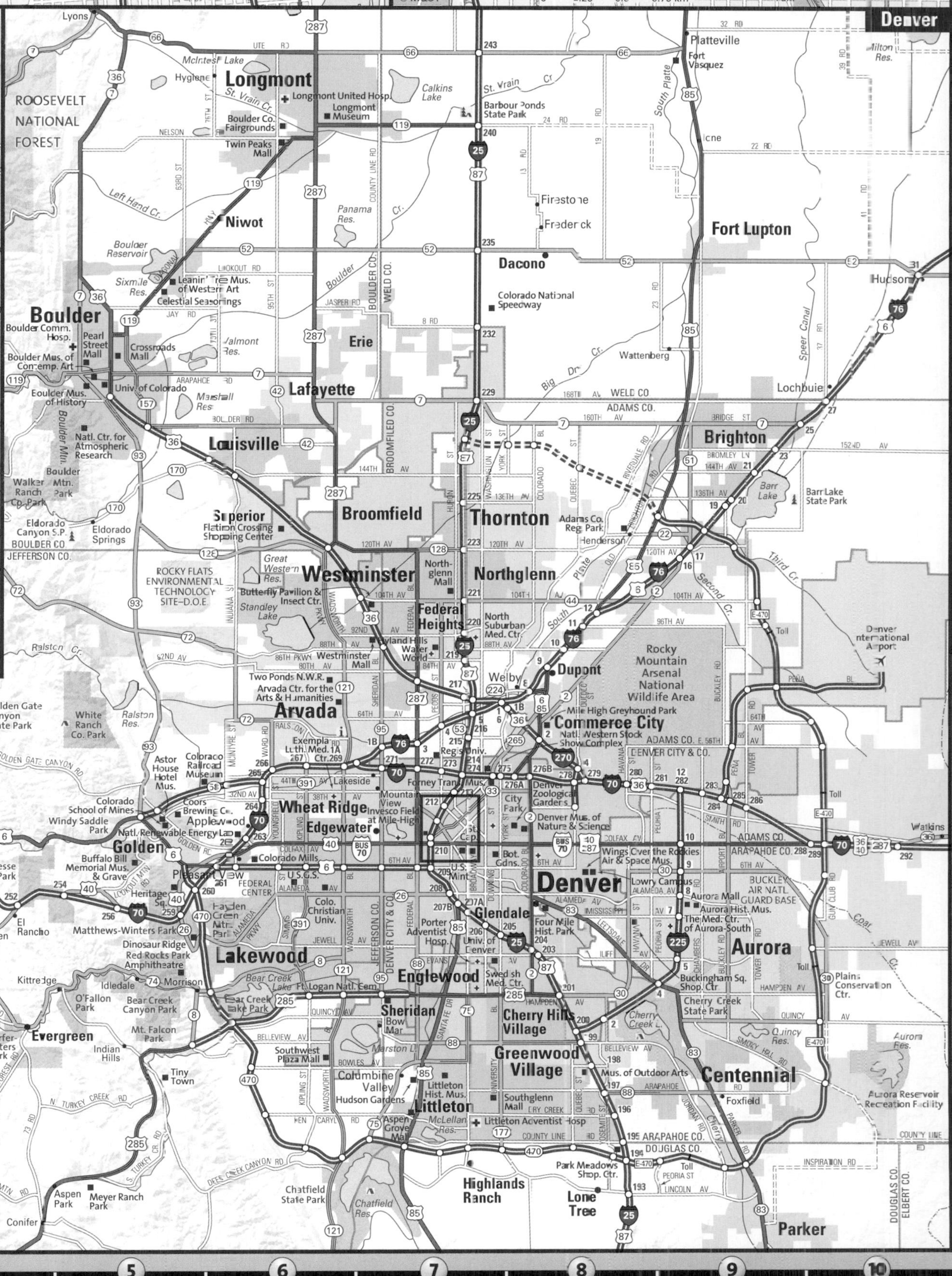
Denver
Lyons
Longmont
Longmont United Hosp.
Longmont Museum
Boulder Co. Fairgrounds
Twin Peaks Mall
Calkins Lake
Barbour Ponds State Park
St. Vrain Cr.
Platteville
Fort Vasquez
Roosevelt National Forest
Niwot
Boulder Reservoir
Panama Res.
Firestone
Frederick
Dacono
Fort Lupton
Colorado National Speedway
Leanin' Tree Mus. of Western Art
Celestial Seasonings
Boulder
Boulder Comm. Hosp.
Pearl Street Mall
Crossroads Mall
Boulder Mus. of Contemp. Art
Boulder Mus. of History
Univ. of Colorado
Natl. Ctr. for Atmospheric Research
Erie
Lafayette
Louisville
Wattenberg
Hudson
Lochbuie
Brighton
Barr Lake State Park
Superior
Flatiron Crossing Shopping Center
Eldorado Canyon S.P.
Eldorado Springs
Broomfield
Thornton
Adams Co. Reg. Park
Henderson
Westminster
Northglenn
Federal Heights
North Suburban Med. Ctr.
Rocky Flats Environmental Technology Site-D.O.E.
Great Western Res.
Butterfly Pavilion & Insect Ctr.
Standley Lake
Westminster Mall
Rocky Mountain Arsenal National Wildlife Area
Denver International Airport
Dupont
Welby
Commerce City
Mile High Greyhound Park
Natl. Western Stock Show Complex
Two Ponds N.W.R.
Arvada Ctr. for the Arts & Humanities
Arvada
White Ranch Co. Park
Golden Gate Canyon State Park
National Historic District Central City
Black Hawk
Casinos
St. Mary's Glacier
Arapaho Natl. Forest
Empire
Dumont
Lawson
Argo Gold Mine, Mill & Mus.
Idaho Springs
Astor House Hotel Mus.
Colorado Railroad Museum
Coors Brewing Co.
Colorado School of Mines
Windy Saddle Park
Golden
Natl. Renewable Energy Lab
Wheat Ridge
Edgewater
Lakeside
Invesco Field at Mile High
Denver Zoological Gardens
City Park
Denver Mus. of Nature & Science
Wings Over the Rockies Air & Space Mus.
Lowry Campus
Aurora Mall
Buckley Air Natl. Guard Base
Aurora Hist. Mus.
The Med. Ctr. of Aurora-South
Aurora
Denver
Bot. Gdns.
U. of Denver
Glendale
Four Mile Hist. Park
Hamill House and Hotel de Paris Mus.
Georgetown
Georgetown Loop R.R.
Genesee Park
Buffalo Bill Memorial Mus. & Grave
Pleasant View
Heritage Sq.
Colo. Christian Univ.
Lakewood
Porter Adventist Hosp.
Swedish Med. Ctr.
Englewood
Matthews-Winters Park
Dinosaur Ridge
Red Rocks Park Amphitheatre
Morrison
Bergen Park
El Rancho
Elk Meadow Park
Kittredge
Idledale
O'Fallon Park
Bear Creek Canyon Park
Bear Creek Lake Park
Logan Natl. Cem.
Sheridan
Cherry Hills Village
Greenwood Village
Buckingham Sq. Shop. Ctr.
Plains Conservation Ctr.
Cherry Creek State Park
Quincy Res.
Aurora Res.
Centennial
Foxfield
Aurora Reservoir Recreation Facility
Echo Lake
Mt. Goliath Natural Area
Mt. Evans 14,264
Highest Road in the U.S.
Mt. Evans Wilderness
Evergreen
Alderfer-3 Sisters Park
Mt. Falcon Park
Indian Hills
Tiny Town
Southwest Plaza Mall
Columbine Valley
Hudson Gardens
Littleton
Littleton Hist. Mus.
Southglenn Mall
Littleton Adventist Hosp.
Mus. of Outdoor Arts
Aspen Grove Mall
McLellan Res.
Brook Forest Estates
Park Meadows Shop. Ctr.
Highlands Ranch
Lone Tree
Chatfield State Park
Chatfield Res.
Aspen Park
Meyer Ranch Park
Conifer
Harris Park
Parker
Pike Natl. Forest
Arapaho Natl. Forest
Watkins
Toll
Jefferson Co.
Douglas Co.
Elbert Co.
0 2 4 6 mi
0 2 4 6 8 km
© MOST
A B C D E F G H J K L M N
1 2 3 4 5 6 7 8 9 10

Tourism: 800/265-6723
Road Conditions: 303/639-1111
Road Construction: 303/757-9341

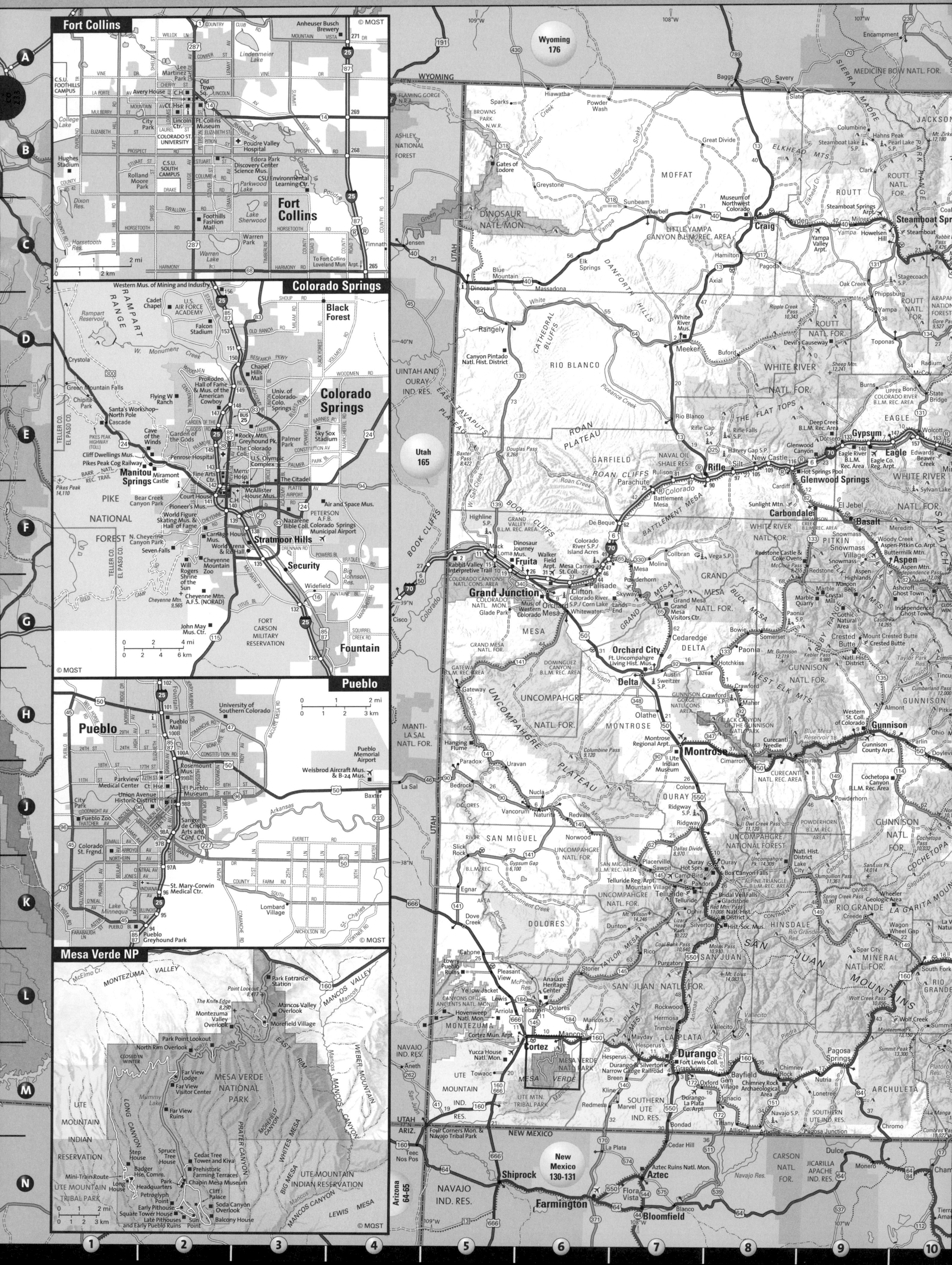

DRIVING DISTANCES IN MILES	ALAMOSA	ASPEN	BOULDER	BURLINGTON	COLORADO SPRINGS	CRAIG	DENVER	DURANGO	ESTES PARK	FORT COLLINS	GLENWOOD SPRINGS	GRAND JUNCTION	GREELEY	LAMAR	MONTROSE	PUEBLO	STERLING	TRINIDAD
COLORADO SPRINGS	162	157	97	152		270	70	314	134	133	226	318	133	161	236	43	194	127
DENVER	230	164	27	168	70	203		337	64	64	158	250	64	208	277	111	130	196
DURANGO	152	244	366	461	314	321	337		402	399	226	169	399	354	107	271	465	260
GRAND JUNCTION	261	135	254	418	318	152	250	169	291	311	92		311	458	62	360	377	444
PUEBLO	119	185	139	191	43	312	111	271	175	175	268	360	175	119	229		236	84

Tourism: 800/282-6863
Road Conditions: 860/594-2650

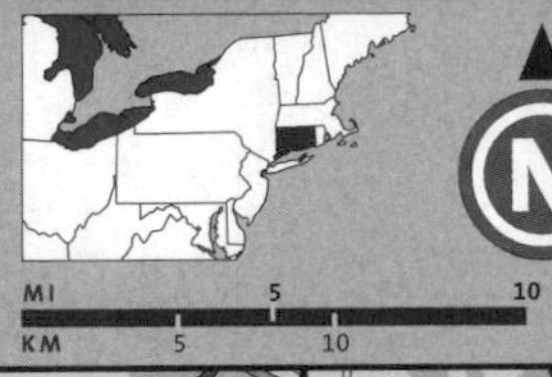

DRIVING DISTANCES IN MILES	BRIDGEPORT	DANBURY	HARTFORD	MERIDEN	MIDDLETOWN	NEW HAVEN	NEW LONDON	NEW YORK, NY	NORWICH	PROVIDENCE, RI	PUTNAM	SPRINGFIELD, MA	STAMFORD	STORRS	TORRINGTON	WATERBURY	WILLIMANTIC	WINDSOR LOCKS
BRIDGEPORT		31	56	37	44	19	64	60	72	118	100	81	21	75	54	33	79	68
HARTFORD	56	57		21	16	39	46	115	38	73	46	25	77	21	25	30	25	13
NEW LONDON	64	81	46	50	40	46		124	15	58	51	71	85	41	72	65	29	59
TORRINGTON	54	40	25	40	40	50	72	107	64	98	71	50	74	46		21	51	38
WATERBURY	33	31	30	20	25	30	65	99	60	118	76	55	53	51	21		56	43

Tourism: 800/441-8846
Road Conditions: 302/760-2080

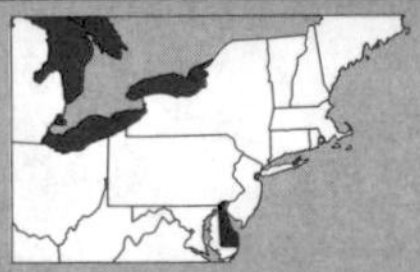

DRIVING DISTANCES IN MILES	BETHANY BEACH	DOVER	GEORGETOWN	HARRINGTON	LEWES	MILFORD	NEWARK	PHILADELPHIA, PA	REHOBOTH BEACH	SALISBURY, MD	SEAFORD	WILMINGTON
DOVER	55		38	17	42	21	41	74	43	56	36	44
NEWARK	94	41	78	57	81	60		44	83	97	76	14
REHOBOTH BEACH	13	43	18	31	10	24	83	116		46	35	86
SEAFORD	37	36	17	19	34	26	76	110	35	21		80
WILMINGTON	98	44	81	61	85	64	14	30	86	101	80	

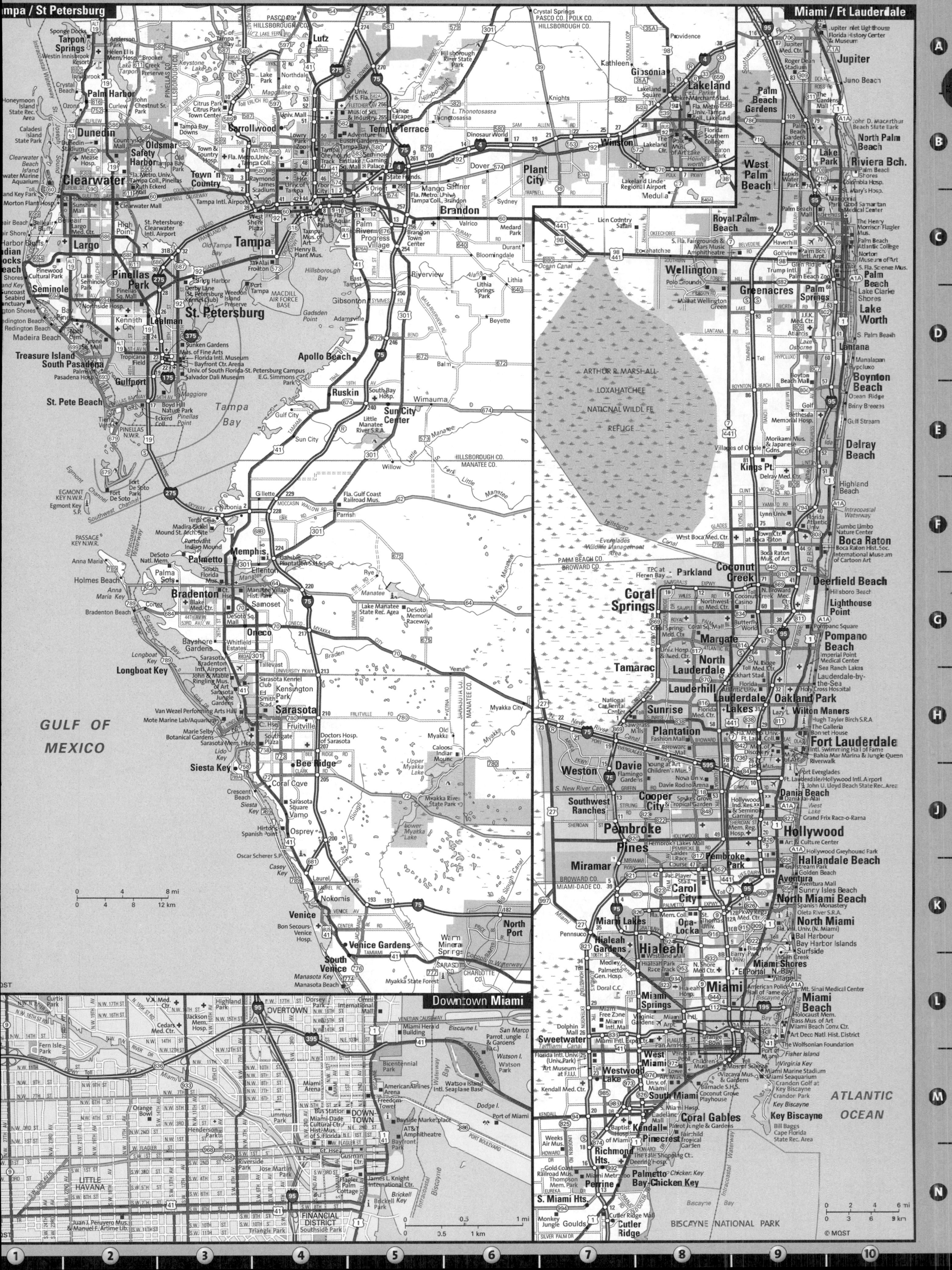
Tampa / St Petersburg
Miami / Ft Lauderdale
Downtown Miami
GULF OF MEXICO
ATLANTIC OCEAN
Tampa Bay
Clearwater
Tampa
St. Petersburg
Largo
Pinellas Park
Dunedin
Palm Harbor
Tarpon Springs
Oldsmar
Safety Harbor
Seminole
Brandon
Lakeland
Plant City
Bradenton
Palmetto
Sarasota
Venice
North Port
Siesta Key
Longboat Key
Apollo Beach
Ruskin
Sun City Center
Temple Terrace
Lutz
Gulfport
St. Pete Beach
Treasure Island
South Pasadena
Jupiter
Palm Beach Gardens
West Palm Beach
Riviera Bch.
North Palm Beach
Lake Worth
Boynton Beach
Delray Beach
Boca Raton
Deerfield Beach
Pompano Beach
Coral Springs
Margate
Tamarac
Fort Lauderdale
Plantation
Sunrise
Davie
Weston
Hollywood
Hallandale Beach
Pembroke Pines
Miramar
Hialeah
Miami
Miami Beach
North Miami Beach
Coral Gables
Kendall
Key Biscayne
Wellington
Greenacres
ARTHUR R. MARSHALL LOXAHATCHEE NATIONAL WILDLIFE REFUGE
BISCAYNE NATIONAL PARK
LITTLE HAVANA
OVERTOWN
DOWNTOWN
FINANCIAL DISTRICT
0 4 8 mi
0 4 8 12 km
© MQST

Tourism: 888/735-2872
Road Conditions: 800/475-0044

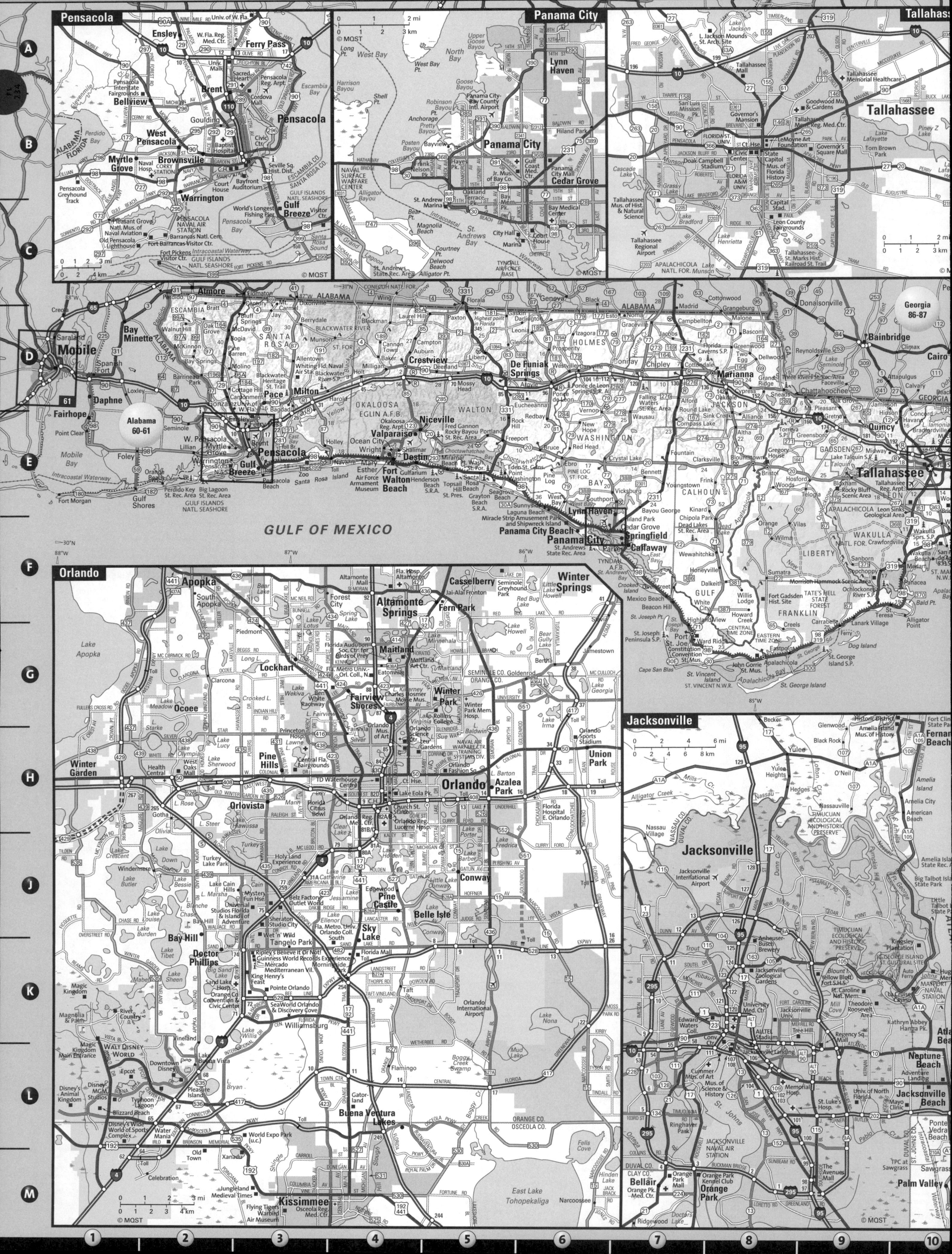

DRIVING DISTANCES IN MILES

	DAYTONA BEACH	FORT MYERS	FORT PIERCE	FORT WALTON BEACH	GAINESVILLE	JACKSONVILLE	LAKE CITY	LAKELAND	MELBOURNE	MIAMI	OCALA	ORLANDO	PANAMA CITY	PENSACOLA	ST. AUGUSTINE	TALLAHASSEE	TAMPA	TITUSVILLE
JACKSONVILLE	91	295	223	328	70		62	197	175	345	101	141	267	363	41	166	196	133
ORLANDO	56	155	120	425	117	141	157	56	72	232	80		364	460	103	262	82	40
PENSACOLA	455	589	567	39	349	363	306	471	526	681	383	460	102		405	200	474	497
TALLAHASSEE	258	392	369	166	152	166	109	274	329	483	186	262	104	200	207		277	300
TAMPA	138	123	172	440	132	196	172	37	142	274	95	82	378	474	185	277		121

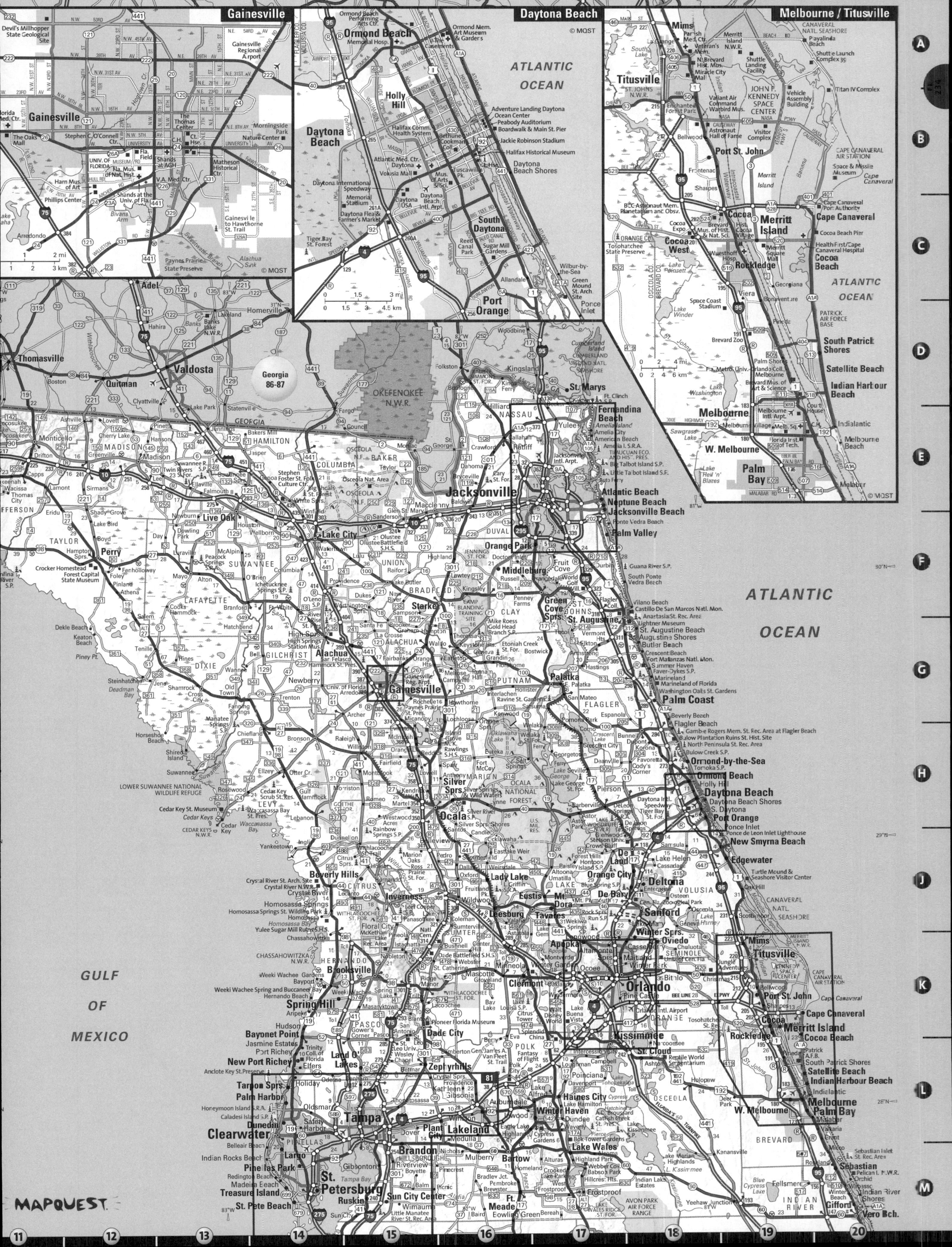

Tourism: 888/735-2872
Road Conditions: 800/475-0044

DRIVING DISTANCES IN MILES	FORT LAUDERDALE	FORT MYERS	FORT PIERCE	KEY WEST	LAKELAND	MELBOURNE	MIAMI	ORLANDO	ST. PETERSBURG	SARASOTA	TAMPA	WEST PALM BEACH
FORT MYERS	139		126	308	113	178	155	155	108	74	123	125
FORT PIERCE	102	126		288	122	57	122	120	197	150	172	57
MIAMI	23	155	122	168	236	179		232	259	225	274	67
ORLANDO	216	155	120	398	56	72	232		107	130	82	169
TAMPA	257	123	172	426	37	142	274	82	25	60		223

Atlanta
Acworth
Kennesaw
Marietta
Smyrna
Powder Springs
Austell
Mableton
Douglasville (part)
Alpharetta
Roswell
Sandy Plains
Sandy Springs
Dunwoody
Norcross
Duluth
Doraville
Chamblee
North Atlanta
Brookhaven
Tucker
Lilburn
Clarkston
Stone Mountain
Druid Hills
N. Decatur
Scottdale
Decatur
Belvedere
Avondale Estates
Pine Lake
Gresham Park
Panthersville
East Point
Hapeville
College Park
Forest Park
Riverdale
Union City
Fairburn
Red Oak
Campbellton
Ben Hill
Fair Oaks
Vinings
Chattahoochee River N.R.A.
Kennesaw Mountain National Battlefield Park
Hartsfield Atlanta International Airport
Stone Mountain Park
Fernbank Mus. of Nat. Hist.
Jimmy Carter Pres. Center
Martin Luther King Jr. N.H.S.
Turner Field
State Capitol
© MOST
0 1 2 3 mi
0 1 2 3 4 km

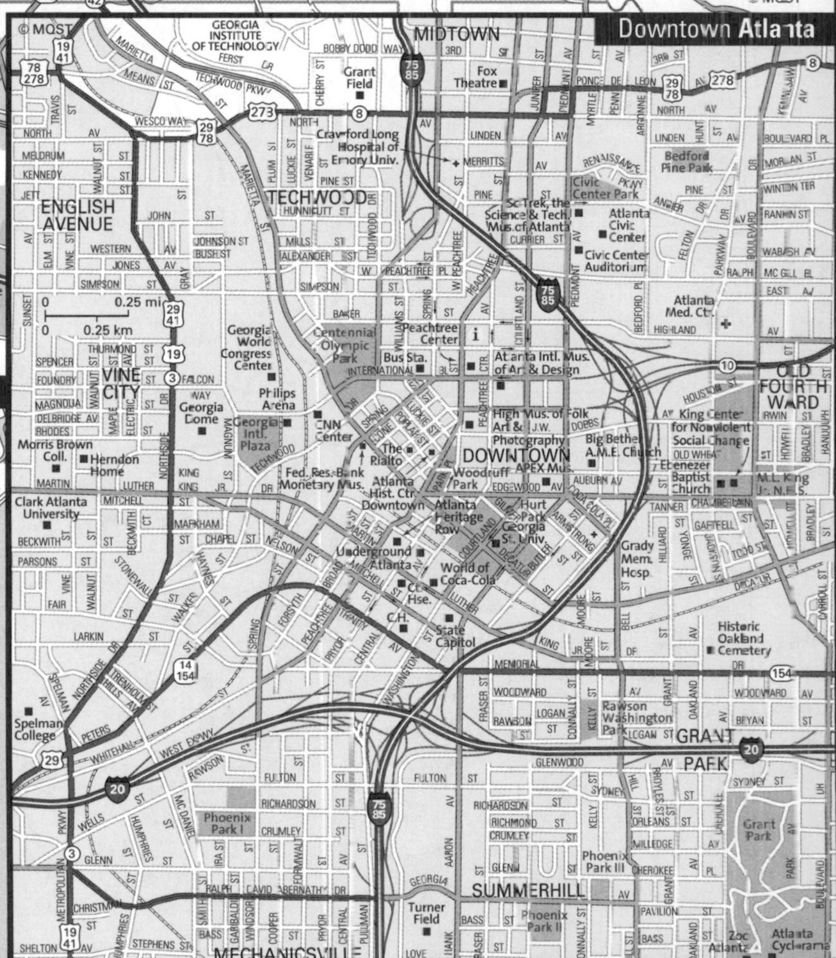
Downtown Atlanta
MIDTOWN
Georgia Institute of Technology
TECHWOOD
ENGLISH AVENUE
VINE CITY
DOWNTOWN
OLD FOURTH WARD
GRANT PARK
SUMMERHILL
MECHANICSVILLE
Georgia Dome
Georgia World Congress Center
Philips Arena
CNN Center
Centennial Olympic Park
Underground Atlanta
World of Coca-Cola
State Capitol
Turner Field
Clark Atlanta University
Morris Brown Coll.
Spelman College
Grady Mem. Hosp.
Historic Oakland Cemetery
King Center for Nonviolent Social Change
Fox Theatre
Atlanta Civic Center
Grant Park
Zoo Atlanta
Atlanta Cyclorama
© MOST
0 0.25 mi
0 0.25 km

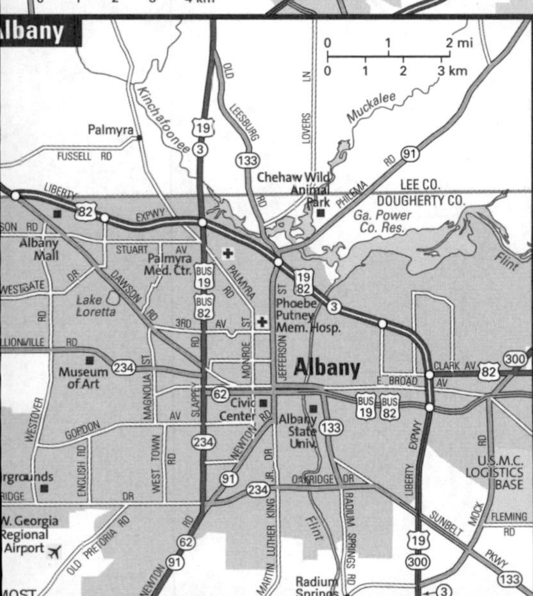
Albany
Palmyra
Albany Mall
Lake Worth
Museum of Art
Phoebe Putney Mem. Hosp.
Albany State Univ.
Chehaw Wild Animal Park
Muckalee Cr.
Flint
DOUGHERTY CO.
LEE CO.
U.S.M.C. Logistics Base
SW Georgia Regional Airport
Radium Springs
0 1 2 mi
0 1 2 3 km

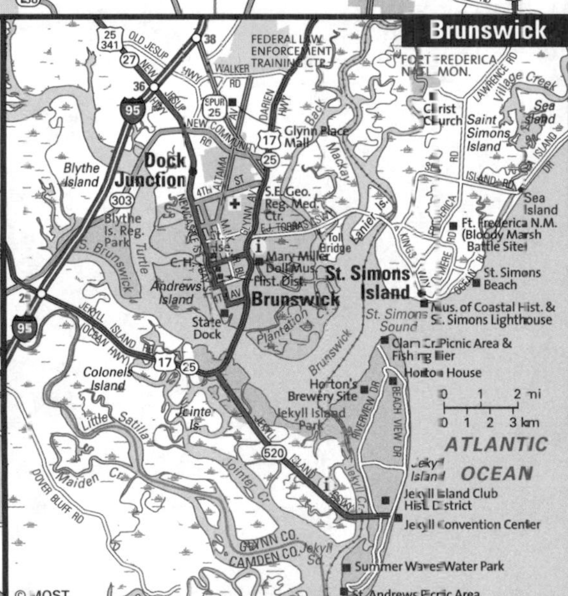
Brunswick
Dock Junction
Brunswick
St. Simons Island
Sea Island
Blythe Island
Andrews Island
Colonels Island
Jekyll Island
Fort Frederica Nat. Mon.
Ft. Frederica N.M. (Bloody Marsh Battle Site)
Mus. of Coastal Hist. & St. Simons Lighthouse
St. Simons Sound
Jekyll Island Club Hist. District
Jekyll Island Convention Center
Summer Waves Water Park
St. Andrews Picnic Area
ATLANTIC OCEAN
© MOST
0 1 2 mi
0 1 2 3 km

Tourism: 800/847-4842
Road Conditions: 404/656-5267

DRIVING DISTANCES IN MILES	ALBANY	AMERICUS	ATHENS	ATLANTA	AUGUSTA	BAINBRIDGE	BRUNSWICK	CHATTANOOGA, TN	COLUMBUS	DUBLIN	GAINESVILLE	LA GRANGE	MACON	ROME	SAVANNAH	STATESBORO	VALDOSTA	WAYCROSS
ATLANTA	180	129	70		149	236	308	113	106	139	56	69	84	66	249	211	228	253
AUGUSTA	226	206	97	149		282	194	266	249	95	136	212	123	219	135	81	274	184
MACON	102	83	89	84	123	159	225	201	95	55	142	114		154	165	127	151	159
SAVANNAH	246	226	225	249	135	248	78	366	244	114	307	279	165	319		53	168	106
VALDOSTA	90	119	239	228	274	80	120	346	183	139	287	226	151	298	168	173		62

Tourism: 808/973-2255
Road Construction: 808/536-6566

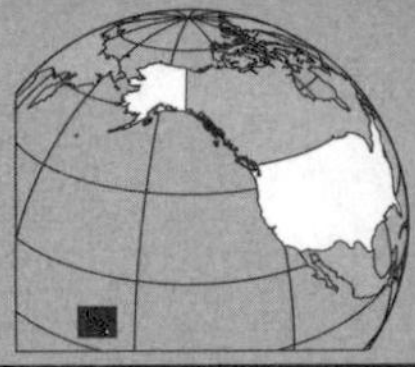

DRIVING DISTANCES IN MILES	HANA	HILO	HONOLULU	HOOLEHUA	KAHULUI	KAILUA	KAILUA-KONA	LAHAINA	LANAI CITY	LIHUE	WAHIAWA	WAIMEA
HILO	149*		217*	169*	121*	235*	88	142*	155*	319*	234*	54
HONOLULU	129*	217*		54*	101*	14	185*	92*	74*	102*	23	172*
KAHULUI	42	121*	101*	76		119*	109*	23	57	202*	118*	79*
KAILUA-KONA	137*	88	185*	157*	109*	203*		132*	143*	285*	202*	39
LIHUE	230*	319*	102*	156*	202*	120*	285*	225*	176*		119*	174*

* DISTANCE INCLUDES AIR TRAVEL

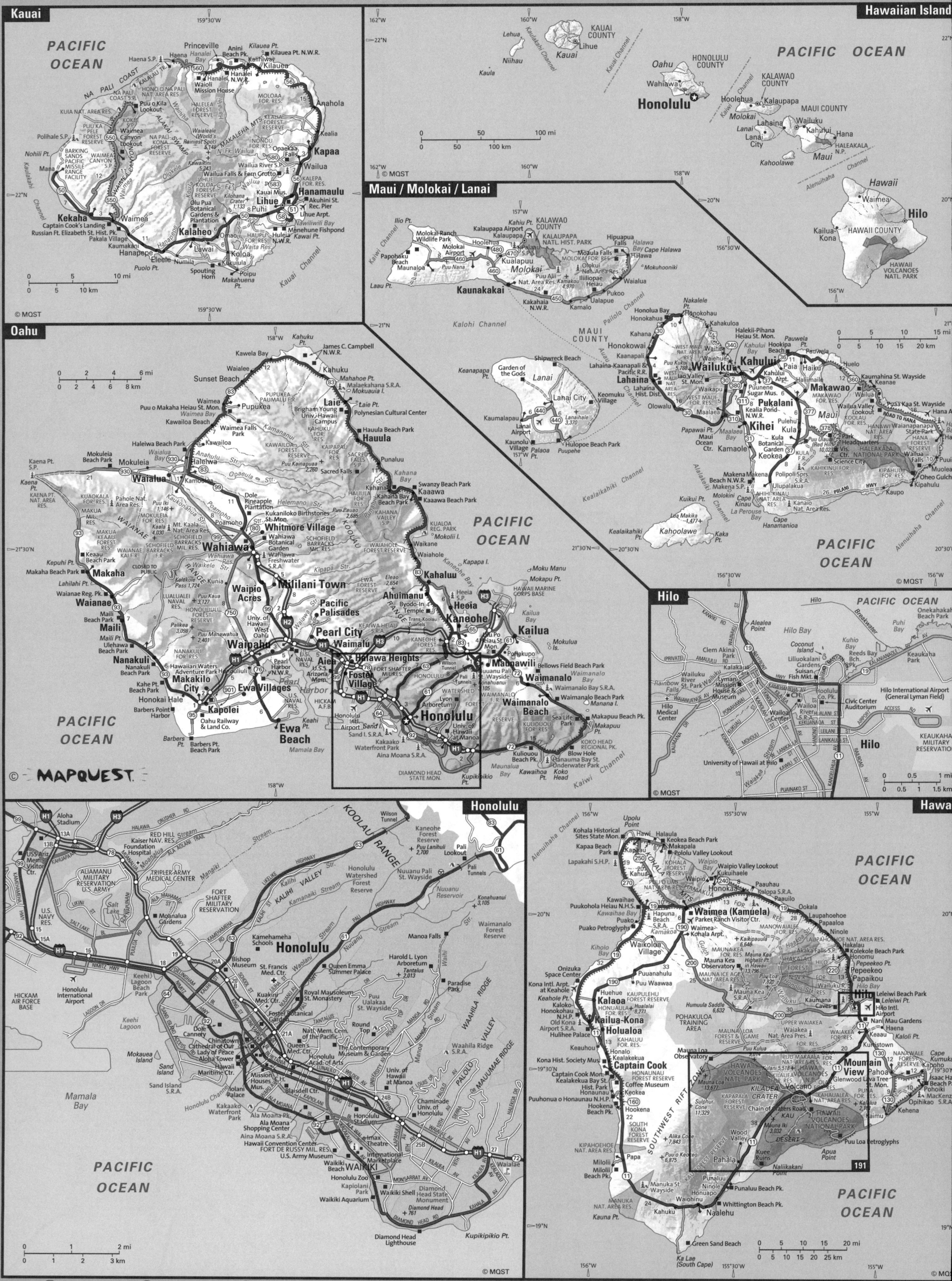

DRIVING DISTANCES IN MILES	BOISE	COEUR D'ALENE	GRANGEVILLE	IDAHO FALLS	KETCHUM	LEWISTON	MISSOULA, MT	MOUNTAIN HOME	POCATELLO	SALMON	SANDPOINT	TWIN FALLS
BOISE		406	202	288	163	270	374	49	241	247	452	134
COEUR D'ALENE	406	476	186	476	485	118	167	499	526	307	48	584
IDAHO FALLS	288	118	483		153	532	311	240	53	168	523	162
LEWISTON	270	526	74	532	477		221	363	555	337	166	448
POCATELLO	241		440	53	190	555	360	193		217	572	116

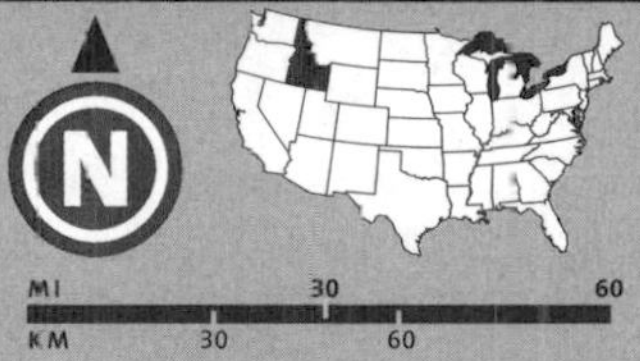

Tourism: 800/847-4843
Road Conditions: 208/336-6600
Road Construction: 208/334-8888

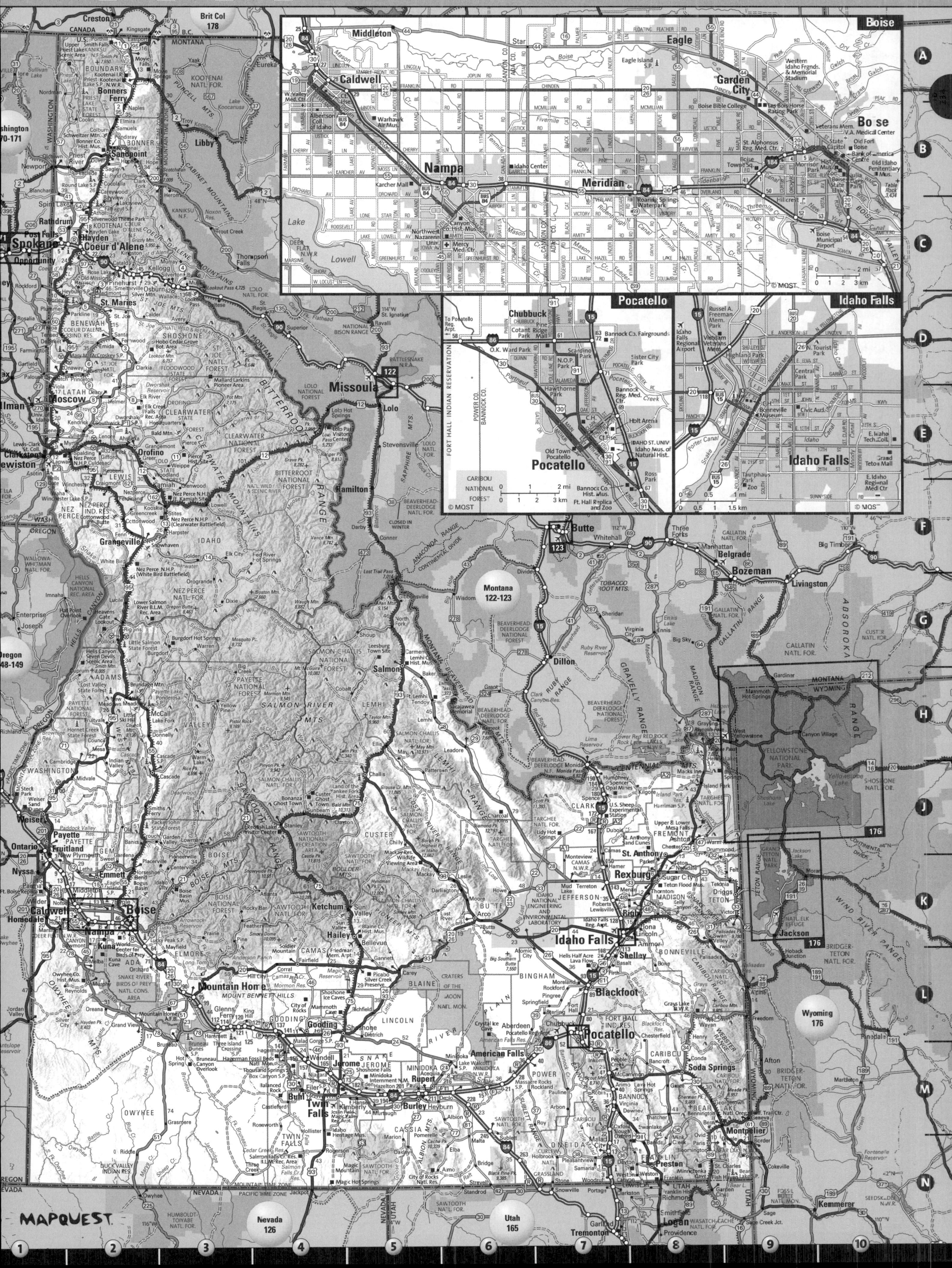

Tourism: 800/226-6632
Road Conditions: 312/368-4636

DRIVING DISTANCES IN MILES	BLOOMINGTON	CAIRO	CARBONDALE	CHAMPAIGN	CHICAGO	DECATUR	DUBUQUE, IA	EFFINGHAM	GALESBURG	JOLIET	KANKAKEE	MOUNT VERNON	PEORIA	QUINCY	ROCKFORD	ROCK ISLAND	ST. LOUIS, MO	SPRINGFIELD
CHAMPAIGN	54	241	199		141	52	263	77	141	115	79	145	94	197	189	191	179	87
CHICAGO	135	376	334	141		186	180	212	198	40	61	280	168	306	86	169	294	197
ROCKFORD	134	424	382	189	86	184	93	260	153	99	139	328	135	272		124	293	196
ST. LOUIS, MO	160	156	105	179	294	116	342	103	220	257	252	81	172	131	293	270		97
SPRINGFIELD	63	254	182	87	197	40	245	89	123	160	152	158	75	110	195	173	97	

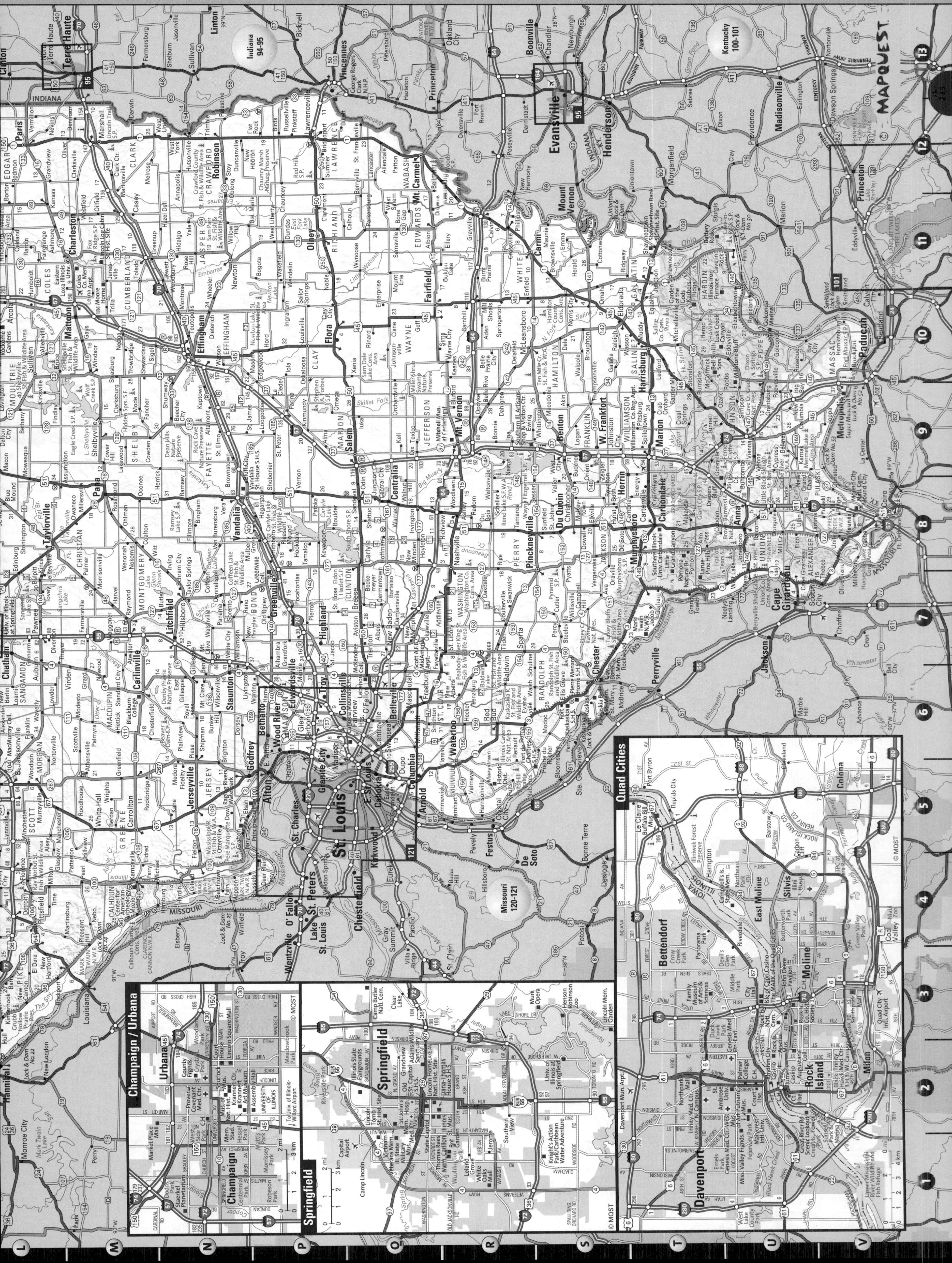

LAKE
MICHIGAN
Chicago
Waukegan
North Chicago
Gurnee
Lake Bluff
Lake Forest
Highwood
Highland Park
Deerfield
Glencoe
Winnetka
Wilmette
Evanston
Skokie
Northbrook
Glenview
Northfield
Lincolnwood
Niles
Morton Grove
Park Ridge
Des Plaines
Mount Prospect
Arlington Heights
Wheeling
Buffalo Grove
Lincolnshire
Libertyville
Mundelein
Vernon Hills
Round Lake Beach
Fox Lake
Lake Villa
Lindenhurst
Grayslake
Wauconda
Island Lake
Johnsburg
McHenry
Crystal Lake
Cary
Lake Zurich
Long Grove
Palatine
Inverness
Barrington
Algonquin
Carpentersville
West Dundee
Elgin
Hoffman Estates
Schaumburg
Streamwood
Bartlett
Hanover Park
Roselle
Itasca
Wood Dale
Elk Grove Village
Bensenville
Addison
Glendale Heights
Carol Stream
Bloomingdale
West Chicago
St. Charles
Geneva
Batavia
Aurora
North Aurora
Winfield
Wheaton
Glen Ellyn
Lombard
Villa Park
Elmhurst
Oak Brook
Westchester
Hillside
Maywood
Melrose Park
Oak Park
Forest Park
Berwyn
Cicero
Broadview
La Grange
Western Springs
Hinsdale
Clarendon Hills
Downers Grove
Westmont
Lisle
Naperville
Woodridge
Darien
Willowbrook
Burr Ridge
Countryside
Summit
Justice
Burbank
Bridgeview
Hickory Hills
Oak Lawn
Evergreen Park
Chicago Ridge
Palos Hills
Worth
Alsip
Blue Island
Calumet Park
Riverdale
Dolton
Calumet City
Harvey
Markham
Oak Forest
Midlothian
Crestwood
Palos Heights
Orland Park
Orland Hills
Tinley Park
Country Club Hills
Hazel Crest
South Holland
Lansing
Homewood
Flossmoor
Glenwood
Chicago Heights
Matteson
Richton Park
Park Forest
Steger
Crete
Sauk Village
University Park
Frankfort
Mokena
New Lenox
Joliet
Lockport
Crest Hill
Shorewood
Plainfield
Romeoville
Bolingbrook
Lemont
Homer Glen
Montgomery
Oswego
Boulder Hill
Hammond
East Chicago
Munster
Whiting
Dyer
Schererville
St. John

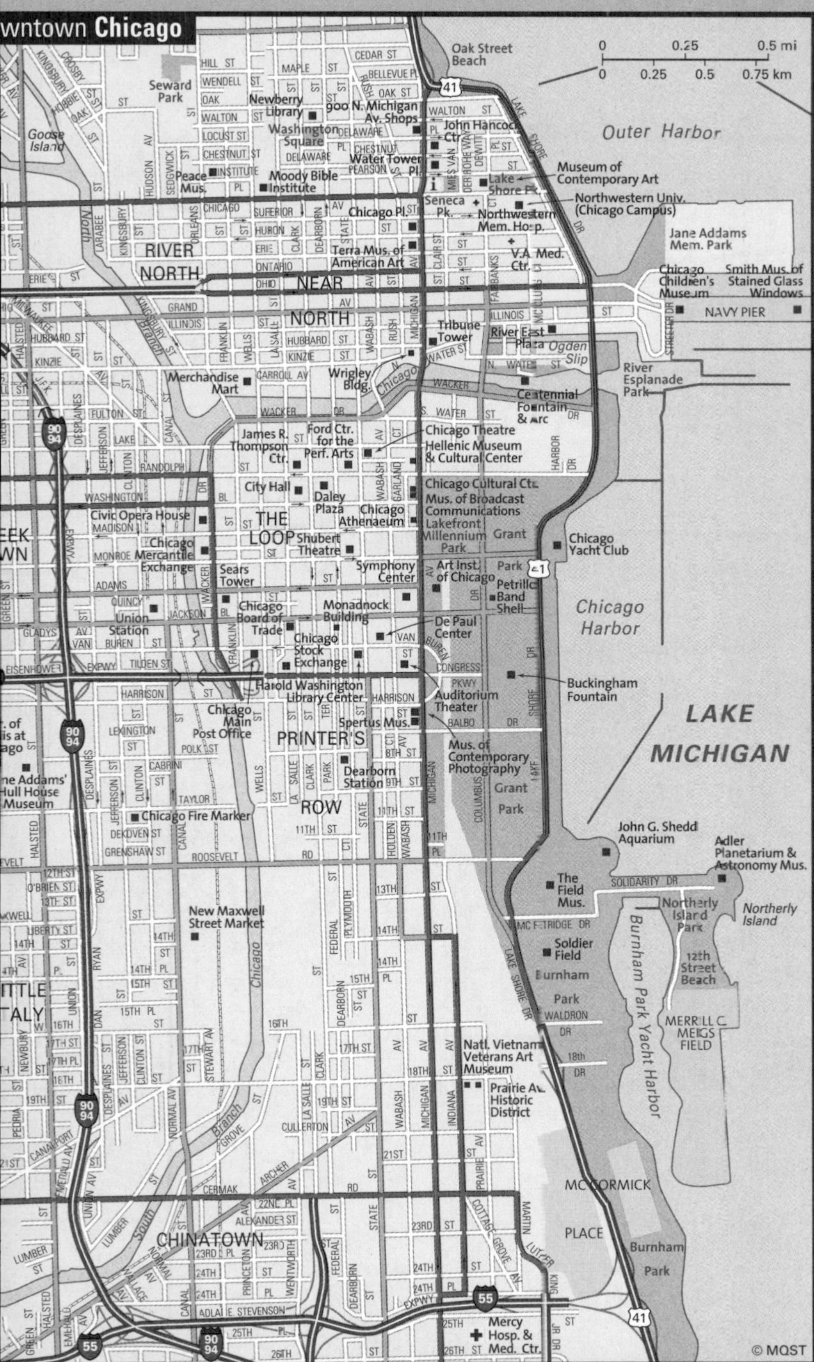
Downtown Chicago
LAKE MICHIGAN
Chicago Harbor
Outer Harbor
NAVY PIER
RIVER NORTH
NEAR NORTH
THE LOOP
PRINTER'S ROW
CHINATOWN
McCORMICK PLACE
Burnham Park
Grant Park
Burnham Park Yacht Harbor
Northerly Island
MERRILL C. MEIGS FIELD
© MQST

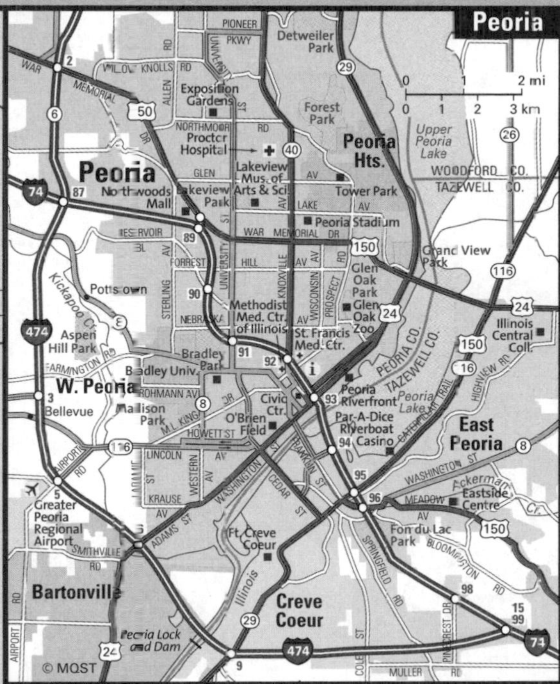
Peoria
Peoria
Peoria Hts.
W. Peoria
East Peoria
Creve Coeur
Bartonville
Bellevue
Upper Peoria Lake
© MQST

South Bend
South Bend
Mishawaka
Granger
Bertrand
MICH.
IND.
© MQST

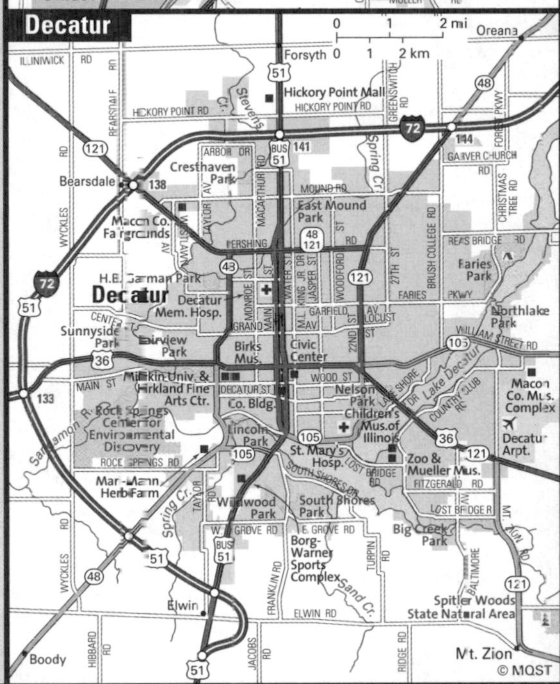
Decatur
Decatur
Forsyth
Oreana
Bearsdale
Elwin
Mt. Zion
Boody
© MQST

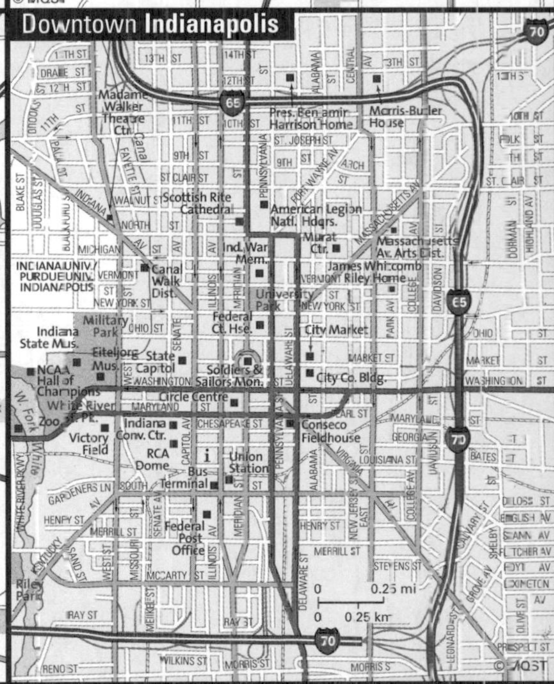
Downtown Indianapolis
Circle Centre
Union Station
RCA Dome
City Market
© MQST

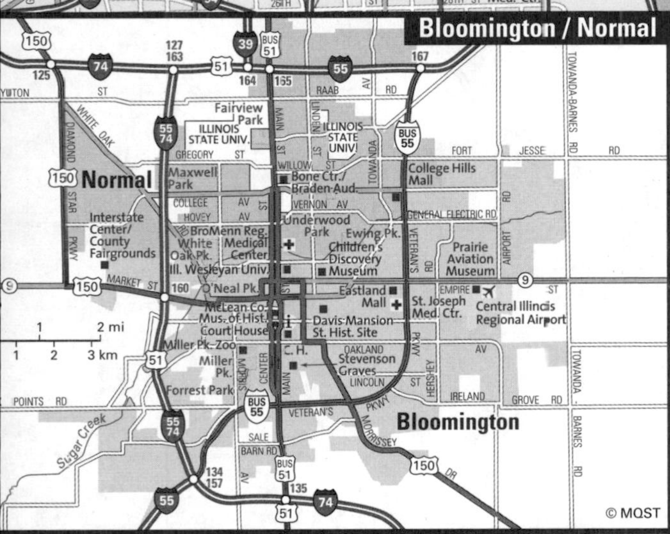
Bloomington / Normal
Normal
Bloomington
© MQST

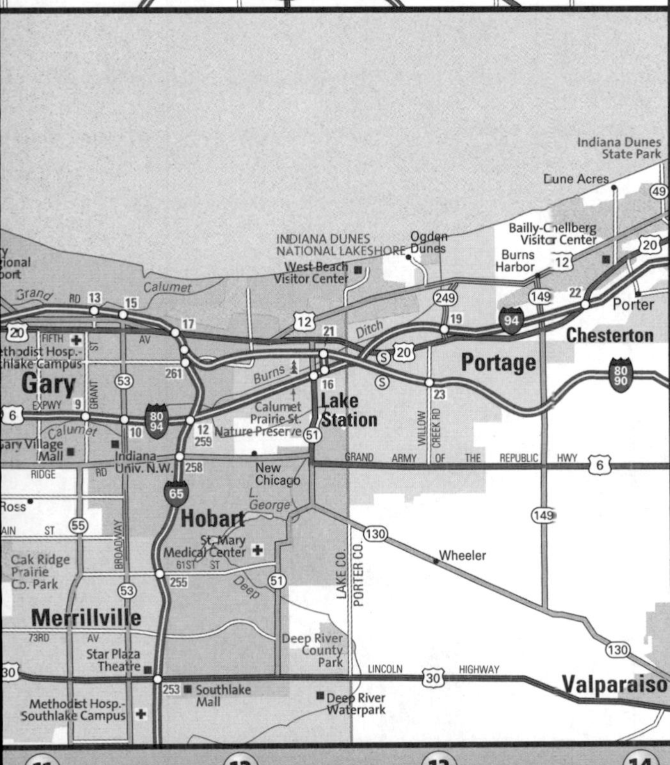
Gary
Portage
Chesterton
Porter
Lake Station
Hobart
Merrillville
Valparaiso
INDIANA DUNES NATIONAL LAKESHORE
Indiana Dunes State Park
Wheeler

Indianapolis
Indianapolis
Carmel
Fishers
Zionsville
Lawrence
Speedway
Brownsburg
Avon
Plainfield
Beech Grove
Cumberland
Clermont
Indianapolis International Airport
© MQST

Tourism: 800/759-9191
Road Conditions: 317/232-8300

DRIVING DISTANCES IN MILES	ANDERSON	BLOOMINGTON	COLUMBUS	CRAWFORDSVILLE	EVANSVILLE	FORT WAYNE	GARY	GREENSBURG	INDIANAPOLIS	KOKOMO	LAFAYETTE	LOUISVILLE, KY	MUNCIE	PLYMOUTH	RICHMOND	SOUTH BEND	TERRE HAUTE	VINCENNES
EVANSVILLE	211	117	175	164		296	324	195	166	219	194	114	228	281	241	305	107	51
FORT WAYNE	86	175	169	163	296		143	149	128	85	116	236	75	65	95	79	207	253
GARY	180	192	200	122	324	143		210	153	127	91	268	198	66	226	62	161	268
INDIANAPOLIS	43	47	45	47	166	128	153	55		52	66	112	61	114	74	138	77	123
SOUTH BEND	129	187	187	136	305	79	62	187	138	86	104	255	141	24	172		217	263

Tourism: 800/345-4692
Road Conditions: 515/288-1047

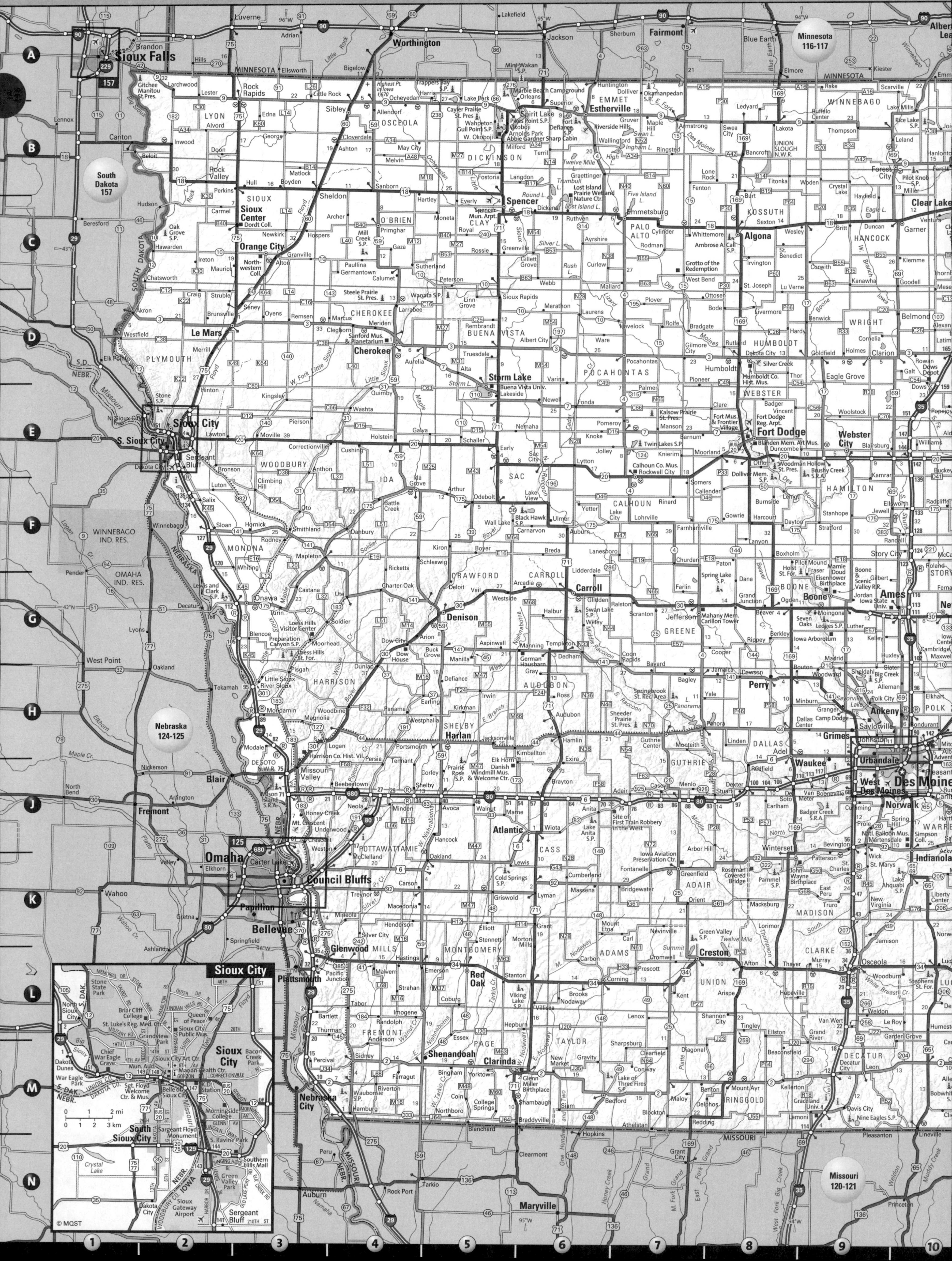

DRIVING DISTANCES IN MILES	AMES	BURLINGTON	CARROLL	CEDAR RAPIDS	COUNCIL BLUFFS	CRESTON	DAVENPORT	DECORAH	DES MOINES	DUBUQUE	FORT DODGE	IOWA CITY	MARSHALLTOWN	MASON CITY	OTTUMWA	SIOUX CITY	SPENCER	WATERLOO
COUNCIL BLUFFS	165	323	101	261		99	303	347	130	327	160	245	181	258	216	101	157	238
DES MOINES	34	157	90	129	130	81	171	215		196	94	113	49	126	85	202	188	106
IOWA CITY	136	82	195	28	245	195	59	131	113	84	196		98	157	83	316	267	78
SIOUX CITY	171	394	105	332	101	189	375	303	202	321	120	316	252	218	287		103	228
WATERLOO	95	157	160	53	238	189	137	79	106	93	108	78	58	79	125	228	189	

Tourism: 800/252-6727
Road Conditions: 800/459-7623

DRIVING DISTANCES IN MILES	ARKANSAS CITY	ATCHISON	COLBY	DODGE CITY	EMPORIA	GARDEN CITY	GREAT BEND	HAYS	HUTCHINSON	INDEPENDENCE	IOLA	KANSAS CITY	LAWRENCE	LIBERAL	MANHATTAN	SALINA	TOPEKA	WICHITA
DODGE CITY	141	107	315		238	52	83	106	120	270	264	333	298	83	232	164	271	153
KANSAS CITY	247	50	369	333	106	373	250	261	240	162	105		35	402	117	172	61	192
SALINA	151	160	200	164	118	204	81	93	68	206	187	172	137	247	72		111	92
TOPEKA	193	49	308	271	58	311	188	200	178	135	100	61	26	347	55	111		137
WICHITA	61	186	289	153	85	205	119	181	51	118	112	192	159	210	131	92	137	

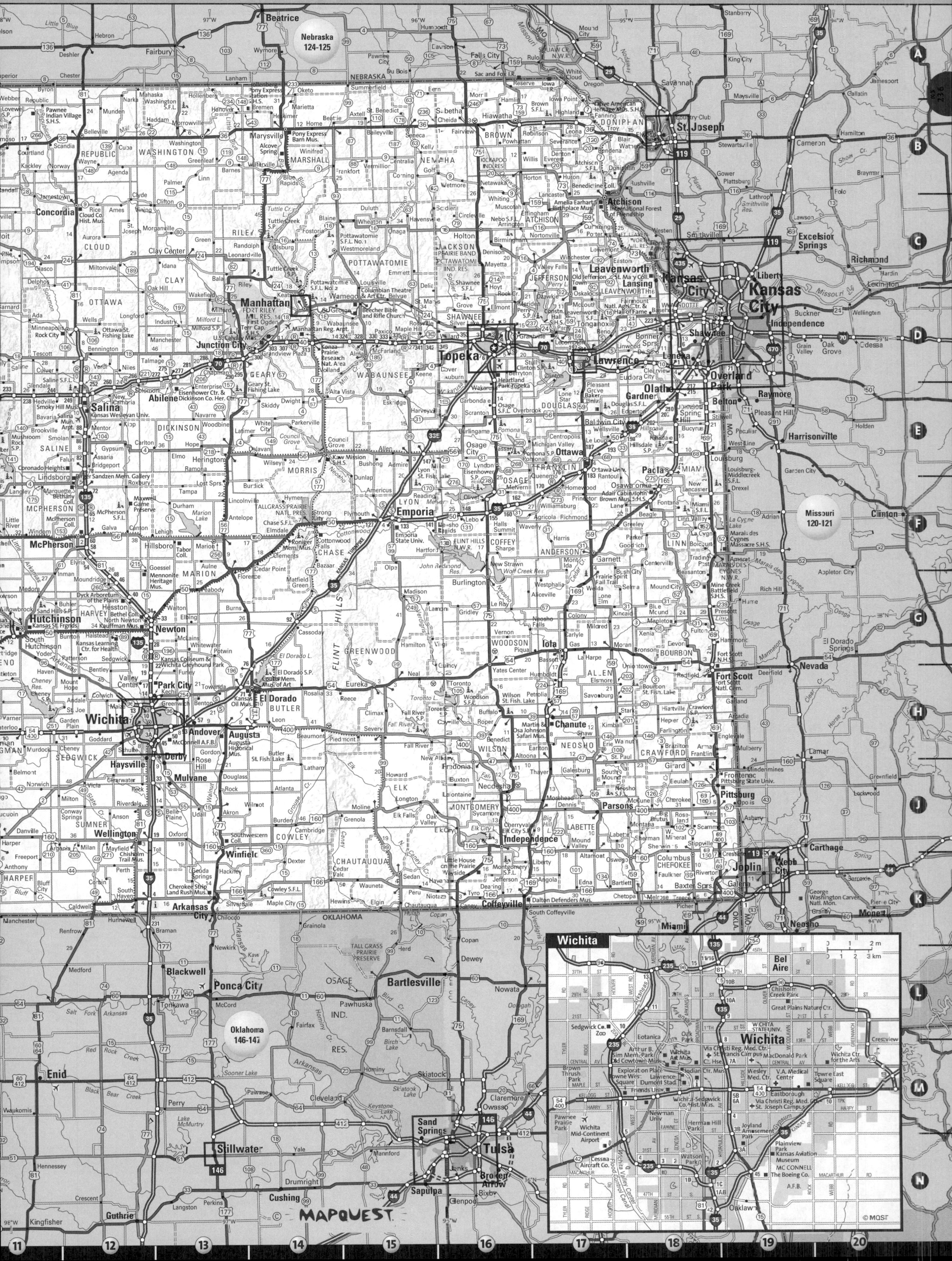

Tourism: 800/225-8747
Road Conditions: 800/459-7623

DRIVING DISTANCES IN MILES

	ASHLAND	BOWLING GREEN	CINCINNATI, OH	ELIZABETHTOWN	FRANKFORT	GLASGOW	HAZARD	HENDERSON	HOPKINSVILLE	LEXINGTON	LONDON	LOUISVILLE	MAYFIELD	MAYSVILLE	MIDDLESBORO	OWENSBORO	PADUCAH	PIKEVILLE
BOWLING GREEN	274		212	70	161	36	200	107	63	157	145	112	146	222	203	76	135	265
LEXINGTON	119	157	85	89	29	138	120	201	215		77	80	273	67	136	183	262	142
LOUISVILLE	194	112	100	44	54	92	194	123	170	80	156		228	141	214	109	217	217
OWENSBORO	300	76	206	95	161	111	275	30	80	183	221	109	138	248	279		127	323
PADUCAH	379	135	317	175	266	173	337	121	72	262	283	217	24	327	373	127		402

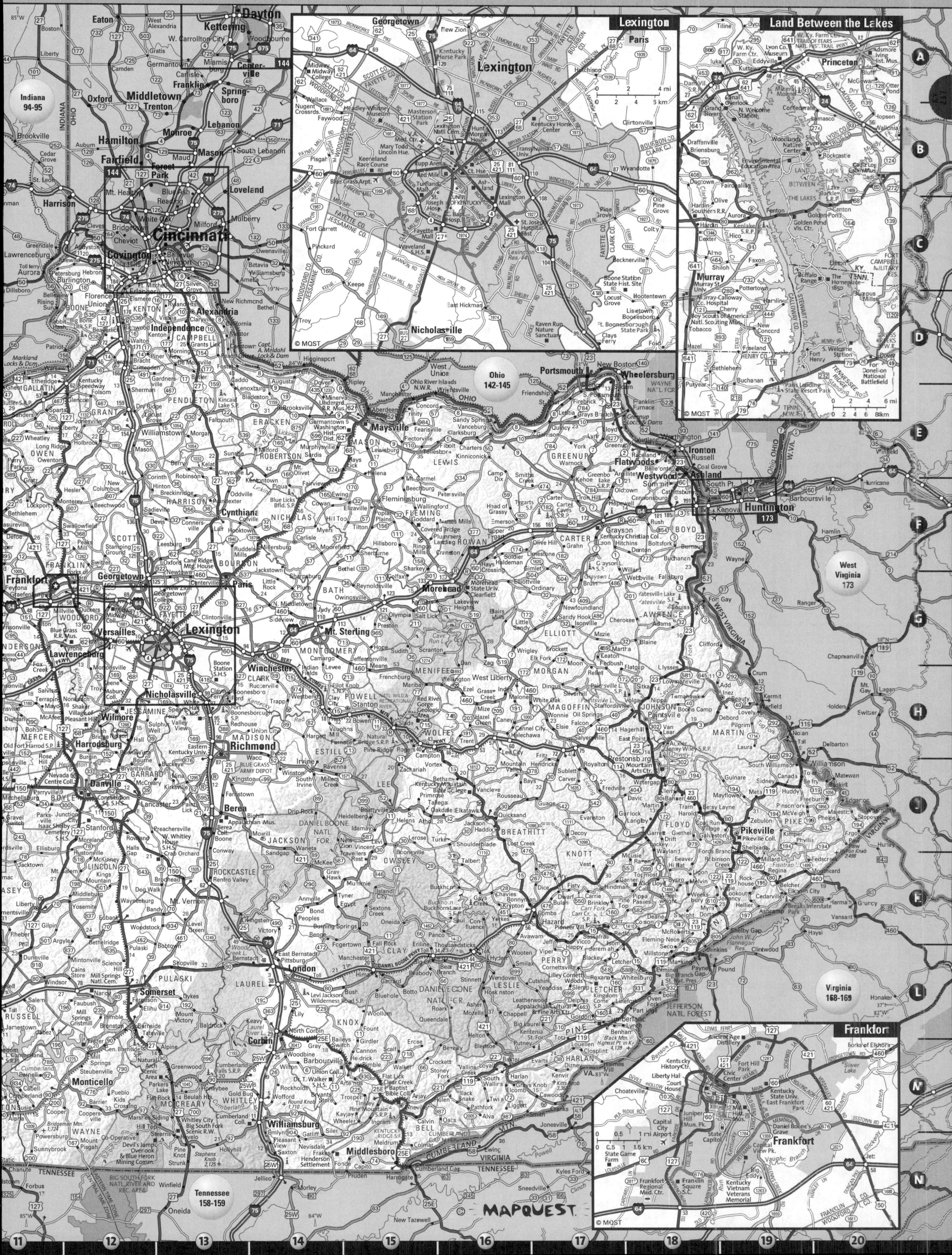

Tourism: 800/695-4064
Road Conditions: 225/379-1100

DRIVING DISTANCES IN MILES	ALEXANDRIA	BATON ROUGE	DE RIDDER	FERRIDAY	HAMMOND	HOUMA	LAFAYETTE	LAKE CHARLES	MONROE	NATCHITOCHES	NEW IBERIA	NEW ORLEANS	OPELOUSAS	RUSTON	SHREVEPORT	SLIDELL	TALLULAH	WINNFIELD
BATON ROUGE	140		176	104	51	101	60	132	188	195	79	91	80	233	251	97	163	188
LAFAYETTE	87	60	119	152	106	101		76	183	142	20	147	27	180	208	152	214	135
MONROE	96	188	170	85	248	283	183	196		100	202	302	156	37	103	298	55	64
NEW ORLEANS	227	91	262	191	57	57	147	219	302	282	166		167	339	348	31	247	275
SHREVEPORT	121	261	137	188	308	309	208	186	103	73	227	348	182	71		354	158	105

Tourism: 888/624-6345
Road Conditions: 207/624-3000

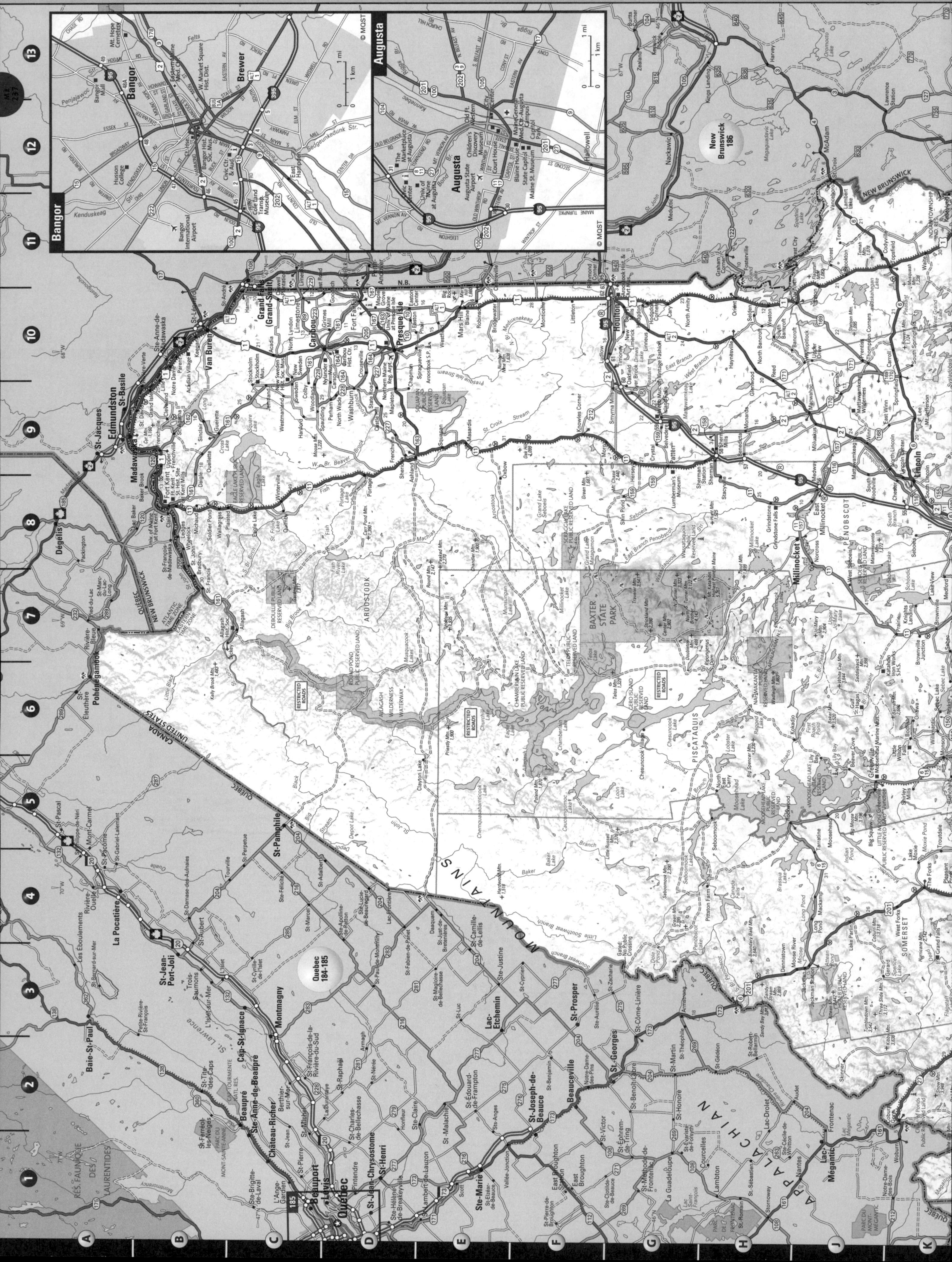

DRIVING DISTANCES IN MILES	AUGUSTA	BANGOR	BAR HARBOR	BRUNSWICK	CALAIS	FARMINGTON	FORT KENT	GREENVILLE	HOULTON	LEWISTON	MACHIAS	MILLINOCKET	PORTLAND	PORTSMOUTH, NH	PRESQUE ISLE	ROCKLAND	SACO	WATERVILLE
AUGUSTA		77	120	32	173	65	269	99	196	35	161	149	58	110	236	43	74	20
BANGOR	77		45	106	97	80	195	74	122	108	85	75	131	184	162	58	147	56
CALAIS	173	97	112	203		177	189	160	91	205	55	112	228	281	133	155	244	153
HOULTON	196	122	166	226	91	200	98	155		228	126	73	251	304	42	182	267	176
PORTLAND	58	131	175	27	228	81	324	153	251	36	216	203		53	291	78	16	84

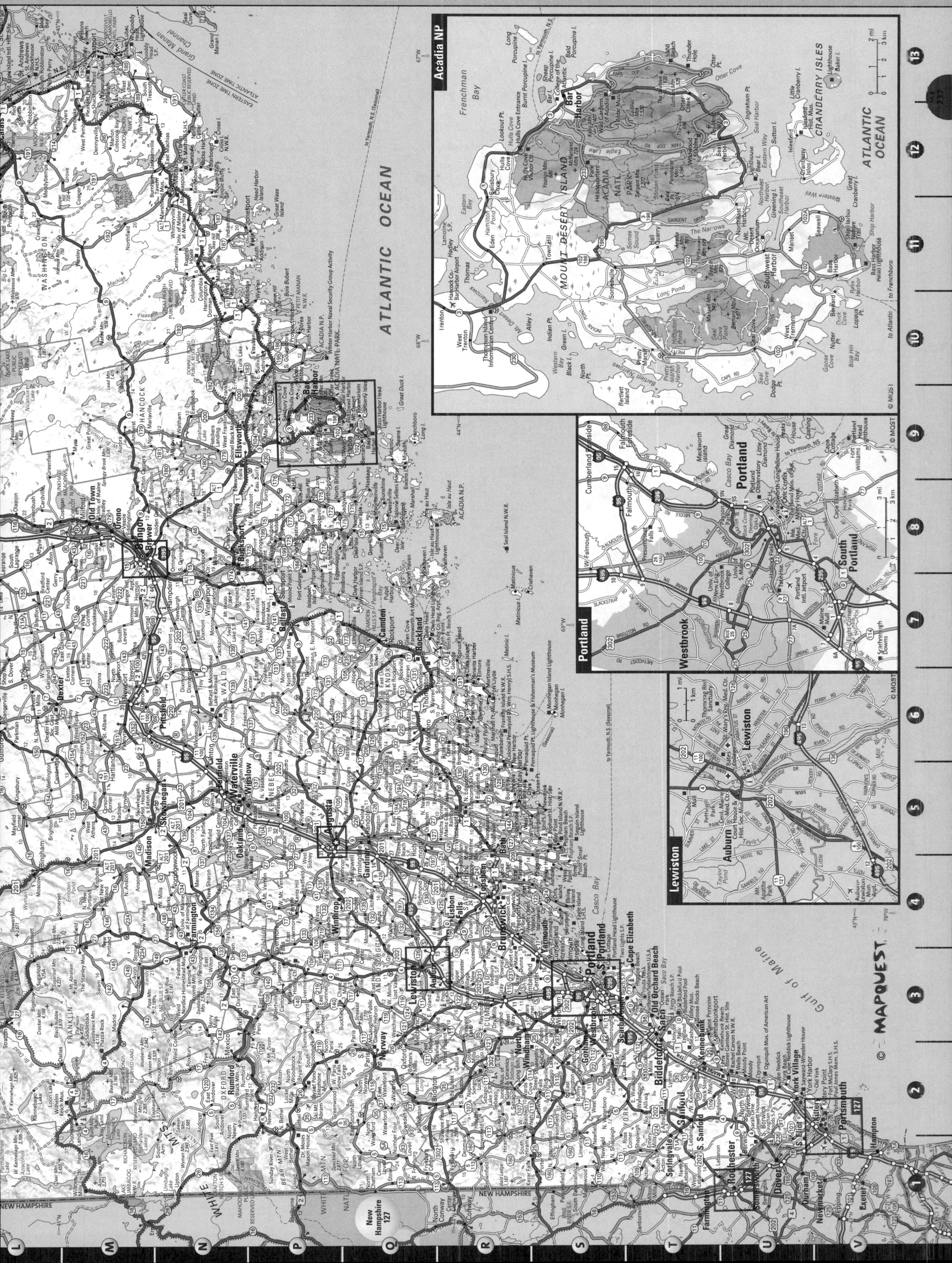

Tourism: 800/634-7386
Road Conditions: 800/327-3125

DRIVING DISTANCES IN MILES	ABERDEEN	ANNAPOLIS	BALTIMORE	CAMBRIDGE	CHESTERTOWN	CUMBERLAND	EASTON	FREDERICK	HAGERSTOWN	HANCOCK	LEXINGTON PARK	OCEAN CITY	POCOMOKE CITY	ROCKVILLE	ST. CHARLES	SALISBURY	WASHINGTON, DC	WESTMINSTER
ANNAPOLIS	54		25	55	45	162	38	73	98	124	66	108	112	47	47	83	31	56
BALTIMORE	35	25		78	68	140	61	51	76	102	95	131	135	45	57	106	38	39
HAGERSTOWN	109	98	76	153	143	67	136	28		29	142	206	211	54	103	182	70	50
SALISBURY	124	83	106	32	81	246	47	156	182	207	149	30	29	130	130		115	138
WASHINGTON, DC	71	31	38	87	76	134	70	44	70	96	63	139	144	19	25	115		53

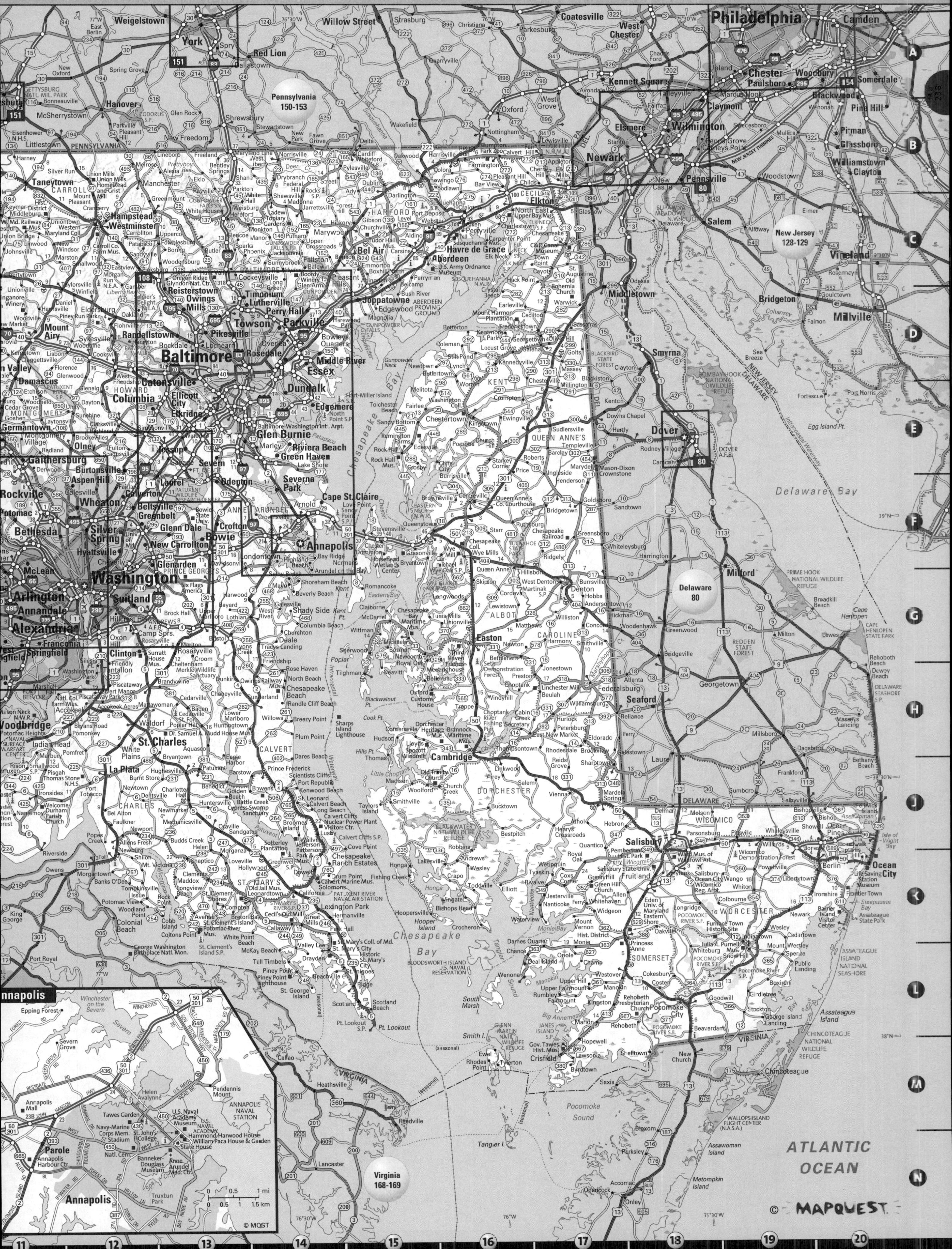

Downtown Baltimore
Baltimore
Towson
Reisterstown
Owings Mills
Pikesville
Randallstown
Cockeysville
Timonium
Lutherville
Parkville
Overlea
Carney
Perry Hall
White Marsh
Rosedale
Essex
Middle River
Dundalk
Edgemere
Catonsville
Woodlawn
Ellicott City
Columbia
Elkridge
Arbutus
Halethorpe
Lansdowne
Baltimore Highlands
Brooklyn Park
Linthicum
Ferndale
Glen Burnie
Jessup
Savage
Maryland City
Laurel
Severn
Odenton
Pasadena
Riviera Beach
Severna Park
Arnold
Cape St. Claire
Parole
Annapolis
Baltimore Washington International Airport
Chesapeake Bay
Patapsco
Upton
Otterbein
Little Italy
Fells Point
Federal Hill
© MQST

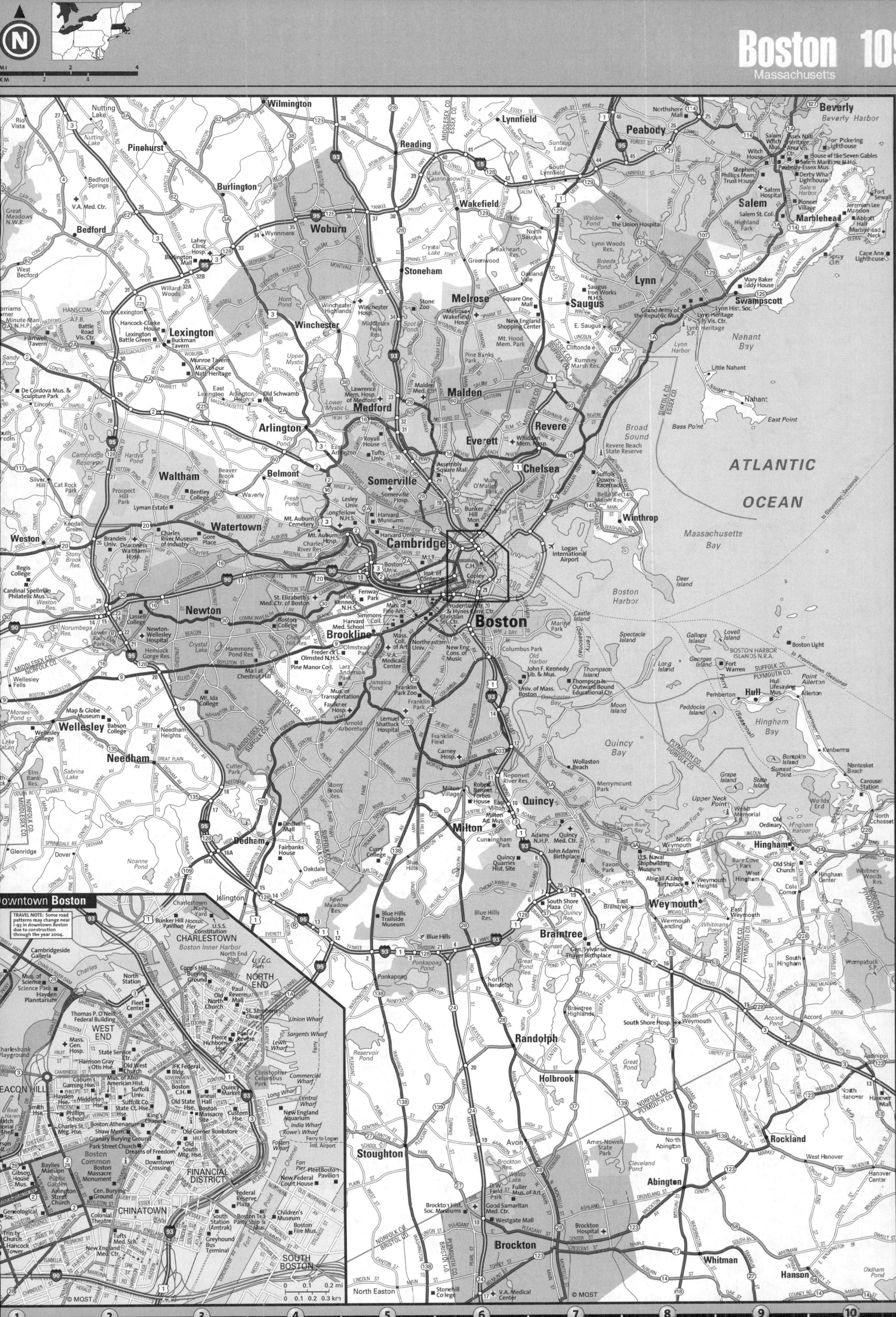
Wilmington
Lynnfield
Peabody
Beverly
Beverly Harbor
Reading
Pinehurst
Burlington
Woburn
Wakefield
Salem
Marblehead
Bedford
Stoneham
Melrose
Saugus
Lynn
Swampscott
Lexington
Winchester
Nahant Bay
Nahant
Medford
Malden
Arlington
Everett
Revere
Chelsea
Broad Sound
ATLANTIC OCEAN
Waltham
Belmont
Somerville
Winthrop
Watertown
Cambridge
Weston
Logan International Airport
Massachusetts Bay
Newton
Boston
Boston Harbor
Brookline
Wellesley
Needham
Hull
Hingham Bay
Quincy Bay
Quincy
Milton
Dedham
Hingham
Weymouth
Braintree
Randolph
Holbrook
Stoughton
Rockland
Abington
Brockton
Whitman
Hanson
North Easton
Downtown Boston
TRAVEL NOTE: Some road patterns may change near I-93 in downtown Boston due to construction through the year 2004.
CHARLESTOWN
NORTH END
WEST END
BEACON HILL
FINANCIAL DISTRICT
CHINATOWN
SOUTH BOSTON
© MQST

Tourism: 800/227-6277
Road Conditions: 617/374-1234

DRIVING DISTANCES IN MILES	BOSTON	BROCKTON	FALL RIVER	FALMOUTH	FITCHBURG	GLOUCESTER	GREENFIELD	HYANNIS	LOWELL	NEW BEDFORD	NORTH ADAMS	NORTHAMPTON	PITTSFIELD	PLYMOUTH	PROVIDENCE, RI	PROVINCETOWN	SPRINGFIELD	WORCESTER
BOSTON		26	53	72	49	35	93	72	31	60	133	105	140	41	52	117	95	46
NEW BEDFORD	60	38	16	41	101	95	136	45	86		189	137	172	43	33	91	127	78
PITTSFIELD	140	153	153	189	101	174	52	193	142	172	17	41		166	138	239	55	101
SPRINGFIELD	95	108	92	143	85	129	40	148	96	127	72	18	55	120	75	193		55
WORCESTER	46	59	58	95	31	80	58	99	44	78	97	65	101	72	43	144	55	

Tourism: 888/784-7328
Road Conditions: 800/381-8477

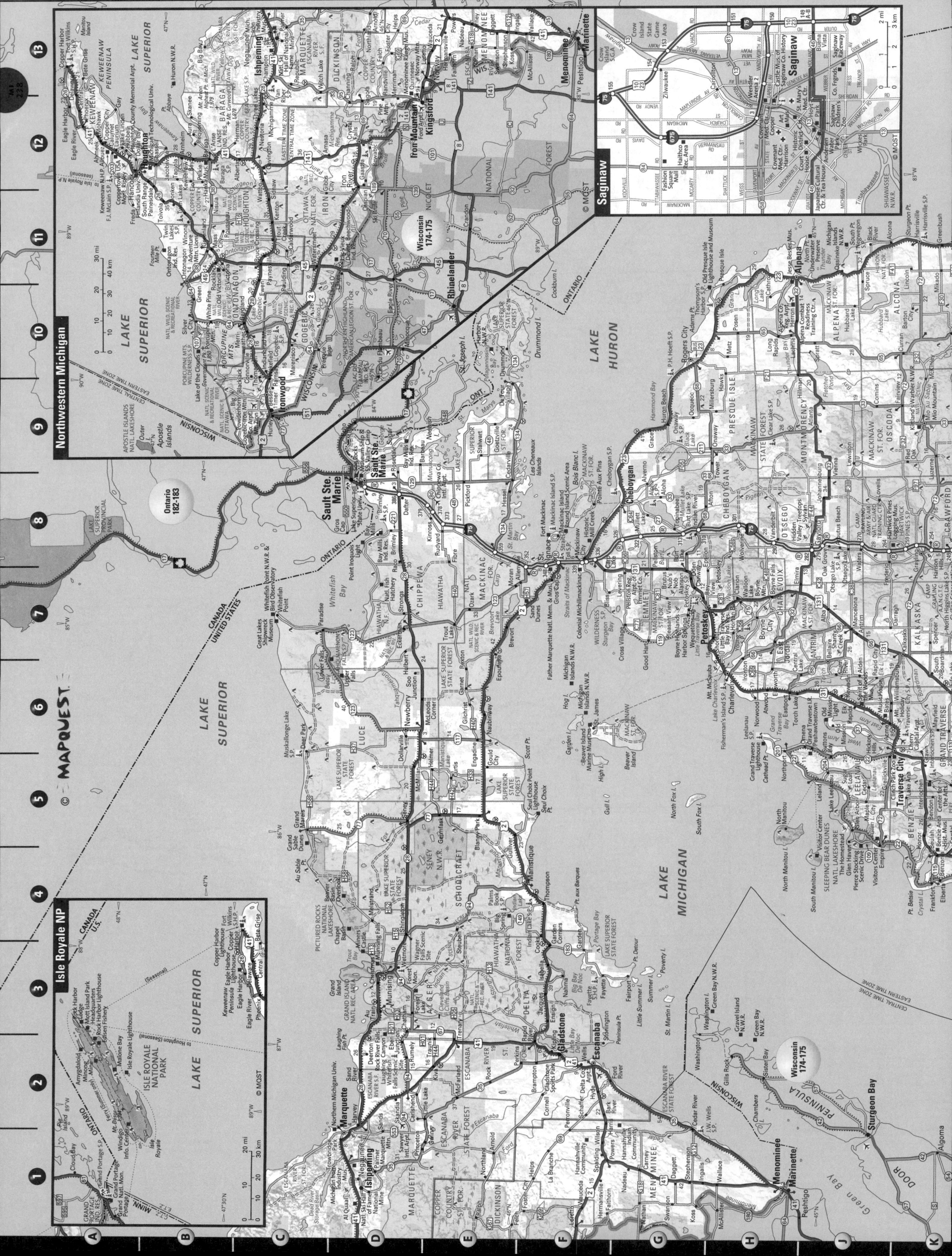

DRIVING DISTANCES IN MILES	ALPENA	ANN ARBOR	BENTON HARBOR	CADILLAC	DETROIT	ESCANABA	FLINT	GRAND RAPIDS	HOUGHTON	KALAMAZOO	LANSING	MACKINAW CITY	MARQUETTE	MUSKEGON	PORT HURON	SAGINAW	SAULT STE. MARIE	TRAVERSE CITY
DETROIT	242	42	186	209		438	62	153	556	136	86	291	455	191	58	97	346	257
GRAND RAPIDS	261	129	78	99	153	391	112		510	53	67	244	408	40	176	144	299	141
LANSING	230	63	126	131	86	375	53	67	493	76		228	391	105	117	86	282	173
MACKINAW CITY	94	281	323	145	291	149	230	244	268	302	228		166	248	293	198	57	106
MARQUETTE	257	444	487	309	455	65	393	408	102	466	391	166		412	457	361	163	269

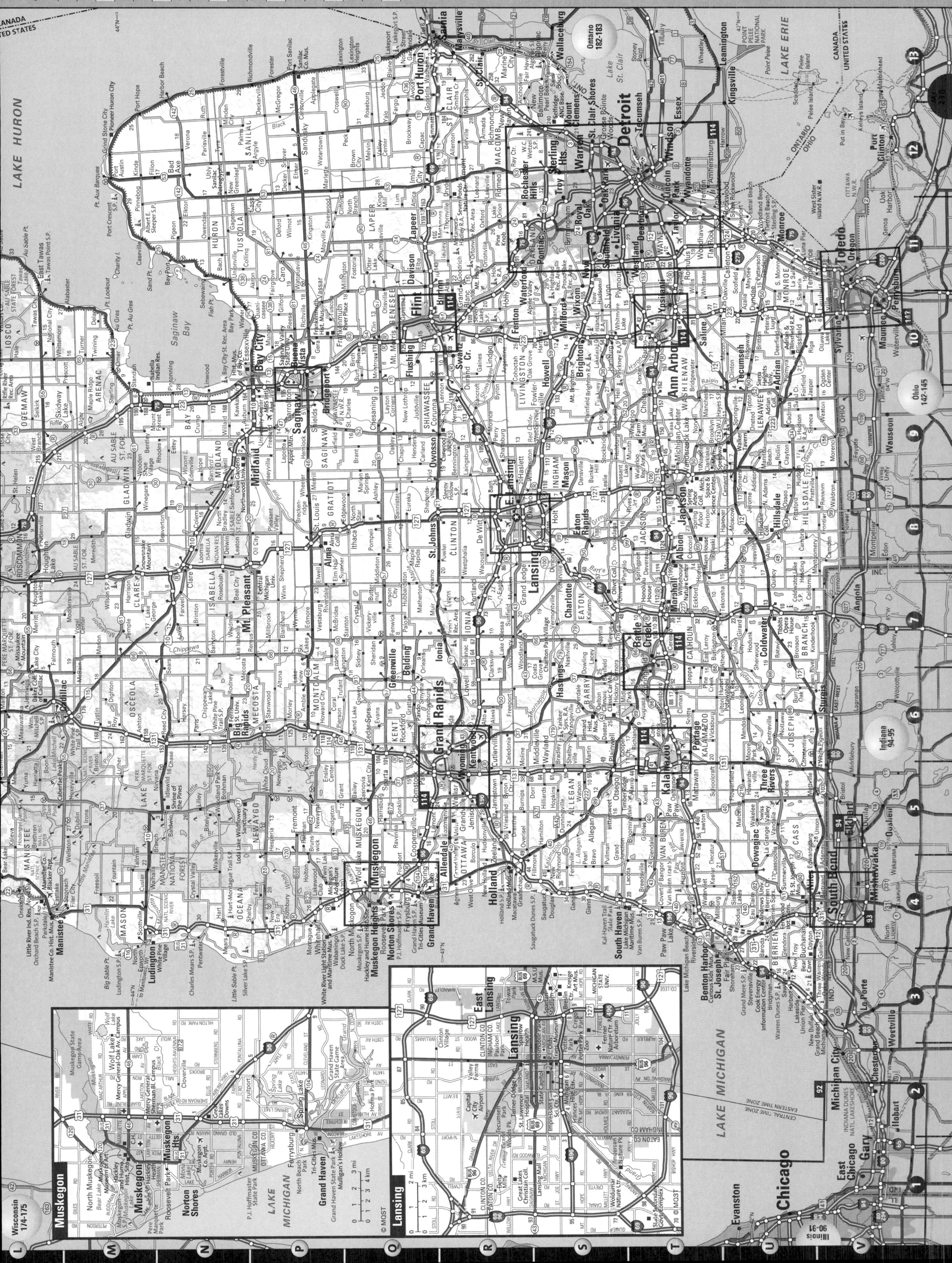

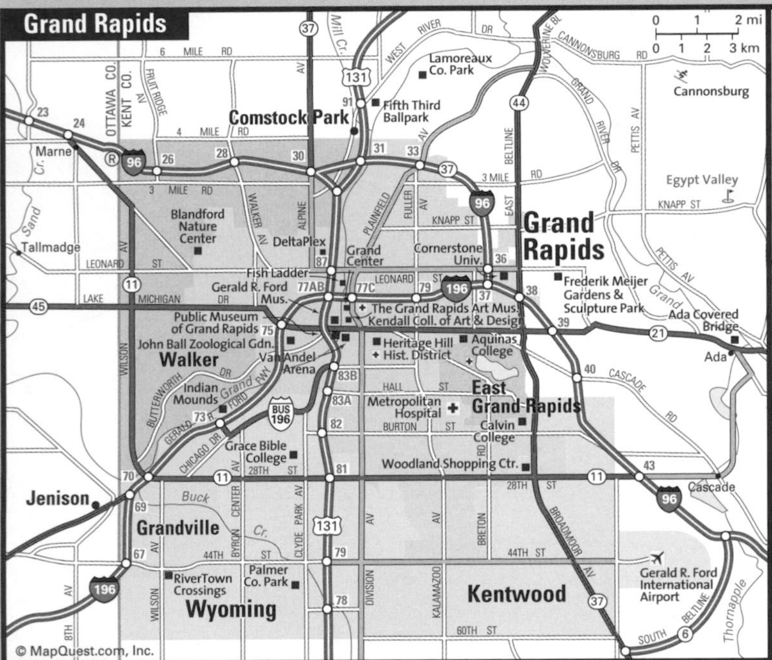
Grand Rapids
Comstock Park
Grand Rapids
Walker
Jenison
Grandville
Wyoming
Kentwood
East Grand Rapids
Cascade
Cannonsburg
Ada
Marne
Tallmadge
Gerald R. Ford International Airport
© MapQuest.com, Inc.

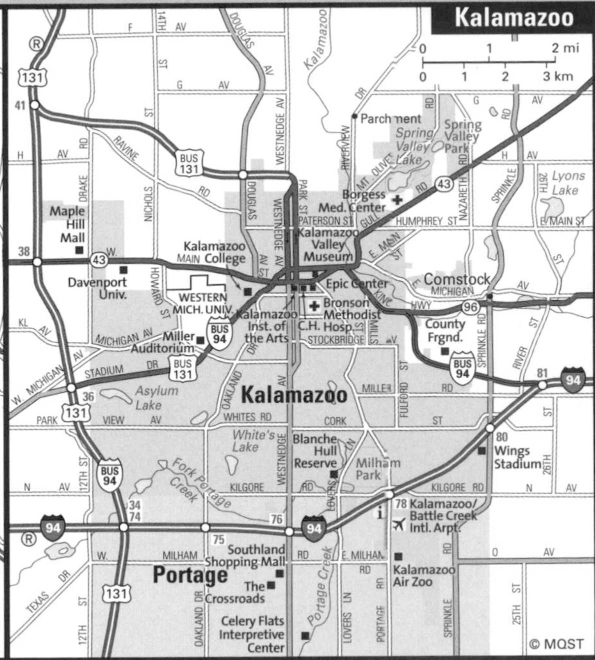
Kalamazoo
Kalamazoo
Portage
Comstock
Western Mich. Univ.
Kalamazoo/Battle Creek Intl. Arpt.
© MQST

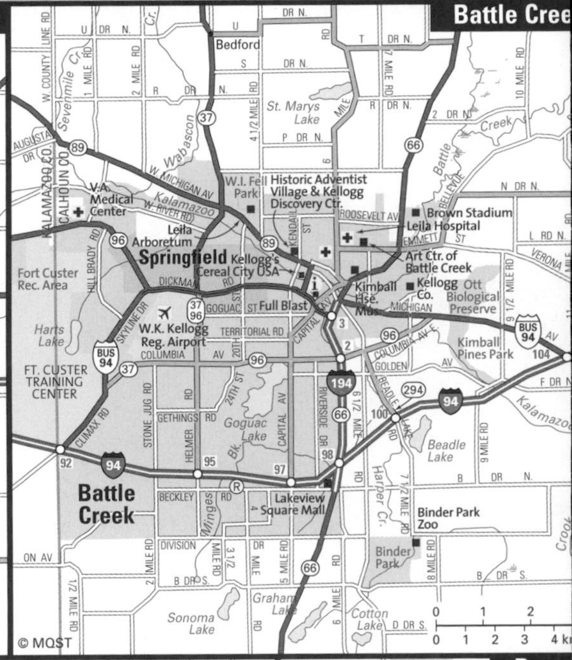
Battle Creek
Battle Creek
Springfield
Bedford
W.K. Kellogg Reg. Airport
© MQST

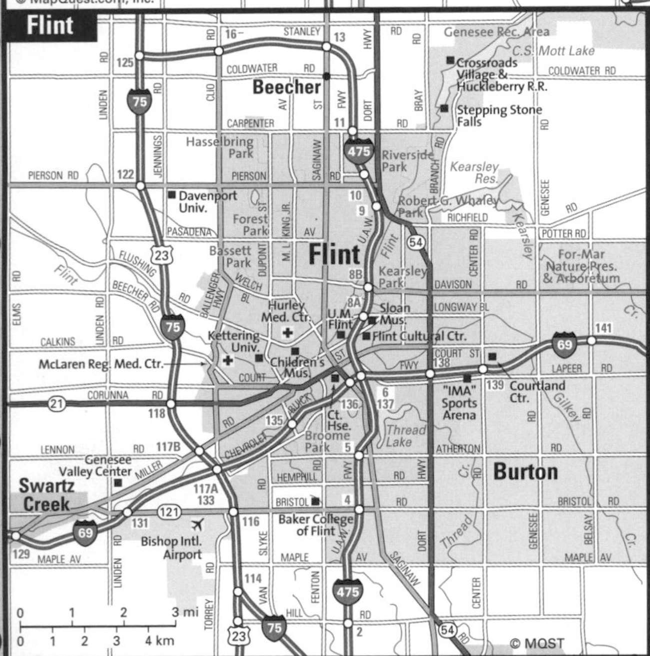
Flint
Beecher
Flint
Burton
Swartz Creek
Bishop Intl. Airport
© MQST

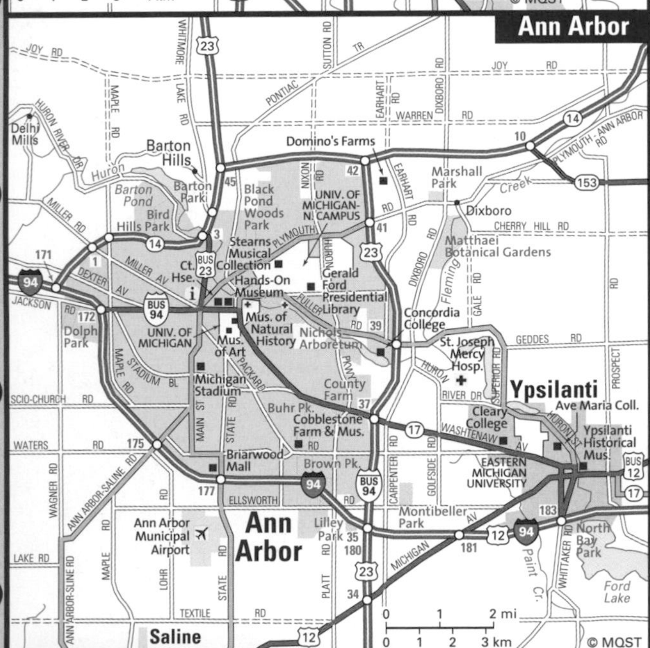
Ann Arbor
Barton Hills
Ann Arbor
Ypsilanti
Saline
Delhi Mills
Ann Arbor Municipal Airport
© MQST

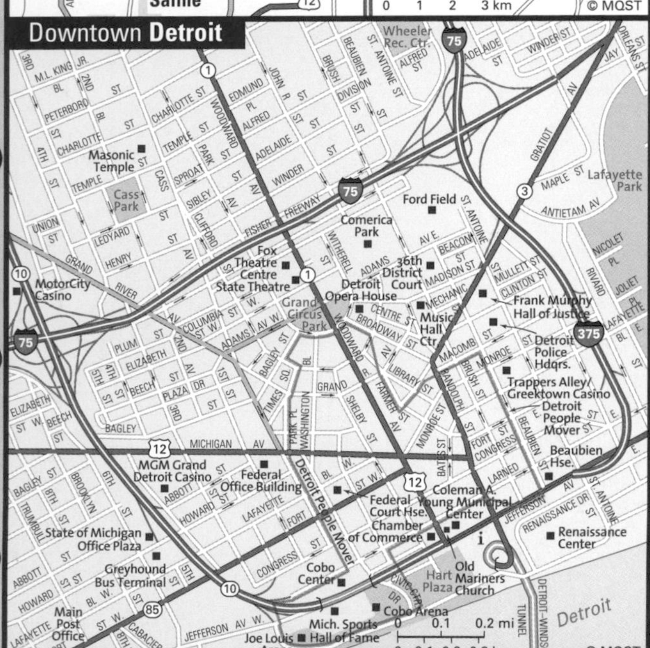
Downtown Detroit
Ford Field
Comerica Park
Fox Theatre
Cobo Center
Greektown Casino
MGM Grand Detroit Casino
MotorCity Casino
© MQST

Detroit
Waterford
Clarkston
Pontiac
Drayton Plains
Auburn Hills
Rochester
Rochester Hills
Union Lake
Swartz Creek
Sterling Heights
Troy
Birmingham
Clawson
Madison Heights
Walled Lake
Farmington Hills
Novi
Farmington
Southfield
Royal Oak
Warren
Roseville
Fraser
St. Clair Shores
Center Line
Hazel Park
Oak Park
Ferndale
Northville
Livonia
Redford
Plymouth
Westland
Garden City
Dearborn Heights
Detroit
Highland Park
Hamtramck
Dearborn
Inkster
Wayne
Romulus
Taylor
Allen Park
Melvindale
Lincoln Park
River Rouge
Ecorse
Southgate
Wyandotte
Riverview
Trenton
Woodhaven
Flat Rock
Grosse Ile
Gibraltar
Eastpointe
Harper Woods
Grosse Pointe
Windsor
La Salle
Amherstburg
Essex
Tecumseh
Sandwich South-Tecumseh-St. Clair Beach
Macomb
Utica
Washington
Mount Clemens
Detroit Metro. Wayne County Airport
© MQST

Ramsey
Anoka
Andover
Ham Lake
Dayton
Champlin
Coon Rapids
Blaine
Lino Lakes
Hugo
Brooklyn Park
Maple Grove
Osseo
Spring Lake Park
Mounds View
Shoreview
Brooklyn Center
Fridley
North Oaks
Vadnais Heights
Mahtomedi
White Bear Lake
Stillwater
Oak Park Heights
Plymouth
New Hope
Crystal
Robbinsdale
Columbia Hts.
New Brighton
St. Anthony
Roseville
Little Canada
Maplewood
North St. Paul
Golden Valley
Falcon Heights
Lauderdale
Oakdale
Lake Elmo
St. Louis Park
St. Paul
Minnetonka
Deephaven
Hopkins
Minneapolis
Woodbury
Edina
Richfield
Mendota Heights
West St. Paul
South St. Paul
Eden Prairie
Bloomington
Eagan
Inver Grove Heights
Newport
St. Paul Park
Cottage Grove
Shakopee
Burnsville
Savage
Prior Lake
Apple Valley
Rosemount
Lakeville
Hastings
Coates
Downtown Minneapolis
Downtown St Paul
© MQST

Tourism: 800/657-3700
Road Conditions: 800/542-0220

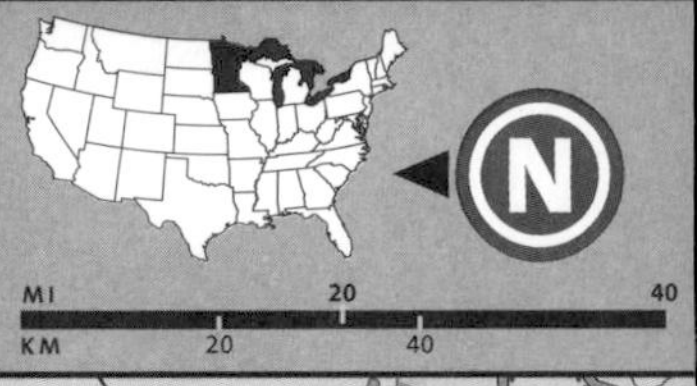

DRIVING DISTANCES IN MILES	ALBERT LEA	BEMIDJI	BRAINERD	DULUTH	FERGUS FALLS	GRAND FORKS, ND	INTERNATIONAL FALLS	MANKATO	MARSHALL	MINNEAPOLIS	MOORHEAD	ROCHESTER	ST. CLOUD	ST. PAUL	VIRGINIA	WILLMAR	WINONA	WORTHINGTON
DULUTH	251	153	116		210	264	157	239	274	158	257	239	149	154	61	206	216	362
MINNEAPOLIS	96	225	129	158	176	312	290	78	148		230	88	64	10	193	92	120	207
MOORHEAD	325	133	141	257	55	80	242	294	220	230		317	172	239	229	168	351	298
ROCHESTER	62	311	215	239	262	399	371	80	185	88	317		151	80	274	177	51	174
ST. CLOUD	159	157	62	149	117	254	251	128	131	64	172	151		73	184	63	185	201

Tourism: 800/927-6378
Road Conditions: 601/359-7017

DRIVING DISTANCES IN MILES	BILOXI	COLUMBUS	GREENVILLE	HATTIESBURG	JACKSON	MEMPHIS, TN	MERIDIAN	NATCHEZ	NEW ORLEANS, LA	TUPELO	VICKSBURG	WINONA
BILOXI		262	297	82	172	379	171	231	93	317	214	262
GREENVILLE	297	164		215	125	148	216	157	310	172	89	82
JACKSON	172	153	125	90		211	91	102	185	175	42	94
MERIDIAN	171	91	216	89	91	234		194	201	146	133	113
TUPELO	317	66	172	235	175	109	146	269	347		213	99

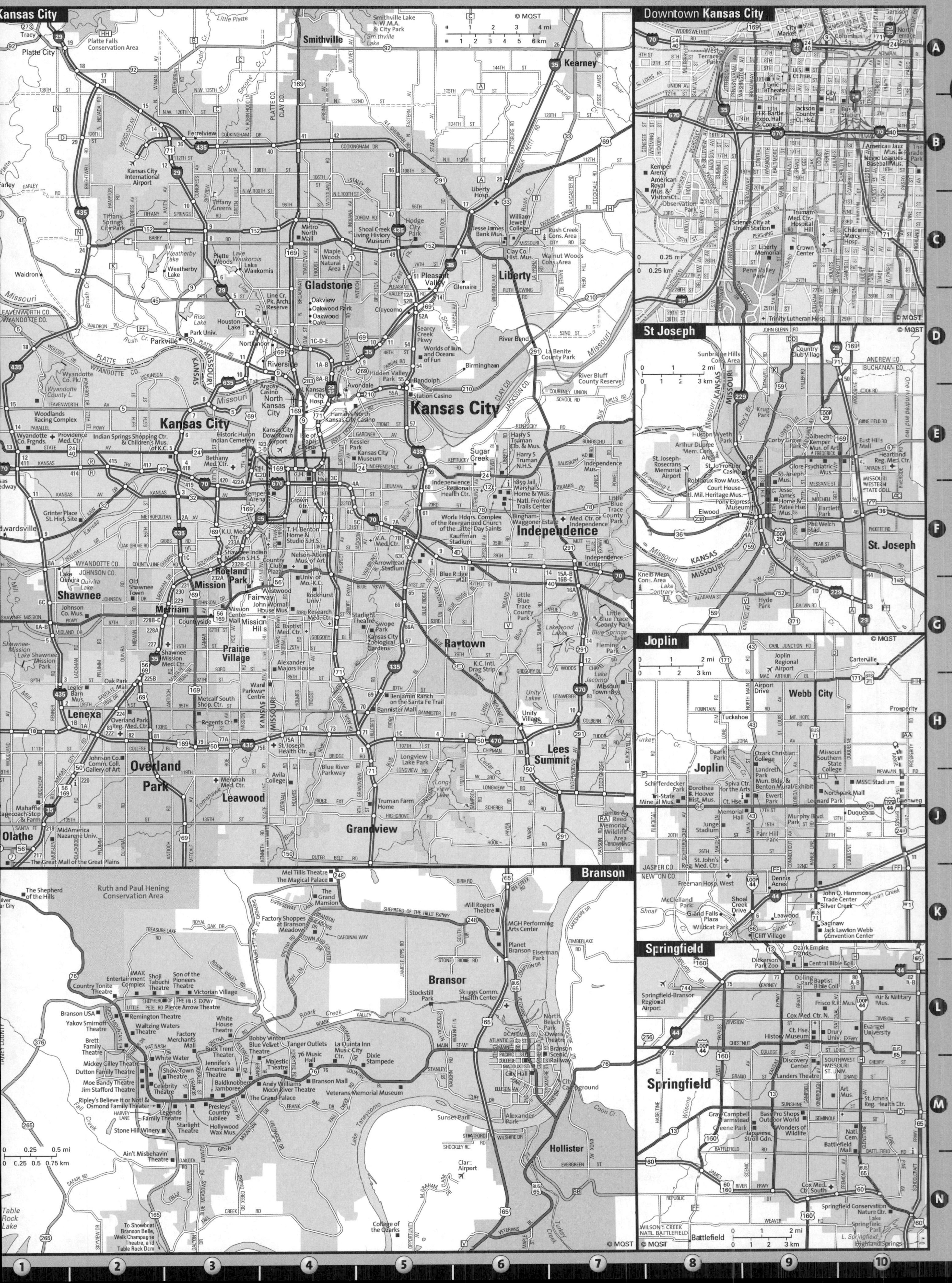
Kansas City
Downtown Kansas City
St Joseph
Joplin
Springfield
Branson
Smithville
Kearney
Gladstone
Liberty
Kansas City
Independence
Shawnee
Lenexa
Overland Park
Olathe
Leawood
Raytown
Grandview
Lees Summit
Prairie Village
Mission
Merriam
Roeland Park
St. Joseph
Webb City
Joplin
Springfield
Branson
Hollister
© MQST

Tourism: 573/526-5900
Road Conditions: 800/222-6400

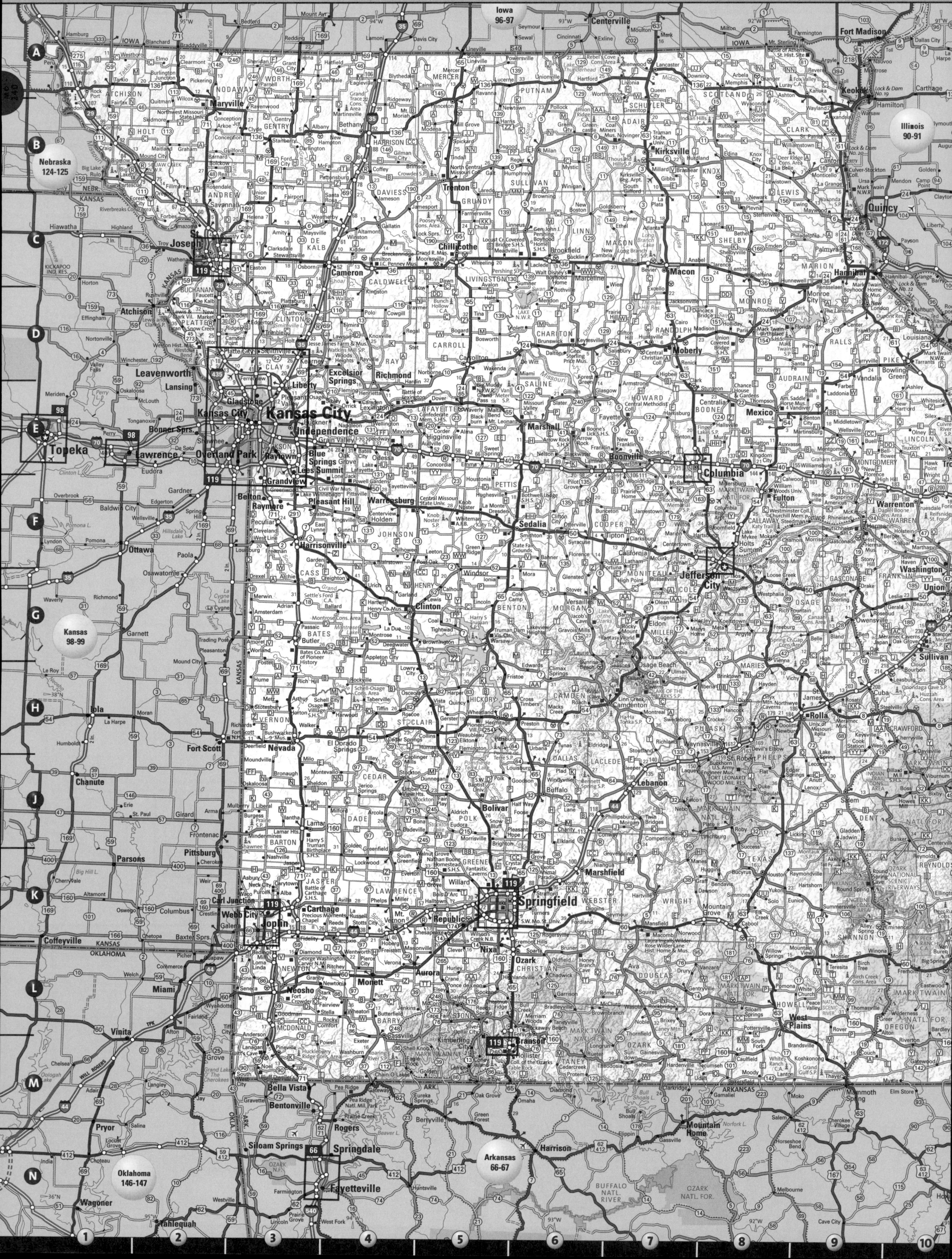

DRIVING DISTANCES IN MILES	BRANSON	CAPE GIRARDEAU	CHILLICOTHE	COLUMBIA	HANNIBAL	JEFFERSON CITY	JOPLIN	KANSAS CITY	KIRKSVILLE	NEVADA	POPLAR BLUFF	ROLLA	ST. JOSEPH	ST. LOUIS	SEDALIA	SIKESTON	SPRINGFIELD	WEST PLAINS
CAPE GIRARDEAU	347		357	234	228	243	382	363	322	374	75	205	419	120	303	36	307	175
COLUMBIA	203	234	124		101	32	238	129	89	206	269	97	185	123	69	265	153	194
KANSAS CITY	210	363	92	129	230	161	165		161	104	398	226	56	252	97	394	169	278
ST. LOUIS	249	120	247	123	117	132	284	252	212	276	156	107	308		192	151	209	204
SPRINGFIELD	41	307	200	163	241	131	70	169	251	95	191	110	225	209	108	238		109

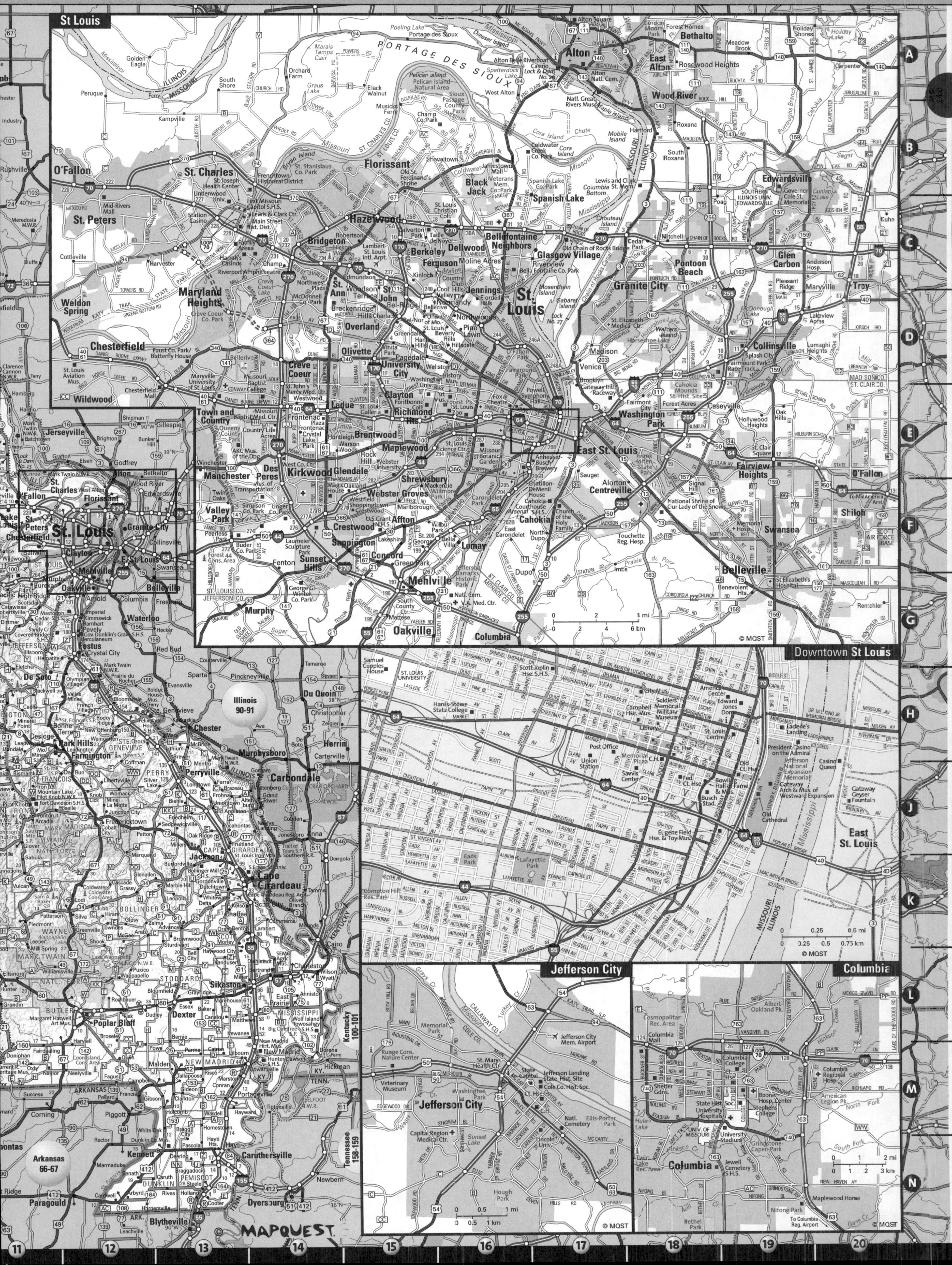

Tourism: 800/847-4868
Road Conditions: 800/332-6171

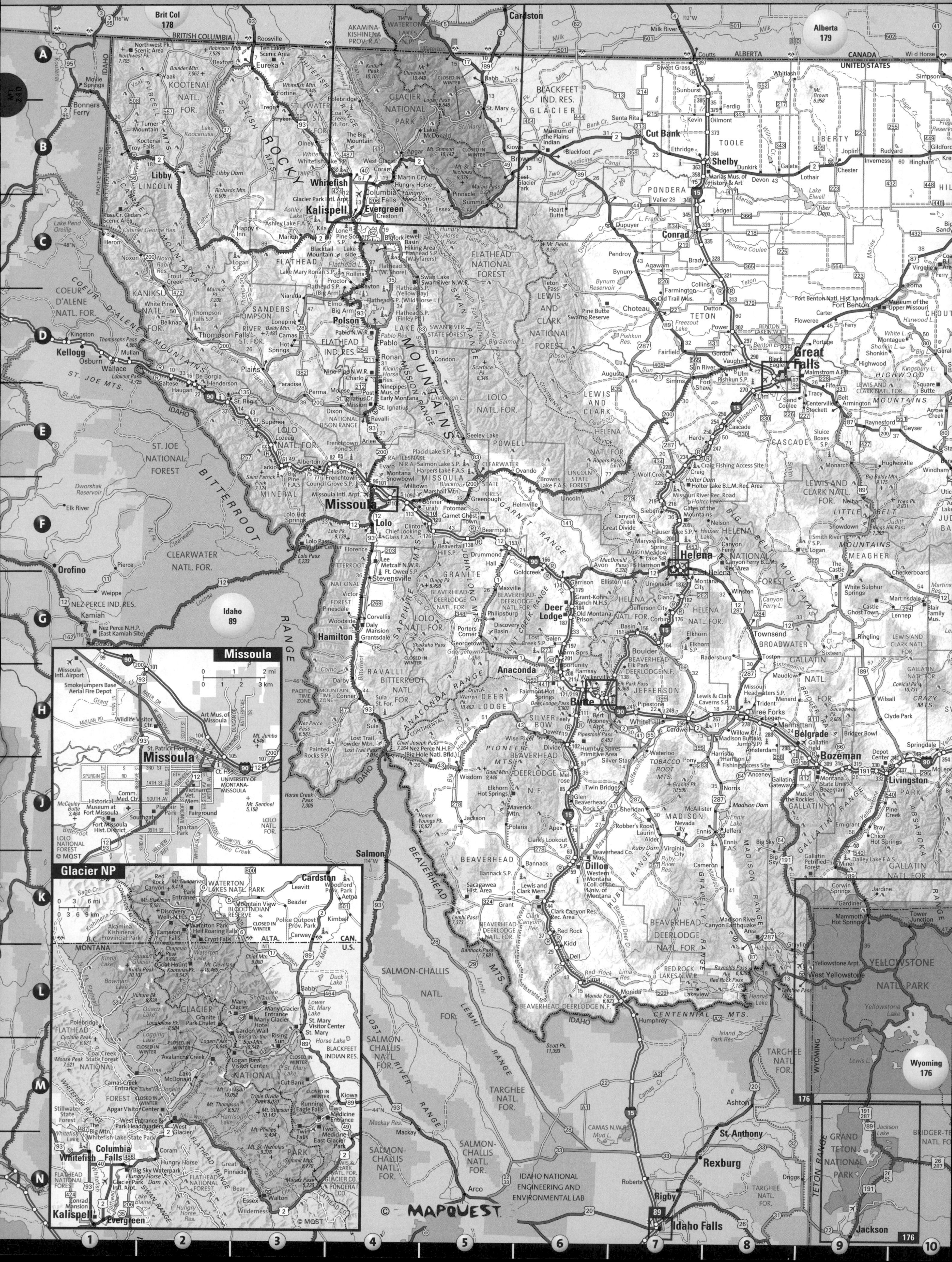

DRIVING DISTANCES IN MILES	BILLINGS	BOZEMAN	BROWNING	BUTTE	DILLON	GLASGOW	GLENDIVE	GREAT FALLS	HAVRE	HELENA	KALISPELL	LEWISTOWN	MILES CITY	MISSOULA	SHELBY	SHERIDAN, WY	WEST GLACIER	WEST YELLOWSTONE
BILLINGS		141	346	223	253	277	217	222	249	235	454	125	144	340	304	131	474	232
BUTTE	223	81	241		63	430	439	153	271	71	232	247	367	118	235	354	252	162
GREAT FALLS	222	176	124	153	215	277	351		118	85	222	109	329	199	82	353	192	257
HELENA	235	94	174	71	132	362	452	85	203		195	192	379	114	168	366	216	174
MISSOULA	340	199	201	118	171	476	557	199	317	114	116	306	484		227	471	136	279

Tourism: 877/632-7275
Road Conditions: 402/471-4533
Road Construction: 402/479-4512

DRIVING DISTANCES IN MILES	ALLIANCE	BEATRICE	CHADRON	COLUMBUS	GRAND ISLAND	HASTINGS	KEARNEY	LINCOLN	MC COOK	NEBRASKA CITY	NORFOLK	NORTH PLATTE	OGALLALA	OMAHA	O'NEILL	SCOTTSBLUFF	SOUTH SIOUX CITY	VALENTINE
GRAND ISLAND	317	135	373	64		23	49	95	147	144	105	143	196	150	111	318	179	210
LINCOLN	397	40	453	77	95	102	129		226	49	119	223	275	58	207	397	154	302
NORTH PLATTE	174	262	230	207	143	150	98	223	67	271	248		53	278	203	175	374	131
OMAHA	452	97	508	84	150	157	184	58	281	50	115	278	330		188	452	99	298
SCOTTSBLUFF	55	437	96	382	318	325	273	397	242	446	423	175	122	452	324		549	214

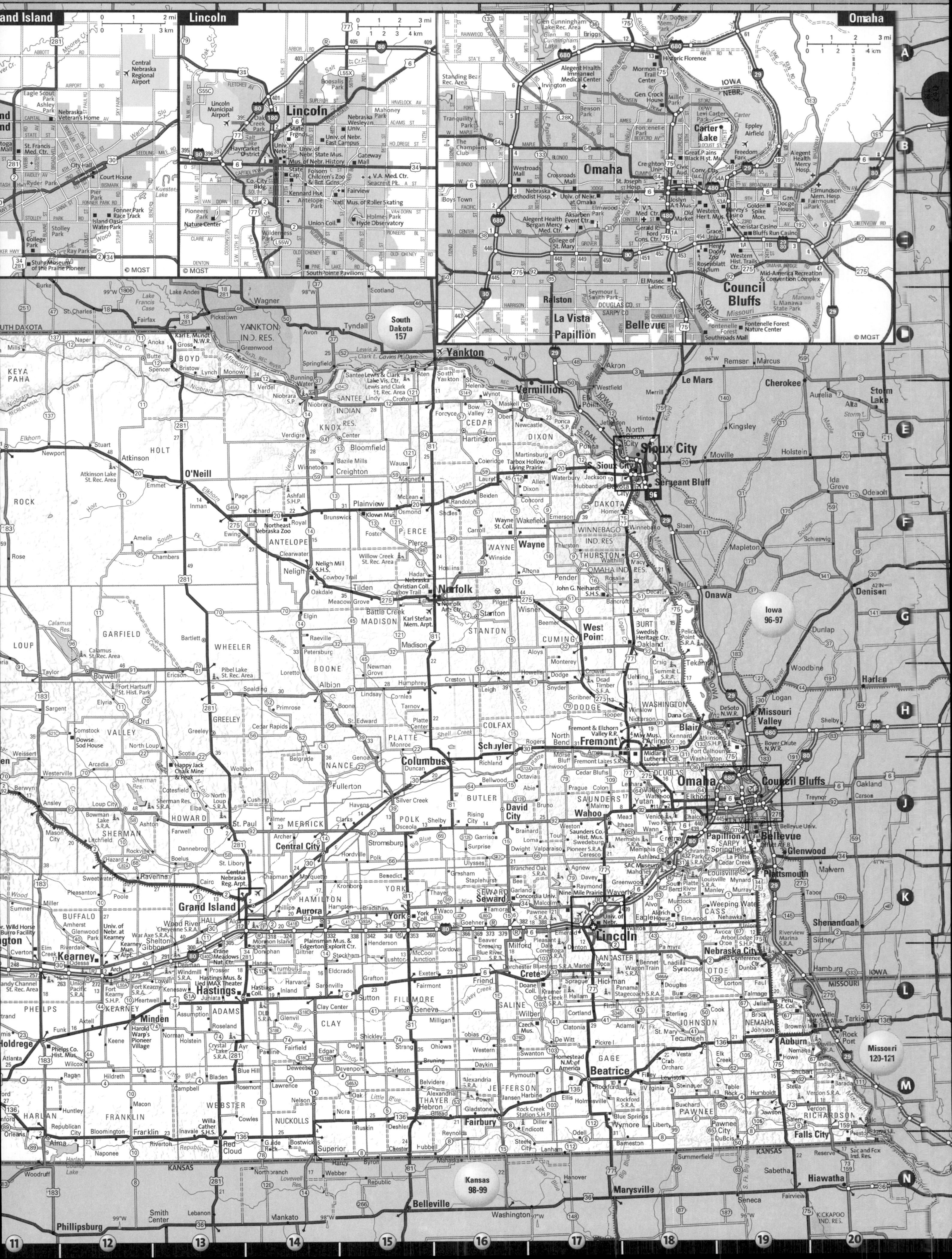

Tourism: 800/638-2328
Road Conditions: 877/687-6237

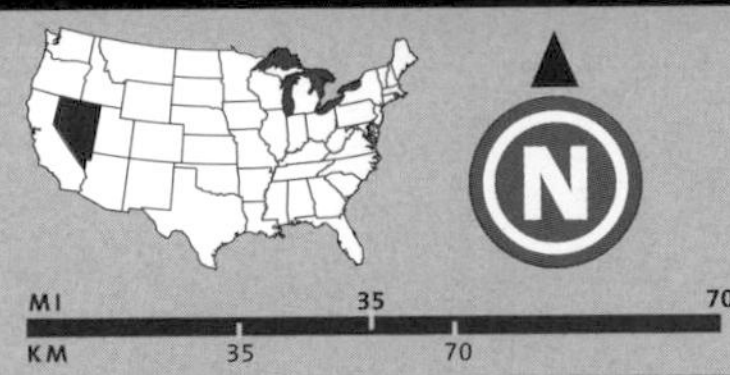

DRIVING DISTANCES IN MILES	BEATTY	CARSON CITY	ELKO	ELY	FALLON	HAWTHORNE	LAS VEGAS	LAUGHLIN	RENO	TONOPAH	WEST WENDOVER	WINNEMUCCA
CARSON CITY	316		320	319	62	128	429	522	30	232	431	194
ELKO	349	320		180	255	300	424	517	291	257	111	127
ELY	259	319	180		257	299	244	338	317	167	120	273
LAS VEGAS	113	429	424	244	381	309		94	442	205	364	465
RENO	329	30	291	317	61	133	442	536		237	402	166

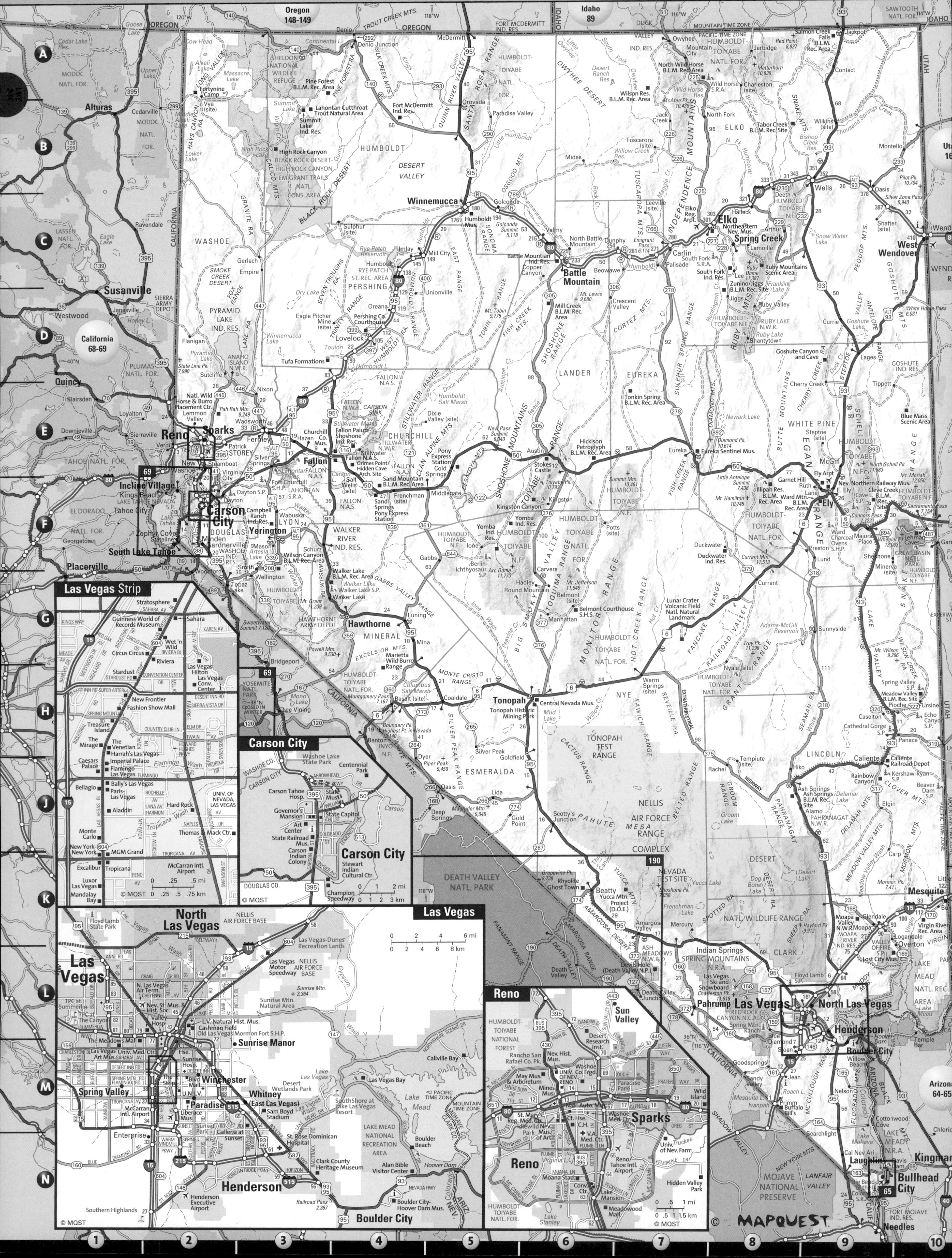

DRIVING DISTANCES IN MILES	BERLIN	CONCORD	CONWAY	KEENE	LACONIA	LEBANON	LITTLETON	MANCHESTER	NASHUA	PLYMOUTH	PORTSMOUTH	ROCHESTER
BERLIN		112	42	161	100	114	42	130	144	72	119	96
CONCORD	112		74	50	26	56	84	19	33	41	47	35
LEBANON	114	56	87	66	56		72	71	85	41	102	90
MANCHESTER	130	19	92	51	44	71	102		16	59	45	46
PORTSMOUTH	119	47	77	96	59	102	129	45	56	86		22

Tourism: 603/271-2665
Road Conditions: 603/271-6900

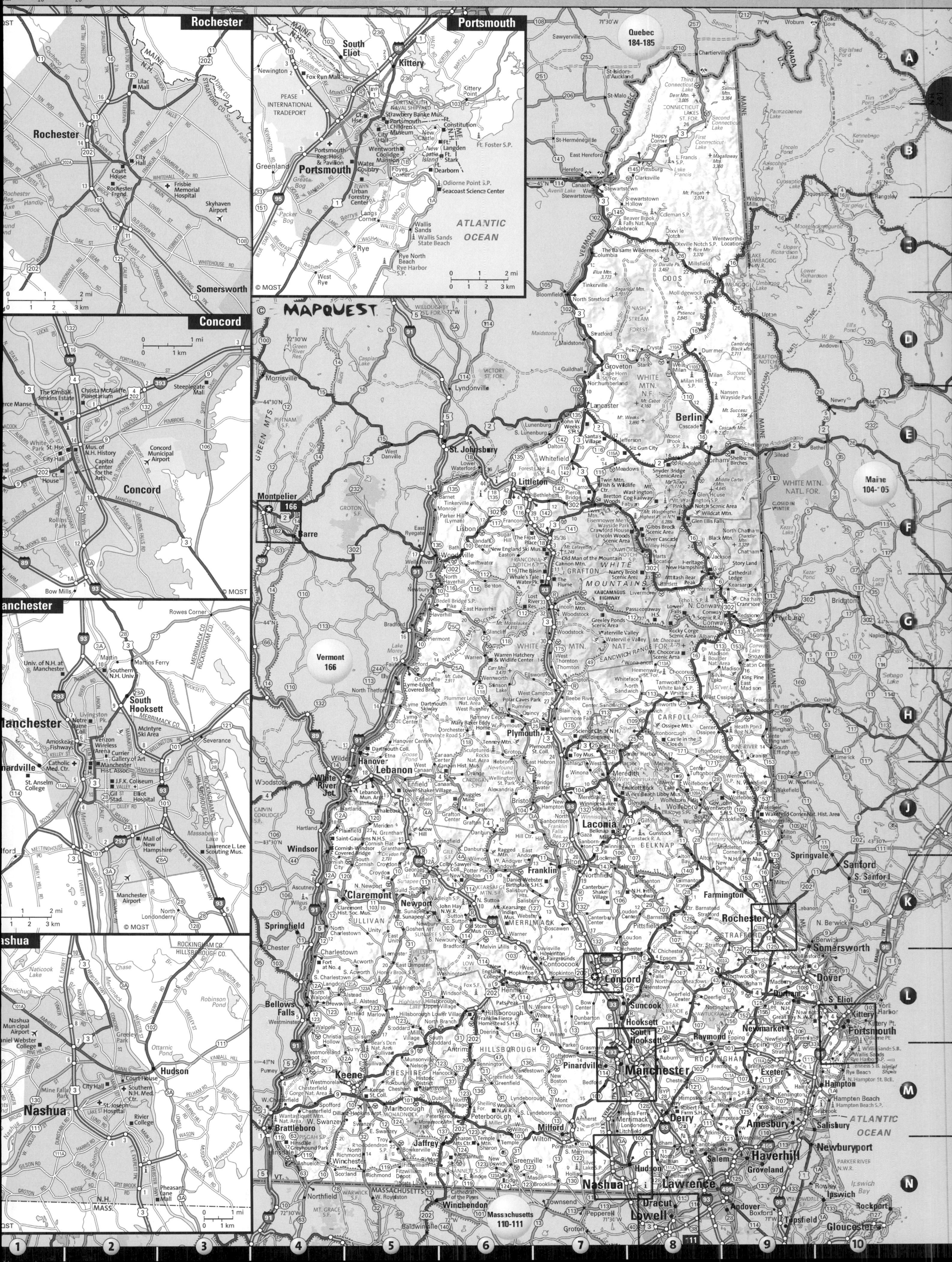

Tourism: 609/272-2470
Road Conditions: 732/247-0900

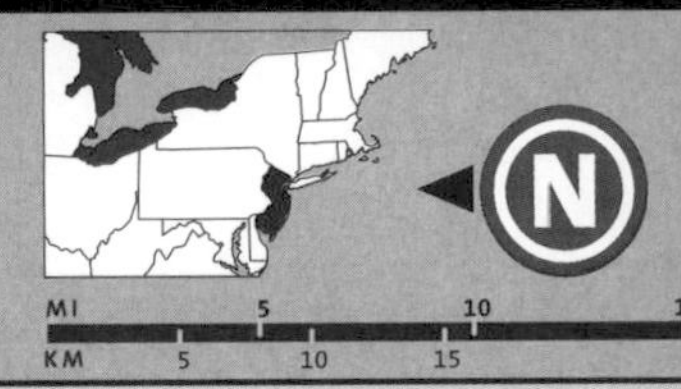

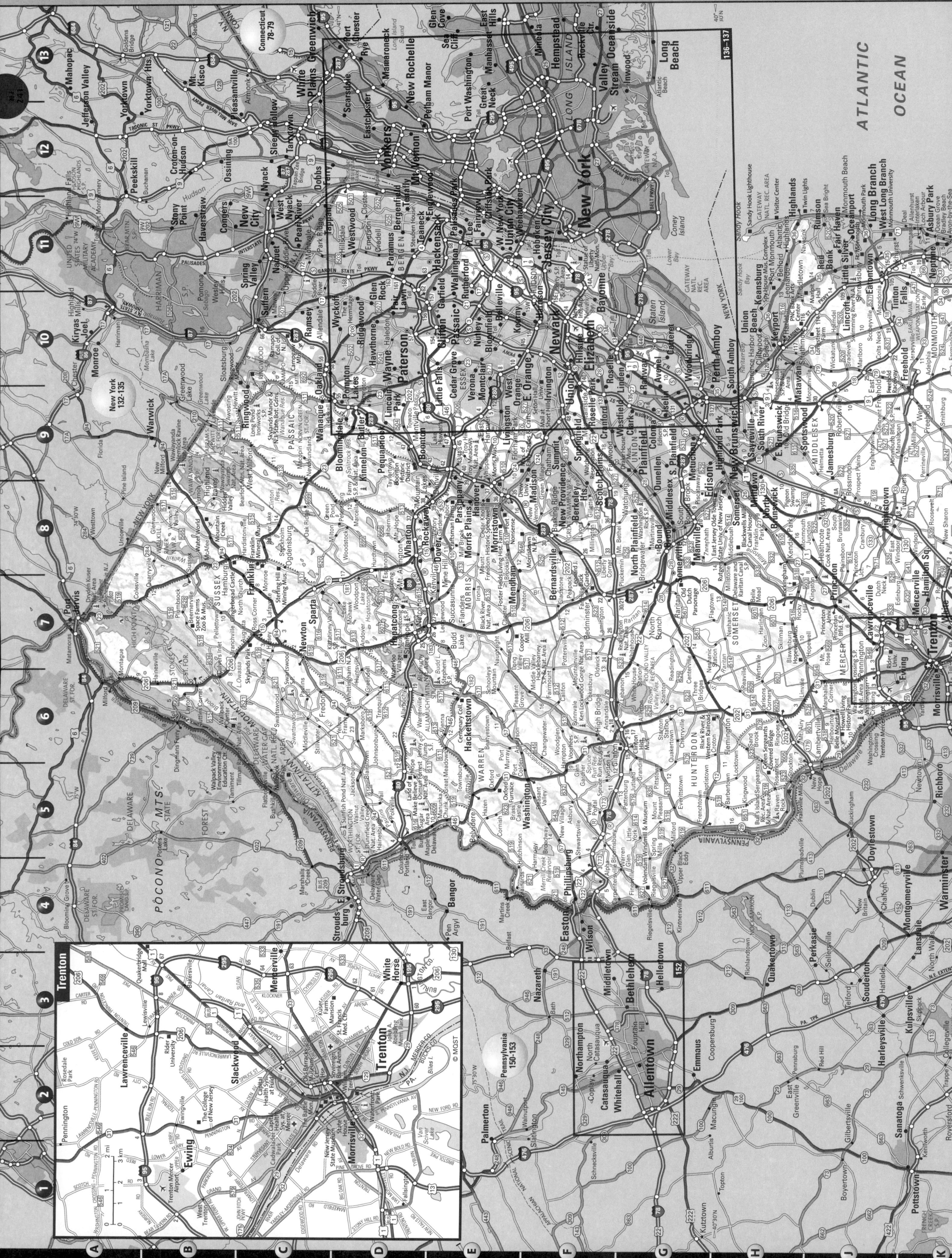

DRIVING DISTANCES IN MILES	ATLANTIC CITY	CAMDEN	CAPE MAY	HACKENSACK	JERSEY CITY	LONG BRANCH	MORRISTOWN	NEW BRUNSWICK	NEW YORK, NY	NEWARK	NEWTON	PATERSON	PHILADELPHIA, PA	PHILLIPSBURG	TOMS RIVER	TRENTON	VINELAND	WILMINGTON, DE
ATLANTIC CITY		61	41	133	120	82	126	94	125	114	159	128	62	120	54	77	47	86
NEW YORK, NY	125	92	155	12	5	55	32	34		11	54	16	91	67	75	55	119	120
NEWARK	114	82	144	15	5	45	18	23	11		51	18	80	57	65	45	109	109
PHILADELPHIA, PA	62	2	92	98	86	77	82	55	91	80	94	94		58	58	34	36	30
TRENTON	77	35	107	63	50	53	47	22	55	45	63	58	34	50	48		68	68

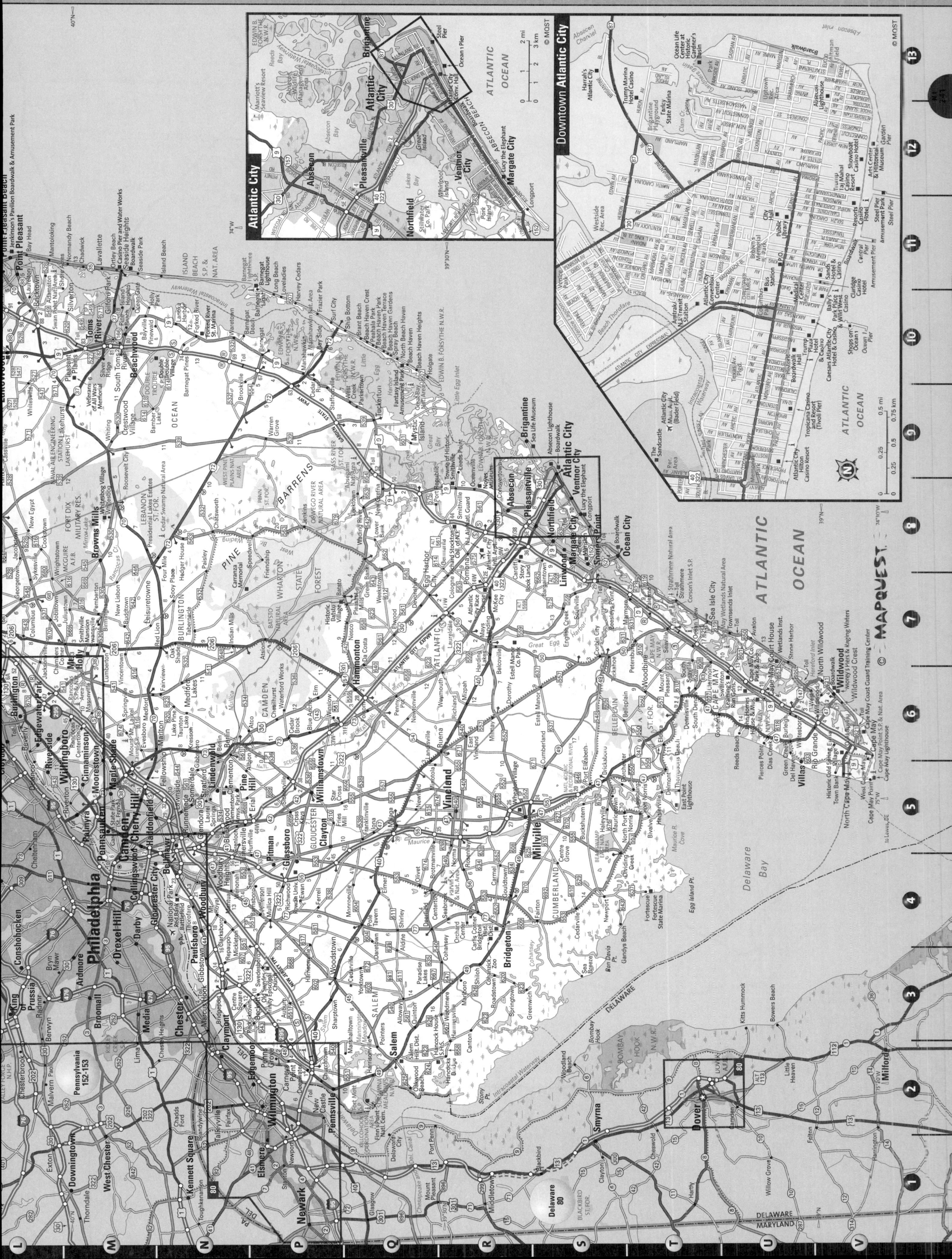

Tourism: 800/733-6396
Road Conditions: 800/432-4269

DRIVING DISTANCES IN MILES	ALAMOGORDO	ALBUQUERQUE	CARLSBAD	CLOVIS	EL PASO, TX	FARMINGTON	GALLUP	HOBBS	LAS CRUCES	LAS VEGAS	LOS ALAMOS	RATON	ROSWELL	SANTA FE	SILVER CITY	SOCORRO	TAOS	TUCUMCARI
ALBUQUERQUE	213		275	220	263	181	141	316	220	115	92	221	199	55	234	77	123	174
FARMINGTON	399	181	455	401	450		120	496	407	264	196	300	379	205	361	263	211	355
LAS CRUCES	65	220	203	293	42	407	338	250		333	312	441	182	275	111	146	343	394
ROSWELL	117	199	76	110	203	379	340	117	182	178	228	284		191	293	164	248	161
SANTA FE	220	55	267	213	319	205	197	308	275	65	37	171	191		290	132	68	167

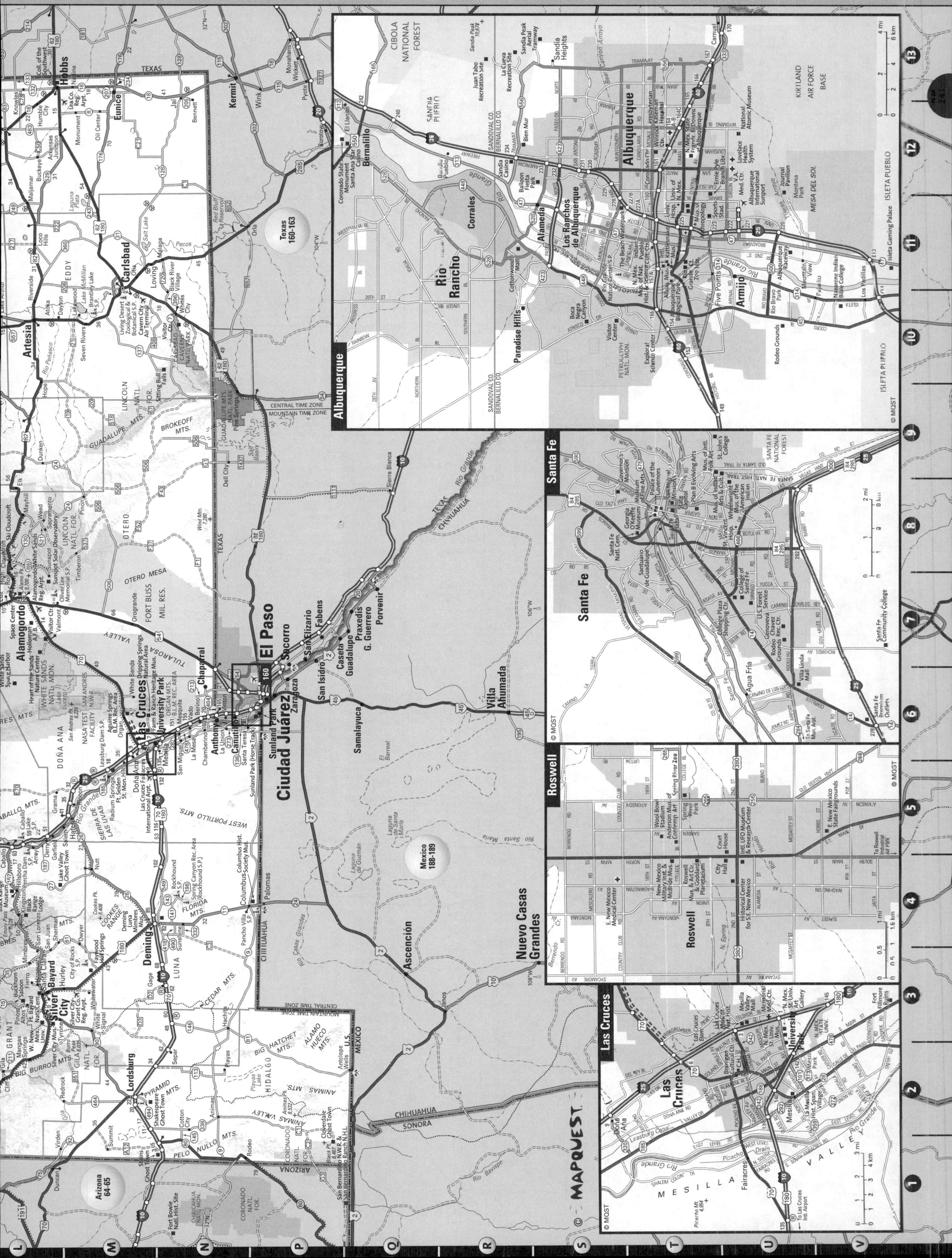

Tourism: 800/225-5697
Road Conditions: 800/847-8929

MI 0 15 30
KM 0 15 30

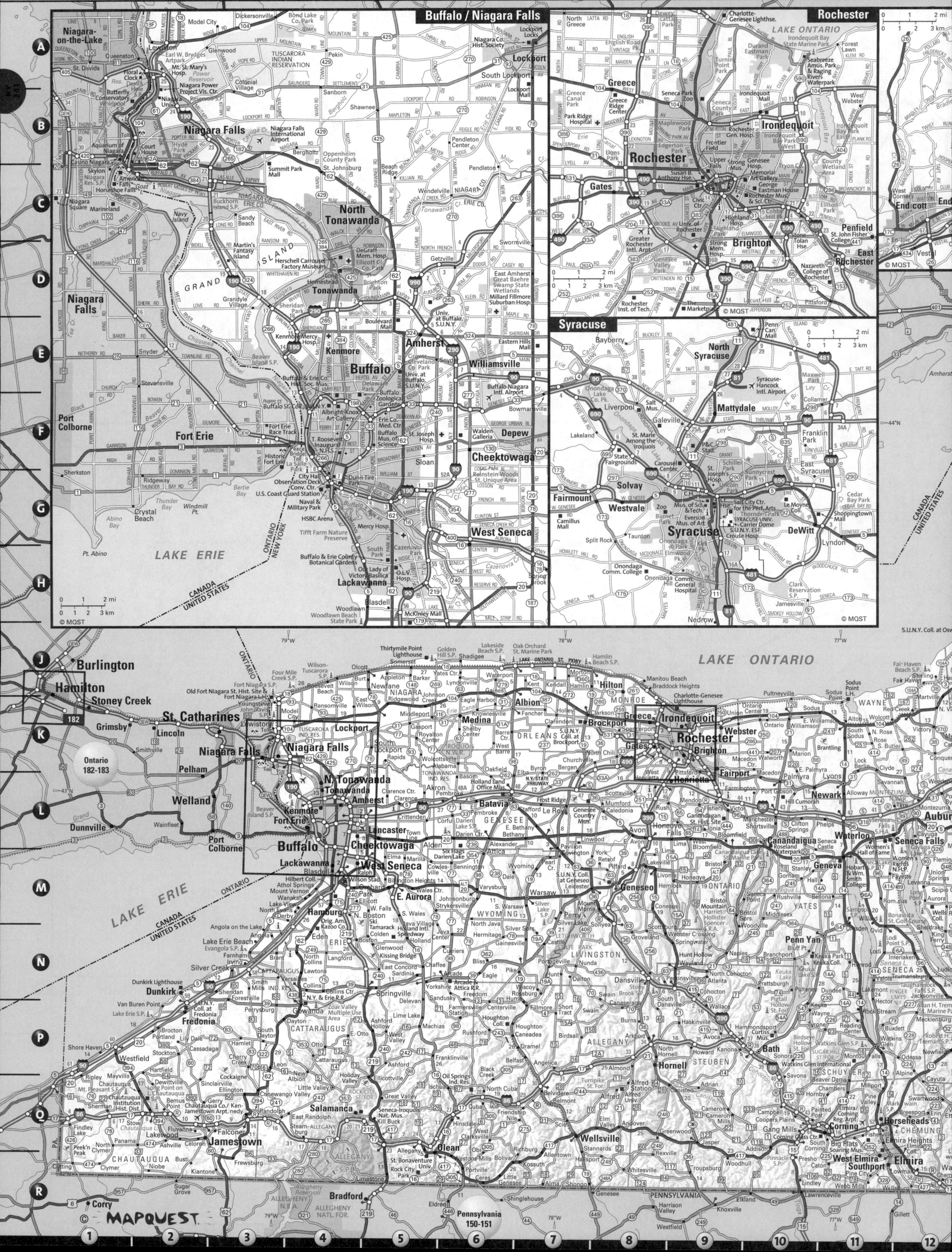

DRIVING DISTANCES IN MILES	ALBANY	BINGHAMTON	BUFFALO	COOPERSTOWN	GENEVA	ITHACA	JAMESTOWN	KINGSTON	LAKE PLACID	NEW YORK	NIAGARA FALLS	OLEAN	PLATTSBURGH	ROCHESTER	SARATOGA SPRINGS	SYRACUSE	UTICA	WATERTOWN
ALBANY		135	292	89	197	186	361	56	138	151	306	297	160	228	32	146	94	179
BINGHAMTON	135		225	78	97	53	214	125	253	176	239	164	276	161	160	76	95	139
BUFFALO	292	225		239	103	153	74	346	337	400	20	74	374	74	293	152	199	210
ROCHESTER	228	161	74	175	39	89	142	282	273	336	88	113	310		229	88	135	146
SYRACUSE	146	76	152	93	56	59	220	201	192	250	166	163	228	88	147		53	65

Tourism: 800/225-5697
Road Conditions: 800/847-8929

DRIVING DISTANCES IN MILES	ALBANY	BINGHAMTON	BUFFALO	HEMPSTEAD	KINGSTON	MIDDLETOWN	MONTAUK	MONTICELLO	NEWBURGH	NEW YORK	PEEKSKILL	PORT JEFFERSON	PORT JERVIS	POUGHKEEPSIE	RIVERHEAD	ROCHESTER	SYRACUSE	WHITE PLAINS
ALBANY		135	292	182	56	105	276	103	89	15[illegible]	107	214	121	79	234	228	146	148
BINGHAMTON	135		225	203	125	116	296	87	134	17[illegible]	144	235	117	127	254	161	76	167
KINGSTON	56	125	346	132		55	225	53	39	10[illegible]	57	164	71	20	183	282	201	98
NEWBURGH	89	134	357	74	39	26	167	47		56	18	106	42	22	125	294	208	42
NEW YORK	151	176	400	26	101	72	120	95	56		45	58	87	96	78	336	250	29

Bloomingdale
Oakland
Waldwick
Woodcliff Lake
Hillsdale
Old Tappan
Palisades
Dobbs Ferry
Ardsley
Butler
Pompton Lakes
Riverdale
Franklin Lakes
Wyckoff
Midland Park
Ho-Ho-Kus
Westwood
Norwood
Northvale
Rockleigh
Harrington Park
Hastings-on-Hudson
Kinnelon
Pompton Plains
North Haledon
Ridgewood
Washington Township
Emerson
Oradell
Closter
Hawthorne
Glen Rock
Haworth
Demarest
Dumont
Prospect Pk.
Fair Lawn
Paramus
New Milford
Bergenfield
Cresskill
Tenafly
Alpine
Wayne
Haledon
Paterson
Elmwood Park
River Edge
Yonkers
Lincoln Park
Totowa
Rochelle Park
Maywood
Saddle Brook
Englewood
West Paterson
Garfield
Hackensack
Teaneck
Lodi
Bogota
Englewood Cliffs
Fairfield
Little Falls
North Caldwell
Clifton
Passaic
Hasbrouck Hts.
Leonia
Wood-Ridge
Wallington
Ridgefield Park
Little Ferry
Palisades Park
Fort Lee
Cedar Grove
West Caldwell
Caldwell
Verona
East Rutherford
Rutherford
Carlstadt
Moonachie
Ridgefield
Cliffside Park
Edgewater
Roseland
Montclair
Nutley
Lyndhurst
North Bergen
Fairview
Bronx
West Orange
Glen Ridge
Bloomfield
Belleville
North Arlington
Secaucus
Guttenberg
West New York
Livingston
Orange
East Orange
Kearny
Weehawken
Union City
South Orange
Harrison
Hoboken
Manhattan
Maplewood
Irvington
Millburn
Summit
Springfield
Union
Hillside
Newark
Jersey City
New York
Brooklyn
Mountainside
Kenilworth
Elizabeth
Bayonne
Westfield
Cranford
Roselle Park
Roselle
Garwood
Linden
Clark
Rahway
Staten Island
Colonia
Iselin
Avenel
Carteret
Woodbridge
Port Reading
Sewaren
Fords
Keasbey
Perth Amboy
South Amboy
Sayreville
Upper New York Bay
Lower New York Bay
Raritan Bay
Jamaica Bay
Rockaway Inlet
Rockaway Pt.
NEW YORK
NEW JERSEY

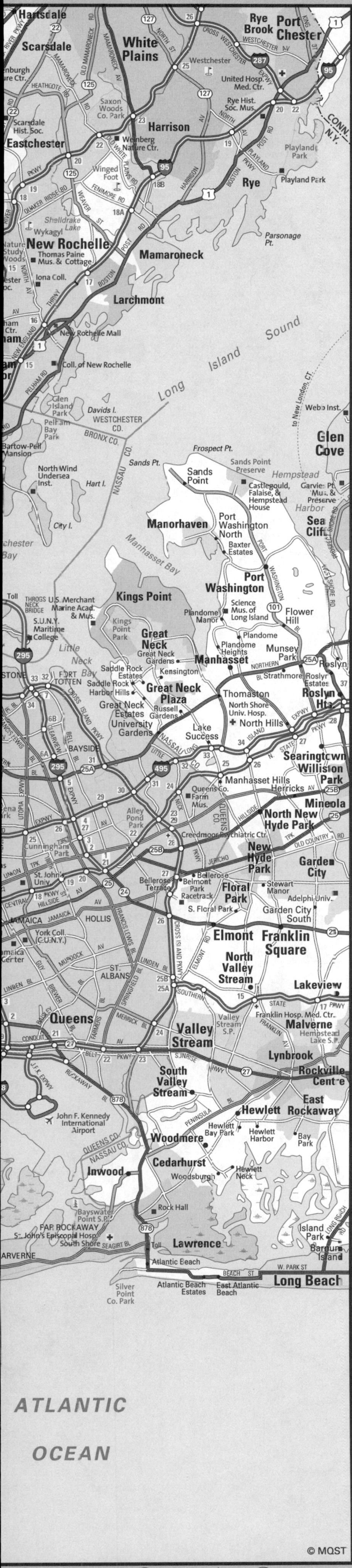
Hartsdale
Scarsdale
White Plains
Rye Brook
Port Chester
Harrison
Eastchester
Rye
New Rochelle
Mamaroneck
Larchmont
Long Island Sound
Glen Cove
Sands Point
Manorhaven
Port Washington
Kings Point
Great Neck
Manhasset
Great Neck Plaza
Roslyn Hts.
Searingtown
Williston Park
Mineola
North New Hyde Park
New Hyde Park
Garden City
Floral Park
Elmont
Franklin Square
North Valley Stream
Lakeview
Queens
Valley Stream
Malverne
Lynbrook
Rockville Centre
South Valley Stream
Hewlett
East Rockaway
Woodmere
Cedarhurst
Inwood
Lawrence
Long Beach
John F. Kennedy International Airport
ATLANTIC
OCEAN
© MQST

Manhattan
West New York
Union City
Weehawken
Hudson
NEW JERSEY
NEW YORK
UPPER WEST SIDE
Central Park
UPPER EAST SIDE
THEATER DISTRICT
CLINTON
MIDTOWN
TURTLE BAY
FASHION CENTER
MURRAY HILL
CHELSEA
Manhattan
GRAMERCY PARK
WEST VILLAGE
GREENWICH VILLAGE
STUYVESANT TOWN
SOHO
EAST VILLAGE
LITTLE ITALY
TRIBECA
CHINATOWN
LOWER EAST SIDE
BATTERY PARK CITY
FINANCIAL DISTRICT
Brooklyn
BROOKLYN NAVY YARD
BROOKLYN HEIGHTS
FORT GREENE
Queens
LONG ISLAND CITY
GREENPOINT
WILLIAMSBURG
0 0.25 0.5 mi
0 0.25 0.5 0.75 km
© MOST
A
B
C
D
E
F
G
H
J
K
L
M
N
11
12
13
14
15
16
17
18
19
20

Tourism: 800/847-4862
Road Conditions: 877/368-4968

DRIVING DISTANCES IN MILES	ASHEVILLE	BOONE	CHARLOTTE	DURHAM	ELIZABETH CITY	FAYETTEVILLE	GREENSBORO	GREENVILLE	HICKORY	JACKSONVILLE	KINSTON	MOREHEAD CITY	NAGS HEAD	RALEIGH	ROCKINGHAM	ROCKY MOUNT	WILMINGTON	WINSTON-SALEM
ASHEVILLE		198	116	224	404	264	176	324	78	354	316	383	444	242	190	297	368	146
CHARLOTTE	116	95		139	319	139	91	239	48	269	232	298	359	158	74	213	205	79
GREENSBORO	176	117	91	49	228	90		148	98	179	141	207	268	67	83	122	193	30
RALEIGH	242	183	158	24	160	62	67	80	164	113	76	142	200		96	54	127	96
WILMINGTON	368	309	205	150	211	92	193	123	290	52	93	95	241	127	131	153		222

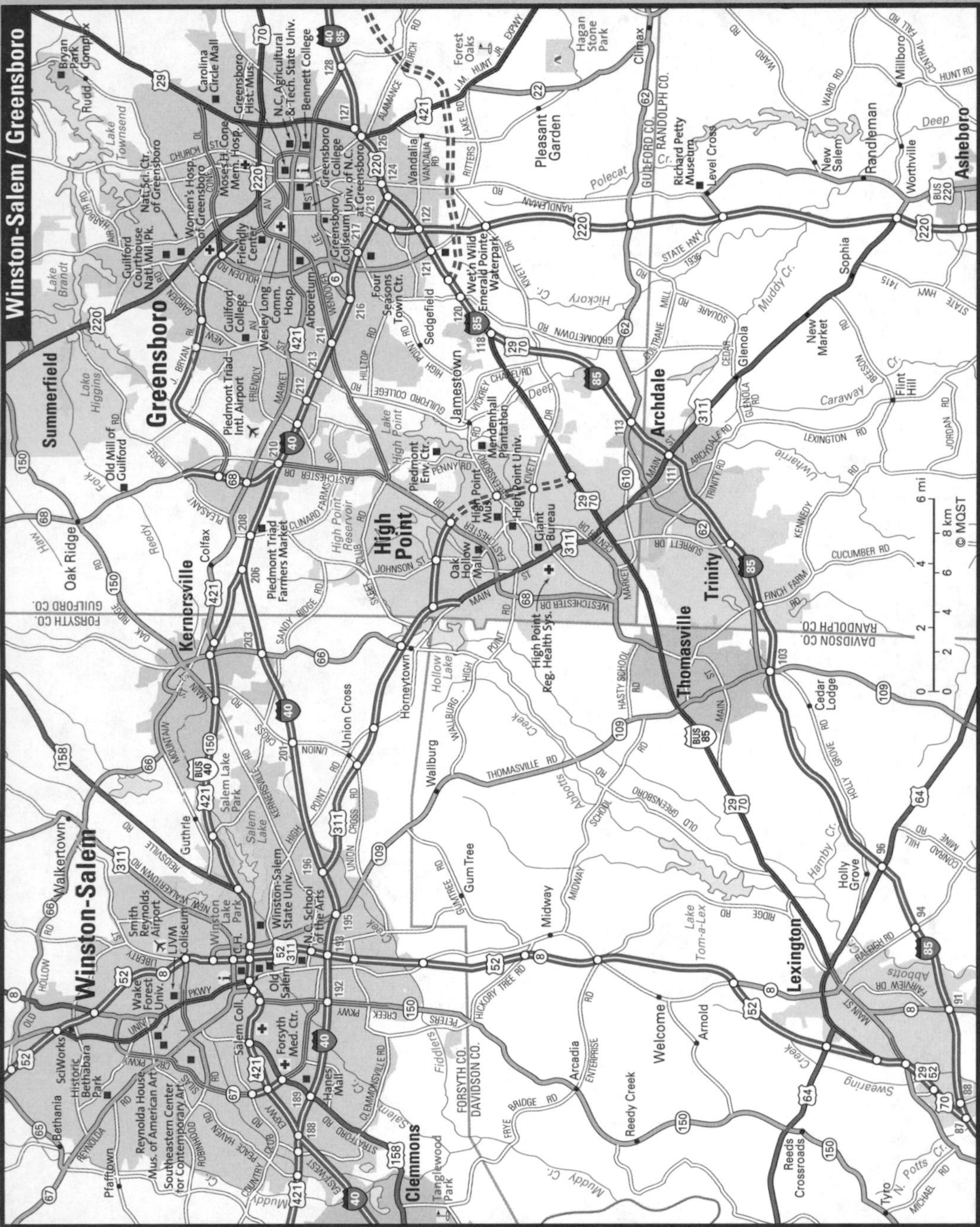
Winston-Salem / Greensboro

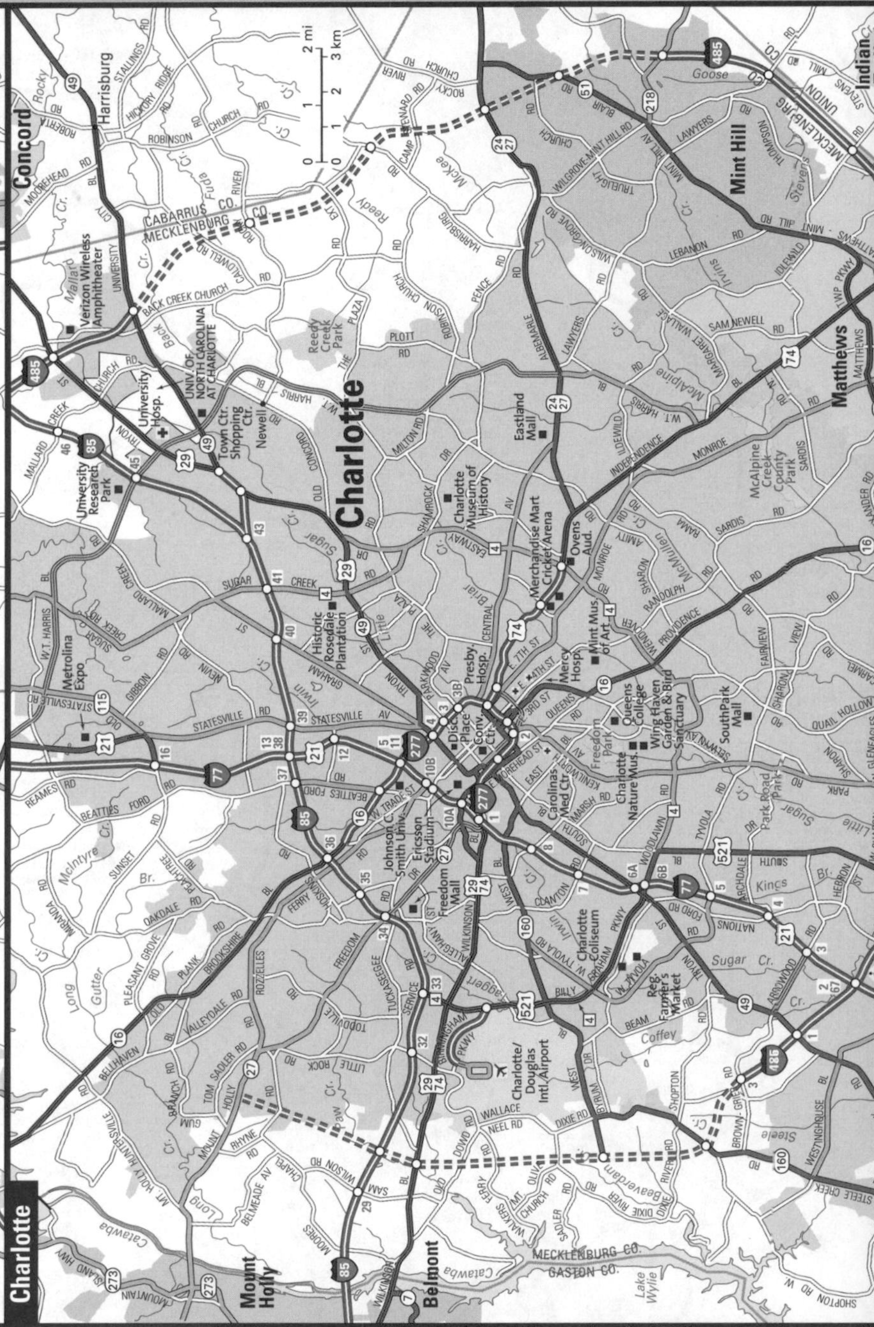
Charlotte

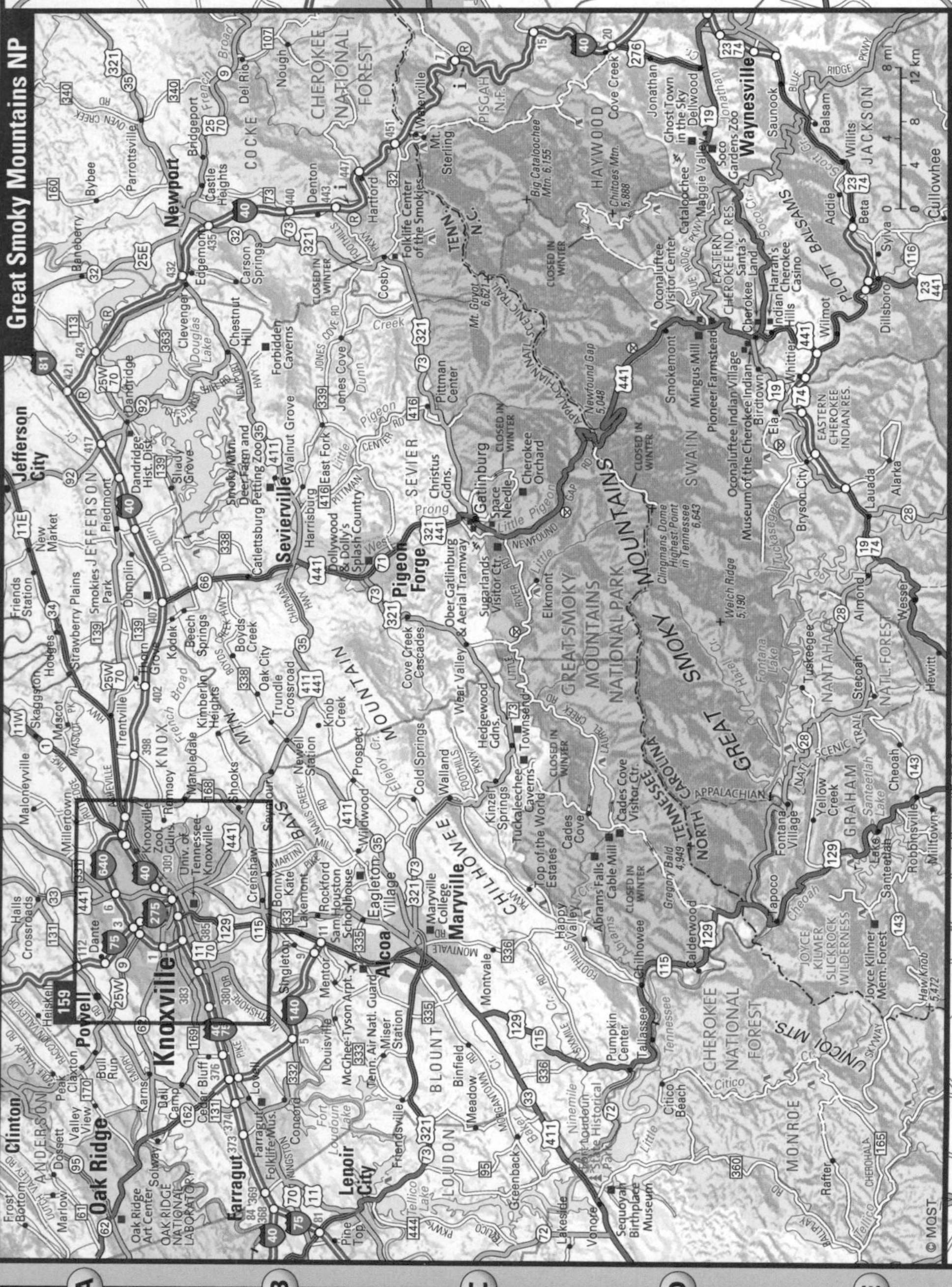
Great Smoky Mountains NP

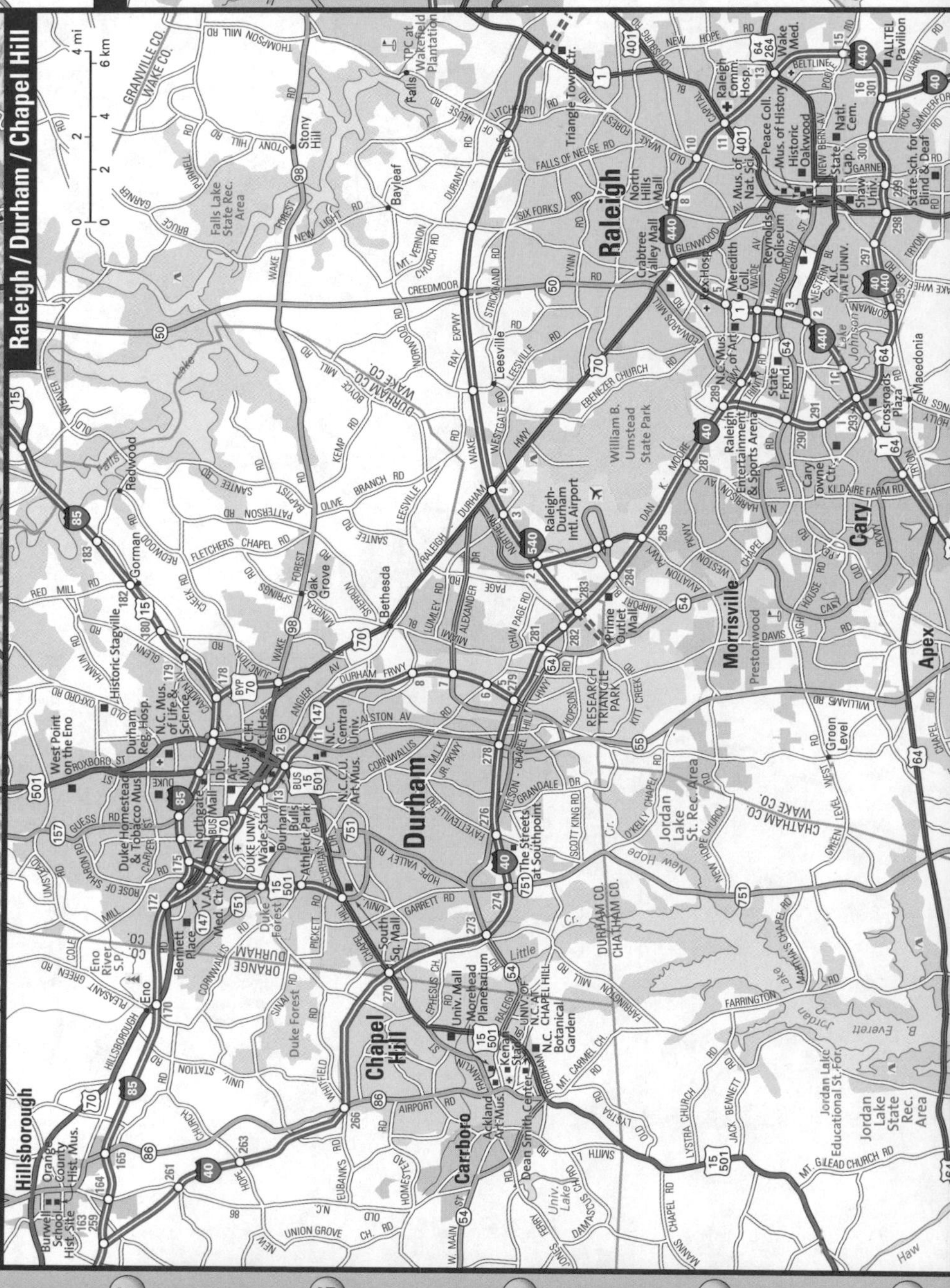
Raleigh / Durham / Chapel Hill

Tourism: 800/435-5663
Road Conditions: 701/328-7623

DRIVING DISTANCES IN MILES

	BISMARCK	DEVILS LAKE	DICKINSON	FARGO	GRAND FORKS	JAMESTOWN	MINOT	PEMBINA	RUGBY	VALLEY CITY	WAHPETON	WILLISTON
BISMARCK		186	97	199	274	105	116	347	153	141	249	229
DICKINSON	97	278		291	367	197	178	440	245	234	341	133
FARGO	193	163	291		79	97	268	152	221	58	45	424
GRAND FORKS	274	91	367	79		173	212	77	148	133	130	340
MINOT	116	122	178	268	212	171		238	64	210	318	128

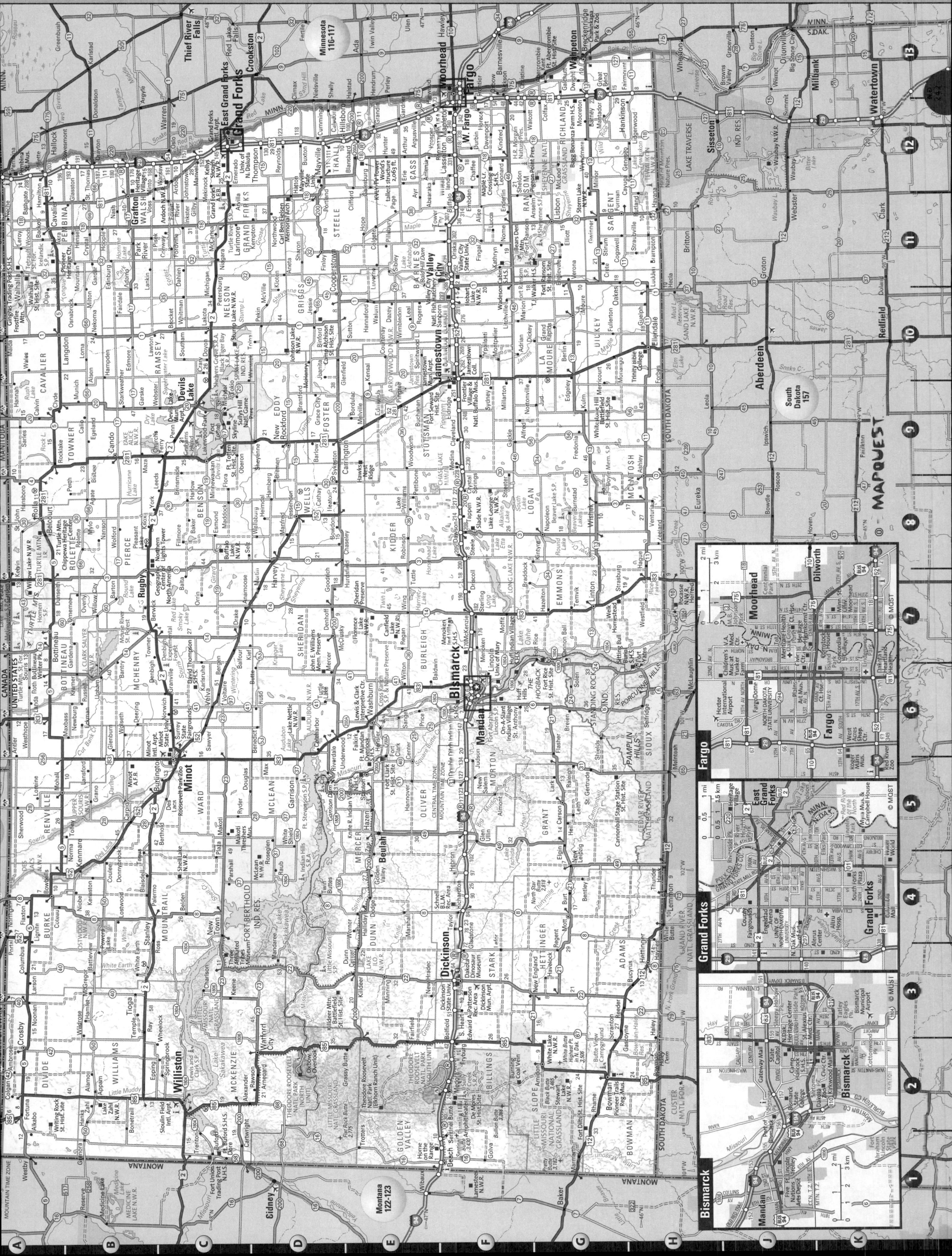

Tourism: 800/282-5393
Road Conditions: 614/644-7031

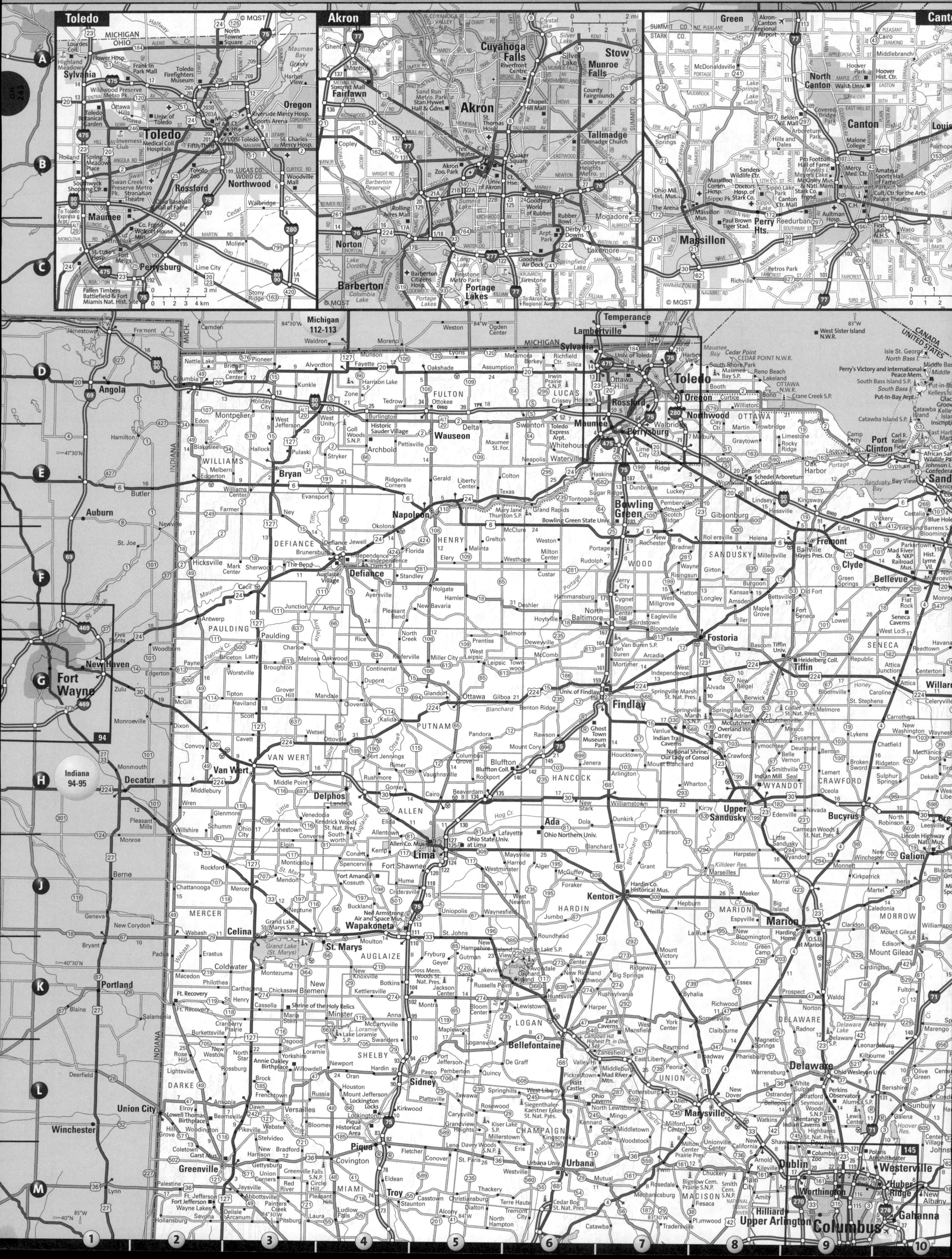

DRIVING DISTANCES IN MILES	AKRON	CAMBRIDGE	CANTON	CHILLICOTHE	CINCINNATI	CLEVELAND	COLUMBUS	DAYTON	DEFIANCE	FINDLAY	LIMA	MANSFIELD	MARION	NEW PHILADELPHIA	SANDUSKY	SPRINGFIELD	TOLEDO	YOUNGSTOWN
AKRON		83	23	184	243	38	129	198	186	140	157	66	101	46	84	172	142	49
CAMBRIDGE	83		61	98	187	124	80	155	228	178	175	108	126	37	169	128	228	129
CLEVELAND	38	124	64	199	259		144	213	163	126	163	81	116	87	61	187	119	75
COLUMBUS	129	80	143	47	110	144		70	146	101	96	67	50	117	119	44	148	175
TOLEDO	142	228	168	189	209	119	148	156	63	51	83	105	100	191	62	169		179

Tourism: 800/282-5393
Road Conditions: 614/644-7031

DRIVING DISTANCES IN MILES	AKRON	ATHENS	CAMBRIDGE	CHILLICOTHE	CINCINNATI	CLEVELAND	COLUMBUS	DAYTON	GALLIPOLIS	HILLSBORO	HUNTINGTON, WV	LANCASTER	MARIETTA	PORTSMOUTH	SPRINGFIELD	TOLEDO	WHEELING, WV	ZANESVILLE
CAMBRIDGE	83	81		98	187	124	80	155	128	145	185	63	49	142	128	228	50	23
CHILLICOTHE	184	57	98		108	199	47	77	69	40	89	35	107	44	85	189	147	75
CINCINNATI	243	152	187	108		259	110	53	154	61	148	134	236	104	79	209	236	164
COLUMBUS	129	74	80	47	110	144		70	114	69	135	30	129	91	44	148	130	58
DAYTON	198	146	155	77	53	213	70		145	57	160	102	204	116	26	156	204	132

Tourism: 800/652-6552
Road Conditions: 405/425-2385
Road Construction: 405/521-2554

DRIVING DISTANCES IN MILES	ARDMORE	BARTLESVILLE	DALLAS, TX	DURANT	ELK CITY	ENID	FORT SMITH, AR	GUYMON	HUGO	LAWTON	MC ALESTER	MIAMI	MUSKOGEE	OKLAHOMA CITY	PONCA CITY	STILLWATER	TULSA	WOODWARD
ENID	183	141	292	238	148		242	219	282	142	210	207	168	84	69	66	117	88
LAWTON	103	243	197	158	115	142	270	297	224		211	283	223	85	192	152	194	175
MC ALESTER	117	141	169	77	245	210	114	407	75	211		160	68	133	186	154	93	276
OKLAHOMA CITY	99	157	209	154	112	84	191	274	205	85	133	198	144		107	67	109	143
TULSA	206	48	259	168	221	117	125	336	165	194	93	91	52	109	93	71		205

Tourism: 800/547-7842
Road Conditions: 503/588-2941

DRIVING DISTANCES IN MILES	ASTORIA	BAKER CITY	BEND	BURNS	COOS BAY	CORVALLIS	CRATER LAKE N.P.	EUGENE	GRANTS PASS	KLAMATH FALLS	LAKEVIEW	MEDFORD	NEWPORT	ONTARIO	PENDLETON	PORTLAND	SALEM	THE DALLES
BEND	252	228		142	227	128	110	115	196	139	177	178	183	272	246	158	134	137
EUGENE	216	423	115	257	105	46	146		137	175	265	164	101	491	328	112	65	198
MEDFORD	375	406	178	311	170	205	80	164	28	76	171		260	441	487	271	224	357
PENDLETON	307	96	246	195	440	298	355	328	460	385	335	487	328	164		212	265	131
PORTLAND	97	307	158	299	224	82	253	112	244	282	335	271	116	375	212		48	82

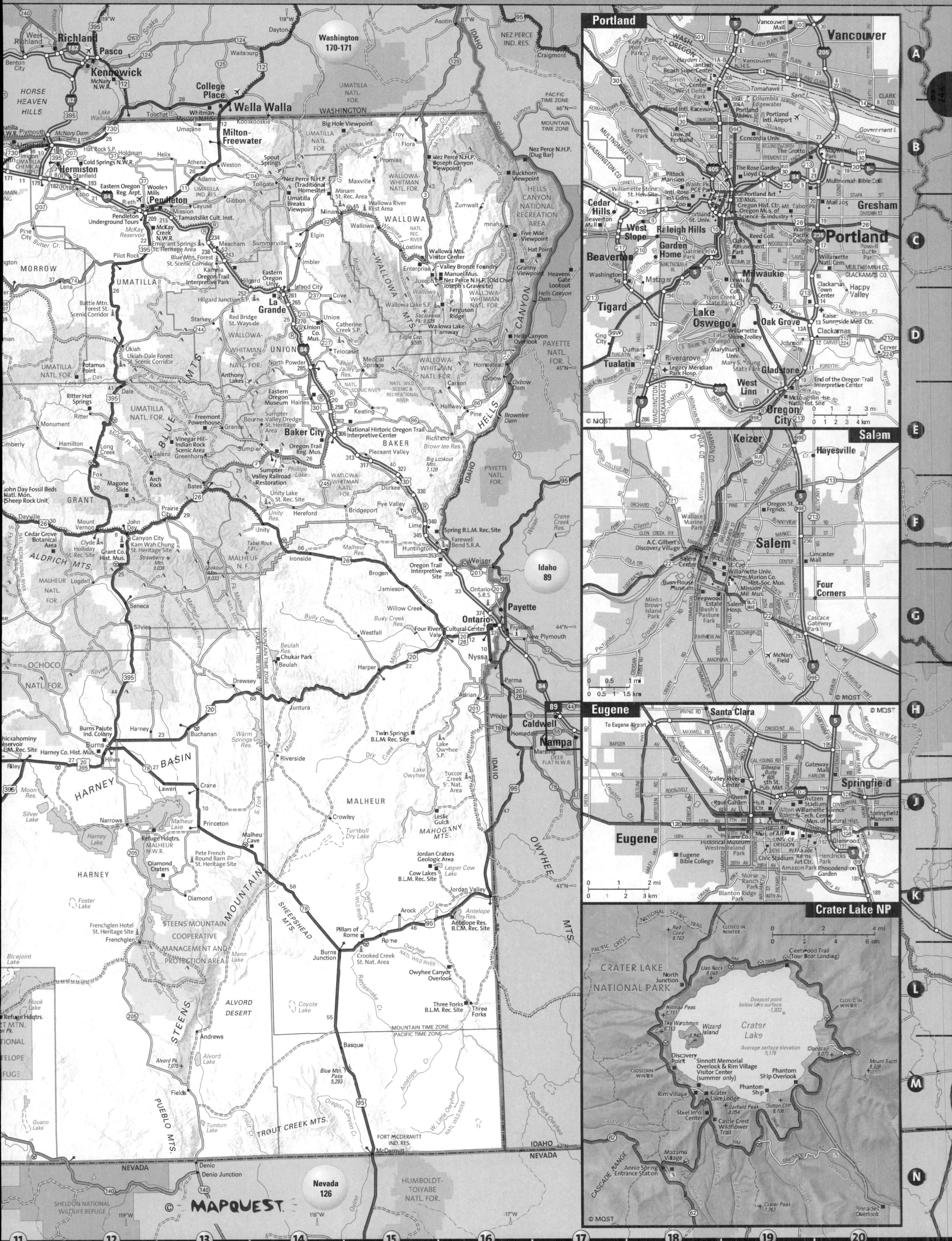

Tourism: 717/787-5453
Road Conditions: 800/331-3414
Road Construction: 888/783-6783

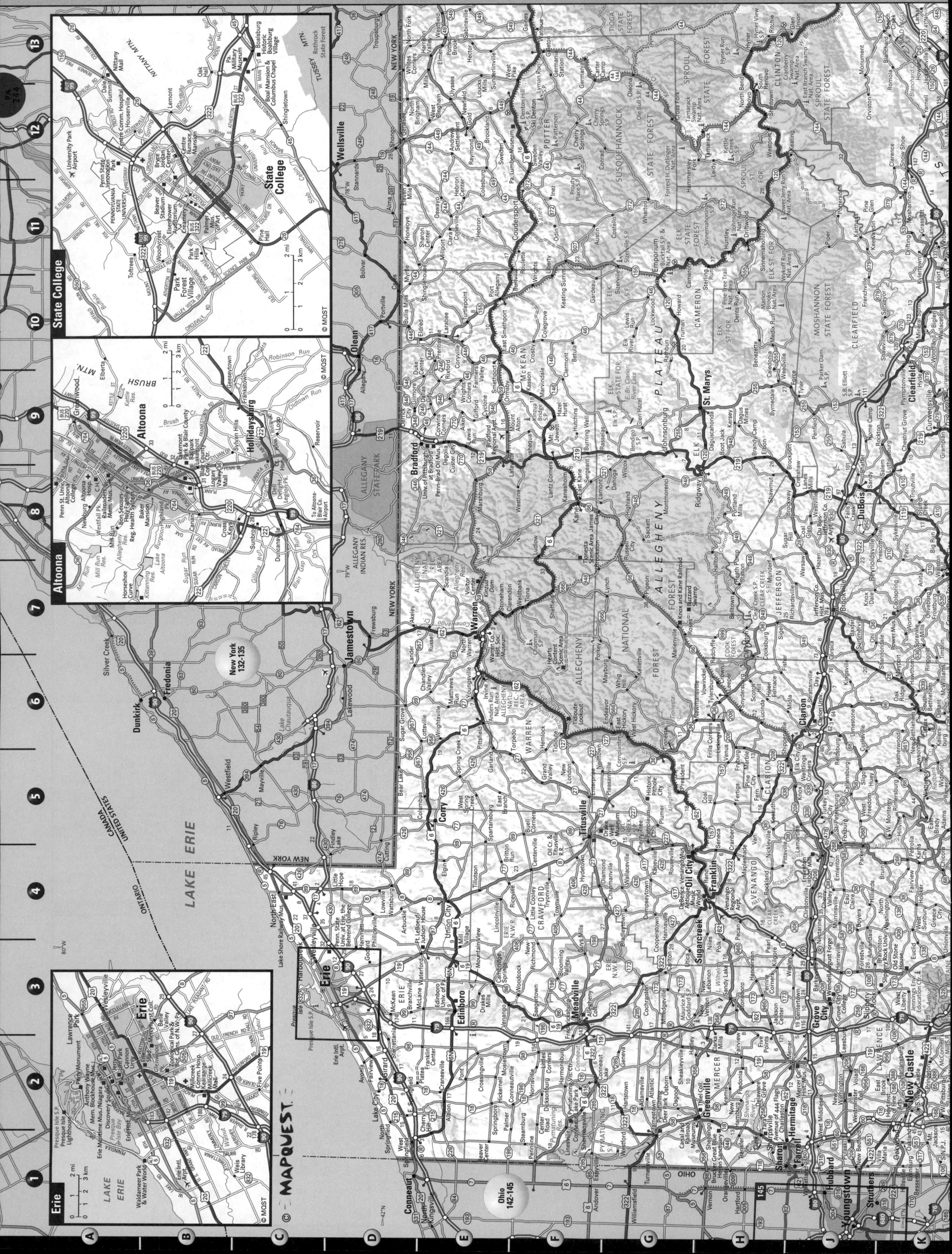

DRIVING DISTANCES IN MILES	ALLENTOWN	ALTOONA	CHAMBERSBURG	ERIE	HARRISBURG	INDIANA	JOHNSTOWN	LEWISTOWN	MEADVILLE	NEW CASTLE	PHILADELPHIA	PITTSBURGH	SCRANTON	STATE COLLEGE	UNIONTOWN	WARREN	WASHINGTON	WILLIAMSPORT
ALTOONA	218		95	205	140	55	48	71	168	129	241	99	185	40	109	147	123	99
ERIE	361	205	282		298	150	195	242	40	95	405	126	317	210	183	66	153	259
HARRISBURG	82	140	54	298		179	138	58	261	250	109	205	119	88	200	224	213	83
PITTSBURGH	284	99	160	126	205	56	73	155	88	49	306		301	139	48	145	30	215
STATE COLLEGE	165	40	105	210	88	95	87	32	172	167	195	139	149		148	136	163	63

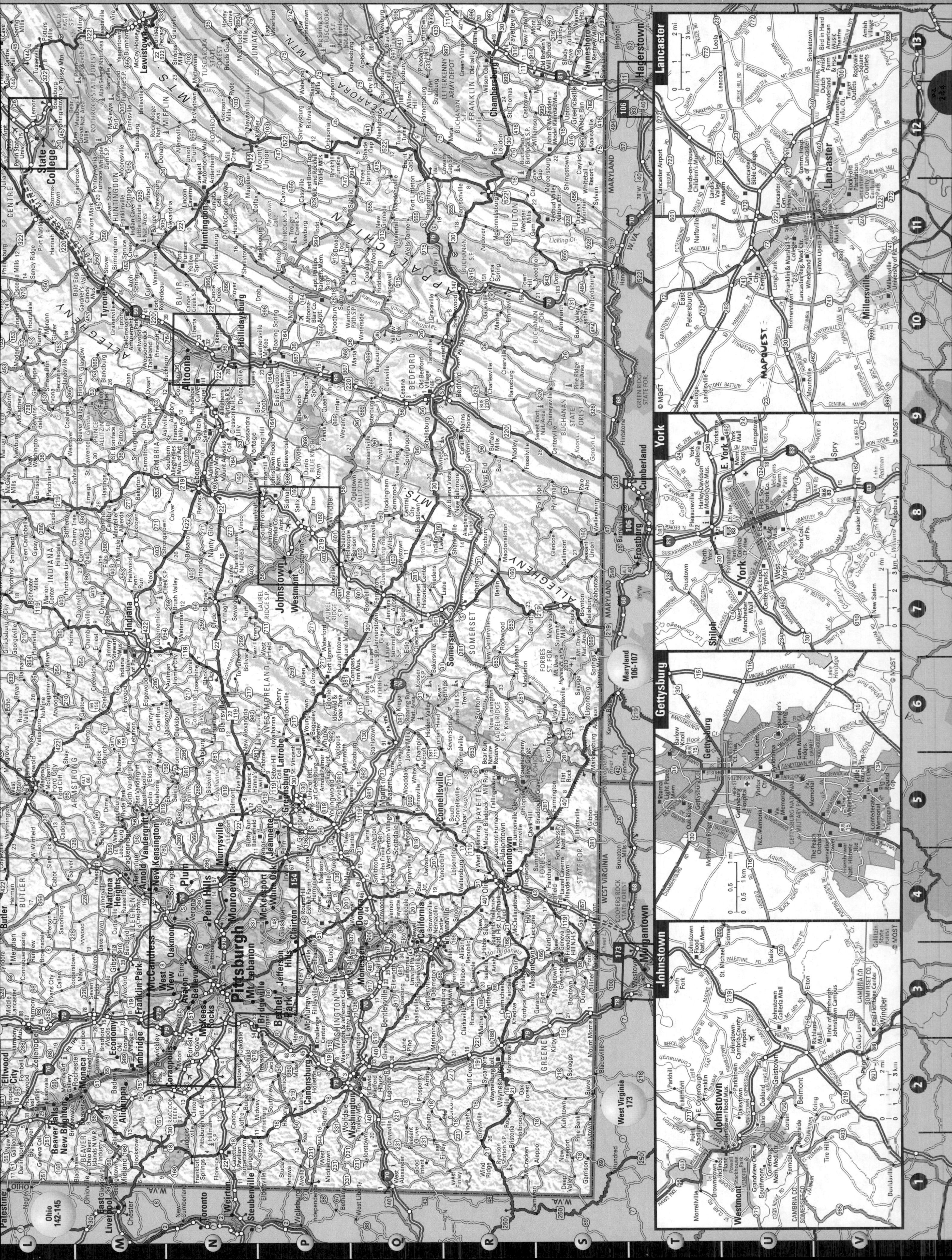

Pennsylvania

Tourism: 717/787-5453
Road Conditions: 800/331-3414
Road Construction: 888/783-6783

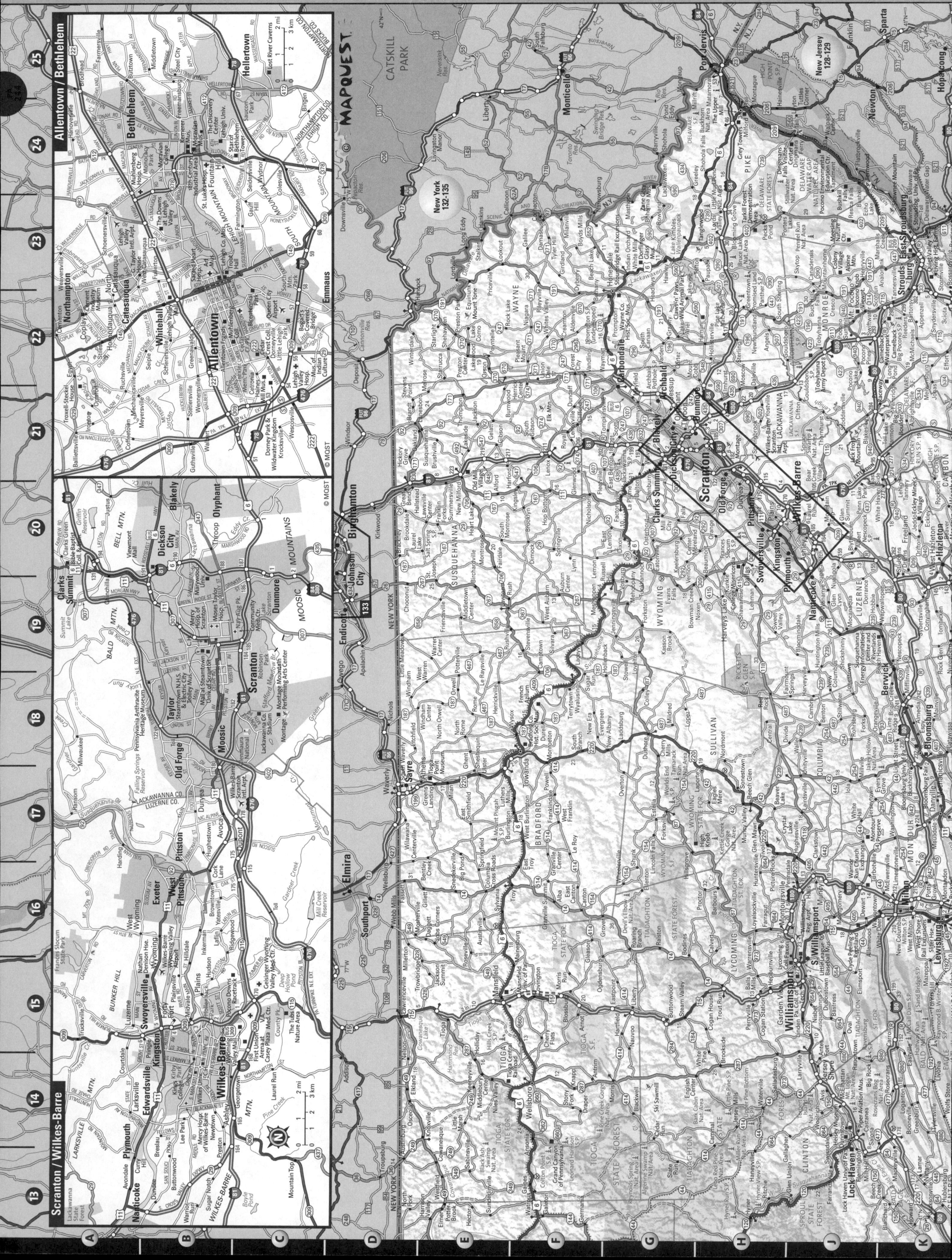

DRIVING DISTANCES IN MILES

	ALLENTOWN	ALTOONA	CHAMBERSBURG	EAST STROUDSBURG	ERIE	GETTYSBURG	HARRISBURG	LANCASTER	LEWISTOWN	PHILADELPHIA	PITTSBURGH	READING	SCRANTON	STATE COLLEGE	SUNBURY	WILKES-BARRE	WILLIAMSPORT	YORK
ALLENTOWN		218	133	39	361	125	82	71	137	63	284	37	76	165	93	64	116	91
HARRISBURG	82	140	54	121	298	42		44	58	105	205	65	119	88	52	105	83	25
PHILADELPHIA	63	241	154	87	405	131	109	79	164		306	63	128	195	144	117	169	100
SCRANTON	76	185	170	50	317	162	119	130	130	128	301	103		149	84	17	83	143
WILLIAMSPORT	116	99	134	118	259	125	83	124	83	169	215	110	83	63	34	66		108

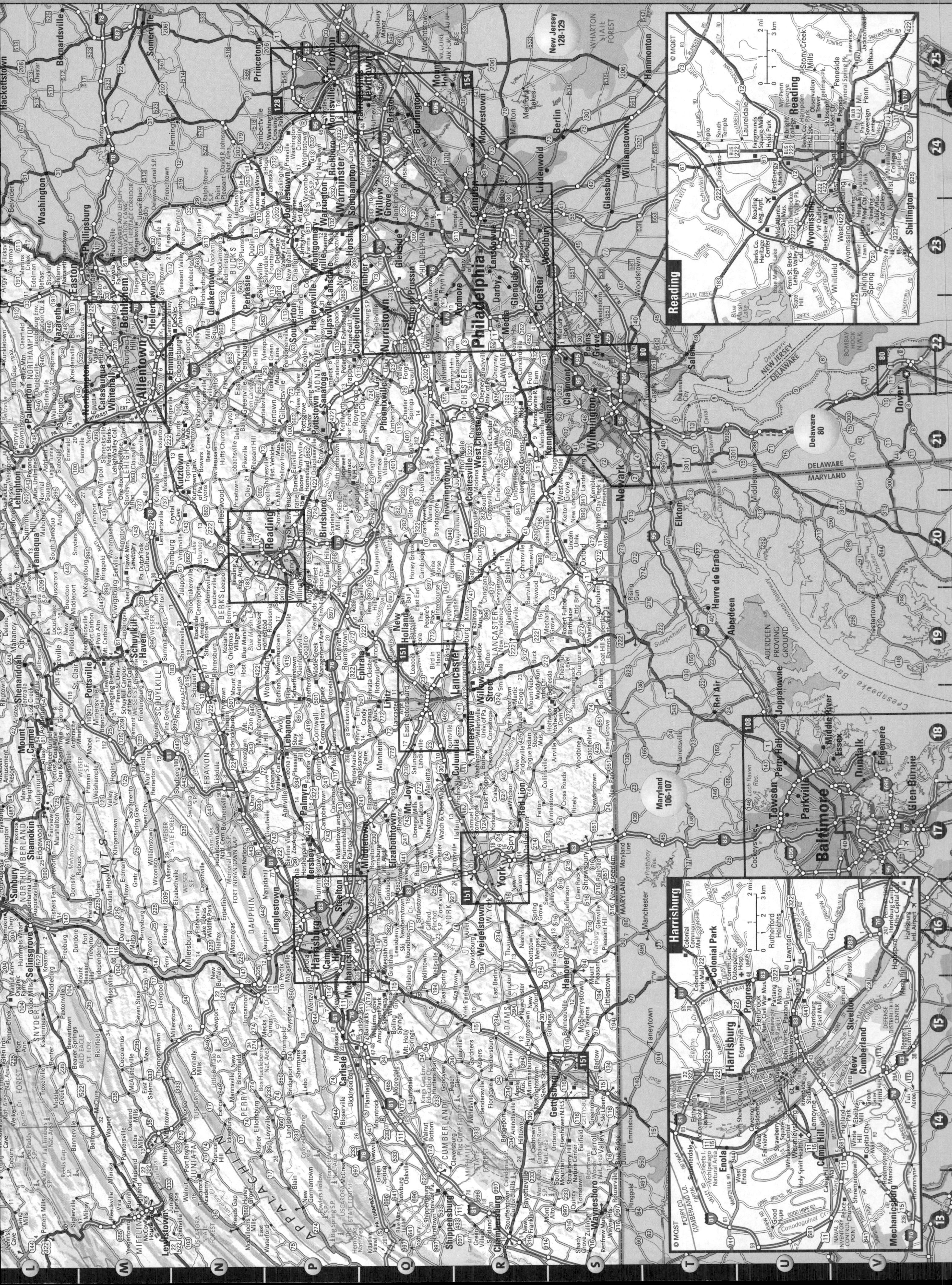

MI 10 20
KM 10 20 30

Tourism: 401/222-2601
Road Conditions: 401/222-2481

DRIVING DISTANCES IN MILES	BOSTON, MA	BRISTOL	EAST GREENWICH	FALL RIVER, MA	HOPE VALLEY	KINGSTON	NEWPORT	PROVIDENCE	WARWICK	WESTERLY	WICKFORD	WOONSOCKET
NEWPORT	73	14	20	20	28	17		33	27	41	13	46
PROVIDENCE	52	16	12	17	30	29	33		12	46	20	16
WARWICK	63	25	6	26	24	23	27	12		40	14	26
WESTERLY	97	60	41	61	17	26	41	46	40		34	59
WOONSOCKET	52	30	26	31	43	42	46	16	26	59	33	

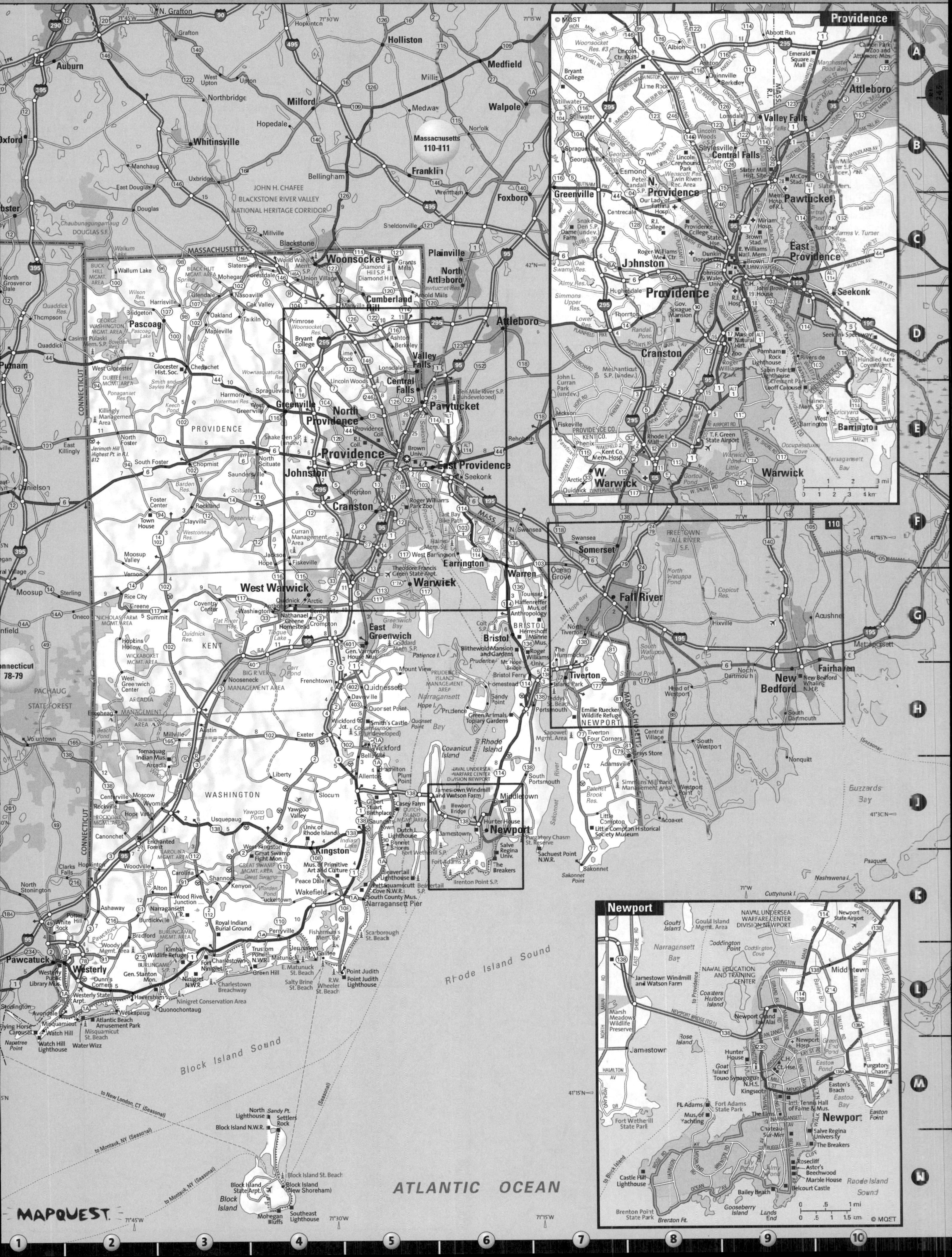

Tourism: 800/810-5700
Road Conditions: 803/869-9621

DRIVING DISTANCES IN MILES	AUGUSTA, GA	CHARLOTTE, NC	CHARLESTON	COLUMBIA	FLORENCE	GREENVILLE	HILTON HEAD ISLAND	MYRTLE BEACH	ROCK HILL	SAVANNAH, GA	SPARTANBURG	SUMTER
CHARLESTON	142	204		110	127	205	95	92	183	107	200	100
COLUMBIA	70	91	110		80	97	152	146	70	159	92	45
FLORENCE	147	107	127	80		174	170	66	115	176	169	39
GREENVILLE	110	96	205	97	174		248	241	88	255	30	142
MYRTLE BEACH	213	173	92	146	66	241	190		181	197	235	93

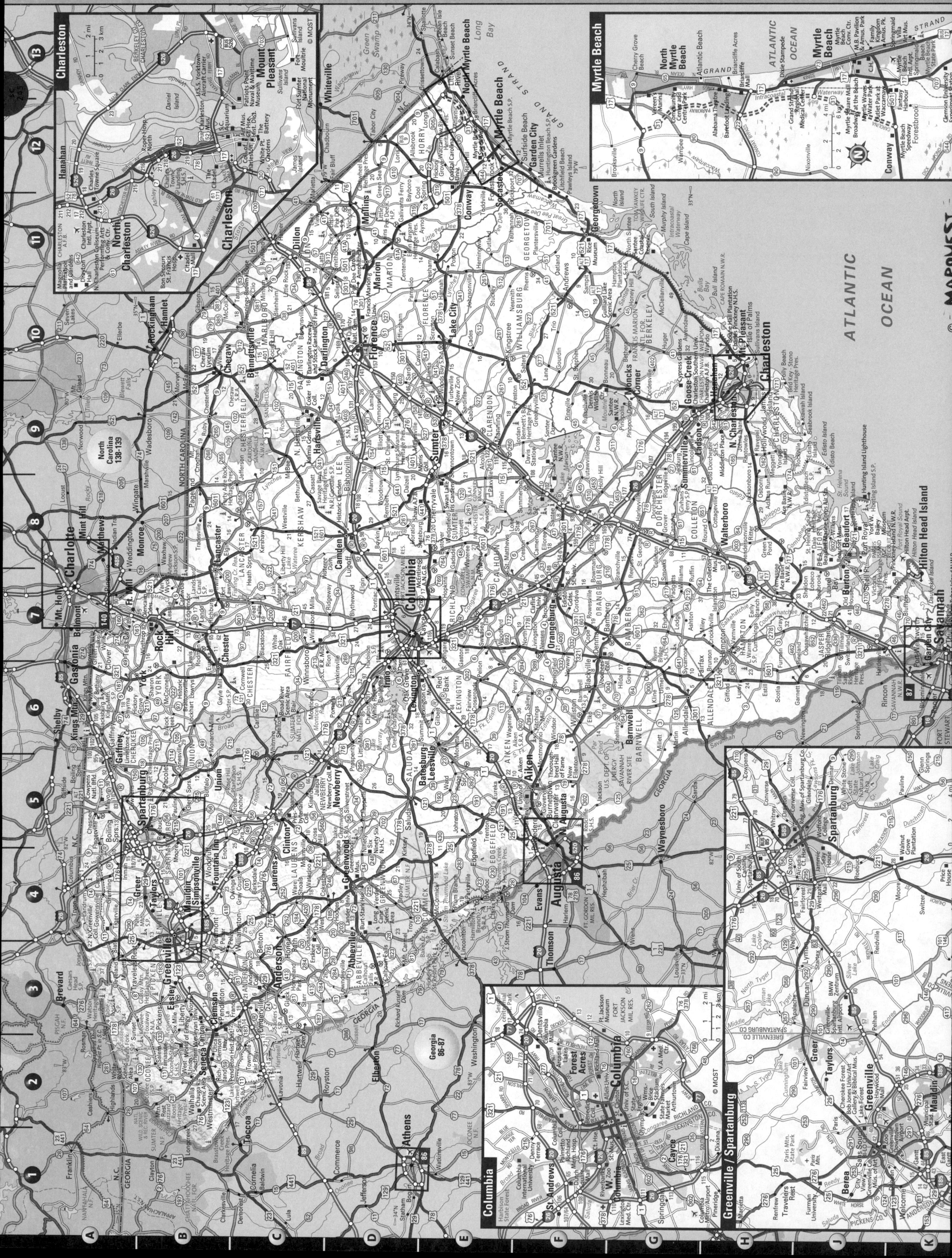

Tourism: 800/732-5682
Road Conditions: 605/367-5707

DRIVING DISTANCES IN MILES

	ABERDEEN	BELLE FOURCHE	BROOKINGS	HOT SPRINGS	HURON	MITCHELL	MOBRIDGE	PIERRE	RAPID CITY	SIOUX FALLS	WATERTOWN	YANKTON
ABERDEEN		310	150	412	90	146	99	160	357	204	98	231
PIERRE	160	247	188	247	115	155	107		193	226	189	240
RAPID CITY	357	56	390	56	313	275	243	193		346	436	360
SIOUX FALLS	204	401	57	401	127	73	303	226	346		103	80
WATERTOWN	98	360	49	490	86	162	196	189	436	103		179

Tourism: 615/741-2159
Road Conditions: 800/342-3258

DRIVING DISTANCES IN MILES	BRISTOL	CHATTANOOGA	CLARKSVILLE	COLUMBIA	COOKEVILLE	DYERSBURG	FAYETTEVILLE	GATLINBURG	JACKSON	JOHNSON CITY	KNOXVILLE	MANCHESTER	MEMPHIS	MORRISTOWN	MURFREESBORO	NASHVILLE	OAK RIDGE	UNION CITY
CHATTANOOGA	233		177	158	89	308	97	156	262	222	116	69	346	164	102	131	110	311
JOHNSON CITY	24	222	336	337	213	469	317	108	423		107	289	507	69	285	290	126	471
KNOXVILLE	117	116	230	231	107	363	211	40	317	107		183	401	48	179	184	24	365
MEMPHIS	518	346	213	210	296	81	268	441	91	507	401	279		449	246	215	383	113
NASHVILLE	301	131	46	49	79	178	91	223	132	290	184	64	215	232	31		166	181

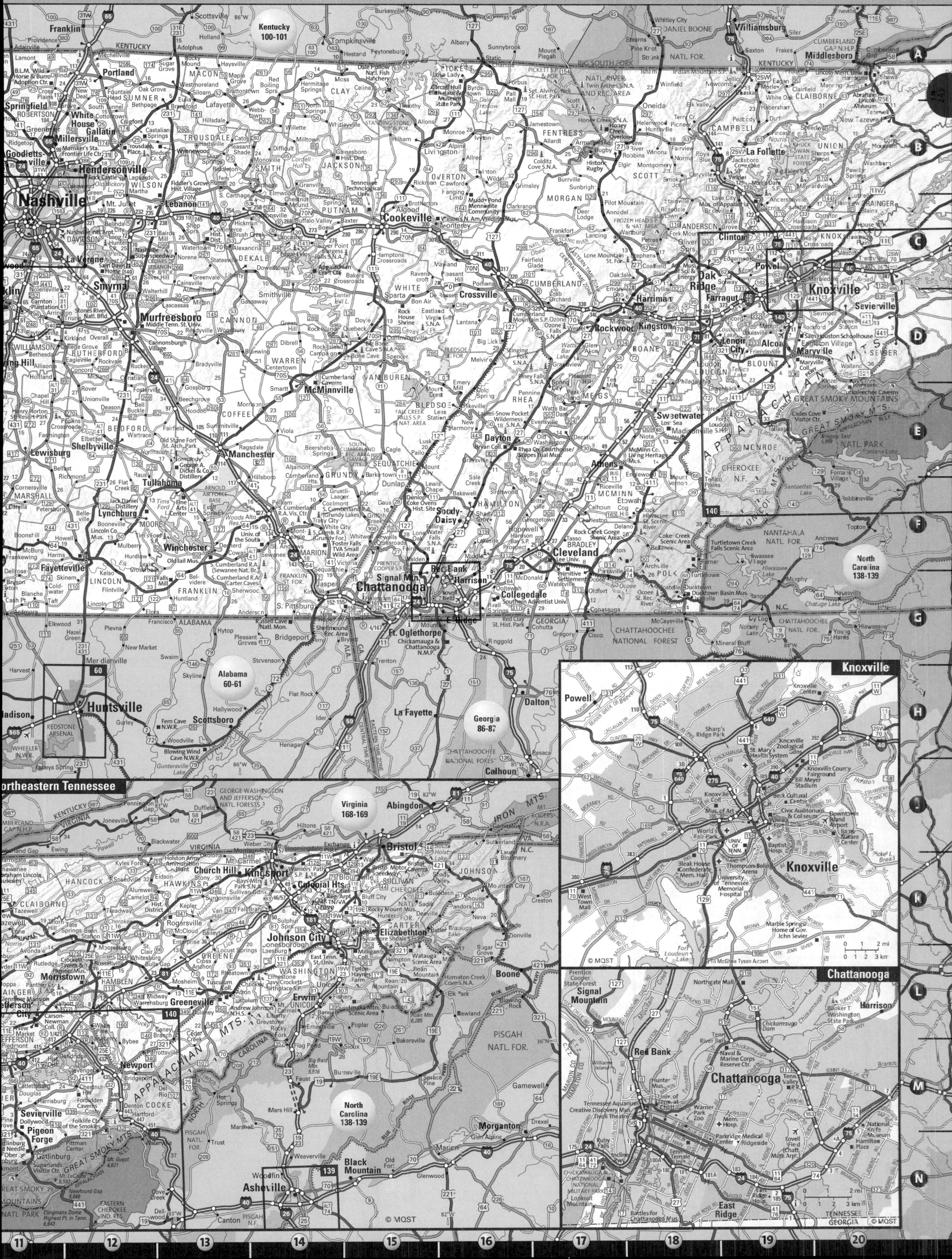

Tourism: 800/888-8839
Road Conditions: 800/452-9292

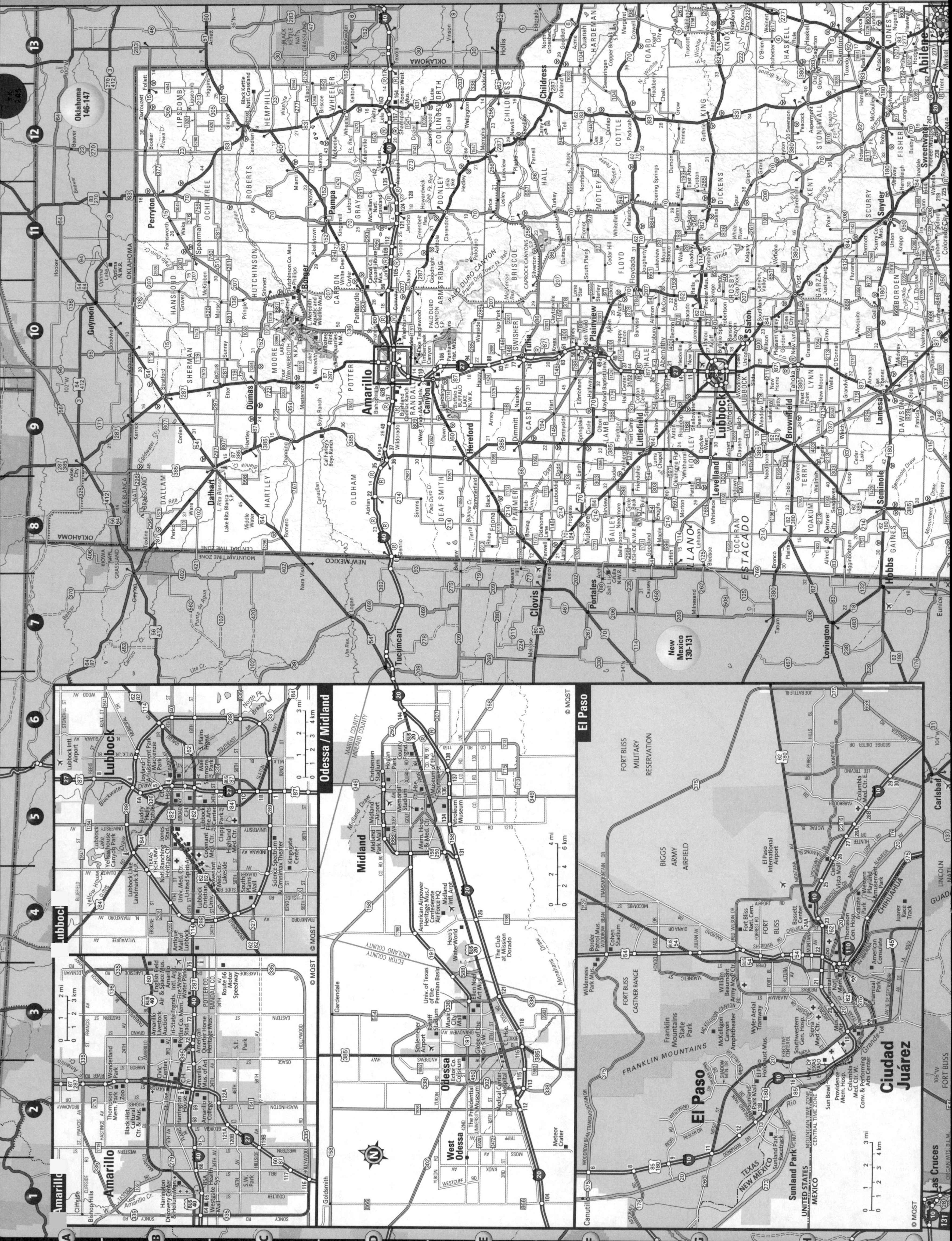

DRIVING DISTANCES IN MILES	ABILENE	ALPINE	AMARILLO	BIG BEND N.P.	BIG SPRING	CHILDRESS	DALHART	DALLAS	DEL RIO	EL PASO	FORT STOCKTON	LUBBOCK	ODESSA	PECOS	SAN ANGELO	SAN ANTONIO	VAN HORN	WICHITA FALLS
AMARILLO	290	414		472	230	118	87	470	462	438	349	124	266	340	308	513	427	228
EL PASO	459	232	438	329	347	558	420	647	425		241	341	285	209	416	556	122	596
LUBBOCK	166	291	124	349	106	144	211	354	338	341	226		142	217	185	389	303	207
ODESSA	176	151	266	209	65	276	353	364	246	285	86	142		76	134	342	163	314
SAN ANGELO	91	230	308	287	87	238	395	265	156	416	164	185	134	208		208	235	232

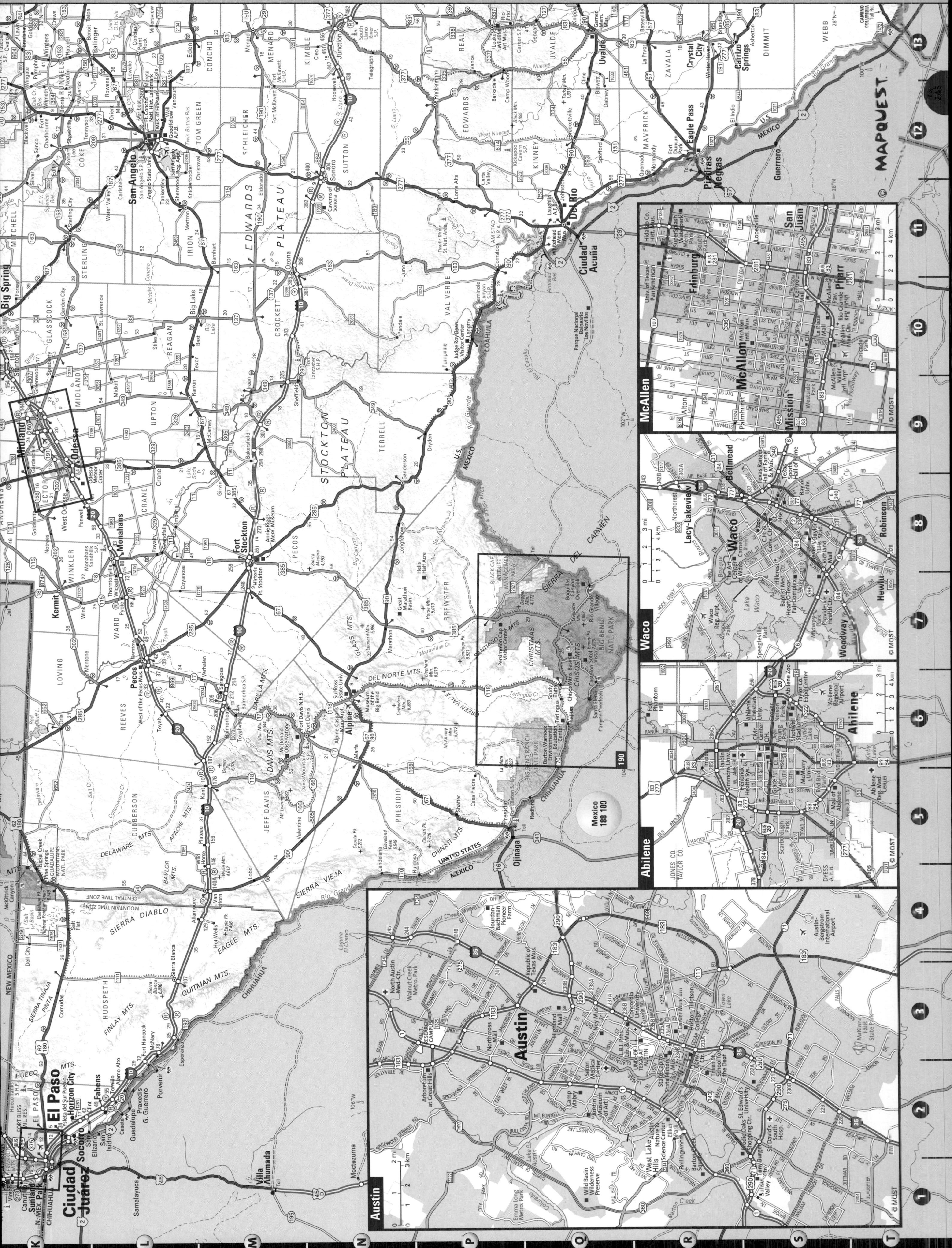

Tourism: 800/888-8839
Road Conditions: 800/452-9292

DRIVING DISTANCES IN MILES	ABILENE	AUSTIN	BEAUMONT	BROWNSVILLE	COLLEGE STATION	CORPUS CHRISTI	DALLAS	DEL RIO	FORT WORTH	HOUSTON	LAREDO	MC ALLEN	SAN ANGELO	SAN ANTONIO	TEXARKANA	TYLER	WACO	WICHITA FALLS
AUSTIN	217		250	350	108	217	195	229	187	166	238	313	207	78	375	229	105	301
CORPUS CHRISTI	411	217	293	157	254		411	272	403	211	141	152	362	147	591	445	321	517
DALLAS	191	195	323	544	184	411		422	32	241	432	507	265	271	179	100	94	141
HOUSTON	425	166	84	351	106	211	241	349	275		355	346	410	200	290	202	283	382
SAN ANTONIO	258	78	284	279	171	147	271	152	264	200	157	243	208		452	305	182	378

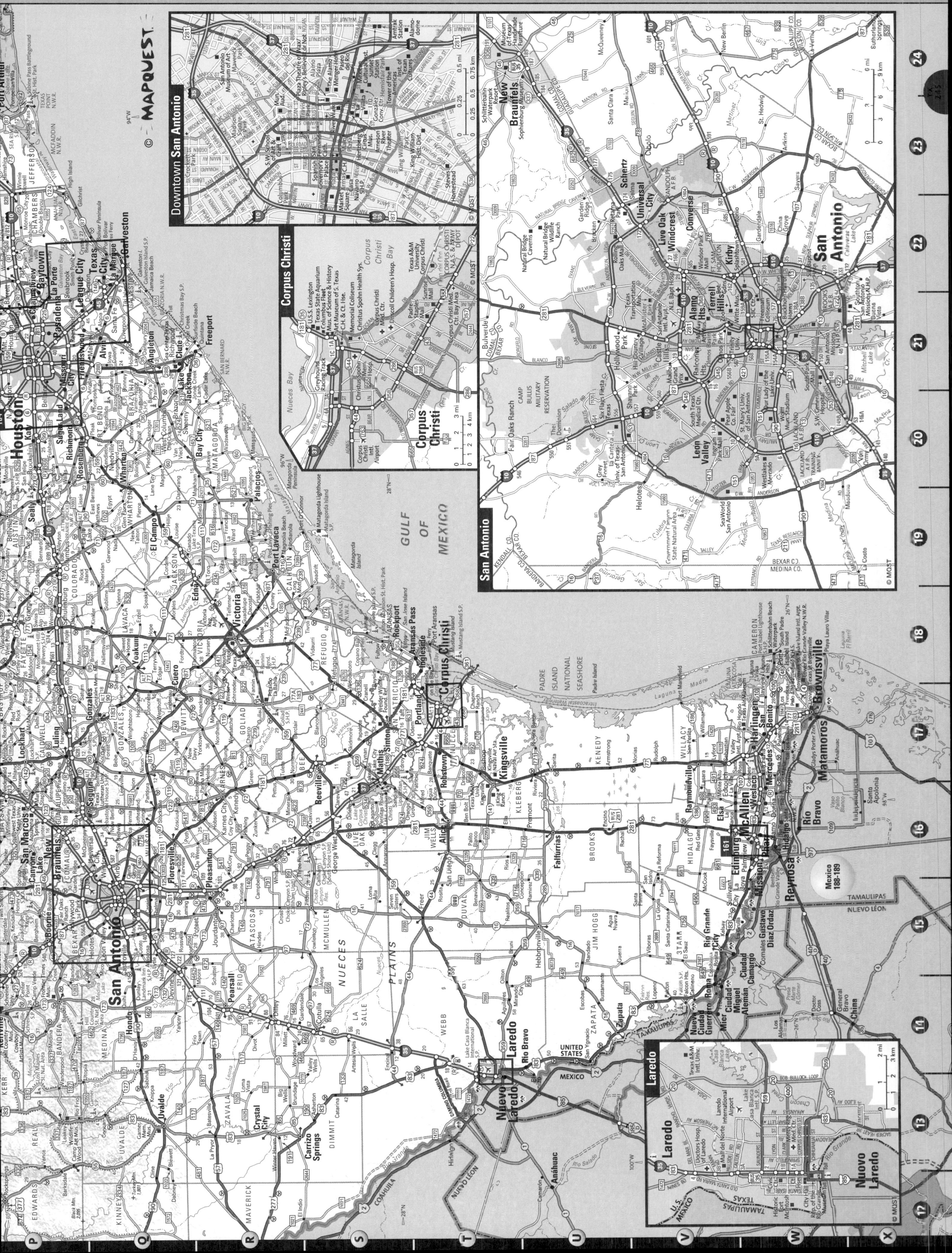

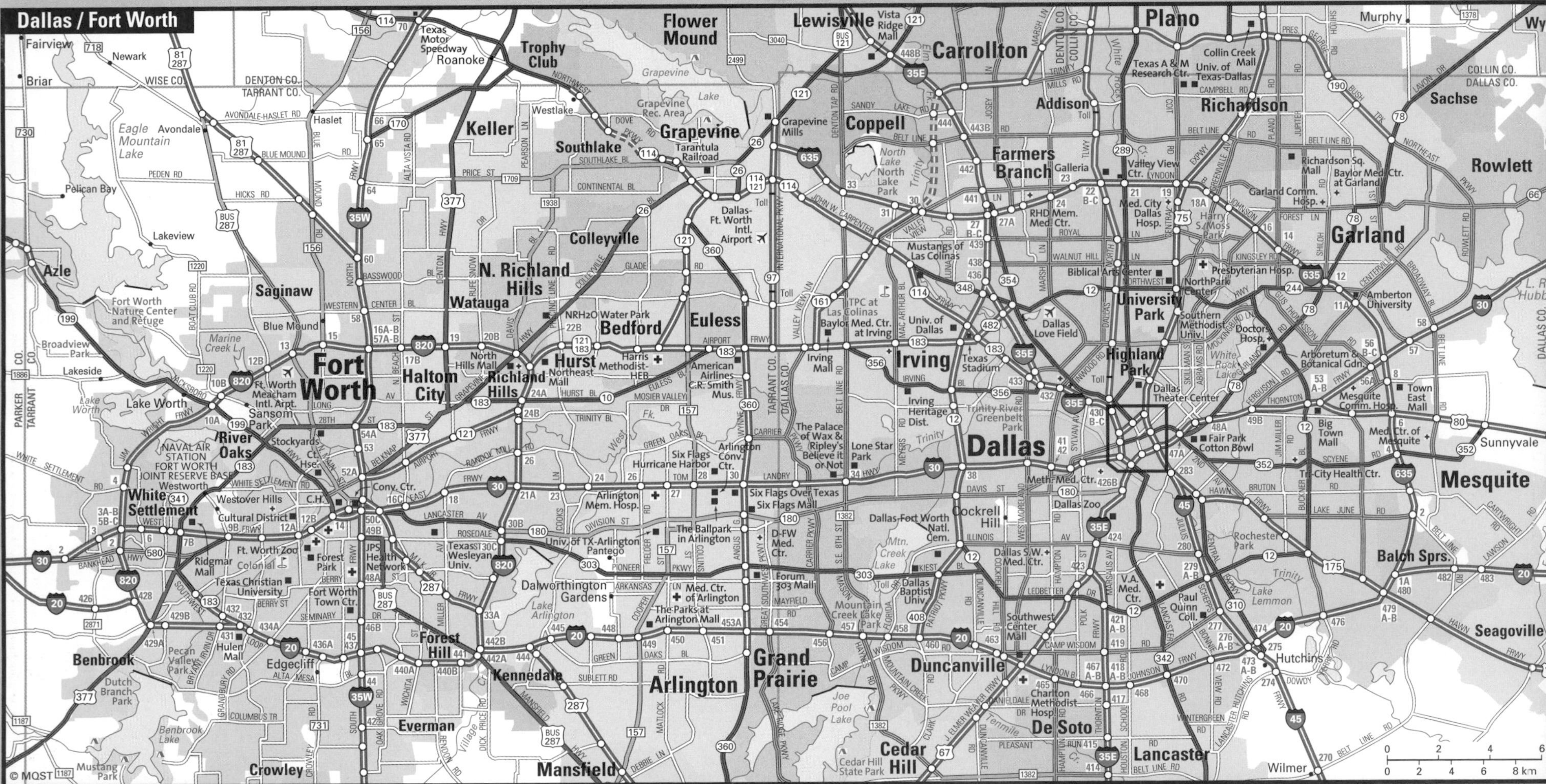
Dallas / Fort Worth
Fairview
Newark
Briar
Flower Mound
Lewisville
Carrollton
Plano
Murphy
Trophy Club
Roanoke
Texas Motor Speedway
Keller
Southlake
Grapevine
Coppell
Farmers Branch
Addison
Richardson
Sachse
Rowlett
Garland
Colleyville
N. Richland Hills
Watauga
Saginaw
Azle
Lakeview
Pelican Bay
Eagle Mountain Lake
Haslet
Avondale
Euless
Bedford
Hurst
Irving
Highland Park
University Park
Fort Worth
Haltom City
Richland Hills
Lake Worth
Sansom Park
River Oaks
White Settlement
Westworth
Dallas
Mesquite
Sunnyvale
Benbrook
Edgecliff
Forest Hill
Kennedale
Everman
Crowley
Mansfield
Arlington
Grand Prairie
Duncanville
De Soto
Cedar Hill
Lancaster
Hutchins
Seagoville
Balch Sprs.
Wilmer
Dalworthington Gardens
Pantego
© MQST

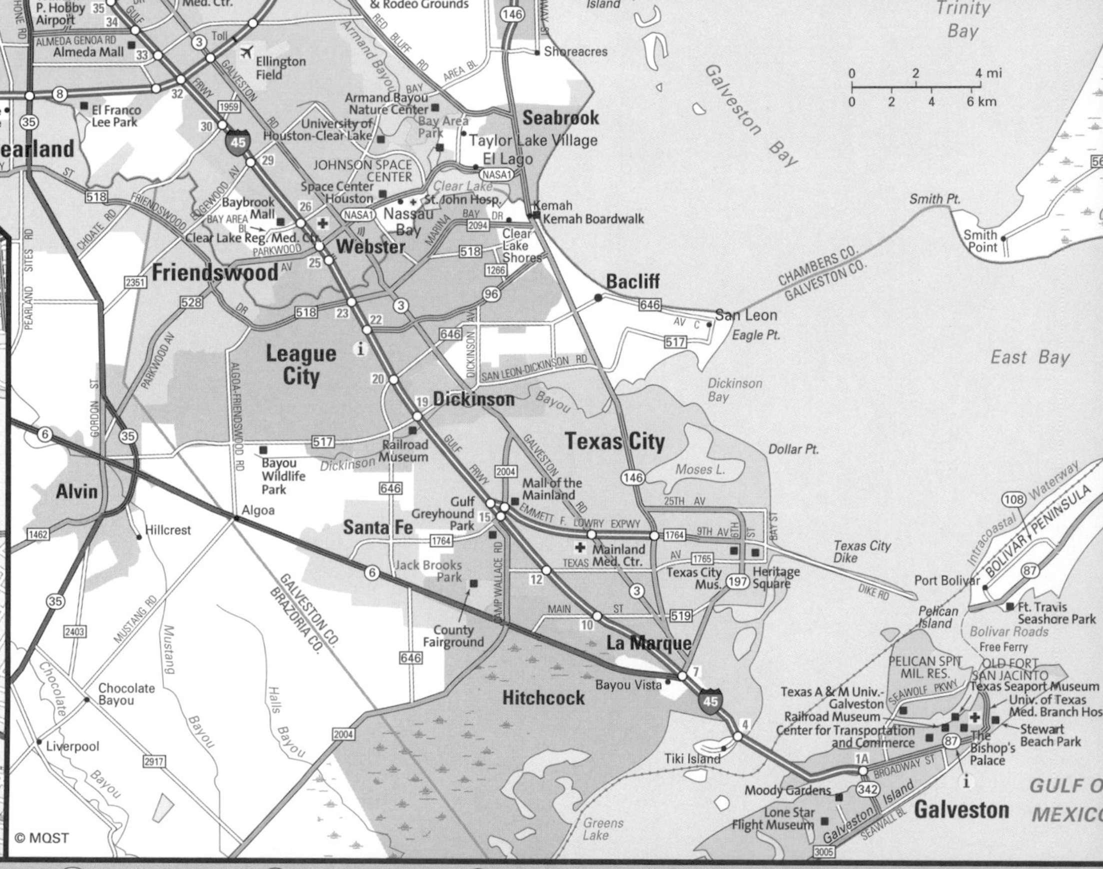
Houston / Galveston
Cypress
Humble
Aldine
Jersey Village
North Houston
Houston
Crosby
Barrett
Highlands
Channelview
Cloverleaf
Jacinto City
Galena Park
Pasadena
Deer Park
La Porte
South Houston
Bellaire
West University Place
Hunters Creek Village
Piney Point Village
Bunker Hill Village
Spring Valley
Hilshire Village
Mission Bend
Meadows Place
Sugar Land
Stafford
Missouri City
Four Corners
Pearland
Friendswood
Webster
Nassau Bay
El Lago
Taylor Lake Village
Seabrook
Shoreacres
Kemah
Clear Lake Shores
Bacliff
San Leon
League City
Dickinson
Texas City
La Marque
Santa Fe
Alvin
Hitchcock
Galveston
Trinity Bay
Galveston Bay
East Bay
Gulf of Mexico
Bolivar Peninsula
© MQST

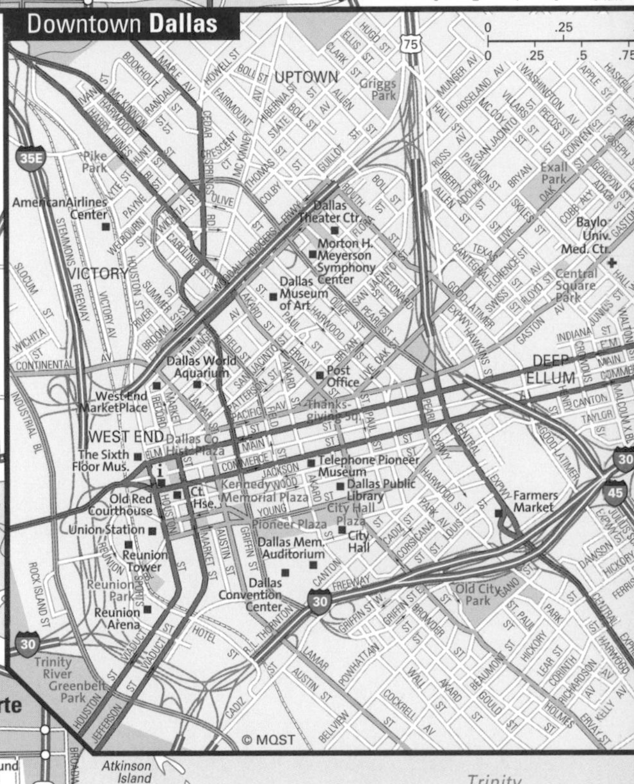
Downtown Dallas
Uptown
Victory
West End
Deep Ellum
Farmers Market
Dallas Convention Center
Union Station
Dallas City Hall
© MQST

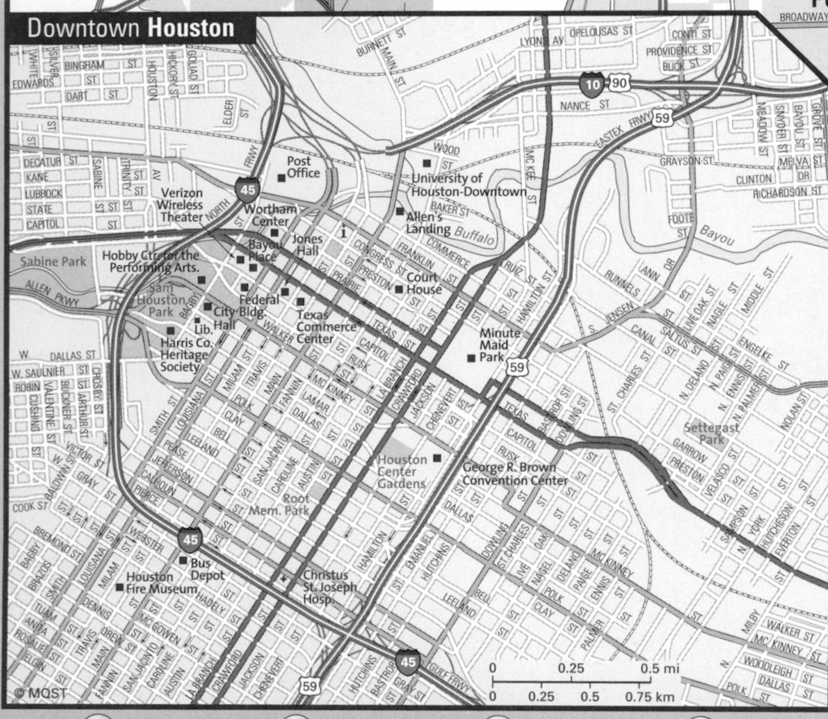
Downtown Houston
University of Houston-Downtown
Wortham Center
Jones Hall
City Hall
Minute Maid Park
George R. Brown Convention Center
Houston Center Gardens
Sam Houston Park
© MQST

Tourism: 800/882-4386
Road Conditions: 801/964-6000

DRIVING DISTANCES IN MILES

	CEDAR CITY	GREEN RIVER	LOGAN	MOAB	OGDEN	PRICE	PROVO	RICHFIELD	ST. GEORGE	SALT LAKE CITY	VERNAL	ZION N.P.
CEDAR CITY		235	325	289	283	234	204	111	53	247	346	66
GREEN RIVER	235		259	54	217	62	137	124	287	180	175	300
LOGAN	325	259		313	46	195	125	233	377	78	252	390
PROVO	204	137	125	192	83	74		111	256	47	155	269
SALT LAKE CITY	247	80	78	235	37	117	47	154	299		173	312

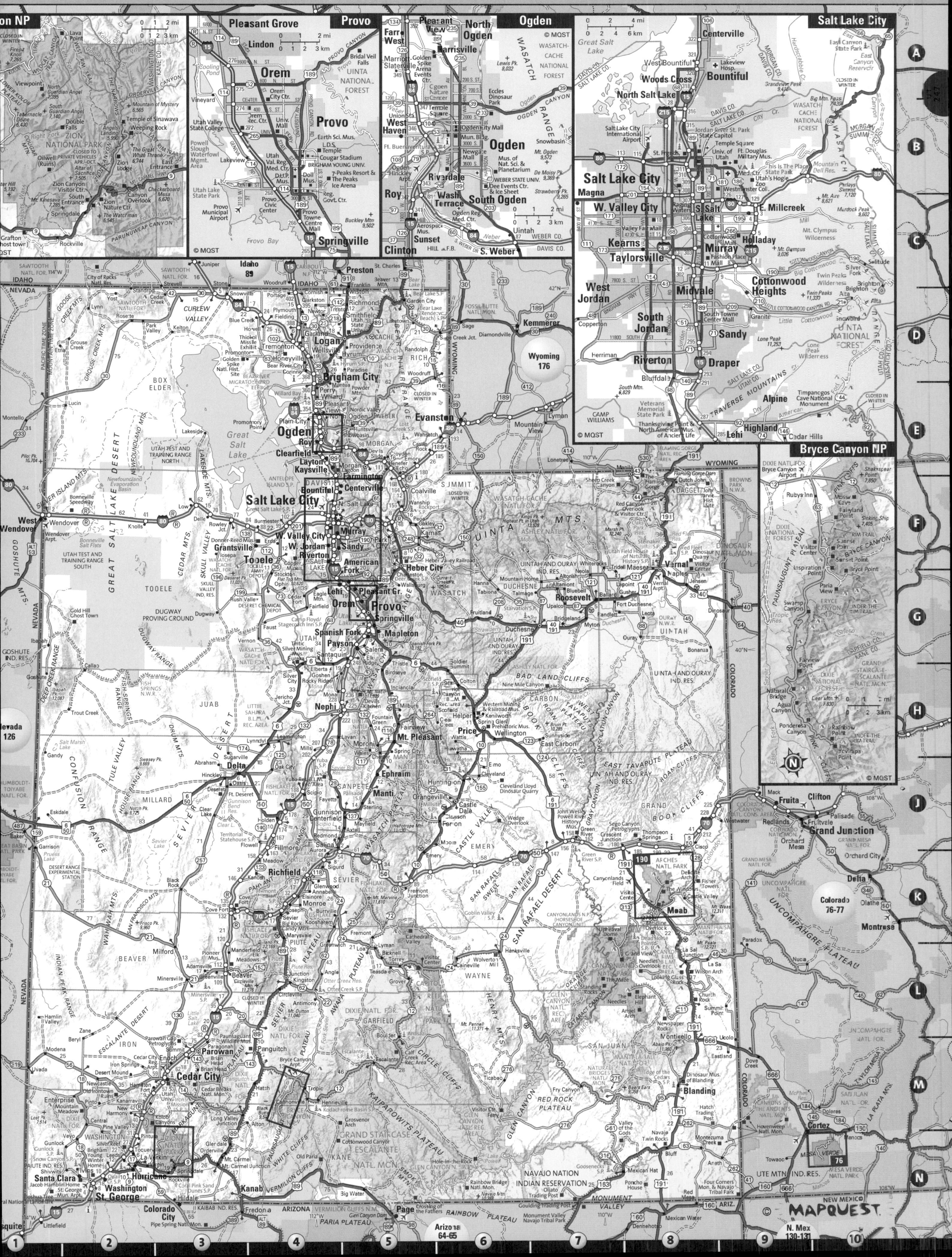

Tourism: 800/837-6668
Road Conditions: 800/429-7623

DRIVING DISTANCES IN MILES	BENNINGTON	BRATTLEBORO	BURLINGTON	MIDDLEBURY	MONTPELIER	NEWPORT	RUTLAND	ST. ALBANS	ST. JOHNSBURY	SPRINGFIELD	VERGENNES	WHITE RIVER JCT.
BENNINGTON		38	127	91	124	200	58	150	161	63	105	98
BURLINGTON	127	148		36	39	81	69	23	76	120	22	91
MONTPELIER	124	112	39	56		64	66	60	37	84	58	54
RUTLAND	58	72	69	33	66	129		93	107	39	47	44
WHITE RIVER JCT.	98	62	91	66	54	104	44	112	65	34	80	

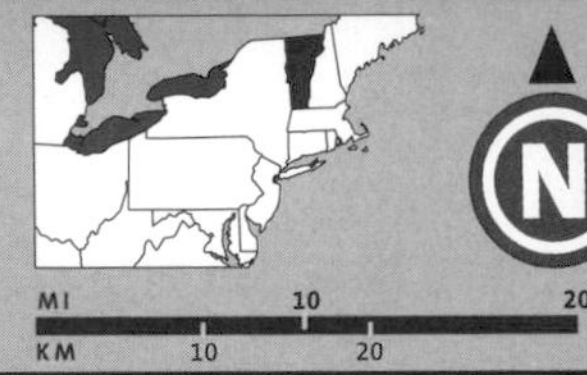

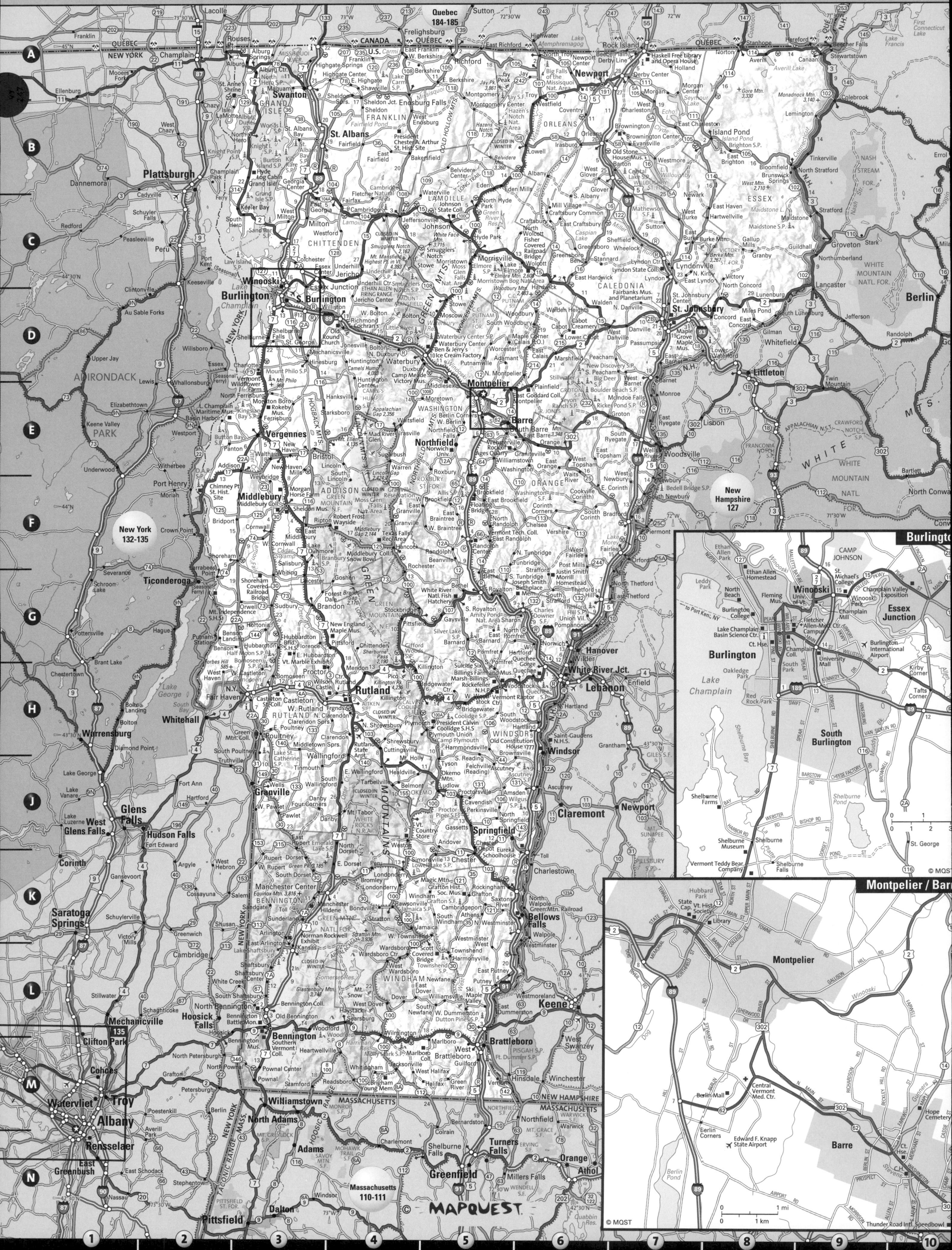

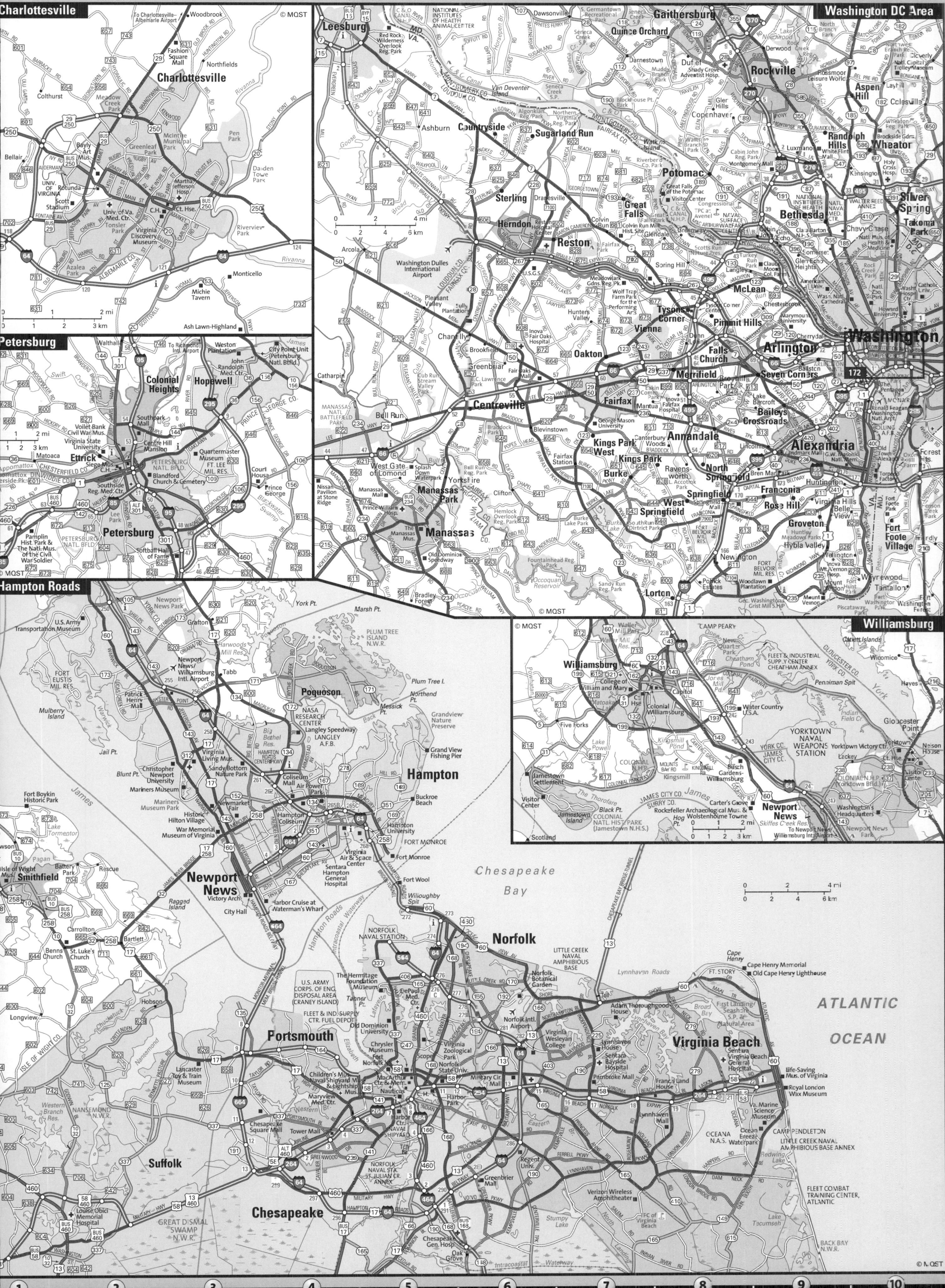
Charlottesville
Petersburg
Washington DC Area
Williamsburg
Hampton Roads
Charlottesville
Colonial Heights
Hopewell
Petersburg
Leesburg
Gaithersburg
Rockville
Bethesda
Silver Spring
Takoma Park
Herndon
Reston
McLean
Vienna
Tysons Corner
Arlington
Washington
Falls Church
Fairfax
Centreville
Annandale
Alexandria
Springfield
Burke
Manassas
Manassas Park
Lorton
Williamsburg
Newport News
Poquoson
Hampton
Norfolk
Portsmouth
Virginia Beach
Chesapeake
Suffolk
Smithfield
Chesapeake Bay
ATLANTIC OCEAN
© MQST

Tourism: 804/786-4484
Road Conditions: 800/367-7623

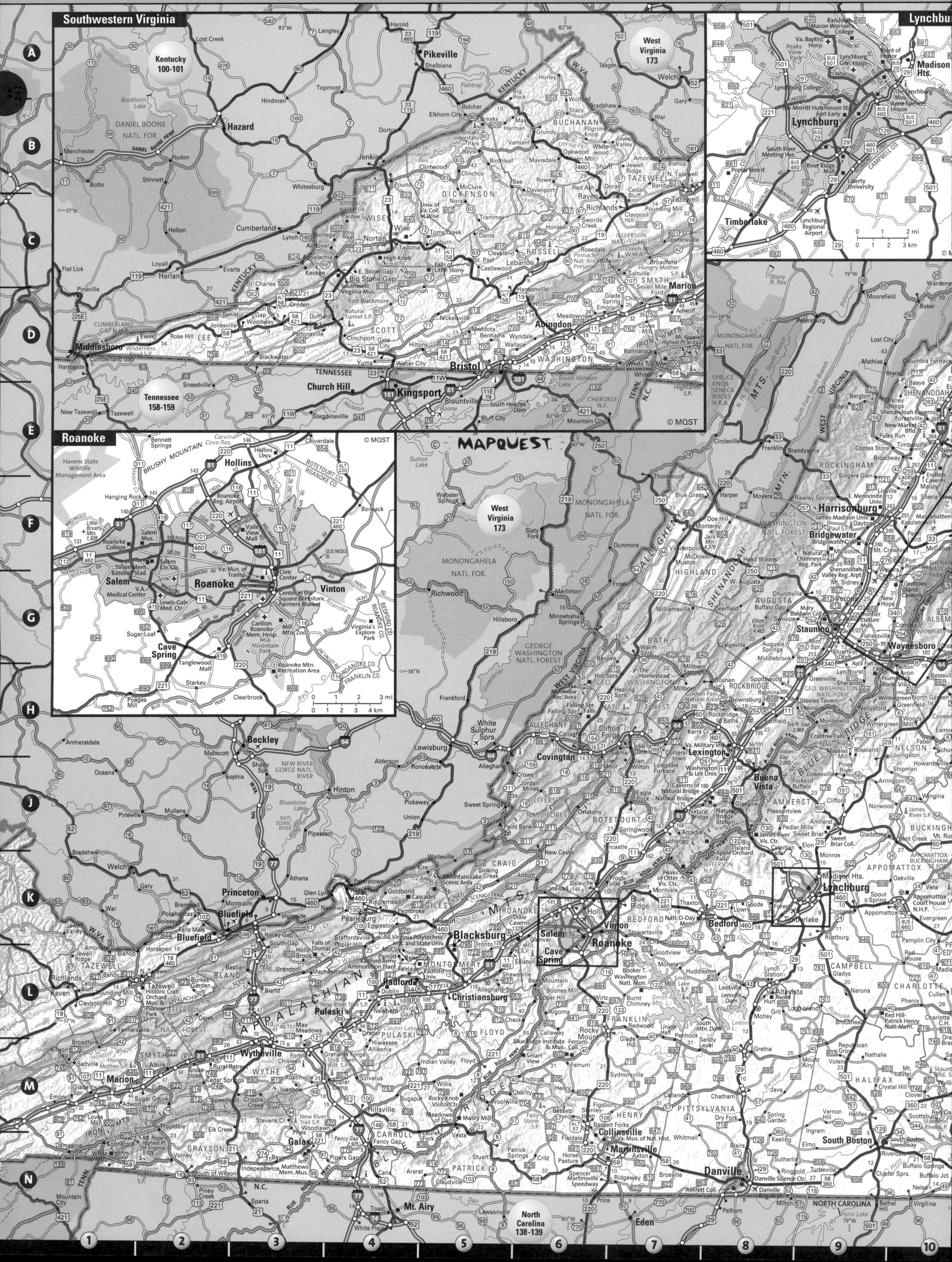

DRIVING DISTANCES IN MILES	BRISTOL	CHARLOTTESVILLE	CHINCOTEAGUE	DANVILLE	EMPORIA	FREDERICKSBURG	HARRISONBURG	LEXINGTON	LYNCHBURG	NORFOLK	PETERSBURG	RICHMOND	ROANOKE	VIRGINIA BEACH	WASHINGTON, DC	WILLIAMSBURG	WINCHESTER	WYTHEVILLE
CHARLOTTESVILLE	258		255	131	140	70	62	69	67	164	95	71	123	180	118	122	100	187
NORFOLK	420	164	101	191	78	145	225	231	203		79	91	285	18	196	43	235	350
RICHMOND	327	71	182	160	69	57	131	138	114	91	24		192	107	108	49	147	256
ROANOKE	149	123	377	83	180	192	117	54	55	285	216	192		301	245	243	184	78
WASHINGTON, DC	380	118	158	268	177	54	131	191	183	196	133	108	245	212		153	92	309

Tourism: 800/544-1800
Road Conditions: 800/695-7623

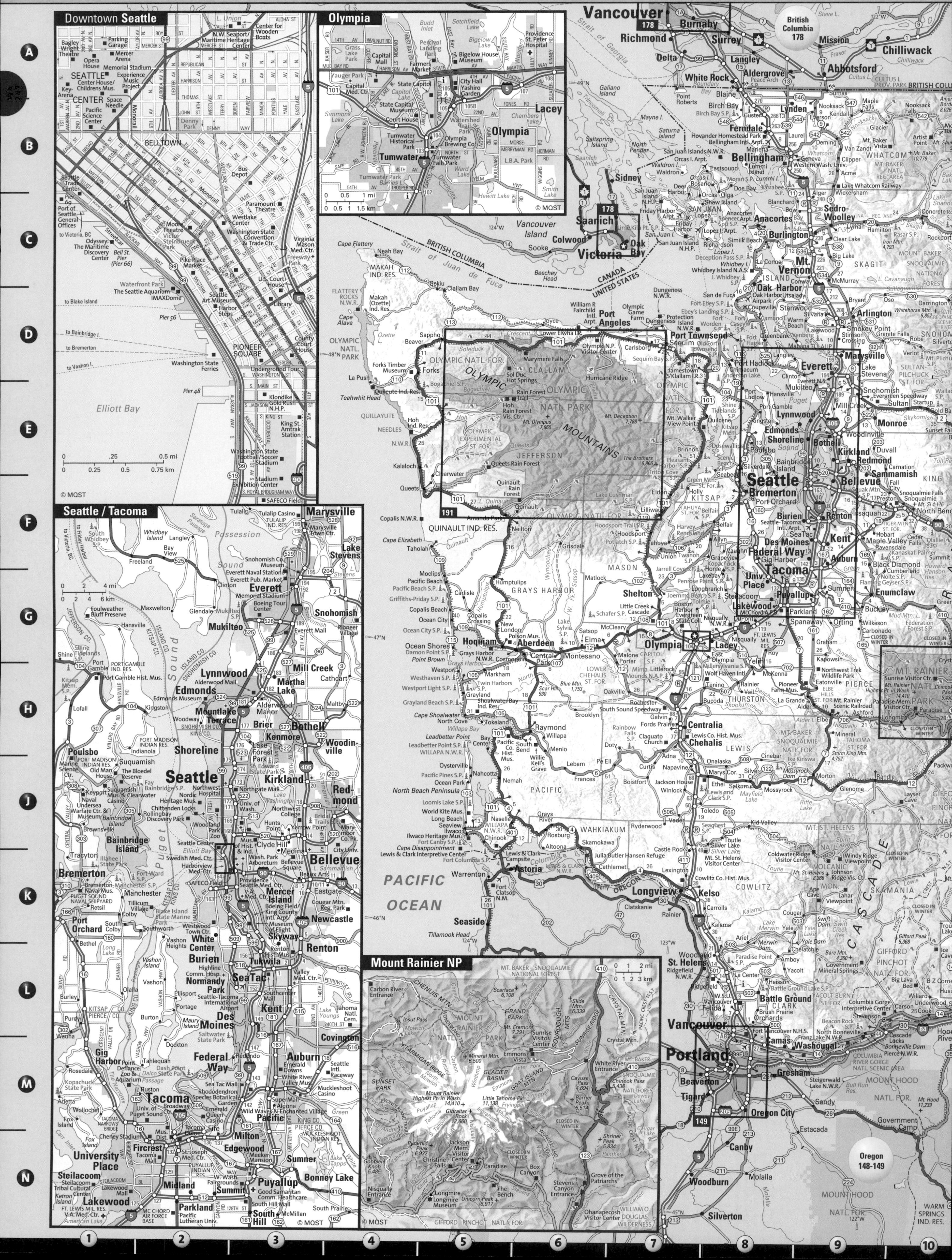

DRIVING DISTANCES IN MILES	ABERDEEN	BELLINGHAM	EVERETT	KENNEWICK	LEWISTON, ID	LONGVIEW	MOUNT RAINIER N.P.	OKANOGAN	OLYMPIA	PORT ANGELES	PORTLAND, OR	PULLMAN	SEATTLE	SPOKANE	TACOMA	WALLA WALLA	WENATCHEE	YAKIMA
BELLINGHAM	196		61	307	420	215	186	195	147	127*	261	390	88	360	122	353	185	221
OLYMPIA	49	147	86	275	387	68	73	282		117	114	358	56	327	27	320	196	188
SEATTLE	105	88	28	226	338	124	96	223	56	83*	170	309		278	31	271	148	140
SPOKANE	376	360	299	139	103	395	290	148	327	362*	351	73	278		303	167	171	203
YAKIMA	237	221	161	86	214	170	87	194	188	223*	187	233	140	203	164	132	115	

* DISTANCE INCLUDES FERRY TRAVEL

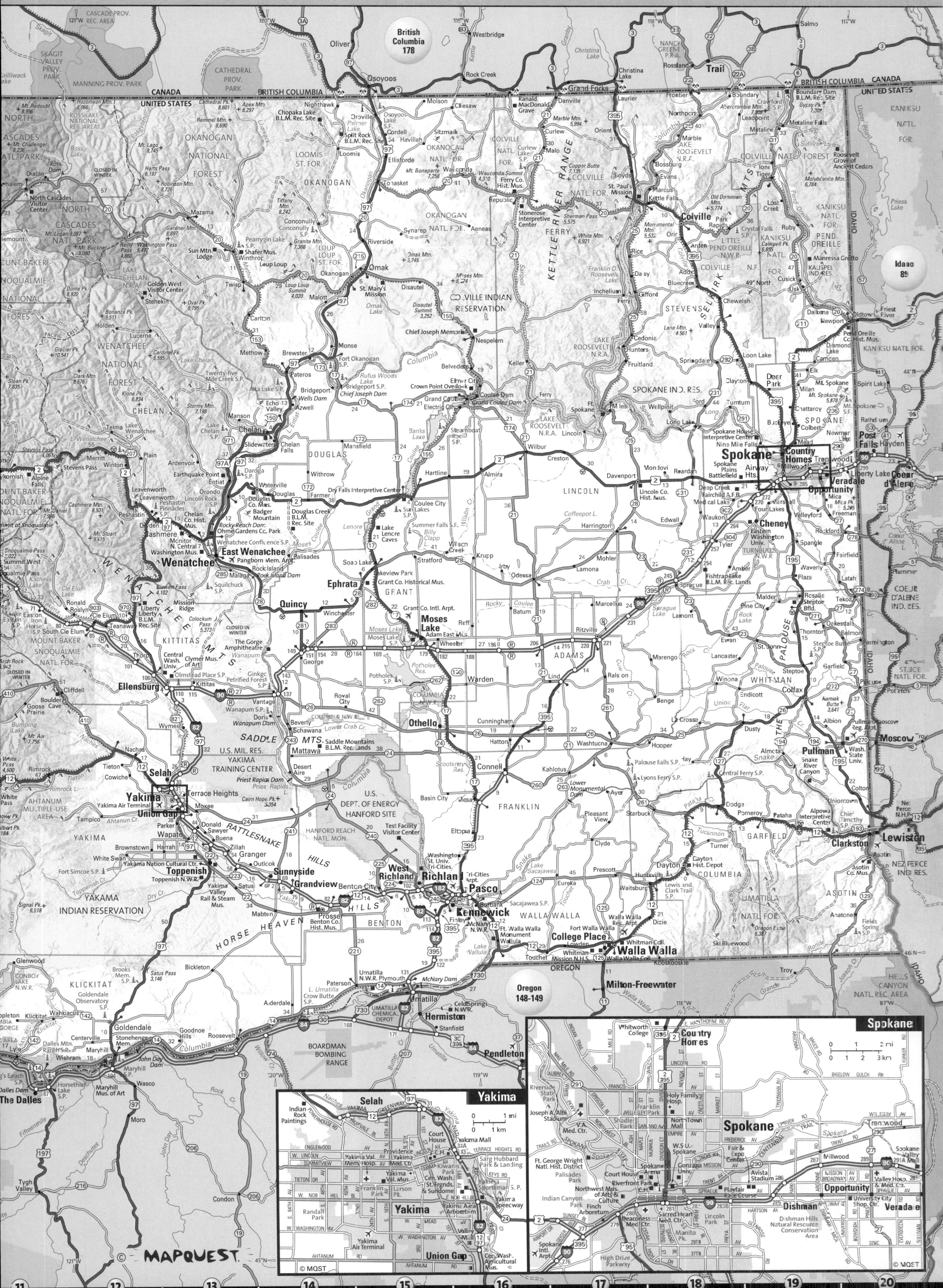

Tourism: 800/422-8644
Road Conditions: 202/673-6813

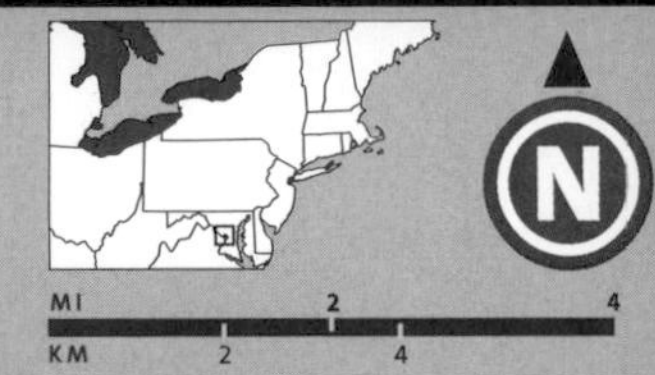

MI 0 15 30
KM 0 15 30

DRIVING DISTANCES IN MILES	BECKLEY	BLUEFIELD	CHARLESTON	CLARKSBURG	ELKINS	HUNTINGTON	LEWISBURG	MARTINSBURG	MORGANTOWN	PARKERSBURG	WHEELING	WILLIAMSON
BECKLEY		49	60	129	142	113	52	270	158	133	237	90
CHARLESTON	60	108		113	131	52	115	283	142	73	175	76
HUNTINGTON	113	161	52	165	184		167	335	195	125	228	62
MORGANTOWN	158	207	142	36	62	195	164	153		104	76	218
WHEELING	237	285	176	109	137	228	237	232	76	106		252

Tourism: 800/225-5982
Road Conditions: 877/982-7623

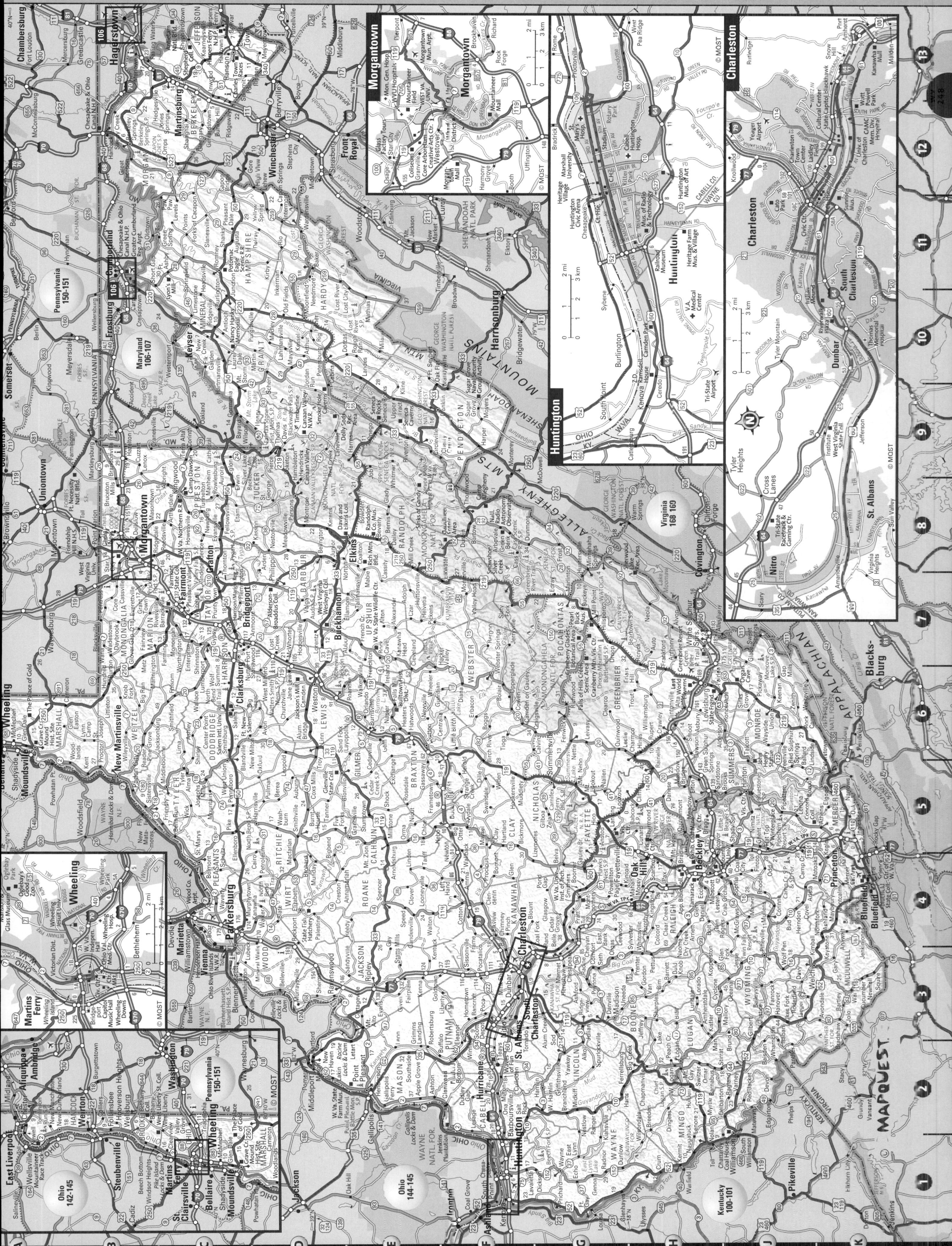

Tourism: 800/432-8747
Road Conditions: 800/762-3947

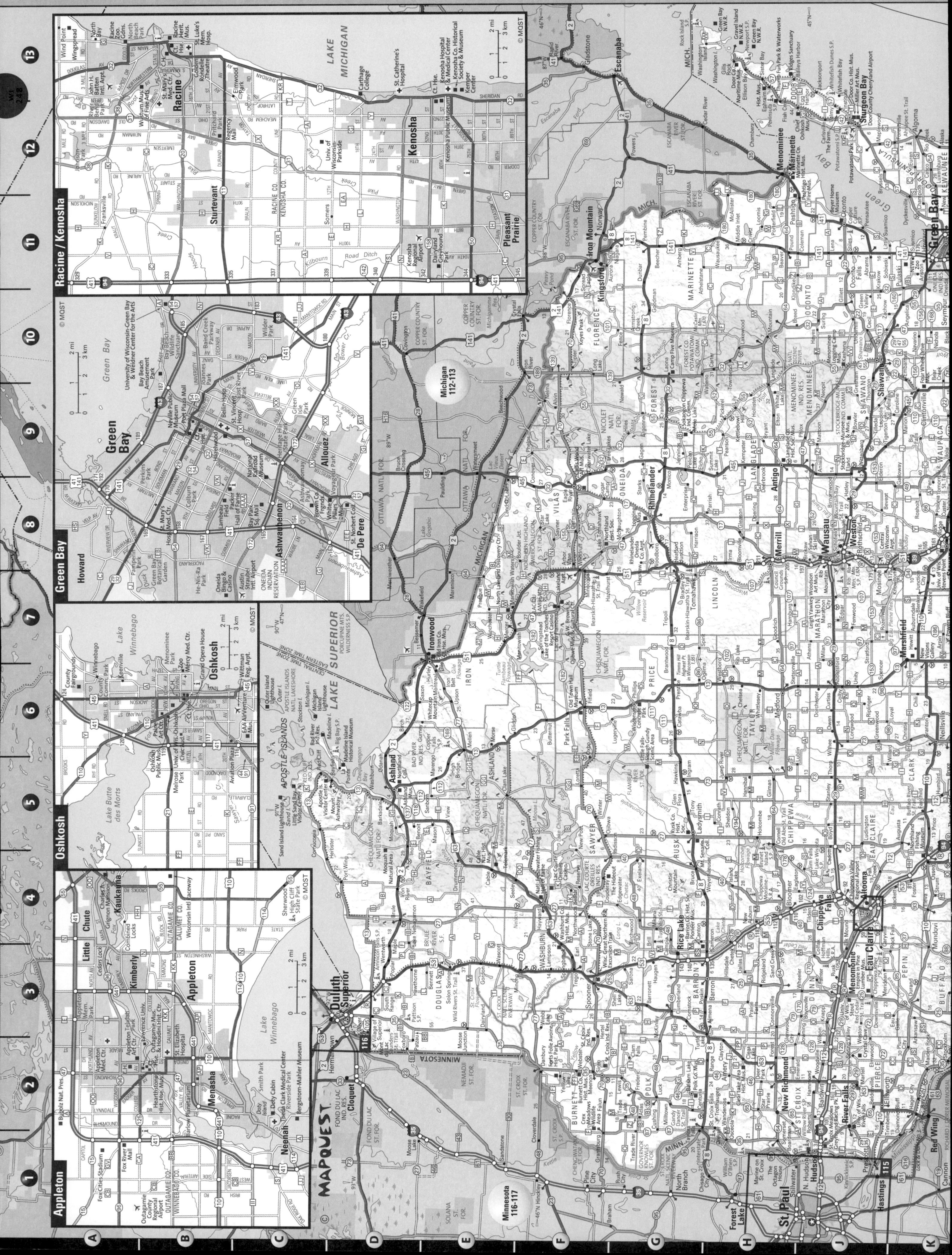

DRIVING DISTANCES IN MILES	APPLETON	ASHLAND	BELOIT	EAU CLAIRE	GREEN BAY	KENOSHA	LA CROSSE	MADISON	MARINETTE	MILWAUKEE	OSHKOSH	PORTAGE	PRAIRIE DU CHIEN	RHINELANDER	ST. PAUL, MN	SHEBOYGAN	SUPERIOR	WAUSAU
EAU CLAIRE	178	163	225		192	284	81	176	211	246	80	147	151	151	83	227	155	99
GREEN BAY	31	245	189	192		154	205	135	54	115	50	120	234	124	268	61	308	93
MADISON	104	305	56	176	135	116	141		184	78	36	36	102	197	258	132	327	141
MILWAUKEE	105	375	74	246	115	39	211	78	170		37	106	180	239	328	54	397	211
WAUSAU	90	165	190	99	93	249	146	141	112	211	11	105	193	58	174	153	223	

Tourism: 800/225-5996
Road Conditions: 307/772-0824

DRIVING DISTANCES IN MILES	CASPER	CHEYENNE	CODY	EVANSTON	GILLETTE	JACKSON	LANDER	LARAMIE	RAWLINS	ROCK SPRINGS	SHERIDAN	YELLOWSTONE N.P.
CASPER		175	215	308	127	282	144	148	117	214	149	298
CHEYENNE	175		390	353	243	433	276	52	151	260	324	455
JACKSON	282	433	181	195	412		163	383	283	177	376	80
ROCK SPRINGS	214	260	281	97	341	177	118	210	110		363	259
SHERIDAN	149	324	150	457	102	376	238	297	266	363		337

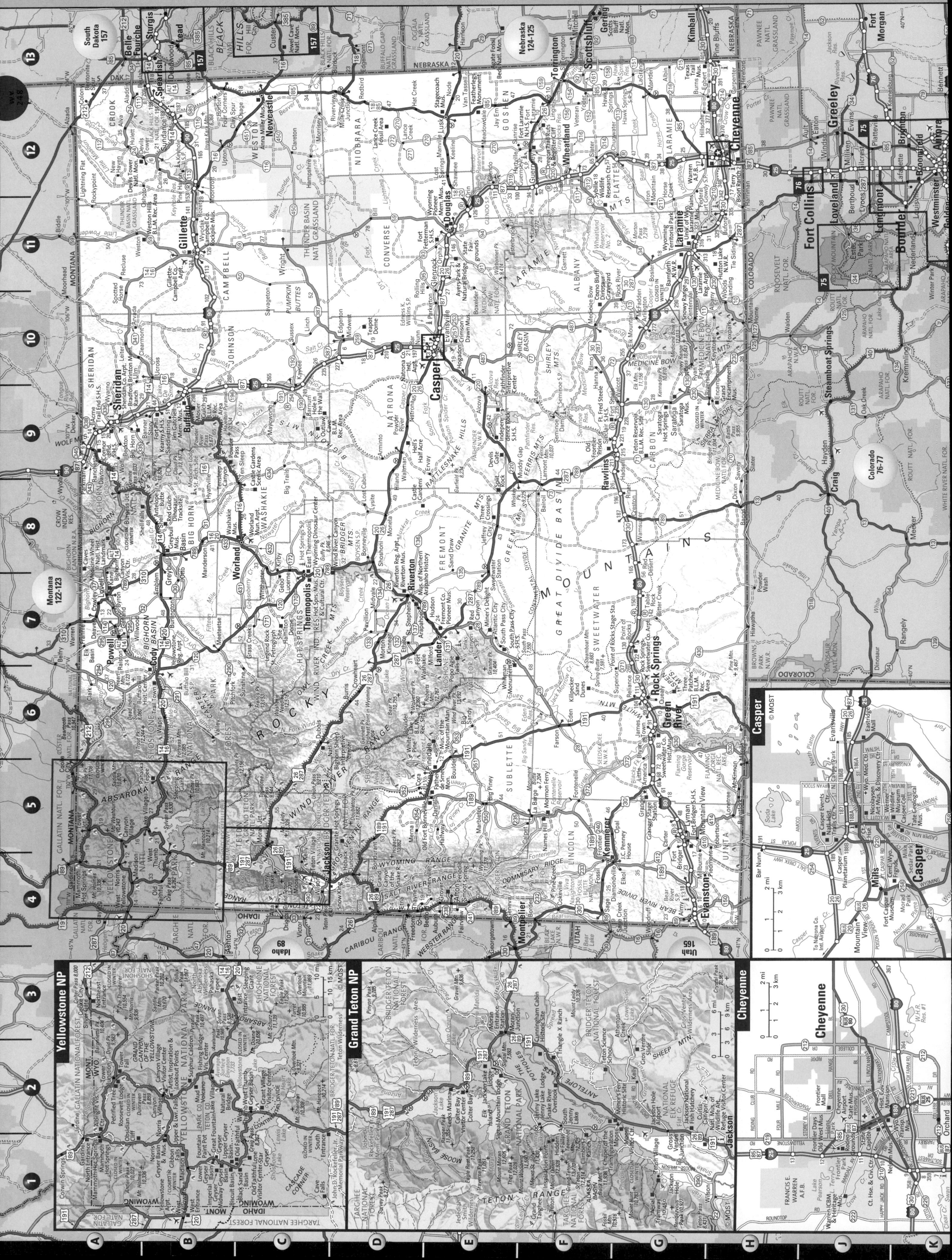

BANFF, AB	4434	1234	128	4681	2811	1001	412	4432	4802	1648	2156	3652	4104	3137	3500	637	3888	856	6032	729	2725	977	2105	3642	819	874	2219	3280	1429
BOSTON, MA		3220	4318	1049	1614	4950	4353	690	1149	2639	2280	504	346	1036	665	5093	634	3577	2379	3840	1572	4941	2187	917	5156	5235	6268	1181	3006
BRANDON, MB			1117	3468	1598	1749	1152	3217	3589	434	943	2438	2889	1923	2287	1894	2675	377	4817	639	1510	2041	892	2427	2016	2108	3067	2066	216
CALGARY, AB				4566	2696	885	296	4315	4686	1530	2041	3536	3986	3021	3384	755	3772	740	5914	613	2607	1093	1989	3524	900	991	2203	3162	1313
CHARLOTTETOWN, PE					2382	5198	4601	354	322	3035	3048	1030	1381	1574	1204	5841	819	3825	1376	4088	1997	5708	2583	1561	5924	6003	6516	1925	3241
CHICAGO, IL						3328	2731	2134	2504	1577	658	1353	1283	1138	1252	3471	1604	1955	3734	2216	896	3318	1521	821	3534	3613	4646	460	1384
DAWSON CREEK, BC							597	4947	5319	2165	2673	4168	4620	3653	4017	406	4405	1373	6548	1112	3241	1283	2622	4158	1184	1181	1318	3796	1946
EDMONTON, AB								4350	4722	1566	2076	3571	4022	3056	3420	740	3806	776	5950	513	2642	1308	2024	3560	1115	1207	1915	3198	1347
FREDERICTON, NB									452	2784	2797	779	1022	1323	953	5092	568	3574	1688	3837	1746	5457	2333	1310	5673	5752	6265	1674	2990
HALIFAX, NS										3156	3169	1151	1481	1695	1324	5462	940	3946	1402	4208	2118	5829	2704	1682	6045	6123	6637	2045	3362
KENORA, ON											668	2005	2622	1489	1854	2308	2240	792	4384	1052	1077	2456	459	1814	2432	2522	3483	1640	208
MINNEAPOLIS, MN												2020	1949	1802	1918	2816	2271	1299	4398	1561	1173	2662	547	1487	2877	2956	3989	1125	727
MONTRÉAL, QC													616	544	194	4311	250	2795	2379	3058	967	4678	1553	531	4894	4973	5486	895	2211
NEW YORK, NY														999	703	4764	838	3248	2710	3508	1545	4609	2171	816	4825	4905	5938	1001	2675
NORTH BAY, ON															364	3796	795	2280	2924	2541	423	4464	1072	336	3920	4012	4971	679	1696
OTTAWA, ON																4160	444	2644	2552	2906	787	4578	1401	431	4792	4873	5335	793	2060
PRINCE GEORGE, BC																	4548	1516	6691	1255	3384	922	2765	4302	778	821	1580	3940	2089
QUÉBEC, QC																		3032	2168	3293	1218	4929	1790	782	5143	5224	5723	1144	2448
REGINA, SK																			5176	261	1868	1664	1249	2786	1640	1732	2691	2424	573
ST. JOHN'S, NF																				5436	3346	7058	3933	2910	7272	7353	7866	3273	4590
SASKATOON, SK																					2129	1823	1511	3046	1630	1722	2430	2684	834
SAULT STE. MARIE, ON																						4223	649	674	3508	3598	4559	563	1283
SEATTLE, WA																							2913	4147	225	177	2504	3787	2237
THUNDER BAY, ON																								1355	2889	2980	3940	1699	665
TORONTO, ON																									4363	4443	5476	364	2213
VANCOUVER, BC																										93	2311	4001	2213
VICTORIA, BC																											2401	4081	2305
WHITEHORSE, YT																												5114	3264
WINDSOR, ON																													1852
WINNIPEG, MB																													

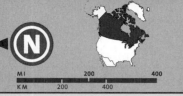

Tourism: 800/663-6000
Road Conditions: 604/420-4997

DRIVING DISTANCES IN KILOMETERS	BANFF, AB	CRANBROOK	DAWSON CREEK	JASPER, AB	KAMLOOPS	KELOWNA	NANAIMO	PRINCE GEORGE	PRINCE RUPERT	REVELSTOKE	VANCOUVER	VICTORIA
CRANBROOK	265		985	504	600	513	845*	838	1562	196	765	882*
KAMLOOPS	479	600	931	444		163	359*	525	1249	206	340	396*
KELOWNA	476	513	1094	597	163		383*	688	1409	192	378	420*
PRINCE GEORGE	637	838	406	376	525	688	784*		724	693	778	821*
VANCOUVER	819	765	1184	784	340	378	109*	778	1502	546		93*

* DISTANCE INCLUDES FERRY TRAVEL

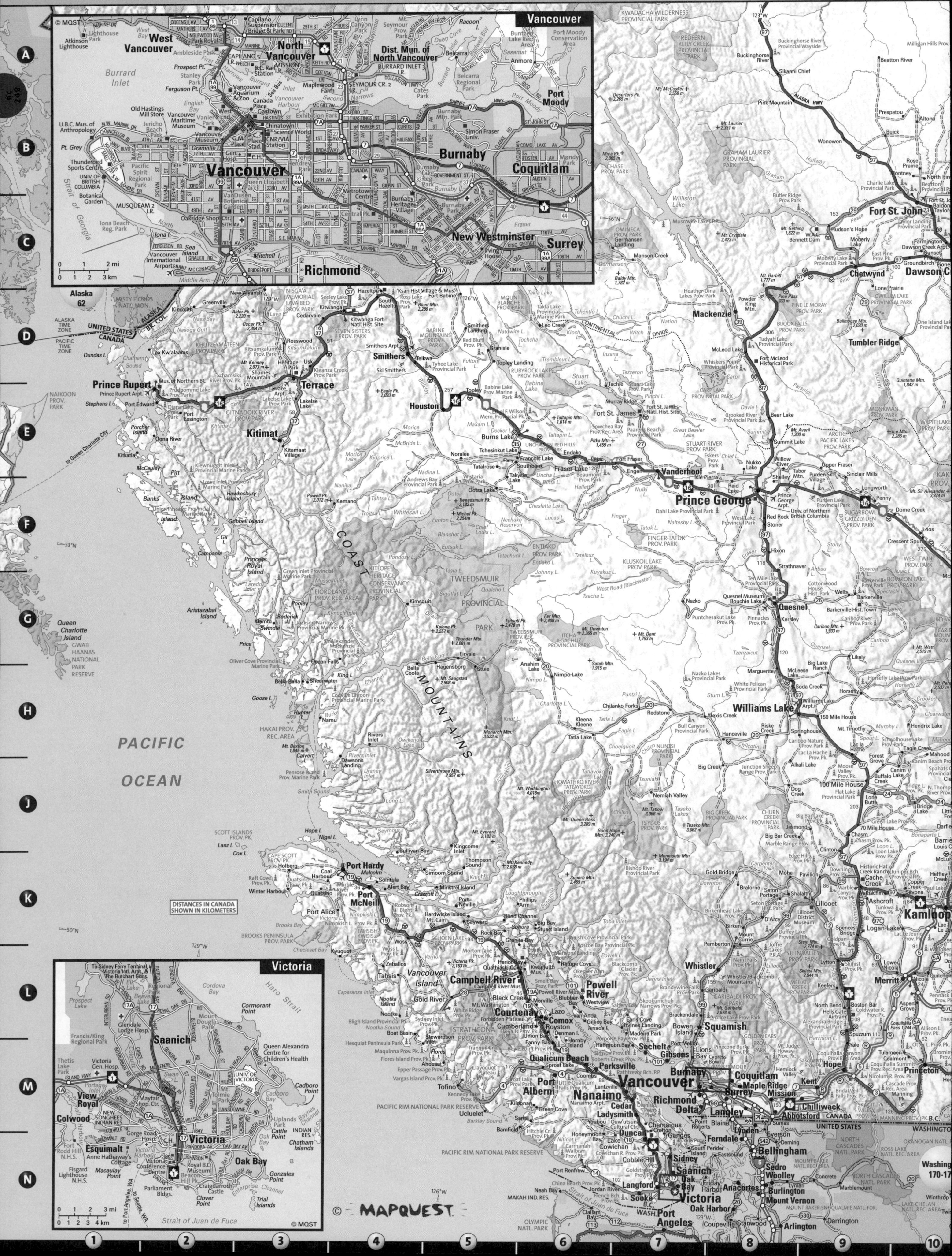

Tourism: 800/661-888
Road Conditions: 403/246-5853

DRIVING DISTANCES IN KILOMETERS	BANFF	CALGARY	CRANBROOK, BC	DAWSON CREEK, BC	EDMONTON	FORT MC MURRAY	GRANDE PRAIRIE	JASPER	LETHBRIDGE	LLOYDMINSTER	MEDICINE HAT	RED DEER
CALGARY	128		383	885	296	726	750	396	216	534	285	145
EDMONTON	412	296	679	597		439	462	367	512	238	579	150
GRANDE PRAIRIE	665	750	861	124	462	756		397	965	700	1033	603
LETHBRIDGE	344	215	296	1101	512	943	965	612		605	164	360
MEDICINE HAT	413	285	460	1168	579	931	1033	681	164	480		430

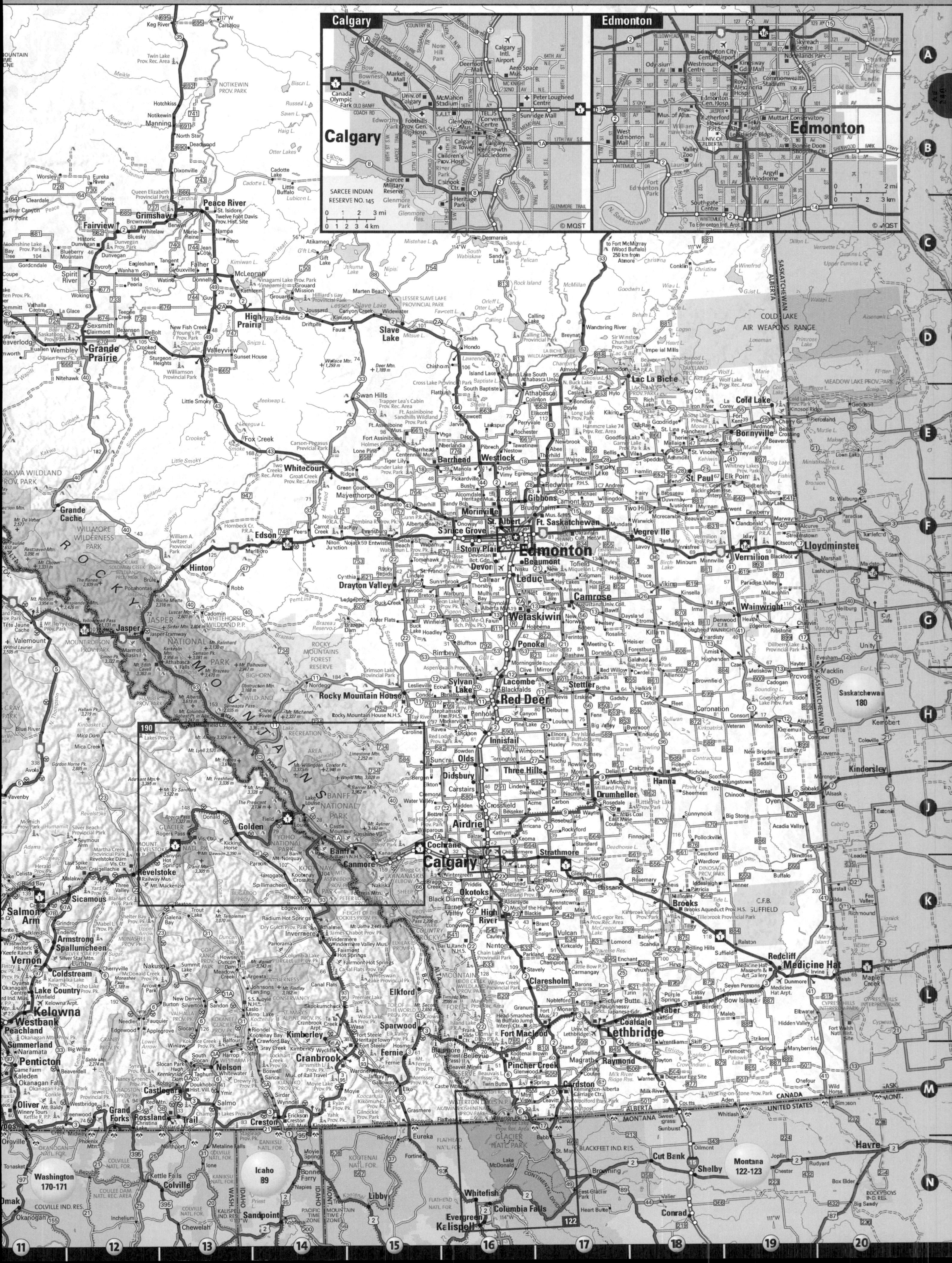

Tourism: 800/667-7191
Road Conditions: 306/787-7623

DRIVING DISTANCES IN KILOMETERS	BRANDON, MB	ESTEVAN	FLIN FLON, MB	LLOYDMINSTER	MEDICINE HAT, AB	MOOSE JAW	NORTH BATTLEFORD	PRINCE ALBERT	REGINA	SASKATOON	SWIFT CURRENT	YORKTON
PRINCE ALBERT	670	570	375	336	618	356	196		374	141	408	391
REGINA	377	196	748	537	455	68	397	374		261	241	195
SASKATOON	639	455	508	275	486	224	137	141	261		267	331
SWIFT CURRENT	598	401	989	441	218	174	301	408	241	267		436
YORKTON	270	289	553	608	650	262	468	391	195	331	436	

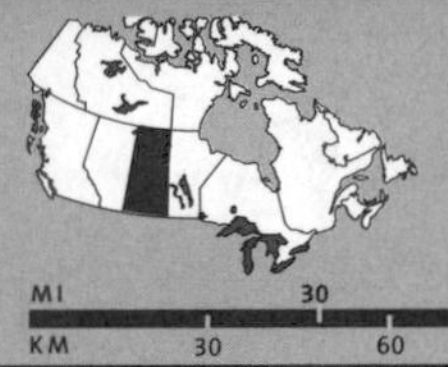

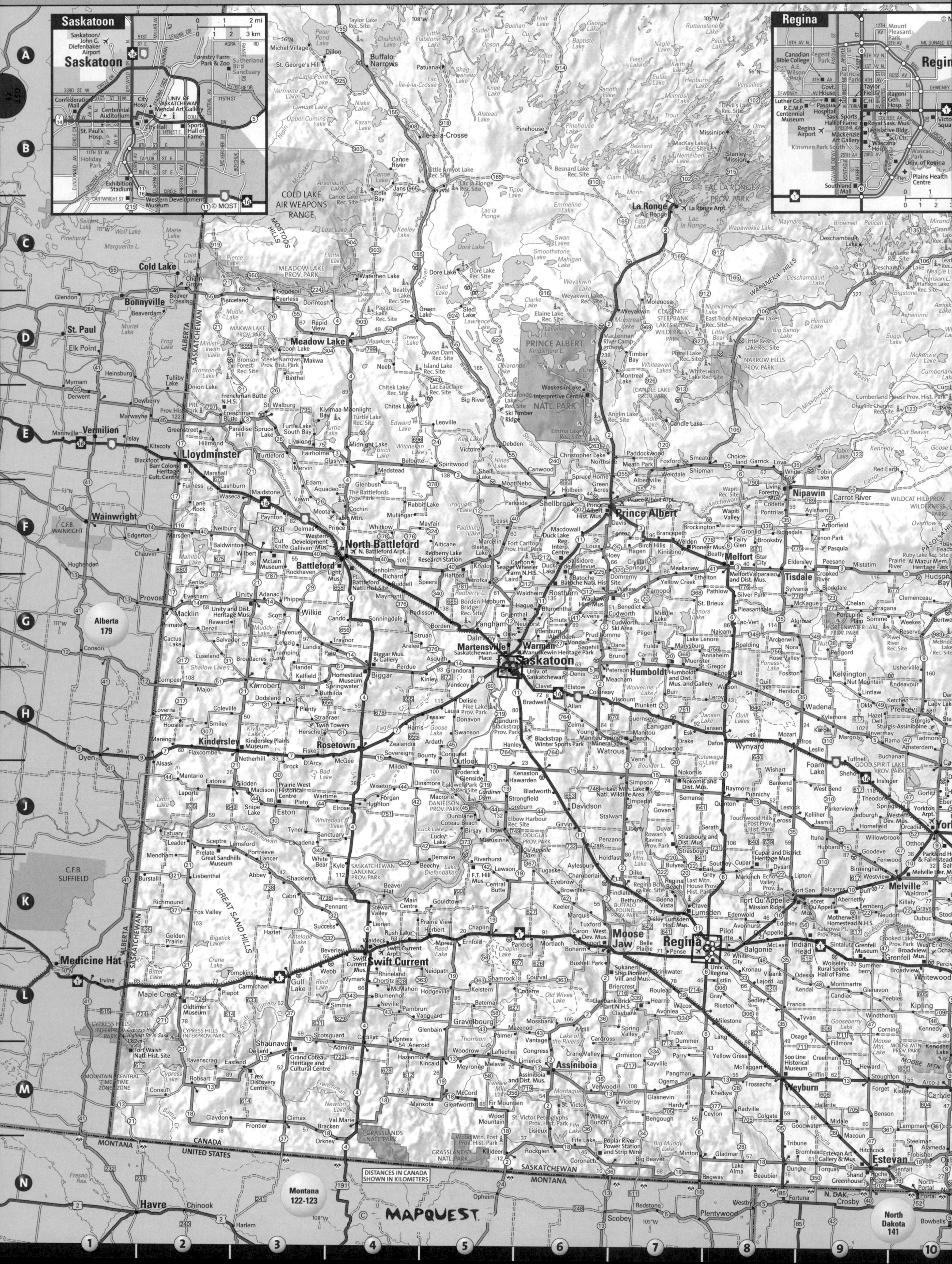

Tourism: 204/945-3777
Road Conditions: 204/945-3704

DRIVING DISTANCES IN KILOMETERS

	BRANDON	DAUPHIN	FLIN FLON	GIMLI	GRAND RAPIDS	KENORA, ON	PORTAGE LA PRAIRIE	SWAN RIVER	THOMPSON	WINKLER	WINNIPEG	YORKTON, SK
BRANDON		166	676	291	525	434	134	333	855	227	216	276
DAUPHIN	166		510	298	403	541	241	167	776	341	322	171
FLIN FLON	676	510		734	389	1051	751	372	380	880	757	553
PORTAGE LA PRAIRIE	134	241	751	164	448	301		407	778	113	82	360
WINNIPEG	216	322	757	88	430	208	82	489	769	118		442

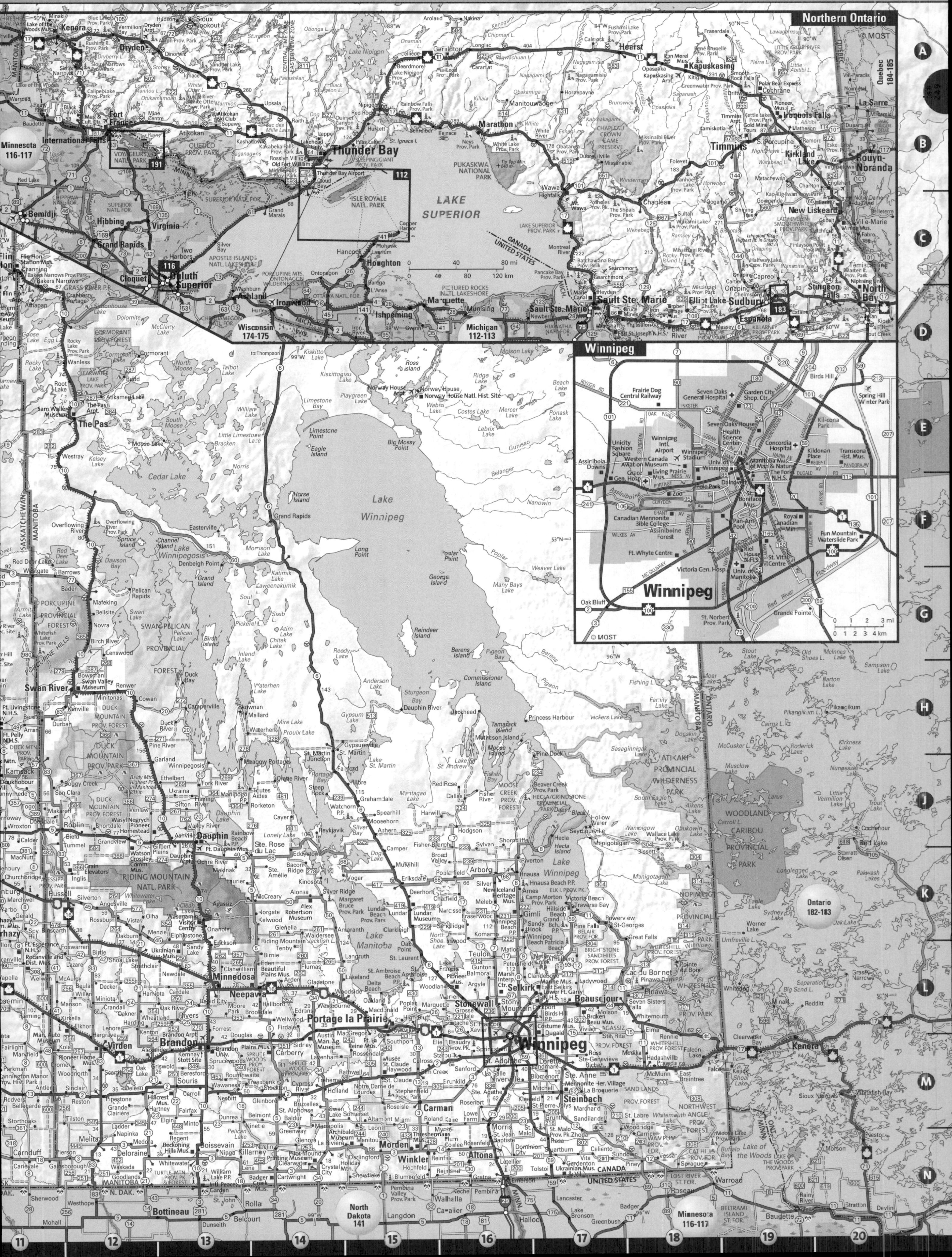

Tourism: 800/668-2746
Road Conditions: 416/235-1110

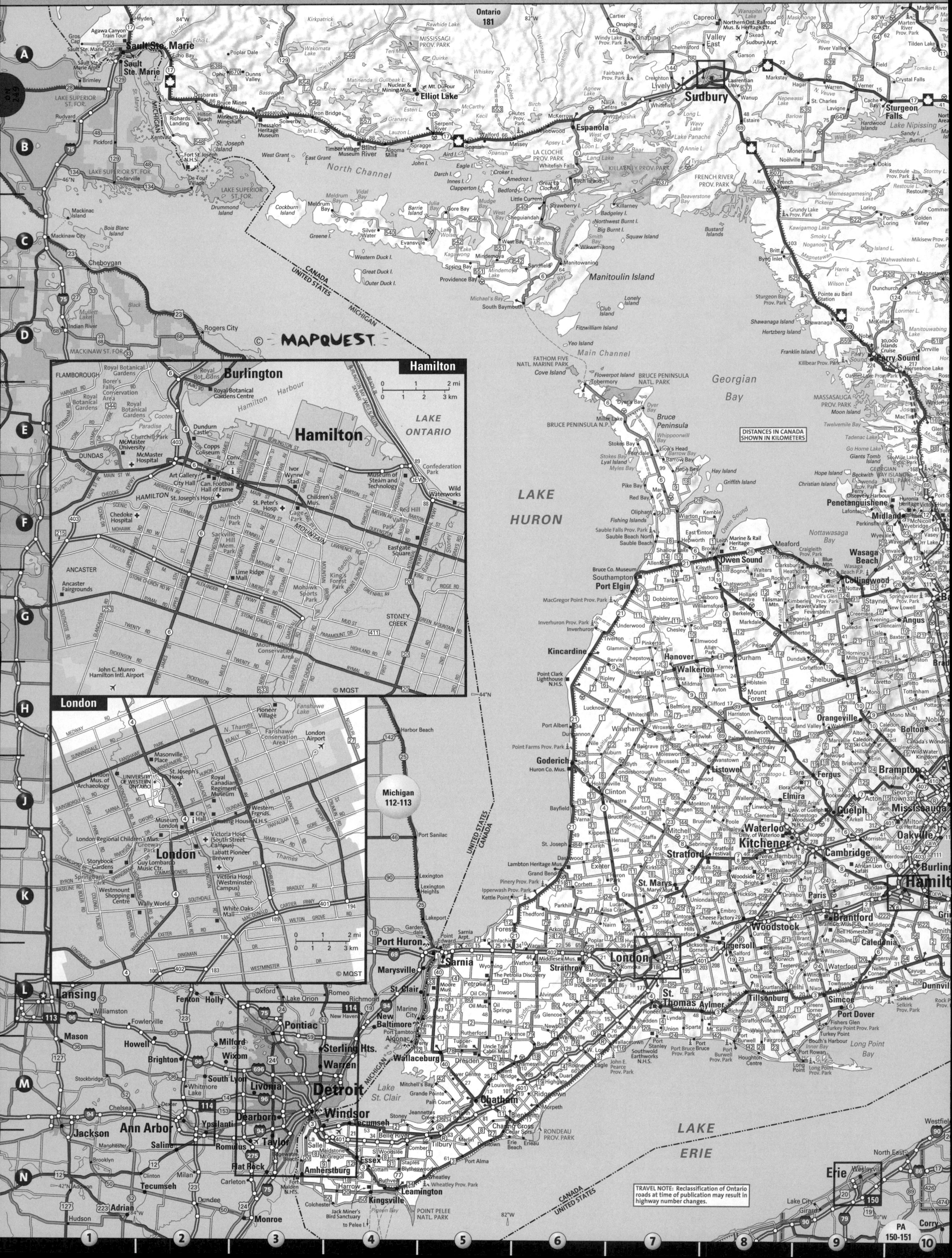

DRIVING DISTANCES IN KILOMETERS

	BARRIE	HAMILTON	KENORA	KINGSTON	KITCHENER	LONDON	NIAGARA FALLS	NORTH BAY	OTTAWA	OWEN SOUND	PETERBOROUGH	SARNIA	SAULT STE. MARIE	SUDBURY	THUNDER BAY	TIMMINS	TORONTO	WINDSOR
LONDON	248	134	1926	434	105		227	499	613	208	309	109	818	570	1467	840	183	195
OTTAWA	442	504	1854	179	496	613	574	364		558	265	714	787	488	1401	705	431	793
SUDBURY	319	462	1407	600	453	570	533	124	488	435	404	673	299		948	290	407	751
THUNDER BAY	1219	1410	459	1548	1401	1467	1481	1072	1401	1335	1371	1621	649	948		735	1355	1699
TORONTO	105	74	1814	251	104	183	145	336	431	183	127	285	674	407	1355	677		364

Tourism: 800/363-7777
Road Conditions: 418/643-6864

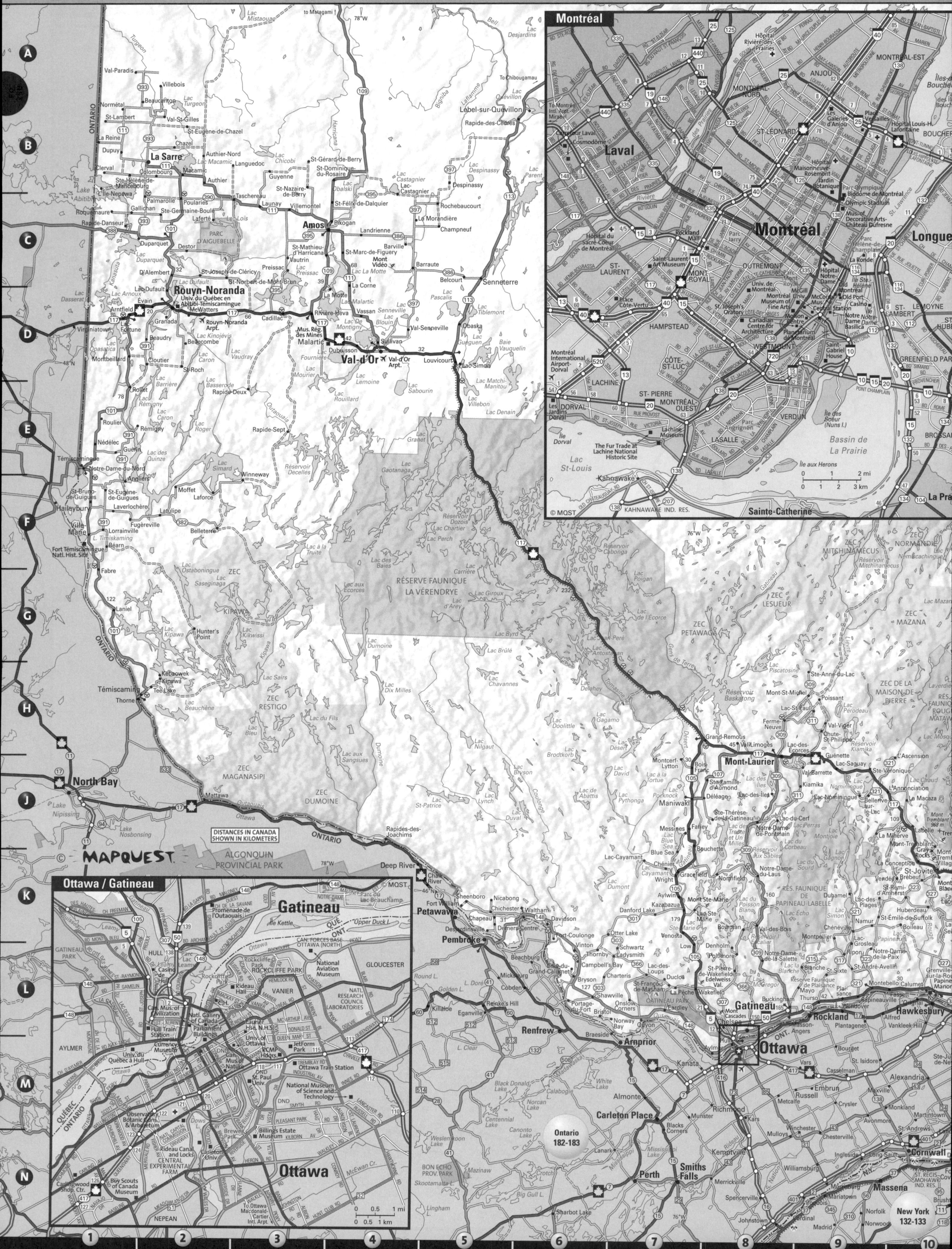

DRIVING DISTANCES IN KILOMETERS	BAIE-COMEAU	CHICOUTIMI	DRUMMONDVILLE	GASPÉ	MONT-LAURIER	MONTRÉAL	OTTAWA, ON	QUÉBEC	RIMOUSKI	RIVIÈRE-DU-LOUP	ROBERVAL	ROUYN-NORANDA	ST-GEORGES	SEPT-ÎLES	SHERBROOKE	SOREL	TROIS-RIVIÈRES	VICTORIAVILLE
MONTRÉAL	663	461	116	898	230		194	250	535	426	448	616	325	887	143	87	146	164
QUÉBEC	400	211	151	668	439	250	444		305	196	253	879	102	624	233	204	135	114
RIVIÈRE-DU-LOUP	230*	154*	328	472	656	426	620	196	109		249*	1042	272	454*	401	381	333	291
SHERBROOKE	633	444	82	873	373	143	337	233	510	401	417	759	148	857		142	158	97
TROIS-RIVIÈRES	535	346	68	804	376	146	340	135	441	333	296	762	214	759	158	82		65

* DISTANCE INCLUDES FERRY TRAVEL

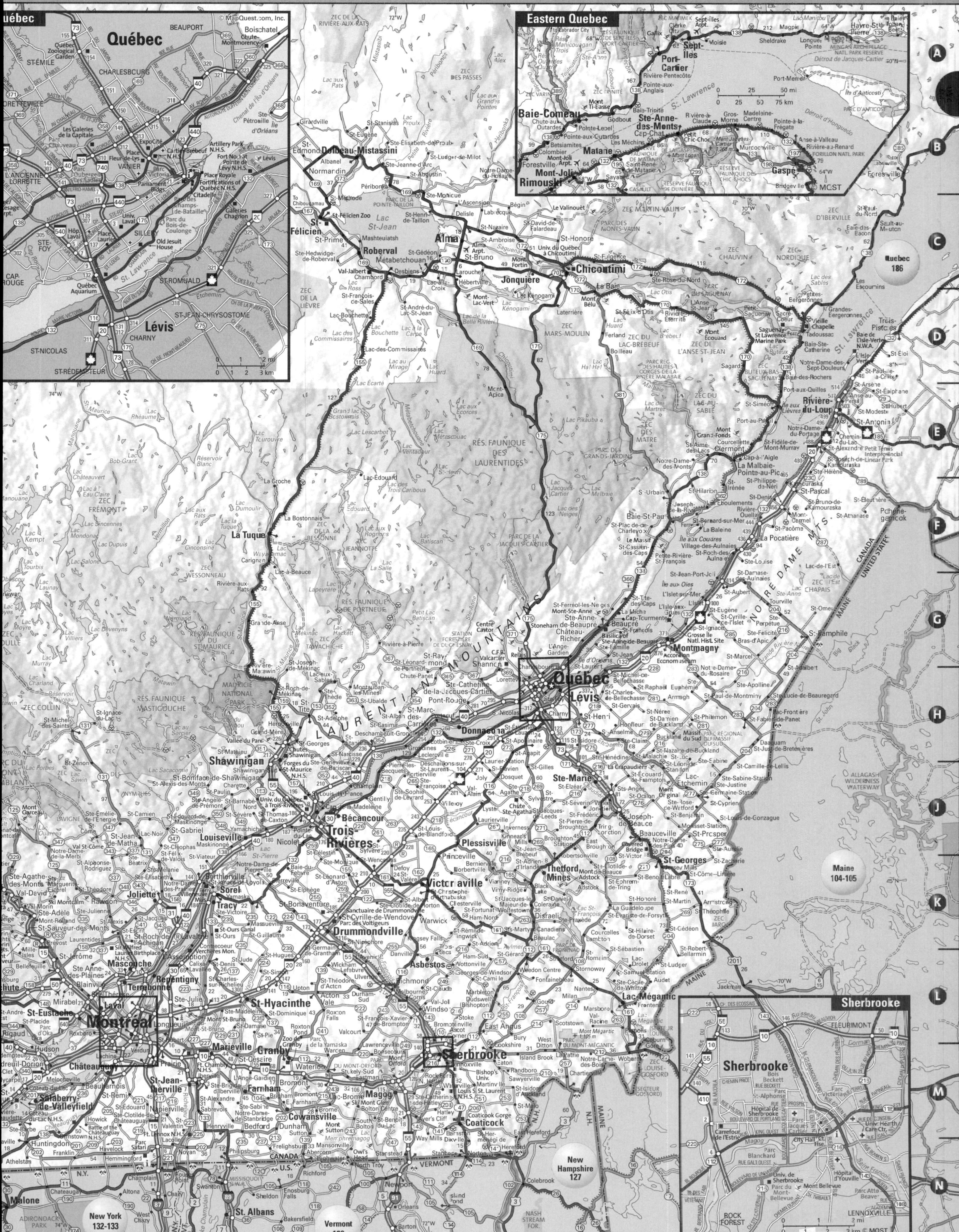

DRIVING DISTANCES IN KILOMETERS	BATHURST, NB	CAMPBELLTON, NB	CHARLOTTETOWN, PE	DIGBY, NS	EDMUNDSTON, NB	FREDERICTON, NB	GASPÉ, QC	HALIFAX, NS	LUNENBURG, NS	MIRAMICHI, NB	MONCTON, NB	NEW GLASGOW, NS	PORT HAWKESBURY, NS	RIMOUSKI, QC	RIVIÈRE-DU-LOUP, QC	SAINT JOHN, NB	ST. STEPHEN, NB	SYDNEY, NS	TRURO, NS	WOODSTOCK, NB	YARMOUTH, NS
CHARLOTTETOWN, PE	328	434		539	629	354	730	322	419	258	162	110*	224*	620	749	312	417	374*	233	457	616
FREDERICTON, NB	245	351	354	669	275		647	452	549	175	192	425	539	445	395	105	123	689	363	103	746
HALIFAX, NS	452	558	322	217	727	452	854		97	382	260	151	265	744	847	410	515	415	89	555	294
SAINT JOHN, NB	350	456	312	82*	380	105	752	410	258*	280	150	383	497	550	500		105	647	321	208	176*
SYDNEY, NS	689	795	374*	632	964	689	1091	415	512	619	497	264	123	981	1084	647	752		326	792	709

* DISTANCE INCLUDES FERRY TRAVEL

New Brunswick
Tourism: 800/561-0123
Road Conditions: 800/561-4063

Prince Edward Island
Tourism: 800/463-4734
Road Conditions: 902/368-4770

Nova Scotia
Tourism: 800/565-0000
Road Conditions: 902/424-3933

Newfoundland
Tourism: 800/563-6353
Road Conditions: 709/729-2391

Tourism: 800/446-3942
Road Conditions: 800/800-0713

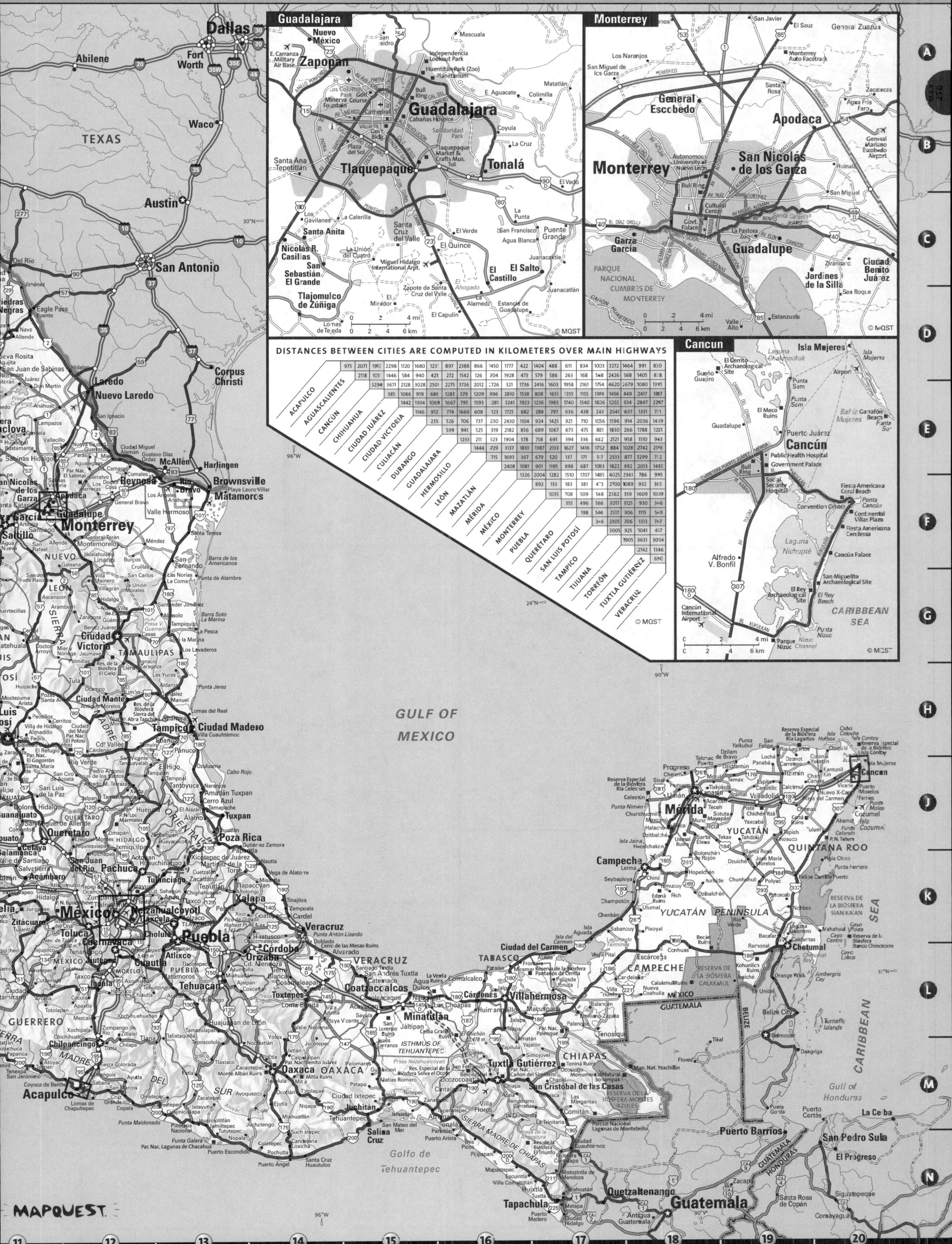

DISTANCES BETWEEN CITIES ARE COMPUTED IN KILOMETERS OVER MAIN HIGHWAYS

	AGUASCALIENTES	CANCÚN	CHIHUAHUA	CIUDAD JUÁREZ	CIUDAD VICTORIA	CULIACÁN	DURANGO	GUADALAJARA	HERMOSILLO	LEÓN	MAZATLÁN	MÉRIDA	MÉXICO	MONTERREY	PUEBLA	QUERÉTARO	SAN LUIS POTOSÍ	TAMPICO	TIJUANA	TORREÓN	TUXTLA GUTIÉRREZ	VERACRUZ
ACAPULCO	973	2071	1913	2298	1120	1680	1231	897	2388	866	1450	1777	422	1404	488	611	834	1003	3272	1464	991	830
AGUASCALIENTES		2118	1057	1446	584	940	421	272	1542	126	704	1928	473	579	586	263	168	548	2426	568	1405	838
CANCÚN			3290	3671	2128	3028	2501	2275	3736	2012	1726	321	1736	2416	1603	1958	2161	1754	4620	2679	1080	1395
CHIHUAHUA				385	1086	919	686	1283	579	1209	896	2810	1538	808	1651	1355	1155	1374	1456	449	2417	1817
CIUDAD JUÁREZ					1442	1304	1069	1667	795	1593	281	3241	1923	1236	1983	1740	1540	1806	1202	334	2847	2247
CIUDAD VICTORIA						1146	912	774	1666	608	123	1725	682	288	797	636	438	243	2641	637	1331	731
CULIACÁN							235	526	706	737	230	2430	1104	924	1425	921	710	1056	1596	914	2036	1459
DURANGO								599	941	525	319	2182	856	689	1067	673	475	821	1830	266	1788	1221
GUADALAJARA									1233	211	523	1904	578	758	691	394	336	682	2121	958	1510	943
HERMOSILLO										1444	729	3137	1810	1387	2133	1627	1416	1752	884	1028	2742	2176
LEÓN											715	1693	367	679	520	137	171	517	2333	877	1299	722
MAZATLÁN												2408	1081	901	1195	898	687	1083	1822	392	2013	1447
MÉRIDA													1326	2004	1282	1510	1707	1435	4025	2361	786	995
MÉXICO														892	133	183	381	473	2700	1089	932	365
MONTERREY															1035	708	509	568	2362	359	1609	1009
PUEBLA																355	496	586	3017	1125	930	346
QUERÉTARO																	198	544	2517	306	1115	549
SAN LUIS POTOSÍ																		346	2305	706	1313	747
TAMPICO																			3005	925	1041	457
TIJUANA																				1905	3631	3054
TORREÓN																					2142	1346
TUXTLA GUTIÉRREZ																						690

© MQST

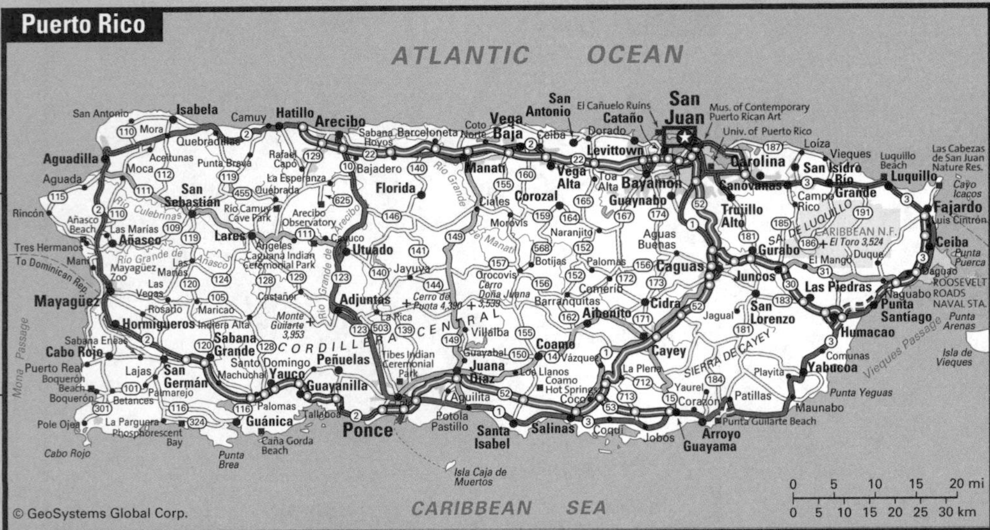
Puerto Rico
ATLANTIC OCEAN
CARIBBEAN SEA
San Juan
Isabela
Hatillo
Arecibo
Vega Baja
Cataño
Bayamón
Carolina
Luquillo
Fajardo
Ceiba
Aguadilla
Mayagüez
Cabo Rojo
San Germán
Yauco
Guánica
Ponce
Guayanilla
Peñuelas
Utuado
Adjuntas
Jayuya
Lares
Manatí
Corozal
Cayey
Caguas
Humacao
Yabucoa
Guayama
Arroyo
Salinas
Santa Isabel
Juana Díaz
Vieques
Culebra
CORDILLERA CENTRAL
Isla Caja de Muertos
Cerro de Punta 4,390
© GeoSystems Global Corp.
0 5 10 15 20 mi
0 5 10 15 20 25 30 km

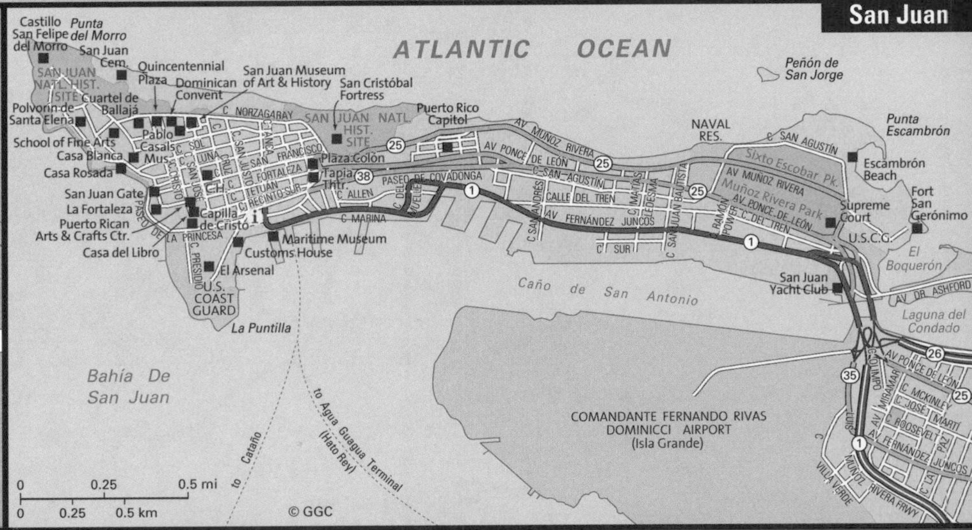
San Juan
ATLANTIC OCEAN
Castillo San Felipe del Morro
San Juan Cem.
Quincentennial Plaza
Dominican Convent
San Juan Museum of Art & History
San Cristóbal Fortress
Puerto Rico Capitol
SAN JUAN NATL. HIST. SITE
Cuartel de Ballajá
Casa Blanca
La Fortaleza
Puerto Rican Arts & Crafts Ctr.
Casa del Libro
Capilla de Cristo
El Arsenal
Maritime Museum
Customs House
La Puntilla
U.S. COAST GUARD
Bahía De San Juan
Caño de San Antonio
Plaza Colón
San Juan Yacht Club
Escambrón Beach
Fort San Gerónimo
Punta Escambrón
Peñón de San Jorge
NAVAL RES.
Supreme Court
COMANDANTE FERNANDO RIVAS DOMINICCI AIRPORT (Isla Grande)
0 0.25 0.5 mi
0 0.25 0.5 km
© GGC

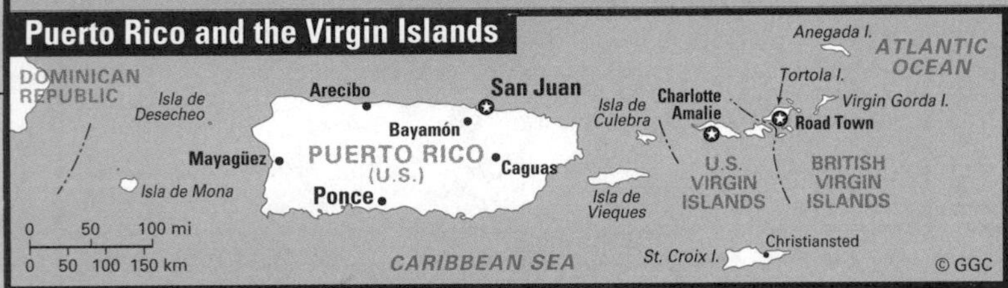
Puerto Rico and the Virgin Islands
DOMINICAN REPUBLIC
Isla de Desecheo
Arecibo
San Juan
Bayamón
Caguas
Mayagüez
PUERTO RICO (U.S.)
Ponce
Isla de Mona
Isla de Culebra
Isla de Vieques
Charlotte Amalie
Road Town
U.S. VIRGIN ISLANDS
BRITISH VIRGIN ISLANDS
Anegada I.
Tortola I.
Virgin Gorda I.
St. Croix I.
Christiansted
ATLANTIC OCEAN
CARIBBEAN SEA
0 50 100 mi
0 50 100 150 km
© GGC

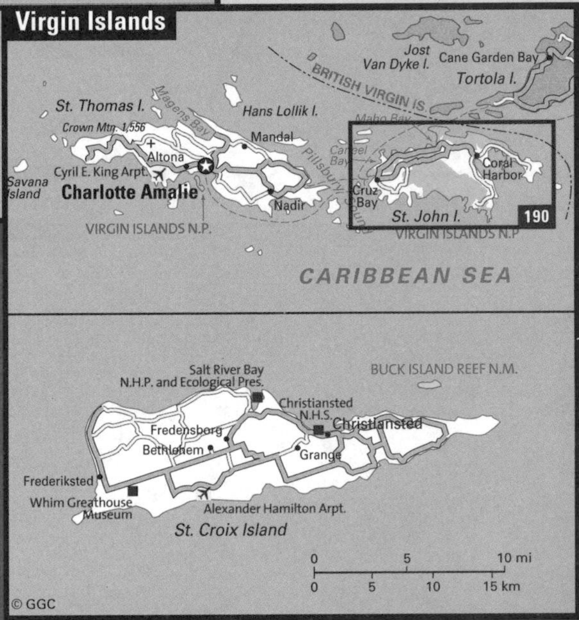
Virgin Islands
St. Thomas I.
Crown Mtn. 1,556
Charlotte Amalie
Cyril E. King Arpt.
Savana Island
Hans Lollik I.
Jost Van Dyke I.
Tortola I.
BRITISH VIRGIN IS.
St. John I.
VIRGIN ISLANDS N.P.
CARIBBEAN SEA
190
Salt River Bay N.H.P. and Ecological Pres.
BUCK ISLAND REEF N.M.
Christiansted N.H.S.
Christiansted
Fredensborg
Bethlehem
Grange
Frederiksted
Whim Greathouse Museum
Alexander Hamilton Arpt.
St. Croix Island
0 5 10 mi
0 5 10 15 km
© GGC

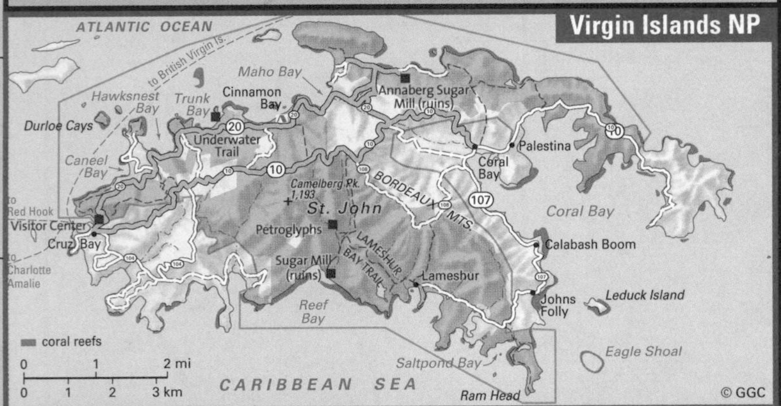
Virgin Islands NP
ATLANTIC OCEAN
Maho Bay
Hawksnest Bay
Trunk Bay
Cinnamon Bay
Annaberg Sugar Mill (ruins)
Durloe Cays
Underwater Trail
Caneel Bay
Coral Bay
Palestina
Red Hook
Visitor Center
Cruz Bay
Camelberg Pk. 1,193
St. John
Petroglyphs
BORDEAUX MTS.
Sugar Mill (ruins)
Lameshur
Reef Bay
Calabash Boom
Leduck Island
Johns Folly
Saltpond Bay
Eagle Shoal
Ram Head
coral reefs
CARIBBEAN SEA
0 1 2 mi
0 1 2 3 km
© GGC

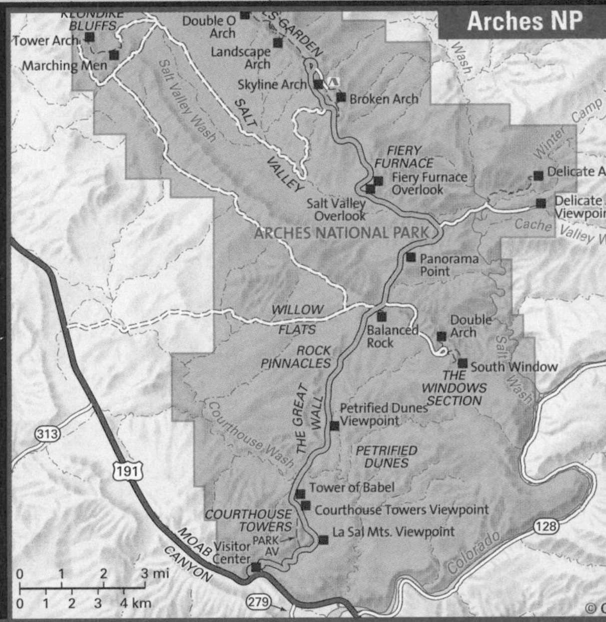
Arches NP
Klondike Bluffs
Tower Arch
Marching Men
Double O Arch
Landscape Arch
Skyline Arch
Broken Arch
FIERY FURNACE
Fiery Furnace Overlook
Salt Valley Overlook
ARCHES NATIONAL PARK
Delicate Arch
Delicate Arch Viewpoint
Panorama Point
WILLOW FLATS
Balanced Rock
Double Arch
ROCK PINNACLES
South Window
THE WINDOWS SECTION
Petrified Dunes Viewpoint
PETRIFIED DUNES
THE GREAT WALL
Tower of Babel
Courthouse Towers Viewpoint
COURTHOUSE TOWERS
La Sal Mts. Viewpoint
Visitor Center
MOAB CANYON
191
313
128
279
0 1 2 3 mi
0 1 2 3 4 km

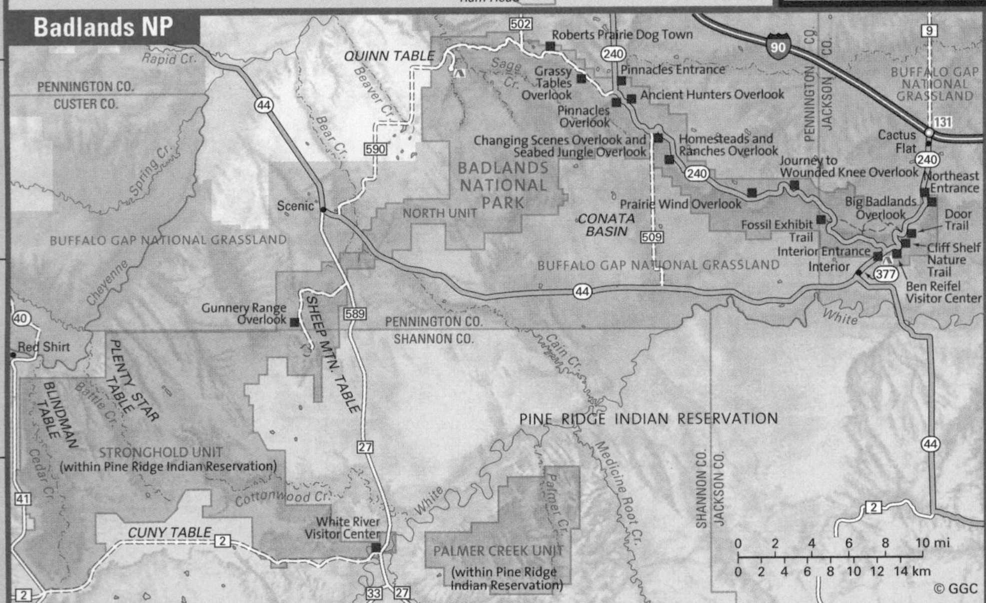
Badlands NP
Roberts Prairie Dog Town
QUINN TABLE
Pinnacles Entrance
Grassy Tables Overlook
Ancient Hunters Overlook
Pinnacles Overlook
BUFFALO GAP NATIONAL GRASSLAND
Changing Scenes Overlook and Seabed Jungle Overlook
Homesteads and Ranches Overlook
Journey to Wounded Knee Overlook
Cactus Flat
Northeast Entrance
BADLANDS NATIONAL PARK
NORTH UNIT
Prairie Wind Overlook
Big Badlands Overlook
Door Trail
Scenic
CONATA BASIN
Fossil Exhibit Trail
Interior Entrance
Cliff Shelf Nature Trail
Interior
Ben Reifel Visitor Center
PENNINGTON CO.
CUSTER CO.
SHANNON CO.
JACKSON CO.
Gunnery Range Overlook
SHEEP MTN. TABLE
Red Shirt
PLENTY STAR TABLE
BLINDMAN TABLE
STRONGHOLD UNIT (within Pine Ridge Indian Reservation)
PINE RIDGE INDIAN RESERVATION
CUNY TABLE
White River Visitor Center
PALMER CREEK UNIT (within Pine Ridge Indian Reservation)
0 2 4 6 8 10 mi
0 2 4 6 8 10 12 14 km
© GGC

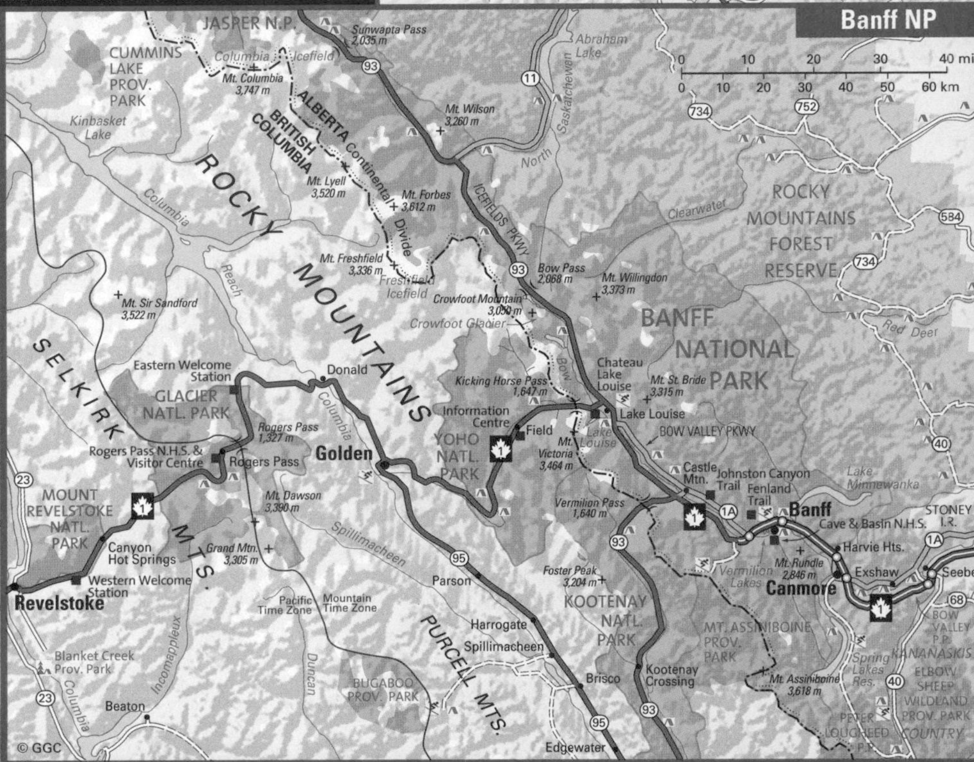
Banff NP
JASPER N.P.
Sunwapta Pass 2,035 m
CUMMINS LAKE PROV. PARK
Kinbasket Lake
Mt. Columbia 3,747 m
ALBERTA
BRITISH COLUMBIA
Continental Divide
Mt. Wilson 3,260 m
Mt. Lyell 3,520 m
Mt. Forbes 3,612 m
ROCKY MOUNTAINS
Mt. Freshfield 3,336 m
Bow Pass 2,068 m
Mt. Willingdon 3,373 m
ROCKY MOUNTAINS FOREST RESERVE
Mt. Sir Sandford 3,522 m
Crowfoot Mountain
BANFF NATIONAL PARK
SELKIRK MTS.
Eastern Welcome Station
GLACIER NATL. PARK
Donald
Kicking Horse Pass 1,647 m
Chateau Lake Louise
Mt. St. Bride 3,315 m
Lake Louise
BOW VALLEY PKWY.
Rogers Pass 1,327 m
Rogers Pass N.H.S. & Visitor Centre
Golden
Information Centre
Field
YOHO NATL. PARK
Mt. Victoria 3,464 m
MOUNT REVELSTOKE NATL. PARK
Mt. Dawson 3,390 m
Vermilion Pass 1,640 m
Castle Mtn.
Johnston Canyon
Banff
Cave & Basin N.H.S.
Harvie Hts.
Canyon Hot Springs
Grand Mtn. 3,305 m
Western Welcome Station
Revelstoke
Parson
Foster Peak 3,204 m
Exshaw
Canmore
KOOTENAY NATL. PARK
Harrogate
Spillimacheen
MT. ASSINIBOINE PROV. PARK
Mt. Assiniboine 3,618 m
PURCELL MTS.
Blanket Creek Prov. Park
Beaton
BUGABOO PROV. PARK
Brisco
Kootenay Crossing
Edgewater
0 10 20 30 40 mi
0 10 20 30 40 50 60 km
© GGC

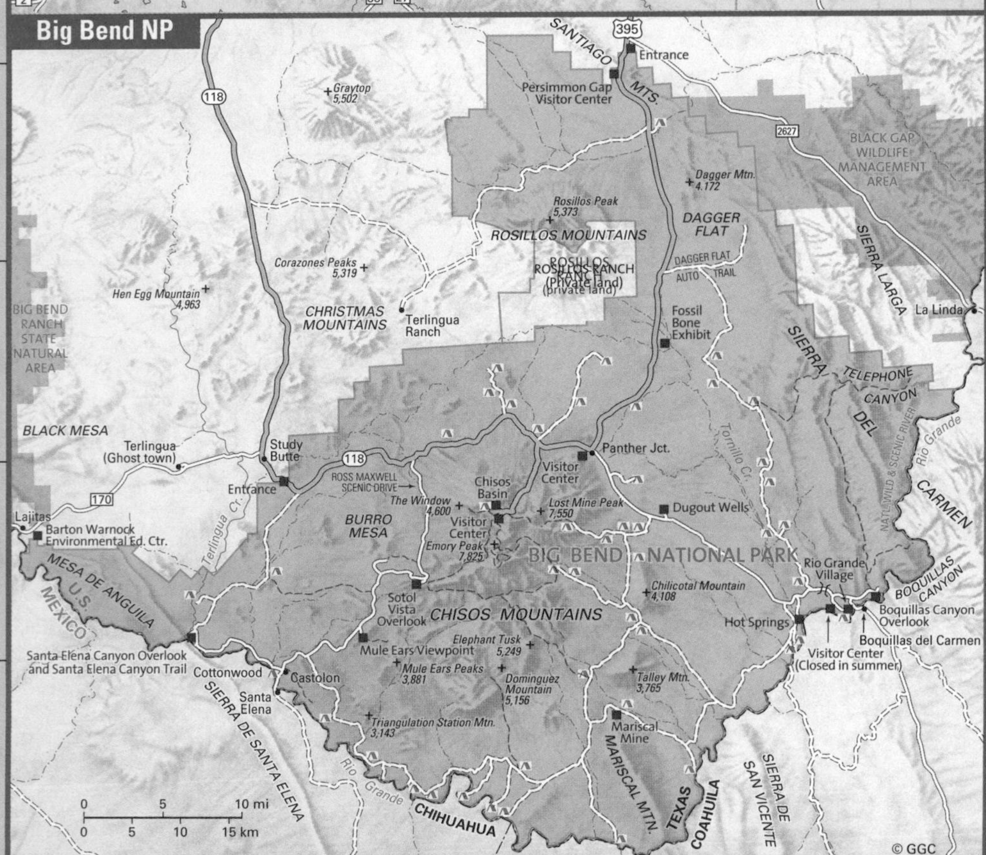
Big Bend NP
Entrance
SANTIAGO MTS.
Persimmon Gap Visitor Center
Graytop 5,502
BLACK GAP WILDLIFE MANAGEMENT AREA
Dagger Mtn. 4,172
Rosillos Peak 5,373
ROSILLOS MOUNTAINS
DAGGER FLAT
Corazones Peaks 5,319
ROSILLOS RANCH (Private Land)
Hen Egg Mountain 4,963
CHRISTMAS MOUNTAINS
Terlingua Ranch
Fossil Bone Exhibit
SIERRA LARGA
La Linda
BIG BEND RANCH STATE NATURAL AREA
SIERRA DEL CARMEN
TELEPHONE CANYON
BLACK MESA
Terlingua (Ghost town)
Study Butte
Panther Jct.
Entrance
Visitor Center
Lost Mine Peak 7,550
Dugout Wells
Chisos Basin
BURRO MESA
Lajitas
Barton Warnock Environmental Ed. Ctr.
MESA DE ANGUILA
BIG BEND NATIONAL PARK
Rio Grande Village
Emory Peak 7,825
Sotol Vista Overlook
CHISOS MOUNTAINS
Boquillas Canyon Overlook
Hot Springs
Boquillas del Carmen
Visitor Center (Closed in summer)
Mule Ears Viewpoint
Santa Elena Canyon Overlook and Santa Elena Canyon Trail
Cottonwood
Castolon
Santa Elena
SIERRA DE SANTA ELENA
MEXICO
U.S.
CHIHUAHUA
COAHUILA
TEXAS
MARISCAL MTN.
Mariscal Mine
SIERRA DE SAN VICENTE
0 5 10 mi
0 5 10 15 km
© GGC

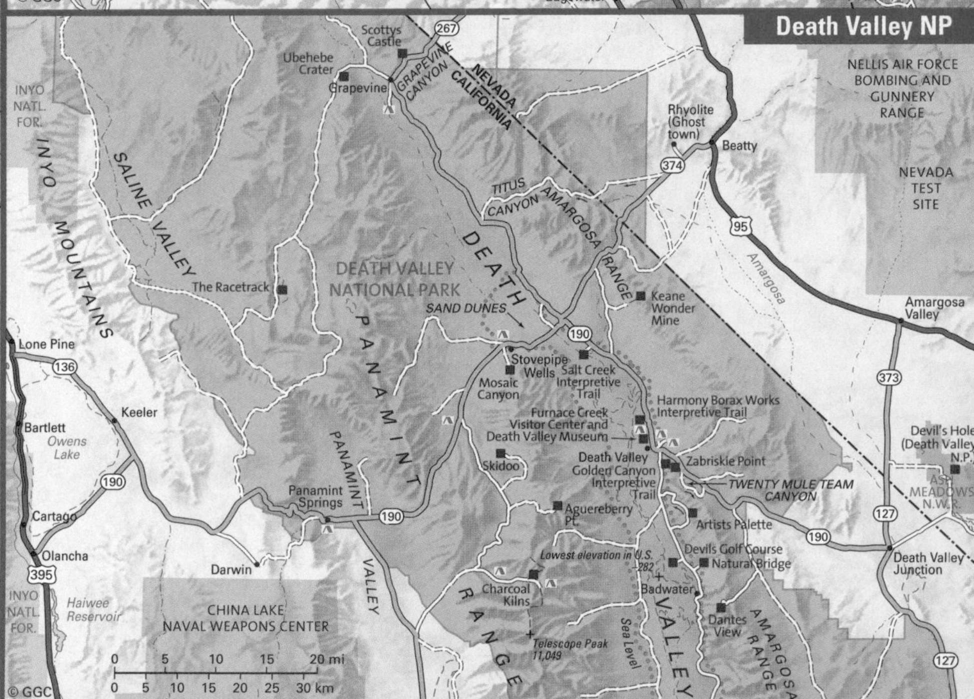
Death Valley NP
Scottys Castle
Ubehebe Crater
Grapevine
GRAPEVINE CANYON
NEVADA
CALIFORNIA
NELLIS AIR FORCE BOMBING AND GUNNERY RANGE
Rhyolite (Ghost town)
Beatty
NEVADA TEST SITE
INYO NATL. FOR.
INYO MOUNTAINS
SALINE VALLEY
TITUS CANYON
AMARGOSA RANGE
DEATH VALLEY NATIONAL PARK
The Racetrack
SAND DUNES
Keane Wonder Mine
Amargosa Valley
Lone Pine
Stovepipe Wells
Salt Creek Interpretive Trail
Mosaic Canyon
Harmony Borax Works Interpretive Trail
Furnace Creek Visitor Center and Death Valley Museum
Keeler
Bartlett
Owens Lake
Skidoo
Death Valley Golden Canyon Interpretive Trail
Zabriskie Point
TWENTY MULE TEAM CANYON
Devil's Hole (Death Valley N.P.)
Artists Palette
Panamint Springs
PANAMINT RANGE
Aguereberry Point
Devils Golf Course
Natural Bridge
Death Valley Junction
Cartago
Olancha
Lowest elevation in U.S. 282 ft.
Badwater
Charcoal Kilns
Dantes View
Darwin
CHINA LAKE NAVAL WEAPONS CENTER
Telescope Peak 11,049
0 5 10 15 20 mi
0 5 10 15 20 25 30 km
© GGC

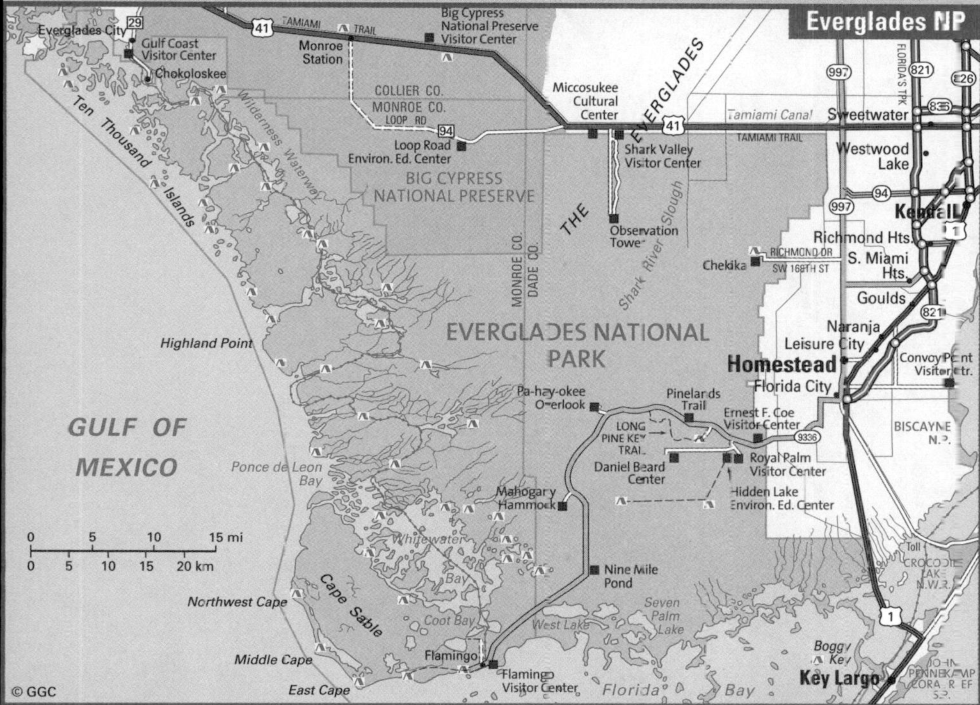
Everglades NP
Everglades City
Gulf Coast Visitor Center
Chokoloskee
Big Cypress National Preserve Visitor Center
Monroe Station
Miccosukee Cultural Center
THE EVERGLADES
Sweetwater
Tamiami Canal
Loop Road Environ. Ed. Center
BIG CYPRESS NATIONAL PRESERVE
Shark Valley Visitor Center
Westwood Lake
Observation Tower
Kendall
Richmond Hts.
S. Miami Hts.
Goulds
Chekika
Ten Thousand Islands
Highland Point
EVERGLADES NATIONAL PARK
Naranja
Leisure City
Homestead
Florida City
Convoy Point Visitor Ctr.
GULF OF MEXICO
Pa-hay-okee Overlook
Pinelands Trail
Ernest F. Coe Visitor Center
Royal Palm Visitor Center
Daniel Beard Center
Hidden Lake Environ. Ed. Center
BISCAYNE N.P.
Ponce de Leon Bay
Mahogany Hammock
Nine Mile Pond
Northwest Cape
Cape Sable
Middle Cape
East Cape
Flamingo
Flamingo Visitor Center
Florida Bay
Key Largo
© GGC

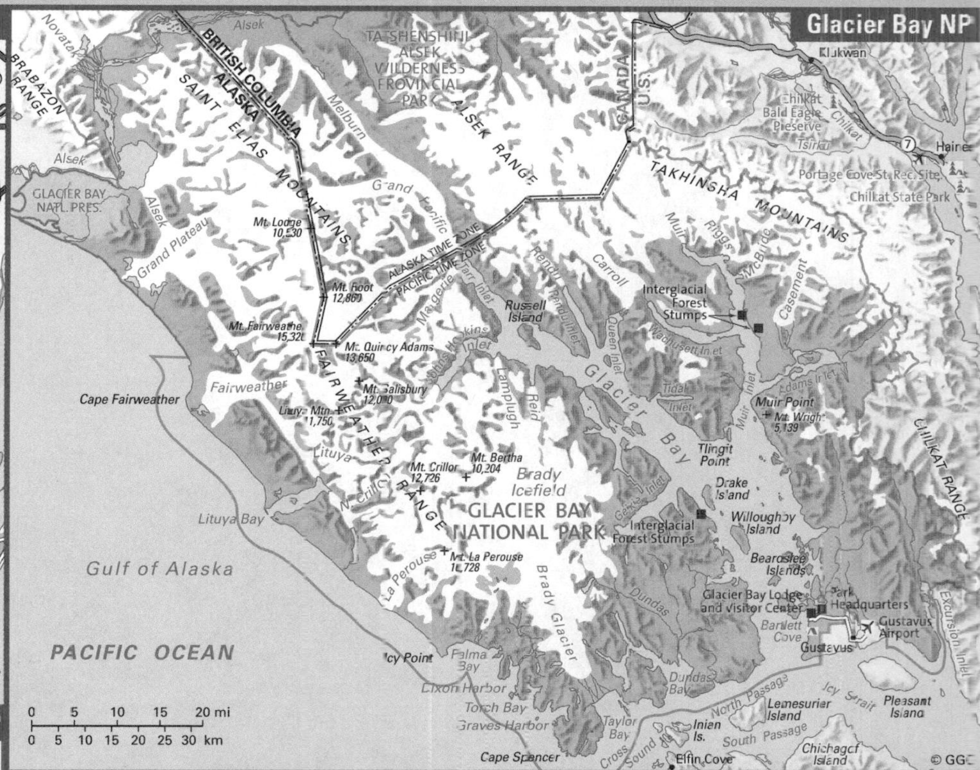
Glacier Bay NP
BRITISH COLUMBIA
ALASKA
SAINT ELIAS MOUNTAINS
TATSHENSHINI-ALSEK WILDERNESS PROVINCIAL PARK
ALSEK RANGE
CANADA
U.S.
Klukwan
Chilkat Bald Eagle Preserve
Haines
TAKHINSHA MOUNTAINS
GLACIER BAY NATL. PRES.
Mt. Fairweather 15,320
Mt. Quincy Adams
Mt. Salisbury
Cape Fairweather
Mt. Crillon 12,726
Mt. Bertha 10,204
Brady Icefield
GLACIER BAY NATIONAL PARK
Lituya Bay
Mt. La Perouse 10,728
Gulf of Alaska
Glacier Bay
Gustavus
Gustavus Airport
Glacier Bay Lodge and Visitor Center
Park Headquarters
Bartlett Cove
PACIFIC OCEAN
Icy Point
Elfin Cove
Cape Spencer
© GGC

Hawaii Volcanoes NP
MAUNA LOA FOREST RESERVE
Mauna Loa Observatory
NORTHEAST RIFT ZONE
HAWAII VOLCANOES N.P.
Mauna Loa Cabin
Mokuaweoweo Caldera
SOUTHWEST RIFT ZONE
KAPAPALA FOREST RESERVE
Glenwood
Volcano
Kilauea Caldera
Thurston Lava Tube
Kilauea Iki Crater
Devastation Trail
EAST RIFT ZONE
HAWAII VOLCANOES N.P.
KAU DESERT
Napua Crater
Hilina Pali Overlook Shelter
Puu Loa Petroglyphs
Holei Sea Arch
KAU FOREST RESERVE
Wood Valley
PACIFIC OCEAN
© GGC

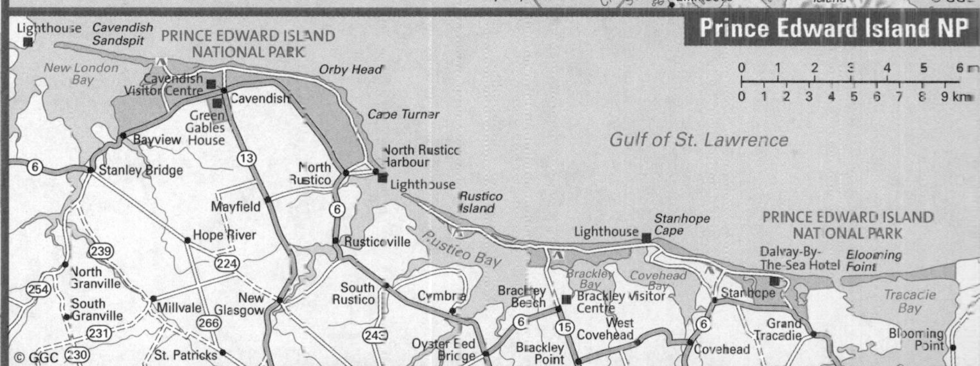
Prince Edward Island NP
Lighthouse
Cavendish Sandspit
PRINCE EDWARD ISLAND NATIONAL PARK
Cavendish
Green Gables House
Orby Head
Cape Turner
Gulf of St. Lawrence
North Rustico Harbour
Stanley Bridge
Rustico Island
Hope River
Rusticoville
Rustico Bay
Stanhope Cape
PRINCE EDWARD ISLAND NATIONAL PARK
Dalvay-By-The-Sea Hotel
Brackley Beach
North Granville
South Granville
Millvale
New Glasgow
South Rustico
Oyster Bed Bridge
Brackley Point
West Covehead
Grand Tracadie
Blooming Point
St. Patricks
© GGC

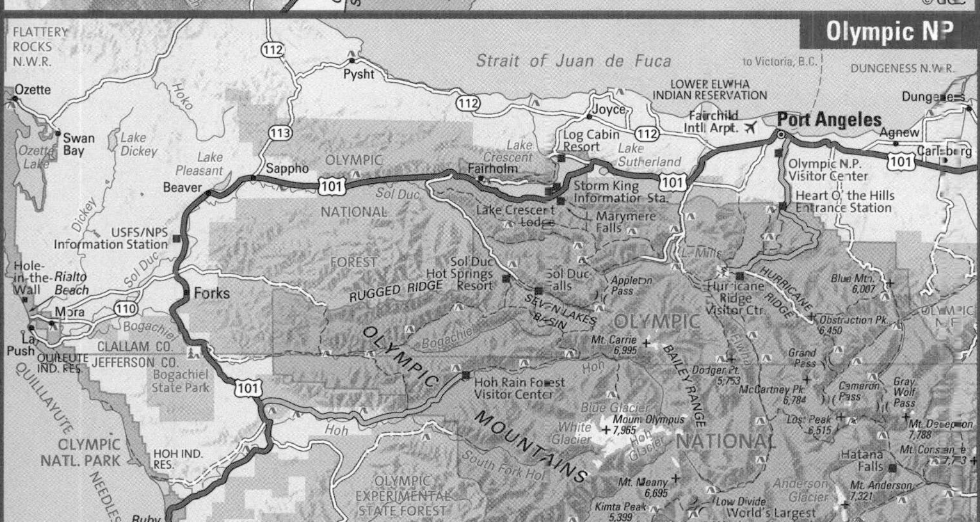
Olympic NP
FLATTERY ROCKS N.W.R.
Ozette
Pysht
Strait of Juan de Fuca
LOWER ELWHA INDIAN RESERVATION
Port Angeles
DUNGENESS N.W.R.
Lake Crescent
Fairholm
Storm King Information Sta.
Olympic N.P. Visitor Center
Heart O' the Hills Entrance Station
Forks
OLYMPIC NATIONAL FOREST
Sol Duc Hot Springs Resort
Hurricane Ridge
OLYMPIC MOUNTAINS
OLYMPIC NATIONAL PARK
Hoh Rain Forest Visitor Center
Mount Olympus 7,965
OLYMPIC EXPERIMENTAL STATE FOREST
Kalaloch Information Station
PACIFIC OCEAN
Lake Quinault
QUINAULT INDIAN RESERVATION
© GGC

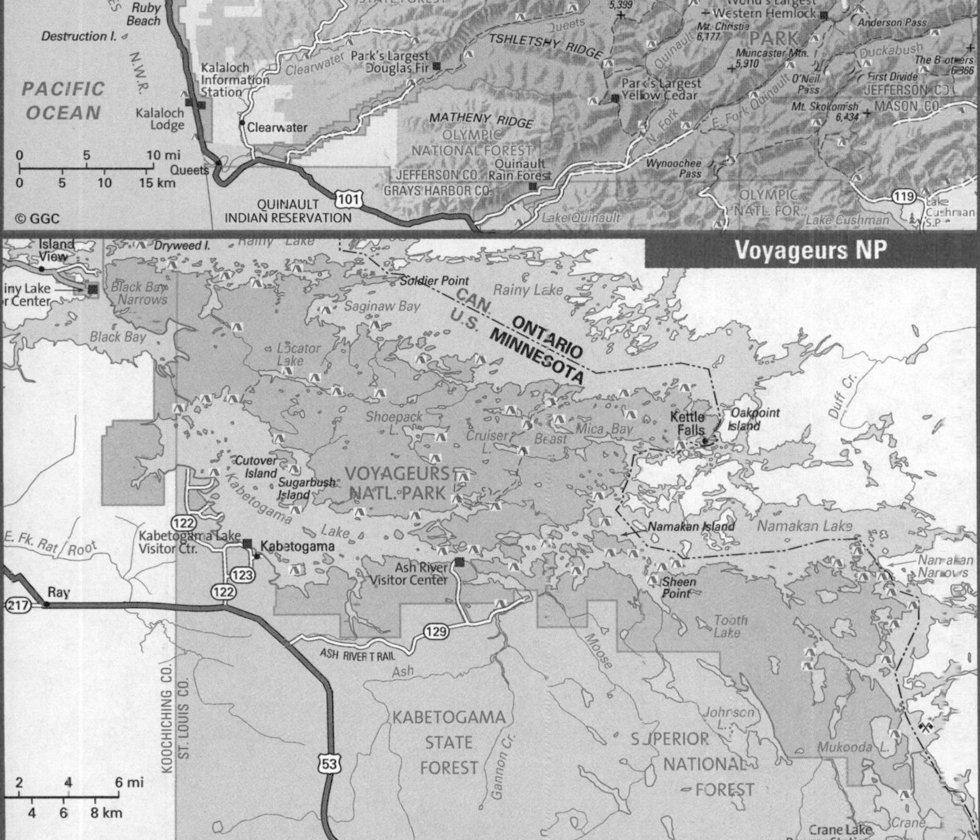
Voyageurs NP
Rainy Lake
CAN.
U.S.
ONTARIO
MINNESOTA
Black Bay
Kettle Falls
VOYAGEURS NATL. PARK
Kabetogama Lake
Kabetogama Lake Visitor Ctr.
Kabetogama
Ash River Visitor Center
Namakan Lake
Ray
KABETOGAMA STATE FOREST
SUPERIOR NATIONAL FOREST
Crane Lake Ranger Station

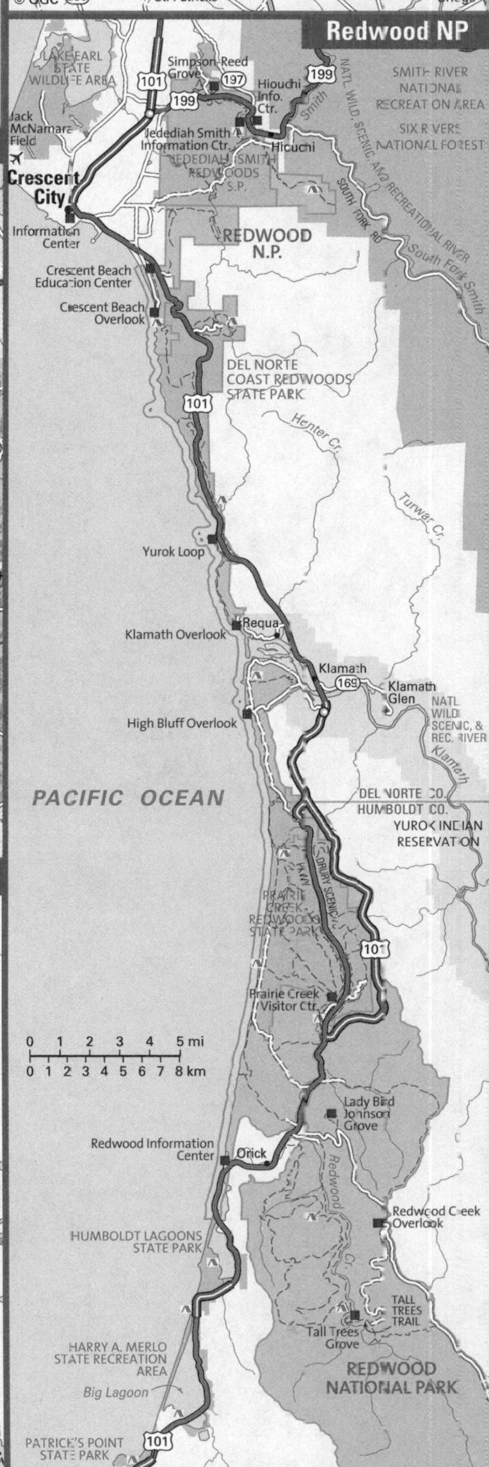
Redwood NP
LAKE EARL STATE WILDLIFE AREA
Hiouchi Info. Ctr.
SMITH RIVER NATIONAL RECREATION AREA
Jedediah Smith Information Ctr.
JEDEDIAH SMITH REDWOODS S.P.
Crescent City
Information Center
Crescent Beach Education Center
Crescent Beach Overlook
REDWOOD N.P.
DEL NORTE COAST REDWOODS STATE PARK
Yurok Loop
Requa
Klamath Overlook
Klamath
Klamath Glen
High Bluff Overlook
PACIFIC OCEAN
DEL NORTE CO.
HUMBOLDT CO.
YUROK INDIAN RESERVATION
PRAIRIE CREEK REDWOODS STATE PARK
Prairie Creek Visitor Ctr.
Lady Bird Johnson Grove
Redwood Information Center
Orick
Redwood Creek Overlook
HUMBOLDT LAGOONS STATE PARK
Tall Trees Grove
HARRY A. MERLO STATE RECREATION AREA
Big Lagoon
REDWOOD NATIONAL PARK
PATRICK'S POINT STATE PARK
© GGC

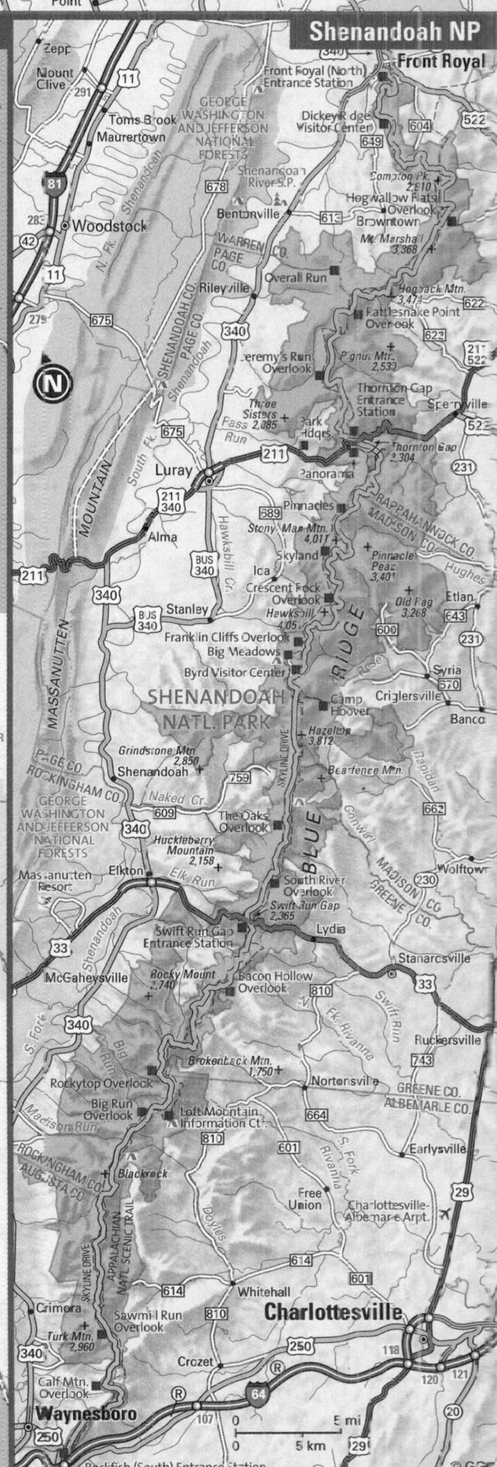
Shenandoah NP
Front Royal
Front Royal (North) Entrance Station
Dickey Ridge Visitor Center
Toms Brook
Maurertown
Woodstock
GEORGE WASHINGTON AND JEFFERSON NATIONAL FORESTS
Bentonville
Overall Run
Thornton Gap Entrance Station
Luray
Skyland
Byrd Visitor Center
Stanley
SHENANDOAH NATL. PARK
MASSANUTTEN MOUNTAIN
BLUE RIDGE
Elkton
Swift Run Gap Entrance Station
Stanardsville
McGaheysville
Loft Mountain Information Ctr.
Charlottesville
Charlottesville-Albemarle Arpt.
Crimora
Waynesboro
Rockfish (South) Entrance Station
Crozet
© GGC

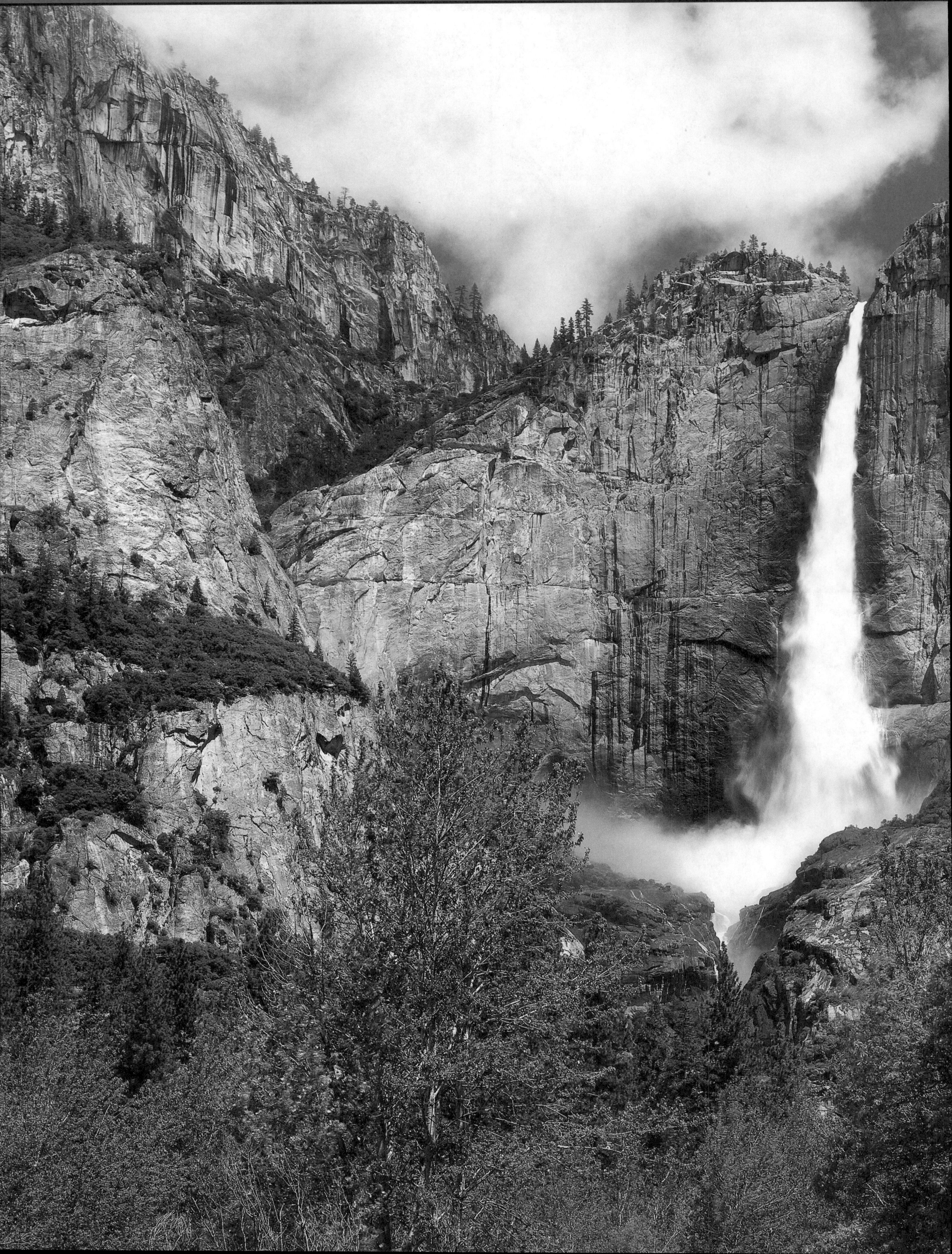

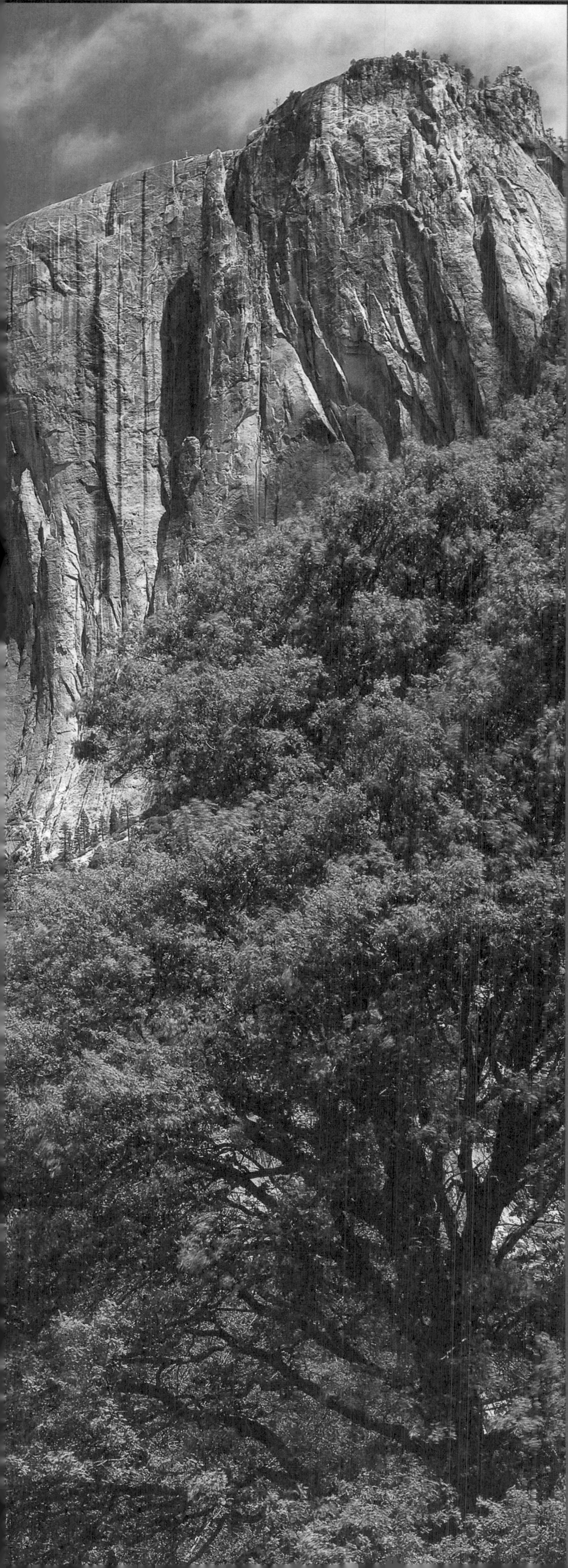

NATIONAL PARKS

Yosemite Falls

Mount Desert Island

Red and orange sandstone of "Devil's Garden"

Spires, steep canyons, and buttes

Peyto Lake

Acadia Maine

Coastal Maine
Established Jan 19, 1929
47,633 acres

Headquarters
Acadia National Park
P.O. Box 177 Eagle Lake Road
Bar Harbor, ME 4609
207.288.3338
www.nps.gov/acad

Visitor Centers
Hulls Cove is open daily mid-Apr-Oct. The Sieur de Monts is open weekends only from May-Sept.

Entrance Fees
$10/vehicle for 7 days.
$5/walk-in for 7 days.

Accommodations
The Blackwoods Campgrounds (800/365-CAMP) are open year-round. Seawall Campground (207/283-3338) is first-come, first-served and open from mid-May-mid-Sept.

When to Go
Visit Acadia Sept-early Oct, the days are warm, the nights are crisp, and congestion is less than in summer.

With waves crashing against a rocky coastline, thick woodlands filled with wildlife, and mountains scraping the sky, Acadia National Park is the Maine of storybooks. Occupying nearly half of Mount Desert Island, with smaller areas on Isle au Haut, Little Cranberry Island, Baker Island, Little Moose Island, and part of the main and at Schoodic Point, Acadia amazes visitors. It is a sea-lashed granite coastal area of forested valleys, lakes, and mountains, all created by the force of ancient glaciers. Acadia is small compared to other national parks; however, it is one of the most visited national parks in the United States.

A 27-mile loop road connects the park's eastern sights on Mount Desert Island, and ferry services take travelers to some of the smaller islands. Visitors can explore 1,530-foot Cadillac Mountain, the highest point on the Atlantic Coast of the United States; watch waves crash against Thunder Hole, a narrow cleft on the rocky coast, creating a thunderous boom; or watch harbor seals sunning during low tide. A road to the summit of Cadillac provides views of Frenchman, Blue Hill, and Penobscot bays. Fir, pine, spruce, many hardwoods, and hundreds of varieties of wildflowers thrive. Nature lovers and hikers will be delighted with the more than 120 miles of trails; park rangers take visitors on various walks and cruises, pointing out and explaining the natural, cultural, and historical features of the park. Forty-five miles of carriage roads offer bicyclists scenic rides through Acadia. Copies of ranger-led programs and trail maps are available at all five of the park's visitor centers. There is saltwater swimming at Sand Beach and freshwater swimming at Echo Lake. Snowmobiles are allowed in some areas and cross-country skiing is available in winter.

BUDGET TIP You can purchase an Acadia Pass—good for entrance into Acadia National Park for one vehicle for one year from date of purchase—for $20.

ME 104
PARK 105

Arches Utah

Eastern Utah
Established Nov 12, 1971
76,519 acres

Headquarters
Arches National Park
P.O. Box 907
Moab, UT 84532
435.719.2299
www.nps.gov/arch

Visitor Centers
The Arches Visitor Center is open daily with the exception of Dec 25.

Entrance Fees
$10/vehicle for 7 days.
$5/walk-in for 7 days.

Accommodations
Devils Garden Campground is available year-round on a first-come, first-served basis.

When to Go
The best time to go is in spring or fall when daytime temperatures are between 60 and 80°F and nights are cool.

This timeless, natural landscape of giant stone arches, pinnacles, spires, fins, and windows was once the bed of an ancient sea. Over time, erosion laid bare the skeletal structure of the earth, making this area a spectacular outdoor museum. This wilderness, which contains the greatest density of natural arches in the world, was named a national monument in 1929 and a national park in 1971. More than 2,000 arches have been cataloged, ranging in size from 3 feet wide to the 105-foot-high, 306-foot-wide Landscape Arch. The arches, fascinating rock formations, and views of the Colorado River canyon, with the peaks of the LaSal Mountains in the distance, can be easily reached by car, but the maze of hiking trails are strongly recommended alternatives. Petroglyphs (drawings) from the primitive peoples who roamed this section of Utah from 700-1200 A.D. can be seen at the Delicate Arch trailhead; the trail itself is three miles round trip, and the destination makes it well worth the trip. Devils Garden Primitive Loop is the longest trail at 7.2 miles round trip and leads to great views of eight arches. A number of shorter, easier trails of less than one mile, such as the Balanced Arch trail, take the hiker up to, around, and through spectacular arches, canyons, and rock formations. Be sure to bring plenty of water.

This is a wildlife sanctuary; no hunting is permitted. There are no bike trails and no bike lanes on the roads. Backcountry permits are required for backpacking and pets are not allowed. The Devils Garden campground is located 18 miles from the park entrance.

BUDGET TIP Consider if the $25 local pass is worth the investment. It is good for entry into Arches and Canyonlands National Parks, as well as Natural Bridges and Hovenweep National Monuments, for one year.

UT 165
PARK 190

Badlands South Dakota

Southern South Dakota
Established Nov 10, 1978
242,756 acres

Headquarters
Badlands National Park
P.O. Box 6
Interior, SD 57750
605.433.5361
www.nps.gov/badl

Visitor Centers
The Ben Riefel Visitor Center is open daily. The White River Visitor Center is open from late May-late Aug only.

Entrance Fees
$10/vehicle for 7 days.
$5/walk-in for 7 days.

Accommodations
There are two campgrounds open year-round on a first-come, first-served basis.

When to Go
Oct is usually pleasant. Winter arrives in the Badlands during Nov and lasts until Feb. Spring and early summer can be very wet, with torrential storms. July-Sept can be hot and dry.

A fantastic, painted landscape of eroded buttes, steep canyons, spires, and razor-edged ridges provides a sharp contrast to the rest of this park which is the largest protected mixed grass prairie in the U.S. The sculpted figures are a stark and simple illustration of geologic processes; they have beauty. Soft clays and sandstones were deposited as sediments during the Eocene and Oligocene epochs, 23 to 37 million years ago. The broad marshy plain of that time was etched by streams from the Black Hills, inhabited by the saber-toothed cat, the rhinoceros-like brontothere, and ancestors of the present-day camel and horse. Their fossilized bones make the area an enormous prehistoric graveyard, entombed in hundreds of feet of a whitish layer of ash blown from ancient volcanoes to the west and southwest. About 500,000 years ago streams began carving the present structures, leaving gullies and multicolored canyons. The current annual rainfall of about 16 inches is just enough to sustain the prairie grasslands.

Herds of bison, gone for many years, roam the area again. Pronghorn antelope, mule deer, prairie dogs, and Rocky Mountain bighorn sheep can also be seen. The park offers a number of hiking trails, the longest being the 10-mile Castle Trail, seldom used but offering great wildlife viewing opportunities and quiet solitude. Most of the other trails in the park are less than a mile long.

Digging and/or moving fossils or artifacts is prohibited and the prohibition is enforced. The Ben Reifel Visitor Center with exhibits and an audiovisual program is open year-round at Cedar Pass. The "Touch Room" is open to children of all ages. Evening programs and activities conducted by ranger-naturalists are offered during the summer.

BUDGET TIP Camp for no fee at Sage Creek Campground.

SD 157
PARK 190

Banff Alberta

Western Alberta
Established Feb 27, 1905
6,641 square kilometres
(2,564 square miles)

Headquarters
Banff National Park
P.O. Box 900
Banff, AB T1L 1K2
403.762.1550
www.worldweb.com/ParksCanada-Banff/

Visitor Centers
The Banff Visitor Center and the Lake Louise Visitor Center are open daily.

Entrance Fees
$6/person/day.

Accommodations
Banff has 10 first-come, first-served campsites. Most are open from mid-June-mid-Sept, but Lake Louise and Mosquito Creek Campgrounds are open year-round.

When to Go
The park's peak season is July-Aug, when the weather is the warmest. Winters are frigid and snowy, but offer a variety of activities.

Banff National Park was Canada's first national park and just the third national park in the world, behind the United States' Yellowstone National Park and Australia's Royal National Park. The Canadian park traces its beginnings back to the building of the transcontinental railroad. The hot springs at the base of Sulphur Mountain were a big attraction to the railroad workers then and remain a popular spot for travelers today. Covering over 2,500 square miles, the park is traversed by the Trans-Canada Highway and miles of towering peaks of the Icefields Parkway, which adjoins Jasper National Park.

Located in the heart of the Canadian Rockies, Banff National Park is famous for its glacially carved mountains—Mt. Forbes at 11,850 feet is the highest—hundreds of alpine glaciers, caves, and mountain reflections glancing off the blue-green waters of Lake Louise. With hundreds of miles of hiking and horseback riding trails, the park allows visitors to observe its abundant wildlife, including black and grizzly bears, elk, bighorn sheep, mountain goats, moose, wolves and many small mammals, such as marmots, pikas and martens. Caribou may be spotted in the northern reaches of the park.

Banff, the highest town in Canada at 4,537 feet, comes alive each summer with a music and drama festival at Banff Centre. Its local pubs, lively bars, and gourmet eateries offer exciting nightlife and Western barbecues are popular throughout the town. Outlying areas add other pleasures: sightseeing at the Cave and Basin National Historic Site, shopping at the Banff Indian Trading Post, gondola rides, boat and raft tours, concerts, art galleries, museums, hot springs, ice field tours, hiking and trail rides. In winter the Canadian Rockies provide some of the best skiing in North American, including heli-copter downhill, and cross-country.

BUDGET TIP Although the weather is best from mid-June to mid-September, you can avoid crowds and save on lodgings by scheduling your visit outside this peak season.

AB 179
PARK 190

Boquillas Canyon and the Rio Grande

Sunrise on the famous Pink Cliffs

Colorado River as seen from the White Rim

South Desert Overlook

Big Bend Texas

Southern Texas
Established June 12, 1944
801,163 acres

Headquarters
Big Bend National Park
P.O. Box 129
Big Bend National Park, TX 79834
915.477.2251
www.nps.gov/bibe

Visitor Centers
The Panther Junction Visitor Center is open daily, excluding Dec 25.

Entrance Fees
$10/vehicle for 7 days.

Accommodations
There are four first-come, first-served, year-round campgrounds. The Chisos Mountain Lodge (915/477-2291) is open year-round.

When to Go
Visitation is highest in Mar and Apr when the weather is pleasant. The park is crowded from mid-late Mar. Visitation is lowest in Aug and Sept. Winters are generally mild.

This is truly a land of contrasts, from daily extremes of hot and cold temperatures to towering mountain peaks and deep canyons and from Chihuahan desert cactus to mountain aspens, this is a park that commands both respect and awe. These contrasts also bring unparalleled diversity in both flora and fauna; Big Bend boasts more than 1,200 species of plants, particularly cacti in the lowest areas and juniper, piñon, oak, and scattered stands of Arizona pine, Douglas fir, Arizona cypress, and aspen in the uplands. More than 400 bird species may be found amid scenery as stark and magnificent as anywhere in the United States. The Chisos Mountains dominate the Texas landscape, while Sierra del Carmen and other mountain ranges visible from the park are across the border in Mexico.

The upper 69 miles of the Rio Grande River courses its way through the Chihuahan Desert, delivering along the way spectacular canyons rising 1,500 feet above the water, unimpeded by impoundments or other man-made diversions. Of particular note are the canyons of Santa Elena, Mariscal, and Boquillas. Designated a Wild and Scenic River by Congress in 1978, the Rio Grande forms the U.S. border with Mexico and includes the "big bend" to the northeast that gives the national park its name.

The visitor center at Panther Junction contains orientation exhibits for visitors; at Persimmon Gap, the entrance from Marathon, there is also a visitor contact station. Permits are required for all overnight trips. Plan on a minimum of two days to see the park from the main roads. Commercial outfitters outside of the park offer Rio Grande float trips.

BUDGET TIP Camping not your cup of tea? The Chisos Mountain Lodge the only lodging inside the park, offers reasonable room rates. The cottages are furnished with three double beds, and perfect for large families on a limited budget.

TX 160
PARK 190

Bryce Canyon Utah

South Central Utah
Established Sept 15, 1928
35,835 acres

Headquarters
Bryce Canyon National Park
P.O. Box 170001
Bryce Canyon, UT 84717
435.834.5322
www.nps.gov/brca

Visitor Centers
The Visitor Center is open daily, excluding Thanksgiving Day, Dec 25, and Jan 1.

Entrance Fees
$20/vehicle for 7 days.

Accommodations
North Campground is available year-round on a first-come, first-served basis. Sunset Campground is open from May-mid-Oct. The Bryce Canyon Lodge (435/834-5361) is open from Apr-Oct.

When to Go
Summer days are pleasant. Spring and fall can be unpredictable. Winter is a popular time to visit; however nights can fall below freezing.

Bryce Canyon is a wonderland of colorful, fantastic cliffs, spires, pinnacles and mazes created by millions of years of erosion. Towering rocks worn to odd, sculptured shapes stand grouped in striking sequences. The Paiute, who once lived nearby, called this "the place where red rocks stand like men in a bowl-shaped canyon." Although termed a canyon, Bryce is actually a series of "breaks" in 12 large amphitheaters—some plunging as deep as 1,000 feet into the multicolored limestone. The formations appear to change color as the sunlight strikes from different angles and seem incandescent in the late afternoon. The famous Pink Cliffs were carved from the Claron Formation; shades of red, orange, white, gray, purple, brown, and soft yellow appear in the strata. Park Road follows 17 miles along the eastern edge of the Paunsaugunt Plateau, where the natural amphitheaters are spread out below and plateaus covered with evergreens and valleys filled with sagebrush stretch away into the distance.

Among the trails that drop down below the canyon rim are Fairyland Trail (8 miles), Peekaboo Loop (5.5 miles), Queen's Garden (1.8 miles), and Navajo Loop (1.3 miles) – all mileages are round trip. The Under-the-Rim trail is 23 miles long and has 8 backcountry campsites (permit required). Be prepared for steep sections, wear hiking boots and bring plenty of water. Tent and trailer camping sites are also available.

The original Bryce Canyon Lodge was built in 1924, the same year that the park achieved national park status, and it still serves park visitors today. The visitor center at the entrance station has complete information on the park, including orientation shows, geologic displays, and detailed maps.

BUDGET TIP On your way to Bryce Canyon, stop to see the magnificent shapes and deep red colors of Red Canyon. There is no entrance fee, and there are camping facilities and shops on site.

UT 165
PARK 165

Canyonlands Utah

Southeastern Utah
Established Sept 12, 1964
337,598 acres

Headquarters
Canyonlands National Park
2282 S. West Resource Blvd
Moab, UT 84532
435.719.2313
www.nps.gov/cany

Visitor Centers
Island in the Sky is open daily.

Entrance Fees
$10/vehicle for 7 days.
$5/person for 7 days.

Accommodations
Squaw Flat and Willow Flat Campgrounds are open daily, and are first-come, first-served. Each campsite typically fills every day from late Mar-June and early Sept-mid-Oct.

When to Go
The best time to visit is in the spring when daytime temperatures are usually 60 to 80°F and nights are cool.

Like other Utah parks, the highlight of Canyonlands is the spectacular mesas, buttes, arches, spires, and of course, canyons that grace the landscape. Pictograph panels and ancestral Puebloan ruins combine with beautiful desert flora to further enhance the magical feeling of the park. Set aside by Congress in 1964 as a national park, the area is largely undeveloped. It is dissected by the Colorado and Green Rivers that have effectively divided the park into four districts that are not directly linked by any roads, so make your visitation plans carefully. The Islands in the Sky district is the most accessible (40 minutes to the visitor center from Moab), with numerous overlooks and short hiking trails; the other districts have attractions that are reached by boating, hiking or via a four-wheel-drive vehicle.

At the southeast corner of the park, the Needles district gets its name from the sandstone spires that dominate the area. Long day hikes and overnights in Needles will take the adventurer to Tower Ruin, Confluence Overlook, Chesler Park and Druid Arch. Permits are required for all overnight trips in the backcountry and campgrounds and group sites are available in the area on a first-come, first-served basis. The rivers themselves form the third district and the Maze, primarily for backcountry enthusiasts using unimproved roads, is the fourth district.

Hiking is not the only major recreational opportunity; the terrain is also well suited for mountain biking, particularly the 100 mile White Rim Road located in the Island in the Sky district. Above the confluence of the Colorado and Green rivers are miles of flat water canoeing and kayaking; Cataract Canyon below the confluence is another matter, with powerful Class III through V whitewater along one 14-mile stretch.

BUDGET TIP Make sure your car is up for the trip—towing charges are very expensive. Visitors caught in the backcountry with disabled vehicles can expect towing fees in excess of $1,000.

UT 165

Capitol Reef Utah

South Central Utah
Established Dec 18, 1971
241,904 acres

Headquarters
Capitol Reef National Park
HC 70 Box 15
Torrey, UT 84775
435.425.3791
www.nps.gov/care

Visitor Centers
The Capitol Reef Visitor Center is open daily, with the exception of Dec 25.

Entrance Fees
$5/vehicle for 7 days.

Accommodations
The park has three campgrounds (435/425-3791) open year-round on a first-come, first-served basis.

When to Go
The best time to visit is fall, particularly Oct and Nov, when temperatures remain warm enough, but not so hot you are constantly looking for shade.

Capitol Reef was so named because the rocks formed a natural barrier to pioneer travel and the white sandstone domes resemble the dome of the U.S. Capitol. In the heart of Utah's slickrock country, the park is located on a 100-mile warp in the earth's crust formed 50-70 million years ago. Through a combination of movements of ancient faults and subsequent erosion, elevations range from 3,900–8,800 feet. Erosion of the tilted rock also left basins in the rock that collect thousands of gallons of water each time it rains—thus the name for the geology of the area—Waterpocket Fold. A visit to Cathedral Valley will reveal colorful sedimentary rock inclines, with soft rock layers eroded into free standing monoliths, or temples Vehicles with good ground clearance can negotiate a 60-mile loop drive through the valley that starts at River Ford, 12 miles east of the visitor center on UT 24. Thousand Lake Mountain Road (unpaved) provides another drive that offers panoramic views of the Painted Desert, climbing 2,700 feet along the way.

A 10-mile scenic drive (additional fee) on paved road starts at the park Visitor Center and provides views to Grand Wash, Capitol Gorge, Pleasant Creek, and the South Draw Road. Southern stretches of the park can be accessed via a 125-mile loop tour that begins at the visitor center on UT 24. Short day hikes off of Notom-Bullfrog Road will take you to Surprise and Headquarters Canyons.

Mountain biking and hiking are other popular modes of taking in the scenic wonders of the park. There are numerous day hiking trailheads along UT 24. Primitive camping is available and the more developed Fruita campground has 70 sites (no reservation required).

BUDGET TIP From May to September, the park offers a variety of ranger-guided programs at no charge. These include guided walks, talks, and evening programs at the campground amphitheater.

UT 165

The Chinese Theater

Mount Scott

Stovepipe Wells's sand dune

Mount McKinley and Wonder Lake

Carlsbad Caverns New Mexico

Southeastern New Mexico
Established May 14, 1930
46,766 acres

Headquarters
Carlsbad Caverns National Park
3225 National Parks Highway
Carlsbad, NM 88220
505.885.8884
www.nps.gov/cave

Visitor Centers
The Carlsbad Caverns Visitor Center is open daily and located 7 miles from the park's entrance.

Entrance Fees
$6 for 3 days; various fees apply for cave tours.

Accommodations
Only backcountry permit is available; a free permit is required.

When to Go
The climate in the caves rarely varies from 56°. The best time to avoid the crowds is between Labor Day and Memorial Day.

One of the largest and most remarkable in the world, this cavern extends approximately 30 miles and has the deepest cave in the U.S., Lechugilla Cave, 1,567 feet below the surface. Carlsbad Caverns was once known as Bat Cave because of the spectacular bat flights that still occur daily at sunset during the warmer months. The bats migrate to Mexico in October/November and return in April/May. There is a bat flight program (free) given at the cavern entrance at dusk; cameras are not permitted.

Carlsbad Cavern was formed by the dissolving action of acidic water in a fossil reef dating back to the Permian age. When geologic uplift drained the cavern, mineral-laden water dripping from the ceiling formed the stalactites and stalagmites. The main cavern has two self-guided tours, the Big Room Route and the Natural Entrance Route. Guided tours include the Kings Palace tour and five others (fees are additional to entrance fees). The "Cavern Guide," an audio tour rented at the visitor center, enhances self-guided tours with interpretations of the caverns, interviews, and historic recreations. Also available are tours in two backcountry caves: Slaughter Canyon Cave and Spider Cave. All guided tours require reservations. Since the temperature in the cavern is always 56°F, be sure to carry a jacket even if it is hot outside; comfortable rubber-soled shoes are also recommended for safety. Photography, including flash and time exposures, is permitted on self-guided trips and some guided tours. Rangers patrol the cave. A scenic 9-1/2 mile loop drive, hiking trails, an observation tower and exhibits can be found on the surface, along with a restaurant.

BUDGET TIP Make every moment of your trip count by preplanning your visit. Decide what tours you want to take and call ahead to make reservations.

NM 130

Crater Lake Oregon

Southern Oregon
Established May 22, 1902
183,224 acres

Headquarters
Crater Lake National Park
P.O. Box 7
Crater Lake, OR 97604
541.594.3100
www.nps.gov/crla

Visitor Centers
The Steel Visitor Center is open daily and the Rim Village Visitor Center is open June-Sept only.

Entrance Fees
$10/vehicle for 7 days.

Accommodations
Two campgrounds in the park are available on a first-come, first-served basis; Lost Creek is open July-Oct, while Mazama operates mid-June-early Oct.

When to Go
July to September

Crater Lake's former name, Lake Majesty, comes close to describing the feeling visitors get from the deep blue waters in the caldera of dormant Mount Mazama. More than 7,700 years ago the volcano collapsed and formed a deep basin. Rain and snow accumulated in the empty caldera, forming the deepest lake in the United States (1,932 ft). Surrounded by 25 miles of jagged rim rock, the 21-square-mile lake is broken only by Wizard and Phantom Ship islands. Entrance by road from any direction brings you to the 33-mile Rim Drive (July-mid-October or first snow) leading to all observation points, park headquarters, and a visitor center at Rim Village (June-September, daily).

The park can be explored by following spurs and trails extending from Rim Drive. Going clockwise from Rim Village, to the west, The Watchman Peak is reached by a one-mile trail that takes the hiker 1,800 feet above the lake with a full view in all directions; Mount Shasta in California, 105 miles away, is visible on a clear day. On the northeast side, Cleetwood Trail descends one mile to the shore and a boat landing where two-hour launch trips depart hourly each day in summer. Six miles farther on Rim Drive, still going clockwise, is the start of a 2-1/2-mile hiking trail, 1,230 feet to Mount Scott, at 8,926 feet the highest point in the park. Four miles beyond this point, a road leads seven miles from Rim Drive to The Pinnacles, pumice spires rising like stone needles from the canyon of Wheeler Creek. In winter, the south and west entrance roads are kept clear in spite of the annual 45-foot snowfall; the north entrance road and Rim Drive are closed from mid-October to June, depending on snow conditions.

BUDGET TIP For the price of admission, you can enjoy a number of ranger-led activities, including boat tours, interpretive walks and talks, and in-depth presentations of various topics relating to the natural and cultural history of Crater Lake.

OR 148
PARK 149

Death Valley California

Southwestern California
Established Oct 31, 1994
3,340,410 acres

Headquarters
Death Valley National Park
P.O. Box 579
Death Valley, CA 92328
760.786.3200
www.nps.gov/deva

Visitor Centers
Scotty's Castle, the Gas House Museum, the Beatty Information Center, and the Furnace Creek Visitor Center and Museum are open daily.

Entrance Fees
$10/vehicle for $7. $5/walk-in for 7 days.

Accommodations
The park has nine campgrounds in all. Texas Spring (760/786-3247) and Furnace Creek (800/365-CAMP) are available for reservations. Mahgony Flat and Thorndike are open Mar-Nov.

When to Go
November to April.

Located approximately 300 miles northeast of Los Angeles, on more than 3,340,410 acres of rugged desert, peaks, and depressions lies an unusual and colorful landscape. The park is one vast geological museum, revealing secrets of ages gone by. Millions of years ago, Death Valley was part of the Pacific Ocean; then violent uplifts of the earth occurred, creating mountain ranges and draining water to the west. Today, 200 square miles of the valley are at or below sea level. The lowest point on the continent (282 feet below sea level) is located next to Telescope Peak (11,049 feet), which towers above this famous spot. The valley itself is about 140 miles long and 4 to 16 miles wide. The average rainfall is less than two inches a year. From October until May the climate is very pleasant. In summer it is extremely hot; a maximum temperature of 134°F in the shade has been recorded. This is, in fact, the lowest, hottest, and driest area in North America.

Death Valley was named in 1849 when a party of gold hunters was stranded here for several weeks awaiting help. The discovery and subsequent mining of borax, hauled out by the 20-mule teams that gave the product its commercial name, led to development of the valley as a tourist attraction. Guided walks, evening programs and talks are offered between November and April. In the summer months it can be dangerous venturing off paved roads in this area. Obey all National Park Service signs and regulations. Make sure your vehicle has plenty of gas and oil. Carry extra water when you explore this park, especially in hot weather.

BUDGET TIP Various campgrounds within Death Valley are free: Emigrant, Mahogany Flat, and Wildrose.

CA 70
NV 126
PARK 190

Denali Alaska

Central Alaska
Established Feb 26, 1917
6,075,030 acres

Headquarters
Denali National Park
Superintendent's Office
P.O. Box 9
Denali Park, AK 99755
907.683.2294
www.nps.gov/dena

Visitor Centers
The Visitor Center is open daily from late Apr-Sept. Eielson Visitor Center is open daily June-mid-Sept.

Entrance Fees
$10/vehicle for 7 days. $5/walk-in for 7 days. There is a $150 climber fee.

Accommodations
There are six campgrounds, three for hikers only, on a first-come, first-served basis. All are open May-Sept, except Riley Creek, which is open year-round.

When to Go
May to September.

Covering an area larger than the state of Massachusetts, Denali National Park and Preserve features spectacular landscapes and Arctic wildlife, including grizzly bears, wolves, Dall sheep, bald eagles, caribou, and moose. It is also home to North America's highest mountain, the 20,320-foot Mount McKinley, known as Denali, which translates as "the high one" in the Athabaskan language.

First established as a wildlife refuge in 1917 to protect its large mammals, the area was given National Park status largely through the efforts of naturalist, hunter and conservationist Charles Sheldon. In 1980, the park's boundary was increased by 4 million acres and it was redesignated Denali National Park and Preserve. There is only one road into the park, and most of it is closed to the public. Private vehicles are restricted by lottery to 400 a day and those are restricted to the first 14 miles of the 85-mile road; those who want to go further take park buses. Denali's unspoiled wilderness is preserved by keeping the park essentially trailess and roadless. Nevertheless, a number of year-round outdoor activities are permitted: wildlife watching, mountaineering ($150 permit and many regulations), backpacking, hiking, cross-country skiing, sled dog mushing, snow shoeing, and snowmobiling. More exotic adventures such as aerial tours, rafting, and horseback trips can be arranged through one of the many tour operators in the area.

BUDGET TIP Take advantage of interpretive programs offered by the park, including talks and guided walks. They offer an excellent introduction to the park and its backcountry, and most are free of charge.

AK 62
PARK 62

FloridaRoyal Palm Area

Swiftcurrent Lake

Vast and breathtaking chasm

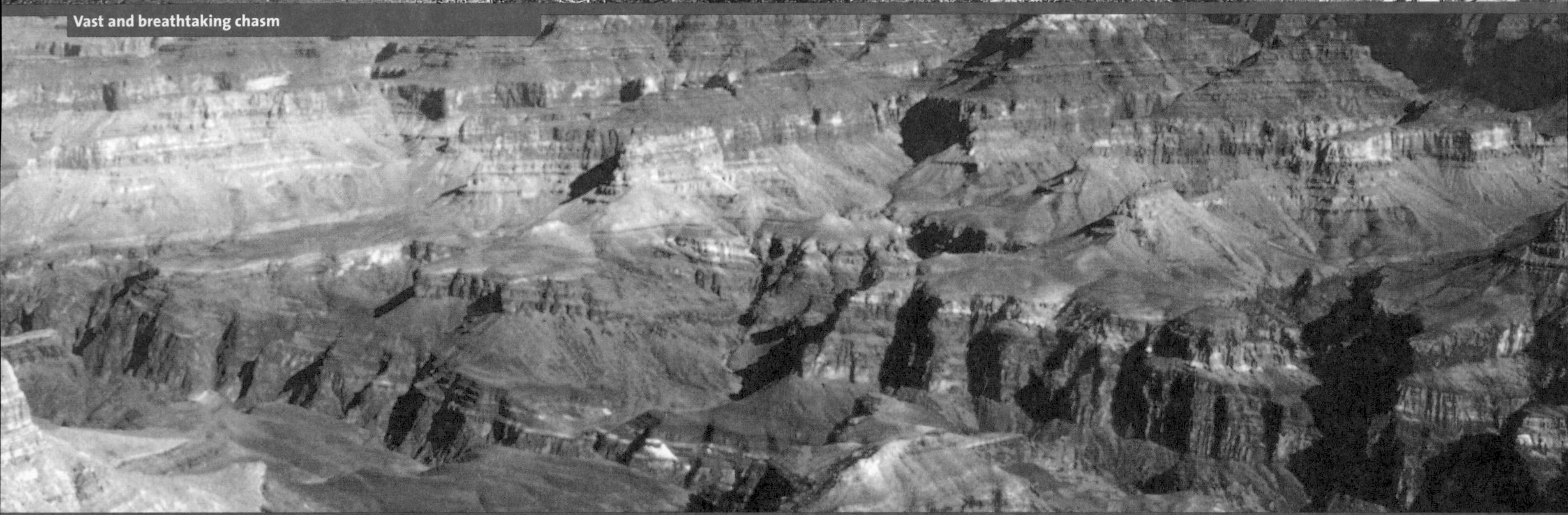

Oxbow Bend

Everglades Florida

Southern Florida
Established Dec 6, 1947
1,508,529 acres

Headquarters
Everglades National Park
40001 State Road 9336
Homestead, FL 33034
305.242.7700
www.nps.gov/ever

Visitor Centers
The Ernest F. Coe Visitor Center, the Flamingo Visitor Center, and the Gulf Coast Visitor Center are open daily.

Entrance Fees
$10/vehicle for 7 days.
$5/walk-in for 7 days

Accommodations
The Flamingo and the Lone Pine Key Campgrounds (800/365-CAMP) are open year-round. The Flamingo Lodge (800/600-3813) is also open year-round.

When to Go
Winters are warm, sunny, and breezy. This is the best time to see the largest variety of wading birds.

The largest subtropical wilderness in North America, the park preserves the spectacular half-land, half-water Everglades that once covered most of the southern third of the Florida peninsula. At the northern reaches of the park, much of the glades have been drained and tamed, leaving an incredibly rich blue-black soil in which to raise sugar, citrus, and winter vegetable crops. In addition to the national park, the remaining area of the Everglades, larger than the state of Delaware, has been developed into a huge recreation area with hunting fishing, boating, camping, and sightseeing. Easily reached from cities along Florida's east coast are 34 access sites, located along the canals and levees that have been constructed to protect 18 counties from flooding. Nowhere else in the world is there an area comparable to this huge, water-sodden wetland with its prairies of saw grass, stands of dwarf cypress, hammocks of cabbage palm, West Indies mahogany, strangler figs, and wild orchids. The entire expanse teems with water birds, alligators, snakes, marsh rabbits, deer, raccoons, bobcats, turtles, largemouth bass, garfish, and panfish. (Wildlife is visible mainly during the winter months.) This is also part of the traditional domain of the Seminole and Miccosukee.

Much of the Everglades is an immense sea of sedges that shoot up ten feet with barbed blades and needle-sharp edges, appropriately called saw grass. These grassy waters are broken only by clusters of trees and dense vegetation called hammocks. The saw grass glades give way along the coast to huge, shadowy mangrove swamps interlaced by tranquil winding water lanes. Much of the national park is impenetrable except with an experienced guide; however, the National Park Service has set up trails (all improved or marked), exhibits, and facilities that make a safe excursion into the Everglades possible for any visitor.

BUDGET TIP Get the most out of your trip—ask for a copy of Parks and Preserves, a free newspaper that's filled with up-to-date information about goings-on in the Everglades.

FL 84
PARK 191

Glacier-Waterton Alberta/Montana

Northwestern Montana
Established May 11, 1910
1,013,572 acres

Headquarters
Glacier National Park
Park Headquarters
West Glacier, MT 59936
406.888.7800
www.nps.gov/glac

Visitor Centers
Apgar Visitor Center is open daily during the summer, and weekends only Nov-Mar. Logan Pass Visitor Center is open early June-mid-Oct.

Entrance Fees
$10/vehicle for 7 days.
$5/walk-in for 7 days.

Accommodations
Glacier Park has 13 campgrounds. Fish Creek and St. Mary Campgrounds (800/365-CAMP) may be reserved in advance. All others are first-come, first-served.

When to Go
Late June-Aug is a lovely time to visit. Fall colors begin to change from late Sept-mid-Oct.

Waterton Lakes National Park in Alberta and Glacier National Park in Montana were designated Waterton-Glacier International Peace Park in 1932 as an acknowledgement of the long standing friendship and goodwill between the two countries. This spectacular section of the Northern Rockies was formed by collisions of the Earth's crust in a geologic process similar to those that created the Himalayan and Andes Mountains, then further carved and polished by the crushing force of vast glaciers thousands of feet thick. Magnificent views of these glaciated mountain peaks and valleys can be found all along the breathtaking Going-to-the-Sun Road. The road can be traversed in two or three hours by car, but can be easily turned into a full day by hiking on the adjoining trails. In particular, Sun Point Nature Trail follows windblown slopes to Baring Falls; Hidden Lake Nature Trail takes the hiker into an alpine wonderland covered by a carpet of flowers; Trail of the Cedars offers a different view of the park, through the dark and damp understory. Day trip hikes and shorter hikes can also originate at Many Glacier, home to the historic Many Glacier Hotel, or Two Medicine, which offers the option of a boat cruise on Lake McDonald and St. Mary Lake. Keep your eyes out for bear, elk and cougars. The Apgar Visitor Center is the park headquarters and can be reached via U.S. 2 at the southwestern end of the park.

While in Waterton Lakes on the Alberta side of the park, be sure to visit the Prince of Wales Hotel, built in 1927 in a Swiss architectural form. The Red Rock Parkway goes from the town of Waterton Park to Red Rock Canyon after branching off Alberta Highway 5. Also from the town of Waterton Park, you can drive to Cameron Lake via the Akamina Parkway.

BUDGET TIP Pick up The Waterton/Glacier Guide a joint International Peace Park newspaper, which provides information on wildlife, safety, new initiatives, special events and services. These free publications are available at the Park Gate, the Visitor Reception Centre, and the Heritage Centre.

MT 122
AB 179
PARK 122

Grand Canyon Arizona

Northern Arizona
Established Feb 26, 1919
1,217,403 acres

Headquarters
Grand Canyon National Park
P.O. Box 129
Grand Canyon, AZ 86023
928.638.7888
www.nps.gov/grca

Visitor Centers
Canyon View and Desert View Information Centers are open daily. The North Rim Visitor Center is open mid-May-Oct daily.

Entrance Fees
$20/vehicle for 7 days.

Accommodations
Camping reservations are strongly suggested Apr-Nov. Mather Campground (800/365-2267), which is open year-round, and North Rim Campgrounds (800/365-2267), open from mid-May-mid-Oct, accept advance reservations.

When to Go
The ideal time to hike the inner canyon is Apr.

Every minute of the day, the light changes the colors of the awesome gorge we call the Grand Canyon. Sunrises and sunsets are particularly breathtaking in the park, visited by more than 5 million people a year. Scenic overlooks at Desert View Drive, Hermet Road, as well as at the Yavapai Observation Station at Yavapai Point offer especially magnificent views of the canyon.

The canyon cut by the Colorado River is 4 to 18 miles wide and nearly a mile deep. Multicolored layers of rock in the canyon walls record more than 2 million years of geologic time. The vivid colors for which the Grand Canyon is famous are due to small amounts of many different minerals in the rock.

The South Rim (altitude 7,000 feet), open all year, has the greatest number of services and is the most popular to visit. The Colorado River is some 4,600 feet below. A trip to the bottom of the canyon from the South Rim is seven miles via the South Kaibab Trail and nine miles via the Bright Angel Trail. The North Rim (altitude 8,100 feet), blocked by heavy snows in winter, is open from approximately mid-May through mid-October.

There are many ways to enjoy a trip to the canyon. A number of scenic air tour operators are based outside the park, and offer both fixed-wing and helicopter tours of the region. For a real adventure, there are whitewater rafting trips through the canyon that last from one day to 30 days. Also available are mule trips from both the North and South Rim, trail rides, and twilight campfire and wagon rides.

BUDGET TIP With no admission fee, the Yavapai Observation Station, located 5 miles north of the park's south entrance, offers a panoramic view of the canyon, and exhibits about the fossil record at the Grand Canyon.

AZ 64
PARK 65

Grand Teton Wyoming

Northwestern Wyoming
Established Feb 26, 1929
309,994 acres

Headquarters
Grand Teton National Park
P.O. Drawer 170
Moose, WY 83012
307.739.3300
www.nps.gov/grte

Visitor Centers
The Moose Visitor Center is open daily, with the exception of Dec 25. Colter Bay and Jenny Lake Visitor Centers are open June-Sept.

Entrance Fees
$20/vehicle for 7 days.

Accommodations
Of the six campgrounds in the national park, only Flagg Ranch (800/443-2311) accepts reservations. All campsites are open mid-May-mid-Sept.

When to Go
There are three optimal times to visit—summer, autumn, and winter. The days are clear and humidity is low.

These rugged, block-faulted mountains began to rise about nine million years ago, making them some of the youngest on the continent. Geologic and glacial forces combined to buckle and sculpt the landscape into a dramatic setting of canyons, cirques, and craggy peaks that cast their reflections across numerous clear alpine lakes. Grand Teton Peak is the tallest in the range, but there are twelve others that are over 12,000 feet. The Snake River winds gracefully through Jackson Hole ("hole" being the old fur trapper's term for a high-altitude valley surrounded by mountains). Hiking, climbing, backpacking, fishing and wildlife viewing are favored activities. The area provides habitat for elk, moose, bison, black and grizzly bear; good observation points include Oxbow Bend, Timbered Island, Cascade Canyon and along the Snake River.

Hiking opportunities are abundant, with more than 200 miles of trails. Ranger-led hikes in the Moose and Jenny Lake areas and Colter Bay are available. Climbers can also tackle summits via routes of varying difficulty; the more ambitious may take advantage of Exum School of Mountaineering and Jackson Hole Mountain Guides classes that range from a beginner's course to an attempt at conquering Grand Teton Mountain.

Corrals at Jackson Lake Lodge and Colter Bay have strings of horses accustomed to rocky trails; pack trips can be arranged. Boaters and anglers can enjoy placid lakes or wild streams; the Colter Bay, Signal Mountain, and Leek's marinas have ramps, guides, facilities, and rentals. Five different campgrounds serve the park on a first-come, first-served basis. There are three visitor centers with interpretive displays: Moose Visitor Center; Colter Bay Visitor Center & Indian Arts Museum; and Jenny Lake Visitor Center (June-Labor Day).

BUDGET TIP If you expect to visit neighboring Yellowstone as well as Grand Teton more than once a year, buy a $20 annual permit (admission is good for both).

WY 176
PARK 176

Blue Ridge Mountain chain

Effects of a recent lava flow

Gulpha Gorge

The famous quartz monzonite boulders

Great Smoky Mountains North Carolina/Tennessee

Eastern Tennessee/Western North Carolina
Established June 15, 1934
521,490 acres

Headquarters
Great Smoky Mountains National Park
107 Park Headquarters Road
Gatlinburg, TN 37738
865.436.1200
www.nps.gov/grsm

Visitor Centers
Cades Cove, Oconaluftee, and Sugarlands are open daily.

Entrance Fees
Free admission.

Accommodations
Smokemount and Cedar Cove Campgrounds (865/436-1231) are open year-round.

When to Go
Summer offers lush greenery and warm temperatures. Oct offers a splendid array of fall colors.

The Appalachian Mountains, product of a slow uplift of ancient sediments that took place more than 200 million years ago, stand tall and regal in this park that is 95% forested. Red spruce, basswood, eastern hemlock, yellow birch, white ash, cucumber trees, silverbells, Fraser fir, tulip poplar, red maple, Fraser magnolias, and dogwood tower above hundreds of other species of flowering plants. Perhaps the most spectacular of these are the purple rhododendron, mountain laurel, and flame azalea, in bloom from early June to mid-July. The moist climate has helped make this a rich wilderness. From early spring to late fall the "coves" (as the open valleys surrounded by peaks are called) and forest floors are covered with a succession of flowers with colorful variety.

Including the Appalachian Trail, which follows the Tennessee-North Carolina state line along a ridge for 70 miles, the park has over 850 miles of foot trails. Among the more popular and scenic are Alum Cave Trail (4.4 miles), Chimney Tops (strenuous 4 miles) and Andrews Bald (moderate, 3.6 miles), but backpacking trips could take the hiker into the back country for a week. Other outdoor activities include horseback riding (five horse camps require reservations), swimming, picnicking, biking and numerous outdoor programs.

In the lowlands are the cabins, barns and mills of the mountain people whose ancestors came years ago from England and Scotland. Cades Cove, a 6,800-acre valley eight miles from Townsend, Tennessee, provides the most popular view into the cultural and natural heritage of the park, including its time as part of the Cherokee Nation prior to 1819. The valley can be driven via an eleven-mile loop road, but the many historic structures and wayside exhibits can also be experienced via bicycle, hay wagon, and numerous foot trails.

BUDGET TIP Due to deed restrictions imposed when the Park was established, there are no entrance fees.

NC 138
TN 158
PARK 140

Hawaii Volcanoes Hawaii

Island of Hawaii
Established Aug 1, 1916
209,695 acres

Headquarters
Hawaii Volcanoes National Park
P.O. Box 52
Hawaii National Park, HI 96718
808.985.6000
www.nps.gov/havo

Visitor Centers
The Kilauea Visitor Center and the Thomas A. Jaggar Museum are open daily.

Entrance Fees
$10/vehicle/day. $5/walk-in/day.

Accommodations
Camping at Namakani and Paio Kulanaokuaiki (808/985-6011) is free and operated on a first-come, first-served basis.

When to Go
Anytime is a good time to visit this national park though the weather can be unpredictable. The park has distinct climate zones that vary according to elevation.

Volcanoes have continuously built the entire Hawaiian Island chain over the course of the last 70 million years. The largest of the islands, Hawaii, is comprised of five major volcanoes, two of which are the world's most active – Kilauea and Mauna Loa. Hawaii Volcanoes National Park was created to preserve the natural setting of these two great mountain masses. First established in 1916, the park was expanded to include the forests of Mauna Loa, the Ka'u Desert, and the rain forest of Ola'a. It was given its current name in 1961. The volcanic eruptions of Kilauea and Mauna Loa have created a continually-changing landscape. Standing just less than 4,200 feet tall, Kilauea is the most active volcano on earth. Its sister, Mauna Loa, the most massive mountain on earth, stands at 13,677 feet and has been erupting for some 100,000 years. It caused Hawaii's largest recorded earthquake in 1868.

Visitors—especially campers and hikers—should be prepared for a wide range of weather conditions. Many of the trails cross deserts, rain forests, beaches, and in the winter, snow. The most popular drive is Crater Rim Drive, an 11-mile road that circles Kilauea's summit caldera, passes through the Ka'u Desert and a tropical rain forest, and provides visitors with a number of scenic stops. Highlights along the loop include Sulfur Banks, Steam Vents and Steaming Bluff, and the walk-through Thurston Lava Tube. Intersecting with Crater Rim Drive is Chain of Craters Road, which descends 3,700 feet to the coast, and ends where a 1994 lava flow crossed the road. A viewing area at the end of the road allows visitors to take a close-up look at pit craters and other spectacular volcanic formations.

BUDGET TIP The only campground accessible by car, Namakani Paio, is free and requires no reservations.

HI 88
PARK 191

Hot Springs Arkansas

Central Arkansas
Established Mar 4, 1921
5,550 acres

Headquarters
Hot Springs National Park
P.O. Box 1860
Hot Springs, AR 71902
501.623.2824
www.nps.gov/hosp

Visitor Centers
The Hot Springs Visitor Center is open daily, year-round but closed on Jan 1, Thanksgiving Day, Dec 25.

Entrance Fees
None, a $10 fee is charged for camping only.

Accommodations
Gulpha Gorge Campground is open year-round and available on a first-come, first-served basis

When to Go
The park is open year-round. Summers are hot and very humid. Spring and fall are mild, but humid. Winters are usually comfortable.

Hot Springs was first created a "reservation" in 1832 by President Andrew Jackson to protect the thermal waters flowing from the Ouachita Mountains. Eight historic bathhouses in the town of Hot Springs, known as "Bathhouse Row," are also on the National Register of Historic Places.

One of the most popular spas and resorts in the United States, the park is partially surrounded by the town of Hot Springs. Approximately one million gallons of thermal water flow daily from 47 springs within the park. The springs have been administered by the federal government since 1832. At an average temperature of 143°F, the water flows to a reservoir under the headquarters building; here it is distributed to bathhouses through insulated pipes. Some of the water is cooled to 90°F without being exposed to air or mixed with other water. Bathhouses mix cooled and hot thermal water to regulate bath temperatures. The Libbey Memorial Physical Medicine Center specializes in hydrotherapy treatments given under the supervision of a registered physical therapist. Patients may be referred to this center for treatments by their doctors. Visitors can get a standard bath there without a referral. The Fordyce Bathhouse now functions as the park's visitor center.

Hot Springs National Park is, however, more than a spa. It is a well-loved resort visited by travelers from all over the world who appreciate its beautiful wooded hills and day-trails for hiking—a good hiking goal is the Hot Water Cascade, a natural thermal waterfall. Swimming, boating, and water sports are available at nearby Catherine, Hamilton, and Ouachita lakes. All three also offer good year-round fishing for bream, crappie, bass, and rainbow trout.

BUDGET TIP Take a free, self-guided tour of Fordyce Bathhouse (park's visitor center) to learn about the geological history of the waters, and how the 800,000-plus gallons of water that pass through the springs are used.

AR 66
PARK 66

Joshua Tree California

Southern California
Established June 16, 1905
1,018,122 acres

Headquarters
Joshua Tree National Park
74485 National Park Drive
Twentynine Palms, CA 92277
760.367.5500
www.nps.gov/jotr

Visitor Centers
The Black Rock Nature Center, the Cottonwood Visitor Center, and the Oasis Visitor Center are open daily.

Entrance Fees
$10/vehicle for 7 days.
$5/walk-in for 7 days.

Accommodations
There are six camping sites on a first-come, first-served basis. Black Rock, Indian Cove, and Sheep Pass can be reserved (800/365-CAMP). All campgrounds are open daily.

When to Go
Temperatures are most comfortable in the spring and fall.

This park preserves a section of two desert ecosystems: the Mojave and the Colorado. Below 3,000 feet and located in the eastern and southern reaches of the park, the Colorado desert vegetation is marked by creosote bush, cholla cactus and ocotillo. In the northern and western section of the park, the higher elevations of the Mohave Desert are slightly moister and cooler and feature the park's namesake, the Joshua tree. The Joshua tree was given its name by the Mormons because of its up stretched "arms." A member of the lily family, this giant yucca attains heights of more than 40 feet.

The geology of the area is both interesting and diverse. Located at the eastern end of southern California's Transverse Range, much of the land is at an elevation of 4,000 feet, with a range of 1,000 to 5,000 feet. Sand dunes, dry lakes, granite monoliths, alluvial fans, canyons, earthquake faults and even a few palm oases add to the stark beauty of the sweeping desert landscape. As in all environments, however harsh, the park visitor will also discover a surprising array of wildlife, from bighorn sheep, coyotes and jack rabbits to a variety of snakes, lizards and rodents. Many varieties of migratory birds can also be found in the spring and fall, as the park is along the Pacific flyway.

Water is available only at the Black Rock Canyon Visitor Center/Campground, Cottonwood Campground, the Indian Cove Ranger Station, and the Twenty-nine Palms Visitor Center. Guided tours and campfire programs are available in the period from February-May and October-December. Picnicking is permitted in designated areas and campgrounds, but no fires may be built outside the campgrounds.

BUDGET TIP If visiting Joshua Tree National Park in the summer, visit neighboring Palm Springs; hotel prices here are usually 50% less in summer than in winter and early spring.

CA 71

An exotic array of stalactites

The Cliff House ruins

Alpenglow on Mount Rainier at sunset

A glimpse of the Hoh rain forest section

Mammoth Cave Kentucky

South Central Kentucky
Established July 1, 1941
52,830 acres

Headquarters
Mammoth Cave National Park
P.O. Box 7
Mammoth Cave, KY 42259
270.758.2251
www.nps.gov/maca

Visitor Centers
The Mammoth Cave Visitor Center is open daily, with the exception of Dec 25.

Entrance Fees
Admission is free.

Accommodations
Maple Springs and Headquarters (800/967-2283) are open from Mar-Nov; reservations are required for Maple Springs and recommended for Headquarters. Houchins Ferry is open on a first-come, first-served basis.

When to Go
Spring is a popular time to visit. Summers are hot and sultry. Winters are mild.

Sandstone ridges on the surface of the park contain a number of sinkholes, but otherwise provide no hint of the largest known underground cave system on earth. This enormous underground complex of intertwining passages, totaling more than 350 miles in length, was carved by mildly acidic water trickling for thousands of years through limestone. Species of colorless, eyeless fish, crayfish, and other creatures make their home within. Such a unique environment has lent itself to several odd commercial pursuits over the years. Visible still are the remains of a crude system developed to mine 400,000 pounds of nitrate used for gunpowder in the War of 1812. The cave was later the scene of an experimental cure for tuberculosis and mushroom farming.

An orientation movie is offered at the visitor center. Evening programs are conducted by park interpreters (summer, daily; spring and fall, weekends). The park offers about 10 different underground walking tours of varying difficulty and length led by Park Service interpreters. The outings range from the 1/4 mile Travertine Tour to the six hour, six mile, extremely strenuous Wild Cave Tour. Fees apply and reservations are strongly recommended between April and October. Most tours involve steps. Proper footwear is recommended (no sandals) and a sweater is also advised.

Don't forget the above-ground activities. There are over 70 miles of trails that course their way among bluffs, valleys, and ridge tops. Drive the scenic Houchins Ferry Road and Little Jordan Road. The visitor center area also offers six miles of woodland trails with sinkhole views, along with educational programs and campfire activities. Limited campsites are available at the park.

BUDGET TIP Take advantage of the many free activities of EARTHSPEAK!, a series of special events running from April through October, highlighting the natural world and the human history of the land in and around Mammoth Cave National Park.

KY 100
PARK 100

Mesa Verde Colorado

Southwestern Colorado
Established June 29, 1906
52,122 acres

Headquarters
Mesa Verde National Park
P.O. Box 8
Mesa Verde National Park, CO 81330
970.529.4465
www.nps.gov/meve

Visitor Centers
The Far View Visitor Center and the Chapin Mesa Archeological Museum are open daily from Apr-mid-Oct.

Entrance Fees
$10/vehicle for 7 days.
$2.25/person for ranger-guided tours.

Accommodations
Morefield Campground (800/449-2288) is available on a first-come, first-served basis from mid-Apr-mid-Oct. The Far View Lodge (800/449-2288) is open late Mar-early Nov.

When to Go
The park attracts the majority of its visitors during spring, summer, and fall.

Mesa Verde, Spanish for "green table," is a large plateau towering 1,500 to 2,000 feet above the Montezuma and Mancos Valleys. The site provides a vivid historic record of the cultural and physical lives of the Ancestral Pueblo people who inhabited these communities between 600 A.D. and 1300 A.D. Mesa Verde is marked by a series of canyons whose various alcoves and overhanging cliffs provided shelter and ultimately the creation of bustling villages, referred to today as "cliff dwellings." These cliff dwellings were mostly built and inhabited during the 1200s, but subsequently abandoned for reasons that remain unknown. Primarily farmers whose crops included corn, beans and squash, the Ancestral Pueblo supplemented their diet by hunting local game. Everyday life was apparently lived at their doorstep; the refuse heaps at the foot of their houses have provided much of what is now known about their daily lives.

Entrance into the park is made at its north end, off of U.S 160. The park headquarters at Chapin Mesa is 21 miles from the entrance and includes exhibits and guided tours that offer insights into the arts and crafts and archaeology of the area. The Far View visitor center is located 15 miles into the park. It includes a restaurant at the motor lodge and is the only location where one can purchase tickets to ranger-guided tours. Several loop roads on Chapin Mesa will take the visitor to three of the major cliff dwellings: Balcony House, Cliff Palace, and Spruce Tree House.

Because of the fragile nature of the cliff dwellings, one regulation is rigidly enforced: the cliff dwellings are entered only while rangers are on duty (all year, weather permitting).

BUDGET TIP Free ranger-guided tours of Spruce Tree House—the third largest cliff dwelling within the park boundaries—are offered three times daily in winter.

CO 76
PARK 76

Mount Rainier Washington

Central Washington
Established Mar 2, 1899
235,625 acres

Headquarters
Mount Rainier National Park
Tahoma Woods, Star Route
Ashford, WA 98304
360.569.2211
www.nps.gov/mora

Visitor Centers
Jackson Visitor Center is open daily late Apr-mid-Oct. Ohanapecosh Visitor Center is open late May- early Sept.

Entrance Fees
$10/vehicle for 7 days.
$5/walk-in for 7 days.

Accommodations
Ohanapecosh and Cougar Rock (800/365-CAMP) are open late May-mid-Oct. Sunshine Point and Ipsut Creek are open daily and available on a first-come, first-served basis.

When to Go
Visit in May and Oct. The rest of the year the weather can be unpredictable.

Majestic Mount Rainier, towering 14,411 feet above sea level and 8,000 feet above the surrounding mountains, is the largest volcano in the Cascade Range, which extends from Mount Garibaldi in southwestern British Columbia to Lassen Peak in northern California. A young volcano by geologic standards, Mount Rainier was once a fairly symmetrical mountain rising about 16,000 feet above sea level. But glaciers and further volcanic activity shaped the mountain into an irregular mass of rock. The glaciation continues today, as Mount Rainier supports the largest glacier system in the contiguous United States, with 35 square miles of ice and 26 named glaciers. Steam emissions often form caves in the summit ice cap and usually melt the snow along the rims of the twin craters. Eruptions occurred at Mount Rainier as recently as the mid-1800s.

The park's various "life zones," which change at different elevations, support a wide array of plant and animal life. Douglas fir, red cedar, and western hemlock, some rising 200 feet into the air, thrive in the old-growth forests. In the summer, the subalpine meadows come alive with brilliant, multi-colored wildflowers. These areas are home to more than 130 species of birds and 50 species of mammals. Mountain goats, chipmunks, and marmots are favorites among visitors, but deer, elk, bears, mountain lions, wolves, and other animals can also be seen here. Winters at Mount Rainier are legendary. Moist air masses moving eastward across the Pacific Ocean are intercepted by the mountain. As a result, some areas on the mountain receive 50 or more feet of snow each winter.

Mount Rainier offers excellent opportunities for scenic drives, nature walks, hiking, mountain climbing, and skiing. Although the park is open year-round, access is limited in winter. During this time, the Nisqually Entrance at the southwest corner of the park is the only point of entry.

BUDGET TIP Get the best views for your money at the Sunrise area, also called Yakima Park—the highest point at which you can drive into the park.

WA 170
PARK 170

Olympic Washington

Northwestern Washington
Established June 29, 1938
922,651 acres

Headquarters
Olympic National Park
600 East Park Avenue
Port Angeles, WA 98362
360.565.3130
www.nps.gov/olym

Visitor Centers
Visitor Centers are located in Port Angeles, Hurricane Ridge, and the Hoh rain forest.

Entrance Fees
$10/vehicle for 7 days.
$5/walk-in for 7 days.

Accommodations
This national park operates a total of 16 campgrounds all available on a first-come, first-served basis.

When to Go
Summers are most popular and most crowded, as the weather is warm and dry. The winters in the park are generally mild.

The diversity of ecosystems encapsulated in this extreme northwest corner of the continental U.S. is incredible. It begins with the rugged Pacific coast, reaches through the temperate rain forest of the Quinault, Queets and Hoh rivers, and is capped by the snow-cloaked Olympic Mountains. And yet the northeast part of the park is the driest area on the west coast outside of southern California. Glaciers and rain forests; pounding surf and soaring mountains; elk and seals and salmon; this is the variety that one can only experience in Olympic National Park

Giant spruce, Douglas fir, red cedar, and hemlock thrive in the rain forest on the western slope of the park, with trees growing to as much as 300 feet tall and 23 feet in circumference. Lichens and ferns flourish on the forest floor and club moss drips from the branches, well watered by the 12 to 14 feet of rain that falls in the rain forest every year. Highway 101 provides the main access to the west side of the park; stop at the Visitor Center at the end of the Hoh road to find out about hiking trails. Nearby lodging is available at Kalaloch Lodge and Lake Quinault Lodge, both within the park.

On the north side of the park trails ranging from 1 mile to 8 miles round trip can be found near the Lake Crescent Lodge. Spectacular views and great hiking in the subalpine high country are the reward for driving the Hurricane Ridge Road. Mount Olympus, the highest peak (7,965 feet) and the others in view have been etched by glaciers for thousands of years. About 60 glaciers are still actively eroding these mountains—the largest three are on Mount Olympus.

BUDGET TIP A Frequent Hiker Pass is available for $30 per person per year. This is an annual pass, good for twelve months from the date of issue. It covers all wilderness use fees for the pass holder.

WA 170
PARK 191

An example of petrified wood

Grasses in Bowley Pond

Hallet Creek Basin

Most well-known cactus in the world

Petrified Forest Arizona

Northeastern Arizona
Established Dec 9, 1962
93,533 acres

Headquarters
Petrified Forest National Park
P.O. Box 2217
Petrified National Forest, AZ 86028
928.524.6228
www.nps.gov/pefo

Visitor Centers
Painted Desert Inn National Historic Lodge, Painted Desert Visitor Center, and Rainbow Forest Museum are open daily, except on Dec 25.

Entrance Fees
$10/vehicle for 7 days.
$5/walk-in/bicyclist for 7 days.

Accommodations
No campgrounds or lodging are available in the park, but nearby communities offer full service accommodations.

When to Go
Summer days are generally hot, but nights can be cool. Winter temperatures are mild.

This park includes some of the most spectacular displays of petrified wood in the world. The trees of the original forest may have grown in upland areas and then were washed down onto a floodplain by rivers. Subsequently, the trees were buried under sediment and volcanic ash, causing the organic wood to be filled gradually with mineral compounds, especially quartz. The grain, now multicolored by these compounds, is still visible in some specimens. Prehistoric Pueblo inhabitants left countless petroglyphs (drawings) of animals, figures, and symbols carved on sandstone that can be seen throughout the park.

The park also contains a portion of the Painted Desert, an amazing stretch extending 200 miles along the north bank of the Little Colorado River. This highly eroded region of mesas, pinnacles, washes, and canyons is part of the Chinle formation, a soft shale, clay, and sandstone stratum of the Triassic age. Sunlight and clouds passing over this colorful scenery create an effect of constant, kaleidoscopic change.

The visitor center is located at the entrance off I-40. The Rainbow Forest Museum (off US 180) depicts the paleontology and geology of the Triassic Era. Picnicking facilities can be found at Rainbow Forest and at Chinde Point on the rim of the Painted Desert. A non-stop drive through the park takes 45 minutes. The average length of stay is 2 hours but remaining all day is also common. The park is locked at night and visitors must be in their cars and driving towards an exit at closing time. It is forbidden to take even the smallest piece of petrified wood or any other object from the park. Nearby curio shops sell wood taken from areas outside the park.

BUDGET TIP Save time and gas. If traveling east, take U.S. 180 from Holbrook to the south park entrance, drive north to rejoin Interstate 40. If traveling west on Interstate 40, exit # 311, drive south through the park to U.S. 180. Turn west to Holbrook where you will return to Interstate 40.

AZ 64

Prince Edward Island Prince Edward Island

Prince Edward Island
Established Apr 20, 1905
18 square kilometers acres

Headquarters
Prince Edward Island
2 Palmers Lane
Charlottetown, PEI C1A 5V6
902.672.6350
parkscanada.pch.gc.ca

Visitor Centers
Cavendish and Greenwich are open late May-Oct, while Brackley is open mid-June-late Sept.

Entrance Fees
$4/person/day, $7/person for 2 days.

Accommodations
Reservations (800/414-6765) are accepted for Robinsons Island, Stanhope, and Cavendish.

When to Go
July and Aug is when the park is most visited.

Established in 1937, Prince Edward Island National Park hugs about 25 miles of the north shore of the island, facing the wind and seas of the Gulf of St. Lawrence. Long inhabited by native people, the French were the first Europeans to settle on the island in the early 1700's, but they ceded it to the British in 1758. The arrival of the British led to changes in land use, adding extensive agriculture to the existing fishing and timber industries. In recent times, much agricultural land has reverted back to forest land, leaving the island with a fascinating patchwork of farms, woodlots, wetlands, and rugged coastal landscapes.

The park itself offers miles of white sand beaches backed by sand dunes, salt marshes, fresh water ponds and sandstone cliffs along the headlands, accompanied by a rich assortment of ducks and shorebirds. There are several supervised beach areas for swimmers and miles of secluded shoreline to walk and explore. Seaside villages dot a landscape that is highlighted by the Green Gables House, the famous setting for several novels written by local native Lucy Maud Montgomery, most notably Anne of Green Gables, published in 1908. Daily walks are offered around the house and grounds. Also be sure to see the Dalvay-by-the-Sea mansion, a National Historic Site built in 1895.

Most tourists visit the area in the two month summer season. In addition to golf, tennis, bicycling, and picnicking, the park offers an interpretation program highlighting the natural and cultural features and stories of the area. Hotels, restaurants, and other amenities can be found in nearby Cavendish and Stanhope.

BUDGET TIP Visiting historical sites while in the area? Purchase a Discovery Package, one of Parks Canada's National Passes. It offers unlimited visits to all Canadian National Parks and Historic Sites for one year, and saves time by allowing pass holders faster entry.

PE 186
PARK 191

Rocky Mountain Colorado

North Central Colorado
Established Jan 26, 1915
265,769 acres

Headquarters
Rocky Mountain National Park
1000 Highway 36
Estes Park, CO 80517
970.586.1206
www.nps.gov/romo

Visitor Centers
Beaver Meadows and Kawuneeche are open daily. Alpine, Fall River, and Lily Lake close for the winter.

Entrance Fees
$15/vehicle for 7 days.
$5/walk-in for 7 days.

Accommodations
Moraine Park (970/586-1206) accepts reservations during the peak season. Aspenglen and Glacier Basin are open mid-May-late Sept. Three other sites stay open year-round.

When to Go
June and July are prime months to visit. The winters are dismal and unpopular.

Described by Albert Bierstadt, one of the great 19th-century landscape artists of the West, as America's finest composition for the painter, the land west of where Joel Estes settled was set aside as Rocky Mountain National Park in 1915. Estes' settlement became what is now Estes Park, the gateway to the park itself. Straddling the Continental Divide, with valleys 8,000 feet in elevation and 114 named peaks more than 10,000 feet high, the park contains a staggering profusion of peaks, upland meadows, sheer canyons, glacial streams, and lakes. The few remaining glaciers offer only a small hint of the tremendous scouring and deposition effects that the ice age glaciers had on the current form of the park's mountain ridges, cirques, and valleys. Dominating the scene is Longs Peak, with its east face towering 14,255 feet above sea level. The park's forests and meadows provide sanctuary for more than 750 varieties of wildflowers, more than 260 species of birds, and such indigenous mammals as deer, American elk, bighorn sheep, beaver, mountain lions, and coyotes.

The park is a hiker's dream, with over 350 miles of trails that offer beautiful views and a glimpse of some of the wildlife. Favored lake hikes include Bear Lake (easy interpretive trail), Cub Lake and Mills Lake trails (moderately difficult). Several suggested waterfall hikes have trailheads at Glacier George Junction at the end of Bear Lake Rd.

Trail Ridge Road (closed in winter) is a breathtaking 19 mile drive, much of it above tree line, which crosses the Continental Divide. The Alpine Visitor Center at 11,796 feet offers a nice rest stop with a snack bar.

BUDGET TIP In summer, a free national park shuttle bus runs from the Glacier Basin parking area to Bear Lake, with departures every 15 to 30 minutes.

CO 76
PARK 75

Saguaro Arizona

Southern Arizona
Established June 16, 1905
91,446 acres

Headquarters
Saguaro National Park
3693 South Old Spanish Trail
Tucson, AZ 85730
520.733.5100
www.nps.gov/sagu

Visitor Centers
Rincon Mountain District and Tucson Mountain District Visitor Centers are open daily, excluding Dec 25.

Entrance Fees
Rincon Mountain District, $6/vehicle for 7 days. No fee for Tucson Mountain District.

Accommodations
Backcountry camping is allowed in the Saguaro Wilderness Area. A free permit is required. There are six wilderness campgrounds accessible by foot or horse.

When to Go
Winters are delightful with warm, mild days. Summers are hot and crowded.

Located outside of Tucson in the harsh and vast Sonoran Desert, the park is the home of what is probably the most recognizable cactus in the world, the majestic saguaro.

The saguaro (sah-WAH-ro) cactus may grow as high as 50 feet and live to be 200 years old. The fluted columns, spined with sharp, tough needles, may branch into fantastic shapes. During the two rainy seasons—January through March and July through September—large saguaros absorb enough water to sustain themselves during the dry season. The saguaro's waxy, white blossoms (Arizona's state flower), which open at night and close the following afternoon, bloom in May and June; the red fruit ripens in July. The Tohono O'Odham eat this fruit fresh and dried; they also use it to make jellies, jams, and wines.

Wildlife in the park, of necessity is well adapted to hot, dry days and cool nights. Gila woodpeckers and gilded flickers drill nest holes in the saguaro trunks. Once vacated, these holes become home to many other species of birds, including the tiny elf owl. Peccaries (nocturnal pig relatives), coyotes, and mule deer are often seen. Yuccas, agaves, prickly pears, mesquite, and paloverde trees are among the desert plants that thrive here.

The Rincon Mountain District offers nature trails, guided nature walks (winter), an eight-mile self-guided drive (fee), mountain hiking, bridle trails, picnicking (no water), and backcountry camping. The Rincon Mountain District visitor center has a museum and orientation film. The Tucson Mountain District offers nature trails, a six-mile self-guided drive, hiking and bridle trails, five picnic areas (no water) and a visitor center that includes exhibits and a slide program.

BUDGET TIP There is no entrance fee for Saguaro West, which embraces a variety of Sonora Desert life against the backdrop of the rugged Tucson Mountains.

AZ 64

The Giant Forest

View from Skyline Drive, Blue Ridge Mountains

South Unit Theodore Roosevelt Wilderness

Cherry Creek in Locator Lake

Sequoia/Kings Canyon California

Southwestern California
Established Sept 25, 1890
864,411 acres

HEADQUARTERS
Sequoia National Park
47050 Generals Highway
Three Rivers, CA 93271
559.565.3341
www.nps.gov/seki

VISITOR CENTERS
Foothills, Grant Grove, and Giant Forest Museum are open daily. Lodgepole is open daily during summer, but closed Tues-Thurs in winter.

ENTRANCE FEES
$10/vehicle for 7 days.
$5/walk-in for 7 days

ACCOMMODATIONS
All but two campgrounds are first-come, first-served. Lodgepole and Dorst (800/365-CAMP) take reservations in summer.

WHEN TO GO
Summer, while short, is the best time to visit. Winter can be bitter.

Lying across the heart of the Sierra Nevada in east central California, Kings Canyon and Sequoia National Parks offer huge trees, massive granite mountains, steep glacially carved canyons, alpine lakes, and caves. Be sure to see the banded marble and large rooms of Crystal Cave, Lilburn Cave with its displays of green malachite and blue azurite, and restored Soldiers Cave. The habitat is extremely varied, as one would expect in a park with elevation ranges from 1,500 feet in the rolling foothills to the 14,495 feet of Mt. Whitney, the highest point in the lower 48 states. Giant sequoias reach their greatest size and are found in the largest numbers in the park. The chemical composition of the wood and its thick bark make sequoias resistant to fire, disease and decay and enables them to live for centuries. The General Grant tree, found in Grant Grove, is the only living memorial to an American who served in war The tree is over 267 feet tall and 107 feet around; age estimates run from 1,500 to 2,000 years old. While in the area of the Grant Grove visitor center, drive to Big Stump Basin, 2-1/2 miles southeast on Hwy 180 and walk the 1-mile loop. Or take the 2-mile drive to Panoramic Point (not recommended for trailers and RVs) and see spectacular vistas of the Sierra Nevada Mountains (closed to vehicles in winter).

Cedar Grove, located on Hwy 180, lies in the spectacular U-shaped Kings Canyon, with its granite cliffs, waterfalls, and the Kings River. A canyon viewpoint is located on the main road, 1 mile east of Cedar Grove village. There are numerous hiking paths in the area, ranging from five minutes (Roaring River Falls) to one hour loops (Zumwalt Meadow) to a day-long 13-mile hike on the Don Cecil Trail to Lookout Peak.

BUDGET TIP Depending on your destination, road closures may force you to drive around outside the parks to another entrance. To prevent this inconvenience and to save time and gas, call the parks from the Fresno or Visalia areas just prior to arrival to check on road conditions.

CA 70
PARK 69

Shenandoah Virginia

Central Virginia
Established Dec 26, 1935
196,149 acres

HEADQUARTERS
Shenandoah National Park
3655 U.S. Highway 211 East
Luray, VA 22835
540.999.3500
www.nps.gov/shen

VISITOR CENTERS
Dickey Ridge and Harry F. Byrd are open daily mid-Apr-late Nov. Loft Mountain Information Center is open Fri-Tue late May-early Nov.

ENTRANCE FEES
$10/vehicle for 7 days.
$5/walk-in for 7 days.

ACCOMMODATIONS
Reservations are required at Big Meadows (800/365-CAMP) and Dundo Group (540/298-9625). Both campgrounds are open mid-May-Nov.

WHEN TO GO
Summers are mild and pleasant. The mountains average 10° cool than the valley.

About 450 million years ago the Blue Ridge Mountains were at the bottom of a sea. Today they average about 2,000 feet above sea level and form the eastern flank of the Appalachian Mountains. Some 300 square miles of the loveliest parts of the Blue Ridge are included in Shenandoah National Park. The park is 80 miles long and from 2 to 13 miles wide. Running its full length is the 105-mile Skyline Drive. The Drive, twisting and turning along the crest of the Blue Ridge, is one of the finest scenic trips in the East. Approximately 70 overlooks give views of the Blue Ridge, the Piedmont to the east, and, to the west, the Shenandoah Valley and the Alleghenies. Exploration on the 500 miles of trails, including 101 miles of the Appalachian Trail, leads to panoramic views, waterfalls and canyons. Most of the area is wooded, predominantly in white, red, and chestnut oak, with hickory, birch, maple, hemlock, tulip poplar, and nearly 100 other species scattered here and there. At the head of Whiteoak Canyon are hemlocks more than 300 years old. The park bursts with color and contrast in the fall, which makes this season particularly popular with visitors. The park is a sanctuary for deer, bear, fox, and bobcat, along with more than 200 varieties of birds.

Skyline Drive is occasionally closed for short periods during November-March. Main entrances are the North Entrance (Front Royal), from I-66, US 340, US 522, and VA 55; Thornton Gap Entrance (31.5 miles south), from US 211; Swift Run Gap Entrance (65.7 miles south), from US 33; and the South Entrance (Rockfish Gap), from I-64, US 250, and the Blue Ridge Parkway (see p. 223).

BUDGET TIP Pick up a free copy of the park's newspaper, The Shenandoah Overlook, at any entrance station, visitor center, park campground, any concession or at Park Headquarters. It provides seasonal information about the park and can help you plan your activities.

VA 168
PARK 191

Theodore Roosevelt North Dakota

Western North Dakota
Established Nov 10, 1978
70,447 acres

HEADQUARTERS
Theodore Roosevelt National Park
P.O. Box 7
Medora, ND 58645
701.623.4466
www.nps.gov/thro

VISITOR CENTERS
The Medora Visitor Center and North Unit Visitor Center are open daily.

ENTRANCE FEES
$10/vehicle for 7 days.
$5/walk-in for 7 days.

ACCOMMODATIONS
Two of the park's three campgrounds are open on a first-come, first-served basis. The Roundup (701/623-4466) is open mid-May-mid-Oct.

WHEN TO GO
Early fall is particularly appealing—the weather is mild and there are few visitors.

General Sully, during his campaign against the Sioux in 1864, described this area as "hell with the fires out . . . grand, dismal, and majestic." Wind and water have carved from a thick series of flat-lying sedimentary rocks, curiously sculptured formations, tablelands, buttes, canyons, and rugged hills. Exposed in eroded hillsides are thick, dark layers of lignite coal that sometimes are fired by lightning and burn slowly for many years, often baking adjacent clay layers into a red, brick-like substance called scoria or clinker.

This spectacular badlands is a monument to Theodore Roosevelt, the 26th president who, in addition to all of his other vigorous pursuits, was the nation's champion for conservation of natural resources. Roosevelt became interested in the open-range cattle industry and purchased interest in the Maltese Cross Ranch near Medora. He returned the next year and established another ranch, the Elkhorn, about 35 miles north of Medora. He eventually abandoned his ranching ventures, but the park preserves the landscape and wildlife much as Roosevelt knew it. The park is comprised of three different areas, the South Unit, Elkhorn Ranch and the North Unit. Visitors heading west toward the park on Interstate 94 get their first panoramic landscape view at Painted Canyon Overlook seven miles east of Medora. The South Unit visitor center is located in Medora (keep your eyes out for wild horses). Behind the visitor center is Roosevelt's Maltese Cross Cabin. A 36-mile loop road shows the area's history and natural features. The Elkhorn Ranch unit is located 35 north of Medora and the North Unit is located 50 miles north of Interstate 94 on U.S. 85. When at the North Unit, find time to take the 14-mile scenic drive to Oxbow Overlook.

BUDGET TIP Purchase a Golden Eagle or Golden Age Park Pass for free entry into the park (and all national parks), and the use of camping facilities for half-price for up to one year.

ND 141

Voyageurs Minnesota

Northern Minnesota
Established Apr 8, 1975
218,200 acres

HEADQUARTERS
Voyageurs National Park
3131 Highway 53 South
International Falls, MN 56649
218.283.9821
www.nps.gov/voya

VISITOR CENTERS
Ash River and Kabetogma Lake are open daily, but close during the winter. Rainy Lake is open year-round.

ENTRANCE FEES
Free admission, but $10/day boat charge.

ACCOMMODATIONS
Various campgrounds (218/283-9821), accessible only by boat, are offered throughout the park year-round on a first-come, first-served basis.

WHEN TO GO
Summer at Voyageurs is mild and inviting.

Voyageurs is made of forested lake country, punctuated by bogs, beaver ponds, and swamps. The park is named for the Voyageurs, French-Canadian fur traders and adventurers of the early to mid-1800's who used the water as their highway. A rich historic record has been discovered by underwater archaeologists who have recovered parts of voyageur canoes, muzzle-loading rifles, beads intended for Indian trade, and other artifacts.

Lying 15 miles east of International Falls and 300 miles north of Minneapolis-St Paul, the park comes close to the border with Ontario. The park is irregular in shape, measuring about 40 miles from east to west and varying in width from 3 to 15 miles. It includes numerous islands and more than 100 lakes. The main body of land, Kabetogama Peninsula, covers 75,000 heavy forested acres and is accessible principally by water. Surrounding the peninsula are waters ranging from narrows less than 100 feet in width to lakes several miles across, dotted with islands, accented with rocky points.

Four lakes dominate the area within the park: Namakan, Kabetogama, Rainy, and Sand Point. Rainy Lake, the largest, covers 350 square miles. In the summer, conducted boat trips, nature walks, campfire programs, and self-guiding trails are available to explain the natural and historic attractions. The Vermillion River tumbles through Crane Lake Gorge, a narrow chasm between high vertical rock walls, before it flows into Crane Lake. There are trails on both sides of the canyon. Wherever you are going in the park, observe the variety of mosses, ferns, and lichens covering the rocks as well as the forest floor. Wild rice grows in shallow bays and streams, and cranberry bogs are common.

An existing link to a more recent era is the Kettle Falls Hotel at the extreme east end of Rainy Lake. Built in 1913, the hotel served trappers, traders, fishermen, and lumberjacks and is remarkably well preserved.

BUDGET TIP Take advantage of free, ranger-led activities, such as campfire programs, canoe trips, and hikes.

MN 116
PARK 191

Display of boxwork cave formations

Geyser at Yellowstone

Yosemite Falls above Yosemite Valley

The Watchman

Wind Cave South Dakota

Southwestern South Dakota
Established Jan 9, 1903
28,295 acres

Headquarters
Wind Cave National Park
RR1, Box 190
Hot Springs, SD 57747
605.745.4600
www.nps.gov/wica

Visitor Centers
The visitor center is open daily, except Thanksgiving and Dec 25.

Entrance Fees
Cave tours range in price from $6-$20/person.

Accommodations
Elk Mountain has flush toilets and running water during the summer. There is a limit of 14 days occupancy.

When to Go
Spring and fall offer the mildest weather. Also, it is less crowded during these seasons.

One of many caves in the ring of limestone surrounding the Black Hills, Wind Cave is a maze of subterranean passages known to extend more than 79 miles. The park got its name from the strong currents of wind that blow in or out of its entrances according to atmospheric pressure. When the pressure is decreasing, the wind blows outward; when it increases the wind blows in. It was the rushing sound of air coming out of its entrance that led to its discovery in 1881. The cave is a constant 53° F, so a sweater or jacket is recommended. More than just a cave, the park also offers prairie grasslands, a forest and wildlife preserve that is home to bison, pronghorn, elk, deer, prairie dogs, and others. Trails range in length from 1 to 8.6 miles of varying difficulty, several of which offer panoramic views of the park and the Black Hills; birdwatchers might find bluebirds, red-headed and Lewis woodpeckers, great horned owls, golden eagles, and kestrels.

Among the many cave tours, the Garden of Eden Cave tour is one hour long and offers a great sampling of the wonders of the cave, including boxwork, a formation of thin calcite fins resembling honeycomb, popcorn, and flowstone. Expect about 150 stairs. The Nature Entrance Cave tour is moderately strenuous, 1-1/4 hour tour (300 stairs). If getting away from the developed trails sounds appealing, try the Wind Cave tour, and expect a four hour trip, that will include some crawling—hardhats provided. Evening campfire talks are given at the Elk Mountain campground (admission on first-come, first-served basis).

BUDGET TIP Wind Cave is a relatively inexpensive destination; there is no entrance fee to the park, and cave tours start at $4. There are also free exhibits in the Visitor Center, guided hikes, and campfire programs.

SD 157

Yellowstone Wyoming

Northwestern Wyoming
Established Mar 1, 1872
2,219,791 acres

Headquarters
Yellowstone National Park
P.O. Box 168
Yellowstone National Park, WY 82190
307.344.7381
www.nps.gov/yell

Visitor Centers
Albright is open daily. Canyon Village and Fishing Bridge are open late May-early Oct. Grant Village is open late May-Sept, and Old Faithful is open late Apr-early Nov.

Entrance Fees
$20/vehicle for 7 days, $10/walk-in for 7 days.

Accommodations
Six campgrounds are available mid-May-Sept on a first-come, first-served basis.

When to Go
Summer, autumn, and winter are the best times to visit. Humidity is low, days are bright, and nights are clear.

In 1872, the US Congress established Yellowstone as the world's first national park. It offers a marvelous list of sights, attractions, and facilities: a large freshwater lake, the highest in the nation (7,733 feet); a waterfall almost twice as high as Niagara; a dramatic, 1,200-foot-deep river canyon; and the world's most famous geyser—Old Faithful. Most of the park has been left in its natural state, preserving the area's beauty and delicate ecological balance. Yellowstone is one of the world's most successful wildlife sanctuaries. Within its boundaries live a variety of species, including grizzly and black bears, elk, deer, pronghorn, and bison.

The Grand Loop Road, a main access way within the park, winds approximately 140 miles past many major points of interest. Five miles south of the North Entrance is Mammoth Hot Springs, the park headquarters, visitor center, and museum. The Norris Geyser Basin is 21 miles south of Mammoth Hot Springs. The hottest thermal basin in the world, it provides a multitude of displays; springs, geysers, mud pots, and steam vents hiss, bubble, and erupt in a showcase of thermal forces at work. Old Faithful has not missed a performance in the more than 100 years since eruptions were first recorded. Eruptions occur on the average of every 75 minutes, although intervals have varied from 30 to 120 minutes. Yellowstone Lake, the highest natural freshwater lake in the United States, is drained by the Yellowstone River which in turn has carved the colorful Grand Canyon of the Yellowstone River.

Hundreds of miles of hiking trails of varying difficulty and length meander through all sections of the park. Camping is available in a number of areas, many of which require reservations. Old Faithful Inn and other lodges, cabins and hotels require reservations.

BUDGET TIP If driving to Yellowstone National Park from the Black Hills of South Dakota, take a brief detour in Eastern Wyoming to a unique natural phenomenon. With no price for admission, see the Devil's Tower, which towers over the prairie just as it did in Steven Spielberg's movie, "Close Encounters of the Third Kind."

WY 176
PARK 176

Yosemite California

North Central California
Established Oct 1, 1890
761,266 acres

Headquarters
Yosemite National Park
Superintendent
P.O. Box 577
Yosemite National Park, CA 95389
209.372.0200
www.nps.gov/yose

Visitor Centers
Yosemite Valley is open year-round, while Tuolumne Meadows is open during the summer only.

Entrance Fees
$20/vehicle for 7 days.
$10/person for 7 days.

Accommodations
Reservations for seven of the thirteen campgrounds are available five months in advance (800/436-PARK).

When to Go
Spring and summer have the most to offer the park visitor.

John Muir, the naturalist instrumental in the founding of this national park, wrote that here are "the most songful streams in the world . . . the noblest forests, the loftiest granite domes, the deepest ice sculptured canyons." Yosemite is a treasure of natural splendor that includes lofty waterfalls, sheer cliffs, alpine meadows, and giant sequoias.

The heart of the park is Yosemite Valley. Most of the falls that tumble into the valley are best viewed in spring. Yosemite Falls (at 2,425 feet the world's fifth tallest), Bridalveil Fall (620 feet), Nevada Fall (594 feet), and Vernal Fall (317 feet), however, all flow throughout the year. Also in the Yosemite Valley, the visitor can learn about the area's cultural history at the Yosemite Museum, the Leconte Memorial Lodge, the Ansel Adams Gallery, and the Ahwahnee Hotel, built in 1927 and containing outstanding paintings, tapestries and stained glass windows.

Spectacular vistas can be found at Glacier Point, a 3,200-foot-high elevation stretching over the forests and meadows around the Merced river. It provides views of Yosemite Valley, Half Dome Mountain, and several of the waterfalls. The road is open by early June and remains open into November. Visitors will recognize Tunnel View as one of the most famous views in Yosemite. From here one can see the largest granite monolith in the world, El Capitan, as well as Bridalveil Fall and Half Dome. It is located at the east end of the Wawona Tunnel on Wawona Road (Hwy 41). In the Valley itself, full views can be obtained from Bridalveil Meadow, El Capitan Meadow Valley View, Sentinel Bridge and others.

Mariposa Grove contains the largest stand of sequoias in Yosemite. The Tioga Road leads into the backcountry past granite domes, meadows, lakes and peaks. The roads to Mariposa Grove and The Tioga are closed from October or November to May or June, due to snow.

BUDGET TIP Does Yosemite inspire the artist in you? The Art Activity Center offers free, informal art classes in various mediums for adults.

CA 68
PARK 69

Zion Utah

Southwestern Utah
Established Apr 2, 1905
146,592 acres

Headquarters
Zion National Park SR 9
Springdale, UT 84767
435.772.3256
www.nps.gov/zion

Visitor Centers
Kolob Canyons and Zion Canyons are open daily.

Entrance Fees
$20/vehicle for 7 days.
$10/walk-in for 7 days.

Accommodations
The Watchman Campground (800/365-CAMP) is open year-round. South Campground, open Apr-Oct, and Lava Point Campground, open June-mid-Oct are available on a first-come, first-served basis.

When to Go
The most mild and pleasant temperatures occur from May-Oct.

Like many national parks of the southwest, Zion is a geologic wonderland. Over a span of 240 million years, the area has undergone a metamorphosis from a flat basin near sea level, through massive regional uplifting to elevations of 10,000 feet, and the erosion effects created by streams cutting down through the uplifted rock. Uplifting continues today, as evidenced by a magnitude 5.8 earthquake in 1992, centered just outside the south entrance to the park.

The Virgin River runs through the interior of the park, and Zion Canyon, with its deep, narrow chasm and multicolored, vertical walls, cuts through the middle, with smaller canyons branching from it like fingers. Zion Canyon drive is a 7-mile trip, surrounded by massive rock formations in awe-inspiring colors that change with the light, ending at the Temple of Sinawava, a natural amphitheater. The formations, described as temples, cathedrals, and thrones, rise to great heights—the loftiest reaching 8,726 feet. The drive is only accessible by shuttle during the months of April-October. Another route, an extension of UT 9, cuts through the park in an east-west direction, taking visitors through the mile-long Zion-Mount Carmel Tunnel, then descends through a series of switchbacks with viewpoints above Pine Creek Canyon. Short hikes to Lower Emerald Pool and Weeping Rock are accessible via shuttle as are longer and more strenuous hikes to Watchman, Hidden Canyon, Angels Landing, and others. Zion Narrows offers a memorable hike with natural springs, hanging gardens and high canyon walls. The trail can be reached by shuttle, but monitor the weather–flash floods can happen at any time.

Zion's main visitor center is near the south entrance; the short trip from Springdale is serviced by frequent shuttle service.

BUDGET TIP The Kolob Canyons Visitor Center provides a free, seven-mile hike to the Kolob Arch, the world's largest, with a span of 310 feet.

UT 165
PARK 165

National Parks Locator Map

Abbreviations

IHS	International Historic Site
NB	National Battlefield
NBP	National Battlefield Park
NBS	National Battlefield Site
NHP	National Historical Park
NHP & PRES	National Historical Park & Preserve
NH RES	National Historical Reserve
NHS	National Historic Site
NL	National Lakeshore
NM	National Monument
NM & PRES	National Monument & Preserve
NMP	National Military Park
N MEM	National Memorial
NP	National Park
NP & PRES	National Park & Preserve
N PRES	National Preserve
NR	National River
NRA	National Recreation Area
NRR	National Recreational River
NRRA	National River & Recreation Area
N RES	National Reserve
NS	National Seashore
NSR	National Scenic River/Riverway
NST	National Scenic Trail
PKWY	Parkway
SRR	Scenic and Recreational River
WR	Wild River
WSR	Wild & Scenic River

National Park System Guide

The National Park System protects areas of natural and historical importance across the U.S., from scenic rivers, lakeshores, and seashores to historic battlefields and buildings. Included here is a list of administrative offices as well as a complete list of the National Parks.

Remember to plan ahead and contact parks in advance about reservations, permits, regulations, activities, and services. A note on reservations: The National Park Service's central reservation system has been temporarily suspended. To make reservations at indicated campgrounds, contact respective parks directly.

National Park Service Offices

National Park Service
Office of Public Inquiries
P.O. Box 37127
Washington, D.C. 20013
202.208.4747

Alaska Region
National Park Service
2525 Gambell St., Rm. 107
Anchorage, AK 99503
907.271.2737 (tourist information), 907.257.2696

Intermountain Region
National Park Service
P.O. Box 25287
Denver, CO 80225
303.969.2000

Midwest Region
National Park Service
1709 Jackson St.
Omaha, NE 68102
402.221.3471

National Capital Region
National Park Service
1100 Ohio Dr. SW
Washington, D.C. 20242
202.619.7222

Northeast Region
National Park Service
200 Chestnut St.
Philadelphia, PA 19106
215.597.7018

Pacific West Region
National Park Service
600 Harrison St., Ste. 600
San Francisco, CA 94107
415.556.0560

Southeast Region
National Park Service
Building 1924
100 Alabama St.
Atlanta, GA 30303
404.562.3123

National Parks

Acadia National Park
P.O. Box 177
Bar Harbor, ME 04609
207.288.3338

Arches National Park
P.O. Box 907
Moab, UT 84532
435.259.8161

Badlands National Park
P.O. Box 6
Interior, SD 57750
605.433.5361

Big Bend National Park
P.O. Box 129
Big Bend National Park, TX 79834
915.477.2251

Biscayne National Park
P.O. Box 1369
Homestead, FL 33090
305.230.7275

Bryce Canyon National Park
P.O. Box 170001
Bryce Canyon, UT 84717
435.834.5322

Canyonlands National Park
2282 S. West Resource Blvd.
Moab, UT 84532
435.259.7164

Capitol Reef National Park
HC 70 Box 15
Torrey, UT 84775
435.425.3791

Carlsbad Caverns National Park
3225 National Parks Hwy.
Carlsbad, NM 88220
505.785.2232

Channel Islands National Park
1901 Spinnaker Dr.
Ventura, CA 93001
805.658.5730

Crater Lake National Park
P.O. Box 7
Crater Lake, OR 97604
541.594.2211

Death Valley National Park
P.O. Box 579
Death Valley, CA 92328
760.786.2331

Denali National Park & Preserve
P.O. Box 9
Denali Park, AK 99755
907.683.2294

Dry Tortugas National Park
P.O. Box 6208
Key West, FL 33041
305.242.7700

Everglades National Park
40001 State Rd. 9336
Homestead, FL 33034
305.242.7700

Gates of the Arctic National Park & Preserve
P.O. Box 74680
Fairbanks, AK 99707
907.692.5494

Glacier Bay National Park & Preserve
P.O. Box 140
Gustavus, AK 99826
907.697.2230

Glacier National Park
P.O. Box 128
West Glacier, MT 59936
406.888.7800

Grand Canyon National Park
P.O. Box 129
Grand Canyon, AZ 86023
520.638.7888

Grand Teton National Park
P.O. Drawer 170
Moose, WY 83012
307.739.3300

Boston Area
Adams NHS
Boston African American NHS
Boston Harbor Islands NRA
Boston NHP
Frederick Law Olmstead NHS
John F. Kennedy NHS
Longfellow NHS
Lowell NHP
Minute Man NHP
Salem Maritime NHS
Saugus Iron Works NHS

New York City Area
Castle Clinton NM
Edison NHS
Federal Hall N MEM
General Grant N MEM
Hamilton Grange N MEM
Sagamore Hill NHS
Saint Paul's Church NHS
Statue of Liberty NM
Theodore Roosevelt Birthplace NHS

Philadelphia Area
Edgar Allan Poe NHS
Independence NHP
Thaddeus Kosciuszko N MEM

Baltimore Area
Ft. McHenry NM and Historic Shrine
Hampton NHS

District of Columbia
Constitution Gardens
Ford's Theatre NHS
Franklin Delano Roosevelt Memorial
Frederick Douglass NHS
Korean War Veterans Memorial
Lincoln Memorial
L.B. Johnson Memorial Grove
Mary McLeod Bethune Council House NHS
National Mall
Pennsylvania Avenue NHS
Rock Creek Park
Theodore Roosevelt Island
Thomas Jefferson Memorial
Vietnam Veterans Memorial
Washington Monument
White House

Maryland
Chesapeake and Ohio Canal NHP
Clara Barton NHS
Fort Washington Park
Greenbelt Park
Monocacy NB
Piscataway Park
Potomac Heritage NST

Virginia
Arlington House
George Washington Memorial PKWY
Wolf Trap Farm Park

The National Park of American Samoa and the War in the Pacific NHP are also administered by the National Park Service but are not shown on this map.

Great Basin National Park
Baker, NV 89311
702.234.7331

Great Smoky Mountains National Park
107 Park Headquarters Rd.
Gatlinburg, TN 37738
423.436.1200

Guadalupe Mountains National Park
HC 60 Box 400
Salt Flat, TX 79847
915.828.3251

Haleakala National Park
P.O. Box 369
Makawao, HI 96768
808.572.9306

Hawaii Volcanoes National Park
P.O. Box 52
Hawaii National Park, HI 96718
808.985.6000

Hot Springs National Park
P.O. Box 1860
Hot Springs, AR 71902
501.624.3383

Isle Royale National Park
800 E. Lakeshore Dr.
Houghton, MI 49931
906.482.0984

Joshua Tree National Park
74485 National Park Dr.
Twentynine Palms, CA 92277
760.367.5500

Katmai National Park & Preserve
P.O. Box 7
King Salmon, AK 99613
907.246.3305

Kenai Fjords National Park
P.O. Box 1727
Seward, AK 99664
907.224.2132

Kobuk Valley National Park
P.O. Box 1029
Kotzebue, AK 99752
907.442.3830

Lake Clark National Park & Preserve
4230 University Dr., Ste. 311
Anchorage, AK 99508
907.781.2218

Lassen Volcanic National Park
38050 Hwy. 36 E
Mineral, CA 96063
916.595.4444

Mammoth Cave National Park
P.O. Box 7
Mammoth Cave, KY 42259
502.758.2328

Mesa Verde National Park
P.O. Box 8
Mesa Verde National Park, CO 81330
970.529.4465

Mount Rainier National Park
Tahoma Woods, Star Rte.
Ashford, WA 98304
360.569.2211

National Park of American Samoa
Pago Pago, AS 96799
684.633.7082

North Cascades National Park
2105 State Rte. 20
Sedro Woolley, WA 98284
360.856.5700

Olympic National Park
600 E. Park Ave.
Port Angeles, WA 98362
360.452.4501

Petrified Forest National Park
P.O. Box 2217
Petrified Forest National Park, AZ 86028
520.524.6228

Redwood National Park
1111 Second St.
Crescent City, CA 95531
707.464.6101

Rocky Mountain National Park
Estes Park, CO 80517
970.586.1206

Saguaro National Park
3693 S. Old Spanish Trail
Tucson, AZ 85730
520.733.5153

Sequoia & Kings Canyon National Parks
Three Rivers, CA 93271
209.565.3341

Shenandoah National Park
3655 U.S. Highway 211 E
Luray, VA 22835
540.999.3500

Theodore Roosevelt National Park
P.O. Box 7
Medora, ND 58645
701.623.4466

Virgin Islands National Park
6310 Estate Nazareth,
Charlotte Amalie,
St. Thomas, VI 00802
340.775.6238

Voyageurs National Park
3131 Hwy. 53
International Falls, MN 56649
218.233.9821

Wind Cave National Park
RR 1, Box 190
Hot Springs, SD 57747
605.745.4600

Wrangell-St. Elias National Park & Preserve
P.O. Box 439
Copper Center, AK 99573
907.822.5234

Yellowstone National Park
P.O. Box 168
Yellowstone National Park, WY 82190
307.344.7381

Yosemite National Park
P.O. Box 577
Yosemite, CA 95389
209.372.0200

Zion National Park
Springdale, UT 84767
801.772.3256

SCENIC DRIVES

AMERICA'S BYWAYS

Drive information provided in cooperation with the National Scenic Byways Program. For more information on America's Byways, please visit *www.byways.org*

Teton Range and Snake River

Alabama — Talladega Scenic Drive

DISTANCE	TIME	BEST SEASONS
29 miles	Allow 1.5 to 2 hours	Spring and fall

FOR STARTERS... Running through the heart of Talladega National Forest, this short, but multifaceted drive provides the best views of the regions' natural seasonal highlights. Bring plenty of film along to catch the fruit trees, dogwoods and redbuds in spring; the blue haze and smoky condensation in summer; the gum, oak, maple and sycamore leaves in fall and the winter light on the ridges. These, and the roaming white-tailed deer and bobcats, make this drive a photographer's heaven.

Most travelers start at the northern end of the byway, near Heflin, at US 78.

The first of three entry points for Pinhoti National Recreational Trail begins at the northern terminus just west of Heflin off US 78. These well-marked trails offer hiking opportunities in which a careful observer may catch a glimpse of a white-tailed deer, the endangered red-cockaded woodpecker. The area offers treats along the path: huckleberries, blueberries, blackberries, wild cherries, wild strawberries, gooseberries, black walnuts, and persimmons. But be on the lookout for poisonous snakes, dry trail sections, and hunting season.

Wind south on AL 281 over the state's highest peak in Cheaha State Park, through scenic woodlands in the Talladega National Forest and along the southern spine of the celebrated Appalachian Trail to Millerville. At mile 16 is the Oxford/Cheaha Overlook where visitors to the area will get their first glimpse of Cheaha State Park and Talladega National Forest.

Alabama's highest point, Cheaha Mountain (2,407 feet high) is at mile 21. This state park offers the best views in the state and hiking, boating, swimming, fishing or camping, as well as rental cabins or chalets. Drive up a paved road (RVs are welcome) and enjoy a meal at the restaurant or stay at the lodge.

Talladega National Forest

At mile 24 is the Lake Chinnabee Recreational Area—the turnoff is 3 miles off the byway. Hikers can walk to the lake via the Chinnabee Silent Trail just one mile from the recreation area or camp, picnic, fish, hunt, or take photographs.

The Cheaha Wilderness which surrounds the drive is off limits to cars, trucks and bicycles but off-road vehicles are welcome at several spots in the national forest.

Your byway journey ends at the South Terminus at Adams Gap.

Contact: National Forests in Alabama **334/241-8128.**

Alaska — The Seward Highway

DISTANCE	TIME	BEST SEASONS
127 miles	2.5 to 8 hours	Summer end/early fall

FOR STARTERS... Following a trail blazed over thousands of years by native Alaskans, sled dog teams and gold rush miners, this drive leads the traveler from the cultural center of the state in Alaska's rugged interior to the coastal waters of Resurrection Bay through a corridor of diverse topography and wildlife. The character of the road traces archeological and human history, changing with every mile to offer picture-postcard views of glacial lakes, breathtaking mountain peaks—and the occasional moose.

On clear days you may glimpse 20,320-foot Mt. McKinley rising over the mountains encircling the city of Anchorage as you begin this trail south toward Seward. Much of the first 30 miles of State Highway 1 (known only as the Seward Highway here) traces the boundary between the woods of Chugach State Park and Turnagain Arm, a long, glacier-carved fjord now filled with ocean waters and Beluga whales.

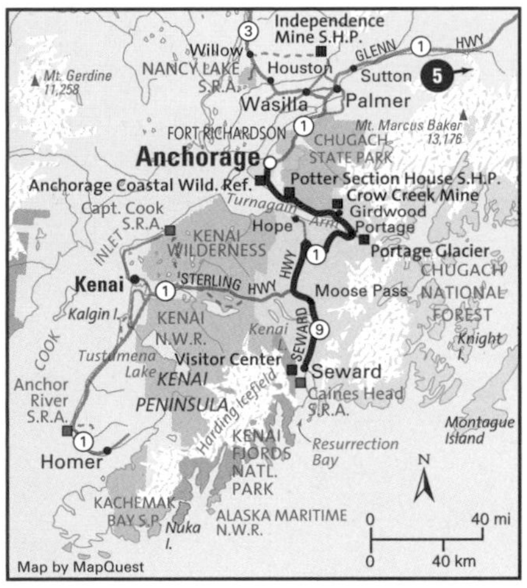

At mile 37 of your journey, stop in the former mining town of Girdwood to learn to prospect for gold. Approximately 10 miles further is the turn-off east for the Portage Highway; a five-mile detour lets you get up close to Portage Glacier. From these sea-level mudflats, the road rises to Turnagain Pass, a 900-foot-high valley with pullouts for spectacular views of the surrounding lowlands. Continue 30 miles south to Upper and Lower Summit Lakes for more scenic vistas, as well as the chance to see how mountain towns prepare for avalanches.

Ten miles further, a pullout one mile off the highway on the north shore of Tern Lake is a goldmine for lovers of wildlife, as is Ptarmigan Creek Recreation Site, 14 miles further south. Here the main attraction in late summer is the rush of spawning red salmon struggling upstream. Less than a mile down the road from the park, a small turnout above Kenai Lake shows off the startling blue of glacial water. One last stop before Seward at Grayling Lake Trailhead offers scenes of distant hanging glaciers and an easy two-mile hike to the lake through spruce forests and meadows.

Mt. McKinley

End your drive in Seward with a boat cruise along the rugged coast of Kenai Fjords National Park. The tour ends at the foot of a 500-foot glacier, where the low moan and popping of calving ice announce a new iceberg before it crashes to the sea.

Contact: Alaska Dept. of Transportation **907/269-0770.**

Arizona — Kaibab Plateau-North Rim Parkway

DISTANCE	TIME	BEST SEASON
43 miles	1 to 6 hours	Fall

FOR STARTERS... Though one of the briefest of the designated scenic drives, this trail to the North Rim of the Grand Canyon may be one of the most striking. "Kaibab" comes from the language of the nomadic native people of the area, meaning "mountain lying down"—though this landscape is far from low. The North Rim, 1,000 feet higher than the South Rim, offers stunning vistas of the canyon walls, the world's greatest example of both erosion and astounding natural beauty.

From Jacob Lake, the entirety of the drive to the Grand Canyon is on State Highway 67. Most of this short but stunning drive is within the Kaibab National Forest, protected lands surrounding the plateau of the same name. The plateau reaches 9,000 feet above sea level, an island of Ponderosa pine, spruce, aspen and juniper. Its steep, grassy lower elevations reach into the Grand Canyon on the plateau's south border; at its east and west are tributaries of the Colorado River. Look north over your shoulder for a glance of Utah's Grand Staircase, a series of sandstone cliffs stretching in order of increasing age. To the east, look for the namesake hue of Vermillion Cliffs.

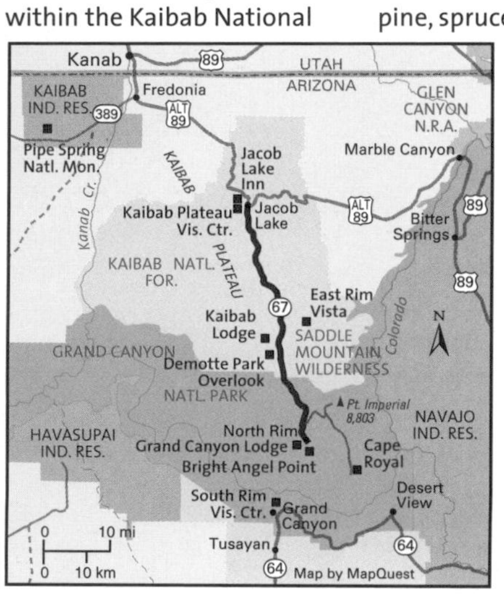

North Rim of the Grand Canyon

Deer, coyote and numerous species of birds—including the endangered California condor soaring overhead—make their home in the park. Demotte is one of the largest meadows on the plateau. To the east of this area is the Saddle Mountain Wilderness and a three-mile spur to the Eastern Viewpoint. The developed and handicapped-accessible overlook provides views of canyon, valley, and forest.

As the road nears the most awe-inspiring of natural wonders in the world, look for the wildlife that calls the area home. Twenty-two miles from the start of the drive is the Demotte Park Overlook.

Just 20 miles further south, the scenic parkway ends at the North Rim of the Grand Canyon National Park. View mile-high panoramas from the historic North Rim Lodge overlooking the canyon. Try a mule ride for an authentic canyon adventure. A half-mile paved trail to Bright Angel Point offers dramatic views of the stratified slopes. Hiking trails lead deeper into the canyon. If you travel to the bottom, the Colorado River (invisible from the overlooks) will carry you through white water on a raft as it continues to chisel away at the canyon walls, as it has for 2 billion years.

Contact: North Kaibab Ranger District **928/643-7395.**

AL 232
AL 60
AK 232
AK 62
AZ 232
AZ 64

AR 232
AR 66

Arkansas

Crowley's Ridge Parkway

DISTANCE	TIME	BEST SEASONS
198 miles	5 hours	Spring and fall

FOR STARTERS... This eastern Arkansas byway, named for the first white-skinned settler here—Benjamin Crowley—follows a series of two-lane highways along the narrow ribbon of Crowley's Ridge. It wends through unusual plant life rooted in a diversity of soil types, ancient geological formations, Native American history and Delta region culture. Home of five state parks and a national forest, travelers can feast their eyes on an immense variety of wildflowers from the car window or stop for many recreational choices.

Starting in St. Francis, cross US 62 to AR 141 past the towns of Piggot and McDougal then follow parkway signs for 34 miles via AR 135 to Paragould. It is 10 miles to your first parkway stop: Crowley's Ridge State Park. Head west on AR 412 to the park turnoff at AR 168 near Wolcott. Visitors will get a taste of 1900s Arkansas life through the log and stone structures of Benjamin Crowley's boyhood home. Crowley's Ridge is actually a geological formation believed to be formed by the erosion of water, ice, and wind action over 50 million years—the closest land form to this one is found in Siberia.

From the state park, follow signs 20 miles south to Jonesboro to the Arkansas State University Museum. Its bell tower can be seen from anywhere in Jonesboro and it houses detailed exhibitions about the natural and human achievement in northwest Arkansas and the Delta region.

Head south about 45 miles along AR 163 for a short side trip to Parkin Archeological State Park. Turn west at US 64 near Wynne. It's 10 miles to the park where travelers can learn about the planned village dating back to 1000 AD visited by Hernando de Soto's expedition in 1541.

Returning to the main route, turn south on US 284 and head 18 miles to Forrest City, home of Arkansas' largest state park, Village Creek State Park. From here it is about 18 miles through Marianna to the entrance of St. Francis National Forest, which takes its name from the river lying along the forests' eastern boundary. It's open year round for camping at Bear Creek Lake, with RV and tent sites.

In 25 miles, visitors reach the route's end in Helena, home of numerous Delta region cultural stops and where the ridge meets the Mississippi River.

Contact: Arkansas Delta Byways **870/910-8082**

Autumn in Arkansas

CA 70

California

Route 1, Big Sur Coast Highway

DISTANCE	TIME	BEST SEASONS
72 miles	2 to 5 hours	Spring, summer and fall

FOR STARTERS... Truly one of America's most breathtaking drives, this highway hugs the rugged Pacific coastline between Carmel and San Luis Obispo County, showcasing the best of California's natural beauty: steep cliffs, brilliant blue seas with pounding surf, ancient redwoods, secluded beaches, mountain meadows and abundant bird and animal life. While the road is narrow and twisting, there are ample turn-offs for taking in the wild and dramatic vistas. High season is summer, but almost any time of year proves enchanting.

Although a relatively short drive, you could easily plan a full week's vacation visiting the natural attractions along California's Route 1. Start in Carmel, home to one of the 18th century Spanish missions, and head south, following the well-marked signs.

In two miles you'll reach Point Lobos State Reserve, often called the crown jewel in the State Park System, and the inspiration for Robert Louis Stevenson's Treasure Island.

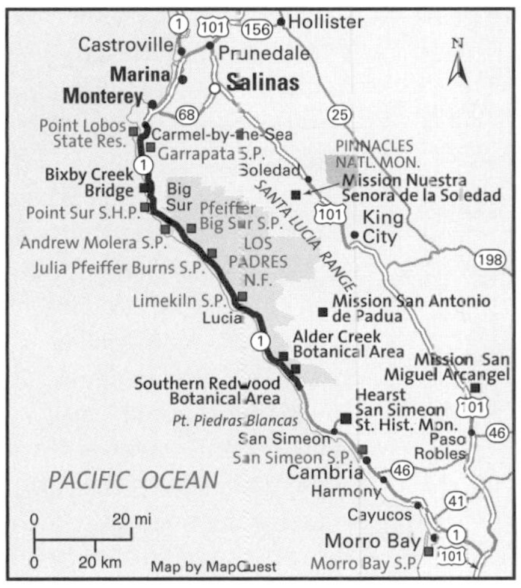

Three miles further down the pristine coastline begins Garrapata State Park. Access is via turn-outs, numbered 1 to 16, at intervals on the right-hand side of the road which can be easily missed if driving too fast. Stop and soak in the postcard-perfect rocky coastline or do a little whale-watching—blue whales June to October and gray whales December to May.

Bixby Creek Bridge

At mile 19 is Point Sur State Historic Park, home of the oldest lighthouse on the California coast. Still operational, guided tours are offered on weekends. Mile 22 brings you to Andrew Molera State Park, the area's largest, which offers camping, and hiking, bike and horseback trails.

Next you'll enter the Big Sur Valley area, considered the heart of Big Sur. Check out the Henry Miller Library, named for one of the many writers and artists who made the area home.

At this point, you may want to get out of the car. Pfeiffer Big Sur State Park to the east has a beautiful waterfall accessible by trail and Pfeiffer Beach, to the west, offers some of the best coastal access.

Further down the coast, you can view the redwood forests in all their primeval splendor—at both Limekiln State Park and the Southern Redwood Botanical Area.

While the drive officially ends at mile 72, you may want to continue down Route 1 to San Simeon and visit the famously extravagant Hearst Castle before continuing on your California journey.

Contact: Route One, Big Sur Coast **831/667-2105.**

CO 76

Colorado

San Juan Skyway

DISTANCE	TIME	BEST SEASONS
232 miles	7 hours to 2 to 3 days	Summer and fall

FOR STARTERS... The San Juan Skyway is an interactive monument to the expansiveness and diversity of the West. The 14,000-foot, iron-red San Juan mountains—which this 232-mile drive loops—sprawl over an area larger than the state of Vermont. Five million acres of undisturbed forest, rich Pueblo history, well-preserved old mining towns, steaming hot springs and deer and elk crossings are in this drive's mix of attractions along with arts festivals, world-class recreational opportunities, and dramatically changing altitudes.

Driving from Durango north on CO 550 towards Silverton, visitors will be transported back in time by the sight of the steely black locomotives of the Durango & Silverton Narrow Gauge Railroad. The trains still run, even in the height of winter offering steam-powered adventures through the San Juan Mountains to Silverton.

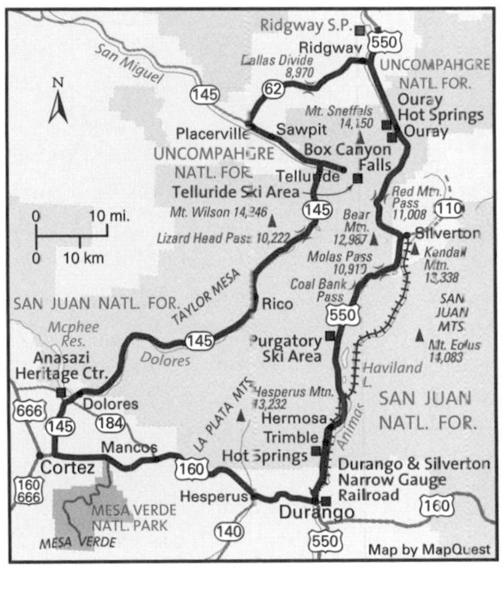

Silverton (so named because silver existed here "by the ton") is a thriving mining and national landmarked town 48 miles north on CO 550. It is a must-see for its beautiful location in a high mountain valley with lovely hiking and camping opportunities.

The 23 mile stretch of skyway from Silverton to Ouray on CO 550 is known as the "Million Dollar Highway" for Red Mountains, the Uncompahgre Gorge, and numerous waterfalls. Ouray is a delightful alpine village reminiscent of a Swiss town. As you enter, you'll see signs for Box Canyon Falls, a plummeting waterfall into a deep cave-like canyon. Visit the hot springs, rent a four-wheeler to the gold and silver mines, and visit an 1880s ghost town.

From Ouray take CO 550 west toward Ridgeway, used as the film location for How the West Was Won. Don't miss the magnificent view at

San Juan Mountains

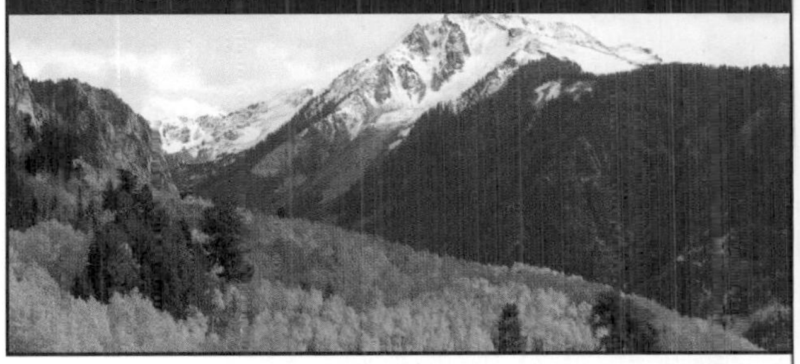

Sneffles Range. At Placerville, head southeast on CO 145 to Telluride. This is Robert Leroy Parker—alias Butch Cassidy—territory and the setting for world class skiing and "jeeping," as well as music, film, wine, balloon and hang gliding festivals.

About ninety-five miles from Telluride, southwest on CO 145 to CO 160 east, is the Mesa Verde National Park entrance, making a terrific end to this treat of a skyway. The park is home to the densest collection of prehistoric ruins in the United States, including fabulous cliff dwellings. It also has snowshoeing trails and abundant wildlife.

Contact: San Juan Skyway, Office of Community Services **970/247-7310.**

Colorado

Trail Ridge/Beaver Meadow Road

DISTANCE	TIME	BEST SEASONS
48 miles	Half day	May to mid-October

FOR STARTERS . . . The trail that skims the rooftop of the Rocky Mountains is the nation's highest continuously paved road. As the peaks rise to the level of alpine tundra, the road offers vistas of hundreds of miles of mountain chain, as well as a glimpse of plants and wildlife normally only found in the Arctic Circle. Contained entirely within the pristine, protected lands of Rocky Mountain National Park and a national forest, this route is itself a national treasure. Park entry fees.

Begin the trail in Estes Park and enter Rocky Mountain National Park by heading straight west on U.S. 36 by way of Beaver Meadows, or take the more wandering route of U.S. 34 north and west. The roads meet at Deer Ridge Junction, continuing westward as U.S. 34, or Trail Ridge Road.

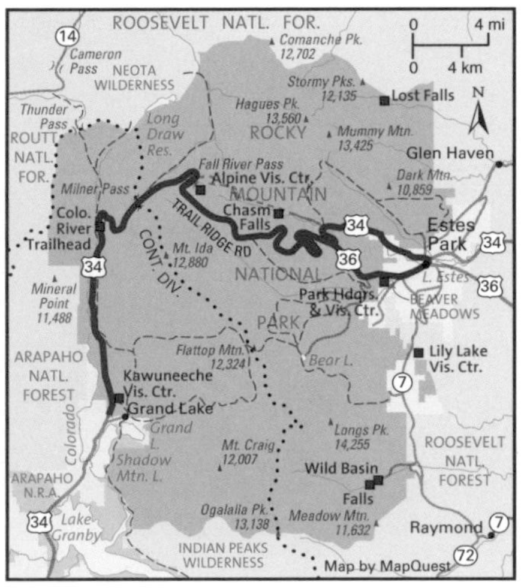

The spectacular beauty of Colorado—its 14,000-foot-high peaks, spruce and fir forests, wildflower gardens and alpine lakes—is apparent from the road, but the trail also offers almost constant opportunities to stop and enjoy the sights. Many Parks Curve, 3.5 miles from the junction, overlooks a number of "parks," or mountain-enclosed meadows. Four circuitous miles later, Rainbow Curve is nearly 11,000 feet—more than 2 vertical miles—high. Here at the upper edge of the treeline, wind, ice and grit urge the trees into strange, low and twisted knots whose branches only survive on the down-wind side of the trunk.

Stream in Beaver Meadow

Continue 3 miles west to the overlook at Forest Canyon; a short walk leads to a panoramic view of this canyon, as well as those of Hayden Gorge and Gorge Lake. Two miles west at Rock Cut, winds can exceed 150 miles an hour. But an elevation of 12,110 feet makes this harsh spot the rooftop of the range and a wonderful vantage point from which to see alpine wonders south of the Arctic Circle, including 100 species of tundra flowering plants.

The road meanders 10.5 miles to Milner Pass and the Continental Divide, the point at which water pulls toward either the Pacific or the Atlantic. Thread your way through several loops of trail to meet up with the Colorado River, the same ancient river that carved the Grand Canyon, and the stunning Kawuneeche Valley. Take a look at views from one of the many hiking trailheads as the road follows the river valley to the tour's end in Grand Lake. **Contact:** Rocky Mountain National Park **970/586-1363.**

Florida

Tamiami Trail Scenic Highway

DISTANCE	TIME	BEST SEASON
50 miles	3 to 4 hours	Summer

FOR STARTERS . . . This section of the Tampa to Miami road (hence the name, a combination of the two termini cities) takes you through one of the last remaining tropical wilderness areas in the continental United States. Built in 1928 to open up Florida's "frontier"—its vast swampy interior—this two-lane road bisects an area of 80% publicly held land to offer unobstructed views and one of the best ways to experience Florida's unique ecosystems and wildlife habitats.

Start southeast of Naples at Collier Seminole State Park, which features 6,423 acres of dense vegetation typical of the Everglades region. As you continue southeast, note the canal that runs alongside the north side of the trail, a natural magnet for alligators, ducks and heron.

In 4 ½ miles, you'll reach Fakahatchee Strand State Park, home to the largest concentration and variety of orchids in North America. A few miles past the park is Route 29. Take it south to Everglades City for access to both Ten Thousand Islands and Everglades National Parks, where you can see the largest mangrove forest in the U.S. and abundant wildlife, including otters and manatee.

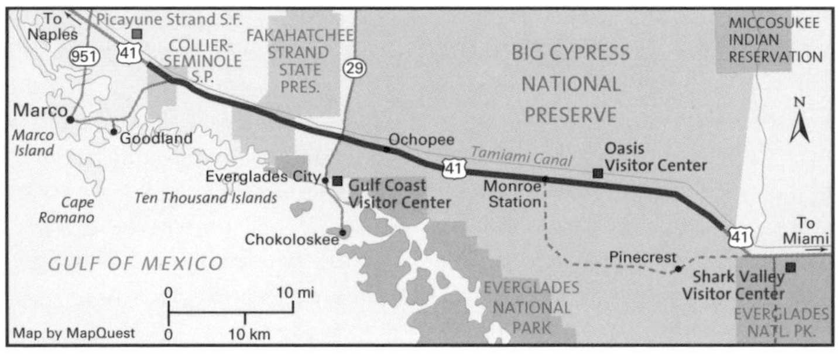

Just 4 ½ miles from Everglades City (heading back north on 29 then east on 41) is the town of Ochopee, which boasts "the smallest post office in the US." It's located within Big Cypress National Reserve, a 729,000 acre park with soaring cypress trees and a 2,400 acre swamp. Stop here and walk, canoe or bicycle to better view the marshes and mangrove forests, every kind of subtropical plant, bald eagles, herons, ibis and, of course, alligators.

If you're interested in the history of the Miccosukee Native American tribe—one of the region's original inhabitants, along with the Calusa and Seminole peoples—you might want to stop at the Miccosukee Cultural Center at mile 35 ½. Another good stop is at the Oasis Visitor Center, 22 miles east of Route 29, where there are 29.7 miles of hiking trails, as well as movies about the area's natural attractions.

The drive ends 13 miles later at another entrance to Everglades National Park. Take your time viewing its natural treasures, especially the sawgrass prairies and more than 350 bird species. Making this drive in early

Tamiami Trail and Canal

summer offers you the lushest landscapes, but it's accessible year-round. Avoid hurricane season (late summer/fall). **Contact:** Everglades Area Chamber of Commerce **941/695-3941.**

Illinois

Ohio River Scenic Route

DISTANCE	TIME	BEST SEASON
188 miles	8 to 10 hours	Year-round

FOR STARTERS . . . The link to the undiscovered west, this section of the Ohio River helped build the young nation and played a significant role in the lives of prehistoric and early European settlers, as well as in the strategies of the Civil War and the tragic resettlement of 1800s Native Americans. With a history closely tied to the people and industries that have shared the bounty of the river, these last miles of the Ohio may be the river's most beautiful.

Whether crossing the toe of Indiana (on Indiana 62/Illinois 141) or bridging the Ohio River from Kentucky (on Illinois 13), the trail quickly leads to the Shawnee National Forest. Once mostly homestead farms, the area has been returned to woodlands. Both paths meet near Shawneetown and continue west, then south, on Illinois 1. At Ponds Hollow Road (county road 9/4) to Karbers

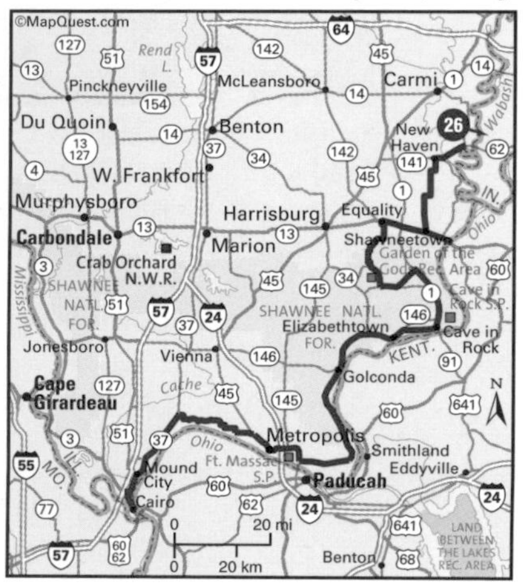

Ridge, a spur of 10 miles leads to Garden of the Gods, an area of rock formations caused by geological shifts and years of weather erosion. Back on Route 1 and six miles south is Cave-in-Rock State Park, home of a great limestone cavern on the Ohio. Once a hideout for river pirates, the popular attraction now looks out on modern river traffic.

The trail follows Illinois 146 west from this park through the portion of the Shawnee National Forest crossed by the 15,000 Cherokee Indians forced to march the "Trail of Tears." The Buell House in Golconda is the former home of a generous family who shared their crops with the starving Indians. From Golconda, the drive traces the river valley on county roads for 30 miles to Fort Massac State Park, where reconstructed 1700s forts bring re-enacted battles to life and trails on the river and in shady woods offer short hikes. At Brookport, take U.S. 45 toward Metropolis, a town that takes its superhero name seriously, protecting its square with a 15-ft. Superman statue.

Shawnee National Forest

The next 35 miles of the trail arch west on county roads 5 and 2, then Illinois 37 past Mounds City and its national cemetery, where soldiers from both sides of the Civil War rest side-by-side. Just seven miles later by way of U.S. 51, the drive ends in Cairo. From the vantage of Fort Defiance Park, the confluence of the two rivers reveals the Ohio's determination: its blue currents are visible far down the muddy Mississippi. **Contact:** Southernmost Illinois Tourism Bureau **800/248-4373.**

Iowa — Loess Hills Scenic Byway

DISTANCE	TIME	BEST SEASON
220 miles	7 hours	Fall

FOR STARTERS . . . There's only one other place on earth that shares the same natural features as Western Iowa's Loess Hills region: China's Yellow River Valley. With a rugged landscape formed by windblown silt deposits, Loess (pronounced "luss") Hills possesses some of America's most fascinating geologic and archeological treasures, including evidence of civilizations more than 12,000 years old. As this drive meanders through the Missouri River Valley, you'll also see a nearly lost American landscape of prairies, grasslands, and rare plants and animals.

Begin south of Akron on Highway12 at the Broken Kettle Grasslands, which features the largest remaining section of the prairies that once covered most of Iowa. Five miles south is an equally fine example of unbroken prairie at Five Ridge Prairie.

Follow the well-marked scenic byway signs, as the route travels a number of highways. In a nutshell: Go south on Highway 12 to Highway 98 south of Sioux City, then take Highway 175 from Onawa. Between Magnolia and Logan the byway follows Highway 127, and between Soldier and Council Bluffs it becomes Highway 183. From there, the byway follows Highway 275 to its endpoint in Hamburg.

Some of the more interesting stops include the riverboat museum at the Sergeant Floyd Welcome Center, mile 27; the Harrison County Historical Village and Iowa Welcome Center at mile 130, with its agricultural displays and artifacts from Native American tribes; the DeSoto Bend National Wildlife Refuge at mile 140 which attracts a half-million migrating geese every November; and the Todd House Museum at mile 194, a former stop on the Underground Railroad.

A trip highlight is the Turin Man Archeological Site three miles south of Castana, where in 1955 the remains of four humans buried 5,500 years ago were found, indicating the ancient heritage of this area.

Loess Hills

Because much of the region's appeal lies in its one-of-a-kind ridged landscape, make time to visit the parks: Loess Hills Wildlife Area, mile 77, for bird- and animal-watching; Lewis and Clark State Park, mile 95, along the Missouri River; Pony Creek Park, mile 196, for fishing, hiking and picnicking; and Wabonsie State Park near the byway's end for exceptional fall colors.

Some of the best views along the way are at the Murray Hill Scenic Overlook, mile 110.

Contact: Loess Hills Scenic Byway Council **712/482-3029.**

IA 236
IA 96

Louisiana — Creole Nature Trail

DISTANCE	TIME	BEST SEASON
180 miles	4 to 8 hours	Spring

FOR STARTERS . . . The word "creole" can refer to a combination of cultures that makes a new culture, and that's exactly what you'll find on Louisiana's Creole Nature Trail. Not only in the inhabitants' mixed French, Spanish and African heritage, but also in the region's distinctive food, architecture, music and attitudes. Along the trail you'll also find acres of untouched wetlands, stunning beaches, and colorful birds, flowers and wildlife—all making this a unique region in the US.

With five entrances to the trail, you can map out a fairly personalized itinerary. Most visitors start on Highway 27 in Sulphur and head south. Ten miles after crossing Interstate 10, you'll reach the intercoastal waterway, then enter Cameron Parish (county) with its more than 700,000 acres of wetlands. As you head south, through untamed wilderness that residents call the "Louisiana Outback," be sure to stop near Hackenberry to sample its famous seafood. By mile 21 you'll reach Sabine National Wildlife Refuge, a winter home for migrating ducks and geese and considered one of the top 40 birding spots in North America. For close-ups of the complex marsh ecosystem, visit the refuge's Wetland Walkway four miles south.

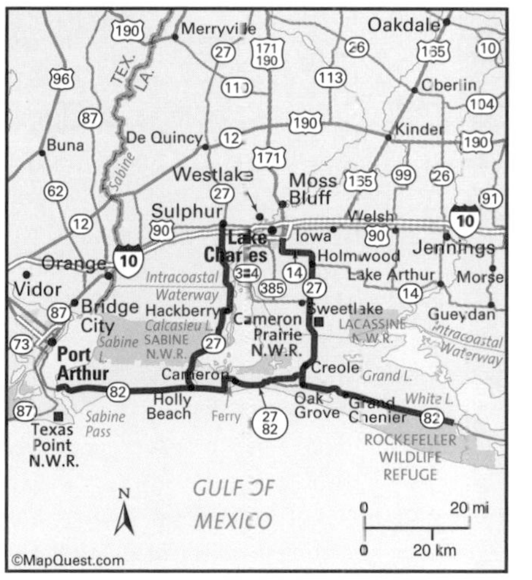

Migrating birds

Seven miles further south is the "Cajun Riviera," the beaches lining the Gulf of Mexico. A popular stop for locals and visitors alike is Holly Beach. From there you can either follow 82 toward Texas or head east toward New Orleans. If you go west, check out the Peveto Woods Bird and Butterfly Sanctuary with its migrating hummingbirds, warblers and monish butterflies, and the Civil War-era Sabine Pass Lighthouse at trail's end.

If you go east on 82, be prepared to take the public ferry across the Calcasieu Ship Channel before entering the town of Cameron. In 4-5 miles, you'll reach a Y in the road where you can take Highway 27 up to Lake Charles through the Cameron-Prairie National Wildlife Refuge. Along this route, the Gibbstown Bridge offers excellent views of the surrounding wetlands.

If you continue straight east you'll pass by numerous beaches where you can fish, picnic, camp, beachcomb or watch the omnipresent birdlife. The trail ends in Grand Chenier, its name referring to the beach ridges typical of the landscape, where you can visit the Rockefeller Wildlife Refuge, internationally recognized for its study of prominent local residents: alligators.

Contact: Southwest Louisiana Convention & Visitors Bureau **800/456-7952.**

LA 237
LA 102

Maine — Acadia Byway

DISTANCE	TIME	BEST SEASONS
40 miles	3 hours	April through October

FOR STARTERS . . . Named for its pink granite-topped peaks, Mount Desert Island is home to Acadia National Park (see page 195), a lush and very undesert-like collection of land parcels protected as an undeveloped masterpiece of nature. Once a vacation getaway for weary city dwellers, the island has benefited from wealthy supporters, such as John D. Rockefeller, Jr., the oil heir who created the island's signature carriage roads. These paths still forbid carriages of the horseless variety, offering miles of safe recreation for modern visitors.

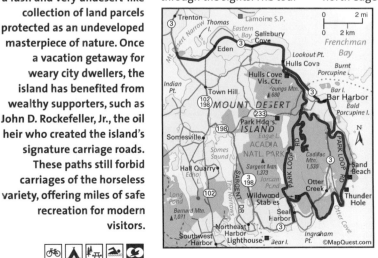

Protection of this idyllic island keeps parking at a premium; leave your car behind and let the island's free bus system take you through the sights. The tour begins by crossing the Thompson Island Bridge over the Desert Narrows onto Mount Desert Island. The first 18 miles travel ME 3 along the north edge of the island to Hulls Cove and its panoramic views of Frenchman Bay and the Porcupine Island chain. Continue on 3 through Bar Harbor (where you can take a ferry to Yarmouth, Nova Scotia) to Acadia National Park, where you pick up its historic Park Loop Road.

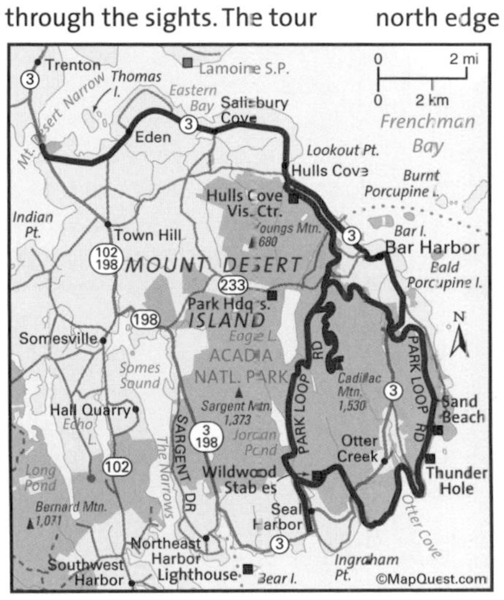

The 26.2-mile, mostly one-way loop around the island cuts a natural path along the rocky coast, offering spectacular views of nearby islands skipping across the Atlantic Ocean. Stop just beyond the Champlain Trailhead at the overlook to see the Egg Rock lighthouse (look for signs). At Otter Cliff, drivers have a clear view of an expanse of ocean and Acadia's coastal mountains from a high road and a low one. (Rockefeller created the then-two-way road to offer panoramas in both directions.)

Curve with the Loop Road around Otter Cove and Day Mountain to Wildwood Stables, where two-way traffic resumes. About a mile north, stop at Jordan Pond House to take part in the long-standing tradition of tea and popovers; take your tea on the lawn to overlook Jordan Pond and the Bubble Mountains. Take a stroll along the motor-free carriage roads. These 57 miles of hiking, biking and horseback riding splendor are the best example of broken stone roads left in America.

Before finishing the loop, a side trip up Cadillac Mountain Road to the top of the 1,530-foot "desert" peak offers a breathtaking vista of the island's lush forests and the crashing waves beyond that continue to shape the island.

Contact: Acadia National Park **207/288-3338.**

Mount Desert Island

ME 237
ME 104

ME 237
ME 104

Maine

Old Canada Road Scenic Byway

DISTANCE	TIME	BEST SEASON
79 miles	2.5 hours	Spring

For starters... It was the "Route des Etats" (or Road to the States) for French Canadians who traveled south to the U.S. searching for agricultural jobs and "Old Canada Road" for Maine farmers looking to open up northern markets to the Kennebec Valley. Today the Old Canada Road Scenic Byway is a mecca for white-water rafters, hikers, campers and snowmobilers as well as those wanting to sift through 1800s artifacts or meander the scenic route to Quebec.

Your journey through this northern mountain-ridged slice of Maine to Canada officially begins in the old-time village of Solon, on ME 201, just 45 miles northwest of Augusta.

For a cultural start to your trip, visit the South Solon Meeting House on South Solon Road, a restored 1842 Greek revival meeting house whose walls have been frescoed by WPA muralists. (Open year round.)

Rivers dominate the southern portion of this route, revealing undeveloped ridges and tiny islands punctuated with white birch trees. Around the 31-mile marker is The Forks, where the Dead River flows into the Kennebec. This area is nationally recognized for its wild whitewater: Several rafting outfitters are located here providing access to the most challenging runs in the northeast United States. The Dead River offers the longest continuous stretch—16 miles—in the East, beginning at Grand Falls and ending at The Forks.

Picnic at the bridge over the Kennebec or hike to one of Maine's highest waterfalls (96-foot drop) two miles north of The Forks and down a one-mile path. This beautiful wooded area contains a network of delightful hiking trails.

From here the byway rises in elevation, highlighting the spectacular Boundary Mountains and Attean/Holeb chain of lakes. These mountains extend between Rangely and Jackman with an average height of 1000 feet. Twenty-three miles north you'll reach the Attean Overlook, where you can see all the way to Canada. Watch out though for frequent moose crossings along this section of the road.

Follow the signs for the Jackman-Moose River Historical Society in Jackman, three miles north for an excellent collection of photos and artifacts dating to the early 1800s to rifle through, including old-time lumbering tools and World War II prisoner-of-war camp artifacts. The actively inclined can head just 2 miles further to Moose River for numerous kayaking, canoeing and snowmobiling opportunities.

Contact: Maine Office of Tourism **800/533-9595.**

Kennebec River

MN 239
MN 117

Minnesota

Great River Road

DISTANCE	TIME	BEST SEASONS
575 miles	19 hours–several days	Summer and fall

For starters... This drive begins where the mighty Mississippi is a tidy trickle of water and follows the river's growth as it passes its first 572 miles. Created from a twisting path of existing roads, this trail traverses a varied landscape as it tours both small towns and the Twin Cities and the sights that have made Minnesota a destination for a century: giant red and white pine forests, swampy wetlands, bluffs and, of course, a few of those 10,000 lakes.

The Mississippi River begins its 2,552-mile journey as an ankle-deep stream in Itasca State Park, where a few stones at the headwaters bridge this tame spot. Request a map to get through the myriad roads this route follows, starting with County Rd. 2 north toward Bemidji. Legend says that Paul Bunyan's big blue ox created numerous lakes here with its heavy hooves. Leave Bemidji by County Rd. 8 west through the Chippewa National Forest, the first national forest east of the Mississippi. Chippewa has 1.6 million acres of bogs, lakes and forests,

Minnehaha Falls

including the Lost Forty, an area of virgin pine untouched because of a mapping error.

Turn southwest on MN 3 at Grand Rapids; 53 miles later at Aitkin, take 210 west to loop north to Brainerd. Peruse MN 371 for 31 miles to Charles Lindbergh, Jr.'s boyhood home of Little Falls. Here, Charles Lindbergh State Park honors the pilot's father, a former state Congressman.

The Great River Road uses small, river-hugging roads to enter the Twin Cities. Follow the byway's signage downtown to view the skyline, the old milling district, and St. Anthony Falls (best seen from the Stone Arch pedestrian bridge).

Return to small town Minnesota (US 61 to I494, exit at MN 56, loop around Lock and Dam #2 to MN 361, then back to US 61) by strolling Red Wing for bargains on its brand of shoes and a look at its shoe museum. Only 50 miles from the Twin Cities, Frontenac State Park on Lake Pepin is one of the best spots in the country for birdwaching. In Winona, 45 miles south, Sugarloaf Mountain is a night-time spectacle of lights. The man-made formation resulted from quarrying done to build a road over the Mississippi. MN 26 leads to the state line; the road continues into Iowa along the river.

Contact: Minnesota Mississippi River Parkway Commission **763/212-2560.**

TN 245
MS 239
AL 232
TN 158
MS 118
AL 60

Mississippi/ Alabama/ Tennessee

Natchez Trace Parkway

DISTANCE	TIME	BEST SEASONS
444 miles	10 hours	Spring to fall

For starters... Not a fixed route but a series of hunter's paths that evolved into a connected trail from the Mississippi River to the Tennessee Valley, the Trace has been a useful path as well as a beautiful one. It served the Choctaw and Chickasaw Indians and in the 1780s expanded the markets of northern merchants, who floated their wares down the Mississippi to Natchez, where they sold everything including the boat and walked back home along the pathway.

The Natchez Trace begins off TN 100 outside of Nashville in pastoral lands intertwined with streams and creeks. Look for wild turkeys and deer as the trail crosses Duck River, and stop at Water Valley Overlook for a view of the valley the Duck River floods occasionally.

Continue south to the site of the grave of famed adventurer Meriwether Lewis. About twenty miles from this area, explore the Glenrock Branch, a stream flowing through a small valley along the trace.

Cross the state line into Alabama, passing the site of Colbert Ferry, where the ferryman tried to charge Andrew Jackson $75,000 to get his returning army across the river after the Battle of New Orleans.

While only in Alabama for a short distance, the Natchez Trace cuts through the heart of Mississippi for 310 miles. Just inside the state line is Bear Creek Mound, the first of seven Native American burial mounds and ceremonial sites along this route. North of Tupelo is another kind of burial ground, for soldiers. One of the bloodiest Civil War battles occurred south of the city; it is commemorated as the Tupelo National Battlefield. The Trace passes through the Tombigbee National Forest and skims the edge of the Rose Barnett Reservoir outside Jackson—both rich areas for outdoor activities. Here the trail is unfinished; use I-55, I-220 and I-20 to circumvent Jackson and return to the Trace.

Stop at the formerly bustling town of Rocky Springs for a reminder of the history of the Trace, and 13 miles further, look for a chance to walk the original footpath, now sunken by years of use. Emerald Mound, an 8-acre ceremonial mound 32 miles south, was built by ancestors of the Natchez Indians around 1400. End the tour in Natchez with a visit to the Grand Village of the Natchez State Historic Site, the former center of life for the now-extinct Indian nation.

Contact: National Park Service **800/305-7417.**

Winding Natchez Trace Parkway

Nevada — Lake Tahoe—Eastshore Drive

DISTANCE	TIME	BEST SEASON
28 miles	45 minutes	Year-round

FOR STARTERS . . . The largest alpine lake in North America (193 square miles) and one of the deepest in the world (1,645 at its deepest point), Lake Tahoe combines sapphire blue yet remarkably clear water with white sand beaches. It is set against dense green forests and the snow-capped Sierra Nevada mountains, creating an unforgettable picture of pristine beauty. Eastshore Drive offers a knockout view of this famed recreation area that features winter skiing, summer sailing and spectacular hiking year-round.

A good starting point is Stateline, on the border between California and Nevada, the states that surround Lake Tahoe. Head north through Nevada along US Highway 50. At mile 2, you'll reach the Tahoe Douglas Visitor's Center, which offers a good introduction to the region with a video and cultural/historical displays.

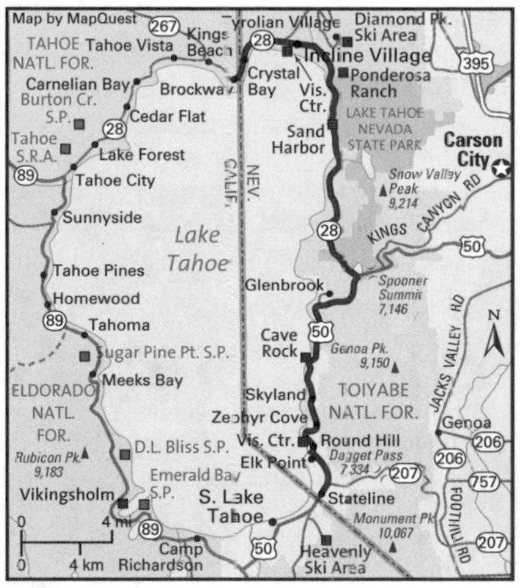

Zephyr Cove Marina, mile 4 is popular for fishing, camping, sailing and—along the mountain trails—snowmobiling. Next, check out Cave Rock, mile 12, where the highway passes through 75 feet of solid stone. This is a holy spot for the native Washoe Indians—some of the region's original inhabitants.

As you climb higher toward the Spooner Summit, elevation 7,146 feet, you'll find increasingly wide and beautiful views. Pull off at any of the dozens of Vista Points. You might want to think about the Pony Express riders who followed this same route to California.

Lake Tahoe

After reaching the summit of the drive, the road becomes State Highway 28. This part of the road passes many state parks and beaches, including Lake Tahoe Nevada State Park, a recreation mecca. Here you may see some of the wildlife that inhabit the region, such as coyotes, porcupines, owls, bald eagles, and osprey. During August, you also may want to visit Sand Harbor State Park, home to a month-long annual Shakespeare festival. Its perfect mile-long white sand beach allows you to see the rocks and geological formations that shaped the lake at any time of year.

Popular culture buffs might want to tour the Ponderosa Ranch, just off mile 25, where the TV series Gunsmoke was taped. The drive ends at Crystal Bay at the California border, a celebrated dining spot and home to Lake Tahoe's first Casino, built in 1928.

Contact: Tahoe Douglas Chamber of Commerce and Visitor's Center **775/588-4591.**

NV 241
NV 126

Nevada — The Las Vegas Strip

DISTANCE	TIME	BEST SEASON
4.5 miles	.5–several hours	Any, but go at night

FOR STARTERS . . . Envisioned by a mobster, immortalized by Hollywood, visited by 32 million annually, the Las Vegas Strip must be seen to be believed. Unlike other scenic drives, the best time to take this one is at night, when the Strip lives up to its other moniker, the "neon trail." In fact, this might be the only scenic drive better undertaken on foot to more easily absorb the people, sights and sounds of this surreal and energetic interpretation of the American dream.

From the time gambling was legalized in Nevada in 1931, Las Vegas has continued to reinvent itself. Today, this desert city has become a vacation destination for people worldwide—featuring more hotel rooms at a single intersection than the entire city of San Francisco.

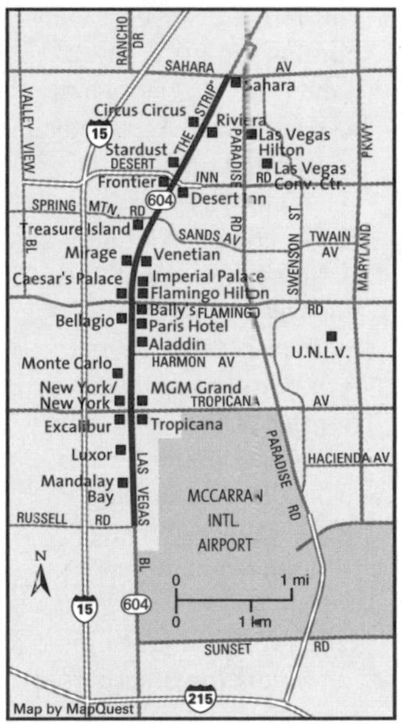

Start on the south end of the Strip (State Highway 604) at Russell Road and head north to see why Las Vegas is known as the entertainment capitol of the world. Flanking both sides of the road are glittering signs, oversized casinos, outrageous architecture, to-scale models of great cities, and hotels that feature world-class art galleries, 4-star restaurants and top-caliber shows.

Park in any of the hotel garages and take to the sidewalks and pedestrian overpasses to view water shows, light spectaculars and the more than 200,000 visitors on any given night. Within a short period of time you can watch an erupting volcano, a pirate ship fight and circus performers, walk through a rain forest and visit reproductions of famous landmarks—at no charge. If you get tired, jump on the free monorail that runs between properties.

Other attractions include the Little Church of the West at Russell Street, included on the National Register of Historic Places as the oldest structure on the Strip; two Guggenheim galleries at the Venetian, about three miles up the Strip on the east side; and the Liberace Museum, 10 minutes east of the strip on Tropicana. As for excursions, try Red Rock Canyon, 20 minutes away. Go south to Blue Diamond, then west till you reach it. Or from the airport adjacent to the Strip, you can take a 2-3 hour helicopter ride over the Grand Canyon.

The bustling Vegas strip

The Strip ends at Sahara Avenue, but you may want to turn around and retrace your route south to better experience the scenery on the other side of this only-in-America street of dreams.

Contact: Las Vegas Convention and Visitor's Bureau **800/332-5333.**

NV 241
NV 126

New Hampshire — White Mountain Trail

DISTANCE	TIME	BEST SEASON
108 miles	2.5 hours	Year-round

FOR STARTERS . . . Hiking enthusiasts, railroad historians and leaf-watchers unite in their enthusiasm for the roadways that curve through the White Mountain National Forest. Under the towering granite cliffs and Presidential Mountains (named for Washington, Adams, Jefferson, Monroe and Madison) and through mountain passes, covered bridges and forgotten logging villages, this trail travels the spectrum of New Hampshire scenery—the same scenes striking enough to inspire the White Mountain school of landscape painters and a salon of transcendental writers.

From Lincoln, go west to North Woodstock and take US 3 north to Franconia Notch State Park, home of several stunning natural wonders. Start with the Flume Gorge, 5.5 miles into the journey. A walk through the natural 800-foot gorge leads past waterfalls and mountain vistas. Less than 2 miles north of this spot is the Basin, a deep glacial pothole at the foot of a waterfall.

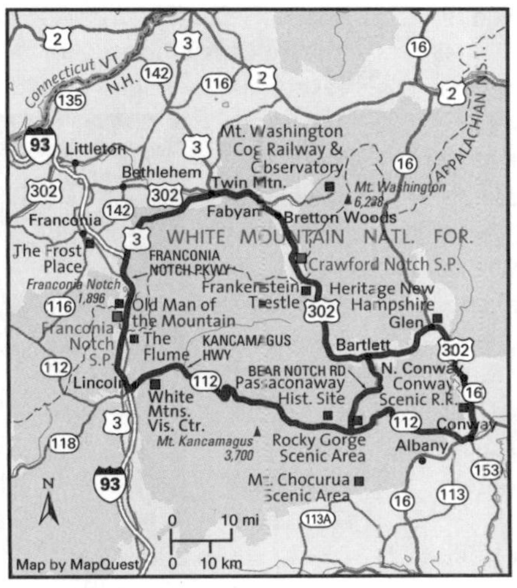

But the best reason to stop at this beautiful park is the man who watches over it: The Old Man of the Mountain is a natural rock profile, the most famous face of the White Mountains. View this spot from Exit 2 (3.6 miles north of the Basin) as you stop for a ride on the Cannon Mountain Aerial Tramway.

At Exit 35, take US 3 north to the town of Twin Mountain and turn east onto US 302. Ten miles along the trail is Crawford Notch State Park. Look for the Elephant Head rock formation overhead and a viewpoint from which to see Flume Cascade and Silver Cascade, just two of the waterfalls along this stretch.

The railroad trestle on Frankenstein Cliff (5 miles southeast) is a reminder of the lumber industry that shaped this area. Turn at Sawyer River Road to visit Livermore, an abandoned logging town. Or continue on 302 past Bartlett Covered Bridge to the junction with NH 16. Take this road 4 miles south to the Intervale Scenic Vista. This low-lying flood-plain is a great place to take in the view of Mt. Washington.

White Mountain National Forest

In North Conway, home of the historic Conway Scenic Railroad train station, catch a ride in a restored locomotive from yesteryear. Continue south through Conway to the Kancamagus Scenic Highway (NH 112), visiting the 1800s covered bridge 6 miles west of NH 16 on Dugway Road in Albany. Enjoy the scenery—exceptional for fall colors—as the road climbs to nearly 3,000 feet along the flank of Mt. Kancamagus near Lincoln.

Contact: White Mountain Attraction **800/346-3687**

NH 241
NH 127

New Mexico — El Camino Real

DISTANCE	TIME	BEST SEASONS
299 miles	9 hours	Spring and fall

NM 241
NM 130

For starters...
From Santa Fe to the Texas and Mexico border, a visitor to El Camino Real will discover a landscape steeped with culture, history and archeological wonders. There are 250 days a year of sunshine (don't forget your sunscreen) to visit prehistoric rock etchings, explore evidence of Tyrannosaurus Rex, observe Pueblo villages and colonial missions, or savor spicy delicacies made with the chile pepper introduced to the US via this very road by Spanish settlers.

The drive begins in Santa Fe, a culturally rich city well worth a walking tour

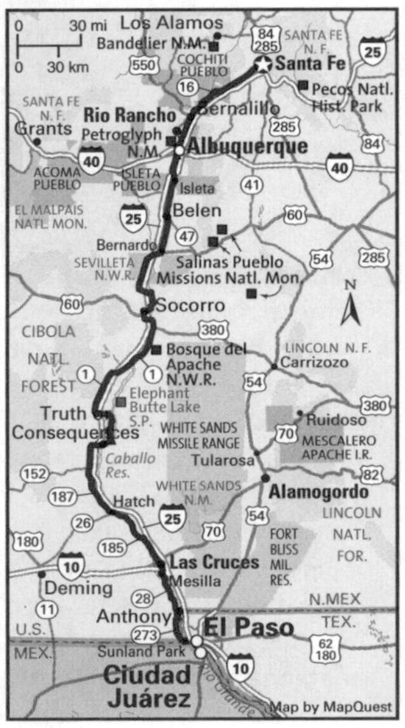

before setting off on your southwestern journey. From here El Camino Real corridor twists on and off US Highway I-25, allowing visitors both a fast track to their desired destination or a meandering one.

Seventy-four miles south on I-25 you reach downtown Albuquerque. Visitors will want to stop at the Petroglyth National Monument (from the junction of I-25 and I-40 in Alburquerque, take I-40 west four miles to Unser Boulevard and then turn north for 3 miles to the visitor's center). More than 15,000 prehistoric Native American etchings in rock are stretched over a 17-mile area.

From the monument, take Unser south to I-40, take I-40 east to I-25 south, then I-25 south to Rio Bravo Boulevard. Go west two miles and take a left on Broadway (NM-47). From here it is approximately 10 miles to the Isleta Pueblo Mission, a beautiful pueblo situated on top of a mesa hundreds of feet above land (nick-named Sky City).

Cathedral of St. Francis

From Isleta take NM 47 south to Belen where you pick up I-25 again. Head south for 43 miles to Socorro, continue 18 more miles and take the exit marked Bosque del Apache National Wildlife Refuge. This 57,000-acre winter sanctuary for Canadian Geese, snow geese, sandhill cranes and endangered whopping cranes offers nature trails and wilderness picnic sites.

Forty-five miles further south on I-25 is Elephant Butte Lake State Park. Forty miles long and one mile wide, it is the largest lake in New Mexico and is named for an island whose profile resembles an elephant. Stop at the visitor center to learn about Butte Dam and the archeological evidence of Tyrannosaurus Rex in the region.

The historic town of La Mesilla in Las Cruces (65 miles south of the state park) is worth a stop for spicy food, shopping, and a spectacular view of the Organ Mountains. The byway ends in Sunland Park, near El Paso. **Contact:** Albuquerque Chamber of Commerce **505/842-9003.**

New Mexico — Santa Fe Trail

DISTANCE	TIME	BEST SEASONS
381 miles	8 hours	Spring, summer and fall

NM 241
NM 130

For starters...
One of America's first great trade routes, the Santa Fe Trail played a major role in the westward expansion of the US. Along the way, you can even see wheel ruts from the covered wagons that traveled the trail more than 150 years ago. You'll actually see much the same scenery that the pioneers did: the rugged Sangre de Cristo mountains to the west, the Chihuahuan desert to the south and vast grasslands and plains north and east.

Start in Santa Fe, .4 of a mile south of the capitol at Museum Plaza. These four museums, Museum of Indian Arts and Culture, Museum of International Folk Art, Museum of Spanish Colonial Art, and Wheelwright Museum of the American Indian, with their astonishing array of regional art and cultural artifacts, are definitely worth a visit.

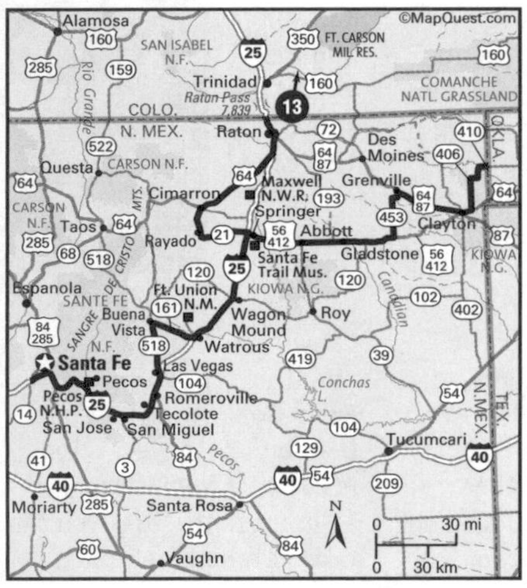

As you drive east just a few miles, the Old Pecos Trail and Old Santa Fe Trails meet and you can view the original dirt trail complete with wagon ruts.

Less than a mile on I-25 you'll reach exit 299 at Glorietta. Take State Road 50 to Pecos

Beautiful adobe buildings

National Historic Park, rich with the region's history, including ancient pueblos of the Pecos, two Spanish Colonial Missions and a Civil War battle site.

Consider making Las Vegas National Wildlife Refuge, located north of Romeroville, your next stop. Exit at State Road 104, travel east for one mile, then south on State Highway 281 for four miles. This former Native American hunting ground is now a habitat for migratory birds, bald eagles, ducks, antelope, badger and bobcat.

Back on I-25, look for exit 366 to go to Fort Union National Monument, the ruins of the largest US military installation on the 19th century southwestern frontier. At the exit, follow State Road 161 for 8 miles.

Back on I-25 heading north, you'll be driving through plains, home to buffalo and gamma grass. When you reach the Cimarron Cutoff, the trail splits in two directions. You can follow it northwest along State Highway 21 and US 64 toward Colorado to visit the Sugarite Canyon State Park with its mountain meadows full of wildflowers or you can travel east on US 56/412 toward Oklahoma and visit the Kiowa National Grasslands, 5 miles south of Abbott on Route 39.

Whatever route you choose, be sure to visit the Santa Fe Trail Museum at Cimarron Cutoff, which features art exhibits and artifacts that tell the story of this trail and the pioneers who traveled it. **Contact:** New Mexico Department of Tourism and Santa Fe Visitor's Center **800/545-2040.**

New York — Seaway Trail

DISTANCE	TIME	BEST SEASONS
454 miles	Allow 4 days	Summer through fall

NY 241
NY 132

For starters...
Seaway Trail follows a series of well-marked signs along state and county roads paralleling the St. Lawrence River, Lake Ontario, Niagara River, and Lake Erie at the northern border of New York state. Rife with history, culture and natural wonders, it offers a breathtaking alternative to interstate highways and toll roads. Niagara Falls is at the west end of the drive, a magnificent six-story castle is at the east end, and 26 historic lighthouses and other cultural attractions dot the shoreline in between.

The journey starts in Dunkirk. Be sure to check out the lighthouse that was constructed in 1875. From there head east to Buffalo and Niagara Falls, a feast for the senses. Now a cultural icon, the falls were once believed to be the sacred dwelling place of the Native American Thunder Being "Heron." Take in the plunging power of the falls from the Goat Island overlook, photo-

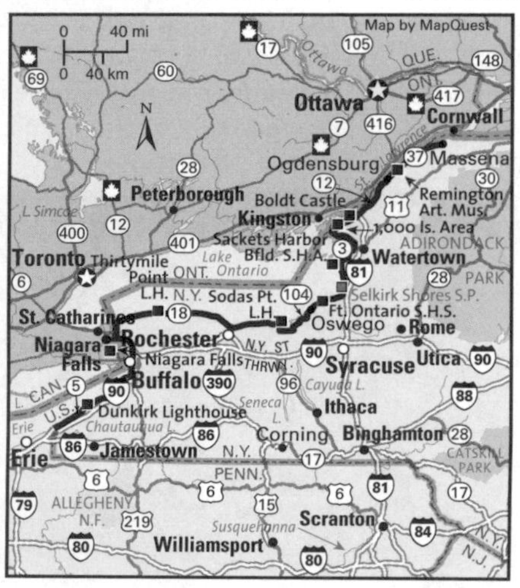

graph them from the Maid of the Mist, or stroll around the gardens and aquarium in Niagara Falls State Park, where the falls are situated.

The city of Rochester, packed with beautiful city parks and more than a handful of museums, is 91 miles east of the falls and makes an excellent overnight stopover.

Follow seaway trail signs north, then east around to the southern edge of Lake Ontario to the Old Sodas Point Lighthouse at Sodas Point about 30 miles from Rochester. This 1800s lighthouse—one of several worth seeing along the Seaway—harkens back to a time when navigation in bad weather was completely dependent on the beacons of these small towers to get home. Old Sodas Point Lighthouse is a not-to-be- missed spot for boaters, campers, fishing fans and picnickers.

From here, follow trail signs to Sackets Harbor, just 90 miles north, where many travelers stop at the Seaway Trail Discovery Center (at the corner of Ray and West Main streets) to map out their trip. From Sackets Harbor, take the trail left off Route 3 toward Cape Vincent, turn east and follow signs to Alexandria Bay, 60 miles. You'll discover an island oasis, Boldt Castle, a grandiose, six-story Rhineland fantasy. Millionaire George C. Boldt, proprietor of New York's Waldorf Astoria hotel, built it for his wife, who tragically died before the building was completed.

Niagara Falls

The trip end is in Massena, which is the eastern terminus of the Seaway Trail. **Contact:** Seaway Trail Discovery Center **800/732-9298.**

North Carolina/Virginia

Blue Ridge Parkway

For starters . . .
Set among the abandoned cabins and old cemeteries of Appalachian mountain families, this parkway earns its name by following the crest of the Blue Ridge Mountains. Once as tall as the Sierras, the weathered Appalachians are the world's oldest range. Time has also been a factor in the construction of the parkway: Planned by trained engineers and architects left unemployed by the Great Depression, the Blue Ridge Parkway was not completed until 1987.

DISTANCE	TIME	BEST SEASONS
469 miles	12 hours or several days.	June through October

The parkway's first 217 miles through Virginia, start at the southern end of

the Shenandoah National Park. Just 5.8 miles south from the park, Humpback Rocks offers a glimpse into the lives of Appalachian families. Access the 2,144-mile Appalachian Trail and a number of easy hiking paths at the Peaks of Otter, 80 miles further. Thirty-four miles south, a scenic 4-mile one-way road loops over Roanoke Mountain, affording stunning views of the city and valley. Stop at popular Mabry Mill for a picnic next to an early 1900s gristmill.

Cross into North Carolina near Cumberland Knob, a spot for strolls through fields and woodlands. Follow the winding curves of the parkway southeast 43 miles to Jumpinoff Rocks, where a short hike opens to a beautiful vista. Save film for the picturesque forest foothills at The Lump, 4 miles further. At Milepost 285.1, modern travelers meet up with the trail blazed by Daniel Boone.

Seven miles later, hikers will find 25 miles of carriage roads at the Moses H. Cone Memorial Park and more trails at Julian Price Memorial Park next door. But the highlight of any tour of the Blue Ridge Parkway is the Linn Cove Viaduct, a feat of engineering 6.4 miles south of the parks. The suspended viaduct—completed 52 years after the route's groundbreaking—skirts the perimeter of Grandfather Mountain (a designated biosphere, home to 47 rare or endangered species) with little disturbance to the area.

Meandering in the Blue Ridge Mtns

Save time for the sights near Asheville, including the traditional crafts of the Appalachian region at the Folk Art Center and the 250-room Biltmore Estate 4 miles off the parkway on NC 25 North. Enter the Pisgah National Forest, enjoying a scenic 42 miles to Waterrock Knob, where a 360-degree panorama of the trademark haze of the Great Smoky Mountains awaits. The parkway ends in the Great Smoky Mountain National Park as the road intersects with US 441.

Contact: Blue Ridge Parkway information line **828/298-0398.**

Ohio

Ohio River Scenic Route

For starters . . .
This trail promises both natural beauty and a history lesson on the early leaders, frontier spirit and industrial expansion of the young United States—all at the same gentle pace of the river below. The route traces the Civil War boundary between North and South, the dividing line between slavery and freedom. With every whim of the water, the road curves through 14 counties as it offers nearly continuous views of the waterway that helped build a nation.

DISTANCE	TIME	BEST SEASONS
462 miles	10 hours to 2 days	Spring and summer

From East Liverpool, take Ohio 7 south past Steubenville and its reconstructed Fort Steuben, a headquarters for 1700s exploration. Forty miles later in Tiltonsville, a Native American burial mound is just one of the 11,000 earthworks left behind by early inhabitants. Many of the 77 miles between Wheeling and the steamboat town of Marietta curl through the lush growth of the Wayne National Forest, home to covered bridges and a variety of wildlife.

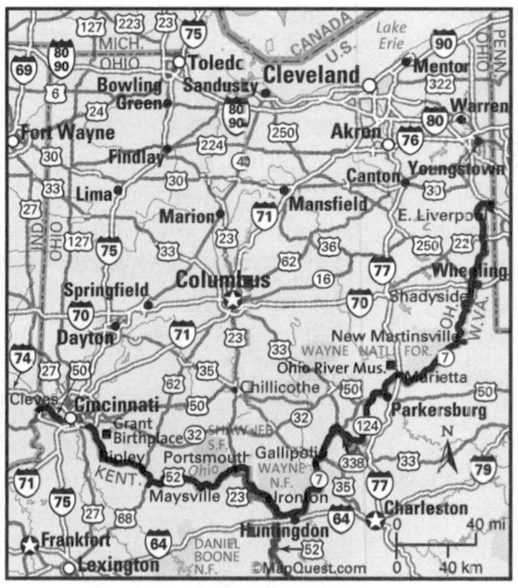

Take Ohio 124 at Little Hocking; 45 curvy miles south, the loop of 338 dips deep into West Virginia and back to124, then north on 33 back to 7—which leads 19 miles later to the architecture of Gallipolis, inspired by the town's French settlement history. At the state's southernmost tip, the path takes up with U.S. 52, while the scenery across the river turns to Kentucky bluegrass. Follow the road through 42 miles of rolling hills to Portsmouth, where a single artist has created 53 murals on the river flood wall, or continue for another 46 miles to Rankin House in Ripley. The1800s residence sheltered 2,000 slaves in their bid for freedom on the Underground Railroad.

The last segment of the trail traces the footsteps of leaders. The birthplace of Ulysses S. Grant in Point Pleasant is a three-room cottage once exhibited around the country on a railroad flat car. Cincinnati offers the Harriet Beecher Stowe House (Exit 3 north on U.S. 71), where the author wrote her anti-slavery classic *Uncle Tom's Cabin*, and the boyhood home of 27th U.S. President William Howard Taft (Exit 28 north on U.S. 75). Just six miles before this

Ohio River

journey ends at the state border, one last Executive Branch monument beckons. The 60-foot obelisk in North Bend is William Henry Harrison Tomb, a memorial to the ninth President—who caught pneumonia at his own inauguration and died after serving only a month of his term.

Contact: Ohio Department of Travel and Tourism **800/282-5393.**

Oregon

Hells Canyon Scenic Byway

For starters . . .
The region encircled by this byway has seen its share of travelers. More than 300,000 pioneers passed this way on the Oregon Trail, and ranching, timber production and gold have drawn more generations. But the real goldmine of this area is its namesake, Hells Canyon. Carved over a million years by the Snake River, the canyon goes as deep as 8,000 feet in places, making it the deepest river gorge in North America— and the reason modern travelers come calling.

DISTANCE	TIME	BEST SEASONS
218 miles	8 hours	May to October

Start in Baker City, driving east on OR 86 until I-84, where the National Historic Oregon Trail Interpretive Center explains the importance of the area in the settlement of the northwest; a short walk from the center, look for the still-visible wagon wheel ruts of trail riders.

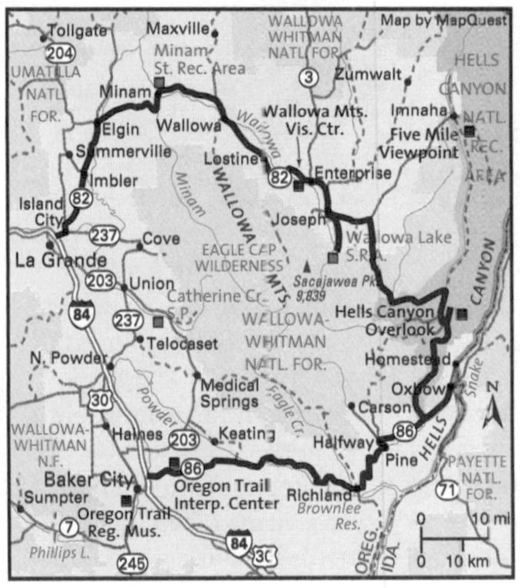

Continue 15 miles on OR 86 to an overlook at the site of Hole-in-the-Wall Landslide, which now covers the original road. Thirty miles east of the Slide, a visit to Copperfield gets you close to the master carver of the Hells Canyon Gorge, the Snake River. Go back to the junction of 86 and Forest

Thistles along the Snake River

Road 39 and take that road 16 miles north. Look for Forest Road 3965 and follow the signs to the east to the Hells Canyon overlook. From a perch on the 5,400-foot high canyon rim, visitors are treated to sweeping vistas of the rugged Seven Devils Mountain Range.

Return to 39 and into the Wallowa Whitman National Forest and the wilderness area surrounding Eagle Cap, elevation 9,595 feet. To the northwest, the snow-capped Wallowa Mountains, some of the oldest and most dramatic peaks in the region, were the inspiration for the area's nickname, Little Switzerland. Turn west onto OR 82 toward Joseph; one mile out of town, Wallowa Lake offers yurt camping rentals and a tram to the top of Mt. Howard. Back on the trail, the Wallowa River (named for the Nez Perce word for the tripod used to support fishing nets) offers opportunities for anglers.

Follow OR 82 as the road loops around the mountains to La Grande, a popular rest stop during the days of the Oregon Trail. To finish the trip, look for the Ladd Marsh Wildlife Preserve just south of the city off I-84. One of the largest wetlands in the region, the refuge offers superb viewing of 116 species of birds and other wildlife.

Contact: Eastern Oregon Visitor Association **800/523-1235.**

NC 242
VA 247
NC 138
VA 168
OH 144
OR 148

OR 244
OR 148

Oregon — Historic Columbia River Highway

DISTANCE	TIME	BEST SEASON
70 miles	3 to 5 hours	Spring/Summer

For starters . . . Steep gorges, dramatic views, 56 hiking trails and the largest aggregation of waterfalls outside of Yosemite make this drive one of the most scenic in the US. The highway itself has been designated both a National Historic Landmark and a National Historic Civil Engineering Landmark, so you'll literally be driving on history. Go in the spring and early summer when the waterfalls and rivers are fullest.

Start in Troutdale, accessing the highway from I-84, and head east. For the entire drive, follow the brown signs for the Historic Columbia River Highway because the drive switches among several main roads. The first major scenic vista pops up just east of Corbett: the Portland Women's Forum State Scenic Viewpoint, offering magnificent views of Crown Point, Vista House and the 4,000-foot deep Columbia River Gorge.

Over the next few miles you'll encounter many of the waterfalls that make this drive so special—Latoureel, Sheppard's Dell, Wahkeena and Bridal Veil—as well as the most-visited natural attraction in Oregon: Multnomah Falls, its name referring to the Chinookan Native American tribe who inhabited the region. For a closer look at this 650-foot double cascade, hike up the Benson Bridge.

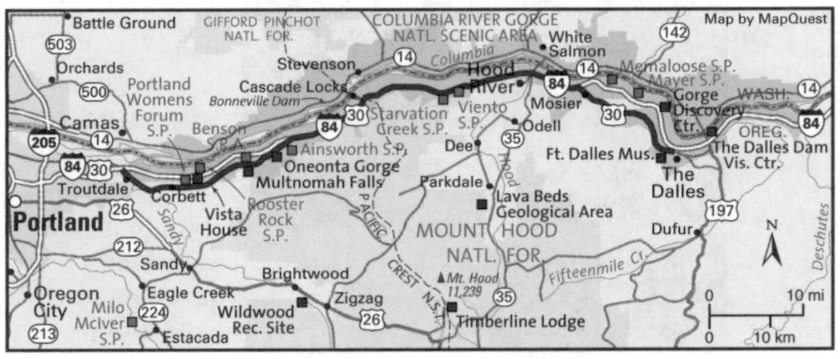

At mile 20 is Oneonta Gorge, a good hiking spot. Eleven miles later, you'll reach the Bride of the Gods at Cascade Locks, which links Oregon to Washington. Besides waterfalls, other natural attractions abound on the highway: rainforests, wildflowers and rare plant species, bald eagles, peregrine falcons and salmon.

Mile 51 brings you to Hood River, the windsurfing capitol of the world. Here you can watch the windsurfers from the many overlooks or hike the stretch between Hood River and Mosier that has been converted to a state trail. Evidence of the original highway is visible, which was part of the Oregon Trail and the last leg of the Lewis and Clark Expedition. When the existing highway was designed in 1913, it was considered one of the greatest engineering feats of the modern age.

Between Rowena and the highway's end at the Dalles you'll experience some of this remarkable engineering by navigating hairpin turns and switchback loops. For a last stop, consider the Gorge Discovery Center and Wasco County Museum, which offer exhibits on the human and natural history of the area. **Contact:** Oregon District 2C, **503/665-4514**.

Columbia River Gorge

OR 244
OR 148

Oregon — Pacific Coast Scenic Byway

DISTANCE	TIME	BEST SEASONS
350 miles	10 to 12 hours	Spring to fall

For starters . . . From the rocky viewpoints of exposed seaside cliffs to graceful, majestic sand dunes and from the famous Tillamook cheese dairy pastures to a forest of giant redwoods, this diverse stretch of the Pacific Coast is America at its most striking. Millions of settlers and tourists have made the trip since Lewis and Clark acclaimed the merits of this territory. And Oregon's dedication to preservation means that tourists today can take in many of the same wondrous views the expedition did.

The Oregon portion of this byway on US 101 starts in Astoria, the oldest American settlement west of the Rockies, where the Astoria-Megler Bridge spans the gaping mouth of the Columbia River. This is the wild northwest territory explored by Lewis and Clark. The Lewis and Clark Salt Cairn 20 miles south in Seaside commemorates the spot where the expedition made salt from seawater.

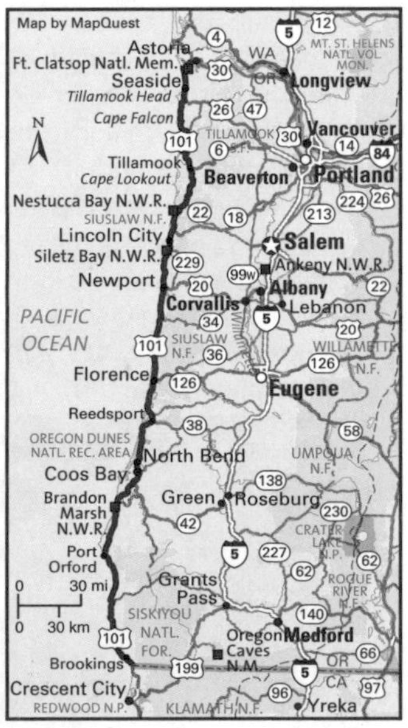

Don't be so dazzled by the Siuslaw National Forest over your shoulder and the sparkling ocean to the west that you forget to stop for the churning waves of the Devil's Punch Bowl just south of Depoe Bay. Take a whale-watching cruise from the bay in Newport at Milepost 141 or continue one mile south to Yaquina Bay to one of many historic lighthouses along the highway. Just a short distance away are the Hatfield Marine Science Center and the Oregon Coast Aquarium, great places to see, and even touch, some marine life.

At Cape Perpetua Viewpoint 25 miles further south, take the climbing road of US 101 to a vista of the coastal expanse so good that the spot served as a lookout for enemy invasions during World War II. Get a look at the lighthouse keeper's life 11 miles further along the trail at Heceta Head Lighthouse Scenic Viewpoint. A short walk through this little cove leads to the keeper's home and the lighthouse itself. The largest sea caves in the world and the only remaining mainland home of wild Stellar sea lions are one mile south.

The next 40 miles in the Oregon Dunes National Recreation Area offer hiking trails and other activities among the towering, shifting sand dunes. Pass the Umpqua Lighthouse, and at Cape Blanco, 79 miles further down the coast, a short drive out to the ocean places you at the westernmost point in Oregon. This byway ends in redwood country at the California state line near Brookings. **Contact:** Oregon Coast Visitors Association **888/628-2101.**

Pacific Coast foliage and flora

SC 245
SC 156

South Carolina — Ashley River Road

DISTANCE	TIME	BEST SEASON
11 miles	.5 hour to 2 days	Spring

For starters . . . You can travel the Ashley River Road in less than an hour, but why would you want to? Driving it is like immersing yourself in a snapshot of South Carolina history, and the more time you spend, the more you learn about this quixotic state. Along the road you'll not only pass three historic landmarks—Old St. Andrews Church, Drayton Hall and Middleton Place—but a National Register Historic District that traces the history of European and African settlement, commerce and industry from our country's infancy to the present.

One of the first scenic automobile touring routes in America and a key connection for the settlement and commercial development of South Carolina, the Ashley River Road Scenic Byway starts just outside of historic Charleston and follows the Ashley River north along State Highway 61. The road, built along former Native American paths, was funded by the area's rice plantation owners and built by slave labor.

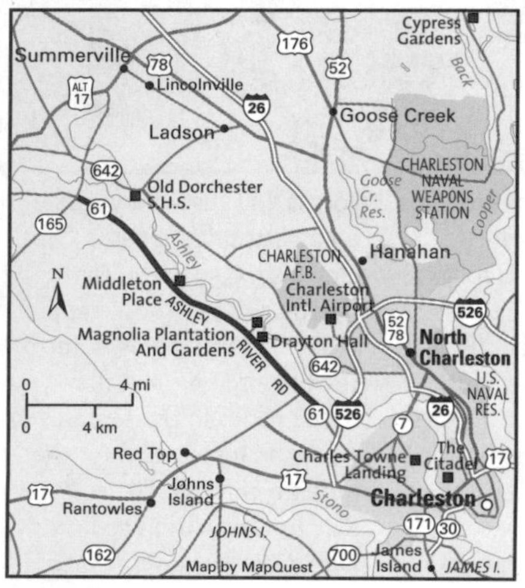

Begin at milepost 5.84 at Church Creek. The ancient oak trees and hanging Spanish moss lining the road create an atmosphere of a bygone Southern era. In about 3 miles you'll reach the first of three plantations open to the public: Drayton Hall, on the east side of the road. The only pre-Revolutionary plantation still standing in the area, it is also one of the finest surviving examples of Georgian Palladian architecture in the South.

Drayton Hall

As you cross Bee's Ferry, you'll encounter Fort Bull Confederate Earthworks, a civil war defense constructed in 1863. In less than a mile you'll reach Magnolia Gardens, a restored plantation with gardens showcasing indigenous trees and flowers. By milepost 12, you'll arrive at Middleton Place, another exquisitely preserved 18th century plantation featuring America's oldest landscaped gardens. Touring all three will give you a sense of how the plantation business, fueled by African slavery, shaped this region.

North of the plantation district are two historic churches. Old Saint Andrews Church, built in 1706, is the oldest surviving church in the Carolinas. The tombstones in the adjoining churchyard name the region's first colonial settlers. End your drive at Springfield Baptist Church. Established in 1863 as one of the first freely organized Black Baptist congregations, it played an important role in the transition from slavery to freedom. **Contact:** Charleston Visitor Reception Center **843/853-8000.**

South Dakota

Peter Norbeck Scenic Byway

DISTANCE	TIME	BEST SEASONS
68 miles	1 day	Spring through fall

For starters . . . Most visitors who take this drive come for Mt. Rushmore and stay for the scenery. While the monument is a stunning artistic and engineering achievement, it's often dwarfed by its surroundings: granite spires, Ponderosa pines, spectacular vistas. The byway is named for the conservationist and legislator who first envisioned it as a way of making the extraordinary beauty of the Black Hills accessible. Note: Due to the rock tunnels, spiral "pigtail" bridges and steep grades, campers and RVs are discouraged. Fees for Mt. Rushmore and Custer State Park.

Start in Custer and drive east on 16A. At Highway 87, also known as Needles Highway, proceed north. Not only will you travel through rock tunnels and canyons, but as you climb, you'll enter the Ponderosa pine ecosystem.

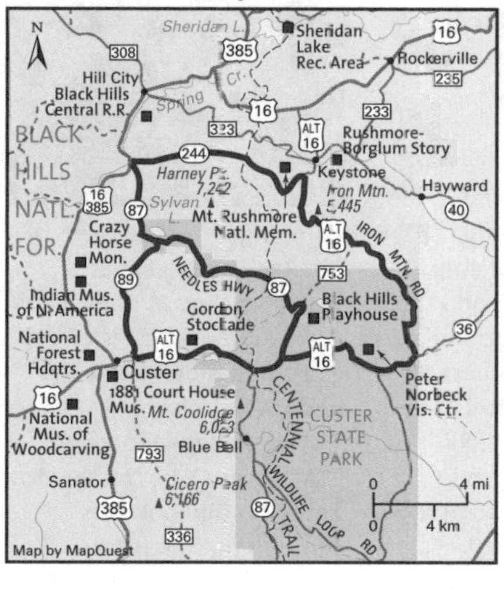

Upon cresting the rise, Cathedral Spires—the granite needles typical of the Black Hills—jut in the near distance. Here there are several good, short hiking trails. After exiting the longest rock tunnel on the route, you'll then see the Needle's Eye. For best views, pull into the parking area.

Continuing west on 87, you'll reach Sylvan Lake, a recreation and picnic spot. One of the hiking trails here takes you to Harney Peak, the tallest east of the Rockies. Pass the junction with 89, continuing until you reach Highway 16/385. Turn right. In 200 yards, turn right again onto 244 East.

At Horsethief Lake, 6 miles down the road, is a short handicapped-accessible boardwalk trail. In another mile, Breezy Point picnic grounds offers one of the most spectacular panoramic views on the drive.

As you approach Mt Rushmore, stop at the Washington Profile overlook and look behind you to see our first president's profile. In 1/4 mile you'll reach the monument itself. For best views, follow the President's Trail to the base of the monument. Don't overlook the two nearby museums either—one is a hands-on museum for kids, the other is in the carvers' workshop and displays the original models for the monument.

Mount Rushmore

When highway 16A becomes Iron Mountain Road, be sure to go the posted speed limit. Between the pigtail bridges, switchbacks and single-lane tunnels every precaution is necessary. On this section of the drive, however, you can see just how well the road blends with—and respects—its natural surroundings. The Peter Norbeck Visitor's Center, 3 miles past the 36 junction, provides more detail on this achievement.

The drive's final leg passes through Custer State Park, where you might see buffalo, wild donkeys, bighorn sheep and deer, before returning to Custer.

Contact: Black Hills National Forest 605/673-9200.

SD 245
SD 157

Tennessee/ North Carolina

Cherohala Skyway

DISTANCE	TIME	BEST SEASON
51 miles	1.5 to 2 hrs	Fall

For starters . . . Cherohala Skyway winds along dense virgin forest, spectacular 4,000-foot scenic overlooks, pounding waterfalls and shimmering lakes. This former Cherokee Indian trading route southwest of the Great Smoky Mountains reaches—quite literally—above the clouds allowing for front-row seats for glorious sunsets from dramatic, mile-high ridges. There are no gas stations, restrooms or water spigots along this rather primitive wilderness drive and few passing zones, so stock up on rations before you leave Tellico Plains.

Traversing two national forests — the Cherokee and the Nantahala (where the skyway got its name) — and two states (Tennessee and North Carolina) this skyway is rich with relatively untouched natural beauty framed by gentle elevation changes. Most travelers start on Tennessee 165 in the town of Tellico Plains where the Tellico River parallels the Appalachian Trail at an elevation of 1,000 feet. At five miles, look for signs for the area's most majestic waterfalls, Bald River Falls and head southeast about seven miles on Forest Service Road 210 where you can view the falls from your car. Back onto TN 165, heading east, you'll want to stop at Indian Boundary Lake and Campground, located just 16.5 miles off the skyway on Forest Service Road 345. The area offers a great spot for a picnic lunch or overnight campout. Just 10 miles later, you'll reach Beech Gap, the state line and highest point on the Tennessee side of the skyway at 4,490 feet. (Unicoi Crest, just under a mile later on the NC side, has the best overlook.) Across the state line, TN 165 becomes NC 143 and the drive reaches its highest height of 5,390 feet at Santeelah in North Carolina where you can picnic as you take in the mile-high overlook. The drive officially ends at Santeelah Gap in Graham County, 12 miles from Robbinsville, NC. It's two miles north on NC 1127 to the state's most impressive timber forest, Joyce Kilmer National Forest. One hundred-foot-high and 20-foot-wide trees remain here as one of the few tracts of virgin hardwood left in the Appalachians. Visitors can walk a well-marked, two-mile loop for a view of these towering beauties, along a carpet of wildflowers, ferns and enormous moss-covered logs.

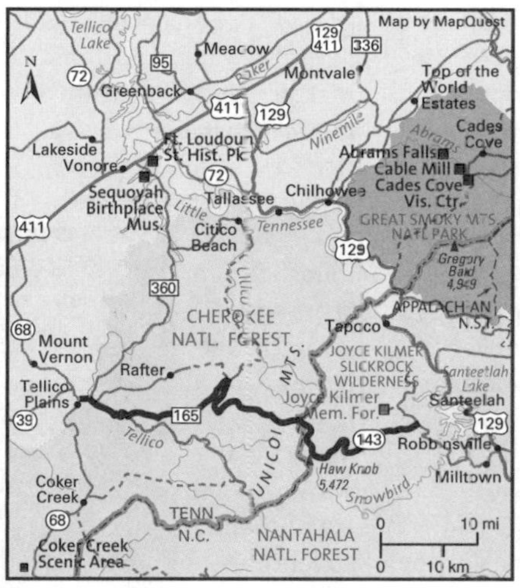

Contact: Monroe County (Tennessee) Tourism Department 800/245-5428.

Unicoi Mountains

NC 138
TN 158

Utah

Flaming Gorge-Uintas Scenic Byway

DISTANCE	TIME	BEST SEASON
82 miles	3 hours	Year-round

For starters . . . The corner of Utah covered by this byway has had a number of influences: Butch Cassidy and other outlaws galloped through, and followers of the Mormon Church settled the area. But this region also honors its Jurassic inhabitants, the dinosaurs—and before that, the elements that laid down this land a billion years ago. Travel this road for a taste of the real west, a walk in the footprints of extinct giants and a glimpse of true geologic power.

Begin this tour with a visit to the Utah Field House of Natural History and Dinosaur Gardens in Vernal to walk among life-sized models of the wooly mammoth, the T-rex, and others. For a short side trip on the same theme, visit Dinosaur National Monument. The largest Jurassic period fossil bone quarry in the world is just 20 miles east of Vernal.

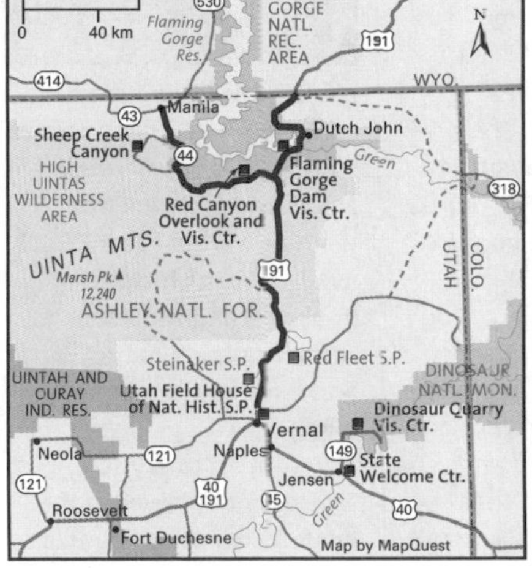

Travel US 191 north from Vernal 9 miles to Steinaker Lake State Park for water activities in a reservoir among petrified sandstone dunes. Or just a mile north, pull off at Red Fleet State Park to see the red Navajo sandstone "ships" protruding from the water. Red Fleet is also the home of a set of dinosaur tracks more than 200 million years old. From here, the road rises into the Ashley National Forest, growing lush green aspen and pine, perfectly suited for modern wildlife. To the west are the Uinta Mountains, the only major east west range in the country. Kings Peak, at 13,528 feet, is the highest point in Utah. Look for the strata that illustrate how the land has shifted over time.

Thirty-five miles north of Vernal, the trail takes two directions. Continue northeast on US 191 through the Flaming Gorge National Recreation Area to Flaming Gorge Dam on the Green River. This route passes near the town of Dutch John and ends at the Wyoming state line with a fantastic view of the rugged red cliffs of Flaming Gorge.

Flaming Gorge Reservoir in Red Canyon at sunset

The second route curls around the western edge of the same crimson cliffs on UT 44. Turn off 4 miles later to view Flaming Gorge and the Green River 1,500 feet below from Red Canyon Overlook. Another vista 14 miles later illustrates the geologic trauma the area was put through 2.5 billion years ago. The route ends at the town of Manila.

Contact: Dinosaurland Travel Board 800/477-5558.

UT 165

WA 247
WA 170

Washington

Chinook Scenic Byway

DISTANCE	TIME	BEST SEASONS
85 miles	2 hours	Late May to late October

For starters . . .
The 53-mile route through Mt. Rainier State Park and the surrounding forestland was designated as Mather Memorial Parkway in 1931 to honor preservationist and park service director, Stephen Mather. This road from Enumclaw to Naches had long been known to locals as Chinook Scenic Byway. Both names are still used today, fittingly, because it has two distinct atmospheric personalities: the east side of Chinook Pass is in the arid rain shadow of Mt. Rainier, the west side is considerably wetter and greener.

State Route 410 takes you through pristine territory where it is still possible to breathe in the piney scent of 1,000-year-old trees, hear the rush of restless river waters, and glimpse the country's largest single-peak glacier system outside of Alaska.

The drive begins in Enumclaw,18 miles due east of Tacoma on WA-164. Heading east along WA-410, you'll pass the White River and Federation Forest State Park; then you will arrive at the spectacular Mt. Rainier Scenic Viewpoint, located after Forest Service 70/Crystal Village (before the Dalles Campground.)

Skookum Flats Trail is at mile 24. On this 12-mile path, visitors will see the White River, small falls, yellow violets, trilliums, salmonberry and vanilla leaf (in spring), and a tangle of fallen trees. You can also venture across a wavering suspension bridge. Stay on the marked trails; park officials take Mather's preservationist vision seriously and won't hesitate to cite visitors for posing a potential threat to the environment.

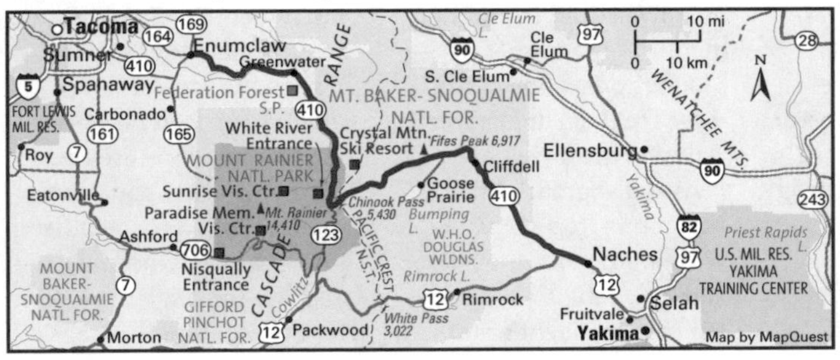

Your next stop is Tipsoo Lake and the Naches Loop Trail, 12 miles southeast off WA-410, within Mt. Rainier State Park. This is a 3.5 mile paved trail with a gentle elevation of 500 feet. Catch the stunning reflective views of Mt. Rainier, considered a young volcano at one million years old. (The trail is wheelchair accessible but no bikes or dogs are allowed.)

Yakima Peak

At the 40 mile mark on WA-410 you'll be crossing the beautiful Chinook Pass through the 5,430-foot Cascade Mountains. Since this area is known as the "snowiest place on earth," the pass is closed in wintertime.

Thirty miles east of the pass along WA-410 is Boulder Cave Nature Trail—a natural stone tunnel and home of the rare Pacific Western Big-Eared Bat. Bring a flashlight, good walking shoes, and a water bottle (as there is no drinking water available on the trail).

From here it is 55 miles to the route's end in Naches. The forest opens up to scrub-brush country, unique basaltic formations and grasslands.

Contact: Yakima Valley Visitor & Convention Center **800/221-0751.**

WA 247
WA 170

Washington

Strait of Juan de Fuca Highway

DISTANCE	TIME	BEST SEASONS
61 miles	2 to 8 hours	Spring and fall

For starters . . .
This remote scenic byway through Washington's Olympic Peninsula, originally built to connect logging camps, combines the wonders of nature with great recreation opportunities. Watch whales and sea otters as you kayak; see glacial fjords and snowcapped mountains as you hike and bike; gape at eagles diving for fish as you meander along the shoreline. Or, simply take in the majestic scenery as you drive through deep forests, coastal cliffs and isolated beaches along the Strait of Juan de Fuca.

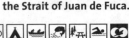

Start about five miles west of Port Angeles heading west along State Road 112 just north of Olympic National Park, internationally recognized for its magnificent old growth forests. The road follows the rugged coastline of the Strait of Juan de Fuca—the glacial fjord that connects Puget Sound to the Pacific Ocean—fairly closely, sometimes with cliffside views, sometimes at sea level. Note that this is a working road, so you'll be sharing it with logging trucks. Take advantage of the safety turnouts provided for slower-moving tourist cars.

In 10 miles you'll reach Joyce, which offers an historical museum, as well as access to Crescent Bay. Six more miles brings you to Lyre River, a campsite with beach and river access.

A popular halfway point is the Merrill and Ring Tree Farm at Pysht, a former logging camp, that features a self-guided tour on resource management, the logging industry and reforestation. Just 11 miles further is Clallam Bay County Park, an ideal picnic ground set on a saltwater beach. On clear days, expect excellent views of Vancouver Island and Sekui Point.

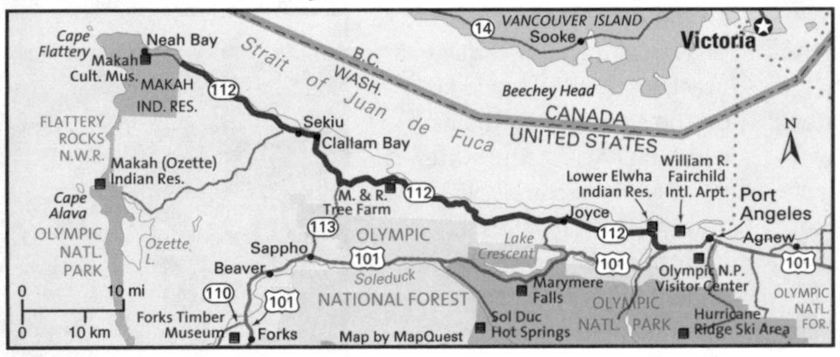

From Sekiu onward, the road travels alongside the water, providing beach access, plenty of hiking trails and world-class salmon and halibut fishing. At the end of the byway, be sure to stop at Sail and Seal Rock, a popular feeding ground for gray whales and otters. You may also want to visit the Makah Cultural Museum on the Makah Indian Reservation to view artifacts of a Native American village covered in a mudslide 500 years ago. Although the byway ends here, for many it's a starting point for further adventures: hiking the Cape Flattery Trail to the most northwest point of the continental US or traveling 21 miles south to Lake Ozette for camping, canoeing, kayaking, sailing or hiking along its famous cedar boardwalk.

Contact: North Olympic Peninsula Visitor and Convention Bureau **800/942-4042.**

Olympic Peninsula

WV 248
WV 173

West Virginia

Highland Scenic Highway

DISTANCE	TIME	BEST SEASONS
43 miles	2 to 4 hours	Summer and fall

For starters . . .
This corridor through West Virginia's Monongahela National Forest, with its clear mountain streams, steep 4,500-foot valleys, sandstone rock formations, and 750 acres of spongy wetlands, is a camping, backpacking, fishing and tree watching paradise. Because of its isolated location, the region has relatively undeveloped natural resources. Back in Civil War days, Americans sought safety here and the area remains an untouched portrait of southeastern wilderness.

This lush West Virginia highway—WV 39/55—climbs slowly east from Richwood to Marlinton through wild cherry and spruce forests and mountainous terrain. Only a few dwellings dot the road and a 45-to 55-mph speed limit is enforced.

From Richwood, take the WV 39/55 twelve miles to the Falls of Hills Creek Scenic Area, right off of the highway. Waterfalls up to 63 feet spill over shale and sandstone rock layers. A paved, three-quarter mile, barrier-free trail allows close access to the falls along a carpet of wildflowers, and is wheelchair accessible. Be prepared, however: The largest falls, the second highest in the state, are located 365 steps down from the trail.

Ten miles east of WV 39/55, where WV 150 intersects, travelers enter the Cranberry Glades Botanical Area, which offers excellent mountain picnic spots, boardwalk views of the largest sprawling area of springy wetlands in the state, and botanical rarities such as carnivorous plants and bog orchids. One mile north is the Cranberry Mountain Nature Center where visitors can take a tour around an exhibit hall that highlights the area's unique history, geology and vegetation.

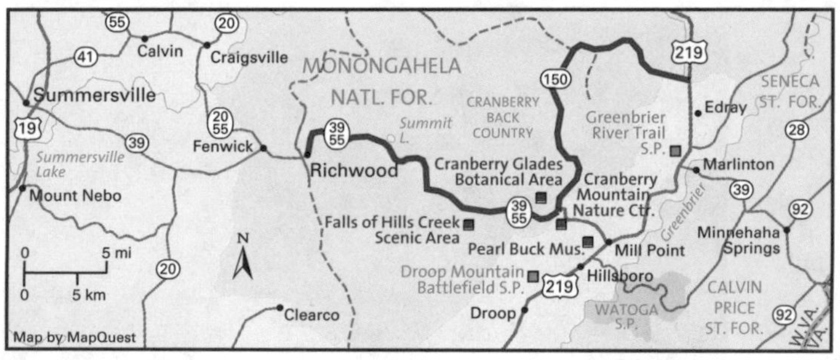

Germany Valley

Hillsboro, WV, just 10 miles south on US 219, is where Nobel and Pulitzer Prize winning author Pearl S. Buck lived. Her 1892 historic house-turned-museum contains period rooms, crafts, and Buck family memorabilia.

Returning to WV 150, which is not plowed in the wintertime, travel 10 miles north to the Williams River, a favorite spot in April and May for trout (rainbow and brook) and bass fishing. One mile north, on Forest Road 86 (also known as Williams River Road) is Tea Creek Campground, a 29-unit site open year round (though not during high water season). Fifteen trailheads ranging in distance from .5 mile to 7 miles begin here.

Contact: Gauley Ranger District **304/846-2695.**

West Virginia

Washington Heritage Trail

For starters . . .
At the time the towns along this trail were being built, the area was still part of Virginia. Now the Eastern Panhandle of West Virginia, the area comprises picturesque towns that George Washington helped survey. Rising over ridges, dipping into lush valleys and running by the rivers and springs that drew Washington and other early settlers to the area, this route is packed with history: an amazing 21 National Register Historic Districts and 126 National Register Sites are located nearby.

DISTANCE	TIME	BEST SEASONS
137 miles	6 to 8 hours	Spring and fall

Start this drive in Berkeley Springs, which was known as the Town of Bath in Washington's day because of its constant 74-degree spring waters. Visit the future leader's favorite spot to relax—his tub—in the Berkeley Springs State Park before heading east on WV 9 through unspoiled country-side toward the Potomac River.

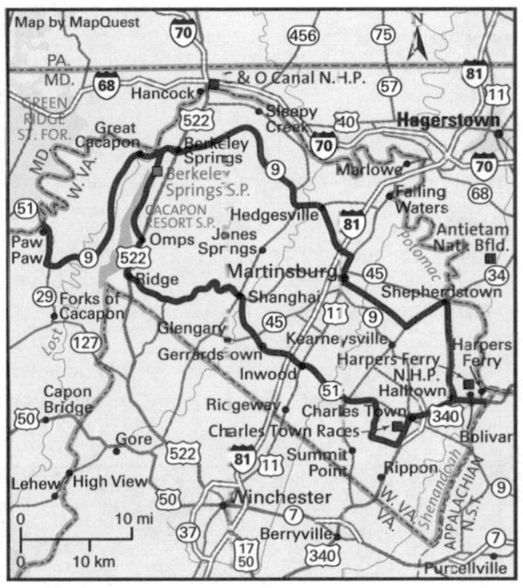

In Martinsburg, connect with WV 45 east toward Shepherdstown, one of the state's oldest towns; here, take WV 230 south. At Halltown, 8.5 miles later, take U.S. 340 east 4 miles to Harpers Ferry. Here in 1859, zealous abolitionist John Brown seized the Federal Armory, fighting (and losing) the first battle over slavery. The armory is now John Brown's Fort; the courthouse and jail where he was convicted of treason still stand. The narrow, hilly streets and the banks where the Potomac and Shenandoah rivers meet remain much the way they looked in the 1800s.

The Washington Heritage Trail

Take 340 west 7 miles to Charles Town. Washington's brother Charles owned this land and planned the town, naming streets after family members (you can visit the corner of George and Washington, for instance). Visit the Zion Episcopal Church cemetery to find many Washington headstones, including at least three later George Washingtons. Many former homes of the family remain: South of Charles Town on CR 13/3, visit Claymont Court, the only Washington home open to the public. West of the town and visible from WV 51 is Harewood, still the private residence of Washington descendants.

The trail crests the ridges of the Appalachians along marked county roads to Ridge; here, take U.S. 522 to return to 9, then take 9 southwest past vistas of the mountain waters of the Cacapon River to the Paw Paw tunnel. The tunnel, 25 miles off the rest of the looped drive, is a feat of engineering worth seeing. It took 14 years to dig by hand and was constructed with 6 million bricks.

Contact: Washington Heritage Trail **800/498-2386.**

Wisconsin

Great River Road

For starters . . .
Melted glaciers from the Ice Age carved this river valley flanking the best-known river in the United States on one side and tall limestone bluffs on the other. Two hundred and fifty miles of leisurely road offers paddle wheeler riverboat rides, picturesque river walks, a car ferry, and an overhead view of working dams and barges. Thirty-one historic river towns reveal the area's cultural influences and riverside parks provide a full range of range of recreational options.

DISTANCE	TIME	BEST SEASONS
249 miles	10 hours	All, but summer is busiest.

Prescott, Wisconsin is the northern gateway to the Great River Road, located at the junction of the Mississippi and St. Croix rivers. Highway 35 takes visitors through the state's western edge as it parallels the Mississippi River.

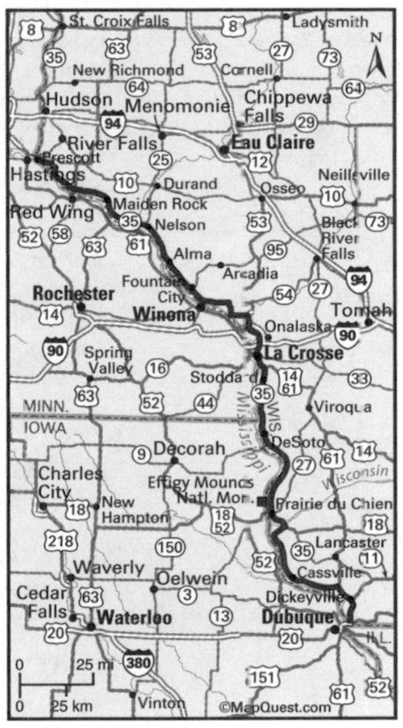

Thirty-five miles south of Prescott is the town of Pepin, worth a stop for a look at Midwest life at the turn of the century, and for a glimpse at the reconstructed cabin home of Laura Ingalls Wilder, author of Little House on the Prairie.

Ten miles later is the town of Alma: Seven miles long and two streets wide, this tiny town is a Swiss settlement nestled in a narrow corridor between the river and 500-foot bluffs. The city's Buena Vista Park provides a panoramic view of the town, its locks and dams, and the valley.

Continuing 60 miles south, Highway 35 turns into Highway 53 which will take you through downtown La Crosse. Hop aboard the popular grand-style river paddle wheeler "La Crosse River Queen" at Riverside Park on Veterans Memorial Drive at the convention and visitor's bureau. There you can also take your bike (or rent from area providers) and ride the La Crosse River Bike Trail—part of the 217 miles of trails found along the road.

At the southern section of the road, 50 miles south of La Crosse, the Wisconsin River

Highway 35 scenery

joins the Mississippi at Wyalusing State Park. This beautiful park boasts great boating and fishing and a chance to see across the river to Iowa. Thirty miles from the state park, look for signs for the car ferry to Iowa in Cassville, formerly a center for steamboat traffic, off Route 133.

There are many entry points to this scenic slice of the Midwest—all allowing for a selection of driving itineraries without covering the same stretch twice.

Contact: LaCrosse Area Convention and Visitor Bureau **800/658-9480.**

Wyoming/Montana

Beartooth Scenic Byway

For starters . . .
When a road's been called the most scenic drive in America by the late "On the Road" correspondent Charles Kuralt, it had better be spectacular. Beartooth doesn't disappoint. From Yellowstone Park to Red Lodge, Montana, this highway travels through three National Forests and past snow-capped peaks, alpine meadows, ice-age crests, and sparkling white-water rivers. This, however, can be a challenging road to drive. For safety, travel east to west in the morning and west to east in the afternoon to cut down on sun glare.

DISTANCE	TIME	BEST SEASON
68.7 miles	3 hours	Summer

One of the wonders of this drive is that it whisks you from lush forests to alpine tundra in a matter of miles. The drive begins at the Northeast Entrance of Yellowstone National Park on Highway 212 heading east. In 7 miles you reach Colter Pass, elevation 8,000 feet, before crossing from Montana into Wyoming.

Take advantage of the scenic overlooks along the drive. Clarks Fork Overlook, for example, offers a vista of the Clarks Fork River. Here you can also see the aftermath of 1988 fires that devastated nearly 400,000 acres. Waterfall lovers will want to pull off at Crazy Creek Cascade, mile 9, for a picnic or an overnight stop. It is one of 12 National Forest campgrounds along the route.

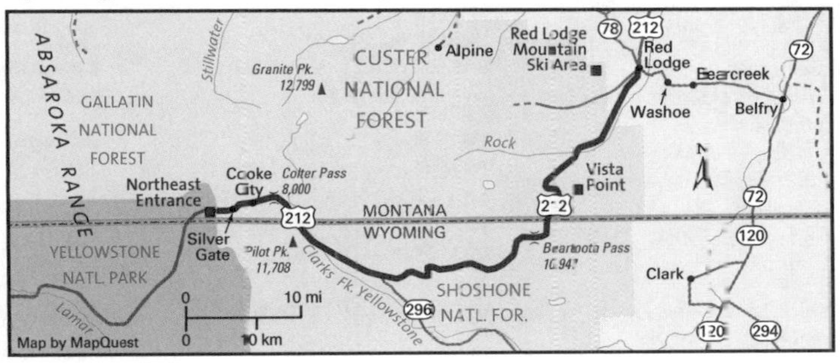

Clay Butte Lookout, mile 33, has panoramic vistas of the Beartooth plateau, where fossils dating back 500 million years have been found, and the Absaroka-Beartooth mountain ranges, which have some of the highest elevations and most rugged terrain in the lower 48 states.

A must-see is the East Summit Overlook, 5 to 6 miles from Beartooth Lake, which offers stunning views of the Bear's Tooth, the glacial spire that gave this road its name. At the Gardner Lake Overlook, mile 44, you can see how glaciers formed the surrounding basins and lakes.

Before going back into Montana, you'll reach Beartooth Pass and cross over the road's highest summit—10,971 feet—where a turnout gives a panoramic view of the area's dramatic landscape. For the curious, Rock Creek Vista Point, mile 52, has a visitors' center with information about the history of the road and the surrounding flora and fauna. The drive ends at Red Lodge, a popular retreat on area where you can ride horses, ski, hike, fish or simply soak up the region's natural beauty.

Contact: Red Lodge Area Chamber of Commerce and Visitor's Center **406/446-1718.**

Beartooth Highway

WV 248
WV 173
WI 174
WY 176
MT 122

UNITED STATES

Alabama
Alabama Bureau of
Tourism & Travel
401 Adams Ave., P.O. Box 4927
Montgomery, AL 36103
800.252.2262, 334.242.4169
www.touralabama.org

Alaska
Alaska Div. of Tourism
P.O. Box 110801
Juneau, AK 99811
907.465.2010
www.state.ak.us/local/akpages/
COMMERCE/tour.htm

Arizona
Arizona Office of Tourism
2702 N. Third St., Ste. 4015
Phoenix, AZ 85004
800.842.8257, 602.230.7733
www.arizonaguide.com

Arkansas
Arkansas Dept. of Parks & Tourism
One Capitol Mall
Little Rock, AR 72201
800.628.8725, 501.682.7777
www.18oonatural.com

California
California Div. of Tourism
P.O. Box 1499
Sacramento, CA 95812
800.862.2543, 916.322.2881
www.gocalif.ca.gov

Colorado
Colorado Travel &
Tourism Authority
707 17th St., Ste. 3500
Denver, CO 80202
800.265.6723, 303.296.3384
www.state.co.us/visit_dir/
visitormenu.html

Connecticut
Connecticut Office of Tourism
505 Hudson St.
Hartford, CT 06106
800.282.6863, 860.270.8080
www.state.ct.us/tourism

Delaware
Delaware Tourism Office
99 Kings Highway
Dover, DE 19901
800.441.8846, 302.739.4271
www.state.de.us/tourism/intro.htm

Florida
Florida Tourism Industry
Marketing Corporation
P.O. Box 1100
Tallahassee, FL 32302
888.735.2872, 850.488.5607
www.flausa.com

Georgia
Georgia Dept. of Industry,
Trade & Tourism
P.O. Box 1776
Atlanta, GA 30301
800.847.4842, 404.656.3590
www.itt.state.ga.us

Hawaii
Hawaii Visitors &
Convention Bureau
2270 Kalakaua Ave., Ste. 801
Honolulu, HI 96815
800.464.2924, 808.923.1181
www.visithawaii.com

Idaho
Idaho Dept. of Commerce
Box 83720
Boise, ID 83720
800.847.4843, 208.334.2470
www.idoc.state.id.us

Illinois
Illinois Bureau of Tourism
100 W. Randolph St., Ste. 3-400
Chicago, IL 60601
800.226.6632, 312.814.4732
www.enjoyillinois.com

Indiana
Indiana Tourism
1 N. Capitol Ave.
Indianapolis, IN 46024
800.759.9191
www.state.in.us/tourism/index.html

Iowa
Iowa Div. of Tourism
200 E. Grand Ave.
Des Moines, IA 50309
800.345.4692, 515.242.4705
www.state.ia.us/tourism/index.html

Kansas
Kansas Travel & Tourism
Development Div.
700 S.W. Harrison, Ste. 1300
Topeka, KS 66603
800.252.6727, 785.296.2009
www.kansascommerce.com

Kentucky
Kentucky Dept. of Travel
Capital Plaza Tower
500 Mero St., Ste. 22
Frankfort, KY 40601
800.225.8747
www.state.ky.us/tour/tour.htm

Louisiana
Louisiana Office of Tourism
P.O. Box 94291
Baton Rouge, LA 70804
800.695.4064, 504.342.8100
www.louisianatravel.com

Maine
Maine Publicity Bureau
P.O. Box 2300
Hallowell, ME 04347
800.533.9595, 207.623.0363
www.visitmaine.com

Maryland
Maryland Office of
Tourism Development
217 E. Redwood St.
Baltimore, MD 21202
800.445.4558, 410.767.3400
www.mdisfun.org

Massachusetts
Massachusetts Office of
Travel & Tourism
100 Cumming Center
Beverly, MA 01915
800.447.6277, 617.727.3201
www.mass-vacation.com

Michigan
Michigan Travel Bureau
P.O. Box 30226
Lansing, MI 48909
888.784.7328, 517.373.0670
www.michigan.org

Minnesota
Minnesota Office of Tourism
500 Metro Square
121 Seventh Place
St. Paul, MN 55101
800.657.3700, 612.296.5029
www.exploreminnesota.com

Mississippi
Mississippi Div. of Tourism
P.O. Box 1705
Ocean Spring, MS 39556
800.927.6378, 601.359.3297
www.decd.state.ms.us/tourism.htm

Missouri
Missouri Div. of Tourism
301 W. High St., P.O. Box 1055
Jefferson City, MO 65102
800.877.1234, 573.751.4133
www.missouritourism.org

Montana
Travel Montana
1424 Ninth Ave.
Helena, MT 59620
800.847.4868, 406.444.2654
www.travel.mt.gov

New Jersey
New Jersey Div. of
Travel & Tourism
20 W. State St., P.O. Box 826
Trenton, NJ 08625
800.537.7397, 609.292.2470
www.state.nj.us/travel

New Mexico
New Mexico Dept. of Tourism
491 Old Santa Fe Trail
Santa Fe, NM 87503
800.545.2040, 800.733.6396
www.newmexico.org

New York
New York State Div. of Tourism
One Commerce Plaza
Albany, NY 12245
800.225.5697, 518.474.4116
www.iloveny.state.ny.us

North Carolina
North Carolina Div. of Tourism,
Film & Sports Development
301 N. Wilmington St.
Raleigh, NC 27601
800.847.4862, 919.733.4171
www.visitnc.com

North Dakota
North Dakota Tourism
604 E. Boulevard Ave.
Bismarck, ND 58505
800.435.5663, 701.328.2525
www.ndtourism.com

Ohio
Ohio Div. of Travel & Tourism
77 S. High St., 29th Fl.
Columbus, OH 43215
800.282.5393
www.ohiotourism.com

Oklahoma
Oklahoma Dept. of
Tourism & Recreation
P.O. Box 60789
Oklahoma City, OK 73146
800.652.6552, 405.521.2409
www.otrd.state.ok.us

Oregon
Oregon Tourism Commission
775 Summer St. NE
Salem, OR 97310
800.547.7842, 503.986.0000
www.traveloregon.com

Pennsylvania
Pennsylvania Office of Travel,
Tourism & Film Promotion
Rm. 404, Forum Building
Harrisburg, PA 17120
800.847.4872, 717.787.5453
www.state.pa.us/visit

Rhode Island
Rhode Island Tourism Div.
1 W. Exchange St.
Providence, RI 02903
800.556.2484
www.visitrhodeisland.com

South Carolina
South Carolina Dept. of
Parks, Recreation & Tourism
P.O. Box 71
Columbia, SC 29201
800.872.3505, 803.734.0122
www.prt.state.sc.us/sc

Inside Passage, Alaska

Nebraska
Nebraska Travel & Tourism
P.O. Box 94666
Lincoln, NE 68509
800.228.4307, 402.471.3796
www.ded.state.ne.us/tourism.html

Nevada
Nevada Commission on Tourism
5151 S. Carson St.
Carson City, NV 89701
800.638.2328, 702.687.4322,
800.237.0774
www.travelnevada.com

New Hampshire
New Hampshire Office of
Travel & Tourism Development
172 Pembroke Rd., P.O. Box 1856
Concord, NH 03302
800.386.4664, 603.271.2666
www.visitnh.gov

South Dakota
South Dakota Dept. of Tourism
711 E. Wells Ave.
Pierre, SD 57501
800.732.5682
www.state.sd.us/state/executive/
tourism/tourism.html

Tennessee
Tennessee Dept. of Tourist Development
320 Sixth Ave. N
Rachel Jackson Building
Nashville, TN 37243
800.836.6200, 615.741.2158
www.state.tn.us/tourdev

Texas
Texas Dept. of Economic
Development, Tourism Div.
P.O. Box 12728
Austin, TX 78711
800.888.8839, 512.462.9191
www.traveltex.com

Utah
Utah Travel Council
Council Hall/Capitol Hill
Salt Lake City, UT 84114
800.200.1160, 801.538.1030
www.utah.com

Vermont
Vermont Dept. of Tourism & Marketing
134 State St., Box 1471
Montpelier, VT 05601
800.837.6668, 802.828.3236
www.travel-vermont.com

Virginia
Virginia Tourism Corporation
901 E. Byrd St.
Richmond, VA 23219
800.932.5827, 804.786.4484
www.virginia.org

Washington
Dept. of Community Trade
& Economic Development,
Washington State Tourism Div.
P.O. Box 42500
Olympia, WA 98504
800.890.5493, 800.544.1800
www.tourism.wa.gov

Taos Indian Pueblo, New Mexico

Washington, D.C.
WCVA Visitors Services
1212 New York Ave. NW, Ste. 600
Washington, D.C. 20005
800.422.8644, 202.789.7000
www.washington.org

West Virginia
West Virginia Div. of Tourism
2101 Washington St. E
Charleston, WV 25305
800.225.5982, 304.558.2286
www.state.wv.us/tourism

Wisconsin
Wisconsin Dept. of Tourism
P.O. Box 7976
Madison, WI 53707
800.432.8747
tourism.state.wi.us

Wyoming
Wyoming Div. of Tourism
I-25 at College Dr.
Cheyenne, WY 82002
800.225.5996, 307.777.7777
www.state.wy.us/state/
tourism/tourism.html

UNITED STATES TERRITORIES

Puerto Rico
Puerto Rico Tourism Company
Old San Juan Station
P.O. Box 4435
San Juan, PR 00902
800.223.6530, 787.721.2400
www.discoverpuertorico.com

Virgin Islands
U.S. Virgin Islands Dept. of Tourism
P.O. Box 6400
St. Thomas, VI 00804
340.774.8784
www.usvi.net

CANADA

Alberta
Travel Alberta
10155 102nd St., 3rd Fl.
Edmonton, AB, Canada T5J 4G8
800.661.8888, 403.427.4321
www.discoveralberta.com

British Columbia
Super, Natural British Columbia
Box 9830
Stn. Prov. Govt.
Victoria, BC, Canada V8W 9W5
800.663.6000, 250.387.1642
www.tbc.gov.bc.ca

Manitoba
Travel Manitoba
7-155 Carlton St.
Winnipeg, MB, Canada R3C 3H8
800.665.0040, ext. SG8,
204.945.3777
www.gov.mb.ca/itt/travel

New Brunswick
Tourism New Brunswick
P.O. Box 12345
Woodstock, NB, Canada E0J 2B0
800.561.0123
www.gov.nb.ca/tourism

Newfoundland
Newfoundland &
Labrador Tourism Marketing
P.O. Box 8730
St. John's, NF, Canada A1B 4K2
800.563.6353, 709.2830
www.gov.nf.ca/tourism

Nova Scotia
Tourism Nova Scotia
P.O. Box 519
Halifax, NS, Canada B3J 2R5
800.565.0000, 902.424.4247
www.explore.gov.ns.ca/virtualns

Ontario
Ontario Tourism
Queen's Park, 900 Bay St.
Toronto, ON, Canada M7A 2E1
800.668.2746,
416.314.0944
www.travelinx.com

Prince Edward Island
Dept. of Economical
Development & Tourism
P.O. Box 940
Charlottetown, PE, Canada C1A 7M5
800.463.4734, 902.368.4444
www.gov.pe.ca/vg/index.asp

Québec
Tourisme Québec
P.O. Box 979
Montréal, PQ, Canada H3C 2W3
800.363.7777, 514.873.2015
www.tourisme.gouv.qc.ca

Saskatchewan
Tourism Saskatchewan
Albert St., Ste. 500
Regina, SK, Canada S4P 4L9
800.667.7191, 306.787.2300
www.sasktourism.com

MEXICO

Mexico Ministry of Tourism
Mariano Escobedo, No. 726
Col. Nueva Anzures
11590 Mexico City, D.F. Mexico
800.446.3942
www.mexico-travel.com

STATE POLICE

Telephone numbers for information on road conditions and construction are available in the Road Map chapter. The numbers below may be used for nonemergency roadside assistance and travel safety advisories. Many state police authorities are divided into districts; in such cases, calls will be referred to the most appropriate local office.

Alabama State Troopers
334.242.4378

Alaska State Troopers
907.428.7200

Arizona Dept. of Public Safety
602.223.2000

Arkansas State Police
501.618.8000

California Highway Patrol
916.445.1865

Colorado State Patrol
303.239-4501

Connecticut Dept. of Public Safety
860.685.8190

Delaware State Police
302.739.5931

Florida Highway Patrol
904.488.5370

Georgia State Patrol
404.657.9300

Hawaii Motor Vehicle Safety Office
808.832.5824

Idaho State Police
208.884.7120

Illinois State Police
217.786.6677

Indiana State Police
317.897.6220

Iowa State Patrol
515.281.5824

Kansas Highway Patrol
785.296.3102

Kentucky State Police
502.695.6300

Louisiana State Police
504.754.8500

Maine State Police
207.624.7000

Maryland State Police
410.653.4200

Massachusetts State Police
508.820.2121

Michigan State Police
517.332.2521

Minnesota Dept. of Public Safety
612.297.3935

Mississippi State Highway Patrol
601.987.1212

Missouri State Highway Patrol
573.751.3313

Montana Highway Patrol
406.444.7000

Nebraska State Police
402.479.4952

Nevada Highway Patrol
702.687.5300

New Hampshire State Police
603.271.3636

New Jersey State Police
609.882.2000

New Mexico State Police
505.827.9300

New York State Police
518.457.6811

North Carolina State Highway Patrol
919.733.7952

North Dakota Highway Patrol
701.328.2455

Ohio State Highway Patrol
614.466.2660

Oklahoma Highway Patrol
405.425.2043

Oregon Dept. of State Police
503.378.2575

Pennsylvania State Police
717.787.7777

Rhode Island State Police
401.444.1000

South Carolina State Patrol
803.896.9621

South Dakota Highway Patrol
605.773.3536

Tennessee Highway Patrol
615.741.2060

Texas Dept. of Public Safety
800.525.5555

Utah Highway Patrol
801.576.8606

Vermont State Police
802.244.8727

Virginia State Police
804.674.2000

Washington State Patrol
360.753.6540

Washington, D.C. Police Dept.
202.727.1010

West Virginia State Police
304.746.2100

Wisconsin State Patrol
608.266.3212

Wyoming Highway Patrol
307.777.4321

Monhegan Island, Maine

WEATHER

Alabama
Birmingham 205.945.7000
Huntsville 205.837.5655
Mobile 334.478.6666

Alaska
Anchorage 907.936.2525
So. AK hwys. 907.936.2626
Fairbanks 907.452.3553
Juneau 907.586.3997

Arizona
Flagstaff 520.774.3301
Phoenix 602.265.5550
Tucson 520.881.3333

Arkansas
Fort Smith 501.785.9000
Little Rock 501.371.7777

California
Eureka (north coast)
707.443.7062
Los Angeles (and Oxnard)
805.988.6610
Monterey (San Francisco Bay area)
408.656.1725
Redding 916.221.5613
Sacramento 916.646.2000
San Diego 619.289.1212
San Francisco 510.562.8573
San Joaquin Valley
805.393.2340
209.584.8047

Colorado
Denver and Boulder
303.398.3964
Grand Junction 970.243.0914
Pueblo 719.948.3371

Connecticut
Southern New England
508.822.0634

Delaware
Mount Holly, NJ (area office)
609.261.6600

Florida
Daytona Beach 904.252.8000
Jacksonville 904.387.4545
Melbourne 407.255.2900
Miami 305.229.4522
Orlando 407.851.7510
Pensacola 904.476.1313
Tallahassee 904.422.1212
Tampa Bay 813.645.2506

Georgia
Atlanta 770.486.8834
Macon 912.755.1300
Savannah 912.964.1700

Hawaii
Honolulu 808.973.4380
Oahu 808.973.4381

Idaho
Boise 208.334.9860
208.342.6569
Lewiston 208.743.3841
Pocatello 208.233.0137

Illinois
Chicago 815.834.0675
Lincoln (central IL)
217.732.3089
Peoria 309.697.8620
Rockford 815.963.8518
Springfield 217.522.0642

Indiana
Fort Wayne 219.424.5050
Indianapolis 317.635.5959
South Bend 219.234.1504

Iowa
Des Moines 515.270.2614
Quad Cities 319.386.3976

Kansas
Dodge City 316.227.3311
Northwest KS 913.899.7119
Topeka 913.234.2592
Wichita 316.942.3102

Kentucky
Jackson 606.666.8000
Louisville 502.968.6025
Paducah 502.744.6331

Louisiana
Baton Rouge 504.387.5411
Lake Charles 318.478.4810
New Orleans 504.828.4000
Shreveport 318.635.7575

Maine
Portland 207.688.3210

Maryland
Washington, D.C. (area office)
703.260.0307
Northern MD and VA mountains
703.260.0705

Massachusetts
Southern New England
508.822.0634

Michigan
Detroit 248.620.2355
Gaylord (north-central lower MI)
517.732.6242
Grand Rapids 616.949.4253
Marquette 906.475.5212

Minnesota
Duluth 218.729.6697
Minneapolis/St. Paul
612.512.1111

Mississippi
Jackson 601.354.3333
Meridian 601.693.5311

Missouri
Kansas City 816.540.6021
Springfield 417.869.4491
St. Louis 314.441.8467

Pennsylvania
Mount Holly, NJ (area office)
609.261.6600
Pittsburgh 412.262.2170

Rhode Island
Southern New England
508.822.0634

South Carolina
Charleston 803.744.3207
Columbia 803.822.8135

South Dakota
Aberdeen 605.225.6173
Rapid City 605.341.7531
Sioux Falls 605.330.4444

Tennessee
Memphis 901.522.8888
Nashville 615.737.2255

Texas
Abilene 915.698.8484
Amarillo 806.354.2278
Brownsville 956.546.5378
Corpus Christi 512.289.1861
El Paso 915.562.4040
Dallas / Fort Worth
972, 817, or 214.787.1111
Galveston 409.740.7272
Houston 713.529.4444
Lubbock 806.745.1058
Midland 915.563.9292
San Angelo 915.949.8586
San Antonio 210.225.0404
Victoria 512.572.9999
Wichita Falls 940.692.9999

Pigeon Forge, Tennessee

Montana
Billings 406.652.1916
Glasgow 406.228.9625
Great Falls 406.453.5469
Helena 406.443.5151
Missoula 406.755.4829

Nebraska
Hastings 402.462.4287
North Platte 308.532.5592
Omaha 402.392.1111

Nevada
Elko 702.738.3018
Ely 702.289.2403
Las Vegas 702.263.9744
Reno and Lake Tahoe
702.831.6677
Winnemucca 702.623.2203

New Hampshire
Portland, ME 207.688.3210

New Jersey
Mount Holly, NJ (area office)
609.261.6600

New Mexico
Albuquerque 505.821.1111
Roswell 505.347.5700

New York
Albany 518.476.1111
Binghamton 607.729.1597
Buffalo 716.565.0204

North Carolina
Morehead City (eastern NC)
919.223.5737

North Dakota
Bismarck 701.223.3700
Grand Forks (eastern ND)
701.772.0720
Williston 701.572.2351

Ohio
Cincinnati 513.241.1010
Cleveland 216.265.2370
Columbus 614.281.8211
Dayton 937.499.1212

Oklahoma
Norman 405.478.3377
Tulsa 918.743.3311

Oregon
Astoria 503.861.2722
Eugene 541.683.9041
Klamath Falls 541.882.5060
Medford 541.779.5990
Pendleton 541.276.0103
Portland 503.243.7575
Salem 503.363.4131

Utah
Salt Lake City 801.575.7246

Vermont
Burlington 802.862.2475

Virginia
Roanoke/Lynchburg
540.552.0497
Richmond 804.268.1212
Washington, D.C. (area office)
703.260.0307
VA mountains and northern MD
703.260.0705

Washington
Olympia 360.357.6453
Seattle 206.526.6087
Spokane 509.244.6395

Washington, D.C.
703.260.0307

West Virginia
Charleston 304.345.2121

Wisconsin
Green Bay 920.494.2363
La Crosse 608.784.7294
Milwaukee / Sullivan
414.744.8000

Wyoming
Cheyenne 307.635.9901

BORDER CROSSING

Canada

Visiting Canada requires neither a passport nor visa; however, individuals should be prepared to demonstrate proof of United States citizenship at the port of entry. They should carry U.S. birth certificates or naturalization papers; medical cards or credit cards accompanied by photo identification may also be accepted. Alien residents of the U.S. must show their Alien Registration Receipt Cards. Individuals under 18 must provide a letter from a legal guardian stating permission for their travel in Canada.

Automobiles entering Canada are admitted free of payments or duty fees for up to 12 months. No special insurance is required; however, motorists are advised to carry vehicle registration cards with them as well as documents establishing proof of insurance and vehicle ownership. A yellow Non-Resident Inter-Provincial Motor Vehicle Liability Insurance Card can be obtained from most U.S. insurance companies. The card indicates the insurance company's agreement to provide the minimum legal coverage required in all Canadian provinces and territories.

United States (from Canada)

Canadian citizens visiting the U.S. are not required to present passports or visas for visits lasting less than six months. Individuals should be prepared however, to demonstrate proof of citizenship at their port of entry. A photo identification accompanied by a valid birth certificate or citizenship card should suffice. For visits exceeding six months valid passports or visas are required, obtainable from the U.S. Immigration and Naturalization Service.

Automobiles may enter the U.S. free of payments or duty fees. Drivers need only provide customs officials with valid proof of vehicle registration, ownership, and insurance.

Mexico

Visiting Mexico requires neither a passport nor visa, but individuals must prove their United States citizenship at border crossing points. Naturalized citizens must show naturalization certificates or a U.S. passport. Alien residents of the U.S. must carry Tourist Cards, which can be obtained from the nearest Mexican Consulate or Mexican Tourist Office.

Vehicles traveling from the U.S. to Mexico require permits if traveling more than 13 miles beyond the border. Permits are not required for travel within the Baja Peninsula, or in Puerto Peñasco and El Golfo de Santa Clara in the State of Sonora. Permit holders must be of 18 years of age. Permits may be obtained from the Mexican Customs Office at border crossing points as long as the original and two copies of the following documents are provided:

- Valid proof of driver's citizenship (passport or birth certificate) or tourist card
- Valid vehicle registration in driver's name
- Valid driver's license in driver's name
- Major U.S.- or Canadian-issued credit card in driver's name (Visa, MasterCard, American Express, Diners Club)

Permits require a fee of U.S. $12.00, payable by credit card only, and are valid for 180 days. They must be returned at the border when leaving Mexico.

U.S. and Canadian auto insurance policies are not valid in Mexico, and buying short-term tourist insurance is required. Many U.S. insurance companies sell Mexican auto insurance. American Automobile Association (for members only) and Sanborn's Mexico Insurance (800.638.9423) are popular companies with offices at most U.S. border crossings.

SUNSHINE

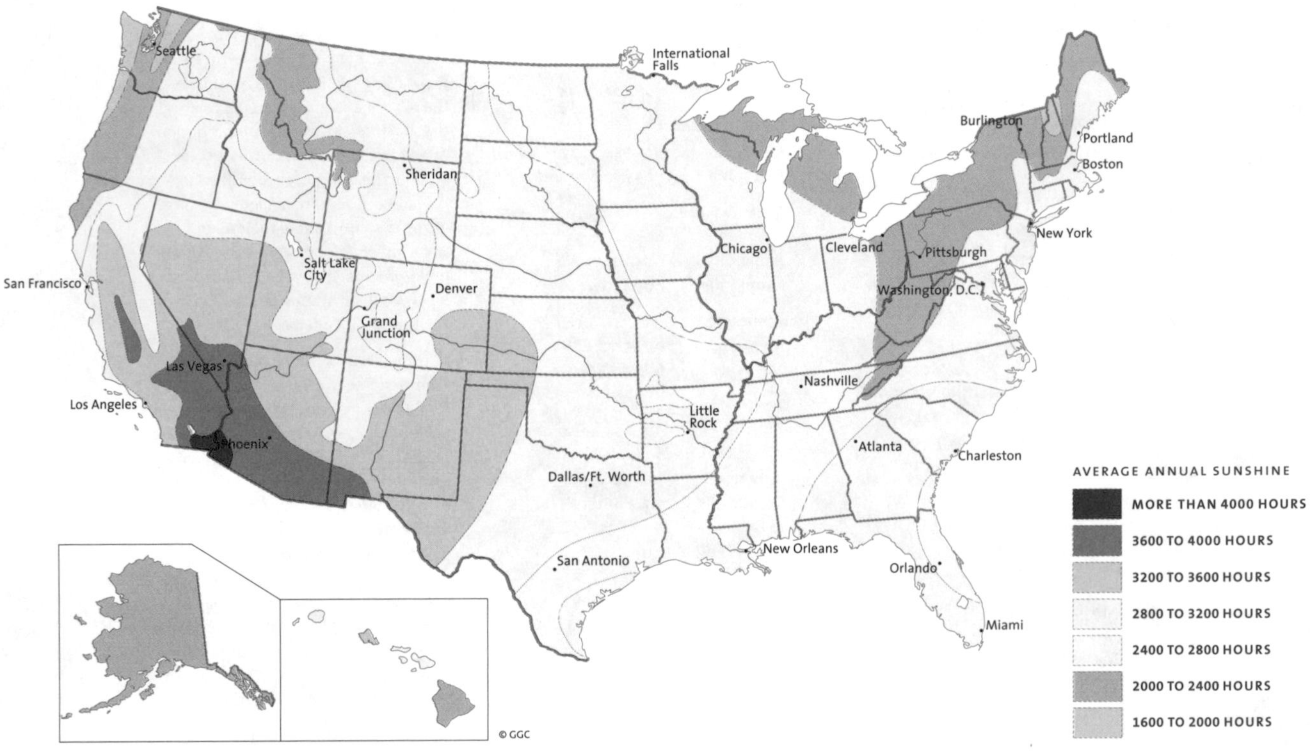

CITY	DAYS OF SUNSHINE
Las Vegas, NV	211.1
Phoenix, AZ	211.0
Los Angeles, CA	186.0
San Francisco, CA	160.3
Grand Junction, CO	136.6
Dallas/Fort Worth, TX	135.5
Salt Lake City, UT	125.0
Little Rock, AR	118.7
Denver, CO	115.2
Atlanta, GA	110.4
New York, NY	106.7
San Antonio, TX	106.1
Nashville, TN	102.9
Charleston, SC	102.3
New Orleans, LA	101.4
Portland, ME	101.3
Boston, MA	98.4
Washington, DC	96.7
Sheridan, WY	95.8
Orlando, FL	89.9
Chicago, IL	83.8
International Falls, MN	76.7
Miami, FL	75.1
Seattle, WA	71.0
Cleveland, OH	66.4
Pittsburgh, PA	58.3
Burlington, VT	57.9

RAINFALL

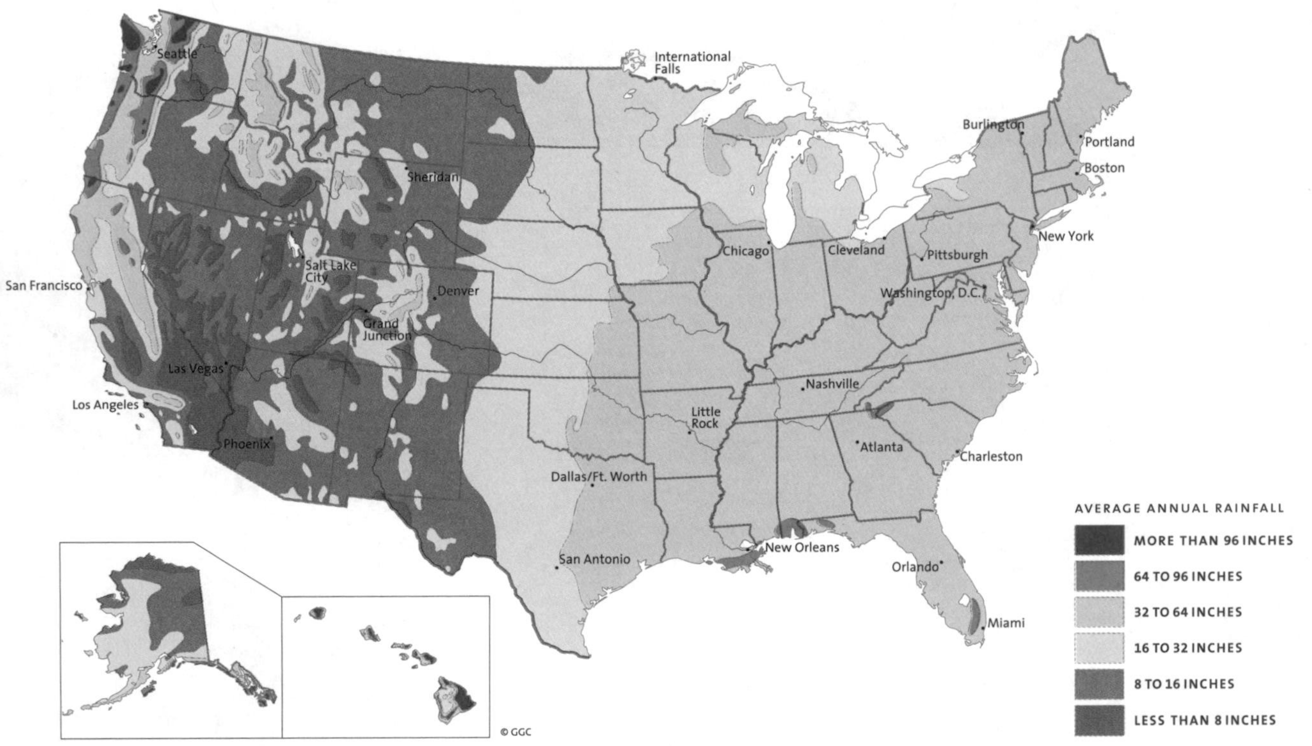

CITY	DAYS OF RAINFALL
Cleveland, OH	156.0
Burlington, VT	154.0
Pittsburgh, PA	153.3
Seattle, WA	150.4
International Falls, MN	131.3
Miami, FL	129.5
Portland, ME	128.5
Boston, MA	126.5
Chicago, IL	126.3
New York, NY	120.6
Nashville, TN	118.6
Orlando, FL	115.8
Atlanta, GA	115.1
New Orleans, LA	114.5
Charleston, SC	112.9
Washington, DC	112.3
Sheridan, WY	106.8
Little Rock, AR	104.5
Salt Lake City, UT	90.6
Denver, CO	89.1
San Antonio, TX	82.1
Dallas/Fort Worth, TX	78.9
Grand Junction, CO	72.8
San Francisco, CA	62.0
Phoenix, AZ	36.5
Los Angeles, CA	35.2
Las Vegas, NV	26.5

SNOWFALL

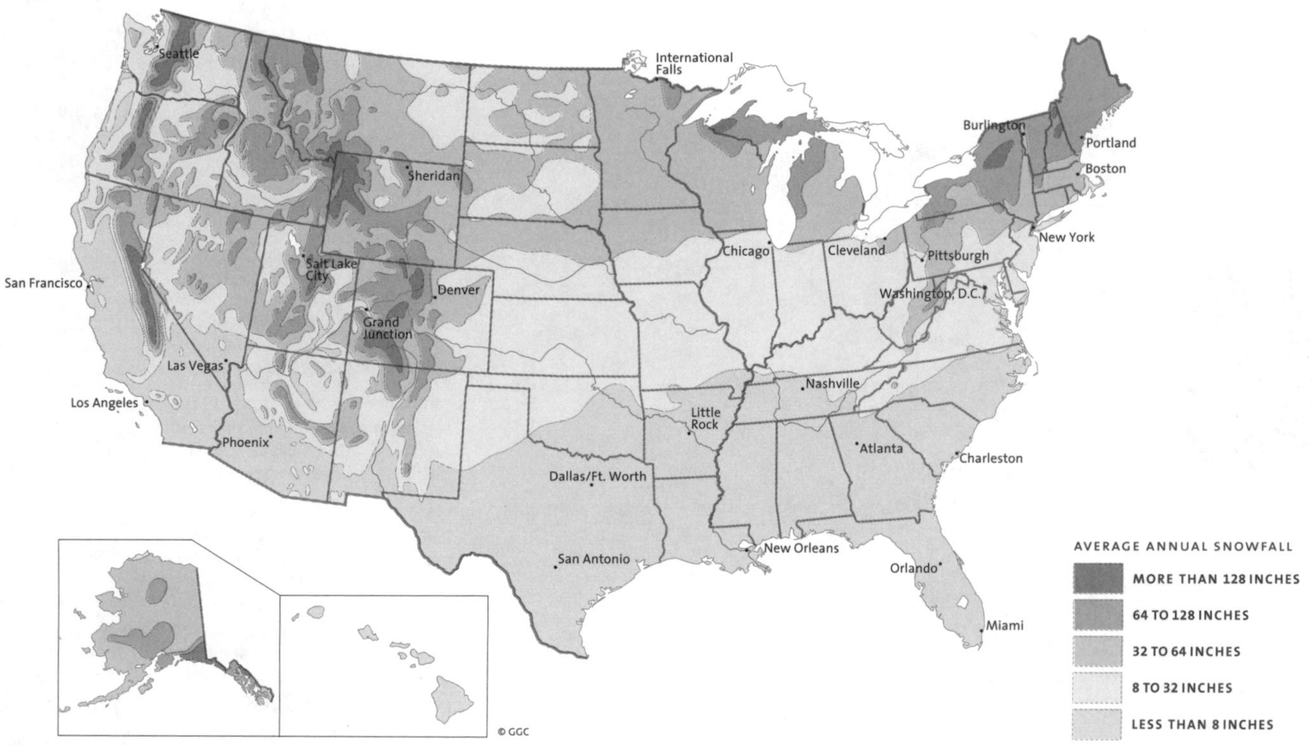

CITY	DAYS OF SNOWFALL
Sheridan, WY	23.6
Burlington, VT	22.0
International Falls, MN	19.5
Cleveland, OH	18.4
Denver, CO	17.9
Salt Lake City, UT	17.8
Portland, ME	17.3
Pittsburgh, PA	12.8
Chicago, IL	11.6
Boston, MA	10.7
Grand Junction, CO	8.7
New York, NY	7.9
Washington, DC	4.6
Nashville, TN	3.5
Seattle, WA	2.4
Little Rock, AR	1.9
Dallas/Fort Worth, TX	1.1
Atlanta, GA	0.6
Las Vegas, NV	0.4
Charleston, SC	0.2
San Antonio, TX	0.2
New Orleans, LA	rare
San Francisco, CA	rare
Los Angeles, CA	0.0
Miami, FL	0.0
Orlando, FL	0.0
Phoenix, AZ	0.0

WINTER HIGHS

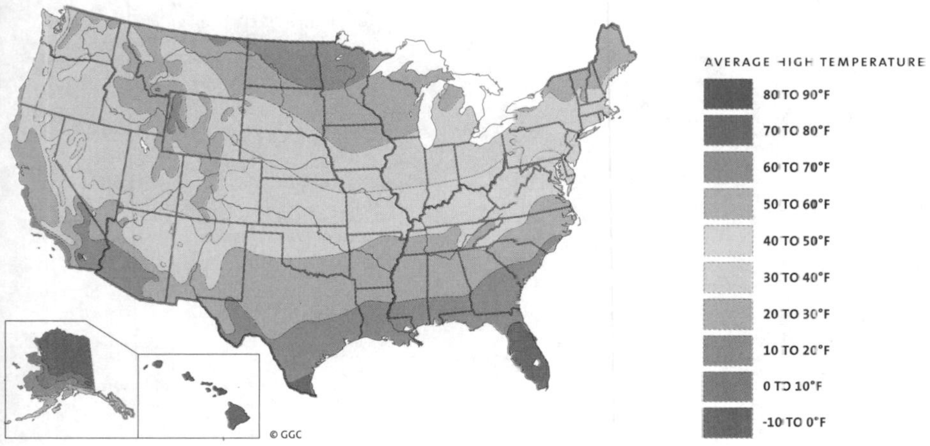

WINTER LOWS

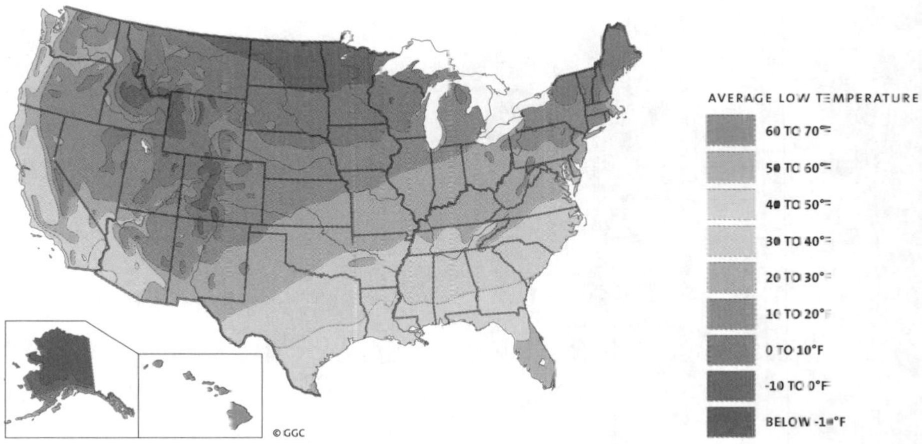

SPRING HIGHS

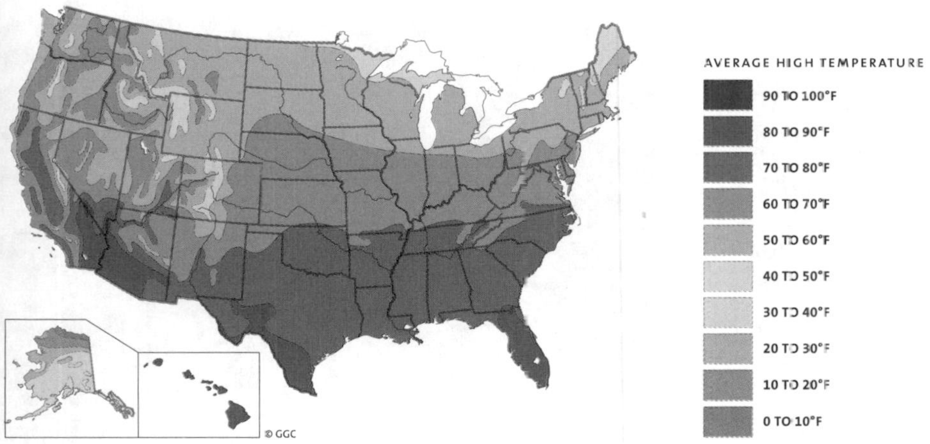

SPRING LOWS

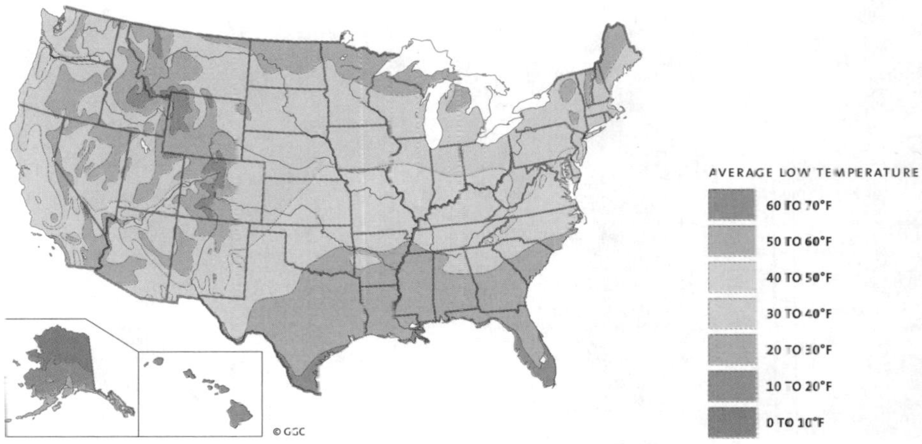

SUMMER HIGHS

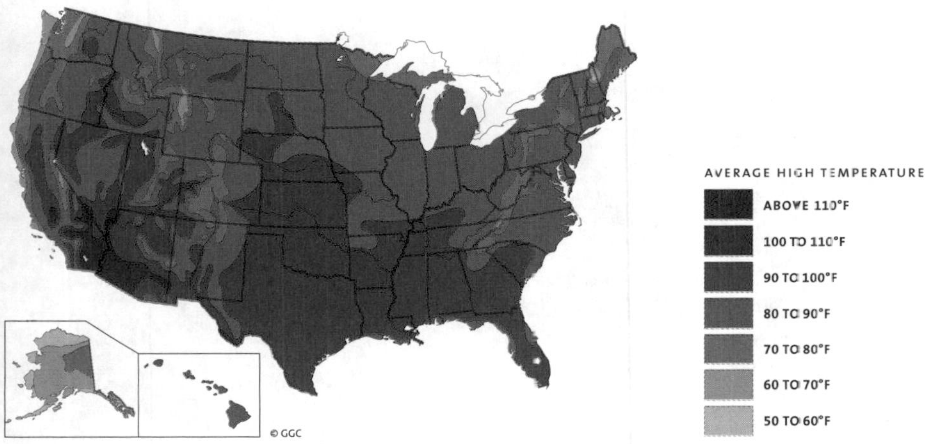

SUMMER LOWS

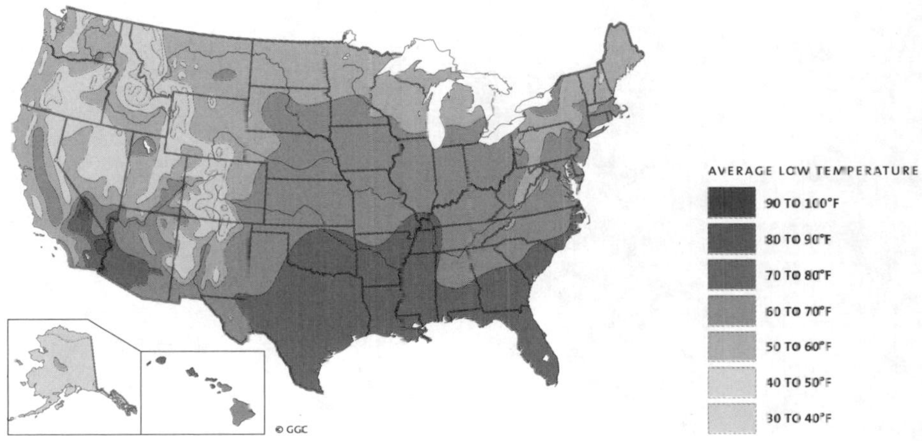

FALL HIGHS

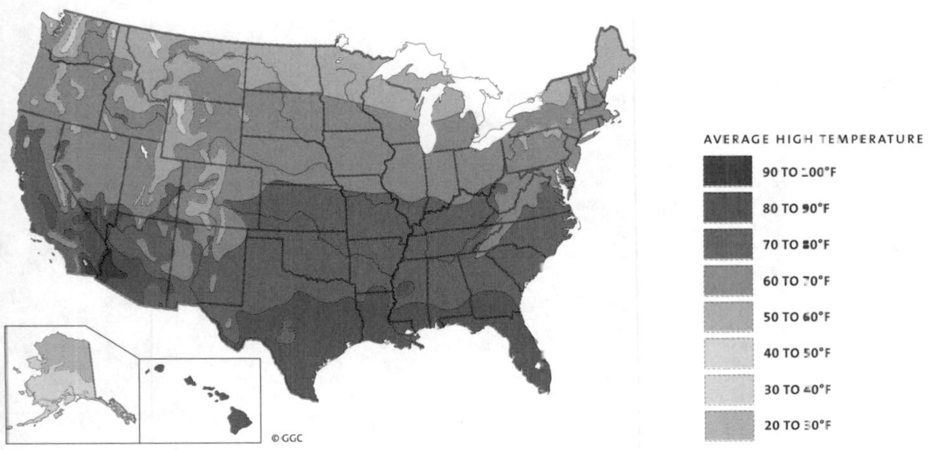

FALL LOWS

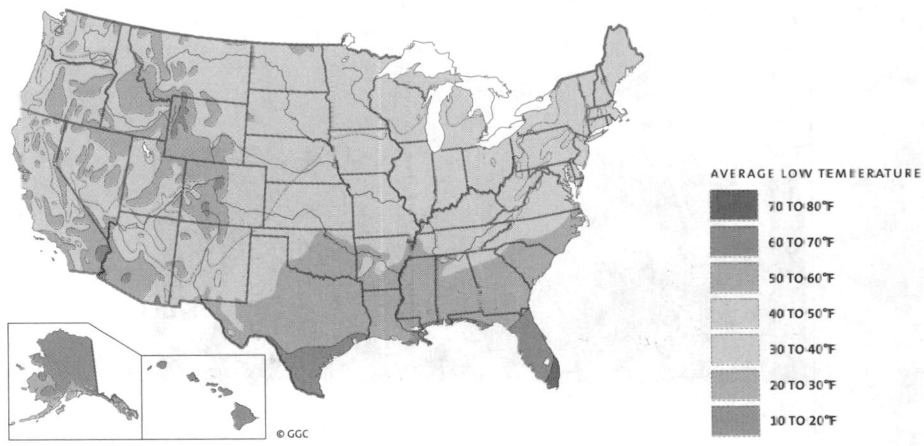

ALABAMA PG. 60-61

CAPITAL
Montgomery

NICKNAME
Heart of Dixie

POPULATION
4,447,100, rank 23

AREA
51,705 sq mi, rank 29

Counties

Cities and Towns

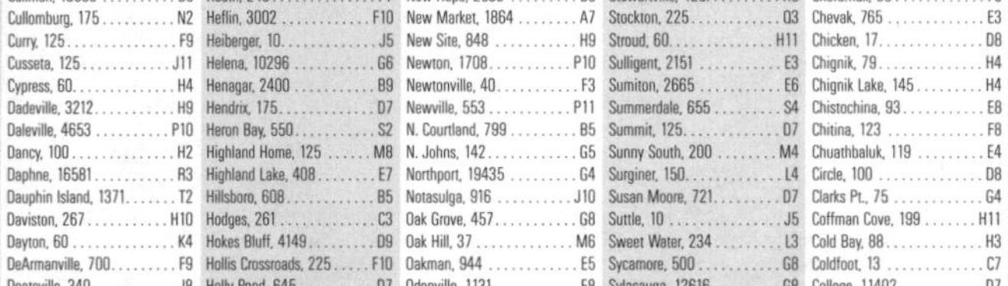

Russell Cave National Monument, Alabama

ALASKA PG. 62

CAPITAL
Juneau

NICKNAME
Great Land

POPULATION
626,932, rank 48

AREA
591,004 sq mi, rank 1

Cities and Towns

ARIZONA PG. 63-65

CAPITAL
Phoenix

NICKNAME
Grand Canyon State

POPULATION
5,130,632, rank 20

AREA
114,000 sq mi, rank 6

Counties

Cities and Towns

Glacier Bay National Monument, Alaska

ARKANSAS PG. 66-67

CAPITAL
Little Rock

NICKNAME
Natural State

POPULATION
2,673,400, rank 33

AREA
53,187 sq mi, rank 27

Counties

Cities and Towns

CALIFORNIA
PG. 68-75

CAPITAL
Sacramento

NICKNAME
Golden State

POPULATION
33,871,648, rank 1

AREA
158,706 sq mi, rank 3

Counties

Cities and Towns

Chaco Culture National Historic Park, New Mexico

COLORADO
PG. 75-77

CAPITAL
Denver

NICKNAME
Centennial State

POPULATION
4,301,261, rank 24

AREA
104,091 sq mi, rank 8

Counties

Cathedral Rock, Arizona

Cities and Towns

CONNECTICUT
PG. 78-79

CAPITAL
Hartford

NICKNAME
Constitution State

POPULATION
3,405,565, rank 29

AREA
5,018 sq mi, rank 48

Counties

Cities and Towns

DELAWARE
PG. 80

CAPITAL
Dover

NICKNAME
First State

POPULATION
783,600, rank 45

AREA
2,044 sq mi, rank 49

DISTRICT OF COLUMBIA
PG. 172

POPULATION
572,059

AREA
69 sq mi

FLORIDA
PG. 81-84

CAPITAL
Tallahassee

NICKNAME
Sunshine State

POPULATION
15,982,378, rank 4

AREA
58,664 sq mi, rank 22

GEORGIA
PG. 85-87

CAPITAL
Atlanta

NICKNAME
Empire State of the South

POPULATION
8,186,453, rank 10

AREA
58,910 sq mi, rank 21

Georgetown, Colorado

HAWAII
PG. 88

CAPITAL
Honolulu

NICKNAME
Aloha State

POPULATION
1,211,537, rank 42

AREA
6,471 sq mi, rank 47

IDAHO
PG. 89

CAPITAL
Boise

NICKNAME
Gem State

POPULATION
1,293,953, rank 39

AREA
83,564 sq mi, rank 13

Muir Woods National Monument, California

IOWA
PG. 96-97

CAPITAL
Des Moines

NICKNAME
Hawkeye State

POPULATION
2,926,324, rank 30

AREA
56,275 sq mi, rank 25

Counties

USS Arizona Memorial, Hawaii

Lewes Harbor, Delaware

KANSAS
PG. 98-99

CAPITAL
Topeka

NICKNAME
Sunflower State

POPULATION
2,688,418, rank 32

AREA
82,277 sq mi, rank 14

Counties

KENTUCKY
PG. 100-101

CAPITAL
Frankfort

NICKNAME
Bluegrass State

POPULATION
4,041,769, rank 25

AREA
40,409 sq mi, rank 37

Counties

South Beach Miami, Florida

LOUISIANA
PG. 102-103

CAPITAL
Baton Rouge

NICKNAME
Pelican State

POPULATION
4,468,976, rank 22

AREA
47,751 sq mi, rank 31

Counties

MAINE
PG. 104-105

CAPITAL
Augusta

NICKNAME
Pine Tree State

POPULATION
1,274,923, rank 40

AREA
33,265 sq mi, rank 39

Counties

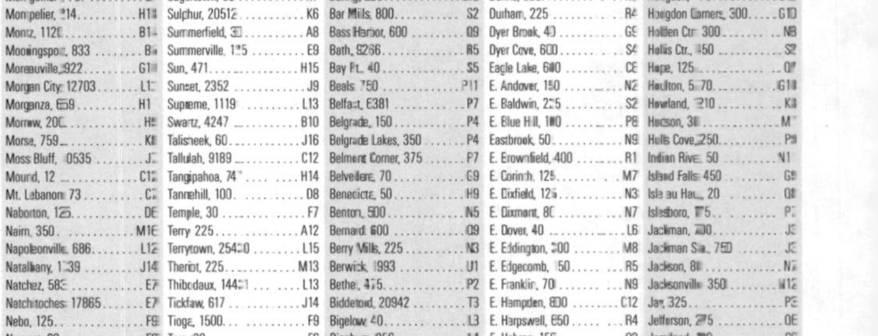
Epcot Spaceship, Orlando, Florida

Livermore Falls, 1626 . . . P3
Locke Mills, 150 . . . P2
Long Beach, 300 . . . R2
Long Cove, 425 . . . R6
Long Pond, 30 . . . J4
Loon Lake, 10 . . . L2
Lovell, 100 . . . Q1
Lubec, 650 . . . M13
Lucerne-in-Maine, 100 . . . N8
Ludlow, 80 . . . G10
Machias, 1376 . . . N12
Machiasport, 100 . . . N12
Macwahoc, 40 . . . J9
Madawaska, 3326 . . . A9
Madison, 2733 . . . M4
Madrid, 90 . . . M3
Mainstream, 40 . . . M5
Manchester, 600 . . . P4
Manset, 700 . . . U11
Maple Grove, 80 . . . D10
Mapleton, 600 . . . D9
Maplewood, 90 . . . S1
Mariaville, 50 . . . N9
Marion, 20 . . . M12
Marlboro, 70 . . . P9
Marshfield, 200 . . . N12
Mars Hill, 1428 . . . E10
Marshville, 200 . . . N11
Martin, 125 . . . R6
Martinsville, 225 . . . R6
Masardis, 40 . . . E9
Matinicus, 60 . . . R7
Mattawamkeag, 400 . . . J9
McFarlands Corner, 70 . . . P6
Mechanic Falls, 2450 . . . Q3
Meddybemps, 20 . . . L12
Medford Ctr., 10 . . . K7
Medway, 650 . . . J8
Mercer, 70 . . . N4
Mexico, 1946 . . . N2
Michaud, 150 . . . B8
Milbridge, 475 . . . P10
Milford, 2197 . . . M8
Millinocket, 5190 . . . J8
Millvale, 125 . . . N8
Milo, 1898 . . . K7
Milton, 40 . . . P2
Minot, 400 . . . Q3
Minturn, 175 . . . Q9
Molunkus, 20 . . . J9
Monarda, 20 . . . H9
Monhegan, 90 . . . S6
Monmouth, 500 . . . Q4
Monroe, 30 . . . N7
Monson, 100 . . . K6
Monticello, 300 . . . F10
Moody, 1000 . . . U2
Moody Pt., 800 . . . U2
Moose River, 175 . . . J3
Moro, 10 . . . F9
Morrill, 175 . . . P7
Moscow, 325 . . . L4
Mountainville, 150 . . . Q8
Mt. Vernon, 175 . . . P4
Muscongus, 150 . . . R6
Naples, 300 . . . R2
Naskeag, 80 . . . Q8
Nequasset, 450 . . . R5
Newagen, 80 . . . S5
Newburgh Ctr., 250 . . . N7
Newcastle, 1751 . . . R5
Newfield, 125 . . . S1
New Gloucester, 500 . . . R3
New Harbor, 225 . . . R5
New Limerick, 40 . . . G10
Newport, 1754 . . . M6
New Portland, 125 . . . M4
Newry, 20 . . . P2
New Sharon, 200 . . . N4
New Sweden, 200 . . . C10
New Vineyard, 150 . . . M4
Nobleboro, 375 . . . Q6
Norridgewock, 1557 . . . N5
N. Alfred, 225 . . . T2
N. Amity, 30 . . . G10
N. Anson, 400 . . . M4
N. Bancroft, 10 . . . H10
N. Berwick, 1580 . . . U2
N. Bethel, 60 . . . P2
N. Bradford, 125 . . . L7
N. Bridgton, 225 . . . Q2
N. Brooklin, 125 . . . P8
N. Brooksville, 80 . . . P8
N. Castine, 175 . . . P8
N. Chesterville, 100 . . . N4
N. Cutler, 20 . . . N12
N. Deer Isle, 200 . . . Q8
N. Dexter, 70 . . . L6
N. Dixmont, 150 . . . N6
Northeast Harbor, 500 . . . Q9
N. Edgecomb, 300 . . . R5
N. Fairfield, 275 . . . N5
Northfield, 40 . . . M11
N. Fryeburg, 125 . . . Q1
N. Guilford, 30 . . . K6
N. Haven, 200 . . . Q7
N. Jay, 350 . . . N3
N. Lebanon, 200 . . . T1
N. Leeds, 100 . . . P4
N. Lincoln, 350 . . . K9
N. Livermore, 100 . . . P3
N. Lovell, 40 . . . Q1
N. Mariaville, 10 . . . M9
N. Monmouth, 600 . . . Q4
N. Newcastle, 250 . . . Q5
N. Newport, 60 . . . M6
N. New Portland, 200 . . . M4
N. Newry, 10 . . . N2
N. Norway, 150 . . . Q2
N. Palermo, 125 . . . P6
N. Paris, 150 . . . P2
N. Parsonsfield, 50 . . . S1
N. Penobscot, 60 . . . P8
N. Perry, 200 . . . L13
Northport, 150 . . . P7

Living History Farms, Iowa

N. Pownal, 125 . . . R3
N. Scarborough, 650 . . . S3
N. Searsmont, 100 . . . P6
N. Sedgwick, 100 . . . P8
N. Shapleigh, 100 . . . S1
N. Turner, 400 . . . P3
N. Vassalboro, 750 . . . P5
N. Waldoboro, 150 . . . Q6
N. Waterboro, 300 . . . S2
N. Waterford, 70 . . . Q2
N. Whitefield, 100 . . . Q5
N. Windham, 4568 . . . R3
N. Woodstock, 125 . . . P2
Norway, 2623 . . . Q2
Notre Dame, 10 . . . B10
Number Four, 175 . . . Q1
Oakfield, 475 . . . G9
Oakland, 2758 . . . N5
Ocean Park, 3100 . . . T3
Ocean Pt., 100 . . . S5
Oceanville, 100 . . . Q8
Ogunquit, 800 . . . U2
Olamon, 175 . . . L8
Old Orchard Beach, 8856 . . . T3
Old Town, 8130 . . . M8
Oquossoc, 50 . . . M2
Orient, 40 . . . H10
Orland, 500 . . . N8
Orono, 8253 . . . M8
Orrington, 325 . . . N8
Orrs Island, 550 . . . S4
Otisfield, 60 . . . R2
Otter Creek, 250 . . . P9
Ouellette, 30 . . . B9
Owls Head, 275 . . . Q7
Oxbow, 50 . . . E8
Oxford, 1300 . . . Q2
Palermo, 200 . . . P6
Palmyra, 200 . . . M6
Parent, 20 . . . B10
Paris, 375 . . . Q2
Parker Head, 150 . . . S5
Parkman, 60 . . . L6
Parsonsfield, 20 . . . S1
Passadumkeag, 100 . . . L8
Patten, 850 . . . G9
Pejepscot, 300 . . . R4
Pemaquid, 125 . . . R5
Pemaquid Pt., 70 . . . R5
Pembroke, 475 . . . M12
Penobscot, 125 . . . P8
Perham, 80 . . . D9
Perry, 125 . . . M13
Peru, 125 . . . P3
Phillips, 600 . . . M3
Phippsburg, 200 . . . S5
Pine Pt., 600 . . . T3
Pittsfield, 3217 . . . M6
Pittston, 350 . . . Q5
Plaisted, 50 . . . B8
Pleasant Pt., 600 . . . M13
Plymouth, 20 . . . N6
Poland, 300 . . . Q3
Popham Beach, 50 . . . S5
Portage, 225 . . . D9
Port Clyde, 300 . . . R6
Porter, 150 . . . S1
Portland, 64249 . . . S3
Pownal Ctr., 175 . . . R3
Prairie, 10 . . . K7
Prentiss, 40 . . . J10
Presque Isle, 9511 . . . D10
Princeton, 125 . . . K11
Pripet, 70 . . . P7
Prospect, 150 . . . N7
Prospect Harbor, 200 . . . P10
Prouts Neck, 80 . . . T3
Quimby, 70 . . . C8
Randolph, 1911 . . . Q5
Rangeley, 450 . . . M2
Raymond, 325 . . . R3
Razorville, 100 . . . Q6
Readfield, 475 . . . P4
Red Beach, 30 . . . L12
Reed, 30 . . . H10
Richmond, 1864 . . . Q5
Richmond Corner, 175 . . . Q4
Richville, 250 . . . S2
Riley, 375 . . . P3
Ripley, 175 . . . M6
Riverside, 250 . . . P5
Robbinston, 125 . . . L13
Robinhood, 100 . . . R5
Robinsons, 125 . . . E10
Rockland, 7609 . . . Q7
Rockport, 900 . . . Q7
Rockville, 225 . . . Q7
Rockwood, 30 . . . H5
Rome, 125 . . . N4
Roque Bluffs, 10 . . . N12
Ross Corner, 125 . . . S2
Round Pond, 325 . . . R6
Roxbury, 40 . . . N2
Rumford, 4795 . . . N2
Rumford Ctr., 125 . . . P2
Rumford Pt., 50 . . . P2
Sabattus, 1200 . . . Q4
Saco, 16822 . . . T3
St. Albans, 200 . . . M6
St. David, 125 . . . A9
St. Francis, 250 . . . B7
St. George, 350 . . . R6
St. John, 50 . . . B8
Salem, 90 . . . M3
Salsbury Cove, 300 . . . P9
Sandy Creek, 125 . . . R2
Sandy Pt., 175 . . . P8
Sanford, 10133 . . . T2
Sangerville, 475 . . . L6
Saponac, 10 . . . L9
Sargentville, 80 . . . Q8
Scarborough, 3867 . . . T3
Seal Cove, 70 . . . U10
Seal Harbor, 300 . . . Q9
Searsmont, 90 . . . P6
Searsport, 1102 . . . P7
Seawall, 125 . . . V11
Sebago, 80 . . . R2
Sebago Lake, 550 . . . S2
Sebec, 100 . . . K7
Seboeis, 10 . . . K8
Sedgwick, 125 . . . Q8
Selden, 10 . . . H10
Shaker Vil., 125 . . . R3
Shapleigh, 150 . . . T1
Sheridan, 250 . . . D9
Sherman, 200 . . . H9
Sherman Mills, 300 . . . H9
Sherman Sta., 150 . . . H9
Shin Pond, 60 . . . G8
Shirley Mills, 150 . . . K5
Sidney, 150 . . . P5
Silvers Mills, 200 . . . L6
Sinclair, 100 . . . B9
Skowhegan, 6696 . . . N5
Small Pt. Beach, 50 . . . S4
Smithfield, 80 . . . N5
Smyrna Mills, 200 . . . G9
Soldier Pond, 100 . . . B8
Solon, 275 . . . M4
Somerset, 60 . . . M4
Somerville, 90 . . . P6
Somesville, 250 . . . P9
Songo Lock, 475 . . . R2
Sorrento, 100 . . . P9
S. Acton, 50 . . . T1
S. Addison, 100 . . . P11
S. Andover, 30 . . . N2
S. Berwick, 2300 . . . U1
S. Bridgton, 150 . . . R2
S. Casco, 650 . . . R2
S. China, 325 . . . P5
S. Dover, 30 . . . L7
S. Eliot, 3445 . . . U1
S. Gardiner, 50 . . . Q5
S. Gouldsboro, 100 . . . P10
S. Gray, 400 . . . R3
S. Hancock, 400 . . . P9
S. Harpswell, 550 . . . S4
S. Hiram, 900 . . . S1
S. Lagrange, 100 . . . L8
S. Lebanon, 350 . . . U1
S. Levant, 125 . . . M7
S. Liberty, 70 . . . P6
S. Limington, 200 . . . S2
S. Lincoln, 150 . . . K8
S. Lubec, 100 . . . M13
S. Monmouth, 300 . . . Q4
S. Orrington, 475 . . . N8
S. Paris, 2237 . . . Q2
S. Parsonsfield, 60 . . . S1
S. Penobscot, 125 . . . P8
S. Portland, 23324 . . . S3
S. Princeton, 30 . . . L11
S. Robbinston, 125 . . . L13
S. Sanford, 4173 . . . T2
S. Sebec, 10 . . . L7
S. Springfield, 10 . . . K10
S. Thomaston, 350 . . . R7
S. Trescott, 40 . . . M13
S. Waldoboro, 225 . . . R6
S. Warren, 250 . . . Q6
S. Waterford, 50 . . . Q2
Southwest Harbor, 950 . . . Q9
S. Windham, 1792 . . . S3
S. Woodstock, 125 . . . P2
Spaulding, 20 . . . C9
Springfield, 100 . . . K10
Springvale, 3488 . . . T2
Spruce Head, 300 . . . R7
Squa Pan, 20 . . . E9
Stacyville, 50 . . . H8
Standish, 600 . . . S2
Starboard, 225 . . . N12
Starks, 30 . . . N4
State Road, 100 . . . D9
Steep Falls, 300 . . . S2
Stetson, 100 . . . M7
Steuben, 150 . . . P10
Stickney Corner, 150 . . . Q6
Stillwater, 1600 . . . M8
Stockholm, 100 . . . C9
Stockton Sprs., 550 . . . P7
Stonington, 850 . . . Q8
Stow, 80 . . . Q1
Stratton, 425 . . . L3
Stricklands, 70 . . . P4
Strong, 550 . . . M3
Sullivan, 175 . . . P9
Sumner, 100 . . . P3
Sunset, 300 . . . Q8
Sunshine, 150 . . . Q8
Surry, 150 . . . P8
Swans Island, 100 . . . Q9
Swanville, 250 . . . P7
Sweden, 125 . . . C9
Sweden, 20 . . . Q2
Temple, 275 . . . N3
Tenants Harbor, 500 . . . R6
The Forks, 20 . . . K4
Thomaston, 2714 . . . Q6
Thompson Corners, 20 . . . J10
Thorndike, 200 . . . N6
Timoney, 80 . . . G10
Topsfield, 60 . . . K11
Topsham, 6271 . . . R4
Trenton, 100 . . . P9
Trevett, 325 . . . R5
Troy, 100 . . . N6
Tunk Lake, 40 . . . N10
Turner, 550 . . . Q3
Turner Ctr., 150 . . . Q3
Union, 475 . . . Q6
Unionville, 60 . . . N10
Unity, 486 . . . N6
Upper Abbot, 125 . . . L6
Upper Frenchville, 125 . . . B9
Upper Gloucester, 475 . . . R3
Upton, 30 . . . N1
Van Buren, 2369 . . . B10
Vanceboro, 60 . . . J12
Vassalboro, 350 . . . P5
Veazie, 1500 . . . M8
Vienna, 125 . . . P4
Vinalhaven, 750 . . . R8
Waite, 80 . . . K11
Waldo, 50 . . . P7
Waldoboro, 1291 . . . Q6
Wales Corner, 150 . . . Q4
Wallagrass, 125 . . . B8
Waltham, 50 . . . N9
Wards Cove, 200 . . . R2
Warren, 900 . . . Q6
Washburn, 800 . . . D9
Washington, 175 . . . Q6
Waterboro, 800 . . . T2
Waterford, 50 . . . Q2
Waterville, 15605 . . . N5
Wayne, 200 . . . P4
Webster Corner, 1000 . . . R4
Weeks Mills, 150 . . . P5
Welchville, 600 . . . Q3
Weld, 200 . . . N3
Weld Corner, 20 . . . N3
Wellington, 50 . . . L5
Wells, 1000 . . . U2
Wells Beach, 500 . . . U2
Wesley, 30 . . . M11
W. Athens, 60 . . . M5
W. Baldwin, 175 . . . R2
W. Bethel, 150 . . . P1
W. Bowdoin, 325 . . . R4
Westbrook, 16142 . . . S3
W. Buxton, 425 . . . S2
W. Charleston, 60 . . . L7
W. Corinth, 175 . . . M7
W. Enfield, 350 . . . K8
W. Falmouth, 950 . . . S8
W. Farmington, 3500 . . . N4
Westfield, 150 . . . E10
W. Forks, 20 . . . K4
W. Franklin, 250 . . . N9
W. Gorham, 475 . . . S2
W. Gray, 225 . . . R3
W. Harrington, 125 . . . N10
W. Kennebunk, 809 . . . T2
W. Lebanon, 350 . . . T1
W. Levant, 40 . . . M7
W. Lubec, 150 . . . M13
W. Mills, 90 . . . N4
W. Minot, 175 . . . Q3
W. Mt. Vernon, 60 . . . P4
W. Newfield, 90 . . . S1
W. Old Town, 20 . . . M8
Weston, 20 . . . H10
W. Paris, 550 . . . P2
W. Pembroke, 300 . . . M12
W. Penobscot, 40 . . . P8
W. Peru, 350 . . . P3
W. Point, 175 . . . S4
W. Poland, 350 . . . R3
W. Princeton, 70 . . . L11
W. Ripley, 20 . . . M6
W. Rockport, 425 . . . Q7
W. Seboeis, 10 . . . J7
W. Sidney, 400 . . . P5
W. Southport, 325 . . . S5
W. Sullivan, 175 . . . P9
W. Sumner, 50 . . . P3
W. Tremont, 225 . . . U10
W. Trenton, 275 . . . R10
W. Washington, 125 . . . Q6
Wheelock, 10 . . . B8
Whitefield, 125 . . . Q5
Whiting, 100 . . . M12
Whitneyville, 150 . . . N11
Willimantic, 50 . . . K6
Wilsons Mills, 20 . . . M1
Wilton, 2290 . . . N3
Windsor, 225 . . . P5
Winn, 150 . . . J9
Winnecook, 90 . . . N6
Winslow, 7743 . . . N5
Winslows Mills, 90 . . . Q6
Winter Harbor, 250 . . . P10
Winterport, 1307 . . . N7
Winterville, 125 . . . C8
Winthrop, 2893 . . . P4
Wiscasset, 1203 . . . R5
Woodland (Baileyville), 1044 . . . L12
Woolwich, 325 . . . R5
Wyman, 200 . . . P10
Wytopitlock, 40 . . . J10
Yarmouth, 3560 . . . S3
York Beach, 1400 . . . U2
York Harbor, 3321 . . . U2
York Vil., 2000 . . . U2

MARYLAND
PG. 106-108

CAPITAL
Annapolis

NICKNAME
Old Line State

POPULATION
5,296,486, rank 19

AREA
10,460 sq mi, rank 42

Counties

Allegany, 74930 . . . B5
Anne Arundel, 489656 . . . F13
Baltimore, 754292 . . . C13
Calvert, 74563 . . . H14
Caroline, 29772 . . . G17
Carroll, 150897 . . . B11
Cecil, 85951 . . . C16
Charles, 120546 . . . J12
Dorchester, 30674 . . . J16
Frederick, 195277 . . . C9
Garrett, 29846 . . . C2
Harford, 218590 . . . C15
Howard, 247842 . . . E12
Kent, 19197 . . . E16
Montgomery, 873341 . . . E11
Prince George's, 801515 . . . G13
Queen Anne's, 40563 . . . E17
St. Mary's, 86211 . . . K13
Somerset, 24747 . . . L18
Talbot, 33812 . . . G16
Washington, 131923 . . . B7
Wicomico, 84644 . . . J18
Worcester, 46543 . . . K19

Cities and Towns

Aberdeen, 13842 . . . C15
Abingdon, 950 . . . C15
Accident, 353 . . . B2
Accokeek, 7349 . . . H12
Accokeek Acres, 1500 . . . H12
Adamstown, 650 . . . D10
Adelphi, 14998 . . . K4
Aldino, 375 . . . C15
Allen, 200 . . . K18
Andrews, 70 . . . K16
Annapolis, 35838 . . . F14
Antietam, 275 . . . D8
Aquasco, 250 . . . H13
Arbutus, 20116 . . . F4
Arden-on-the-Severn, 1971 . . . K6
Arnold, 23422 . . . F14
Arundel on the Bay, 1000 . . . F14
Arundel Vil., 8000 . . . G6
Ashton, 3437 . . . G4
Aspen Hill, 50228 . . . F12
Avenue, 475 . . . K13
Baden, 225 . . . H13
Baldwin, 850 . . . C14
Baltimore, 651154 . . . D13
Baltimore Highlands, 15724 . . . F5
Barclay, 143 . . . E17
Barnesville, 161 . . . E10
Barstow, 750 . . . J14
Barton, 478 . . . C3
Bartonsville, 12529 . . . D10
Bay Ridge, 2300 . . . F14
Beachville, 225 . . . L14
Beallsville, 150 . . . E10
Bel Air, 10080 . . . C15
Bel Alton, 425 . . . J12
Belcamp, 1900 . . . C15
Bellevue, 175 . . . H15
Beltsville, 15690 . . . F12
Belvedere Hts., 7900 . . . K8
Benedict, 450 . . . J13
Benson, 950 . . . C14
Bentley Sprs., 175 . . . B13
Berlin, 3491 . . . K20
Berwyn Hts., 2942 . . . K5
Bethesda, 55277 . . . F11
Bethlehem, 600 . . . G16
Betterton, 376 . . . D16
Beulah, 125 . . . H17
Beverly Beach, 1600 . . . G14
Big Pool, 200 . . . C7
Bishop, 200 . . . J20
Bishopville, 300 . . . J20
Bivalve, 450 . . . K17
Bladensburg, 7661 . . . L5
Bond Mill Park, 3400 . . . H6
Boonsboro, 2803 . . . C9
Boring, 550 . . . C13
Bowie, 50269 . . . F13
Bowleys Quarters, 6314 . . . D14
Bowling Green, 2000 . . . C4
Boxhill North, 2900 . . . C15
Boxiron, 30 . . . L19
Braddock Hts., 4627 . . . D9
Brandywine, 1410 . . . H13
Breezy Pt., 800 . . . H14
Brentwood, 2844 . . . L5
Breton Bay, 750 . . . K13
Bridgeport, 2700 . . . B9
Bridgetown, 100 . . . F17
Brock Hall, 1200 . . . G13
Brookeville, 120 . . . E12
Brooklandville, 2200 . . . B5
Brooklyn Park, 10938 . . . F6
Brookview, 65 . . . H17
Broomes Island, 425 . . . J14
Brownsville, 325 . . . F16
Brunswick, 4894 . . . D9
Bryans Road, 4912 . . . H12
Bryantown, 550 . . . F15
Bryantown, 550 . . . J13
Buckeystown, 425 . . . D10
Bucklodge, 200 . . . E10
Burkittsville, 171 . . . D9
Burrisville, 175 . . . E16
Burrsville, 150 . . . G17
Burtonsville, 7305 . . . E12
Butler, 225 . . . C13
Butlertown, 350 . . . D16
Byrdtown, 475 . . . M17
Cabin Creek, 100 . . . H17
Cabin John, 1734 . . . K2
California, 9307 . . . K14
Callaway, 400 . . . K14
Calvert, 450 . . . B16
Calvert Beach, 2487 . . . J14
Calvert Manor, 650 . . . H12
Calverton, 12610 . . . F12
Cambridge, 10911 . . . H16
Camp Sprs., 17968 . . . G12
Cape St. Claire, 8022 . . . F14
Capitol Hts., 4138 . . . M5
Captains Hill, 600 . . . K20
Cardiff, 650 . . . B15
Carney, 28264 . . . C7
Carpenter Pt., 400 . . . C16
Cascade, 1141 . . . B10
Catonsville, 39820 . . . E13
Cavetown, 1486 . . . B9
Cearfoss, 800 . . . B8
Cecilton, 474 . . . D17
Cedar Grove, 950 . . . E11
Cedar Lawn, 900 . . . K9
Cedartown, 20 . . . K19
Cedarville, 275 . . . H13
Centreville, 1970 . . . F16
Champ, 150 . . . L17
Chance, 377 . . . L16
Chaneyville, 475 . . . H13
Chaptico, 175 . . . K13
Charlestown, 1019 . . . C16
Charlotte Hall, 1214 . . . J13
Chelsea Beach, 4400 . . . J7
Cheltenham, 650 . . . H13
Chesapeake Beach, 3180 . . . H14
Chesapeake City, 787 . . . C17
Chesapeake Ranch Estates, 11503 . . . K14
Chester, 3723 . . . F15
Chestertown, 4746 . . . E16
Cheverly, 6433 . . . F12
Chevy Chase, 2726 . . . K3
Chevy Chase View, 863 . . . K3
Chewsville, 293 . . . C9
Chillum, 34252 . . . L4
Choptank, 250 . . . H16
Church Creek, 85 . . . J16
Church Hill, 530 . . . E16
Churchton, 1800 . . . G14
Churchville, 1200 . . . C15
Claggettsville, 250 . . . D11
Claiborne, 225 . . . G15
Clarksburg, 1834 . . . E11
Clarksville, 900 . . . E12
Clear Spr., 455 . . . B8
Clements, 150 . . . K13
Clinton, 26064 . . . G12
Cloverly, 7835 . . . H4
Cobb Island, 750 . . . K13
Cockeysville, 19388 . . . C13
Cokesbury, 200 . . . L18
Coleman, 250 . . . D16
Colesville, 19810 . . . F12
College Park, 24657 . . . K5
Colmar Manor, 1257 . . . D7
Coltons Pt., 375 . . . K13
Columbia, 88254 . . . E12
Columbia Beach, 700 . . . G14
Cooksville, 125 . . . D12
Coral Hills, 10720 . . . M5
Cordova, 592 . . . G16
Cornersville, 175 . . . H15
Corriganville, 1000 . . . B4
Costen, 80 . . . L18
Cottage City, 1136 . . . D7
Cove Pt., 275 . . . J15
Craigtown, 550 . . . C16
Crapo, 70 . . . K16
Cresaptown, 5884 . . . C4
Crisfield, 2723 . . . M17
Crofton, 20091 . . . F13
Crosby, 300 . . . E15
Crownsville, 1670 . . . F14
Crumpton, 500 . . . E16
Cumberland, 21518 . . . B4
Damascus, 11430 . . . D11
Dames Quarter, 188 . . . L17
Daniel, 650 . . . D12
Dares Beach, 1400 . . . H14
Dargan, 350 . . . D9
Darlington, 350 . . . B15
Darnestown, 6378 . . . E11
Davidsonville, 550 . . . F13
Dayton, 600 . . . E12
Deale, 4796 . . . G14
Deal Island, 578 . . . L16
Deer Park, 405 . . . D2
Delmar, 1859 . . . J18
Denton, 2960 . . . G17
Derwood, 2000 . . . E11
Dickerson, 250 . . . E10
District Hts., 5958 . . . M5
Dominion, 600 . . . F15
Dorsey, 1000 . . . G7
Doubs, 750 . . . D10
Dowell, 750 . . . K14
Downsville, 175 . . . C8
Drum Pt., 11503 . . . K14
Dublin, 650 . . . B15
Dundalk, 62306 . . . E14
Dunkirk, 2363 . . . H13
Eagle Harbor, 55 . . . H13
Earleville, 125 . . . D16
E. New Market, 167 . . . H16
Easton, 11708 . . . G16
Eastview, 650 . . . C12
Eden, 793 . . . K18
Edesville, 275 . . . E15
Edgemere, 9248 . . . E14
Edgewater, 2900 . . . N7
Edgewood, 23378 . . . D15
Edmonston, 959 . . . L5
Eldersburg, 27741 . . . D12
Eldorado, 60 . . . H17
Elkridge, 22042 . . . E13
Elkton, 11893 . . . C17
Ellerslie, 600 . . . B4
Ellicott City, 56397 . . . E13
Elliott, 10 . . . K16
Elvaton, 3500 . . . J6
Emmitsburg, 2290 . . . B10
Emmorton, 4000 . . . C15
Essex, 39078 . . . D14
Etchison, 325 . . . E11
Ewell, 364 . . . M16
Ewingville, 150 . . . E16
Fairland, 21738 . . . F12
Fairlee, 250 . . . E15
Fairmount, 537 . . . L17
Fairmount Hts., 1508 . . . M5
Fallston, 8427 . . . C14
Farmington, 375 . . . B16
Faulkner, 250 . . . J12
Feagaville, 600 . . . N8
Federalsburg, 2620 . . . H17
Ferndale, 16056 . . . G5
Fishing Creek, 300 . . . K15
Flintstone, 275 . . . B5
Flohrville, 950 . . . D12
Forest Hts., 2585 . . . N4
Forestville, 12707 . . . N6
Fowblesburg, 600 . . . C13
Frederick, 52767 . . . D10
Friendly, 10938 . . . G12
Friendship, 425 . . . H14
Friendsville, 539 . . . B1
Frostburg, 7873 . . . B3
Fruitland, 3774 . . . K18
Fullerton, 10100 . . . C8
Fulton, 850 . . . E12
Funkstown, 983 . . . L10
Gaithersburg, 52613 . . . E11
Galena, 428 . . . D17
Galestown, 101 . . . H17
Galesville, 600 . . . G14
Gamber, 1000 . . . C12
Gapland, 325 . . . D9
Garrett Park, 917 . . . J3
Garrison, 7969 . . . B3
Germantown, 55419 . . . E11
Gibson, 650 . . . C15
Girdletree, 117 . . . L19
Glassmanor, 35355 . . . G6
Glenarden, 6318 . . . F12
Glen Arm, 500 . . . D14
Glen Burnie, 38922 . . . E13
Glencoe, 450 . . . C13
Glen Echo, 242 . . . K2
Glenn Dale, 12609 . . . F13
Glenwood, 650 . . . D12
Glyndon, 1200 . . . C13
Golden Beach, 2665 . . . J13
Goldsboro, 216 . . . F17
Goodwill, 150 . . . L18
Gorman, 175 . . . D2
Goshen, 1300 . . . E11
Graceham, 475 . . . C10
Grantsville, 619 . . . B2
Grasonville, 2193 . . . F15
Great Mills, 2600 . . . K14
Greenbelt, 21456 . . . F12
Green Haven, 17415 . . . E14
Green Hill, 50 . . . K17
Greenmount, 600 . . . C12
Greensboro, 1632 . . . F17
Green Valley, 12262 . . . D11
Guilford, 12918 . . . G6
Hack Pt., 400 . . . C17
Hagerstown, 36687 . . . B9
Halethorpe, 150 . . . F4
Halfway, 10065 . . . C8
Hampstead, 5060 . . . C13
Hampton, 5004 . . . B6
Hancock, 1725 . . . B7
Harewood Park, 3400 . . . D15
Harrisville, 600 . . . B16
Harrisville, 475 . . . D11
Havre de Grace, 11331 . . . C16
Hebbville, 10900 . . . D3
Hebron, 807 . . . J18
Helen, 500 . . . J13
Henderson, 118 . . . F17
Herald Harbor, 2313 . . . K6
Hereford, 550 . . . C13
Hermanville, 1100 . . . K14
Highland, 800 . . . E12
Highland Beach, 109 . . . F14
Hillandale, 3054 . . . J4
Hillcrest Hts., 16359 . . . G12
Hillsboro, 163 . . . F16
Hillsmere Shores, 2977 . . . N8
Hobbs, 150 . . . G17
Hollywood, 650 . . . K14
Honga, 225 . . . K15
Hopewell, 550 . . . M17
Hudson, 275 . . . H15
Hughesville, 1537 . . . J13
Huntingtown, 2436 . . . H14
Hurlock, 1874 . . . H17
Hyattstown, 60 . . . D10
Hyattsville, 14733 . . . F12
Ijamsville, 225 . . . D10
Indian Head, 3422 . . . H11
Indiantown, 20 . . . K19
Ingleside, 125 . . . E17
Ironshire, 225 . . . K19
Jacksonville, 900 . . . C14
Jarrettsville, 2756 . . . C14
Jessup, 7865 . . . E13
Jesterville, 225 . . . K17
Jonestown, 475 . . . H17
Joppatowne, 11391 . . . D15
Keedysville, 482 . . . C9
Kennedyville, 175 . . . D16
Kensington, 1873 . . . J3
Kentmore Park, 20 . . . D16
Kenwood, 9800 . . . D8
Kenwood Beach, 600 . . . J14
Kettering, 11008 . . . M6
Keymar, 350 . . . C11
Keysville, 80 . . . C11
Kingston, 175 . . . L17
Kingstown, 1644 . . . E16
Kingsville, 4214 . . . A9
Kitzmiller, 302 . . . D2
Ladiesburg, 275 . . . C11
Lake Shore, 13065 . . . E14
Landover, 22900 . . . L5
Landover Hills, 1534 . . . L5
Langley Park, 16214 . . . K4
Lanham, 18190 . . . L6
Lansdowne, 15724 . . . F5
La Plata, 6551 . . . J12
Largo, 8408 . . . M6
Laurel, 19960 . . . E13
LaVale, 4613 . . . B4
Lawsonia, 1300 . . . M17
Laytonsville, 277 . . . E11
Le Gore, 375 . . . C10
Leitersburg, 523 . . . B9
Leonardtown, 1896 . . . K13
Lewistown, 600 . . . C10
Lewistown, 175 . . . G16
Lexington Park, 11021 . . . K14
Libertytown, 275 . . . C11
Linthicum, 7539 . . . G5
Lochearn, 25269 . . . D13
Loch Lynn Hts., 469 . . . D2
Lonaconing, 1205 . . . C3
Londontown, 7595 . . . F14
Long Beach, 2487 . . . J14
Long Green, 1000 . . . C14
Longridge, 40 . . . K18
Longview Beach, 275 . . . K13
Longwoods, 250 . . . G16
Love Pt., 30 . . . F15
Loveville, 650 . . . K13
Lower Marlboro, 450 . . . H13
Luke, 80 . . . C3
Lusby, 1666 . . . J14
Lynch, 200 . . . D16
Maddox, 225 . . . K13
Madison, 70 . . . J15
Manchester, 3329 . . . B12
Manokin, 100 . . . L17
Marbury, 1200 . . . H11
Mardela Sprs., 364 . . . J17
Marion, 600 . . . L17
Marley, 11200 . . . E14
Marlow Hts., 6059 . . . F7
Marlton, 7798 . . . G13
Martins Additions, 875 . . . K3
Marydel, 147 . . . E17
Maryland City, 6814 . . . H6
Marywood, 6000 . . . C15
Massey, 200 . . . D17
Mattawoman, 3100 . . . H12
Matthews, 100 . . . G16
Maugansville, 2295 . . . B8
Mayo, 3153 . . . G14
Mays Chapel, 11427 . . . A5
McDaniel, 425 . . . G15
McHenry, 250 . . . C2
McKay Beach, 600 . . . L14
Mechanicsville, 750 . . . J13
Melitota, 225 . . . E15
Melrose, 750 . . . B12
Melson, 225 . . . J18
Middleburg, 350 . . . C11
Middle River, 23958 . . . D14
Middletown, 2668 . . . D9
Midland, 473 . . . C3
Milford, 26527 . . . D4
Millington, 416 . . . E17
Monie, 50 . . . L17
Montgomery Vil., 38051 . . . E11
Montpelier, 11800 . . . J6
Montrose, 4800 . . . J2
Morgantown, 275 . . . K12
Morganza, 500 . . . K13
Morningside, 1295 . . . N5
Mt. Aetna, 838 . . . C9
Mountaindale, 325 . . . C10
Mtn. Lake Park, 2248 . . . D2
Mt. Airy, 6425 . . . D11
Mt. Pleasant, 550 . . . C12
Mt. Rainier, 8498 . . . L4
Mt. Savage, 1200 . . . B4
Mt. Vernon, 761 . . . K17
Mt. Westley, 80 . . . L19
Myersville, 1382 . . . C9
Nanjemoy, 300 . . . J11
Nanticoke, 275 . . . K17
Neavitt, 250 . . . H15
Newark, 339 . . . K19
Newburg, 300 . . . K12
New Carrollton, 12589 . . . F12
Newcomb, 600 . . . G15
New Market, 427 . . . D11
Newport, 175 . . . J12
Newton, 250 . . . G16
Newtown, 80 . . . D15
New Windsor, 1303 . . . C11
Nikep, 650 . . . C3
Normans, 650 . . . F15
Norrisville, 300 . . . B14
N. Beach, 1880 . . . H14
N. Brentwood, 469 . . . L5
N. Chevy Chase, 465 . . . K3
North East, 2733 . . . C16
Oakland, 2100 . . . D12
Oakland, 1930 . . . D1
Oakville, 50 . . . K18
Oakwood, 425 . . . B15
Ocean City, 7173 . . . K20
Ocean Pines, 10496 . . . J20
Odenton, 20534 . . . F13
Oldtown, 200 . . . C5
Olivet Hill, 250 . . . D17
Olney, 31438 . . . E12
Orchard Beach, 4400 . . . H7
Orchard Hills, 3844 . . . J9
Oriole, 200 . . . L17
Overlea, 12148 . . . D14
Owings, 1325 . . . H14
Owings Mills, 20193 . . . D13
Oxford, 771 . . . H15
Oxon Hill, 35355 . . . G12
Palmer Park, 7000 . . . L6
Paramount, 2722 . . . J10
Park Hall, 800 . . . K14
Parkville, 31118 . . . D14
Parole, 14031 . . . N11
Parsonsburg, 600 . . . J18
Pasadena, 12093 . . . J6
Perry Hall, 28705 . . . D14
Perryman, 2461 . . . C15
Perryville, 3672 . . . C16
Petersburg, 175 . . . H17
Phoenix, 500 . . . C13
Pikesville, 29123 . . . D13
Piney Pt., 700 . . . L14
Piscataway, 150 . . . H12
Pisgah, 175 . . . J11
Pittsville, 1182 . . . J19
Pleasant Hills, 2851 . . . C14
Pocomoke City, 4098 . . . L18
Pt. of Rocks, 850 . . . E9
Pomona, 150 . . . E16
Pomonkey, 750 . . . H12
Poolesville, 5151 . . . E10
Popes Creek, 125 . . . J12
Port Deposit, 676 . . . C16
Port Tobacco, 15 . . . J12
Potomac, 44822 . . . F11
Potomac Hts., 1154 . . . H11
Potomac Park, 1900 . . . C4
Potomac View, 200 . . . K12
Powellville, 225 . . . K19
Preston, 566 . . . H17
Price, 100 . . . E16
Prince Frederick, 1432 . . . J14
Princess Anne, 2313 . . . K18
Public Landing, 90 . . . L19
Pumphrey, 5317 . . . G5
Pylesville, 350 . . . B14
Quantico, 325 . . . J17
Queen Anne, 176 . . . F16
Queenstown, 617 . . . F15
Quince Orchard, 23044 . . . E11
Randallstown, 30870 . . . D13
Randle Cliff Beach, 800 . . . H14
Randolph Hills, 14300 . . . J3
Rawlings, 750 . . . C4
Redland, 16998 . . . E11
Rehobeth, 50 . . . L18
Reids Grove, 80 . . . J17
Reisterstown, 22438 . . . D13
Reliance, 20 . . . H17
Rhodesdale, 70 . . . H17
Ridge, 400 . . . L15
Ridgely, 1352 . . . F17
Rising Sun, 1702 . . . B16
Riva, 3966 . . . N6
Riverdale Park, 6690 . . . L5
Riviera Beach, 12695 . . . E14
Robbins, 40 . . . J16
Roberts, 100 . . . E16
Rockdale, 16100 . . . D13
Rock Hall, 1396 . . . E15
Rock Pt., 750 . . . K13
Rockville, 47388 . . . F11
Rocky Ridge, 425 . . . C10
Rohrersville, 170 . . . D9
Romancoke, 800 . . . G15
Rosaryville, 12322 . . . G13
Rosedale, 19199 . . . D14
Rose Haven, 1400 . . . H14
Rosemont, 273 . . . D9
Rossmoor Leisure World, 7569 . . . H3
Rossville, 11515 . . . D8
Royal Oak, 750 . . . G15
Rumbley, 96 . . . L17
Ruthsburg, 125 . . . F16
Sabillasville, 350 . . . B10
St. Charles, 33379 . . . H12
St. Clement Shores, 800 . . . K13
St. George Island, 275 . . . L14
St. Inigoes, 650 . . . L15
St. James, 1657 . . . C8
St. Leonard, 536 . . . J14
St. Mary's City, 900 . . . L14
St. Michaels, 1193 . . . G15
Salisbury, 23743 . . . K18
Sandgates, 550 . . . J14
Sandy Spr., 3437 . . . G4
Sandyville, 1000 . . . C12
Sassafras, 100 . . . D17
Savage, 12918 . . . E13
Scientists Cliffs, 500 . . . J14
Scotland, 300 . . . L15
Scotland Beach, 125 . . . L15
Seabrook, 18190 . . . K6
Seat Pleasant, 4885 . . . M5
Secretary, 503 . . . H16
Severn, 35076 . . . E13
Severna Park, 28507 . . . F14
Shady Side, 5559 . . . G14
Sharpsburg, 691 . . . C8
Sharptown, 649 . . . J17
Shawsville, 275 . . . C14
Shelltown, 40 . . . M18
Sherwood, 100 . . . G15
Shiloh, 250 . . . K12
Shoreham Beach, 1300 . . . G14
Showell, 225 . . . J20
Silver Hill, 33515 . . . N5
Silver Spr., 76540 . . . F12
Simpsonville, 4400 . . . E12
Skipton, 200 . . . G16
Smallwood, 950 . . . C12
Smithsburg, 2146 . . . B9
Smithville, 150 . . . G17
Smithville, 30 . . . J15
Snow Hill, 2409 . . . L19
Solomons, 1536 . . . K14
Somerset, 1124 . . . K3
S. Gate, 28672 . . . H6
Sparks, 1800 . . . C13
Spencerville, 2900 . . . H4
Spring Garden Estates, 2400 . . . C10
Stevensville, 5880 . . . F15
Still Pond, 325 . . . D16
Stockton, 143 . . . L19
Sudlersville, 391 . . . E17
Suitland, 33515 . . . G12
Sunderland, 1400 . . . H14
Sunnybrook, 2300 . . . C14
Sykesville, 4197 . . . D12
Takoma Park, 17299 . . . K4
Tall Timbers, 275 . . . L14
Taneytown, 5128 . . . B11
Tantallon, 7900 . . . H12
Taylors Island, 100 . . . J15
Taylorsville, 900 . . . D12
Temple Hills, 7792 . . . N5
Templeville, 80 . . . E17
Thompsontown, 90 . . . H17
Thurmont, 5588 . . . C10
Tilghman, 854 . . . H15
Tilghmanton, 475 . . . C8
Toddville, 150 . . . K16
Tolchester Beach, 175 . . . E15
Tonytank, 3500 . . . K18
Town Pt., 550 . . . C17
Towson, 51793 . . . D14
Trappe, 1146 . . . H16
Tunis Mills, 225 . . . G15
Tyaskin, 250 . . . K17
Union Bridge, 989 . . . C11
Union Mills, 300 . . . B12
Uniontown, 275 . . . C11
Unionville, 175 . . . G16
University Park, 2318 . . . K5
Upper Hill, 175 . . . L17
Upper Marlboro, 648 . . . G13
Urbana, 400 . . . D10
Valley Lee, 400 . . . L14
Vienna, 280 . . . J17
Waldorf, 22312 . . . H12
Walker Mill, 11104 . . . M5
Walkersville, 5192 . . . C10
Warwick, 300 . . . D17
Washington Grove, 515 . . . G2
Waterloo, 900 . . . E13
Waterview, 100 . . . K17
Webster, 1200 . . . C15
Welcome, 175 . . . J11
Wenona, 475 . . . L16
Wesley, 80 . . . K16
W. Denton, 325 . . . G17
Westernport, 2104 . . . C3
W. Friendship, 700 . . . D12
W. Liberty, 325 . . . B14
Westminster, 16731 . . . C12
Westover, 100 . . . L17
Wetipquin, 100 . . . K17
Whaleysville, 250 . . . J19
Wheaton, 57694 . . . F12
Whiteford, 700 . . . B15
White Hall, 300 . . . C13
Whitehaven, 70 . . . K17
White Marsh, 8485 . . . C9
White Oak, 20973 . . . J4
White Plains, 3600 . . . H12
White Pt. Beach, 200 . . . K14
Whiton, 30 . . . K19
Willards, 938 . . . J19
Williamsburg, 60 . . . H17
Williamsport, 1868 . . . C8
Williston, 425 . . . G17
Willows, 900 . . . H14
Wilson, 1885 . . . B8
Wittman, 325 . . . G15
Woodbine, 425 . . . D12
Woodfield, 2500 . . . E11
Woodland Pt., 125 . . . K12
Woodlawn, 36079 . . . D4
Woodlawn, 1600 . . . B16
Woodmore, 6077 . . . L7
Woodsboro, 846 . . . C10
Woolford, 150 . . . J15
Worton, 225 . . . D16
Wye Mills, 325 . . . F16
Yellow Sprs., 1100 . . . C10

MASSACHUSETTS
PG. 109-111

CAPITAL
Boston

NICKNAME
Bay State

POPULATION
6,349,097, rank 13

AREA
8,284 sq mi, rank 45

Counties

Barnstable, 222230 . . . K17
Berkshire, 134953 . . . D2
Bristol, 534678 . . . H13
Dukes, 14987 . . . M17
Essex, 723419 . . . B14
Franklin, 71535 . . . C5
Hampden, 456228 . . . F7
Hampshire, 152251 . . . E4
Middlesex, 1465396 . . . D13
Nantucket, 9520 . . . N19
Norfolk, 650308 . . . F13
Plymouth, 472822 . . . H15
Suffolk, 689807 . . . E14
Worcester, 750963 . . . D9

Cities and Towns

Abington, 14605 . . . G15
Accord, 2300 . . . F15
Acoaxet, 175 . . . L14
Acton, 2700 . . . D12
Acushnet, 3171 . . . K15
Adams, 5784 . . . C3
Adamsville, 200 . . . B5
Agawam, 28144 . . . G6
Alford, 100 . . . F1
Amesbury, 12327 . . . A15
Amherst, 17050 . . . E6
Andover, 7900 . . . C14
Arlington, 42389 . . . D14
Ashburnham, 1000 . . . C9
Ashby, 550 . . . B10
Ashfield, 550 . . . D5
Ashland, 14674 . . . F12
Ashley Falls, 450 . . . G2
Assinippi, 2700 . . . F15
Assonet, 1200 . . . J14
Athol, 8370 . . . C8
Attleboro, 42068 . . . H13
Auburn, 15901 . . . F10
Ayer, 2960 . . . C11
Baldwinville, 1852 . . . C8
Ballardvale, 3500 . . . C14
Bancroft, 125 . . . E3
Barnstable, 47821 . . . K18
Barre, 1150 . . . D8
Barre Plains, 1200 . . . E8
Becket, 350 . . . E3
Becket Ctr., 100 . . . E3
Bedford, 12595 . . . D13
Belchertown, 2626 . . . E7
Bellingham, 4497 . . . G12
Belmont, 24194 . . . E13
Berkley, 850 . . . J14
Berkshire, 400 . . . D2
Berlin, 650 . . . E11
Bernardston, 1000 . . . C6
Beverly, 39862 . . . C15
Billerica, 38981 . . . C13
Blackstone, 2900 . . . G11
Blandford, 400 . . . F4
Bliss Corner, 5466 . . . N12
Bolton, 425 . . . D11
Bondsville, 1876 . . . F7
Boston, 589141 . . . E14
Bourne, 1443 . . . J17
Boxborough, 1400 . . . D12
Boxford, 2340 . . . C14
Braintree, 33698 . . . F14
Brant Rock, 5100 . . . G16
Brewster, 2212 . . . J19
Bridgewater, 6664 . . . G15
Briggsville, 750 . . . B3
Brimfield, 400 . . . G8
Brockton, 94304 . . . G14
Brookfield, 1200 . . . F8
Brookline, 57107 . . . E14
Bryantville, 2600 . . . G15
Buckland, 125 . . . C5
Burlington, 22876 . . . D13
Buzzards Bay, 3549 . . . J17
Byfield, 850 . . . B15
Cambridge, 101355 . . . E14
Canton, 20775 . . . F14
Carlisle, 800 . . . D13
Carver, 900 . . . H16
Centerville, 9200 . . . K18
Central Vil., 600 . . . L14
Chaffinville, 3100 . . . E10
Charlemont, 250 . . . C4
Charlton, 1100 . . . F9
Charlton City, 1400 . . . F9
Charlton Depot, 1200 . . . F9
Chartley, 1600 . . . H13
Chatham, 1667 . . . K20
Chelmsford, 32400 . . . C13
Chelsea, 35080 . . . D14
Cheshire, 1200 . . . C3
Cheshire Harbor, 450 . . . C3
Chester, 800 . . . E4
Chesterfield, 250 . . . E4
Chicopee, 54653 . . . F6
Chilmark, 200 . . . M16
Clayton, 50 . . . G2
Clinton, 7884 . . . D11
Cochituate, 6768 . . . E12
Cohasset, 3300 . . . F16
Cold Spr., 30 . . . F3
Colrain, 200 . . . C5
Concord, 3500 . . . D13
Conway, 350 . . . D5
Cordaville, 2515 . . . E12
Cotuit, 2400 . . . K18
Cummington, 275 . . . D4
Dalton, 4100 . . . D3
Danvers, 25212 . . . C15
Dedham, 23464 . . . F14
Deerfield, 450 . . . C6
Dennis, 2798 . . . J19
Dennis Port, 3612 . . . K19
Dighton, 1200 . . . J14
Douglas, 800 . . . G10
Dover, 2216 . . . F13
Drury, 100 . . . C3
Dudley, 1800 . . . G9
Dunstable, 650 . . . B12
Duxbury, 1426 . . . G16
Dwight, 550 . . . E6
E. Blackstone, 1600 . . . G12
E. Brewster, 850 . . . J20
E. Bridgewater, 4000 . . . G15
E. Brookfield, 1410 . . . F9
E. Dennis, 3299 . . . J19
E. Douglas, 2319 . . . G11
E. Falmouth, 6615 . . . K17
E. Freetown, 1200 . . . J15
Eastham, 1100 . . . J20
Easthampton, 15994 . . . E5
E. Harwich, 4744 . . . J20
E. Leverett, 275 . . . D6
E. Longmeadow, 14100 . . . G6
E. Marion, 550 . . . J16
E. Northfield, 150 . . . B6
E. Orleans, 1800 . . . J20
E. Otis, 200 . . . F3
E. Pepperell, 2034 . . . C11
E. Princeton, 300 . . . D10
E. Sandwich, 3720 . . . J17
E. Templeton, 1200 . . . C9
E. Wareham, 1700 . . . J16
E. Windsor, 80 . . . D4
Edgartown, 1100 . . . M17
Erving, 250 . . . C7
Essex, 1426 . . . C16
Everett, 38037 . . . D6
Fairhaven, 16159 . . . K15
Fall River, 91938 . . . K14
Falmouth, 4115 . . . L17
Farley, 200 . . . C6
Fiskdale, 2156 . . . G8
Fitchburg, 39102 . . . C10
Five Corners, 2100 . . . G14
Florida, 90 . . . C3
Forestdale, 3992 . . . K17
Forge Vil., 2300 . . . C12
Foxboro, 5509 . . . G13
Framingham, 66910 . . . E12
Franklin, 29560 . . . G12
Gardner, 20770 . . . C9
Gay Head, 175 . . . M16
Georgetown, 3000 . . . B14
Gilbertville, 1000 . . . E8
Glendale, 250 . . . E2
Glen Mills, 750 . . . B15
Gloucester, 30273 . . . C16
Goshen, 250 . . . D5
Grafton, 2400 . . . F11
Granby, 1344 . . . F6
Granville, 325 . . . G4
Great Barrington, 2459 . . . F2
Greenbush, 550 . . . F16
Greenfield, 13716 . . . C6
Green Harbor, 2397 . . . G16
Griswoldville, 150 . . . C5
Groton, 1113 . . . C11
Groveland, 2800 . . . B14
Hadley, 1200 . . . E6
Halifax, 1000 . . . G15
Hampden, 500 . . . G7
Hancock, 125 . . . C2
Hanover, 2200 . . . G15
Hanson, 2044 . . . G15
Hardwick, 150 . . . E8
Hartsville, 150 . . . F2
Harvard, 800 . . . D11
Harwich, 1832 . . . K19
Harwich Port, 1809 . . . K19
Hatfield, 1298 . . . E6
Haverhill, 58969 . . . B14
Hawley, 70 . . . C4
Haydenville, 700 . . . E5
Heath, 150 . . . B4
Hingham, 5352 . . . F15
Hinsdale, 750 . . . D3
Hixville, 500 . . . K14
Holbrook, 10785 . . . F14
Holden, 4200 . . . E10
Holland, 1444 . . . G8
Holliston, 3400 . . . F12
Holyoke, 39838 . . . F6
Hopedale, 4158 . . . F12
Hopkinton, 2628 . . . F12
Hortonville, 850 . . . J13
Housatonic, 1335 . . . E1
Hubbardston, 375 . . . D9
Hudson, 14388 . . . E11
Hull, 11050 . . . E15
Humarock, 2000 . . . F16
Huntington, 950 . . . F4
Hyannis, 14100 . . . K18
Hyannis Port, 3100 . . . K18
Interlaken, 225 . . . E2
Ipswich, 4161 . . . B15
Jefferson, 1600 . . . E9
Katama, 125 . . . M17
Kingston, 5380 . . . G16
Knights Corner, 50 . . . E7
Lake Pleasant, 350 . . . C6
Lakeside, 300 . . . K14
Lakeville, 2233 . . . J15
Lancaster, 1700 . . . D11
Lanesboro, 850 . . . D2
Lawrence, 72043 . . . B14
Lee, 2021 . . . E2
Leicester, 2400 . . . F9
Lenox, 1667 . . . E2
Lenox Dale, 1100 . . . E2
Leominster, 41303 . . . D10
Leverett, 500 . . . D6
Lexington, 30355 . . . D13
Lincoln, 650 . . . D1
Lithia, 60 . . . D4
Littleton Common, 2816 . . . C12
Locks Vil., 225 . . . D6
Longmeadow, 15633 . . . G6
Long Pond, 1500 . . . H17
Lowell, 105167 . . . C13
Ludlow, 7400 . . . F6
Ludlow City, 375 . . . F6
Lunenburg, 1695 . . . C10
Lynn, 89050 . . . D15
Lynnfield, 11542 . . . C14
Madaket, 125 . . . N19
Malden, 56340 . . . D14
Manchaug, 850 . . . G10
Manchester-by-the-Sea, 3600 . . . C16
Manomet, 2900 . . . H17
Mansfield, 7320 . . . G13
Marblehead, 20377 . . . D15
Marion, 1202 . . . K16
Marlborough, 36255 . . . E12
Marshfield, 4246 . . . G16
Marshfield Hills, 2369 . . . F16
Marstons Mills, 8000 . . . K18
Mashpee, 901 . . . K17
Mattapoisett, 2966 . . . K15
Maynard, 10433 . . . D12
Medfield, 6670 . . . F13
Medford, 55765 . . . D14
Medway, 4000 . . . F12
Melrose, 27134 . . . C6
Mendon, 1100 . . . G11
Menemsha, 100 . . . M16
Merrimac, 2900 . . . A14
Methuen, 43789 . . . B13
Middleboro, 6913 . . . H15
Middlefield, 80 . . . E3
Middleton, 1200 . . . C14
Milford, 24230 . . . F12
Millbury, 4700 . . . F10
Millers Falls, 1072 . . . C6
Millis, 4607 . . . F13
Mill River, 225 . . . G2
Milton, 26062 . . . F14
Minot, 1100 . . . F16
Monponsett, 1700 . . . G15
Monroe Bridge, 60 . . . B4
Monson, 2103 . . . G7
Montague, 800 . . . C6
Monterey, 250 . . . F2
Montgomery, 150 . . . F4
Montville, 60 . . . F3
Monument Beach, 2438 . . . J17
Morningdale, 2500 . . . K6
Myricks, 600 . . . J14
Nahant, 3632 . . . D15
Nameloc Hts., 1500 . . . J17
Nantucket, 3830 . . . N19
Nashaquitsa, 30 . . . M16
Natick, 32170 . . . E13
Needham, 28911 . . . E13
New Ashford, 150 . . . C2
New Bedford, 93768 . . . K15
New Boston, 200 . . . G3
New Braintree, 250 . . . E8
Newbury Old Town, 475 . . . B15
Newburyport, 17189 . . . A15
New Marlborough, 40 . . . F2
New Salem, 70 . . . D7
Newton, 83829 . . . E13
Nonquitt, 350 . . . L15
Norfolk, 1900 . . . G13
N. Acton, 3000 . . . D12
N. Adams, 14681 . . . B3
N. Amherst, 6019 . . . D6
Northampton, 28978 . . . E5
N. Attleboro, 16796 . . . H13
N. Billerica, 5200 . . . C13
Northborough, 6257 . . . E11
Northbridge, 3000 . . . F11
N. Brookfield, 2527 . . . E8
N. Carver, 700 . . . H16
N. Chatham, 750 . . . J20
N. Chelmsford, 4900 . . . C12
N. Cohasset, 1600 . . . E15
N. Dartmouth, 2200 . . . M11
N. Dighton, 1400 . . . H14
N. Eastham, 1915 . . . H20
N. Easton, 3700 . . . G14
N. Egremont, 200 . . . F1
N. Falmouth, 3355 . . . K17
Northfield, 1141 . . . B6
N. Grafton, 3600 . . . F11
N. Hatfield, 550 . . . D6
N. Leverett, 250 . . . D6
N. Middleboro, 850 . . . H15
N. New Salem, 275 . . . C7
N. Orange, 200 . . . C7
N. Otis, 40 . . . F3
N. Oxford, 1200 . . . F9
N. Pembroke, 2913 . . . G16
N. Plymouth, 3593 . . . H16
N. Plympton, 475 . . . G16
N. Reading, 2800 . . . C14
N. Scituate, 5065 . . . F16
N. Swansea, 1100 . . . J13
N. Tisbury, 200 . . . M16
N. Truro, 550 . . . G19
N. Uxbridge, 4200 . . . G11
Northville, 2400 . . . G15
Norton, 2618 . . . H13
Norwell, 1300 . . . F16
Norwich, 350 . . . E4
Norwood, 28587 . . . F13
Nutting Lake, 5700 . . . A2
Oak Bluffs, 1700 . . . L17
Oakdale, 1100 . . . E10
Oakham, 300 . . . E9
Ocean Bluff, 5100 . . . G16
Ocean Grove, 3012 . . . J13
Onset, 1292 . . . J16
Orange, 3945 . . . C7
Orleans, 1716 . . . J20
Osterville, 2900 . . . K18
Otis, 200 . . . F3
Otter River, 850 . . . C9
Oxford, 5899 . . . G10
Palmer, 3900 . . . F7
Paxton, 1000 . . . E9
Peabody, 48129 . . . D15
Pelham, 125 . . . E7
Pembroke, 2800 . . . G15
Pepperell, 2517 . . . C11
Peru, 150 . . . D3
Petersham, 350 . . . D8
Phillipston, 175 . . . C8
Pigeon Cove, 1700 . . . B16
Pinehurst, 6941 . . . D13
Pittsfield, 45793 . . . D2
Plainfield, 125 . . . D4
Plainville, 3000 . . . G13
Pleasant Lake, 800 . . . J19
Plymouth, 7658 . . . H16
Plympton, 550 . . . H15
Pocasset, 2671 . . . K17
Polpis, 90 . . . M20
Popponesset Beach, 310 . . . K17
Princeton, 225 . . . D9
Princeton Sta., 225 . . . D9
Provincetown, 3192 . . . G19
Quidnet, 10 . . . M20
Quincy, 88025 . . . F14
Randolph, 30963 . . . F14
Raynham, 1900 . . . H14
Raynham Ctr., 3633 . . . H14
Reading, 23708 . . . D14
Rehoboth, 700 . . . J13
Revere, 47283 . . . D14
Richmond, 450 . . . E1
Ringville, 100 . . . E4
Risingdale, 225 . . . F2
Rochdale, 1400 . . . F9
Rochester, 500 . . . J15
Rock, 850 . . . J15
Rockland, 17670 . . . F15
Rockport, 5606 . . . C16
Rowe, 150 . . . B4
Rowley, 1434 . . . B15
Royalston, 60 . . . B8
Russell, 600 . . . F4
Rutland, 2205 . . . E9
Sagamore, 3544 . . . J17
Sagamore Beach, 1200 . . . J17
Salem, 40407 . . . D15
Salisbury, 4484 . . . A15
Salisbury Beach, 1300 . . . A15
Sand Hills, 2400 . . . F16
Sandisfield, 50 . . . G3
Sandwich, 3058 . . . J17
Santuit, 375 . . . K17
Saugus, 26078 . . . D14
Savoy, 125 . . . C3
Scituate, 5069 . . . F16
Scotland, 1900 . . . H14
Sharon, 5941 . . . G14
Shattuckville, 225 . . . C5
Sheffield, 750 . . . G2
Shelburne, 325 . . . C5
Shelburne Falls, 1951 . . . C5
Sheldonville, 500 . . . G12
Sherborn, 1200 . . . F12
Shirley, 1427 . . . C11
Shrewsbury, 31640 . . . E10
Shutesbury, 125 . . . D7
Siasconset, 275 . . . N20
Silver Beach, 500 . . . K16
Silver Lake, 3300 . . . C13
Silver Lake, 1000 . . . G16
Sippewisset, 950 . . . L16
Somerset, 18234 . . . J14
Somerville, 77478 . . . E14
S. Acton, 2700 . . . D12
S. Amherst, 5039 . . . E6
S. Ashburnham, 1013 . . . C9
S. Berlin, 800 . . . E11
Southborough, 1700 . . . E12
Southbridge, 12878 . . . G9
S. Bridgewater, 2600 . . . H15
S. Carver, 375 . . . J16
S. Chatham, 800 . . . K20
S. Dartmouth, 1900 . . . K15
S. Deerfield, 1868 . . . D6
S. Dennis, 3679 . . . K19
S. Duxbury, 3062 . . . G16
S. Easton, 3600 . . . G14
S. Egremont, 450 . . . F1
Southfield, 100 . . . G2
S. Hadley, 3900 . . . E6
S. Hadley Falls, 4300 . . . F6
S. Lancaster, 1742 . . . D11
S. Middleboro, 750 . . . J15
S. Orleans, 1100 . . . J20
S. Royalston, 300 . . . C8
S. Sandisfield, 20 . . . G3
S. Walpole, 1900 . . . G13
S. Wareham, 375 . . . J16
S. Wellfleet, 500 . . . H20

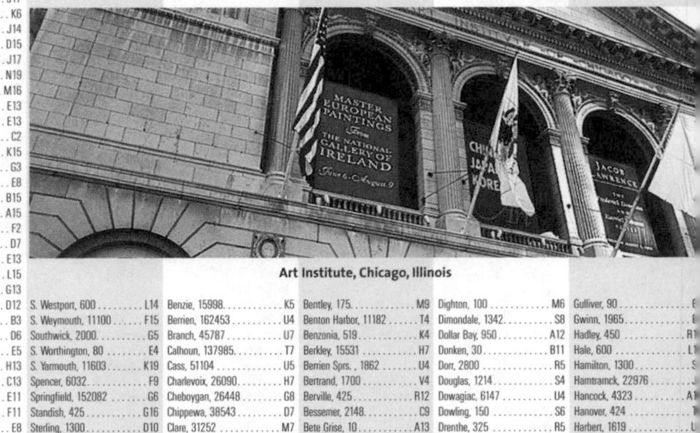

Art Institute, Chicago, Illinois

S. Westport, 600 . . . L14
S. Weymouth, 11100 . . . F15
Southwick, 2000 . . . G5
S. Worthington, 80 . . . E4
S. Yarmouth, 11603 . . . K19
Spencer, 6032 . . . F9
Springfield, 152082 . . . G6
Standish, 425 . . . G16
Sterling, 1300 . . . D10
Still River, 400 . . . D11
Stockbridge, 900 . . . E2
Stoneham, 22219 . . . D14
Stoughton, 11200 . . . F14
Sturbridge, 2047 . . . G8
Sudbury, 2300 . . . E12
Sunderland, 850 . . . D6
Surfside, 175 . . . N19
Sutton, 650 . . . F10
Swampscott, 14412 . . . D15
Swifts Beach, 2700 . . . J16
Taunton, 55976 . . . H14
Teaticket, 1907 . . . L17
Templeton, 800 . . . C8
Tewksbury, 28851 . . . C13
Texas, 1300 . . . F9
Three Rivers, 2939 . . . F7
Topsfield, 2826 . . . C15
Townsend, 1043 . . . C11
Townsend Harbor, 1700 . . . C11
Truro, 400 . . . G20
Tully, 275 . . . C7
Turners Falls, 4441 . . . C6
Tyringham, 80 . . . F2
Upton, 2326 . . . F11
Uxbridge, 3300 . . . G11
Vallersville, 2000 . . . H17
Vineyard Haven, 2048 . . . L17
Wades Corner, 150 . . . H14
Wakeby, 1600 . . . K17
Wakefield, 24804 . . . D14
Wales, 850 . . . G8
Walpole, 5867 . . . F13
Waltham, 59226 . . . E13
Ware, 6174 . . . F8
Wareham, 2874 . . . J16
Warren, 1452 . . . F8
Warrentown, 400 . . . H15
Warwick, 150 . . . B7
Washington, 275 . . . E3
Watertown, 32986 . . . E13
Waterville, 950 . . . B8
Watson, 80 . . . C4
Wauwinet, 10 . . . M20
Wayland, 1300 . . . E12
Webster, 11600 . . . G9
Wellesley, 26613 . . . E13
Wellfleet, 1000 . . . H20
Wendell, 100 . . . C7
Wenham, 2300 . . . C15
W. Barnstable, 1500 . . . J18
W. Becket, 80 . . . E3
Westborough, 3983 . . . E11
W. Boxford, 1200 . . . B14
W. Boylston, 1100 . . . E10
W. Bridgewater, 2400 . . . G14
W. Brimfield, 125 . . . F7
W. Brookfield, 1610 . . . F8
W. Chelmsford, 1400 . . . C12
W. Chesterfield, 100 . . . D4
W. Concord, 5632 . . . D12
W. Cummington, 125 . . . D4
W. Dennis, 2570 . . . K19
W. Falmouth, 1867 . . . K16
Westfield, 40072 . . . G5
W. Granville, 20 . . . G4
W. Groton, 750 . . . C11
Westhampton, 275 . . . E5
W. Hawley, 50 . . . C4
W. Medway, 3500 . . . F12
Westminster, 1300 . . . C9
W. Otis, 125 . . . F3
W. Pelham, 1300 . . . E6
Westport Pt., 350 . . . L14
W. Royalston, 40 . . . B8
W. Springfield, 27899 . . . G5
W. Sterling, 450 . . . D10
W. Stockbridge, 750 . . . E1
W. Sutton, 350 . . . G10
W. Tisbury, 350 . . . M16
W. Townsend, 1300 . . . B10
W. Upton, 2326 . . . F11
W. Wareham, 1908 . . . J16
W. Warren, 1100 . . . F8
Westwood, 14117 . . . F13
W. Yarmouth, 6460 . . . K19
Weymouth, 53988 . . . F15
Whately, 425 . . . D5
Wheelwright, 425 . . . E8
White Horse Beach, 2300 . . . H17
White Island Shores, 2133 . . . J16
Whitinsville, 6340 . . . G11
Whitman, 13882 . . . G15
Wilbraham, 3544 . . . F6
Williamsburg, 550 . . . E5
Williamstown, 4754 . . . B2
Williamsville, 225 . . . D8
Wilmington, 21363 . . . C13
Winchendon, 4246 . . . B9
Winchester, 20810 . . . D14
Windsor, 125 . . . D3
Winnecunnet, 750 . . . H14
Winthrop, 18303 . . . E15
Woburn, 37258 . . . D14
Woods Hole, 925 . . . L16
Woodville, 500 . . . F11
Worcester, 172648 . . . F10
Worthington Corners, 250 . . . D4
Wrentham, 2600 . . . G13
Yarmouth, 2100 . . . J19
Yarmouth Port, 5395 . . . K18
Zoar, 175 . . . C4

MICHIGAN
PG. 112-114

CAPITAL
Lansing

NICKNAME
Great Lakes State

POPULATION
9,938,444, rank 8

AREA
58,527 sq mi, rank 23

Counties

Alcona, 11719 . . . K10
Alger, 9862 . . . E3
Allegan, 105665 . . . S5
Alpena, 31314 . . . J10
Antrim, 23110 . . . J7
Arenac, 17269 . . . M10
Baraga, 8746 . . . B12
Barry, 56755 . . . S6
Bay, 110157 . . . N9
Benzie, 15998 . . . K5
Berrien, 162453 . . . U4
Branch, 45787 . . . U7
Calhoun, 137985 . . . T7
Cass, 51104 . . . U5
Charlevoix, 26090 . . . H7
Cheboygan, 26448 . . . G8
Chippewa, 38543 . . . D7
Clare, 31252 . . . M7
Clinton, 64753 . . . R8
Crawford, 14273 . . . K8
Delta, 38520 . . . F3
Dickinson, 27472 . . . E1
Eaton, 103655 . . . S7
Emmet, 31437 . . . G7
Genesee, 436141 . . . Q10
Gladwin, 26023 . . . M8
Gogebic, 17370 . . . C10
Grand Traverse, 77654 . . . K6
Gratiot, 42285 . . . P8
Hillsdale, 46527 . . . U8
Houghton, 36016 . . . C11
Huron, 36079 . . . N11
Ingham, 279320 . . . S9
Ionia, 61518 . . . R7
Iosco, 27339 . . . L10
Iron, 13138 . . . C11
Isabella, 63351 . . . N7
Jackson, 158422 . . . T8
Kalamazoo, 238603 . . . T6
Kalkaska, 16571 . . . K7
Kent, 574335 . . . Q6
Keweenaw, 2301 . . . A12
Lake, 11333 . . . M5
Lapeer, 87904 . . . Q11
Leelanau, 21119 . . . J5
Lenawee, 98890 . . . U9
Livingston, 156951 . . . S10
Luce, 7024 . . . D6
Mackinac, 11943 . . . E7
Macomb, 788149 . . . R12
Manistee, 24527 . . . L5
Marquette, 64634 . . . D1
Mason, 28274 . . . M4
Mecosta, 40553 . . . P6
Menominee, 25326 . . . G1
Midland, 82874 . . . N9
Missaukee, 14478 . . . L7
Monroe, 145945 . . . U11
Montcalm, 61266 . . . P6
Montmorency, 10315 . . . J9
Muskegon, 170200 . . . Q5
Newaygo, 47874 . . . P5
Oakland, 1194156 . . . S11
Oceana, 26873 . . . N4
Ogemaw, 21645 . . . L9
Ontonagon, 7818 . . . C10
Osceola, 23197 . . . M6
Oscoda, 9418 . . . J9
Otsego, 23301 . . . H8
Ottawa, 238314 . . . R5
Presque Isle, 14411 . . . H9
Roscommon, 25469 . . . L8
Saginaw, 210039 . . . P9
St. Clair, 164235 . . . R12
St. Joseph, 62422 . . . U6
Sanilac, 44547 . . . P12
Schoolcraft, 8903 . . . E4
Shiawassee, 71687 . . . Q9
Tuscola, 58266 . . . P10
Van Buren, 76263 . . . T4
Washtenaw, 322895 . . . T10
Wayne, 2061162 . . . T11
Wexford, 30484 . . . L6

Cities and Towns

Acme, 650 . . . J6
Addison, 627 . . . U9
Adrian, 21574 . . . U9
Afton, 100 . . . G8
Agnew, 275 . . . R4
Ahmeek, 157 . . . A12
Akron, 461 . . . P11
Alabaster, 40 . . . M10
Alamo, 275 . . . T5
Alanson, 785 . . . G7
Alba, 325 . . . J7
Alberta, 150 . . . C12
Albion, 9144 . . . T8
Alcona, 40 . . . J11
Alden, 150 . . . J6
Algonac, 4613 . . . S13
Allegan, 4838 . . . S5
Allen, 225 . . . U8
Allendale, 11555 . . . R5
Allen Park, 29376 . . . L6
Allouez, 225 . . . A12
Alma, 9275 . . . P8
Almont, 2803 . . . R12
Aloha, 175 . . . G8
Alpena, 11304 . . . H11
Alpha, 198 . . . D12
Alto, 300 . . . R6
Alverno, 225 . . . G8
Amasa, 200 . . . D12
Anchorville, 3200 . . . R13
Ann Arbor, 114024 . . . T10
Applegate, 287 . . . P13
Arcadia, 325 . . . K4
Argentine, 2285 . . . R10
Argyle, 125 . . . P12
Armada, 1573 . . . R12
Arnold, 20 . . . E1
Ashley, 526 . . . Q8
Ashton, 200 . . . M6
Assyria, 275 . . . S7
Athens, 1111 . . . U6
Atlanta, 757 . . . J9
Attica, 700 . . . Q11
Atwood, 90 . . . H6
Auburn, 2011 . . . P9
Auburn Hills, 19837 . . . E7
Au Gres, 1028 . . . M10
Augusta, 899 . . . T6
Aura, 150 . . . B12
Au Sable, 1533 . . . L11
Au Train, 225 . . . D3
Avoca, 325 . . . Q13
Bach, 90 . . . N11
Bad Axe, 3462 . . . N12
Baldwin, 1107 . . . N5
Bancroft, 616 . . . R9
Bangor, 1933 . . . T4
Baraga, 1285 . . . B12
Barbeau, 30 . . . D9
Bark River, 425 . . . F2
Baroda, 858 . . . U3
Barryton, 381 . . . N7
Barton City, 250 . . . K10
Barton Hills, 335 . . . T10
Bath, 1200 . . . R8
Battle Creek, 53364 . . . T7
Bay City, 36817 . . . P10
Bay Port, 500 . . . N11
Bay Shore, 550 . . . H7
Beal City, 345 . . . N7
Bear Lake, 318 . . . L4
Beaverton, 1106 . . . N8
Bedford, 600 . . . T6
Beecher, 12793 . . . D2
Beechwood, 90 . . . D11
Belding, 5877 . . . Q6
Bellaire, 1164 . . . J6
Belleville, 3997 . . . T11
Bellevue, 1365 . . . S7
Bentley, 175 . . . M9
Benton Harbor, 11182 . . . T4
Benzonia, 519 . . . K4
Berkley, 15531 . . . H7
Berrien Sprs., 1862 . . . U4
Bertrand, 1700 . . . V4
Berville, 425 . . . R12
Bessemer, 2148 . . . C9
Bete Grise, 10 . . . A13
Beulah, 363 . . . K4
Beverly Hills, 10437 . . . G6
Big Bay, 265 . . . B13
Big Rapids, 10849 . . . N6
Bingham Farms, 1030 . . . G6
Birch Run, 1653 . . . Q10
Birmingham, 19291 . . . S11
Bitely, 125 . . . N5
Black River, 100 . . . J11
Blanchard, 350 . . . P7
Bliss, 70 . . . F7
Blissfield, 3223 . . . U10
Bloomfield Hills, 3940 . . . F6
Bloomingdale, 528 . . . T5
Boon, 150 . . . L6
Boyne City, 3503 . . . H7
Boyne Falls, 370 . . . H7
Brampton, 80 . . . F2
Branch, 150 . . . M5
Breckenridge, 1339 . . . P8
Breedsville, 235 . . . T4
Brethren, 275 . . . L5
Brevort, 20 . . . E7
Bridgeport, 7849 . . . P10
Bridgewater, 175 . . . T10
Bridgman, 2428 . . . U3
Brighton, 6701 . . . S10
Brimley, 450 . . . D8
Brinton, 100 . . . N7
Bristol, 60 . . . M6
Britton, 699 . . . U10
Brohman, 175 . . . N5
Bronson, 2421 . . . U7
Brooklyn, 1176 . . . T9
Brown City, 1334 . . . Q12
Bruce Crossing, 225 . . . C11
Brutus, 175 . . . G7
Buchanan, 4681 . . . U4
Buckley, 550 . . . K5
Buena Vista, 7845 . . . P10
Burlington, 405 . . . T7
Burnips, 375 . . . R5
Burr Oak, 797 . . . U6
Burt, 1122 . . . Q10
Burt Lake, 225 . . . G8
Burton, 30308 . . . Q10
Byron, 595 . . . R10
Byron Ctr., 3777 . . . R5
Cadillac, 10000 . . . L6
Caledonia, 1102 . . . R6
Calumet, 879 . . . A12
Camden, 550 . . . V8
Capac, 1775 . . . Q12
Carleton, 2562 . . . U11
Carlshend, 90 . . . D2
Carney, 225 . . . G1
Caro, 4145 . . . P11
Carp Lake, 150 . . . F7
Carrollton, 6602 . . . P10
Carson City, 1190 . . . Q7
Carsonville, 502 . . . P13
Caseville, 888 . . . M11
Casnovia, 315 . . . Q5
Caspian, 997 . . . D12
Cass City, 2643 . . . N11
Cassopolis, 1740 . . . U5
Cedar, 250 . . . J5
Cedar River, 30 . . . G2
Cedar Sprs., 3112 . . . Q6
Cedarville, 425 . . . E8
Cement City, 452 . . . U9
Center Line, 8531 . . . H8
Central Lake, 990 . . . H6
Centreville, 1579 . . . U6
Champion, 250 . . . C13
Channing, 250 . . . D12
Charlevoix, 2994 . . . H6
Charlotte, 8389 . . . S7
Chase, 275 . . . N5
Chassell, 800 . . . B12
Chatham, 231 . . . D3
Cheboygan, 5295 . . . G8
Chelsea, 4398 . . . T9
Chesaning, 2548 . . . Q9
Chippewa Lake, 125 . . . N6
Christmas, 250 . . . D3
Clare, 3173 . . . N8
Clarklake, 250 . . . T9
Clarkston, 962 . . . D5
Clarksville, 317 . . . R6
Clawson, 12732 . . . G7
Clayton, 326 . . . U9
Clifford, 324 . . . P11
Climax, 791 . . . T6
Clinton, 2293 . . . U10
Clio, 2483 . . . Q10
Cloverdale, 400 . . . S6
Cohoctah, 275 . . . R10
Coldwater, 12697 . . . U7
Coleman, 1296 . . . N8
Coloma, 1595 . . . T4
Colon, 1227 . . . U6
Columbiaville, 815 . . . Q11
Comins, 150 . . . J9
Comstock, 4472 . . . T6
Comstock Park, 10674 . . . Q5
Concord, 1101 . . . T8
Constantine, 2095 . . . U5
Conway, 275 . . . G7
Cooks, 100 . . . F4
Coopersville, 3910 . . . Q5
Copemish, 232 . . . L5
Copper City, 205 . . . A12
Copper Harbor, 50 . . . A13
Cornell, 90 . . . F2
Corunna, 3381 . . . R9
Covert, 650 . . . T4
Covington, 40 . . . C12
Cross Vil., 70 . . . G7
Croswell, 2467 . . . P13
Croton, 275 . . . P5
Crump, 275 . . . N9
Crystal Falls, 1791 . . . D12
Crystal Valley, 175 . . . N4
Curran, 40 . . . K10
Curtis, 250 . . . E5
Curtisville, 50 . . . K10
Custer, 318 . . . M4
Cutlerville, 15114 . . . R5
Dafter, 250 . . . D8
Daggett, 270 . . . G1
Dansville, 429 . . . S9
Darragh, 200 . . . J7
Davison, 5536 . . . Q11
Dearborn, 97775 . . . T11
Dearborn Hts., 58264 . . . K6
Decatur, 1838 . . . T5
Deckerville, 944 . . . P12
Deerfield, 1005 . . . U10
Deerton, 30 . . . D2
Deford, 325 . . . P11
De Tour Vil., 421 . . . E9
Detroit, 951270 . . . T12
Detroit Beach, 2289 . . . U11
De Witt, 4702 . . . R8
Dexter, 2338 . . . T10
Dighton, 100 . . . M6
Dimondale, 1342 . . . S8
Dollar Bay, 950 . . . A12
Donken, 30 . . . B11
Dorr, 2800 . . . R5
Douglas, 1214 . . . S4
Dowagiac, 6147 . . . U4
Dowling, 150 . . . S6
Drenthe, 325 . . . R5
Drummond, 200 . . . E10
Dryden, 815 . . . R12
Dundee, 3522 . . . U10
Dunningville, 150 . . . S5
Durand, 3933 . . . R9
Eagle, 130 . . . R7
Eagle Harbor, 30 . . . A12
Eagle River, 20 . . . A12
E. Grand Rapids, 10764 . . . C3
E. Jordan, 2507 . . . H7
Eastlake, 441 . . . L4
E. Lansing, 46525 . . . R8
E. Leroy, 275 . . . T7
Eastpointe, 34077 . . . H9
Eastport, 200 . . . H6
E. Tawas, 2951 . . . L11
Eaton Rapids, 5330 . . . S8
Eau Claire, 656 . . . U4
Eben Jct., 200 . . . D2
Eckerman, 50 . . . D7
Ecorse, 11229 . . . L7
Edenville, 200 . . . N8
Edgewood, 100 . . . Q8
Edmore, 1244 . . . P7
Edwardsburg, 1147 . . . V4
Elberta, 457 . . . K4
Elk Rapids, 1700 . . . J6
Elkton, 863 . . . N11
Ellsworth, 483 . . . H6
Elmira, 200 . . . H7
Elo, 70 . . . B12
Elsie, 1055 . . . Q8
Elwell, 300 . . . P8
Emmett, 251 . . . Q12
Empire, 378 . . . J5
Engadine, 275 . . . E6
Ensign, 40 . . . F3
Ensley Ctr., 175 . . . P6
Epoufette, 40 . . . E7
Epsilon, 200 . . . G7
Escanaba, 13140 . . . F2
Essexville, 3766 . . . N10
Estey, 150 . . . N9
Estral Beach, 486 . . . U11
Eureka, 300 . . . Q8
Evans, 225 . . . Q6
Evart, 1738 . . . N6
Ewen, 175 . . . C11
Fairgrove, 627 . . . P10
Fair Haven, 1500 . . . R13
Fair Plain, 7828 . . . U4
Fairport, 125 . . . G3
Fairview, 600 . . . K9
Faithorn, 20 . . . F1
Falmouth, 275 . . . L7
Farmington, 10423 . . . H5
Farmington Hills, 82111 . . . G5
Farwell, 855 . . . N7
Fayette, 10 . . . F3
Felch, 80 . . . E1
Fennville, 1459 . . . S4
Fenton, 10582 . . . R10
Ferndale, 22105 . . . H7
Ferry, 250 . . . P4
Ferrysburg, 3040 . . . Q4
Fibre, 20 . . . E8
Fife Lake, 466 . . . K6
Filion, 225 . . . N12
Flat Rock, 8488 . . . T11
Flint, 124943 . . . Q10
Flushing, 8348 . . . Q10
Ford River, 150 . . . F2
Forest Lake, 20 . . . D3
Forestville, 127 . . . N13
Foster City, 60 . . . F1
Fostoria, 600 . . . Q11
Fountain, 175 . . . M4
Fowler, 1136 . . . R8
Fowlerville, 2972 . . . S9
Frankenmuth, 4838 . . . P10
Frankfort, 1513 . . . K4
Franklin, 2937 . . . G6
Fraser, 15297 . . . G9
Freda, 50 . . . A11
Frederic, 425 . . . J8
Freeland, 5147 . . . P9
Freeport, 444 . . . R6
Freesoil, 177 . . . M4
Fremont, 4224 . . . P5
Frontier, 250 . . . V8
Fruitport, 1124 . . . Q4
Fulton, 350 . . . T6
Gaastra, 339 . . . D12
Gagetown, 389 . . . N11
Gaines, 366 . . . R10
Galesburg, 1988 . . . T6
Galien, 593 . . . V3
Garden, 240 . . . F3
Garden City, 30047 . . . K5
Gardendale, 800 . . . Q13
Garnet, 40 . . . E6
Gay, 40 . . . A12
Gaylord, 3681 . . . J8
Genesee, 1800 . . . Q10
Germfask, 125 . . . E5
Gibraltar, 4264 . . . T11
Girard, 275 . . . U7
Gladstone, 5032 . . . F2
Gladwin, 3001 . . . M
Glen Arbor, 200 . . . J
Glendale, 300 . . . T
Glendora, 325 . . . U
Glenn, 325 . . . S
Glennie, 90 . . . K1
Gobles, 815 . . . T
Goetzville, 70 . . . E
Good Hart, 50 . . . G
Goodrich, 1353 . . . R1
Gould City, 80 . . . E
Grace, 40 . . .
Grand Beach, 221 . . . V
Grand Blanc, 8242 . . . R1
Grand Haven, 11168 . . .
Grand Jct., 325 . . . S
Grand Ledge, 7813 . . . R
Grand Marais, 300 . . .
Grand Rapids, 197800 . . . R
Grandville, 16263 . . . R
Grant, 881 . . . P
Grass Lake, 1082 . . . T
Grawn, 1600 . . . K
Grayling, 1952 . . . K
Green, 80 . . . B1
Greenbush, 225 . . . K1
Greenland, 325 . . . B1
Greenville, 7935 . . .
Gregory, 500 . . . S
Greilickville, 1415 . . . J
Grind Stone City, 100 . . . M1
Gros Cap, 90 . . . F
Grosse Ile, 10894 . . . N
Grosse Pointe, 5670 . . . J1
Grosse Pointe Farms, 9764 . . . J1
Grosse Pointe Park, 12443 . . . J
Grosse Pointe Shores, 2823 . . . J1
Grosse Pointe Woods, 17080 . . . S1
Gulliver, 90 . . .
Gwinn, 1965 . . .
Hadley, 450 . . . R1
Hale, 600 . . . L1
Hamilton, 1300 . . . S
Hamtramck, 22976 . . . J
Hancock, 4323 . . . A1
Hanover, 424 . . . T
Harbert, 1619 . . . U
Harbor Beach, 1837 . . . N1
Harbor Sprs., 1567 . . . G
Harper Woods, 14254 . . . J
Harrietta, 169 . . . L
Harrison, 2108 . . . M
Harrisville, 514 . . . K1
Hart, 1950 . . . N
Hartford, 2476 . . .
Hartland, 375 . . . S1
Harvey, 1321 . . . D
Haslett, 11283 . . . R
Hastings, 7095 . . . S
Hawks, 80 . . . H1
Hazel Park, 18963 . . . H
Helmer, 50 . . . E
Helps, 10 . . . F
Hemlock, 1585 . . . P
Herman, 60 . . . C1
Hermansville, 325 . . . F
Hersey, 374 . . . N
Hesperia, 954 . . . P
Hessel, 200 . . . E
Higgins Lake, 60 . . . L
Highland Park, 16746 . . . J
Hillman, 685 . . . H1
Hillsdale, 8233 . . . U
Holland, 35048 . . . R
Holly, 6135 . . . R1
Holt, 11315 . . . S
Holton, 600 . . . P
Homer, 1851 . . . T
Honor, 299 . . . K
Hope, 200 . . . N
Hopkins, 592 . . . S
Houghton, 7010 . . . A1
Houghton Lake, 3749 . . . L
Howard City, 1585 . . . P
Howell, 9232 . . . S1
Hoxeyville, 40 . . . M
Hubbard Lake, 993 . . . J1
Hubbardston, 394 . . . Q
Hubbell, 1105 . . . A1
Hudson, 2499 . . . U
Hudsonville, 7160 . . . R
Hulbert, 80 . . . D
Huntington Woods, 6151 . . . H
Huron Beach, 225 . . . G
Hyde, 275 . . . F
Ida, 1100 . . . U1
Idlewild, 350 . . . N
Imlay City, 3869 . . . Q1
Indian River, 2008 . . . G
Ingalls, 175 . . . G
Inkster, 30115 . . . L
Interlochen, 600 . . . K
Ionia, 10569 . . . R
Iron Mtn., 8154 . . . D1
Iron River, 3386 . . . D1
Irons, 90 . . . M
Ironton, 200 . . . H
Ironwood, 6293 . . . C
Isabella, 40 . . . F
Ishpeming, 6686 . . . D
Ithaca, 3098 . . . Q
Jackson, 36316 . . . T
Jacobsville, 10 . . . B1
Jamestown, 750 . . . R
Jasper, 400 . . . U
Jenison, 17211 . . . R
Johannesburg, 80 . . . J
Jones, 450 . . . U
Jonesville, 2337 . . . U
Kalamazoo, 77145 . . . T
Kaleva, 509 . . . L
Kalkaska, 2226 . . . K
Karlin, 100 . . . K
Kawkawlin, 1600 . . . N1
Keego Harbor, 2769 . . . F
Kent City, 1061 . . . Q
Kenton, 20 . . . C1
Kentwood, 45255 . . . R
Keweenaw Bay, 150 . . . B1
Kinde, 534 . . . M1
Kinderhook, 350 . . . V
Kingsford, 5549 . . . D1
Kingsley, 1469 . . . K
Kingston, 450 . . . P1
Kinross, 175 . . . E
Kipling, 300 . . . F
Kiva, 50 . . . E
Koss, 80 . . . G
La Branche, 10 . . . F
Lachine, 225 . . . H1
Laingsburg, 1223 . . . R
Lake, 475 . . . N
Lake Angelus, 326 . . . E
Lake Ann, 276 . . . K
Lake City, 923 . . . L
Lake George, 400 . . . M
Lake Isabella, 1243 . . . N
Lake Linden, 1081 . . . A1
Lake Michigan Beach, 1509 . . . T
Lake Odessa, 2272 . . . R
Lake Orion, 2715 . . . R1
Lakeport, 700 . . . Q1
Lakeview, 1112 . . . P
Lakewood Club, 1006 . . . P
Lambertville, 9299 . . . V1

Lancaster County covered bridge, Pennsylvania

MISSISSIPPI PG. 118
CAPITAL
Jackson
NICKNAME
Magnolia State
POPULATION
2,844,658, rank 31
AREA
47,639 sq mi, rank 32

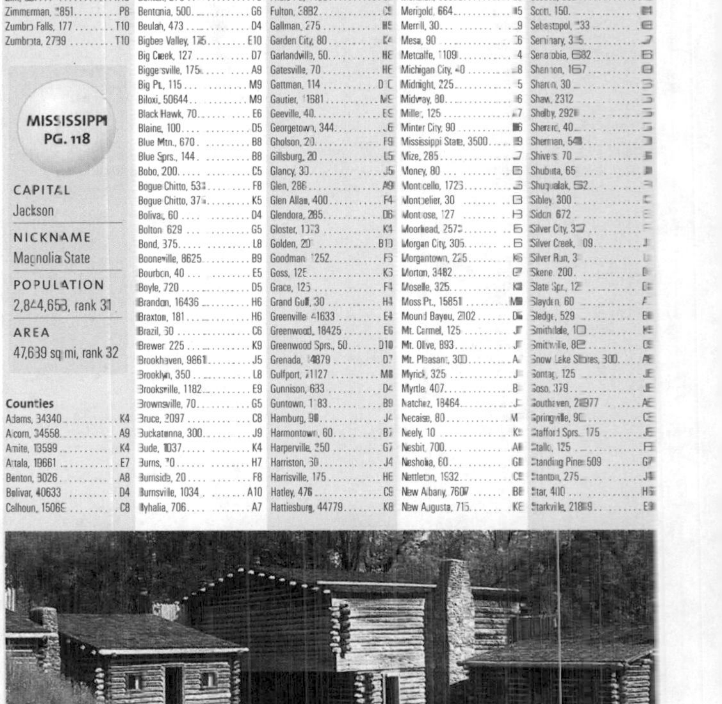

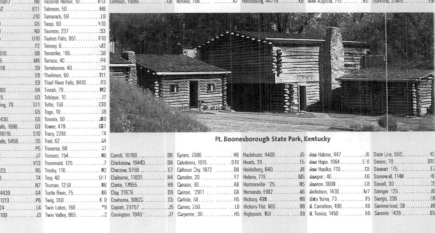

Ft. Boonesborough State Park, Kentucky

Sumner, 407 C6
Sumrall, 1005 K7
Sunflower, 696 E5
Suqualena, 150 G9
Swan Lake, 60 D6
Swiftown, 80 E5
Sylvarena, 120 H7
Talowah, 100 L7
Taylor, 289 C7
Taylorsville, 1341 J7
Tchula, 2332 E6
Terry, 664 H6
Thaxton, 513 C8
Thomastown, 100 F7
Thompson, 30 K5
Thorn, 200 D8
Thornton, 70 F6
Tie Plant, 450 D7
Tilden, 100 C10
Tillatoba, 121 C6
Tinsley, 50 G5
Tiplersville, 100 A8
Tishomingo, 316 B10
Toccopola, 189 C8
Tomnolen, 90 E8
Toomsuba, 175 G9
Trebloc, 40 D9

Mardi Gras Souvenir Mask, New Orleans, Louisiana

Tremont, 390 C10
Troy, 60 C8
Tucker, 534 G8
Tuckers Crossing, 350 J8
Tula, 200 C8
Tunica, 1132 B5
Tupelo, 34211 C9
Tuscola, 125 G7
Tutwiler, 1364 C5
Tylertown, 1910 K6
Tyro, 20 B7
Union, 2021 G8
Union Church, 50 J5
Utica, 966 H5
Vaiden, 840 E7
Valley Park, 60 G5
Vance, 80 C6
Vancleave, 4910 M9
Vardaman, 1065 D8
Vaughan, 60 F6
Verona, 3334 C9
Vicksburg, 26407 G4
Vossburg, 80 H8
Wade, 491 M9
Walls, 200 A6
Walnut, 754 A8
Walnut Grove, 488 G7
Walthall, 170 D8
Wanilla, 90 J6
Washington, 250 J4
Waterford, 90 B7
Water Valley, 3677 C7
Waveland, 6674 M8
Waynesboro, 5197 J9
Wayside, 70 E4
Webb, 587 D6
Weir, 553 E8
Wenasoga, 175 A9
Wesson, 1693 J5
West, 220 E7
W. Point, 12145 D9
Wheeler, 300 B9
White Apple, 80 K4
Whitfield, 90 K8
Wiggins, 3849 L8
Wiggins, 100 G7
Wilkinson, 125 K4
Williamsburg, 90 J7
Williamsville, 400 F7
Winchester, 50 J9
Winona, 5482 E7
Winstonville, 319 D5
Winterville, 175 E4
Woodland, 159 D8
Woodville, 1192 K4
Wyatte, 10 B7
Yazoo City, 14550 F5
Zama, 40 F8

MISSOURI
PG. 119-121

CAPITAL
Jefferson City

NICKNAME
Show Me State

POPULATION
5,595,211, rank 17

AREA
69,697 sq mi, rank 19

Counties

Adair, 24977 B7
Andrew, 16492 B2
Atchison, 6430 A1
Audrain, 25853 D8
Barry, 34010 L4
Barton, 12541 J3
Bates, 16653 G3
Benton, 17180 G5
Bollinger, 12029 K12
Boone, 135454 E8
Buchanan, 85998 D2
Butler, 40867 L11
Caldwell, 8969 C4
Callaway, 40766 F8
Camden, 37051 H6
Cape Girardeau, 68693 J13
Carroll, 10285 D5
Carter, 5941 L11
Cass, 82092 G3
Cedar, 13733 J4
Chariton, 8438 D6
Christian, 54285 L6
Clark, 7416 B9
Clay, 184006 D3
Clinton, 18979 D3
Cole, 71397 G7
Cooper, 16670 F7
Crawford, 22804 H10
Dade, 7923 J4
Dallas, 15661 J6
Daviess, 8016 B4
DeKalb, 11597 C3
Dent, 14927 J9
Douglas, 13084 L7
Dunklin, 33155 N13
Franklin, 93807 G10
Gasconade, 15342 G9
Gentry, 6861 B3
Greene, 240391 K5
Grundy, 10432 C5
Harrison, 8850 B4
Henry, 21997 G4
Hickory, 8940 H6
Holt, 5351 B2
Howard, 10212 E7
Howell, 37238 L9
Iron, 10697 J11
Jackson, 654880 E3
Jasper, 104686 K3
Jefferson, 198099 G11
Johnson, 48258 F4
Knox, 4361 B8
Laclede, 32513 J6
Lafayette, 32960 E5
Lawrence, 35204 K4
Lewis, 10494 B8
Lincoln, 38944 E10
Linn, 13754 C6
Livingston, 14558 C5
Macon, 15762 C7
Madison, 11800 J12
Maries, 8903 H8
Marion, 28289 C9
McDonald, 21681 L3
Mercer, 3757 A5
Miller, 23564 G7
Mississippi, 13427 L14
Moniteau, 14827 G7
Monroe, 9311 D8
Montgomery, 12136 E9
Morgan, 19309 G6
New Madrid, 19760 M13
Newton, 52636 L3
Nodaway, 21912 A2
Oregon, 10344 L10
Osage, 13062 G9
Ozark, 9542 M7
Pemiscot, 20047 N13
Perry, 18132 J13
Pettis, 39403 F5
Phelps, 39825 H8
Pike, 18351 D10
Platte, 73781 D2
Polk, 26992 J5
Pulaski, 41165 J8
Putnam, 5223 A6
Ralls, 9626 D9
Randolph, 24663 D7
Ray, 23354 D4
Reynolds, 6689 K10
Ripley, 13509 L11
St. Charles, 283883 F11
St. Clair, 9652 H5
Ste. Genevieve, 17842 H12
St. Francois, 55641 J12
St. Louis, 1016315 F11
Saline, 23756 E6
Schuyler, 4170 B7
Scotland, 4983 A8
Scott, 40422 L13
Shannon, 8324 K9
Shelby, 6799 C8
Stoddard, 29705 L13
Stone, 28658 L5
Sullivan, 7219 B6
Taney, 39703 M6
Texas, 23003 K8
Vernon, 20454 H3
Warren, 24525 F10
Washington, 23344 H11
Wayne, 13259 K11
Webster, 31045 K6
Worth, 2382 A3
Wright, 17955 K7

Cities and Towns

Adrian, 1780 G3
Advance, 1244 K13
Affton, 20535 F15
Agency, 599 C3
Airport Drive, 622 H9
Akers, 10 K9
Alba, 588 K3
Albany, 1937 B3
Aldrich, 75 J5
Alexandria, 166 B9
Allendale, 54 A4
Alma, 399 E5
Altamont, 218 C4
Altenburg, 309 J14
Alton, 668 L9
Amazonia, 277 C2
Americus, 100 F9
Amity, 70 C3
Amoret, 211 G3
Amsterdam, 281 G3
Anderson, 1856 L3
Annada, 48 E11
Annapolis, 310 K11
Anniston, 285 L14
Appleton City, 1314 G4
Arbela, 40 A8
Arbyrd, 528 N12
Arcadia, 567 J11
Archie, 890 G3
Arcola, 45 J4
Argyle, 164 G8
Arkoe, 58 B2
Armstrong, 287 E7
Arnold, 19965 G12
Arrow Rock, 79 E6
Asbury, 218 K3
Ashburn, 51 D10
Ash Grove, 1430 K5
Ashland, 1869 F8
Ashley, 80 E10
Atlanta, 450 C7
Augusta, 218 F11
Aullville, 86 E5
Aurora, 7014 L5
Auxvasse, 901 E8
Ava, 3021 L7
Avalon, 100 C5
Avilla, 137 K4
Avondale, 529 E4
Baker, 5 L13
Bakersfield, 285 M8
Ballard, 60 G4
Ballwin, 31283 F11
Bardley, 40 L10
Baring, 159 B8
Barnard, 257 B2
Barnett, 207 G7
Barnhart, 6108 G12
Bates City, 245 E4
Battlefield, 2385 N8
Belgrade, 200 H11
Bella Villa, 687 F16
Bell City, 461 K13
Belle, 1344 G9
Bellefontaine Neighbors, 11271 C16
Bellerive, 254 D15
Belleview, 125 J11
Bellflower, 427 E9
Bel-Nor, 1598 D15
Bel-Ridge, 3082 D15
Belton, 21730 F3
Bendavis, 80 K8
Benton, 732 K14
Benton City, 122 E9
Berger, 206 F10
Berkeley, 10063 C15
Bernie, 1777 L13
Bertrand, 740 L14
Bethany, 3087 B4
Bethel, 121 C8
Beverly Hills, 603 D16
Bevier, 723 C7
Biehle, 11 J13
Bigelow, 38 B1
Big Lake, 127 B1
Bigspring, 200 F9
Billings, 1091 K5
Birch Tree, 634 L9
Birmingham, 214 D6
Bismarck, 1470 H11
Bixby, 125 J10
Blackburn, 284 E5
Black Jack, 6792 B16
Blackwater, 199 E6
Blairstown, 141 F4
Bland, 565 G9
Bloomfield, 1952 L13
Bloomsdale, 419 H12
Blue Eye, 129 M5
Blue Sprs., 48080 E3
Blythedale, 233 A4
Bogard, 234 D5
Bois D'Arc, 300 K5
Bolckow, 234 B2
Bolivar, 9143 J5
Bonne Terre, 4039 H11
Bonnots Mill, 275 F8
Boonville, 8202 E7
Boss, 80 J10
Bosworth, 382 D5
Bourbon, 1348 H10
Bowling Green, 3260 D10
Bradleyville, 50 L6
Braggadocio, 200 N13
Bragg City, 189 M13
Brandsville, 174 M9
Branson, 6050 M6
Brashear, 280 B7
Braymer, 910 D4
Breckenridge, 454 C4
Breckenridge Hills, 4817 D15
Brentwood, 7693 E15
Briar, 30 M11
Bridgeton, 15550 C14
Brighton, 225 J5
Brimson, 63 B5
Brixey, 10 L7
Bronaugh, 245 J3
Brookfield, 4769 C6
Broseley, 250 L12
Brownbranch, 10 L6
Browning, 317 B6
Brownington, 119 G5
Brownwood, 150 K13
Brumley, 102 H7
Bruner, 175 L6
Brunswick, 925 D6
Bucklin, 524 C6
Buckner, 2725 E4
Bucyrus, 30 K8
Buell, 100 E9
Buffalo, 2781 J6
Bull Creek, 225 L6
Bunceton, 348 F7
Bunker, 427 J10
Burgess, 70 J3
Burlington Jct., 632 A2
Butler, 4209 G3
Butterfield, 397 L4
Cabool, 2168 K8
Cainsville, 370 A5
Cairo, 293 D7
Caledonia, 158 J11
Calhoun, 491 G5
California, 4005 F7
Callao, 291 C7
Calverton Park, 1322 C15
Camden, 209 E4
Camden Pt., 484 D3
Camdenton, 2779 H7
Cameron, 8312 C4
Campbell, 1883 M13
Canalou, 348 L13
Canton, 2557 B9
Cape Fair, 300 L5
Cape Girardeau, 35349 K14
Caplinger Mills, 50 H4
Cardwell, 789 N12
Carl Jct., 5294 K3
Carrollton, 4122 D5
Carterville, 1850 G10
Carthage, 12668 K3
Caruthersville, 6760 N13
Carytown, 217 K3
Cassville, 2890 L4
Catron, 68 M13
Caulfield, 150 M8
Cave, 7 E10
Cedar Hill, 1703 G11
Cedar Sprs., 50 H4
Center, 644 D9
Centertown, 257 F7
Centerview, 249 F4
Centerville, 171 J10
Centralia, 3774 E8
Chadwick, 10 L6
Chaffee, 3044 K13
Chain of Rocks, 91 E11
Chain-O-Lakes, 127 M5
Chamois, 456 F9
Champ, 12 C14
Charity, 70 J6
Charlack, 1431 D15
Charleston, 4732 L14
Cherryville, 125 H10
Chesapeake, 150 K5
Chesterfield, 46802 F11
Chilhowee, 329 F4
Chillicothe, 8968 C5
Chula, 198 C5
Clarence, 915 C8
Clark, 275 D7
Clarksburg, 375 F7
Clarksdale, 351 C3
Clarksville, 490 D11
Clarkton, 1330 M13
Claycomo, 1267 D5
Clayton, 12825 F12
Clearmont, 191 A2
Cleveland, 592 F3
Clever, 1010 L5
Cliff Vil., 33 K9
Clifton City, 30 F6
Clifton Hill, 124 D7
Climax Sprs., 80 H6
Clinton, 9311 G4
Clyde, 74 B3
Coal, 60 G5
Cobalt City, 189 J12
Coffey, 140 B4
Coffman, 50 H12
Coldwater, 20 K12
Cole Camp, 1028 G6
Collins, 176 H5
Columbia, 84531 E8
Commerce, 110 K14
Competition, 30 J7
Conception Jct., 202 B3
Concord, 16689 F15
Concordia, 2360 E5
Coney Island, 94 M5
Conway, 743 J6
Cook Sta., 30 H9
Cool Valley, 1081 D16
Cooter, 440 N13
Corder, 427 E5
Corning, 21 B1
Cosby, 143 C3
Cottleville, 1928 C12
Couch, 30 M9
Country Club Hills, 1381 D16
Country Club Vil., 1846 C2
Country Life Acres, 81 E14
Cowgill, 247 D4
Craig, 309 B1
Crane, 1390 L5
Creighton, 322 G4
Crestwood, 11863 F15
Creve Coeur, 16500 D14
Crocker, 1033 H8
Cross Timbers, 185 H6
Crystal City, 4247 G12
Crystal Lake Park, 457 E14
Cuba, 3230 H9
Curryville, 251 D9
Dadeville, 224 J5
Dalton, 27 D6
Darlington, 113 B3
Davisville, 20 H10
Dawson, 50 K8
Dearborn, 529 D3
Deepwater, 507 G4
Deerfield, 75 H3
De Kalb, 257 D2
Dellwood, 5255 C16
Delta, 517 K13
Dennis Acres, 68 K9
Denver, 40 A3
Des Arc, 187 K11
Desloge, 4802 H12
De Soto, 6375 H11
Des Peres, 8592 E14
De Witt, 120 D6
Dexter, 7356 L13
Diamond, 807 L3
Diehlstadt, 163 L14
Diggins, 298 K6
Dillard, 10 J10
Dixon, 1570 H8
Doe Run, 475 J12
Doniphan, 1932 M11
Doolittle, 644 H8
Dora, 30 L8
Dover, 108 E5
Downing, 396 A7
Drake, 30 G9
Dresden, 175 F5
Drexel, 1090 G3
Drury, 50 L7
Dudley, 289 L12
Duenweg, 1034 J10
Duncans Bridge, 50 D8
Dunnegan, 125 J5
Duquesne, 1640 J10
Dutchtown, 99 K13
Eagle Rock, 150 M4
Eagleville, 321 A4
E. Lynne, 300 F4
Easton, 258 C3
E. Prairie, 3227 L14
Eastwood, 10 L10
Edgar Sprs., 190 J8
Edgerton, 533 D3
Edina, 1233 B8
Edmundson, 840 C15
Edwards, 30 H6
Eldon, 4895 G7
El Dorado Sprs., 3775 H4
Eldridge, 80 H7
Elk Creek, 30 K8
Elkland, 225 J6
Elkton, 60 H5
Ellington, 1045 K10
Ellsinore, 363 L11
Elmer, 98 C7
Elmira, 82 D4
Elmo, 166 A2
Elsberry, 2047 E11
Elsey, 150 L5
Emden, 70 C8
Eminence, 548 K10
Emma, 243 E5
Eolia, 435 E10
Essex, 524 L13
Ethel, 100 C7
Eugene, 175 G7
Eunice, 50 K9
Eureka, 7676 G11
Everton, 322 K5
Ewing, 464 C9
Excello, 40 D7
Excelsior Sprs., 10847 D4
Exeter, 707 L4
Fagus, 60 M12
Fairdealing, 225 L11
Fairfax, 645 B1
Fair Grove, 1107 K6
Fair Play, 418 J5
Fairport, 80 C3
Fairview, 395 L4
Falcon, 50 J7
Farber, 411 E9
Farley, 226 B1
Farmington, 13924 H12
Faucett, 300 D2
Fayette, 2793 E7
Fayetteville, 90 F5
Fenton, 4360 F14
Ferguson, 22406 C16
Ferrelview, 593 D3
Festus, 9660 G12
Fidelity, 252 K3
Fillmore, 211 B2
Fisk, 363 L12
Flat, 90 J8
Fleming, 122 E4
Flemington, 124 H5
Flordell Hills, 931 D16
Florence, 125 F6
Florida, 9 D9
Florissant, 50497 F12
Foley, 178 E11
Ford City, 30 B3
Fordland, 684 K6
Forest City, 338 C2
Foristell, 331 F10
Forsyth, 1686 L6
Fortescue, 51 B1
Fortuna, 225 F7
Foster, 130 G3
Four Seasons, 1493 G7
Frankford, 351 D10
Franklin, 112 E7
Fredericktown, 3928 J12
Freeburg, 423 G8
Freeman, 521 F3
Freistatt, 184 L4
Fremont, 125 L10
Fremont Hills, 597 K6
Fristoe, 30 H6
Frohna, 192 J13
Frontenac, 3483 E14
Fruitland, 400 J13
Fulton, 12128 F8
Gainesville, 632 M7
Galena, 451 L5
Gallatin, 1789 C4
Galt, 275 B5
Garden City, 1500 F4
Garland, 100 G4
Garrison, 40 L6
Garwood, 20 K11
Gasconade, 267 F9
Gatewood, 50 M10
Gentry, 101 B3
Gentryville, 20 L7
Gerald, 1171 G10
Gerster, 35 H5
Gibbs, 100 B7
Gideon, 1113 M13
Gilliam, 229 E6
Gilman City, 380 B4
Gladden, 30 J9
Gladstone, 26365 E3
Glasgow, 1263 E6
Glasgow Vil., 5234 C17
Glenaire, 553 C6
Glenallen, 145 K13
Glendale, 5767 E15
Glenwood, 203 A7
Glover, 20 J11
Golden, 70 M5
Golden City, 884 K4
Goodman, 1183 L3
Gordonville, 425 K13
Gower, 1399 D3
Graham, 191 B2
Grain Valley, 5160 E4
Granby, 2121 L3
Grand Falls Plaza, 104 K8
Grandin, 236 L11
Grand Pass, 53 E5
Grandview, 24881 F3
Granger, 44 A8
Grant City, 926 A3
Grassy, 50 K12
Gravois Mills, 208 G6
Grayridge, 150 L13
Gray Summit, 2640 G11
Greencastle, 308 B6
Green City, 688 B6
Greendale, 722 D15
Greenfield, 1358 J4
Green Park, 2666 F15
Green Ridge, 445 F5
Greentop, 427 B7
Greenville, 451 K12
Greenwood, 3952 F3
Greer, 50 L10
Grovespring, 125 K7
Guilford, 87 B3
Gunn City, 85 F4
Hale, 473 D5
Half Way, 176 J6
Hallsville, 978 E8
Halltown, 189 K5
Hamilton, 1813 C4
Hanley Hills, 2124 D15
Hannibal, 17757 C9
Hardin, 614 E4
Harris, 105 B5
Harrisburg, 184 E7
Harrisonville, 8946 F3
Hartsburg, 108 F8
Hartshorn, 70 K9
Hartville, 607 K7
Hartwell, 16 G4
Harviell, 125 L12
Harwood, 90 H4
Hawk Pt., 459 E10
Hayti, 3207 N13
Hayti Hts., 771 N13
Hayward, 123 M13
Haywood City, 239 K14
Hazelwood, 26206 C15
Hematite, 275 G12
Henrietta, 457 E4
Herculaneum, 2805 G12
Hermann, 2674 F9
Hermitage, 406 H5
Higbee, 623 D7
Higginsville, 4682 E5
High Hill, 231 F9
Highlandville, 872 L5
High Pt., 80 G7
High Ridge, 4236 G11
Hillsboro, 1675 G11
Hillsdale, 1477 D16
Hoberg, 60 K4
Holcomb, 696 M13
Holden, 2510 F4
Holland, 246 N13
Holliday, 129 D8
Hollister, 3867 M6
Holt, 405 D3
Holts Summit, 2935 F8
Homestown, 181 M13
Hopkins, 579 A2
Hornersville, 686 N12
Horton, 40 H3
Houston, 1992 K8
Houstonia, 275 F5
Houston Lake, 284 D3
Howardville, 342 M14
Howes Mill, 10 J10
Hughesville, 174 F6
Humansville, 946 H5
Hume, 337 H3
Humphreys, 164 B5
Hunnewell, 227 C8
Hunter, 20 L11
Huntleigh, 323 E14
Huntsville, 1553 D7
Hurdland, 239 B8
Hurley, 157 L5
Iantha, 125 J3
Iatan, 54 D2
Iberia, 605 H8
Imperial, 4373 G12
Independence, 113288 E3
Ionia, 108 G5
Irena, 33 A3
Irondale, 437 H11
Iron Mtn. Lake, 693 J11
Ironton, 1471 J11
Irwin, 50 J3
Jackson, 11947 J13
Jacksonville, 163 D7
Jameson, 120 C4
Jamesport, 505 C4
Jamestown, 382 F7
Jane, 200 M3
Jasper, 1011 K3
Jefferson City, 39636 F8
Jenkins, 50 L5
Jennings, 15469 D16
Jerico Sprs., 259 J4
Jonesburg, 695 F10
Joplin, 45504 K3
Junction City, 319 J12
Kahoka, 2241 A9
Kaiser, 500 H7
Kansas City, 441545 E3
Kearney, 5472 D3
Kelso, 527 K14
Kennett, 11260 N13
Kewanee, 175 L14
Keysville, 30 H9
Keytesville, 533 D6
Kidder, 271 C4
Kimberling City, 2253 M5
Kimmswick, 94 G12
King City, 1012 B3
Kingdom City, 121 E8
Kingston, 287 C4
Kingsville, 257 F4
Kinloch, 449 C15
Kirksville, 16988 B7
Kirkwood, 27324 E14
Knob Lick, 200 J12
Knob Noster, 2462 F5
Knox City, 223 B8
Knoxville, 50 D4
Koshkonong, 205 M9
Labadie, 225 F11
La Belle, 669 B8
Laclede, 415 C6
Laddonia, 620 E9
Ladue, 8645 E15
La Due, 39 G4
La Grange, 1000 B9
Lake Lafayette, 346 E4
Lake Mykee, 326 F8
Lake Ozark, 1489 G7
Lake St. Louis, 10169 F11
Lakeshire, 1375 F15
Lake Spr., 10 J9
Lake Waukomis, 917 C3
Lake Winnebago, 902 F3
Lamar, 4425 J3
Lamar Hts., 216 J3
Lambert, 49 K14
Lamine, 20 E6
La Monte, 1064 F5
Lanagan, 411 M3
Lancaster, 737 A7
Lanton, 70 M9
La Plata, 1486 B7
Laredo, 250 B5
La Russell, 138 K4
Lathrop, 2092 D3
La Tour, 65 F4
Laurie, 663 G6
Lawson, 2336 D4
Leadington, 206 H12
Leadwood, 1160 H11
Leasburg, 323 H10
Leawood, 904 K9
Lebanon, 12155 J7
Leeper, 60 K11
Lees Summit, 70700 E3
Leeton, 619 F5
Lemay, 17215 F16
Lenox, 125 J9
Leonard, 66 C8
Leslie, 87 G10
Lesterville, 225 J11
Lewis and Clark Vil., 155 D2
Lewistown, 595 B9
Lexington, 4453 E4
Liberal, 779 J3
Liberty, 26232 E3
Libertyville, 70 J12
Licking, 1471 J8
Lilbourn, 1303 M14
Lincoln, 1026 G5
Linn, 1354 G8
Linn Creek, 280 H7
Linneus, 369 C6
Livonia, 114 A7
Lock Sprs., 69 C5
Lockwood, 989 K4
Lodi, 20 K12
Lohman, 168 F7
Loma Linda, 507 L3
Lonedell, 300 G11
Lone Jack, 528 F4
Longrun, 10 M7
Longtown, 76 J13
Loose Creek, 80 G8
Louisburg, 147 J6
Louisiana, 3863 D10
Lowry City, 728 H5
Lucerne, 92 A6
Ludlow, 204 C5
Lupus, 29 F7
Luray, 102 A8
Lynchburg, 20 J8
Mackenzie, 137 F15
Macks Creek, 267 H6
Macon, 5538 C7
Madison, 586 D8
Maitland, 342 B2
Malden, 4782 M13
Malta Bend, 249 E5
Manchester, 19161 E13
Manes, 100 K7
Mansfield, 1349 K7
Maplewood, 9228 E15
Marble Hill, 1502 K13
Marceline, 2558 C6
Marion, 60 F7
Marionville, 2113 L5
Marlborough, 2235 F15
Marquand, 251 J12
Marshall, 12433 E6
Marshfield, 5720 K6
Marston, 610 M13
Marthasville, 837 F10
Martinsburg, 326 E9
Martinsville, 30 B4
Maryland Hts., 25756 D13
Marys Home, 80 G7
Maryville, 10581 B2
Matthews, 605 L14
Maysville, 1212 C3
Mayview, 294 E4
Maywood, 225 C9
McBaine, 17 F7
McBride, 40 H13
McCord Bend, 292 L5
McFall, 135 B4
McGee, 20 K12
McKittrick, 72 F9
Meadville, 457 C5
Mehlville, 28822 F12
Memphis, 2061 A8
Mendon, 208 D6
Menfro, 60 H13
Mercer, 342 A5
Merriam Woods, 1142 L6
Merwin, 83 G3
Meta, 249 G8
Metz, 67 H3
Mexico, 11320 E8
Miami, 160 D6
Middletown, 199 E9
Milan, 1958 B6
Milford, 52 J4
Millard, 75 B7
Miller, 754 K4
Millersburg, 175 F8
Millersville, 250 J13
Mill Grove, 50 B5
Mill Spr., 219 K11
Milo, 84 J3
Mindenmines, 409 J3
Mine La Motte, 100 J12
Miner, 1056 L14
Mineral Pt., 363 H11
Moberly, 11945 D7
Mokane, 188 F8
Moline Acres, 2662 C16
Monett, 7396 L4
Monroe City, 2588 D9
Montevallo, 30 J4
Montgomery City, 2442 E9
Monticello, 126 B9
Montrose, 417 G4
Moody, 125 M8
Mooresville, 89 C5
Morehouse, 1015 L14
Morgan, 90 J7
Morley, 792 K14
Morrison, 123 F9
Morrisville, 344 J5
Mosby, 242 D3
Moscow Mills, 1742 E11
Mound City, 1193 B2
Moundville, 103 J3
Mtn. Grove, 4574 K8
Mtn. View, 2430 L9
Mt. Leonard, 123 E5
Mt. Moriah, 143 B5
Mt. Sterling, 20 G9
Mt. Vernon, 4017 K4
Murphy, 9048 G12
Myrtle, 90 M10
Napoleon, 208 E4
Nashville, 60 K3
Naylor, 610 M11
Neck City, 119 K3
Neelys Landing, 20 J14
Neelyville, 487 M12
Nelson, 212 E6
Neosho, 10505 L3
Nevada, 8607 H3
Newark, 100 C8
New Bloomfield, 599 F8
New Boston, 40 C6
Newburg, 484 H8
New Cambria, 222 C7
New Florence, 764 E9
New Franklin, 1145 E7
New Hampton, 349 B4
New Haven, 1867 F10
New London, 1001 D9
New Madrid, 3334 M14
New Melle, 124 F11
Newtonia, 231 L4
Newtown, 209 B5
Niangua, 445 K6
Nixa, 12124 K5
Noel, 1480 M3
Norborne, 805 D5
Normandy, 5153 D16
N. Kansas City, 4714 E4
Northmoor, 399 D4
Northview, 125 K6
Northwoods, 4643 D16
Northwye, 550 H9
Norwood, 552 K7
Novelty, 119 C8
Novinger, 534 B7
Oak Grove, 5535 E4
Oak Grove, 382 G10
Oak Hill, 60 G9
Oakland, 1540 F15
Oak Ridge, 202 J13
Oaks, 136 D4
Oakview, 386 D4
Oakville, 35309 G12
Oakwood, 197 D4
Oakwood Park, 183 D4
Odessa, 4818 E4
O'Fallon, 46169 F11
Old Appleton, 82 J13
Old Mines, 350 H11
Old Monroe, 250 E11
Olean, 157 G7
Olivette, 7438 D15
Olney, 40 E10
Olympian Vil., 669 H12
Oran, 1264 K13
Orchard Farm, 275 A14
Oregon, 935 C2
Orrick, 889 E4
Osage Beach, 3662 H7
Osage City, 175 F8
Osborn, 455 C3
Osceola, 835 H5
Osgood, 51 B5
Oskaloosa, 40 J3
Otterville, 476 F6
Overland, 16838 D15
Owensville, 2500 G9
Oxly, 175 M11
Ozark, 9665 L6
Pacific, 5482 G11
Pagedale, 3616 D15
Palmyra, 3467 C9
Paris, 1529 D8
Park Hills, 7861 H12
Parkville, 4059 D3
Parkway, 280 G10
Parma, 852 M13
Parnell, 197 A3
Pascola, 138 N13
Passaic, 40 G3
Patterson, 250 K11
Patton, 125 J13
Pattonsburg, 261 B4
Paynesville, 91 E11
Peculiar, 2604 F3
Peerless Park, 80 F13
Perry, 666 D9
Perryville, 7667 J13
Pevely, 3768 G12
Phelps, 90 K4
Phelps City, 40 A1
Philadelphia, 250 C9
Phillipsburg, 201 J7
Pickering, 154 A2
Piedmont, 1992 K11
Pierce City, 1385 L4
Pilot Grove, 723 F6
Pilot Knob, 697 J11
Pine Lawn, 4204 D16
Pineville, 768 M3
Pittsville, 50 F4
Platte City, 3866 D2
Platte Woods, 474 C3
Plattsburg, 2354 D3
Pleasant Hill, 5582 F3
Pleasant Hope, 548 J6
Pleasant Valley, 3321 E3
Plevna, 40 C8
Pocahontas, 127 J13
Pollock, 131 B6
Polo, 582 D4
Pomona, 300 L8
Poplar Bluff, 16651 L12
Portage des Sioux, 351 A15
Portageville, 3295 M13
Portland, 90 F9
Post Oak, 60 F5
Potosi, 2662 H11
Pottersville, 50 L8
Powe, 100 L12
Powersville, 86 A6
Poynor, 90 M11
Prairie Hill, 100 D7
Prairie Home, 220 F7
Preston, 113 H6
Princeton, 1047 A5
Protem, 30 M6
Purcell, 357 K3
Purdin, 223 C6
Purdy, 1103 L4
Puxico, 1145 L12
Queen City, 638 A7
Quincy, 30 H5
Quitman, 46 A2
Qulin, 467 M12
Racine, 200 L3
Randolph, 47 E5
Ravenwood, 448 B3
Raymondville, 442 K9
Raymore, 11146 F3
Raytown, 30388 E3
Rayville, 204 D4
Rea, 56 B3
Readsville, 30 F9
Redings Mill, 159 L3
Reeds, 103 K4
Reeds Spr., 465 L5
Regal, 50 D4
Renick, 221 D7
Rensselaer, 145 C9
Republic, 8438 K5
Revere, 121 A9
Reynolds, 125 K10
Rhineland, 176 F9
Richards, 95 H3
Rich Fountain, 90 G8
Rich Hill, 1461 H3
Richland, 1805 H7
Richmond, 6116 D4
Richmond Hts., 9602 E15
Richwoods, 225 G11
Ridgely, 64 D3
Ridgeway, 530 B4
Risco, 392 M13
Ritchey, 76 L4
River Bend, 10 D6
Riverside, 2979 D4
Riverton, 20 M10
Riverview, 3146 C17
Rives, 88 N13
Roby, 60 J8
Rocheport, 208 E7
Rockaway Beach, 577 L6
Rock Hill, 4765 E15
Rock Port, 1395 A1
Rockville, 162 H4
Rocky Comfort, 175 L4
Rocky Ridge, 350 H12
Rogersville, 1508 K6
Rolla, 16367 H9
Rombauer, 80 L12
Rome, 20 L7
Rosati, 125 H9
Roscoe, 112 H4
Rosebud, 364 G9
Roselle, 100 J12
Rosendale, 180 B2
Rothville, 93 C6
Rover, 60 L9
Rueter, 20 M6
Rush Hill, 130 E9
Rushville, 280 D2
Russellville, 758 G7
Rutledge, 103 B8
Sabula, 30 J11
Saginaw, 276 K9
St. Ann, 13607 C14
St. Charles, 60321 F12
St. Clair, 4390 G10
St. Cloud, 56 G10
Ste. Genevieve, 4476 H12
St. Elizabeth, 297 G8
St. George, 1288 F15
St. James, 3704 H9
St. John, 6871 D15
St. Joseph, 73990 C2
St. Louis, 348189 F12
St. Martins, 1023 F7
St. Mary, 377 H13
St. Paul, 1634 F11
St. Peters, 51381 F11
St. Robert, 2760 H8
St. Thomas, 287 G8
Salem, 4854 J9
Salisbury, 1726 D7
Santa Fe, 70 D9
Sappington, 7287 F15
Sarcoxie, 1354 K4
Savannah, 4762 C2
Schell City, 286 H4
Scotsdale, 211 G11
Scott City, 4591 K14
Sedalia, 20339 F6
Sedgewickville, 197 J13
Seligman, 877 M4
Senath, 1650 N12
Seneca, 2135 L3
Seymour, 1834 K7
Shelbina, 1943 C8
Shelbyville, 682 C8
Sheldon, 529 J3
Shell Knob, 1393 M5
Sheridan, 185 A3
Shirley, 125 H11
Shoal Creek Drive, 346 K8
Shrewsbury, 6644 F15
Sibley, 347 E4
Sikeston, 16992 L14
Silex, 206 E10
Siloam Sprs., 70 L8
Silva, 125 K12
Silver Creek, 608 K9
Silver Lake, 60 J13
Simmons, 30 K8
Skidmore, 342 B2
Slater, 2083 E6
Sleeper, 175 J7
Smithton, 510 F6
Smithville, 5514 D3
S. Fork, 50 M8
S. Gifford, 72 B7
S. Gorin, 143 B8
S. Greenfield, 136 K4
S. Lineville, 37 A5
South West City, 855 M3
Spanish Lake, 21337 B17
Sparta, 1144 L6
Spickard, 315 B5
Spokane, 133 L5
Springfield, 151580 K5
Squires, 20 L7
Stanberry, 1243 B3
Stanton, 225 G10
Stark City, 156 L4
Steele, 2263 N13
Steelville, 1429 H10
Stella, 178 L4
Stewartsville, 759 C3
Stockton, 1960 J4
Stotesbury, 43 H3
Stotts City, 250 K4
Stoutland, 177 H7
Stoutsville, 44 D8
Stover, 968 G6
Strafford, 1845 K6
Strasburg, 136 F4
Sturgeon, 944 E8
Success, 100 J8
Sugar Creek, 3839 E6
Sullivan, 6351 G10
Summersville, 544 K9
Sumner, 142 C6
Sundown, 38 M7
Sunrise Beach, 368 G7
Sunset Hills, 8267 F14
Swedeborg, 250 H7
Sweet Sprs., 1628 E5
Syracuse, 172 F6
Taberville, 50 H4
Tallapoosa, 204 M13
Taneyville, 359 L6
Taos, 870 G8
Tarkio, 1935 A1
Tarrants, 30 D10
Tecumseh, 50 M8
Thayer, 2201 M9
The Landing, 10 D9
Theodosia, 240 M7
Thomasville, 40 L9
Thornfield, 60 L7
Tiff City, 125 L3
Tiffin, 40 H4
Tightwad, 63 G5
Tina, 193 D5
Tindall, 65 B5
Tipton, 3261 F7
Town and Country, 10894 E13
Tracy, 213 A1
Trenton, 6216 B5
Trimble, 451 D3
Triplett, 64 D6
Troy, 6737 E10
Truesdale, 397 F10
Truxton, 96 E10
Tunas, 50 H6
Turney, 155 D3
Tuscumbia, 218 G7
Twin Bridges, 42 J7
Twin Oaks, 362 F13
Umber View Hts., 52 J4
Union, 7757 G10
Union Star, 433 C3
Unionville, 2041 A6
Unity Vil., 140 H6
University City, 37428 D15
Urbana, 407 H6
Urich, 499 G4
Utica, 274 C5
Valles Mines, 275 H12
Valley Park, 6518 F13
Van Buren, 845 L10
Vandalia, 2529 D9
Vandiver, 83 E9
Vanduser, 217 L13
Vanzant, 20 L8
Verona, 714 L4
Versailles, 2565 G6
Viburnum, 825 J10
Vichy, 70 H9
Vienna, 628 G8
Villa Ridge, 2417 G11
Vinita Park, 1924 D15
Vista, 55 H5
Waco, 86 K3
Wakenda, 90 D5
Waldron, 175 C1
Walker, 275 H4
Walnut Grove, 630 J5
Wardell, 278 M13
Wardsville, 976 G8
Warrensburg, 16340 F5
Warrenton, 5281 F10
Warsaw, 2070 G5
Warson Woods, 1983 E14
Washburn, 448 M4
Washington, 13243 F10
Wasola, 90 L7
Watson, 121 A1
Waverly, 806 E5
Wayland, 425 B9
Waynesville, 3507 H8
Weatherby, 123 C4
Weatherby Lake, 1873 C3
Weaubleau, 518 H5
Webb City, 9812 K3
Webster Groves, 23230 F15
Weingarten, 70 H12
Weldon Spr., 5270 D12
Wellington, 784 E4
Wellston, 2460 D16
Wellsville, 1423 E9
Wentworth, 141 L4
Wentzville, 6896 F11
W. Alton, 573 F12
Westboro, 163 A1
W. Line, 95 F3
Weston, 1631 D2
Westphalia, 320 G8
W. Plains, 10866 L9
Westwood, 284 E14
Wheatland, 388 H5
Wheaton, 721 L4
Wheeling, 268 C5
White Church, 50 L9
Whiteside, 67 E10
Whitewater, 113 K13
Wien, 50 C7
Wilbur Park, 475 F15
Wilderness, 40 L10
Wildwood, 32884 F11
Willard, 3193 K5
Williamstown, 100 B9
Williamsville, 379 L12
Willow Sprs., 2147 L8
Wilson City, 165 L14
Wilton, 70 F7
Winchester, 1651 E13
Windsor, 3087 F5
Windyville, 20 J6
Winfield, 723 E11
Winigan, 20 B6
Winona, 1290 L10
Winston, 247 C4
Wittenberg, 30 J14
Woods Hts., 742 D4
Woodson Terrace, 4189 C15
Wooldridge, 47 E7
Worth, 94 A3
Worthington, 89 A7
Wright City, 1532 F10
Wyaconda, 310 B8
Wyatt, 364 L14
Yukon, 60 K8
Zalma, 93 K12
Zanoni, 50 L7

MONTANA
PG. 122-123

CAPITAL
Helena

NICKNAME
Treasure State

POPULATION
902,195, rank 44

AREA
147,046 sq mi, rank 4

Counties

Beaverhead, 9202 K5
Big Horn, 12671 H15
Blaine, 7009 B12
Broadwater, 4385 G8
Carbon, 9552 K12
Carter, 1360 H19
Cascade, 80357 E8
Chouteau, 5970 D10
Custer, 11696 G18
Daniels, 2017 A17
Dawson, 9059 E19
Deer Lodge, 9417 H5
Fallon, 2837 G19
Fergus, 11893 E12
Flathead, 74471 C3
Gallatin, 67831 J8
Garfield, 1279 E16
Glacier, 13247 B6
Golden Valley, 1042 G12
Granite, 2830 G5
Hill, 16673 B10
Jefferson, 10049 H7
Judith Basin, 2329 F10
Lake, 26507 D4
Lewis and Clark, 55716 E6
Liberty, 2158 B9
Lincoln, 18837 B2
Madison, 6851 J7
McCone, 1977 D17
Meagher, 1932 F9
Mineral, 3884 F3
Missoula, 95802 F5
Musselshell, 4497 F13
Park, 15694 J10
Petroleum, 493 E13
Phillips, 4601 B14
Pondera, 6424 B7
Powder River, 1858 J17
Powell, 7180 E5
Prairie, 1199 F17
Ravalli, 36070 H4
Richland, 9667 C19
Roosevelt, 10620 C18
Rosebud, 9383 G16
Sanders, 10227 D3
Sheridan, 4105 B18
Silver Bow, 34606 H6
Stillwater, 8195 H12
Sweet Grass, 3609 H10
Teton, 6445 D7
Toole, 5267 B8
Treasure, 861 G15
Valley, 7675 B15
Wheatland, 2259 G11
Wibaux, 1068 F19
Yellowstone, 129352 G14

Cities and Towns

Absarokee, 1234 J12
Acton, 50 H13
Agawam, 10 C7
Alberton, 374 E3
Albion, 20 J20
Alder, 116 J7
Alzada, 50 K20
Amsterdam, 727 H8
Anaconda, 9417 H6
Anceney, 20 J8
Angela, 10 F17
Antelope, 43 B19
Arlee, 602 E4
Armington, 150 E9
Arrow Creek, 10 E10
Ashland, 464 J17
Augusta, 284 D7
Austin, 10 F7
Avon, 124 F6
Babb, 20 A5
Bainville, 153 C19
Baker, 1695 G20
Ballantine, 346 H14
Bannack, 20 K6
Barber, 10 G12
Basin, 255 G7
Bearcreek, 83 K12
Bearmouth, 10 F5
Beaverton, 20 B15
Belfry, 219 K12
Belgrade, 5728 H8
Belknap, 50 D2
Belt, 633 E9
Benchland, 20 E10
Biddle, 30 K18
Big Arm, 131 D4
Bigfork, 1421 C4
Bighorn, 20 G15
Big Sandy, 703 C10
Big Sky, 1221 K8
Big Timber, 1650 H11
Billings, 89847 H13
Birney, 108 J16
Black Eagle, 914 D8
Blackfoot, 30 B6
Bonner, 1693 F4
Boulder, 1300 G7
Bowdoin, 10 B14
Box Elder, 794 C10
Boyes, 20 J19
Bozeman, 27509 J9
Brady, 150 C7
Brandenberg, 10 H17
Bridger, 745 J12
Broadus, 451 J18
Broadview, 150 H12
Brockton, 245 C18
Brockway, 20 E17
Browning, 1065 B6
Brusett, 30 E15
Buffalo, 10 F11
Busby, 695 J15
Butte, 34606 H6
Bynum, 20 C7
Cameron, 10 K8
Canyon Creek, 10 F7
Cardwell, 40 H7
Carlyle, 10 F20
Carter, 62 D9
Cascade, 819 E8
Cat Creek, 30 E14
Charlo, 439 D4
Checkerboard, 20 G10
Chester, 871 B9
Chico Hot Sprs., 50 J9
Chinook, 1386 B12
Choteau, 1781 D7
Christina, 10 E12
Circle, 644 D17
Clancy, 1406 G7
Clinton, 549 F5
Clyde Park, 310 H9
Coalridge, 50 A19
Coburg, 10 B13
Coffee Creek, 20 E10
Cohagen, 20 E16
Collins, 10 C8
Colstrip, 2346 H16
Columbia Falls, 3645 B4
Columbus, 1748 J12
Comanche, 20 H13
Comertown, 10 A19
Condon, 60 D5
Conner, 40 H4
Conrad, 2753 C7
Cooke City, 140 K11
Coram, 337 B4
Corbin, 100 G7
Corvallis, 443 G4
Corwin Sprs., 20 K9
Craig, 60 E7
Crane, 40 D19
Creston, 125 C4
Crow Agency, 1552 J15
Culbertson, 716 C19
Cushman, 10 G12
Custer, 145 H15
Cut Bank, 3105 B7
Dagmar, 10 B19
Darby, 710 H4
Dayton, 95 D4
De Borgia, 69 D2
Deer Lodge, 3421 G6
Dell, 20 L6
Delphia, 10 G13
Denton, 301 E11
Devon, 10 B8
Dewey, 40 H6
Dillon, 3752 K6
Divide, 30 H6
Dixon, 216 E4
Dodson, 122 B13
Drummond, 318 F5
Dunkirk, 10 B8
Dupuyer, 40 C7
Dutton, 389 D8
E. Glacier Park, 396 B5
E. Helena, 1642 F7
Edgar, 125 J12
Ekalaka, 410 H19
Elliston, 225 G7
Elmo, 143 D4
Emigrant, 10 J9
Enid, 30 D19
Ennis, 840 J8
Epsie, 10 J18
Essex, 10 C5
Ethridge, 10 B7
Eureka, 1017 A3
Evaro, 329 E4
Evergreen, 6215 C4
Fairfield, 659 D7
Fairview, 709 C20
Fallon, 138 F18
Farmington, 30 D7
Fergus, 20 E12
Fife, 10 E9
Fishtail, 60 J11
Flatwillow, 30 F13
Flaxville, 87 A18
Florence, 901 F4
Floweree, 10 D9
Forsyth, 1944 G16
Ft. Belknap Agency, 1262 B12
Ft. Benton, 1594 D9
Fortine, 169 A3
Ft. Peck, 240 C16
Ft. Shaw, 274 D8
Ft. Smith, 122 J14
Four Buttes, 20 A17
Frazer, 452 C17
Frenchtown, 883 E4
Fresno, 10 B10
Froid, 195 B19
Fromberg, 486 J12
Galata, 20 B8
Gallatin Gateway, 350 J8
Gardiner, 851 K9
Garland, 20 H17
Garneill, 10 F11
Garrison, 112 G6
Garryowen, 10 J15
Geraldine, 284 D10
Geyser, 40 E10
Gildford, 185 B10
Glasgow, 3253 C16
Glen, 20 J6
Glendive, 4729 E19
Goldcreek, 40 F6
Grant, 50 K5
Grantsdale, 750 G4
Grass Range, 149 F12
Grayling, 20 L8
Great Falls, 56690 D8
Greycliff, 56 H11
Hall, 150 F5
Hamilton, 3705 G4
Hammond, 30 J19
Hanover, 30 E11
Happy's Inn, 10 C2
Hardin, 3384 H14
Hardy, 50 E7
Harlem, 848 B12
Harlowton, 1062 G11
Harrison, 162 H8
Hathaway, 10 G17
Havre, 9621 B11
Hays, 702 C13
Heart Butte, 698 C6
Heath, 20 F12
Helena, 25780 F7
Helmville, 20 F6
Heron, 149 C1
Highwood, 189 D9
Hilger, 70 E12
Hingham, 157 B10
Hinsdale, 125 B15
Hobson, 244 F11
Hodges, 10 E19
Hogeland, 20 A13
Homestead, 30 B19
Horton, 10 G17
Hot Sprs., 531 D3
Hughesville, 10 E9
Hungry Horse, 934 B4
Huntley, 411 H13
Huson, 125 E4
Hysham, 330 G15
Ingomar, 20 F15
Intake, 10 E19
Inverness, 103 B9
Ismay, 26 F19
Jackson, 10 J5
Jardine, 20 K9
Jeffers, 70 J8
Jefferson City, 295 G7
Joliet, 575 J12
Joplin, 210 B9
Jordan, 364 E15
Judith Gap, 164 F11
Kalispell, 14223 C4
Kevin, 178 B7
Kila, 225 C3
Kinsey, 30 F17
Kiowa, 10 B6
Klein, 188 G13
Kolin, 10 E11
Kremlin, 126 B10
Lakeside, 1679 C4
Lakeview, 10 L7
Lambert, 150 D19
Lame Deer, 2018 J16
Landusky, 200 D13
Laredo, 10 B11
Larslan, 20 B16
Laurel, 6255 J13
Lavina, 209 G12
Ledger, 10 C8
Lennep, 40 G10
Leroy, 40 D12
Lewistown, 5813 E12
Libby, 2626 B2
Lima, 242 L6
Limestone, 10 J11
Lincoln, 1100 F6
Lindsay, 30 E18
Livingston, 6851 J9
Lloyd, 60 C12
Lodge Grass, 510 J15
Lodgepole, 214 C13
Logan, 90 H8
Lohman, 40 B12
Lolo, 3388 F4
Lolo Hot Sprs., 10 F3
Loma, 92 C10
Lonepine, 137 D3
Lothair, 20 B8
Lozeau, 20 E3
Lustre, 10 B17
Luther, 50 J12
Madoc, 10 A18
Malta, 2120 B14
Manhattan, 1396 H8
Marion, 100 C3
Marsh, 20 F19
Martin City, 331 B4
Martinsdale, 20 G10
Marysville, 10 F7
Maudlow, 10 H9
Maxville, 40 G5
McAllister, 150 J8
McCabe, 20 C19
McLeod, 10 J10
Medicine Lake, 269 B19
Melrose, 10 J6
Melstone, 136 F14
Melville, 20 H11
Menard, 20 H8
Mildred, 10 F18
Miles City, 8487 G17
Mill Iron, 20 H20
Milltown, 20 F4
Miner, 10 K9
Missoula, 57053 F4
Moccasin, 40 E11
Moiese, 20 E4
Molt, 10 H12
Monarch, 10 E9
Monida, 10 L7
Montague, 10 D10
Montana City, 2094 G7
Moore, 186 F11
Moorhead, 10 K17
Morgan, 10 A14
Mosby, 30 F14
Musselshell, 60 G14
Nashua, 325 C16
Neihart, 91 F9
Nelson, 10 F8
Niarada, 50 D3
Norris, 20 J8
Noxon, 230 C1
Nye, 30 J11
Oilmont, 20 B8
Olive, 30 J18
Olney, 60 B3
Opheim, 111 A16
Oswego, 60 C17
Otter, 20 J17
Outlook, 82 A18
Ovando, 71 E5
Pablo, 1814 D4
Paradise, 184 E3
Park City, 870 J12
Peerless, 60 A17
Pendroy, 20 C7
Philipsburg, 914 G5
Pinesdale, 742 G4
Pinnacle, 30 B5
Plains, 1126 D3
Plentywood, 2061 A19
Plevna, 138 G19
Polaris, 60 J5
Polson, 4041 D4
Pompeys Pillar, 30 H14
Pony, 40 J7
Poplar, 911 C18
Porters Corner, 10 G5
Post Creek, 70 E4
Potomac, 125 F5
Power, 171 D8
Pray, 50 J9
Proctor, 30 C4
Pryor, 628 J13
Quietus, 10 K17
Radersburg, 70 G8
Rapalje, 70 H12
Ravalli, 119 E4
Raymond, 10 A19
Raynesford, 30 E9
Red Lodge, 2177 K12
Redstone, 40 A18

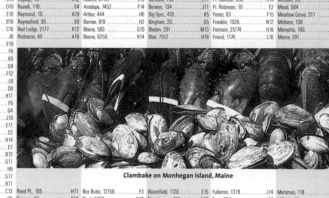

Clambake on Monhegan Island, Maine

Reed Pt., 185 H11
Reserve, 37 B19
Rexford, 151 A2
Richey, 189 D18
Richland, 10 A17
Ridge, 10 K19
Ringling, 20 G9
Roberts, 200 J12
Rock Sprs., 20 F16
Rocky Boy, 175 C11
Rollins, 183 C4
Ronan, 1812 D4
Rosebud, 20 G16
Ross Fork, 20 E11
Rothiemay, 30 G12
Roundup, 1931 G13
Roy, 100 E12
Rudyard, 275 B9
Ryegate, 268 G12
Saco, 224 B15
St. Ignatius, 788 E4
St. Marie, 183 B16
St. Mary, 30 B5
St. Phillip, 10 F20
St. Regis, 315 E2
St. Xavier, 67 J14
Saltese, 10 D2
Sand Coulee, 200 E8
Sanders, 40 G15
Sand Sprs., 40 E15
Santa Rita, 100 B7
Savage, 250 D19
Savoy, 10 B13
Scobey, 1082 A18
Seeley Lake, 1436 E5
Shawmut, 90 G11
Sheffield, 10 G17
Shelby, 3216 B8
Shepherd, 193 H13
Sheridan, 659 J7
Shonkin, 10 D9
Sidney, 4774 D20
Silesia, 20 J12
Silver Gate, 140 K11
Silver Star, 30 J7
Simms, 373 D7
Simpson, 10 A10
Sixteen, 20 G9
Somers, 556 C4
Springdale, 40 H10
Square Butte, 20 D10
Stanford, 454 E10
Stevensville, 1553 G4
Stockett, 200 E9
Stryker, 20 B3
Suffolk, 10 E12
Sula, 10 H4
Sumatra, 10 F14
Sunburst, 415 A7
Sun River, 131 D8
Superior, 893 E3
Sweet Grass, 175 A7
Tampico, 60 C15
Tarkio, 10 E3
Teigen, 10 E13
Terry, 611 F18
Thompson Falls, 1321 D2
Three Forks, 1728 H8
Toston, 105 G8
Townsend, 1867 G8
Tracy, 150 E9
Trego, 10 B3
Trident, 20 H8
Trout Creek, 261 C2
Troy, 957 B1
Turner, 80 A13
Twin Bridges, 400 J7
Twodot, 20 G10
Ulm, 750 E8
Unionville, 175 G7
Utica, 20 F10
Valier, 498 C7
Vananda, 20 G15
Vandalia, 10 B15
Vaughn, 701 D8
Victor, 859 G4
Vida, 10 D18
Virginia City, 130 J7
Volborg, 20 H17
Wagner, 10 B14
Walkerville, 714 H6
Warren, 10 K13
Washoe, 20 K12
Waterloo, 30 H7
Weldon, 10 D17
Westby, 172 A20
W. Glacier, 125 B4
W. Yellowstone, 1177 L9
Whitefish, 5032 B4
Whitehall, 1044 H7
White Pine, 70 D2
White Sulphur Sprs., 984 G9
Whitetail, 30 A18
Whitewater, 40 B14
Whitlash, 10 A8
Wibaux, 567 E20
Willard, 50 G19
Willow Creek, 209 H8
Wilsall, 237 H9
Windham, 50 E10
Winifred, 156 D12
Winnecook, 40 G11
Winnett, 185 F13
Winston, 73 G8
Wisdom, 114 J5
Wise River, 60 H6
Wolf Creek, 10 F7
Wolf Pt., 2663 C17
Woodside, 175 G4
Worden, 506 H14
Wyola, 186 K15
Yaak, 30 A2
Zortman, 175 D13
Zurich, 30 B12

NEBRASKA
PG. 124-125

CAPITAL
Lincoln

NICKNAME
Cornhusker State

POPULATION
1,711,263, rank 38

AREA
77,355 sq mi, rank 15

Counties

Adams, 31151 L13
Antelope, 7452 F14
Arthur, 444 H6
Banner, 819 H2
Blaine, 583 G10
Boone, 6259 H14
Box Butte, 12158 F3
Boyd, 2438 D13
Brown, 3525 F10
Buffalo, 42259 K12
Burt, 7791 G18
Butler, 8767 J16
Cass, 24334 K19
Cedar, 9615 E16
Chase, 4068 L6
Cherry, 6148 E7
Cheyenne, 9830 J3
Clay, 7039 L14
Colfax, 10441 H16
Cuming, 10203 G17
Custer, 11793 J10
Dakota, 20253 F17
Dawes, 9060 E3
Dawson, 24365 K10
Deuel, 2098 J5
Dixon, 6339 E17
Dodge, 36160 H17
Douglas, 463585 J18
Dundy, 2292 M6
Fillmore, 6634 L15
Franklin, 3574 M12
Frontier, 3099 L8
Furnas, 5324 M10
Gage, 22993 M17
Garden, 2292 H4
Garfield, 1902 G12
Gosper, 2143 L10
Grant, 747 G6
Greeley, 2714 H13
Hall, 53534 K13
Hamilton, 9403 K14
Harlan, 3786 M11
Hayes, 1068 L7
Hitchcock, 3111 M7
Holt, 11551 E13
Hooker, 783 G7
Howard, 6567 J13
Jefferson, 8333 M16
Johnson, 4488 L18
Kearney, 6882 L12
Keith, 8875 J6
Keya Paha, 983 D11
Kimball, 4089 J2
Knox, 9374 E14
Lancaster, 250291 L17
Lincoln, 34632 K8
Logan, 774 H9
Loup, 712 G11
Madison, 35226 G15
McPherson, 533 H7
Merrick, 8204 J14
Morrill, 5440 G3
Nance, 4038 J14
Nemaha, 7576 L19
Nuckolls, 5057 M14
Otoe, 15396 L19
Pawnee, 3087 M18
Perkins, 3200 K6
Phelps, 9747 L11
Pierce, 7857 F15
Platte, 31662 H15
Polk, 5639 J15
Red Willow, 11448 M8
Richardson, 9531 M20
Rock, 1756 F11
Saline, 13843 L16
Sarpy, 122595 J18
Saunders, 19830 J17
Scotts Bluff, 36951 G1
Seward, 16496 K16
Sheridan, 6198 F5
Sherman, 3318 J12
Sioux, 1475 E2
Stanton, 6455 G16
Thayer, 6055 M15
Thomas, 729 G8
Thurston, 7171 F17
Valley, 4647 H12
Washington, 18780 H18
Wayne, 9851 F16
Webster, 4061 M13
Wheeler, 886 G13
York, 14598 K15

Cities and Towns

Abie, 108 J17
Adams, 489 L18
Agnew, 100 K17
Ainsworth, 1862 E10
Albion, 1797 H14
Alda, 652 K13
Alexandria, 216 M16
Allen, 411 F17
Alliance, 8959 G4
Alma, 1214 N11
Almeria, 20 G11
Aloys, 50 G17
Altona, 40 G16
Alvo, 142 K18
Amelia, 10 F12
Amherst, 277 K12
Anoka, 10 D12
Anselmo, 159 H10
Ansley, 520 J11
Arapahoe, 1028 M10
Arcadia, 359 J12
Archer, 90 J14
Arlington, 1197 H18
Arnold, 630 J9
Arthur, 145 H6
Ashby, 10 G6
Ashland, 2262 K18
Ashton, 237 J13
Assumption, 70 L13
Atkinson, 1244 E12
Atlanta, 130 M11
Auburn, 3350 L19
Aurora, 4225 K14
Avoca, 270 K19
Axtell, 696 L12
Ayr, 98 M13
Bancroft, 520 G17
Barada, 28 M20
Barneston, 122 N18
Bartlett, 128 G13
Bartley, 355 M9
Bassett, 743 E11
Battle Creek, 1158 G15
Bayard, 1247 G2
Bazile Mills, 26 E14
Beatrice, 12496 M17
Beaver City, 641 M10
Beaver Crossing, 457 K16
Bee, 223 K16
Beemer, 773 G17
Belden, 131 F16
Belgrade, 134 H14
Bellevue, 44382 J19
Bellwood, 446 J16
Belvidere, 98 M15
Benedict, 278 K15
Benkelman, 1006 N6
Bennet, 570 L18
Bennington, 937 J18
Berea, 70 F3
Bertrand, 786 L11
Berwyn, 134 J11
Big Sprs., 418 K5
Bingham, 20 G5
Bladen, 291 M13
Blair, 7512 H18
Bloomfield, 1126 E15
Bloomington, 124 N12
Blue Hill, 867 M13
Blue Sprs., 383 M17
Boelus, 221 K13
Boone, 50 H14
Bostwick, 20 N14
Bow Valley, 125 E16
Boys Town, 818 C16
Bradshaw, 336 K15
Brady, 366 K9
Brainard, 351 J17
Brandon, 10 K5
Brewster, 29 G10
Bridgeport, 1594 H3
Bristow, 88 D13
Broadwater, 140 H3
Brock, 162 L19
Broken Bow, 3491 J11
Brownlee, 10 F8
Brownson, 30 J3
Brownville, 146 L20
Brule, 372 K6
Bruning, 300 M15
Bruno, 112 J17
Brunswick, 179 F14
Burchard, 103 M18
Burr, 66 L18
Burton, 11 D11
Burwell, 1130 H12
Bushnell, 162 J1
Butte, 366 D12
Byron, 144 N15
Cairo, 790 K13
Callaway, 637 J10
Cambridge, 1041 M9
Campbell, 387 M13
Carleton, 136 M15
Carroll, 238 F16
Cedar Bluffs, 615 J17
Cedar Creek, 396 K19
Cedar Rapids, 407 H14
Center, 90 E15
Central City, 2998 K14
Ceresco, 920 K17
Chadron, 5634 D3
Chalco, 10736 J18
Chambers, 333 F13
Champion, 150 L6
Chapman, 341 K14
Chappell, 983 J4
Chester, 294 N15
Clarks, 361 J15
Clarkson, 685 H16
Clatonia, 275 L17
Clay Ctr., 861 L14
Clearwater, 384 F14
Clinton, 30 E5
Cody, 149 D7
Coleridge, 541 E16
Colon, 138 J17
Colton, 10 J3
Columbus, 20971 J16
Comstock, 110 H12
Concord, 160 F16
Cook, 322 L18
Cordova, 127 L16
Cornlea, 41 H15
Cortland, 488 L17
Cotesfield, 66 J13
Cowles, 48 M13
Cozad, 4163 K10
Crab Orchard, 49 M18
Craig, 241 G18
Crawford, 1107 E2
Creighton, 1270 F14
Creston, 215 H16
Crete, 6028 L17
Crofton, 754 E15
Crookston, 98 D8
Crowell, 40 H17
Culbertson, 594 M8
Curtis, 832 L9
Cushing, 31 J14
Dakota City, 1821 F18
Dalton, 332 J3
Danbury, 127 N9
Dannebrog, 352 J13
Darr, 30 K10
Davenport, 339 M15
Davey, 153 K17
David City, 2597 J16
Dawson, 209 M19
Daykin, 177 M16
Decatur, 618 G18
Denman, 30 L13
Denton, 189 L17
Deshler, 879 M15
Deweese, 80 M14
De Witt, 572 M17
Dickens, 20 K8
Diller, 287 M17
Dix, 267 J2
Dixon, 108 F16
Dodge, 700 H17
Doniphan, 763 L14
Dorchester, 615 L16
Douglas, 231 L18
DuBois, 166 N19
Dunbar, 237 L19
Duncan, 359 J15
Dunning, 109 G9
Dwight, 259 K16
Eagle, 1105 K18
Eddyville, 96 K11
Edgar, 539 M14
Edison, 154 M10
Elba, 243 J13
Eldorado, 30 L14
Elgin, 735 G14
Eli, 10 D7
Elk Creek, 112 M19
Elkhorn, 6062 J18
Ellis, 30 M17
Ellsworth, 10 G5
Elm Creek, 894 L11
Elmwood, 668 K18
Elsie, 139 K7
Elsmere, 30 F9
Elwood, 761 L10
Elyria, 54 H12
Emerson, 817 F17
Emmet, 77 F13
Enders, 70 L6
Endicott, 139 M16
Ericson, 104 H13
Eustis, 464 L10
Ewing, 433 F14
Exeter, 712 L16
Fairbury, 4262 M16
Fairfield, 467 M14
Fairmont, 691 L15
Falls City, 4671 M20
Farnam, 223 L9
Farwell, 148 J13
Filley, 174 M18
Firth, 564 L17
Flats, 10 H7
Fordyce, 182 E16
Ft. Calhoun, 856 H19
Ft. Robinson, 10 E2
Foster, 63 F15
Franklin, 1026 N12
Fremont, 25174 H18
Friend, 1174 L16
Fullerton, 1378 J14
Funk, 204 L12
Gandy, 30 H9
Garland, 247 K17
Garrison, 67 J16
Geneva, 2226 L15
Genoa, 981 J15
Gering, 7751 G2
Gibbon, 1759 L13
Gilead, 40 M
Giltner, 389 L
Glenvil, 332 L
Glenwood Park, 550 L
Goehner, 186 K
Gordon, 1756
Gothenburg, 3619
Grafton, 152 L
Grainton, 20
Grand Island, 42940 K
Grant, 1225
Greeley, 531 H
Greenwood, 544 K
Gresham, 270 K
Gretna, 2355 J
Gross, 5 D
Guide Rock, 245 N
Gurley, 228
Hadar, 312 G
Haigler, 211
Hallam, 276 L
Halsey, 59
Hamlet, 54 M
Hampton, 439 K
Hansen, 90 L
Harbine, 56 M
Hardy, 179 N
Harrisburg, 75
Harrison, 279
Hartington, 1640 E
Harvard, 998 L
Hastings, 24064 L
Havens, 10 J
Hayes Ctr., 240
Hay Sprs., 652
Hazard, 66 K
Heartwell, 80 L
Hebron, 1565 M
Hemingford, 993
Henderson, 986 L
Hendley, 38 M
Henry, 162
Herman, 310 H
Hershey, 572
Hickman, 1084 L
Hildreth, 370 M
Holbrook, 225 M
Holdrege, 5636 M
Hollinger, 20 M
Holmesville, 90 M
Holstein, 229 L
Homer, 590 F
Hooper, 827 H
Hordville, 150 K
Hoskins, 283 G
Howe, 50 M
Howells, 632 H
Hubbard, 234 F
Hubbell, 73 N
Humboldt, 941 M
Humphrey, 786 H
Huntley, 67 M
Hyannis, 287
Imperial, 1982
Inavale, 150 N
Indianola, 642 M
Inglewood, 382 J
Inland, 70 L
Inman, 148 F
Irvington, 950 A
Ithaca, 168 J
Jackson, 205 E
Jansen, 143 M
Johnson, 280 L
Johnstown, 53 E
Julian, 63 L
Juniata, 693 L
Kearney, 27431 L
Keene, 30 M
Kenesaw, 873 L
Kennard, 371 H
Keystone, 60
Kilgore, 99
Kimball, 2559
Kramer, 80 L
Kronborg, 40 K
Lakeside, 10
Lamar, 19
Lanham, 40 N
Laurel, 986 F
La Vista, 11699 J
Lawrence, 312 M
Lebanon, 70
Leigh, 442 H
Lemoyne, 60
Leshara, 111 J
Lewellen, 282
Lewiston, 86 M
Lexington, 10011 L
Liberty, 86 M
Lincoln, 225581 K
Lindsay, 276 H
Lindy, 30 E
Linwood, 118 J
Lisco, 30
Litchfield, 280 J
Lodgepole, 348
Loma, 60 J
Long Pine, 341 E
Loomis, 397 L
Lorenzo, 40
Loretto, 20 H
Lorton, 39 L
Louisville, 1046 K
Loup City, 996 J
Lowell, 30 L
Lushton, 33 L
Lyman, 421
Lynch, 269 D
Lyons, 963 G
Macon, 40 M
Macy, 956 F
Madison, 2367 G
Madrid, 265
Magnet, 79 F
Malcolm, 413 K
Malmo, 109 J
Manley, 191 K
Marion, 50
Marquette, 282 K
Marsland, 10
Martinsburg, 103 E
Maskell, 67 E
Mason City, 178 J
Max, 60 M
Maxwell, 315
Maywood, 331
McCook, 7994 M
McCool Jct., 385 L
McGrew, 103 H
McLean, 38 F
Mead, 564 J
Meadow Grove, 311 G
Melbeta, 138
Memphis, 106 J
Merna, 391 H
Merriman, 118 D
Milburn, 10 H1
Milford, 2070 K1
Miller, 156 K1
Milligan, 315 L1
Mills, 10 D1
Minatare, 810 G
Minden, 2964 L1
Mitchell, 1831 G

US Naval Academy, Maryland

NEVADA
PG. 126

CAPITAL
Carson City

NICKNAME
Silver State

POPULATION
1,998,257, rank 35

AREA
110,561 sq mi, rank 7

Counties

Cities and Towns

NEW HAMPSHIRE
PG. 127

CAPITAL
Concord

NICKNAME
Granite State

POPULATION
1,235,786, rank 41

AREA
9,279 sq mi, rank 44

Counties

Cities and Towns

NEW JERSEY
PG. 128-129

CAPITAL
Trenton

NICKNAME
Garden State

POPULATION
8,414,350, rank 9

AREA
7,787 sq mi, rank 46

Counties

Cities and Towns

NEW MEXICO
PG. 130-131

CAPITAL
Santa Fe

NICKNAME
Land of Enchantment

POPULATION
1,819,046, rank 36

AREA
121,593 sq mi, rank 5

Counties

Cities and Towns

Mount Desert Island, Maine

NEW YORK
PG. 132-137

CAPITAL
Albany

NICKNAME
Empire State

POPULATION
18,976,457, rank 3

AREA
49,108 sq mi, rank 30

Counties

Cities and Towns

Au Sable Forks, 670 ...... O23
Averill Park, 1517 ...... N23
Avoca, 1008 ...... P9
Avon, 2977 ...... L8
Babylon, 12615 ...... X25
Bainbridge, 1365 ...... P16
Baiting Hollow, 1449 ...... W27
Bakers Mills, 60 ...... H22
Baldwin, 23455 ...... K14
Baldwin Harbor, 8147 ...... Y24
Baldwinsville, 7053 ...... K13
Ballston Ctr., 400 ...... L22
Ballston Spa, 5556 ...... L22
Balmville, 3339 ...... T22
Bangall, 425 ...... R23
Barker, 577 ...... J5
Barnes Corners, 50 ...... H14
Barneveld, 332 ...... J17
Barnum Island, 2487 ...... L14
Barrytown, 375 ...... R22
Barryville, 125 ...... U19
Batavia, 16256 ...... L6
Bath, 5641 ...... P10
Baxter Estates, 1006 ...... E13
Bay Park, 2300 ...... K13
Bayport, 8662 ...... X26
Bay Shore, 23852 ...... X25
Bayville, 7135 ...... W24
Beacon, 13808 ...... T22
Bedford, 1724 ...... V23
Bedford Hills, 5500 ...... V23
Beekmantown, 550 ...... B23
Belfast, 800 ...... P7
Bellerose, 1173 ...... H12
Bellerose Terrace, 2157 ...... H12
Belle Terre, 832 ...... W26
Bellport, 2363 ...... X26
Belmont, 952 ...... O7
Bemus Pt., 340 ...... Q2
Bergen, 1240 ...... K7
Berkshire, 300 ...... P14
Berlin, 500 ...... M24
Berne, 300 ...... N21
Bethel, 125 ...... T19
Bethlehem Ctr., 2500 ...... T29
Bethpage, 16543 ...... X24
Big Flats, 2482 ...... O11
Billings, 800 ...... S23
Billington Hts., 1691 ...... M5
Binghamton, 47380 ...... O15
Black Brook, 80 ...... C22
Black River, 1285 ...... F15
Blasdell, 2718 ...... M4
Blauvelt, 5207 ...... W22
Bliss, 375 ...... N6
Bloomfield, 1267 ...... L9
Bloomingburg, 353 ...... T20
Blooming Grove, 1200 ...... U21
Bloomington, 1100 ...... R22
Blue Pt., 4407 ...... X26
Blue Ridge, 20 ...... F22
Blue Store, 425 ...... Q23
Boiceville, 350 ...... R21
Bolivar, 1173 ...... R6
Bolton, 175 ...... H23
Bolton Landing, 650 ...... H23
Bombay, 325 ...... A19
Boonville, 2138 ...... H17
Bouquet, 30 ...... D24
Branchport, 375 ...... N10
Brant Lake, 375 ...... G23
Brasher Falls, 1140 ...... B19
Brentwood, 53917 ...... X25
Brewerton, 3453 ...... K14
Brewster, 2162 ...... U23
Brewster Hill, 2226 ...... U24
Briarcliff Manor, 7696 ...... V23
Bridgehampton, 1381 ...... W28
Bridgeport, 1665 ...... K15
Bridgewater, 579 ...... L17
Brier Hill, 200 ...... C16
Brighton, 35584 ...... K9
Brightwaters, 3248 ...... X25
Brinckerhoff, 2734 ...... T22
Briscoe, 175 ...... S19
Broadalbin, 1411 ...... L21
Brockport, 8103 ...... K7
Brocton, 1547 ...... P2
Bronxville, 6543 ...... C10
Brookhaven, 3570 ...... X26
Brookville, 2126 ...... X24
Brownville, 1022 ...... F14
Brushton, 479 ...... B20
Buchanan, 2189 ...... V22
Buffalo, 292648 ...... L4
Bullville, 550 ...... T21
Burdett, 357 ...... P11
Burke, 213 ...... A21
Burlingham, 750 ...... T21
Burnt Hills, 2100 ...... L22
Bushville, 175 ...... S19
Buskirk, 475 ...... L24
Buttonville, 450 ...... S22
Cadyville, 700 ...... B23
Cairo, 1390 ...... P22
Calcium, 3346 ...... F15
Caledonia, 2327 ...... L8
Callicoon, 216 ...... S18
Callicoon Ctr., 175 ...... S18
Calverton, 5704 ...... W27
Cambridge, 1925 ...... L24
Camden, 2330 ...... J15
Camillus, 1249 ...... L13
Campbell Hall, 750 ...... U21
Canaan, 225 ...... N24
Canajoharie, 2257 ...... L19
Canandaigua, 11264 ...... L10
Canaseraga, 594 ...... P8
Canastota, 4425 ...... L16
Candor, 855 ...... O13
Canisteo, 2336 ...... O9
Canton, 5882 ...... C17
Cape Vincent, 760 ...... E13
Carle Place, 5247 ...... G14
Carlisle, 325 ...... M20
Carmel, 5650 ...... U23
Carthage, 3721 ...... F16
Cassadaga, 676 ...... P2
Castile, 1051 ...... N7
Castleton-on-Hudson, 1619 ...... N23
Castorland, 306 ...... F16
Cato, 601 ...... K12
Catskill, 4392 ...... Q22
Cattaraugus, 1075 ...... P4
Cayuga, 509 ...... L12
Cayuga Hts., 3273 ...... P13
Cazenovia, 2614 ...... L15
Cedarhurst, 6164 ...... K13
Cedarville, 325 ...... L18
Celoron, 1295 ...... Q2
Cementon, 350 ...... Q22
Center Berlin, 150 ...... M24
Center Brunswick, 900 ...... M23
Centereach, 27285 ...... X26
Center Moriches, 6655 ...... X27
Centerport, 5446 ...... W25
Centerville, 150 ...... P6
Central Bridge, 900 ...... M21
Central Islip, 31950 ...... X25
Central Square, 1646 ...... J14
Central Valley, 1857 ...... V22
Centre Island, 444 ...... W24
Champlain, 1173 ...... A23
Chappaqua, 9468 ...... V23
Charlton, 700 ...... L22
Chateaugay, 798 ...... B21
Chatham, 1758 ...... P23
Chaumont, 592 ...... F14
Chazy, 600 ...... A23
Chazy Landing, 250 ...... A24
Cheektowaga, 79988 ...... L4
Chelsea, 2300 ...... T22
Chenango Bridge, 4100 ...... O15
Cherry Creek, 551 ...... P3
Cherry Grove, 20 ...... X25
Cherry Plain, 90 ...... N24
Cherry Valley, 592 ...... M19
Chester, 3445 ...... U21
Chestertown, 450 ...... H22
Chestnut Ridge, 7829 ...... V22
Cheviot, 550 ...... Q22
Childwold, 50 ...... D19

Boothbay Harbor, Maine

Pictured Rocks National Lakeshore, Michigan

NORTH CAROLINA PG. 138-140

CAPITAL
Raleigh

NICKNAME
Tar Heel State

POPULATION
8,049,313, rank 11

AREA
52,669 sq mi, rank 28

NORTH DAKOTA PG. 141

CAPITAL
Bismarck

NICKNAME
Flickertail State

POPULATION
642,200, rank 47

AREA
70,703 sq mi, rank 17

Hoover Dam, Nevada

Trump Taj Mahal Casino, New Jersey

OHIO
PG. 142-145

CAPITAL
Columbus

NICKNAME
Buckeye State

POPULATION
11,353,140, rank 7

AREA
41,330 sq mi, rank 35

OKLAHOMA
PG. 146-147

CAPITAL
Oklahoma City

NICKNAME
Sooner State

POPULATION
3,450,654 rank 27

AREA
69,956 sq mi, rank 18

The Balsams, New Hampshire

OREGON
PG. 148-149

CAPITAL
Salem

NICKNAME
Beaver State

POPULATION
3,421,399, rank 28

AREA
97,073 sq mi, rank 10

Counties

Cities and Towns

PENNSYLVANIA
PG. 150-154

CAPITAL
Harrisburg

NICKNAME
Keystone State

POPULATION
12,281,054, rank 6

AREA
45,308 sq mi, rank 33

Counties

Cities and Towns

Owachomo Bridge, Utah

RHODE ISLAND
PG. 155

CAPITAL
Providence

NICKNAME
Ocean State

POPULATION
1,048,319, rank 43

AREA
1,212 sq mi, rank 50

SOUTH CAROLINA
PG. 156

CAPITAL
Columbia

NICKNAME
Palmetto State

POPULATION
4,012,012, rank 26

AREA
31,113 sq mi, rank 40

SOUTH DAKOTA
PG. 157

CAPITAL
Pierre

NICKNAME
Mount Rushmore State

POPULATION
754,844, rank 46

AREA
77,116 sq mi, rank 16

Somesville, Maine

TENNESSEE
PG. 158-159

CAPITAL
Nashville

NICKNAME
Volunteer State

POPULATION
5,689,283, rank 16

AREA
42,144 sq mi, rank 34

TEXAS
PG. 160-164

CAPITAL
Austin

NICKNAME
Lone Star State

POPULATION
20,851,820, rank 2

AREA
266,807 sq mi, rank 2

Allentown Historic District, New York

Gillespie, 20814 N14
Glasscock, 1406 K10
Goliad, 6928 R17
Gonzales, 18628 O17
Gray, 22744 D11
Grayson, 110595 G18
Gregg, 111379 J21
Grimes, 23552 N20
Guadalupe, 89023 P16
Hale, 36602 G10
Hall, 3782 F12
Hamilton, 8229 L16
Hansford, 5369 B10
Hardeman, 4724 F13
Hardin, 48073 N22
Harris, 3400578 P20
Harrison, 62110 J22
Hartley, 5537 C8
Haskell, 6093 H13
Hays, 97589 P16
Hemphill, 3351 C12
Henderson, 73277 K19
Hidalgo, 569463 V16
Hill, 32321 K17
Hockley, 22716 G9
Hood, 41100 J16
Hopkins, 31960 H20
Houston, 23185 L20
Howard, 33627 J10
Hudspeth, 3344 L3
Hunt, 76596 H19
Hutchinson, 23857 C11
Irion, 1771 L11
Jack, 8763 H16
Jackson, 14391 O19
Jasper, 35604 M23
Jeff Davis, 2207 M5
Jefferson, 252051 P23
Jim Hogg, 5281 U15
Jim Wells, 39326 T16
Johnson, 126811 J17
Jones, 20785 J13
Karnes, 15446 R16
Kaufman, 71313 J19
Kendall, 23743 P15
Kenedy, 414 U17
Kent, 859 H11
Kerr, 43653 P14
Kimble, 4468 N13
King, 356 G12
Kinney, 3379 O12
Kleberg, 31549 T17
Knox, 4253 G13
Lamar, 48499 G20
Lamb, 14709 F9
Lampasas, 17762 M16
La Salle, 5866 S14
Lavaca, 19210 O18
Lee, 15657 N18
Leon, 15335 L20
Liberty, 70154 N22
Limestone, 22051 L19
Lipscomb, 3057 B12
Live Oak, 12309 S16
Llano, 17044 N15
Loving, 67 K6
Lubbock, 242628 G9
Lynn, 6550 H9
Madison, 12940 M19
Marion, 10941 H22
Martin, 4746 J9
Mason, 3738 N14
Matagorda, 37957 R20
Maverick, 47297 R12
McCulloch, 8205 M13
McLennan, 213517 L17
McMullen, 851 S15
Medina, 39304 O14
Menard, 2360 M13
Midland, 116009 K9
Milam, 24238 M18
Mills, 5151 L15
Mitchell, 9698 K11
Montague, 19117 G16
Montgomery, 293768 N20
Moore, 20121 C10
Morris, 13048 H22
Motley, 1426 F11
Nacogdoches, 59203 K21
Navarro, 45124 K18
Newton, 15072 M24
Nolan, 15802 J12
Nueces, 313645 T17
Ochiltree, 9006 B11
Oldham, 2185 D8
Orange, 84966 N23
Palo Pinto, 27026 J15
Panola, 22756 K23
Parker, 88495 J17
Parmer, 10016 E8
Pecos, 16809 M8
Polk, 41133 M22
Potter, 113546 D10
Presidio, 7304 N5
Rains, 9139 H20
Randall, 104312 D9
Reagan, 3326 L10
Real, 3047 P13
Red River, 14314 G21
Reeves, 13137 L6
Refugio, 7828 S18
Roberts, 887 C11
Robertson, 16000 M19
Rockwall, 43080 H19
Runnels, 11495 K13
Rusk, 47372 K22
Sabine, 10469 L23
San Augustine, 8946 L23
San Jacinto, 22246 N21
San Patricio, 67138 S17
San Saba, 6186 M14
Schleicher, 2935 M12
Scurry, 16361 J11
Shackelford, 3302 J14
Shelby, 25224 K22
Sherman, 3186 B10
Smith, 174706 J21
Somervell, 6809 K16
Starr, 53597 V15
Stephens, 9674 J15
Sterling, 1393 K11
Stonewall, 1693 H12
Sutton, 4077 N12
Swisher, 8378 E10
Tarrant, 1446219 H17
Taylor, 126555 J13
Terrell, 1081 N9
Terry, 12761 H8
Throckmorton, 1850 H14
Titus, 28118 H21
Tom Green, 104010 M12
Travis, 812280 N16
Trinity, 13779 M21
Tyler, 20871 M22
Upshur, 35291 J21
Upton, 3404 L9
Uvalde, 25926 O13
Val Verde, 44856 P10
Van Zandt, 48140 J20
Victoria, 84088 R18
Walker, 61758 M20
Waller, 32663 P20
Ward, 10909 L7
Washington, 30373 N19
Webb, 193117 S13
Wharton, 41188 O19
Wheeler, 5284 D12
Wichita, 131664 F15
Wilbarger, 14676 G14
Willacy, 20082 V17
Williamson, 249967 M16
Wilson, 32408 O16
Winkler, 7173 K7
Wise, 48793 H17
Wood, 36752 H21
Yoakum, 7322 H8
Young, 17943 H15
Zapata, 12182 U14
Zavala, 11600 R13

Cities and Towns

Abbott, 300 K18
Abernathy, 2839 G10
Abilene, 115930 J13
Ace, 50 N22
Ackerly, 245 J10
Acme, 10 F13
Acuff, 100 G10
Adamsville, 30 L16
Addison, 14166 A7
Admiral, 10 K14
Adrian, 159 D8
Afton, 60 G11
Agnes, 150 H16
Agua Dulce, 737 T16
Agua Nueva, 20 U15
Aiken, 80 K22
Aiken, 40 F10
Alamo, 14760 W16
Alamo Alto, 70 L2
Alamo Hts., 7319 V21
Alanreed, 60 D11
Alba, 430 H20
Albany, 1921 J14
Albion, 80 F21
Aldine, 13979 F4
Aledo, 1726 J17
Alexander, 50 K16
Alfred, 451 T16
Algerita, 70 L15
Algoa, 900 O21
Alice, 19010 T16
Allamoore, 10 M4
Allen, 43554 H18
Allenfarm, 60 N19
Alleyton, 175 P19
Allison, 150 C12
Allmon, 10 G10
Allred, 70 H8
Alma, 302 J19
Aloe, 850 R18
Alpine, 5786 N6
Altair, 125 P19
Alto, 1190 L21
Alton, 4384 R9
Alvarado, 3288 J17
Alvin, 21413 O21
Alvord, 1007 H17
Amarillo, 173627 D10
Ames, 1079 N22
Amherst, 791 F9
Anahuac, 2210 P22
Anderson, 257 N20
Andice, 175 M16
Andrews, 9652 J8
Angleton, 18130 O21
Angus, 334 K19
Anna, 1225 H18
Annarose, 10 S16
Annetta, 1108 J17
Annona, 282 G21
Anson, 2556 J13
Antelope, 50 G15
Anthony, 3850 K1
Anton, 1200 G9
Appleby, 444 K22
Apple Sprs., 200 L21
Aquilla, 136 K17
Aransas Pass, 8138 T18
Archer City, 1848 G15
Arcola, 1048 P21
Argyle, 2365 H17
Arlington, 332969 J18
Arneckeville, 10 R17
Arnett, 40 G9
Arnett, 10 L16
Arney, 10 E9
Arp, 901 J21
Artesia Wells, 50 S14
Arthur City, 125 F20
Arvana, 10 J9
Asherton, 1342 S13
Ashtola, 20 E11
Aspermont, 1021 H12
Athens, 11297 K20
Atlanta, 5745 H22
Aubrey, 1500 H18
Aurora, 853 H17
Austin, 656562 N17
Austonio, 20 L20
Austwell, 192 S18
Avalon, 150 K18
Avery, 462 G21
Avinger, 464 H22
Avoca, 125 H13
Axtell, 350 L18
Azle, 9600 H17
Bacliff, 6962 L8
Bagwell, 100 G21
Bailey, 213 G19
Baileyboro, 10 F8
Bailey's Prairie, 694 O21
Baileyville, 10 M18
Bainer, 20 G9
Baird, 1623 J14
Baker, 10 J17
Bakersfield, 10 M9
Balch, 50 G9
Balch Sprs., 19375 D9
Balcones Hts., 3016 V21
Bald Prairie, 30 L19
Ballinger, 4243 L13
Balmorhea, 527 M6
Bandera, 957 P14
Bandera Falls, 225 P14
Bangs, 1620 L14
Banquete, 850 T17
Bardwell, 583 K18
Barksdale, 20 P13
Barnhart, 100 M11
Barnum, 40 M22
Barrett, 2872 P21
Barry, 209 K18
Barstow, 406 L7
Bartlett, 1675 M17
Bartons Chapel, 40 H16
Barwise, 40 F10
Bassett, 100 G22
Bastrop, 5340 N17
Batesville, 1298 R13
Batson, 150 N22
Bay City, 18667 R20
Bayou Vista, 1644 N8
Bayside, 360 S18
Baytown, 66430 P22
Bayview, 323 W17
Beach City, 1645 P22
Beasley, 590 O20
Beaumont, 113866 N23
Beaumont Place, 4500 G6
Bebe, 10 O17
Beckville, 752 J22
Becton, 60 G10
Bedford, 47152 C4
Bedias, 350 M20
Bee Cave, 656 N16
Beeville, 13129 S17
Belcherville, 20 G16
Belfalls, 70 M17
Bellaire, 15642 P21
Bellevue, 386 G16
Bellmead, 9214 L18
Bells, 1190 G19
Bellville, 3794 P19
Belmont, 20 O17
Belton, 14623 M17
Ben Arnold, 50 M18
Benavides, 1686 T15
Ben Bolt, 450 T16
Benbrook, 20208 E1
Benchley, 70 M19
Bend, 10 M15
Ben Hur, 10 L18
Benjamin, 264 G13
Benoit, 10 K13
Ben Wheeler, 300 J20
Berclair, 150 R17
Berea, 125 H22
Bergheim, 80 P15
Bernardo, 90 P19
Berryville, 891 K20
Bertram, 1122 M16
Bethel, 90 K20
Bettie, 150 H21
Beverly Hills, 2113 S8
Bevil Oaks, 1346 N23
Biardstown, 125 G20
Bigfoot, 304 O15
Big Lake, 2885 M10
Big Sandy, 1288 J21
Big Spr., 25233 K10
Big Wells, 704 R13
Birome, 50 K18
Bishop, 3305 T17
Bishop Hills, 210 D9
Bivins, 250 H22
Black, 20 E8
Blackwell, 360 K12
Blair, 20 J13
Blanco, 1505 P15
Blanconia, 20 S17
Blanket, 402 K15
Bledsoe, 175 G8
Blessing, 861 R19
Blewett, 30 O13
Bloomburg, 375 H23
Blooming Grove, 833 K18
Bloomington, 2562 R18
Blossom, 1439 G20
Blue, 90 N18
Bluegrove, 30 G16
Blue Mound, 2388 C3
Blue Ridge, 672 H19
Bluff Dale, 80 J16
Blum, 399 K17
Blumenthal, 225 N15
Boerne, 6178 P15
Bogata, 1396 G21
Boling, 1271 O20
Bomarton, 10 G14
Bonham, 9990 G19
Bonita, 10 G17
Bonney, 384 O21
Bono, 100 J17
Bon Wier, 300 M24
Booker, 1315 B12
Boonsville, 40 H16
Borger, 14302 C10
Bovina, 1874 E8
Bowie, 5219 G16
Box Church, 60 L19
Boxelder, 10 G21
Boyd, 1099 H17
Boys Ranch, 600 D9
Bozar, 30 L15
Bracken, 150 U22
Brackettville, 1876 O12
Bradford, 50 K20
Bradshaw, 30 K13
Brady, 5523 M14
Brandon, 10 K18
Brashear, 200 H20
Brazoria, 2787 O20
Brazos, 30 J16
Brazos Pt., 60 K17
Breckenridge, 5868 J15
Bremond, 876 M18
Brenham, 13507 N19
Breslau, 60 O18
Briar, 5350 H17
Briarcliff, 895 N16
Brice, 10 E11
Bridge City, 8651 N23
Bridgeport, 4309 H16
Briggs, 50 M16
Briscoe, 10 C12
Bristol, 325 J19
Broaddus, 189 L23
Brock, 90 J16
Bronson, 250 L23
Bronte, 1076 K12
Brookeland, 300 L23
Brookesmith, 20 L14
Brookshire, 3450 P20
Brookside Vil., 1960 K5
Brookston, 175 G20
Browndell, 219 L23
Brownfield, 9488 H9
Brownsboro, 796 J20
Brownsville, 139722 W17
Brownwood, 18813 L14
Bruceville-Eddy, 1490 L17
Brundage, 31 R13
Bruni, 412 T15
Brushy Creek, 40 K20
Bryan, 65660 M19
Bryans Mill, 40 H22
Bryson, 528 H15
Buchanan Dam, 1688 M15
Buckeye, 10 R20
Buckholts, 387 M18
Buda, 2404 P16
Buffalo, 1804 L19
Buffalo Gap, 463 K13
Buffalo Sprs., 493 G10
Buford, 20 J11
Bula, 30 F8
Bulcher, 30 G17
Bullard, 1150 K21
Bulverde, 3761 P15
Buna, 2269 N23
Bunger, 10 H15
Bunker Hill Vil., 3654 H2
Bunyan, 20 K15
Burkburnett, 10927 F15
Burke, 315 L22
Burkeville, 200 M24
Burleson, 20976 J17
Burlington, 100 M18
Burnet, 4735 M16
Burton, 359 N19
Busby, 10 J12
Bushland, 125 D9
Butler, 300 N17
Byers, 517 F16
Bynum, 225 K18
Cactus, 2538 C9
Caddo, 20 J15
Caddo Mills, 1149 H19
Caldwell, 3449 N18
Calf Creek, 10 M14
Call, 125 M23
Calliham, 80 S16
Callisburg, 365 G18
Calvert, 1426 M18
Camden, 10 M22
Cameron, 5634 M18
Campbell, 734 H19
Campbellton, 125 R16
Camp San Saba, 30 M14
Camp Verde, 10 P14
Camp Wood, 822 P13
Canadian, 2233 C12
Candelaria, 150 N4
Caney City, 236 K19
Canton, 3292 J20
Canutillo, 5129 K1
Canyon, 12875 E9
Canyon Lake, 16870 P16
Canyon Valley, 10 G10
Cap Rock, 20 G10
Caps, 100 J13
Carbon, 224 K15
Carlos, 40 N19
Carlsbad, 250 L12
Carlton, 90 K16
Carmine, 228 N19
Carrizo Sprs., 5655 R13
Carrollton, 109576 H18
Carthage, 6664 K22
Casa Piedra, 10 P5
Cash, 300 H19
Cason, 175 H21
Cassin, 475 O15
Castell, 10 M14
Castle Hills, 4202 V21
Castroville, 2664 O15
Catarina, 135 S13
Cat Spr., 40 P19
Cayote, 40 K17
Cayuga, 50 K20
Cedar Creek, 70 P17
Cedar Hill, 32093 E6
Cedar Hill, 10 F11
Cedar Lake, 50 R20
Cedar Lane, 90 R20
Cedar Park, 26049 N16
Cee Vee, 10 F12
Celeste, 817 H19
Celina, 1861 H18
Center, 5678 K23
Center City, 10 L15
Center Pt., 750 P14
Centerville, 903 L20
Centralia, 70 L21
Cestohowa, 50 R16
Chalk, 10 G12
Chalk Mtn., 30 K16
Chandler, 2099 J20
Channelview, 29685 P21
Channing, 356 C9
Chapman, 100 K22
Chapman Ranch, 80 T17
Chappel, 20 M15
Chappell Hill, 425 N19
Charco, 40 R17
Charlie, 125 F15
Charlotte, 1637 R15
Chatfield, 40 K19
Cherokee, 30 M15
Cherry Spr., 40 N14
Chester, 265 M22
Chico, 947 H16
Childress, 6778 F12
Chillicothe, 798 F13
Chilton, 475 L18
China, 1112 N23
China Grove, 1247 O16
China Spr., 400 L17
Chireno, 405 L22
Choate, 100 R17
Chriesman, 40 N18
Christine, 436 R15
Christoval, 422 M12
Cibolo, 3035 V23
Circle, 30 F9
Circle Back, 20 F8
Cisco, 3851 J14
Cistern, 20 P18
Clairette, 50 K16
Clarendon, 1974 E11
Clareville, 30 S16
Clarksville, 3883 G21
Claude, 1313 D10
Clauene, 10 G9
Clay, 125 N19
Clayton, 10 K22
Claytonville, 40 F10
Clear Lake Shores, 1205 K7
Cleburne, 26005 J17
Clegg, 10 S16
Cleo, 50 N13
Cleveland, 7605 N21
Clifton, 3542 K17
Cline, 10 O12
Clint, 980 K2
Close City, 70 H10
Cloverleaf, 23508 H6
Clute, 10424 O21
Clyde, 3345 J13
Coahoma, 932 J10
Cochran, 40 P19
Cockrell Hill, 4443 D7
Coffee City, 193 K20
Coit, 10 L18
Coke, 70 H20
Coldspring, 691 M21
Coleman, 5127 K14
Colfax, 200 J20
Collegeport, 325 R19
College Sta., 67890 M19
Colleyville, 19636 H17
Collinsville, 1235 G18
Colmesneil, 638 M22
Colony, 10 P18
Colorado City, 4281 J11
Columbus, 3916 P19
Comanche, 4482 K15
Combes, 2553 W17
Comfort, 2358 P15
Commerce, 7669 H20
Como, 621 H20
Comstock, 250 P11
Concan, 100 O13
Concepcion, 61 T16
Concho, 30 L13
Concord, 50 K21
Concord, 50 K22
Concrete, 20 O17
Cone, 70 G10
Conlen, 30 B9
Conroe, 36811 N21
Converse, 11508 V22
Conway, 40 D10
Cooks Pt., 80 N19
Cookville, 200 H21
Cool, 162 J16
Coolidge, 848 K18
Cooper, 2150 G20
Copeville, 300 H19
Coppell, 35958 A6
Copperas Cove, 29592 M16
Cordele, 20 O19
Corinth, 11325 H18
Cornudas, 30 K3
Corpus Christi, 277454 T17
Corrigan, 1721 M22
Corsicana, 24485 K19
Coryell City, 60 L17
Cost, 100 O17
Cotton Ctr., 70 F9
Cottondale, 40 H17
Cottonwood, 181 J19
Cottonwood, 60 K14
Cottonwood, 30 M20
Cottonwood Shores, 877 N16
Cotulla, 3614 S14
County Line, 30 G9
Coupland, 200 N17
Courtney, 1500 N20
Cove, 323 P22
Covington, 282 K17
Coyanosa, 138 L7
Coy City, 60 R16
Crandall, 2774 J19
Crane, 3191 L9
Cranell, 175 S17
Cranfills Gap, 335 K16
Crawford, 705 L17
Creedmoor, 211 P17
Cresson, 175 J17
Crews, 10 K13
Crockett, 7141 L21
Crosby, 1714 P21
Crosbyton, 1874 G11
Cross, 30 R15
Cross Cut, 10 K14
Cross Plains, 1068 K14
Cross Roads, 603 H18
Cross Roads, 125 K20
Croton, 10 G11
Crowell, 1141 F13
Crowley, 7467 J17
Crystal Beach, 275 O22
Crystal City, 7190 R13
Crystal Falls, 10 H15
Cuero, 6571 O17
Cumby, 616 H20
Cundiff, 70 H16
Cuney, 145 K21
Cunningham, 125 G20
Curtis, 300 M23
Cushing, 637 K22
Cut, 125 L20
Cut and Shoot, 1158 N21
Cuthbert, 20 J11
Cuyler, 30 D11
Cyclone, 100 M18
Dabney, 20 O12
Dacosta, 70 R18
Daingerfield, 2517 H22
Daisetta, 1034 N22
Dale, 200 P17
Dalhart, 7237 C9
Dallardsville, 30 M22
Dallas, 1188580 J18
Dalworthington Gardens, 2186 D4
Damon, 535 O20
Danbury, 1611 O21
Danciger, 20 O20
Danevang, 325 O19
Darco, 70 J22
Darrouzett, 303 B12
Davilla, 60 M17
Dawn, 30 E9
Dawson, 852 K18
Dayton, 5709 N22
Deadwood, 70 K23
Dean, 341 F15
Dean, 50 G9
Deanville, 70 N18
De Berry, 225 J23
Decatur, 5201 H17
Deer Park, 28520 H6
De Kalb, 1769 G22
De Leon, 2433 K15
Delhi, 10 P17
Dell City, 413 K4
Del Rio, 33867 O11
Del Valle, 1300 S4
Democrat, 20 L15
Denison, 22773 G18
Denning, 20 L23
Dennis, 50 J16
Denton, 80537 H17
Denton, 150 K13
Denver City, 3985 H8
Deport, 718 G21
Derby, 20 R14
Dermott, 20 H11
Dernal, 175 R18
Desdemona, 150 K15
De Soto, 37646 J18
Detroit, 776 G21
Devers, 416 N22
Devine, 4140 O15
Dew, 40 L19
De Wees, 10 R16
Deweyville, 1190 N24
Dexter, 10 G18
D'Hanis, 450 O14
Dialville, 250 K21
Diana, 425 J22
Diboll, 5470 L22
Dickens, 332 G11
Dickinson, 17093 O21
Dike, 60 H20
Dilley, 3674 R14
Dime Box, 80 N18
Dimmitt, 4375 E9
Dinero, 50 S16
Ding Dong, 175 M16
Direct, 20 G20
Divot, 10 R14
Doans, 10 F14
Dobbin, 300 N20
Dodd, 10 F9
Dodd City, 419 G19
Dodge, 70 M21
Dodson, 115 E13
Domino, 52 H23
Donie, 100 L19
Donna, 14768 W16
Doole, 10 L13
Dorchester, 109 G18
Doss, 10 N14
Double Bayou, 100 P22
Doucette, 300 M22
Dougherty, 150 F11
Douglass, 50 K21
Douglassville, 175 H22
Downing, 40 K15
Dozier, 10 D12
Draw, 10 H10
Driftwood, 200 N16
Dripping Sprs., 1548 N16
Driscoll, 825 T17
Dryden, 10 P9
Dublin, 3754 K16
Dudley, 60 K13
Duffau, 80 K16
Dumas, 13747 C9
Dumont, 10 G12
Duncanville, 36081 J18
Dundee, 10 G14
Dunlap, 10 F12
Dunlay, 40 O14
Dunn, 100 J11
Eagle Lake, 3664 P19
Eagle Pass, 22413 R12
Early, 2588 L14
Earth, 1109 F9
E. Afton, 20 G11
E. Bernard, 1729 O20
Easterly, 30 M19
Eastland, 3769 J15
Easton, 524 J22
E. Tawakoni, 775 H19
Echo, 20 K14
Eckert, 10 N15
Ector, 600 G19
Edcouch, 3342 V16
Eden, 2561 M13
Edgar, 20 O18
Edge, 30 M19
Edgecliff, 2550 E3
Edgewood, 1348 J20
Edinburg, 48465 V16
Edith, 10 K12
Edmonson, 123 F9
Edna, 5899 R19
Edna Hill, 10 K16
Edom, 322 J20
Edroy, 420 S17
Egypt, 60 O19
Elbert, 56 H14
El Campo, 10945 O19
El Cenizo, 3545 U14
Eldorado, 1951 M12
Electra, 3168 F14
Elgin, 5700 N17
Eliasville, 40 H15
El Indio, 263 R12
Eliott, 30 M19
Elkhart, 1215 L20
Ella, 50 T16
El Lago, 3075 K7
Ellinger, 200 P18
Elmaton, 50 R20
Elmendorf, 664 O16
Elm Mott, 1200 L18
Elmo, 650 J19
El Paso, 563662 K1
Elsa, 5549 V16
El Sauz, 20 V15
Elwood, 20 M20
Elysian Fields, 175 J23
Emhouse, 159 K19
Emory, 1021 H20
Enchanted Oaks, 357 J19
Encinal, 629 S14
Encino, 177 U16
Energy, 20 K15
Enloe, 125 G20
Ennis, 16045 J18
Enochs, 20 G8
Eola, 125 L13
Era, 150 G17
Escobares, 1954 V15
Escobas, 10 U14
Esperanza, 30 L3
Estelline, 168 E12
Estes, 400 S18
Etoile, 100 L22
Etter, 150 C9
Eula, 125 J13
Euless, 46005 C5
Eureka, 340 K19
Eustace, 798 J19
Evadale, 1430 N23
Evant, 393 L16
Evergreen, 10 N21
Everman, 5836 E3
Ezzell, 30 O18
Fabens, 8043 L2
Fairchilds, 678 O20
Fairfield, 3094 K19
Fairland, 80 N16
Fairlie, 90 H19
Fairmount, 125 L23
Fair Oaks Ranch, 4695 P15
Fairview, 2644 H18
Fairview, 30 O16
Fairview, 20 F8
Fairview, 20 J10
Falcon, 150 V14
Falcon Hts., 335 V14
Falfurrias, 5297 U16
Falls City, 591 R16
Fannett, 1000 P23
Fannin, 30 R18
Fargo, 40 F14
Farmers Branch, 27508 B7
Farmers Valley, 10 F14
Farmersville, 3118 H19
Farnsworth, 150 B11
Farrar, 100 L19
Farrsville, 20 M23
Farwell, 1364 F8
Fashing, 10 R16
Fate, 497 H19
Fayetteville, 261 P18
Faysville, 348 V16
Fedor, 10 N18
Fentress, 250 P17
Ferris, 2175 J18
Fieldton, 20 F9
Fife, 10 L14
Finney, 20 F10
Finney, 20 G12
Fischer, 40 P16
Fisk, 30 L14
Flat, 100 L17
Flatonia, 1377 P18
Flats, 90 H20
Flint, 1200 K21
Flo, 30 L20
Flomot, 10 F11
Florence, 1054 M16
Floresville, 5868 O16
Florey, 20 J8
Flower Mound, 50702 A5
Floydada, 3676 F10
Fluvanna, 80 H11
Flynn, 40 M19
Foard City, 10 G13
Follett, 412 B12
Fordtran, 20 O18
Forest, 30 L21
Forestburg, 20 G17
Forest Hill, 12949 J17
Forney, 5588 J19
Forreston, 250 K18
Forsan, 226 K10
Ft. Chadbourne, 10 K12
Ft. Davis, 1050 N6
Ft. Gates, 800 L17
Ft. Griffin, 10 H14
Ft. Hancock, 1713 L2
Ft. McKavett, 20 M12
Ft. Stockton, 7846 M8
Ft. Worth, 534694 J17
Foster, 10 H9
Fostoria, 20 N21
Four Corners, 2954 J1
Four Way, 100 C9
Fowlerton, 62 S15
Francitas, 50 R19
Franklin, 1470 M19
Frankston, 1209 K20
Fred, 300 M23
Fredericksburg, 8911 N15
Fredonia, 40 M14
Freeport, 12708 R21
Freer, 3241 T15
Friday, 50 M21
Friendship, 30 F8
Friendswood, 29037 P21
Friona, 3854 E8
Frisco, 33714 H18
Fritch, 2235 C10
Fronton, 599 V14
Frost, 648 K18
Fruitland, 70 G16
Fruitvale, 418 J20
Fulshear, 716 P20
Fulton, 1553 S18
Funston, 10 J13
Gail, 70 J10
Gainesville, 15538 G17
Galena Park, 10592 H5
Gallatin, 378 K21
Galveston, 57247 O22
Ganado, 1915 O19
Garden City, 200 K10
Gardendale, 1197 K9
Gardendale, 250 R14
Garden Ridge, 1882 P16
Garfield, 1660 N17
Garland, 215768 H18
Garner, 100 J16
Garrett, 448 J18
Garrison, 844 K22
Garwood, 375 O19
Gary, 303 K22
Gatesville, 15591 L17
Gause, 250 M18
Gay Hill, 60 N19
Geneva, 80 L23
Georgetown, 28339 N17
George West, 2524 S16
Geronimo, 619 P16
Gholson, 922 L17
Giddings, 5105 N18
Gilchrist, 300 P22
Giles, 10 E12
Gillett, 60 O17
Gilliland, 70 G13
Gilmer, 4799 J21
Gilpin, 10 G11
Girard, 62 H12
Girvin, 60 M8
Gladewater, 6078 J21
Glass, 40 K16
Glazier, 40 C12
Glen Cove, 40 K13
Glendale, 100 M21
Glen Flora, 175 O19
Glenn, 10 G11
Glenn Hts., 7224 J18
Glenrio, 20 D8
Glen Rose, 2122 K16
Glenwood, 325 J21
Glidden, 475 P19
Godley, 879 J17
Golden, 250 J20
Goldsboro, 10 K13
Goldsmith, 253 K8
Goldthwaite, 1802 L15
Goliad, 1975 R17
Golinda, 423 L18
Gomez, 20 H9
Gonzales, 7202 O17
Goober Hill, 20 K23
Goodlett, 60 F13
Goodlow, 264 K19
Goodrich, 243 M21
Gordon, 451 J15
Gordon, 10 H10
Gordonville, 200 G18
Goree, 321 G13
Gorman, 1236 K15
Gouldbusk, 20 L14
Graford, 578 H16
Graham, 8716 H15
Graham, 30 H10
Granbury, 5718 J16
Grandfalls, 391 L8
Grand Prairie, 127427 E5
Grand Saline, 3028 J20
Grandview, 1358 K17
Grandview, 20 H9
Granger, 1299 M17
Granite Shoals, 2040 N15
Grapeland, 1451 L20
Grapevine, 42059 H18
Grassland, 60 H10
Gray, 40 H23
Grayback, 20 F14
Grayburg, 250 N22
Grays Prairie, 296 J19
Green, 40 R16
Greenville, 23960 H19
Greenwood, 250 K9
Gregory, 2318 S17
Grey Forest, 418 U20
Grice, 40 H21
Griffith, 40 G8
Grit, 10 M14
Groesbeck, 4291 L19
Groom, 587 D11
Groves, 15733 P23
Groveton, 1107 M21
Gruver, 1162 B10
Guadalupe, 175 R18
Guerra, 8 U15
Gun Barrel City, 5145 J19
Gunsight, 20 J15
Gunter, 1230 G18
Gustine, 457 K15
Guthrie, 10 G12
Guy, 175 O20
Hackberry, 10 G12
Hainesville, 40 J21
Hale Ctr., 2263 F10
Halfway, 80 F9
Hall, 20 L14
Hallettsville, 2345 O18
Hallsburg, 518 L18
Hallsville, 2772 J22
Haltom City, 39018 C3
Hamby, 150 J13
Hamilton, 2977 L16
Hamlin, 2248 H12
Hammond, 40 M18
Hamon, 20 O17
Hamshire, 550 P23
Hankamer, 300 P22
Hanover, 30 M18
Happy, 647 E10
Happy Union, 10 F10
Happy Valley, 10 K12
Hardin, 755 N22
Hare, 20 M17
Hargill, 900 V16
Harker Hts., 17308 M17
Harkeyville, 10 M15
Harleton, 225 J22
Harlingen, 57564 W17
Harper, 1006 N14
Harrold, 125 F14
Hart, 1198 F9
Hart Camp, 10 F9
Hartley, 441 C9
Harwood, 125 P17
Haskell, 3106 H13
Haslet, 1134 A3
Hasse, 125 K15
Hatchel, 20 K13
Hawk Cove, 457 H19
Hawkins, 1331 J21
Hawley, 646 J13
Haynesville, 125 F14
Hearne, 4690 M19
Hebbronville, 4498 U15
Heckville, 50 G10
Hedley, 379 E12
Hedwigs Hill, 10 N14
Hedwig Vil., 2334 H3
Helena, 50 R17
Helotes, 4285 O15
Hemphill, 1106 L23
Hempstead, 4691 N20
Henderson, 11273 K22
Henly, 60 N16
Henrietta, 3264 G16
Hereford, 14597 E9
Hermleigh, 393 J11
Hewitt, 11085 L17
Hico, 1341 K16
Hidalgo, 7322 W16
Higginbotham, 50 H8
Higgins, 425 B13
Highbank, 20 M18
High Island, 500 P23
Highland Haven, 450 N15
Highland Park, 8842 C8
Highlands, 7089 P21
Hill Country Vil., 1028 V21
Hillcrest, 722 M5
Hillister, 175 M22
Hillje, 100 O19
Hillsboro, 8232 K18
Hilltop Lakes, 500 M19
Hilshire Vil., 720 H3
Hindes, 10 R15
Hitchcock, 6386 N7
Hoard, 125 J20
Hobson, 60 R16
Hochheim, 30 O17
Hockley, 175 P20
Hodges, 50 J13
Holiday Lakes, 1095 O21
Holland, 1102 M17
Holliday, 1632 G15
Hollywood Park, 2983 P15
Hondo, 7897 O14
Honey Grove, 1746 G20
Honey Island, 70 N22
Hooks, 2973 G22
Hoover, 10 C11
Hope, 60 O18
Hopewell, 30 L20
Horizon City, 5233 K2
Horseshoe Bay, 3337 N15
Hot Wells, 10 M4
Houston, 1953631 P21
Howardwick, 437 D11
Howe, 2478 G18
Howland, 60 G20
Hub, 30 E8
Hubbard, 1586 K18
Huckabay, 125 J16
Hudson, 3792 L22
Huffman, 475 P21
Hughes Sprs., 1856 H22
Hull, 600 N22
Humble, 14579 P21
Hungerford, 645 O20
Hunt, 275 P14
Hunter, 150 P16
Hunters Creek Vil., 4374 H3
Huntington, 2068 L22
Huntsville, 35078 M20
Huron, 20 K17
Hurst, 36273 C4
Hutchins, 2805 E8
Hutto, 1250 N17
Huxley, 298 K23
Hye, 40 N15
Idalou, 2157 G10
Illinois Bend, 10 G17
Impact, 39 R5
Imperial, 428 L8
Inadale, 40 J11
Independence, 150 N19
Indian Creek, 40 L14
Indian Gap, 10 L15
Indianola, 20 R19
Industry, 304 P19
Inez, 1787 R18
Ingleside, 9388 T18
Ingleside on the Bay, 659 T18
Ingram, 1740 P14
Iola, 325 M19
Iowa Colony, 804 O21
Iowa Park, 6431 F15
Ira, 90 J11
Iraan, 1238 M9
Irby, 30 H13
Iredell, 360 K16
Ireland, 30 L16
Irene, 125 K18
Ironton, 60 K21
Irving, 191615 J18
Italy, 1993 K18
Itasca, 1503 K18
Ivan, 10 H15
Izoro, 10 L16
Jacinto City, 10302 H5
Jacksboro, 4533 H16
Jacksonville, 13868 K21
Jamaica Beach, 1075 O22
James, 175 K23
Jamestown, 90 M23
Jarrell, 275 M17
Jasper, 8247 M23
Jayton, 513 H12
Jean, 80 H15
Jefferson, 2024 H22
Jericho, 30 D11
Jermyn, 40 H15
Jersey Vil., 6880 F2
Jewett, 861 L19
Joaquin, 925 K23
Johnson City, 1191 N15
Johnstone, 50 O11
Johntown, 125 G21
Jolly, 188 G15
Jollyville, 15813 N17
Jonesboro, 100 L16
Jones Creek, 2130 O21
Jonestown, 1681 N16
Joplin, 20 H16
Josephine, 594 H19
Joshua, 4528 J17
Jourdanton, 3732 R15
Joy, 30 G16
Juliff, 40 O21
Junction, 2618 N13
Juno, 20 N11
Justiceburg, 40 H11
Justin, 1891 H17
Kadane Corner, 60 G15
Kalgary, 10 G11
Kamay, 150 G15
Kamey, 10 R18
Kanawha, 20 F21
Karnack, 225 J23
Karnes City, 3457 R16
Katemcy, 40 M14
Katy, 11775 P20
Kaufman, 6490 J19
Keene, 5003 J17
Keller, 27345 H17
Kellerville, 20 D12
Kelsay, 325 V15
Kelton, 40 D12
Kemah, 2330 K7
Kemp, 1133 J19
Kempner, 1004 M16
Kendalia, 20 P15
Kendleton, 466 O20
Kenedy, 3487 R16
Kenefick, 667 N22
Kennard, 317 L21
Kennedale, 5850 E4
Kenney, 100 P19
Kent, 40 M5
Kerens, 1681 K19
Kermit, 5714 K7
Kerrick, 10 B9
Kerrville, 20425 P14
Key, 10 J10
Kildare, 70 H22
Kilgore, 11301 J21
Killeen, 86911 M17
King, 30 L16
Kingsbury, 652 P16
Kingsland, 4584 N15
Kingsmill, 60 D11
Kingston, 200 H19
Kingsville, 25575 T16
Kingwood, 37400 N21
Kinkler, 20 O18
Kirby, 8673 O16
Kirbyville, 2085 M23
Kirk, 10 L18
Kirkland, 20 F13
Kirtley, 50 P18
Kirvin, 122 K19
Klondike, 100 H20
Klondike, 60 J9
Knapp, 10 J11
Knickerbocker, 10 L12
Knippa, 739 O13
Knollwood, 375 G18
Knott, 60 J10
Knox City, 1219 G13
Kopperl, 250 K17
Kosciusko, 100 O16
Kosse, 497 L18
Kountze, 2115 N23
Kress, 826 F10
Krum, 1979 H17
Kurten, 100 M19
Kyle, 5314 P16
La Blanca, 2351 V16
La Coste, 1255 O15
Lacy-Lakeview, 5764 R8
Ladonia, 667 G19
La Feria, 6115 W17
Lagarto, 40 S16
La Gloria, 100 V15
Lago Vista, 4507 N16
La Grange, 4478 P18
La Grulla, 1211 W15
Laguna Hts., 1990 W18
Laguna Park, 600 K17
Laguna Vista, 1658 W18
Laird Hill, 150 J21
Lajitas, 40 O6
La Joya, 3303 W15
Lake Bridgeport, 372 H16
Lake City, 526 S16
Lake Creek, 80 G20
Lake Dallas, 6166 H18
Lakehills, 4668 P14
Lake Jackson, 26386 O21
Lakeport, 861 J22
Lakeside, 1040 C1
Lakeside, 333 S16
Lakeside City, 984 G15
Lakeside Vil., 125 K17
Lake Tanglewood, 825 D10
Laketon, 10 D12
Lake Victor, 40 M16
Lakeview, 152 E11
Lakeview, 40 H9
Lakeview, 20 G11
Lakeway, 8002 N16
Lake Worth, 4618 C2
Lamar, 90 S18
La Marque, 13682 O22
Lamesa, 9952 J9
Lamkin, 10 K16
Lampasas, 6786 M16
Lancaster, 25894 J18
Lane City, 175 O20
Lanely, 30 L19
Laneville, 200 K22
Langtry, 10 P10
La Paloma, 354 W17
La Porte, 31880 P21
La Pryor, 1491 R13
Laredo, 176576 T14
La Reforma, 50 V16
Lariat, 60 F8
Lark, 20 D11
Larue, 175 K20
La Salle, 20 R19
Lasara, 1024 V16
Lassater, 80 H22
Latexo, 272 L20
La Vernia, 931 O16
La Villa, 1305 V16
Lavon, 387 H19
La Ward, 200 R19
Lawn, 353 K13
Lazare, 10 F13
Lazbuddie, 100 F8
League City, 45444 P21
Leakey, 387 P13
Leander, 7596 N16
Leary, 555 G22
Ledbetter, 100 N18
Leesville, 70 O17
Lefors, 559 D11
Leggett, 200 M22
Lehman, 20 G8
Leigh, 70 J23
Lela, 20 D12
Lelia Lake, 60 E11
Leming, 600 O15
Lenorah, 60 J9
Leona, 181 M20
Leonard, 1846 G19
Leon Jct., 70 L17
Leon Valley, 9239 O15
Leroy, 335 L18
Lesley, 10 E11
Levelland, 12866 G9
Lewisville, 77737 H18
Lexington, 1178 N18
Liberty, 8033 N22
Liberty City, 1935 J21
Liberty Hill, 1409 N16
Lilbert, 60 K21
Lillian, 300 J17
Lincoln, 60 N18
Lindale, 2954 J20
Linden, 2256 H22
Lindenau, 50 O17
Lindsay, 788 G17
Lingleville, 80 K15
Linn, 958 V16
Lipan, 425 J16
Lipscomb, 44 B12
Lissie, 100 P19
Little Cypress, 1800 N24
Little Elm, 3646 H18
Littlefield, 6507 F9
Little River-Academy, 1645 M17
Lively, 550 J19
Live Oak, 9156 O16
Liverpool, 404 O21
Livingston, 5433 M21
Llano, 3325 M15
Lobo, 10 M4
Lockett, 100 F14
Lockettville, 10 G9
Lockhart, 11615 P17
Lockney, 2056 F10
Loeb, 250 N23
Log Cabin, 733 K19
Lohn, 40 L14
Lolita, 548 R19
Loma Vista, 50 R13
Lomax, 10 K10
Lometa, 782 L15
London, 50 M13
Lone Camp, 100 J16
Lone Oak, 521 H20
Lone Star, 1631 H22
Lone Star, 50 F10
Long Branch, 20 K22
Long Mott, 20 R18
Longview, 73344 J22
Longworth, 60 J12
Loop, 275 H9
Lopeno, 140 V14
Lopezville, 4476 S11
Loraine, 656 J11
Lorena, 1433 L17
Lorenzo, 1372 G10
Los Fresnos, 4512 W17
Los Indios, 1149 W17
Los Ybanez, 32 J9
Lott, 724 L18
Louise, 977 O19
Lovelady, 608 M21
Loving, 125 H15
Lowake, 20 L13
Loyal Valley, 10 N14
Lubbock, 199564 G9
Lucas, 2890 H18
Lueders, 300 J13
Lufkin, 32709 L22
Luling, 5080 P17
Lumberton, 8731 N23
Lums Chapel, 10 G9
Luther, 20 J10
Lutie, 10 E12
Lydia, 40 G21
Lyford, 1973 V17
Lyons, 80 N19
Lytle, 2383 O15
Mabank, 2151 J19
Mabelle, 10 G14
Macdona, 650 O15
Madisonville, 4159 M20
Magasco, 100 L23
Magnet, 20 O20
Magnolia, 1111 N20
Magnolia Beach, 125 R19
Magnolia Sprs., 70 M23
Malakoff, 2257 K19
Malone, 278 K18
Malta, 300 G22
Manchaca, 1200 N16
Manchester, 20 G21
Manheim, 20 N18
Manor, 1204 N17
Mansfield, 28031 J18
Manvel, 3046 O21
Maple, 50 G8
Marathon, 455 N7
Marble Falls, 4959 N16
Marfa, 2121 N6
Margaret, 60 F13
Marietta, 112 H22
Marion, 1099 V24
Markham, 1138 R20
Markley, 10 H15
Marlin, 6628 L18
Marquez, 220 L19
Marshall, 23935 J22
Mart, 2273 L18
Martindale, 953 P16
Martins Mills, 125 J20
Martinsville, 40 K22
Maryneal, 50 K12
Mason, 2134 M14
Matador, 740 F11
Matagorda, 400 R20
Mathis, 5034 S17
Matthews, 30 O19
Maud, 1028 G22
Mauriceville, 2743 N23
Maverick, 10 K12
Maxwell, 500 P17
May, 175 K15
Maydelle, 200 K21
Mayflower, 20 L24
Maypearl, 746 J18
Maysfield, 90 M18
McAdoo, 60 G11
McAllen, 106414 W16
McCamey, 1805 M9
McCaulley, 100 J12
McCook, 30 V16
McCoy, 20 G10
McCoy, 20 R16
McDade, 325 N17
McFaddin, 30 R18
McGregor, 4727 L17
McKinney, 54369 H18
McLean, 830 D12
McLeod, 175 H23
McMahan, 20 P17
McNary, 40 L3
McQueeney, 2527 P16
Meadow, 658 H9
Meadowlakes, 1293 N16
Meadows Place, 4912 J2
Medicine Mound, 20 F13
Medina, 150 P14
Megargel, 248 G14
Melissa, 1350 H18
Melrose, 100 L22
Melvin, 155 M13
Memphis, 2479 E12
Menard, 1653 M13
Mendoza, 80 P17
Mentone, 20 K6
Mercedes, 13649 W16
Mercers Gap, 10 K15
Mercury, 10 L14
Mereta, 175 L12
Meridian, 1491 K17
Merit, 175 H19
Merkel, 2637 J13
Mertens, 146 K18
Mertzon, 839 L11
Mesquite, 124523 J18
Mesquite, 10 H10
Metcalf Gap, 10 J15
Mexia, 6563 L19
Miami, 588 C12
Midfield, 150 R19
Midkiff, 100 L9
Midland, 94996 K9
Midlothian, 7480 J18
Midway, 288 M20
Midway, 10 J11
Milam, 1329 L23
Milano, 400 M18
Mildred, 405 K19
Miles, 850 L12
Milford, 685 K18
Millersview, 20 L13
Millett, 10 R14
Millican, 108 N19
Millsap, 353 J16
Minden, 125 K22
Mineola, 4550 J20
Mineral, 40 R16
Mineral Wells, 16946 J16
Minerva, 200 M18
Mingus, 246 J15
Mirando City, 493 T14
Mission, 45408 W16
Mission Bend, 30831 J1
Mission Valley, 40 R18
Missouri City, 52913 P21
Mobeetie, 107 D12
Moffat, 350 L17
Monahans, 6821 L8
Monaville, 80 P20
Monkstown, 30 G19
Monroe City, 10 P22
Montague, 225 G16
Montalba, 150 K20
Mont Belvieu, 2324 P22
Monte Alto, 1611 V16
Montgomery, 489 N20
Moody, 1400 L17
Moore, 644 O14
Moore Sta., 184 K20
Mooring, 40 M19
Morales, 30 O18
Moran, 233 J14
Morgan, 485 K17
Morgan Mill, 125 J16
Morgan's Pt. Resort, 2989 M17
Morris Ranch, 20 N14
Morse, 172 C10
Morton, 2249 G8
Morton Valley, 30 J15
Moscow, 225 M22
Mosheim, 40 L17
Moss Hill, 100 N22
Moulton, 944 P18
Mtn. City, 671 P16
Mtn. Home, 30 N14
Mt. Blanco, 20 G11
Mt. Calm, 310 K18
Mt. Enterprise, 525 K22
Mt. Houston, 4400 P21
Mt. Pleasant, 13935 H21
Mt. Selman, 200 K21
Mt. Union, 80 M23
Mt. Vernon, 2286 H21
Muenster, 1556 G17
Muldoon, 20 P18
Muleshoe, 4530 F8
Mullin, 175 L15
Mumford, 60 M19
Muncy, 10 F10
Munday, 1527 G13
Murchison, 592 J20
Murphy, 3099 A9
Murray, 10 H15
Mustang Ridge, 785 P17
Myra, 250 G17
Myrtle Sprs., 350 J20
Nacogdoches, 29914 L22
Nada, 175 O19
Naples, 1410 H22
Naruna, 10 M16
Nash, 2169 G23
Nassau Bay, 4170 K7
Natalia, 1663 O15
Navarro, 191 K19
Navasota, 6789 N19
Nazareth, 356 E9
Necessity, 30 J15
Neches, 250 K20
Nederland, 17422 N23
Needmore, 20 F8
Needmore, 20 H9
Needville, 2609 O20
Negley, 80 G21
Nelsonville, 125 P19
Nesbitt, 302 J22
Nesbitt, 10 M19
Neuville, 100 K23
Newark, 887 H17
New Baden, 90 M19
New Berlin, 467 O16
New Boston, 4808 G22
New Braunfels, 36494 P16
Newburg, 20 K15
Newcastle, 575 H15
New Chapel Hill, 553 J21
New Davy, 40 O17
New Deal, 708 G10
New Fairview, 877 H17
Newgulf, 250 O20
New Home, 320 H9
Newlin, 10 E12
New London, 987 J21
New Lynn, 30 H10
New Moore, 10 H9
Newport, 50 G16
Newsome, 225 H21
New Summerfield, 998 K21

Tsa-la-gi Village Artifacts, Oklahoma

New Sweden, 100 N17
New Taiton, 100 O19
Newton, 2459 M23
New Ulm, 200 P19
New Waverly, 950 N21
New Willard, 150 M22
New York, 60 K20
Neylandville, 56 H19
Nickel Creek, 10 K4
Niederwald, 584 P17
Nineveh, 30 L20
Nixon, 2186 O17
Nocona, 3198 G16
Nolan, 20 K12
Nolanville, 2150 M17
Nome, 515 N22
Noodle, 10 J13
Noonday, 515 J21
Nopal, 10 O17
Nordheim, 323 R17
Norias, 40 V17
Normandy, 70 R12
Normangee, 719 M19
Normanna, 121 R17
N. Cleveland, 263 N21
Northcrest, 1700 R8
Northfield, 10 F12
N. Houston, 4900 P21
N. Richland Hills, 55635 B4
N. Zulch, 275 M19
Norton, 30 K12
Notrees, 10 K8
Novice, 142 K13
Novice, 20 G20
Noxville, 20 N14
Nugent, 50 J13
Nursery, 50 R18
Oakalla, 30 M16
Oak Hill, 400 N16
Oakhurst, 230 M21
Oakland, 50 P18
Oak Ridge, 400 J19
Oak Ridge North, 2991 N21
Oak Trail Shores, 2475 J16
Oak Valley, 401 K19
Oakville, 10 S16
Oakwood, 471 L20
O'Brien, 132 H13
Odell, 80 F14
Odem, 2499 S17
Odessa, 90943 K9
O'Donnell, 1011 H10
Oglesby, 458 L17
Oilton, 310 T14
Oklahoma Flat, 10 G9
Oklahoma Lane, 20 F8
Oklaunion, 40 F14
Olden, 350 J15
Old Glory, 70 H13
Old Ocean, 175 O20
Old River-Winfree, 1364 P22
Olin, 10 K16
Olivia, 90 R19
Olmos, 10 S17
Olmos Park, 2343 V21
Olney, 3396 H15
Olton, 2288 F9
Omaha, 999 H22
Onalaska, 1174 M21
Opdyke West, 188 G9
Oplin, 10 K13
Oran, 20 H16
Orange, 18643 N24
Orange Grove, 1288 S16
Orchard, 408 P20
Ore City, 1106 H22
Orient, 80 L12
Orla, 10 K6
Otto, 40 L18
Ovalo, 150 K13
Overton, 2350 J21
Ovilla, 3405 J18
Owens, 150 K14
Owens, 30 G10
Owentown, 275 J21
Oxford, 20 N15
Oyster Creek, 1192 O21
Ozona, 3436 M11
Paducah, 1498 F12
Paige, 150 N18
Paint Rock, 320 L13
Palacios, 5153 R19
Palestine, 17598 K20
Palisades, 352 D10
Palito Blanco, 70 T16
Palmer, 1774 J18
Palmhurst, 4872 R9
Palmview, 4107 W16
Paloduro, 20 E11
Palo Pinto, 150 J16
Paluxy, 30 K16
Pampa, 17887 D11
Pandora, 70 O16
Panhandle, 2589 D10
Panna Maria, 70 R16
Panola, 125 J23
Pantego, 2318 D4
Papalote, 125 S17
Paradise, 459 H17
Paris, 25898 G20
Parker, 175 K17
Park Sprs., 20 G16
Pasadena, 141674 P21
Patricia, 10 J9
Patroon, 30 K23
Patton Vil., 1391 N21
Pattonville, 125 G20
Pawnee, 201 R16
Paxton, 70 K23
Payne Sprs., 683 J19
Peacock, 40 H12
Pearl, 50 L16
Pearland, 37640 P21
Pearsall, 7157 R14
Peaster, 175 H16
Pecan Gap, 214 G20
Pecos, 9501 L7
Peggy, 10 R16
Pelican Bay, 1505 B1
Penelope, 211 K18
Penitas, 1167 W15
Pennington, 60 L21
Penwell, 20 K8
Pep, 40 G8
Percilla, 90 L21
Perico, 10 B8
Pernitas Pt., 269 S16
Perrin, 100 H16
Perry, 60 L18
Perryton, 7774 B11
Personville, 40 L19
Peters, 100 P19
Petersburg, 1262 G10
Petrolia, 782 F16
Petronila, 83 T17
Petteway, 20 L19
Pettit, 40 G8
Pettus, 608 R17
Petty, 150 G20
Petty, 30 H9
Pflugerville, 16335 N17
Phalba, 80 J19
Pharr, 46660 W16
Phelps, 425 M21
Phillips, 10 C10
Pickton, 150 H20
Pidcoke, 30 L16
Pierce, 40 O19
Pilot Pt., 3538 G18
Pine Forest, 632 N23
Pinehurst, 4266 N20
Pinehurst, 2274 N24
Pine Island, 849 P20
Pineland, 980 L23
Pine Mills, 50 J21
Pine Sprs., 20 K4
Piney Pt. Vil., 3380 H3
Pioneer, 30 K14
Pipe Creek, 60 P14
Pittsburg, 4347 H21
Placedo, 500 R18
Placid, 20 L14
Plains, 1450 H8
Plainview, 22336 F10
Plano, 222030 H18
Pleak, 947 O20
Pleasanton, 8266 R15
Pleasant Valley, 408 F15
Pleasant Valley, 40 H10
Pledger, 100 O20
Plum Grove, 930 N21
Point, 792 H20
Pt. Blank, 559 M21
Pt. Comfort, 781 R19
Polar, 30 H11
Pollok, 175 L22
Ponder, 507 H17
Pontotoc, 20 M14
Poolville, 175 H16
Port Alto, 20 R19
Port Aransas, 3370 T18
Port Arthur, 57755 P23
Port Bolivar, 550 O22
Porter Hts., 1490 N21
Porter Sprs., 30 L20
Port Isabel, 4865 W18
Portland, 14827 T17
Port Lavaca, 12035 R19
Port Mansfield, 415 V17
Port Neches, 13601 N23
Port O'Connor, 600 R19
Posey, 40 G10
Post, 3708 H10
Postoak, 20 G16
Poteet, 3305 O15
Poth, 1850 O16
Potosi, 1664 J13
Pottsboro, 1579 G18
Powderly, 175 G20
Powell, 105 K19
Poynor, 314 K20
Prairie Hill, 80 L18
Prairie Lea, 325 P17
Prairie View, 4410 N20
Prairieville, 100 J19
Premont, 2772 U16
Presidio, 4167 P5
Price, 275 K21
Priddy, 175 L15
Princeton, 3477 H19
Pringle, 50 C10
Pritchett, 325 J21
Proctor, 50 K15
Proffitt, 10 H15
Progreso, 4851 W16
Progress, 125 F8
Prosper, 2097 H18
Pumphrey, 10 K13
Purdon, 60 K18
Purley, 100 H21
Purmela, 10 L16
Purves, 50 K16
Putnam, 88 J14
Pyote, 131 L7
Quail, 33 E12
Quanah, 3022 F13
Queen City, 1613 H23
Quemado, 243 R12
Quihi, 40 O14
Quinlan, 1370 H19
Quintana, 38 R21
Quitaque, 432 F11
Quitman, 2030 H20
Rachal, 80 U16
Rainbow, 250 K17
Raisin, 250 R18
Ralls, 2252 G10
Ramirez, 10 U15
Randado, 10 U15
Randolph, 200 G19
Ranger, 2584 J15
Rankin, 800 L9
Ransom Canyon, 1011 G10
Ratcliff, 90 L21
Ravenna, 215 G19
Rayburn, 175 N22
Rayland, 20 F14
Raymondville, 9733 V17
Reagan, 50 L18
Realitos, 209 T15
Redford, 132 O5
Red Gate, 500 V16
Redland, 100 J20
Red Oak, 4301 J18
Red Rock, 100 P17
Red Sprs., 50 G14
Redwater, 872 G22
Refugio, 2941 S18
Reklaw, 327 K21
Reno, 2767 G20
Reno, 2441 H17
Retreat, 339 K19
Rhea, 20 E8
Rhineland, 90 G13
Rhome, 551 H17
Ricardo, 450 T17
Rice, 798 K19
Richards, 275 N20
Richardson, 91802 A8
Richland, 291 K19
Richland Hills, 8132 C4
Richland Sprs., 350 L14
Richmond, 11081 P20
Richwood, 3012 O21
Ridge, 10 M19
Ridgeway, 125 H20
Riesel, 973 L18
Ringgold, 225 G16
Rio Bravo, 5553 U14
Rio Frio, 100 P13
Rio Grande City, 11923 V15
Rio Grande Vil., 250 O7
Rio Hondo, 1942 W17
Rios, 40 T16
Rio Vista, 656 K17
Rising Star, 835 K14
River Oaks, 6985 C2
Riverside, 425 M21
Riviera, 550 U17
Riviera Beach, 30 U17
Roane, 125 K19
Roanoke, 2810 A4
Roans Prairie, 10 N20
Roaring Sprs., 265 G11
Robbins, 60 L19
Robert Lee, 1171 K12
Robertson, 20 G10
Robinson, 7845 L18
Robstown, 12727 T17
Roby, 673 J12
Rochelle, 30 M14
Rochester, 378 H13
Rockdale, 5439 M18
Rock Island, 225 O19
Rockne, 150 P17
Rockport, 7385 S18
Rocksprings, 1285 P12
Rockwall, 17976 H19
Rocky Mound, 93 H21
Roganville, 50 M23
Rogers, 1117 M17
Rollingwood, 1403 R2
Roma, 9617 V14
Roman Forest, 1279 N21
Romayor, 200 N22
Romero, 10 C8
Romney, 10 K14
Roosevelt, 20 N13
Ropesville, 517 G9
Rosanky, 60 P17
Roscoe, 1378 J12
Rosebud, 1493 M18
Rose City, 519 F24
Rose Hill Acres, 480 N23
Rosenberg, 24043 P20
Rosevine, 70 L23
Rosewood, 150 J21
Rosharon, 450 O21
Rosita, 500 V15
Rosita, 30 T15
Ross, 228 L18
Rosser, 379 J19
Rosston, 30 G17
Rossville, 10 O15
Rotan, 1611 J12
Round Mtn., 111 N16
Round Rock, 61136 N17
Round Top, 77 P18
Roundup, 20 G9
Rowena, 350 L13
Rowlett, 44503 B10
Roxton, 694 G20
Royalty, 30 L8
Royse City, 2957 H19
Rucker, 30 K15
Rudolph, 40 V17
Ruidosa, 40 P4
Rule, 698 H13
Runaway Bay, 1104 H16
Runge, 1080 R17
Rusk, 5085 K21
Rutersville, 60 P18
Rye, 125 N22
Sabinal, 1586 O14
Sabine Pass, 40 P23
Sachse, 9751 A10
Sadler, 404 G18
Sagerton, 10 H13
Saginaw, 12374 B2
St. Francis, 20 D10
St. Hedwig, 1875 O16
St. Jo, 977 G17
St. Lawrence, 40 L10
St. Paul, 630 H18
St. Paul, 542 S17
Salado, 3475 M17
Salesville, 200 H16
Salineno, 304 V14
Salt Flat, 10 K4
Saltillo, 150 H21
Samnorwood, 39 D12
San Angelo, 88439 L12
San Antonio, 1144646 O15
San Augustine, 2475 L23
San Benito, 23444 W17
Sanco, 20 K12
Sanctuary, 256 H17
Sanderson, 861 N8
Sandia, 431 S16
San Diego, 4753 T16
Sandow, 10 N18
Sand Sprs., 800 K10
Sandy, 20 N15
San Elizario, 11046 K2
San Felipe, 868 P20
Sanford, 203 C10
Sanger, 4534 G17
San Isidro, 270 V15
San Juan, 26229 S11
San Leanna, 384 N16
San Leon, 4365 L8
San Marcos, 34733 P16
San Patricio, 318 S17
San Perlita, 680 V17
San Saba, 2637 M15
Sansom Park, 4181 C2
Santa Anna, 1081 L14
Santa Catarina, 30 V15
Santa Clara, 889 U24
Santa Elena, 40 V15
Santa Fe, 9548 O21
Santa Maria, 846 W17
Santa Rosa, 2833 W17
Santo, 225 J16
San Ygnacio, 350 U14
Saragosa, 10 M6
Saratoga, 425 N22
Sargent, 70 R20
Sarita, 20 U17
Satin, 125 L18
Saturn, 30 P17
Savoy, 850 G19
Sayersville, 60 N17
Scallorn, 40 L15
Schertz, 18694 U23
Schroeder, 80 R18
Schulenburg, 2699 P18
Scotland, 438 G15
Scottsville, 263 J22
Scranton, 20 K14
Scurry, 400 J19
Seabrook, 9443 P21
Seadrift, 1352 S19
Seagoville, 10823 J19
Seagraves, 2334 H8
Sealy, 5248 P19
Seaton, 100 M17
Sebastian, 1864 V17
Sebastopol, 80 M21
Segno, 100 M22
Segovia, 10 N13
Seguin, 22011 P16
Selden, 50 K16
Selma, 788 U22
Seminole, 5910 J8
Senate, 30 H16
Seth Ward, 1926 F10
Seven Oaks, 131 M22
Seven Pts., 1145 J19
Seven Sisters, 60 S15
Seymour, 2908 G14
Shafter, 20 P5
Shallowater, 2086 G9
Shamrock, 2029 D12
Shannon, 20 G16
Sharp, 100 M18
Shavano Park, 1754 U21
Sheffield, 225 M9
Shelby, 50 P19
Shelbyville, 100 K23
Sheldon, 1831 G6
Shenandoah, 1503 N21
Shepherd, 2029 N21
Sheridan, 60 O19
Sherman, 35082 G18
Sherwood, 90 L11
Shiloh, 200 L20
Shiloh, 60 L19
Shiloh, 30 N18
Shiner, 2070 O18
Shiro, 20 M20
Shoreacres, 1488 K7
Sidney, 60 K15
Sierra Blanca, 533 L3
Silsbee, 6393 N23
Silver, 10 K11
Silverton, 771 E11
Silver Valley, 20 K13
Simms, 70 G22
Simms, 20 D8
Simonton, 718 P20
Simpsonville, 30 H21
Sinton, 5676 S17
Sipe Sprs., 30 K15
Skellytown, 610 C11
Skidmore, 1013 S17
Slaton, 6109 G10
Slide, 20 G9
Slidell, 175 H17
Slocum, 150 L20
Smiley, 453 O17
Smithland, 175 H23
Smithville, 3901 P18
Smithwick, 10 N16
Smyer, 480 G9
Snook, 568 N19
Snyder, 10783 J11
Socorro, 27152 K2
Somerset, 1550 O15
Somerville, 1704 N19
Sonora, 2924 N11
Sour Lake, 1667 N22
S. Bend, 50 H15
S. Houston, 15833 J5
Southlake, 21519 A4
Southland, 20 H10
Southmayd, 992 G18
S. Padre Island, 2422 W18
S. Plains, 60 F10
Southside Place, 1546 J3
Spade, 100 F9
Spade, 10 K11
Spanish Fort, 60 F17
Sparenberg, 30 J10
Speaks, 30 O18
Spearman, 3021 B11
Splendora, 1275 N21
Spofford, 75 O12
Spraberry, 125 K10
Spring, 36385 N21
Spring Branch, 20 P15
Springlake, 135 F9
Springtown, 2062 H17
Spring Valley, 3611 H3
Spur, 1088 G11
Spurger, 200 M23
Stacy, 10 L13
Stafford, 15681 J2
Stamford, 3636 H13
Stanton, 2556 K10
Star, 60 L16
Stephen Creek, 125 M21
Stephenville, 14921 K16
Sterley, 30 F10
Sterling City, 1081 K11
Stiles, 40 L10
Stinnett, 1936 C10
Stockdale, 1398 O16
Stockman, 60 K22
Stoneburg, 40 G16
Stoneham, 100 N20
Stonewall, 469 N15
Stowell, 1572 P23
Stratford, 1991 B9
Strawn, 739 J15
Streeter, 20 M14
Streetman, 203 K19
String Prairie, 20 P17
Study Butte, 267 O6
Sublime, 60 O18
Sudan, 1039 F8
Sugar Land, 63328 P20
Sullivan City, 3998 V15
Sulphur Bluff, 100 G20
Sulphur Sprs., 14551 H20
Summerfield, 70 E8
Sumner, 60 G20
Sundown, 1505 G8
Sunnyside, 70 F9
Sunnyvale, 2693 C10
Sunray, 1950 C10
Sunrise Beach, 704 N15
Sunset, 339 G16
Sunset Valley, 365 S1
Surfside Beach, 763 R21
Sutherland Sprs., 175 O16
Swearingen, 10 F12
Sweeny, 3624 O20
Sweet Home, 175 O18
Sweetwater, 11415 J12
Swenson, 30 H12
Swiss Alp, 20 P18
Sylvester, 100 J12
Taft, 3396 S17
Tahoka, 2910 H10
Talco, 570 G21
Talpa, 50 K13
Talty, 1028 J19
Tanglewood, 100 N18
Tankersley, 150 L12
Tarpley, 30 P14
Tarzan, 20 J9
Tatum, 1175 J22
Taylor, 13575 N17
Taylor Lake Vil., 3694 K7
Teague, 4557 L19
Tehuacana, 307 K19
Telegraph, 10 N13
Telephone, 20 G19
Telferner, 550 R18
Telico, 175 J19
Tell, 40 F12
Temple, 54514 M17
Tenaha, 1046 K23
Tennessee Colony, 100 K20
Tennyson, 10 L12
Terlingua, 267 O6
Terrell, 13606 J19
Terrell Hills, 5019 V21
Terryville, 30 O18
Texarkana, 34782 G23
Texas City, 41521 O22
Texhoma, 371 B10
Texline, 511 B8
Texon, 40 L10
Thalia, 40 F13
The Colony, 26531 H18
The Grove, 90 L17
The Hills, 1492 N16
Thelma, 375 O15
The Woodlands, 55649 N21
Thicket, 50 N22
Thomaston, 30 R18
Thompsons, 236 O20
Thorndale, 1278 N18
Thornton, 525 L19
Thorntonville, 442 L8
Thorp Spr., 275 J16
Thrall, 710 N17
Three Rivers, 1878 S16
Thrifty, 70 K14
Throckmorton, 905 H14
Tiki Island, 1016 O22
Tilden, 500 S15
Timbercreek Canyon, 406 D10
Timpson, 1094 K22
Tioga, 754 G18
Tira, 248 H20
Tivoli, 450 S18
Toco, 89 G20
Todd Mission, 146 N20
Togo, 10 P18
Tokio, 40 H8
Tolar, 504 J16
Tolbert, 10 F14
Toledo Vil., 30 L24
Tomball, 9089 N20
Tom Bean, 941 G19
Tool, 2275 J19
Topsey, 60 L16
Tornillo, 1609 L2
Tow, 70 M15
Toyah, 100 L6
Toyahvale, 10 M6
Travis, 100 M18
Trawick, 30 K22
Trent, 318 J12
Trenton, 662 G19
Trickham, 10 L14
Trinidad, 1091 K19
Trinity, 2721 M21
Trophy Club, 6350 A4
Troup, 1949 K21
Troy, 1378 M17
Truby, 10 J13
Truscott, 90 G13
Tucker, 175 L20
Tuleta, 292 R17
Tulia, 5117 E10
Tundra, 125 J20
Tunis, 150 N19
Turkey, 494 F11
Turnersville, 60 L17
Turney, 250 K21
Tuscola, 714 K13
Tuxedo, 10 H13
Twin Sisters, 20 P15
Twitty, 20 D12
Tye, 1158 J13
Tyler, 83650 J21
Tynan, 301 S17
Uhland, 386 P17
Umbarger, 125 E9
Uncertain, 150 J23
Union, 100 J11
Union, 50 G10
Union, 30 H9
Union, 30 O16
Union Ctr., 20 K14
Union Grove, 346 J21
Unity, 20 G20
Universal City, 14849 O16
University Park, 23324 B8
Utley, 30 N17
Utopia, 241 P13
Uvalde, 14929 O13
Valentine, 187 M5
Valley Mills, 1123 L17
Valley Spr., 50 M15
Valley View, 737 G17
Valley Wells, 20 S14
Van, 2362 J20
Van Alstyne, 2502 G18
Vance, 10 P13
Vancourt, 20 L12
Vanderbilt, 411 R19
Vanderpool, 20 P13
Vandyke, 50 K15
Van Horn, 2435 M4
Van Vleck, 1411 O20
Vealmoor, 20 J10
Vega, 936 D9
Venus, 910 J18
Vera, 100 G13
Verbena, 60 H11
Verhalen, 30 M6
Vernon, 11660 F14
Viboras, 60 V15
Vick, 10 L13
Victoria, 60603 R18
Vidaurri, 20 S18
Vidor, 11440 N23
Vienna, 10 O18
View, 50 J13
Vigo Park, 20 E10
Village Mills, 60 N22
Vineyard, 20 H16
Vinton, 1892 K1
Voca, 40 M14
Voss, 30 L13
Votaw, 90 N22
Waco, 113726 L18
Wadsworth, 90 R20
Waelder, 947 P17
Waka, 125 B11
Wake, 10 G11
Wakefield, 10 M22
Wake Vil., 5129 G23
Wall, 250 L12
Waller, 2092 P20
Wallis, 1172 P20
Walnut Sprs., 755 K17
Waples, 800 J17
Warda, 30 P18
Ware, 10 B8
Waring, 20 P15
Warren, 475 M22
Washburn, 150 D10
Washington, 80 N19
Waskom, 2068 J23
Wastella, 10 J12
Watauga, 21908 B3
Water Valley, 125 L11
Watson, 10 M16
Waxahachie, 21426 J18
Weatherford, 19000 J16
Weaver, 90 H20
Webster, 9083 L6
Weches, 20 L21
Weedhaven, 40 R19
Weesatche, 20 R17
Weimar, 1981 P18
Weinert, 177 H13
Weir, 591 M17
Welch, 275 H9
Weldon, 60 M20
Wellborn, 300 N19
Wellington, 2275 E12

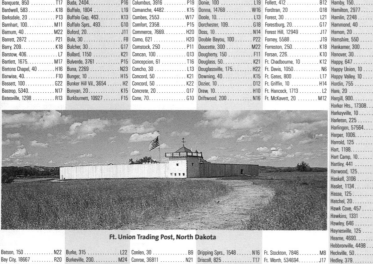

Ft. Union Trading Post, North Dakota

UTAH PG. 165

CAPITAL
Salt Lake City

NICKNAME
Beehive State

POPULATION
2,233,169, rank 34

AREA
84,899 sq mi, rank 11

Counties

Cities and Towns

VERMONT PG. 166

CAPITAL
Montpelier

NICKNAME
Green Mountain State

POPULATION
608,827, rank 49

AREA
9,614 sq mi, rank 43

Counties

Cities and Towns

VIRGINIA PG. 167-169

CAPITAL
Richmond

NICKNAME
Old Dominion

POPULATION
7,078,515, rank 12

AREA
40,767, rank 36

Counties

Cities and Towns

WASHINGTON PG. 170-171

CAPITAL
Olympia

NICKNAME
Evergreen State

POPULATION
5,894,121, rank 15

AREA
68,138 sq mi, rank 20

Counties

Cities and Towns

Stanwood, 3923 D9
Starbuck, 130 J18
Startup, 817 E10
Stehekin, 60 C12
Steilacoom, 6049 G8
Steptoe, 60 G19
Stevenson, 1200 L9
Stimson Crossing, 773 D9
Stratford, 10 F15
Sultan, 3344 E10
Sumas, 960 A9
Summit, 8041 N2
Sumner, 8504 G9
Sunnyside, 13905 J14
Suquamish, 3510 J1
Synarep, 10 C15
Tacoma, 193556 G8
Tahlequah, 225 M2
Taholah, 824 F5
Tahuya, 225 F7
Tampico, 150 J12
Tekoa, 826 G20
Telma, 80 E12
Tenino, 1447 H8
Terrace Hts., 6447 J13
Thornton, 70 G19
Thorp, 273 G12
Tieton, 1154 H12
Tiger, 30 B19
Tokeland, 194 H5
Toledo, 653 J7
Tonasket, 994 B15
Toppenish, 8946 J13
Touchet, 396 K16
Toutle, 125 J8
Tracyton, 3267 K1
Trentwood, 4388 E19
Trout Lake, 494 K10
Tukwila, 17181 L3
Tulalip, 1561 F3
Tumtum, 40 E18
Tumwater, 12698 B4
Turner, 10 J18
Twisp, 938 C13
Tyler, 30 F18
Union, 375 F7
Union Gap, 5621 J13
Uniontown, 345 J20
University Place, 29933 G8
Usk, 100 C19
Vader, 590 J7
Vail, 225 H8
Valley, 125 D18
Vancouver, 143560 L8
Vantage, 70 H14
Van Zandt, 200 B9
Vashon, 10123 L2
Vashon Hts., 1100 K2
Vaughn, 400 F8
Veradale, 9387 E19
Verlot, 170 D10
Waitsburg, 1212 K18
Waldron, 30 B7
Walla Walla, 29686 K17
Wallula, 197 K16
Wapato, 4582 J13
Warden, 2544 G16
Warm Beach, 2040 D9
Washougal, 8595 M8
Washtucna, 260 H17
Waterville, 1163 E14
Wauconda, 30 B16
Waukon, 70 F18
Waverly, 121 F19
Wellpinit, 60 E18
Wenatchee, 27856 F13
Westport, 2137 H5
W. Richland, 8385 J15
Wheeler, 20 G15
White Ctr., 20975 K2
White Salmon, 2193 L10
White Swan, 3033 J12
Wickersham, 125 B9
Wilbur, 914 E16
Wilkeson, 395 G9
Wilson Creek, 227 F15
Winchester, 70 G14
Winlock, 1166 J7
Winona, 40 G18
Winthrop, 349 C13
Wishram, 324 L12
Withrow, 10 E14
Woodinville, 9194 E9
Woodland, 3780 L8
Woodway, 936 H2
Wymer, 20 H13
Yacolt, 1055 L8
Yakima, 71845 J13
Yarrow Pt., 1008 J3
Yelm, 3289 H8
Zillah, 2198 J13

WEST VIRGINIA PG. 173

CAPITAL
Charleston
NICKNAME
Mountain State
POPULATION
1,808,344, rank 37
AREA
24,231 sq mi, rank 41

Counties

Barbour, 15557 D7
Berkeley, 75905 C12
Boone, 25535 G3
Braxton, 14702 E5
Brooke, 25447 B2
Cabell, 96784 F2
Calhoun, 7582 E5
Clay, 10330 F5
Doddridge, 7403 C6
Fayette, 47579 G5
Gilmer, 7160 E5
Grant, 11299 D10
Greenbrier, 34453 H6
Hampshire, 20203 D11
Hancock, 32667 A2
Hardy, 12669 D10
Harrison, 68652 C7
Jackson, 28000 E3
Jefferson, 42190 C13
Kanawha, 200073 F4
Lewis, 16919 D6
Lincoln, 22108 G2
Logan, 37710 H3
Marion, 56598 B7
Marshall, 35519 B6
Mason, 25957 E2
McDowell, 27329 K3
Mercer, 62980 J5
Mineral, 27078 C10
Mingo, 28253 H2
Monongalia, 81866 B7
Monroe, 14583 J6
Morgan, 14943 B12
Nicholas, 26562 G5
Ohio, 47427 A6
Pendleton, 8196 F9
Pleasants, 7514 C4
Pocahontas, 9131 G7
Preston, 29334 C8
Putnam, 51589 F3
Raleigh, 79220 H4
Randolph, 28262 E8
Ritchie, 10343 D5
Roane, 15446 E4
Summers, 12999 J5
Taylor, 16089 C7
Tucker, 7321 D8
Tyler, 9592 C5
Upshur, 23404 E7
Wayne, 42903 G1
Webster, 9719 F7
Wetzel, 17693 B6
Wirt, 5873 D4
Wood, 87986 D3
Wyoming, 25708 J3

Cities and Towns

Abbott, 80 E7
Albright, 247 C8
Alderson, 1091 J6
Alexander, 40 E7
Alma, 60 C5
Alum Bridge, 100 D6
Alum Creek, 1839 G3
Alvon, 50 H7
Amherstdale, 1785 H3
Anawalt, 272 K4
Anmoore, 685 C7
Annamoriah, 90 E4
Ansted, 1576 G5
Anthony, 60 H7
Antioch, 80 C10
Arden, 125 D8
Arista, 225 J4
Arnoldsburg, 60 E5
Arthur, 125 D10
Arthurdale, 950 C8
Asbury, 50 H6
Athens, 1102 K5
Auburn, 103 D5
Augusta, 450 C11
Aurora, 225 C9
Baker, 125 D11
Bald Knob, 40 H3
Bancroft, 367 F3
Barboursville, 3183 F2
Barnabus, 175 H2
Barrackville, 1288 C7
Barrett, 250 H3
Bayard, 299 C9
Beaver, 1378 H4
Beckley, 17254 H4
Beech Bottom, 606 B1
Belington, 1788 D8
Belle, 1259 G3
Belleville, 150 D3
Belmont, 1036 C4
Belva, 225 G4
Bemis, 20 E8
Bens Run, 70 C5
Bergoo, 125 F7
Berkeley Sprs., 663 B12
Bethany, 985 B2
Bethlehem, 2651 B4
Beverly, 651 E8
Big Chimney, 600 F3
Big Creek, 425 H2
Birch River, 150 F5
Blacksville, 175 B7
Blennerhassett, 3225 C3
Bluefield, 11451 K4
Boaz, 1345 C4
Bolair, 225 F6
Bolivar, 1045 C13
Boomer, 1100 G4
Bowden, 70 E8
Bradley, 2371 H4
Bradshaw, 289 K3
Bramwell, 426 K4
Branchland, 350 G2
Brandonville, 102 B8
Brandywine, 30 F9
Bridgeport, 7306 C7
Brohard, 20 D4
Brookhaven, 4734 F13
Brooks, 225 J5
Bruceton Mills, 74 B8
Buckhannon, 5725 D7
Buffalo, 1171 F2
Bunker Hill, 700 C13
Burlington, 200 C10
Burnsville, 481 E6
Cairo, 263 D4
Camden on Gauley, 157 F6
Cameron, 1212 B6
Camp Creek, 30 J5
Capon Bridge, 200 C11
Capon Sprs., 20 D11
Carpendale, 954 B11
Cass, 100 F8
Cassville, 1586 B7
Cedar Grove, 862 G4
Ceredo, 1675 H10
Chapmanville, 1211 H2
Charleston, 53421 F3
Charles Town, 2907 C13
Chattaroy, 1136 J2
Cheat Neck, 950 B8
Chelyan, 1400 G4
Chesapeake, 1643 G3
Chester, 2592 A2
Circleville, 100 E9
Clarksburg, 16743 C7
Clay, 593 F5
Clearco, 10 G6
Clearview, 590 C1
Clendenin, 1116 F4
Cleveland, 60 E7
Clifftop, 70 H5
Clintonville, 125 H6
Coal City, 1905 J4
Coal Fork, 1350 G4
Coalton, 247 E8
Coketon, 100 D9
Colcord, 300 H4
Comfort, 150 G3
Core, 125 B7
Corinth, 275 C9
Cottageville, 750 E3
Cowen, 513 F6
Coxs Mills, 50 D5
Crab Orchard, 2761 J4
Craigsville, 2204 G6
Cranesville, 30 B9
Cross Lanes, 10353 J8
Crum, 125 H1
Culloden, 2940 F2
Cuzzart, 100 B9
Dailey, 350 E8
Danese, 350 H5
Danville, 550 G3
Davis, 624 D9
Davy, 373 J3
Delbarton, 474 J2
Dellslow, 375 B8
Delray, 90 D11
Diana, 125 F6
Dorcas, 175 E10
Dunbar, 8154 F3
Dunlow, 150 G1
Dunmore, 100 F8
Durbin, 262 F8
E. Bank, 933 G4
E. Lynn, 150 G1
Eccles, 700 H4
Edray, 175 G7
Eglon, 175 C9
Eleanor, 1345 F2
Elizabeth, 994 D4
Elk Garden, 217 C10
Elkins, 7032 E8
Elkview, 1182 F4
Ellamore, 150 E7
Ellenboro, 373 C5
Enterprise, 939 C7
Erbacon, 30 F6
Etam, 50 C8
Evans, 750 E3
Evansville, 125 C8
Fairlea, 1706 H6
Fairmont, 19097 C7
Fairview, 435 B7
Falling Waters, 650 B13
Farmington, 387 C7
Fayetteville, 2754 G5
Fellowsville, 175 C8
Fenwick, 400 G6
Ferrellsburg, 500 G2
Fireco, 30 J4
Flatwoods, 348 E6
Flemington, 287 C7
Follansbee, 3115 B2
Folsom, 175 C6
Forks of Cacapon, 90 C12
Ft. Ashby, 1354 C11
Ft. Gay, 819 G1
Frametown, 275 F5
Frankford, 100 H6
Franklin, 797 F9
Frenchton, 250 E7
Friendly, 159 C5
Gandeeville, 150 E4
Gap Mills, 10 J6
Gary, 917 K3
Gassaway, 901 E5
Gauley Bridge, 738 G4
Gerrardstown, 550 C12
Ghent, 325 J5
Gilbert, 417 J3
Gilboa, 275 G5
Glady, 50 E8
Glasgow, 783 G4
Glen Dale, 1552 A6
Glengary, 125 C12
Glenhayes, 30 G1
Glen Rogers, 450 J4
Glenville, 1544 E5
Glenwood, 225 F2
Grafton, 5489 C7
Grantsville, 565 E5
Grant Town, 657 B7
Granville, 778 E12
Great Cacapon, 400 B12
Green Bank, 200 F8
Green Spr., 150 C11
Greenville, 70 J6
Griffithsville, 60 G2
Hacker Valley, 70 E6
Halltown, 400 C13
Hambleton, 246 D8
Hamlin, 1119 G2
Harman, 126 E9
Harpers Ferry, 307 C13
Harrisville, 1842 D5
Hartford, 519 D2
Hartmansville, 250 C10
Harts, 2361 G2
Hazelton, 80 B9
Headsville, 30 C10
Hedgesville, 240 B13
Henderson, 325 E2
Hendricks, 319 D8
Henry, 10 D9
Herndon, 80 J4
Hernshaw, 250 G3
Hillsboro, 243 G7
Hinton, 2880 J5
Hodgesville, 225 D7
Holden, 1105 H2
Hometown, 750 F3
Hooverson Hts., 2909 B2
Howesville, 275 C8
Hundred, 344 B6
Huntington, 51475 F1
Hurricane, 5222 F2
Huttonsville, 217 E8
Iaeger, 358 J3
Independence, 200 C8
Ingleside, 90 K5
Inkerman, 10 D11
Intermont, 30 D11
Inwood, 2084 C13
Ireland, 150 E6
Ivydale, 175 F5
Jane Lew, 406 D6
Jefferson, 567 K9
Jeffrey, 300 H3
Jenkinjones, 350 K4
Jerryville, 20 F7
Jones Sprs., 30 C12
Jordan Run, 100 D9
Junction, 150 C10
Junior, 450 D8
Justice, 325 J3
Kanawha, 500 D4
Kasson, 60 D8
Kearneysville, 650 C13
Kenna, 100 E3
Kenova, 3485 F1
Kerens, 175 D8
Kermit, 209 H1
Kessel, 10 D10
Keyser, 5303 C10
Keystone, 453 K4
Kiahsville, 30 G1
Kimball, 411 K4
Kingston, 60 H4
Kingwood, 2944 C8
Kirby, 60 D11
Kopperston, 500 H3
Lahmansville, 60 D10
Laneville, 10 D9
Laurel Dale, 30 C10
Lavalette, 850 F1
Leewood, 100 G4
Lehew, 70 D12
Lenore, 225 H1
Lenox, 50 B9
Leon, 132 E2
Leopold, 50 D6
Lesage, 125 F2
Lester, 322 J4
Letart, 125 E3
Levels, 20 C11
Lewisburg, 3624 H6
Liberty, 150 F3
Limestone, 300 C10
Lindside, 275 K6
Linn, 125 D6
Littleton, 207 B6
Lizemores, 200 G4
Logan, 1630 H2
Lookout, 175 G5
Looneyville, 50 E4
Lorentz, 250 D7
Lost City, 50 E11
Lost Creek, 467 D7
Lost River, 30 D11
Lubeck, 1303 C3
Lumberport, 937 C7
Maben, 60 J4
Mabscott, 1403 H4
Macfarlan, 70 D4
Madison, 2677 G3
Malden, 750 K13
Mallory, 1143 J3
Man, 770 H3
Manheim, 20 C8
Mannington, 2124 C7
Marlinton, 1204 G7
Marlowe, 1300 B13
Marmet, 1693 G3
Martin, 50 D10
Martinsburg, 14972 C13
Mason, 1064 D2
Masontown, 647 B8
Matewan, 498 J2
Mathias, 80 E10
Matoaka, 317 K4
Maybeury, 550 K4
Maysville, 125 D10
McMechen, 1937 A6
McWhorter, 175 D7
Meadow Bridge, 321 H5
Meadow Creek, 100 H5
Meadowville, 20 D8
Medley, 60 D10
Meyerstown, 100 D13
Middlebourne, 870 C5
Milam, 10 E10
Mill Creek, 662 E8
Millstone, 275 E5
Milton, 2206 F2
Mineral Wells, 1860 D4
Minnehaha Sprs., 20 G8
Monongah, 939 C7
Montcalm, 885 K4
Montgomery, 1942 G4
Montrose, 156 D8
Moorefield, 2375 D10
Morgantown, 26809 B8
Moundsville, 9998 A6
Mt. Gay, 2623 H2
Mt. Hope, 1487 H4
Mt. Nebo, 300 G5
Mt. Storm, 150 C9
Mullens, 1769 J4
Murphytown, 200 C4
Myrtle, 30 H2
Nallen, 125 G5
Needmore, 70 D11
Nestorville, 150 D8
Newburg, 360 C8
New Creek, 275 C10
New Cumberland, 1099 A2
Newell, 1602 A1
New Haven, 1559 D2
New Martinsville, 5984 B5
New Milton, 40 D6
Newton, 80 F4
Nitro, 6824 F3
Northfork, 519 K4
Norton, 275 E8
Nutter Fort, 1686 C7
Oak Hill, 7589 H4
Oakvale, 142 K5
Oceana, 1550 J3
Old Fields, 90 D10
Omps, 125 C12
Onego, 80 E9
Orlando, 125 E6
Orma, 40 E5
Osage, 175 E12
Paden City, 2860 B5
Parkersburg, 33099 C4
Parsons, 1463 D8
Paw Paw, 524 C11
Pax, 174 H4
Peach Creek, 175 H2
Pennsboro, 1199 C5
Petersburg, 2423 D10
Peterstown, 499 K5
Petroleum, 30 D4
Philippi, 2870 D7
Pickens, 30 E7
Piedmont, 1014 C10
Pierce, 90 D9
Pike, 125 C5
Pinch, 2811 F4
Pine Grove, 571 B6
Pineville, 715 J3
Pleasant Dale, 175 C11
Pleasant Valley, 3124 C7
Poca, 1013 F3
Pocatalico, 425 F3
Pt. Pleasant, 4637 E2
Points, 100 C11
Pond Gap, 225 G4
Powellton, 1796 G4
Pratt, 551 G4
Prichard, 325 G1
Princeton, 6347 K5
Proctor, 100 B5
Pruntytown, 600 C7
Pullman, 169 D5
Purgitsville, 80 D10
Quinnimont, 40 H5
Quinwood, 435 G6
Racine, 475 G3
Rainelle, 1545 H5
Rand, 2300 G3
Ranson, 2951 C13
Ravenswood, 4031 D3
Red Creek, 40 D9
Red Jacket, 728 J2
Reedsville, 517 C8
Reedy, 198 E4
Renick, 200 H7
Rhodell, 234 J4
Richwood, 2477 G6
Ridge, 150 C12
Ridgedale, 80 C8
Ridgeley, 762 F4
Ridgeview, 375 G3
Ridgeville, 125 C10
Ridgeway, 750 C12
Rig, 125 D10
Rio, 90 D11
Ripley, 3263 E3
Rippon, 200 D13
Riverton, 80 E9
Rivesville, 913 C7
Robertsburg, 225 E2
Rock Cave, 300 E7
Rock Forge, 1800 F13
Rockport, 30 D4
Romney, 1940 C11
Ronceverte, 1557 J6
Rosedale, 100 E5
Rowlesburg, 613 C8
Rupert, 940 H6
St. Albans, 11567 F3
St. George, 60 D8
St. Marys, 2017 C4
Salem, 2006 C6
Sand Fork (Layopolis), 176 E6
Sandyville, 400 E3
Scarbro, 1700 H4
Scherr, 40 D10
Schultz, 125 C4
Scott Depot, 2600 F3
Seth, 275 G3
Shady Spr., 2078 J5
Shanghai, 100 C12
Shanks, 225 C11
Sharples, 70 H3
Shepherdstown, 803 C13
Shinnston, 2295 C7
Short Gap, 450 C11
Silver Lake, 125 C9
Sissonville, 4399 F3
Sistersville, 1588 B5
Slanesville, 90 C11
Sleepy Creek, 125 B12
Smithburg, 350 C6
Smithers, 904 G4
Smithfield, 177 C6
Smithville, 90 D5
Sophia, 1301 J4
S. Charleston, 13390 F3
Southside, 10 E2
Spencer, 2352 E4
Springfield, 400 C11
Spurlockville, 150 G2
Squire, 100 K3
Star City, 1366 B8
Stirrat, 90 J2
Stonewood, 1815 D7
Strange Creek, 80 F5
Stumptown, 50 E5
Summersville, 3294 G5
Summit Pt., 325 C13
Sutton, 1011 E6
Swandale, 20 F5
Sweet Sprs., 150 J7
Switzer, 1138 H2
Sylvester, 195 H3
Tanner, 100 D5
Teays, 2400 F2
Terra Alta, 1456 C9
Thomas, 452 D9
Thornton, 175 C8
Thornwood, 50 F8
Thurmond, 7 H5
Tioga, 175 F6
Tornado, 1111 F3
Triadelphia, 817 A6
Trout, 50 H6
Tunnelton, 336 C8
Uffington, 400 F12
Union, 548 J6
Upper Tract, 175 E9
Valley Grove, 405 A6
Valley Head, 200 F7
Van, 250 H3
Vienna, 10861 C4
Waiteville, 30 J6
Walker, 80 D4
Walkersville, 50 E6
Wallace, 150 C6
Walton, 250 E4
War, 788 K3
Wardensville, 246 D11
Washington, 1170 C3
Wayne, 1105 G1
Webster Sprs., 808 F6
Weirton, 20411 B2
Welch, 2683 K3
Wellsburg, 2891 B1
W. Hamlin, 696 G2
W. Liberty, 1220 C2
W. Logan, 418 H2
W. Milford, 651 D6
Weston, 4317 D6
Westover, 3941 E12
W. Pea Ridge, 6363 G13
W. Union, 806 C5
Wharncliffe, 150 J2
Wheeling, 31419 A6
Whitehall, 595 C7
White Sulphur Sprs., 2315 H7
Whitesville, 520 H3
Wick, 100 C5
Wiley Ford, 1095 G4
Williamson, 3414 J2
Williamstown, 2996 C4
Windsor Hts., 431 B1
Winfield, 1858 F3
Woodlands, 100 B5
Worthington, 170 C7
Yellow Spr., 60 D11
Zela, 200 G5

WISCONSIN PG. 174-175

CAPITAL
Madison
NICKNAME
Badger State
POPULATION
5,363,675, rank 18
AREA
56,153 sq mi, rank 26

Counties

Adams, 18643 M7
Ashland, 16866 E5
Barron, 44963 G3
Bayfield, 15013 E4
Brown, 226778 L11
Buffalo, 13804 K3
Burnett, 15674 F2
Calumet, 40631 M10
Chippewa, 55195 H5
Clark, 33557 K5
Columbia, 52468 P8
Crawford, 17243 P5
Dane, 426526 P9
Dodge, 85897 N9
Door, 27961 H13
Douglas, 43287 E3
Dunn, 39858 J3
Eau Claire, 93142 J4
Florence, 5088 F10
Fond du Lac, 97296 N9
Forest, 10024 G9
Grant, 49597 Q5
Green, 33647 R7
Green Lake, 19105 M9
Iowa, 22780 Q7
Iron, 6861 E6
Jackson, 19100 L6
Jefferson, 74021 Q9
Juneau, 24316 M6
Kenosha, 149577 R11
Kewaunee, 20187 K12
La Crosse, 107120 M4
Lafayette, 16137 R6
Langlade, 20740 H9
Lincoln, 29641 H7
Manitowoc, 82887 M11
Marathon, 125834 J7
Marinette, 43384 G10
Marquette, 15832 M8
Menominee, 4562 J9
Milwaukee, 940164 Q11
Monroe, 40899 M6
Oconto, 35634 J10
Oneida, 36776 G8
Outagamie, 160971 K10
Ozaukee, 82317 P11
Pepin, 7213 K3
Pierce, 36804 J2
Polk, 41319 G2
Portage, 67182 L8
Price, 15822 G6
Racine, 188831 Q11
Richland, 17924 P6
Rock, 152307 R9
Rusk, 15347 G4
St. Croix, 63155 J2
Sauk, 55225 P7
Sawyer, 16196 F5
Shawano, 40664 J9
Sheboygan, 112646 N11
Taylor, 19680 H6
Trempealeau, 27010 K4
Vernon, 28056 N5
Vilas, 21033 F8
Walworth, 93759 Q10
Washburn, 16036 F3
Washington, 117493 P10
Waukesha, 360767 Q10
Waupaca, 51731 K9
Waushara, 23154 L8
Winnebago, 156763 M9
Wood, 75555 K6

Cities and Towns

Abbotsford, 1956 J6
Abrams, 350 J11
Adams, 1914 M7
Adell, 517 N11
Alaska, 125 K12
Albany, 1191 R8
Algoma, 3357 K12
Allenton, 850 P10
Allenville, 200 L10
Allouez, 15443 C9
Alma, 942 L3
Alma Ctr., 446 K5
Almena, 720 H3
Almond, 459 L8
Alto, 250 N9
Altoona, 6698 J4
Alvin, 10 F9
Amberg, 225 G11
Amery, 2845 H2
Amherst, 964 K8
Amherst Jct., 305 K8
Angelica, 150 K10
Aniwa, 272 J9
Anston, 275 K11
Antigo, 8560 H9
Appleton, 70087 L10
Arbor Vitae, 90 F8
Arcadia, 2402 L4
Arena, 685 P7
Argonne, 175 G9
Argyle, 823 R7
Arkdale, 150 M7
Arlington, 484 P8
Armstrong Creek, 50 G10
Arpin, 337 K7
Ashippun, 500 P10
Ashland, 8620 D5
Ashwaubenon, 17634 K11
Athelstane, 70 G11
Athens, 1095 J7
Auburndale, 738 K7
Augusta, 1460 K5
Aurora, 300 F11
Auroraville, 100 M9
Avalon, 150 R9
Avoca, 608 P6
Babcock, 125 L7
Bagley, 339 Q5
Baileys Harbor, 200 H13
Baldwin, 2667 J2
Balsam Lake, 950 G2
Bancroft, 450 L8
Bangor, 1400 M5
Baraboo, 10711 N7
Barksdale, 125 D5
Barneveld, 1088 Q7
Barron, 3248 H3
Barronett, 125 G3
Batavia, 325 N11
Bay City, 465 K2
Bayfield, 611 D5
Bayside, 4518 R5
Bear Creek, 415 K9
Beaver, 100 H11
Beaver Dam, 15169 N9
Beecher, 150 G11
Beetown, 125 Q5
Belgium, 1678 N11
Bell Ctr., 116 P5
Belleville, 1908 Q8
Bellevue, 11828 K11
Belmont, 871 Q6
Beloit, 35775 R9
Bennett, 50 E3
Benoit, 10 D5
Benton, 976 R6
Berlin, 5305 M9
Bevent, 50 J8
Big Bend, 1278 Q11
Big Falls, 85 K9
Big Spr., 70 N8
Birch, 250 D6
Birchwood, 518 G4
Birnamwood, 795 J8
Biron, 915 L7
Black Creek, 1192 K10
Black Earth, 1320 P7
Black Hawk, 125 P7
Black River Falls, 3618 L5
Blair, 1273 L4
Blanchardville, 806 Q7
Bloom City, 60 N6
Bloomer, 3347 H4
Bloomington, 701 Q5
Bloomville, 125 H8
Blue Mounds, 708 Q7
Blue River, 429 P6
Boardman, 200 H2
Boaz, 137 P6
Bohners Lake, 1952 R10
Bonduel, 1416 J10
Borth, 175 M9
Boscobel, 3047 P5
Boulder Jct., 200 F8
Bowler, 343 J9
Boyceville, 1043 J3
Boyd, 680 J5
Brackett, 150 K4
Bradley, 150 G7
Brandon, 912 N9
Brantwood, 40 G7
Breed, 80 H10
Bridgeport, 125 Q5
Briggsville, 250 N8
Brill, 150 G4
Brillion, 2937 L11
Bristol, 1100 R11
Brodhead, 3180 R8
Brokaw, 107 J8
Brookfield, 38649 Q11
Brooklyn, 916 Q8
Brooks, 125 M8
Brothertown, 350 M10
Brown Deer, 12170 P11
Brownsville, 570 N10
Browntown, 252 R7
Bruce, 787 G4
Brule, 200 D4
Brussels, 275 J12
Bryant, 90 H9
Buffalo, 1040 L3
Burlington, 9936 R10
Burnett, 300 N10
Butler, 1881 T3
Butternut, 407 F6
Cable, 200 E4
Cadott, 1345 J5
Calamine, 80 Q7
Caledonia, 250 Q11
Cambria, 792 N9
Cambridge, 1101 Q9
Cameron, 1546 H3
Campbellsport, 1913 N11
Camp Douglas, 592 M6
Campia, 175 G4
Canton, 150 G4
Carlsville, 175 J12
Carter, 80 H10
Caryville, 80 J3
Cascade, 666 N11
Casco, 572 K12
Cashton, 1005 N5
Cassville, 1085 R5
Cataract, 175 M5
Catawba, 149 G6
Cavour, 50 G10
Cazenovia, 326 N6
Cecil, 466 J10
Cedarburg, 10908 P11
Cedar Grove, 1887 N11
Centuria, 865 G2
Champion, 175 K11
Chaseburg, 306 N5
Chelsea, 125 H6
Chetek, 2180 H4
Chili, 275 K6
Chilton, 3708 M11
Chippewa Falls, 12925 J4
Christie, 125 K6
City Pt., 10 L6
Clam Falls, 70 G2
Clam Lake, 50 E5
Clayton, 507 H2
Clear Lake, 1051 H2
Clearwater Lake, 200 F9
Cleveland, 1361 M12
Clifton, 80 M6
Clinton, 2162 R9
Clintonville, 4736 K9
Clyman, 388 P10
Cobb, 442 Q6
Cochrane, 435 L3
Colby, 1616 J6
Coleman, 716 J11
Colfax, 1136 J3
Collins, 250 M11
Coloma, 461 M8
Columbus, 4479 P9
Combined Locks, 2422 A4
Como, 1870 R10
Comstock, 150 G3
Connorsville, 175 H3
Conover, 30 F8
Conrath, 98 H5
Cooksville, 125 Q8
Coon Valley, 714 N5
Cooperstown, 225 L11
Cornell, 1466 H5
Cornucopia, 100 C5
Couderay, 96 F4
Crandon, 1961 G9
Crivitz, 998 H11
Cross Plains, 3084 P8
Cuba City, 2156 R6
Cudahy, 18429 Q11
Cumberland, 2280 G3
Curtiss, 198 J6
Cushing, 175 G2
Custer, 400 K8
Dairyland, 10 E3
Dale, 500 L10
Daleyville, 150 Q7
Dallas, 356 H3
Dalton, 250 N9
Danbury, 225 F2
Dane, 799 P8
Darien, 1572 R10
Darlington, 2418 R7
Dayton, 175 Q8
Deerbrook, 125 H9
Deerfield, 1971 Q9
Deer Park, 227 H2
De Forest, 7368 P8
Delafield, 6472 Q10
Delavan, 7956 R10
Dellwood, 175 M7
Denmark, 1958 L11
De Pere, 20559 K11
De Soto, 366 N4
Dexterville, 40 L7
Diamond Bluff, 125 K1
Dickeyville, 1043 R6
Dodge, 125 L4
Dodgeville, 4220 Q7
Doering, 40 H8
Dorchester, 827 J6
Dousman, 1584 Q10
Downing, 257 J3
Downsville, 200 J3
Doylestown, 328 P9
Dresser, 732 H2
Drummond, 150 E4
Dunbar, 70 G11
Dundas, 175 L11
Durand, 1968 K3
Dyckesville, 300 K11
Eagle, 1707 Q10
Eagle River, 1443 F8
Eagleton, 150 J4
Earl, 60 F3
Eastman, 437 P5
Easton, 150 M7
E. Troy, 3564 Q10
Eau Claire, 61704 J4
Eau Galle, 175 K3
Eden, 687 N10
Edgar, 1386 J7
Edgerton, 4933 Q9
Edgewater, 80 G4
Egg Harbor, 250 J12
Eland, 251 J9
Elcho, 375 G9
Elderon, 189 J8
Eleva, 635 K4
Elkhart Lake, 1021 M11
Elkhorn, 7305 R10
Elk Mound, 785 J3
Ellison Bay, 200 H13
Ellsworth, 2909 J2
Elm Grove, 6249 T3
Elmwood, 841 J2
Elmwood Park, 474 R11
Elroy, 1578 N6
Elton, 50 H9
Embarrass, 399 K10
Endeavor, 440 N8
Enterprise, 80 G8
Ephraim, 353 H13
Esofea, 30 N5
Ettrick, 521 L4
Euren, 175 K12
Evansville, 4039 Q8
Exeland, 212 G4
Fairchild, 564 K5
Fairwater, 350 N9
Fall Creek, 1236 J4
Fall River, 1097 P9
Falun, 125 F2
Fence, 70 G10
Fennimore, 2387 Q5
Fenwood, 174 J7
Ferryville, 174 P5
Fifield, 250 F6
Finley, 30 L7
Fish Creek, 125 H12
Fitchburg, 20501 Q8
Florence, 750 F10
Fond du Lac, 42203 M10
Footville, 788 R9
Forest, 70 H2
Forest Jct., 450 L11
Forestville, 429 K12
Ft. Atkinson, 11621 Q9
Foster, 125 K4
Fountain City, 983 L3
Foxboro, 20 D2
Fox Lake, 1454 N9
Fox Pt., 7012 P11
Francis Creek, 681 L12
Franklin, 29494 Q11
Franklin, 60 L5
Franksville, 1789 Q11
Frederic, 1262 G2
Fredonia, 1934 N11
Freedom, 1500 L10
Fremont, 666 L9
Friendship, 698 M7
Friesland, 298 N9
Gagen, 10 G9
Galesville, 1427 M4
Galloway, 125 K8
Gays Mills, 625 P5
Genoa, 263 N4
Genoa City, 1949 R10
Germania, 70 M8
Germantown, 18260 P11
Gillett, 1256 J10
Gills Rock, 125 H13
Gilman, 474 H5
Gilmanton, 175 K3
Gleason, 325 H8
Glenbeulah, 378 M11
Glendale, 13367 P11
Glen Flora, 93 G5
Glen Haven, 50 Q5
Glenwood City, 1183 H2
Glidden, 650 E6
Goodman, 275 G10
Goodrich, 40 H7
Gordon, 150 E3
Gotham, 275 P6
Grafton, 10312 P11
Grand Marsh, 150 M7
Grand View, 125 E5
Granton, 406 K6
Grantsburg, 1369 F1
Gratiot, 252 R7
Green Bay, 102313 K11
Greendale, 14405 V3
Greenfield, 35476 V4
Green Lake, 1100 M9
Greenleaf, 650 L11
Green Valley, 175 J10
Greenville, 950 L10
Greenwood, 1079 J6
Gresham, 575 J9
Gurney, 30 D6
Hager City, 300 K2
Hales Corners, 7765 Q11
Hamburg, 100 H7
Hammond, 1153 J2
Hancock, 463 L8
Hannibal, 40 H5
Hanover, 250 R9
Harmony Grove, 550 P8
Harrison, 100 G8
Harrisville, 125 M8
Harshaw, 125 G8
Hartford, 10905 P10
Hartland, 7905 P10
Hatfield, 150 L5
Hatley, 476 J8
Haugen, 287 G3
Haven, 200 M12
Hawkins, 317 G5
Hawthorne, 125 D3
Hayward, 2129 F4
Hazel Green, 1183 R6
Hazelhurst, 250 F7
Heafford Jct., 325 G7
Hebron, 243 Q10
Helenville, 225 Q10
Herbster, 50 C4
Hertel, 90 G2
Hewitt, 670 K7
High Bridge, 90 E5
Highland, 855 Q6
Hilbert, 1089 L11
Hiles, 100 G9
Hillsboro, 1302 N6
Hillsdale, 200 H3
Hixton, 446 L5
Holcombe, 200 H5
Hollandale, 283 Q7
Hollister, 30 H9
Holmen, 6200 M4
Horicon, 3775 N10
Hortonville, 2357 L10
Howard, 13546 K11
Howards Grove, 2792 M11
Hudson, 8775 J1
Humbird, 225 K5
Hurley, 1818 E7
Hustisford, 1135 P10
Hustler, 113 M6
Independence, 1244 L4
Ingram, 76 G5
Ino, 20 D5
Institute, 250 J12
Iola, 1298 K9
Irma, 125 H8
Iron Belt, 225 E6
Iron Ridge, 998 P10
Iron River, 500 D4
Ironton, 250 N7
Island Lake, 80 H4
Ixonia, 642 P10
Jackson, 4938 P11
Jacksonport, 125 J13
Janesville, 59498 R9
Jefferson, 7338 Q9
Jim Falls, 325 J4
Johnsburg, 200 M10
Johnson Creek, 1581 Q9
Johnstown Ctr., 125 R9
Juda, 325 R8
Jump River, 100 H5
Junction City, 440 K7
Juneau, 2485 P10
Kaukauna, 12983 L10
Kekoskee, 169 N10
Kellner, 650 L7
Kellnersville, 374 L11
Kempster, 100 H9
Kendall, 469 M6
Kennan, 171 G6
Kenosha, 90352 R11
Keshena, 1394 J10
Kewaskum, 3274 N11
Kewaunee, 2806 K12
Kiel, 3450 M11
Kimberly, 6146 A3
King, 2215 L9
Kingston, 288 N9
Knapp, 421 J3
Kohler, 1926 N12
Krakow, 275 J10
Lac du Flambeau, 1646 F7
La Crosse, 51818 M4
Ladysmith, 3932 G5
La Farge, 775 N6
La Grange, 100 Q10
Lake Beulah, 200 Q10
Lake Delton, 1982 N7
Lake Geneva, 7148 R10
Lake Mills, 4843 P9
Lake Nebagamon, 1015 D4
Lake Tomahawk, 325 F8
Lakewood, 200 H10
Lamartine, 325 N10
Lampson, 80 F3
Lancaster, 4070 Q5
Land O' Lakes, 225 E8
Langlade, 100 H9
Lannon, 1009 S2
Laona, 700 G10
La Pointe, 60 D5
Larsen, 150 L10
La Valle, 326 N7
Lebanon, 275 P10
Leland, 30 P7
Lena, 510 J11
Leon, 40 M5
Lewis, 150 G2
Leyden, 80 Q9
Liberty Pole, 125 N5
Lily, 80 H9
Lime Ridge, 169 N7
Linden, 615 Q6
Little Chute, 10476 L10
Little Suamico, 225 J11
Livingston, 597 Q6
Lodi, 2882 P8
Loganville, 276 N7
Lohrville, 408 M9
Lomira, 2233 N10
Lone Rock, 929 P6
Long Lake, 90 F10
Longwood, 90 J6
Loretta, 30 F5
Lowell, 366 P9
Loyal, 1308 J6
Loyd, 125 P6
Lublin, 110 H5
Luck, 1210 G2
Ludington, 150 J5
Lugerville, 40 G6
Luxemburg, 1935 K12
Lyndon Sta., 458 N7
Lynxville, 176 P5
Lyons, 600 R10
Mackville, 450 L10
Madison, 208054 Q8
Maiden Rock, 121 K2
Manawa, 1330 K9
Manitowish, 10 F7
Manitowish Waters, 100 E7
Manitowoc, 34053 M12
Maple, 200 D3
Maple Bluff, 1358 Q3
Maplewood, 175 J12
Marathon City, 1640 J7
Marengo, 225 E5
Maribel, 264 L11
Marinette, 11749 H12
Marion, 1297 K9
Markesan, 1396 N9
Marquette, 169 N9
Marshall, 3432 P9
Marshfield, 18800 K7
Martell, 150 J2
Mason, 72 E5
Mather, 40 L6
Mattoon, 466 J9
Mauston, 3740 M7
Mayville, 4902 N10
Mazomanie, 1485 P7
McAllister, 30 H11
McFarland, 6416 Q8
McKinley, 100 G2
McNaughton, 30 G8
Medford, 4350 H6
Medina, 450 L10
Meenon, 250 F2
Mellen, 845 E6
Melrose, 529 L5
Melvina, 93 M5
Menasha, 16331 L10
Menomonee Falls, 32647 P11
Menomonie, 14937 J3
Mequon, 21823 P11
Mercer, 450 E7
Meridean, 40 J3
Merrill, 10146 H8
Merrillan, 585 K5
Merrimac, 416 P8
Merton, 1926 P10
Middle Inlet, 90 H11
Middleton, 15770 P8
Mikana, 100 G4
Milan, 200 J7
Milladore, 268 K7
Millston, 100 L6
Milltown, 888 G2
Milton, 5132 Q9
Milwaukee, 596974 Q11
Mindoro, 200 M5
Mineral Pt., 2617 Q6
Minocqua, 750 F7
Minong, 531 F3
Mishicot, 1422 L12
Modena, 40 K3
Mole Lake, 275 G9
Mondovi, 2634 K3
Monico, 175 G9
Monona, 8018 Q8
Monroe, 10843 R8
Monroe Ctr., 100 M7
Montello, 1397 M8
Montfort, 663 Q6
Monticello, 1146 R8
Montreal, 838 E6
Moose Jct., 30 E3
Moquah, 40 D5
Morse, 30 E6
Mosinee, 4063 J7
Mountain, 200 H10
Mt. Calvary, 956 M10
Mt. Hope, 186 Q5
Mt. Horeb, 5860 Q7
Mt. Sterling, 215 P5
Mt. Tabor, 80 N6
Mt. Zion, 50 P5
Mukwonago, 6162 Q10
Muscoda, 1453 P6
Muskego, 21397 Q11
Navarino, 100 K10
Necedah, 888 M7
Neenah, 24507 L10
Neillsville, 2731 K6
Nekoosa, 2590 L7
Nelma, 70 F9
Nelson, 395 K3
Nelsonville, 191 K8
Neopit, 839 J9
Neosho, 593 P10
Neshkoro, 453 M8
Newald, 125 G9
New Auburn, 562 H4
New Berlin, 38220 Q11
Newburg, 1119 N11
New Diggings, 125 R6
New Franken, 225 K11
New Glarus, 2111 Q8
New Holstein, 3301 M11
New Lisbon, 1436 M7
New London, 7085 L9
New Post, 367 F4
New Richmond, 6310 H2
Newry, 60 N5
Newton, 300 M12
Niagara, 1880 G11
Nichols, 307 K10
N. Bay, 260 Q12
N. Bend, 100 M5
Northfield, 90 K5
N. Fond du Lac, 4557 M10
N. Freedom, 649 N7
N. Hudson, 3463 J1
N. Prairie, 1571 Q10
Northwoods Beach, 300 F4
Norwalk, 653 M6
Oak Creek, 28456 Q11
Oakdale, 297 M6
Oakfield, 1012 N10
Oconomowoc, 12382 P10
Oconto, 4708 J11
Oconto Falls, 2843 J11
Odanah, 254 D6
Ogdensburg, 224 K9
Ogema, 250 G6
Ojibwa, 30 F5
Okauchee, 2100 P10
Oliver, 358 D3
Omro, 3177 M9
Onalaska, 14839 M4
Oneida, 1070 K11
Ontario, 476 N6
Oostburg, 2660 N11
Oregon, 7514 Q8
Orfordville, 1272 R8
Osceola, 2421 H1
Oshkosh, 62916 M10
Osseo, 1669 K4
Owen, 936 J6
Oxford, 536 M8
Paddock Lake, 3012 R11
Palmyra, 1766 Q10
Pardeeville, 1982 N8
Park Falls, 2793 F6
Park Ridge, 488 K8
Parrish, 30 H8
Patch Grove, 166 Q5
Patzau, 80 D2
Pearson, 80 H9
Pelican Lake, 50 G9
Pella, 125 J9
Pell Lake, 2988 R10
Pembine, 175 G11
Pensaukee, 125 J11
Pepin, 878 K2
Peru, 90 K8
Peshtigo, 3357 J11
Pewaukee (city), 11783 T1
Pewaukee (village), 8170 T1
Phelps, 350 F9
Phillips, 1675 G6
Phlox, 150 J9
Pickerel, 100 H9
Pickett, 200 M10
Pigeon Falls, 388 K4
Pilsen, 125 K12
Pipe, 175 M10
Pittsville, 866 K7
Plain, 792 P7
Plainfield, 899 L8
Plainville, 150 N7
Platteville, 9989 R6
Pleasant Prairie, 16136 R11
Plover, 10520 K8
Plum City, 574 K2
Plymouth, 7781 N11
Polonia, 275 K8
Poplar, 552 D3
Portage, 9728 N8
Port Edwards, 1944 L7
Porterfield, 125 H11
Port Washington, 10467 P11
Port Wing, 175 D4
Poskin, 125 G3
Postville, 30 Q7
Potosi, 711 R5
Potter, 223 L11
Pound, 355 H11
Powers Lake, 1500 R10
Poynette, 2266 P8
Poy Sippi, 375 L9
Prairie du Chien, 6018 Q4
Prairie du Sac, 3231 P7
Prairie Farm, 508 H3
Prentice, 626 G6
Prescott, 3764 J1
Presque Isle, 70 E7
Price, 30 K5
Princeton, 1504 M9
Pulaski, 3060 K10
Racine, 81855 Q12
Radisson, 222 F4
Randolph, 1869 N9
Random Lake, 1551 N11
Range, 150 H2
Readstown, 395 N5
Red Cliff, 600 C5
Redgranite, 1040 M9
Reedsburg, 7827 N7
Reedsville, 1187 L11
Reeseville, 703 P9
Reserve, 436 F4
Rewey, 311 Q6
Rhinelander, 7735 G8
Rib Lake, 878 H6
Rice Lake, 8320 G3
Richfield, 500 P11
Richford, 40 M8
Richland Ctr., 5114 P6
Richwood, 100 P9
Ridgeland, 265 H3
Ridgeway, 689 Q7
Ringle, 125 J8
Rio, 938 N8
Rio Creek, 150 K12
Riplinger, 125 J6
Ripon, 6828 M9
River Falls, 12560 J2
River Hills, 1631 S5
Roberts, 969 J2
Rochester, 1149 Q11
Rockbridge, 90 N6
Rockdale, 214 Q9
Rockland, 628 M5
Rock Sprs., 425 N7
Rosendale, 923 M10
Rosholt, 518 K8
Rothschild, 4970 J8
Roxbury, 200 P8
Royalton, 300 L9
Rozellville, 275 J7
Rubicon, 350 P10
Rudolph, 423 K7
Rush Lake, 175 M9
Rusk, 90 J3
St. Cloud, 497 M11
St. Croix Falls, 2033 G2
St. Francis, 8662 V5
St. Germain, 225 F8
St. Nazianz, 749 M11
Sanborn, 60 E5
Sand Creek, 175 H3
Sarona, 100 G3
Sauk City, 3109 P7
Saukville, 4068 P11
Saxeville, 200 L9
Saxon, 125 D6
Sayner, 175 F8
Scandinavia, 349 K9
Schofield, 2117 J8
Seeley, 100 E4
Seneca, 125 P5
Sextonville, 250 P6
Seymour, 3335 K10
Sharon, 1549 R10
Shawano, 8298 J10
Sheboygan, 50792 M12
Sheboygan Falls, 6772 N11
Sheldon, 256 H5
Shell Lake, 1309 G3
Sheridan, 150 L9
Sherwood, 1550 L10
Shiocton, 954 K10
Shorewood, 13763 T5
Shorewood Hills, 1732 Q1
Shullsburg, 1246 R6
Silver Lake, 2341 R11
Siren, 988 F2
Sister Bay, 886 H13
Slinger, 3901 P10
Sobieski, 150 J11
Soldiers Grove, 653 P5
Solon Sprs., 576 E3
Somers, 1100 R11
Somerset, 1556 H1
S. Milwaukee, 21256 Q11
S. Range, 250 D3
S. Wayne, 484 R7
Sparta, 8648 M5
Spencer, 1932 J6
Spirit, 60 G7
Spooner, 2653 F3
Spread Eagle, 250 F11
Springbrook, 50 F3
Spring Green, 1444 P7
Springstead, 60 F7
Spring Valley, 1189 J2
Stanley, 1898 J5
Starks, 90 G8
Star Lake, 20 F8
Star Prairie, 574 H2
Stetsonville, 563 H6
Steuben, 177 P5
Stevens Pt., 24551 K8
Stevenstown, 80 M4
Stiles, 200 J11
Stitzer, 175 Q6
Stockbridge, 649 M10
Stockholm, 97 K2
Stoddard, 815 N4
Stone Lake, 225 F4
Stoughton, 12354 Q9
Stratford, 1523 J7
Strum, 1001 K4
Sturgeon Bay, 9437 J12
Sturtevant, 5287 R11
Suamico, 950 K11
Sugar Bush, 350 K9
Sugar Camp, 90 F8
Sullivan, 688 Q10
Summit Lake, 150 H9
Sun Prairie, 20369 P9
Superior, 27368 D3
Suring, 605 J10
Sussex, 8828 P11
Sylvan, 20 P6
Symco, 175 K9
Taylor, 513 L5
Tennyson, 370 R5
Theresa, 1252 N10
Thiensville, 3254 P11
Thornton, 100 J10
Thorp, 1536 J5
Three Lakes, 600 F9
Tigerton, 764 J9
Tilden, 250 J4
Tilleda, 100 J9
Tipler, 40 F10
Tisch Mills, 275 L12
Tomah, 8419 M6
Tomahawk, 3770 G7
Tony, 105 G5
Townsend, 225 H10
Trade Lake, 100 G2
Trade River, 80 G1
Trego, 200 F3
Trempealeau, 1319 M4
Trimbelle, 175 J2
Tripoli, 40 G7
Tunnel City, 225 M6
Turtle Lake, 1065 H3
Tustin, 150 L9
Twin Lakes, 5124 R11
Two Creeks, 125 L12
Two Rivers, 12639 L12
Union Ctr., 214 N6
Union Grove, 4322 R11
Unity, 368 J6
Upson, 50 E6
Valders, 948 M11
Valmy, 150 J12
Valton, 100 N6
Van Dyne, 250 M10
Verona, 7052 Q8
Vesper, 541 K7
Victory, 90 N4
Village of Superior, 500 D3
Viola, 667 N5
Viroqua, 4335 N5
Wabeno, 475 G10
Waldo, 450 N11
Wales, 2523 Q10
Walworth, 2304 R10
Wanderoos, 200 H2
Warrens, 286 L6
Wascott, 20 E3
Washburn, 2280 D5
Washington Island, 150 H13
Waterford, 4048 Q11
Waterloo, 3259 P9
Watertown, 21598 P10
Waucousta, 200 N10
Waukau, 300 M9
Waukesha, 64825 Q11
Waumandee, 20 L3
Waunakee, 8995 P8
Waupaca, 5676 L9
Waupun, 10718 N9
Wausau, 38426 J8
Wausaukee, 572 H11
Wautoma, 1998 M8
Wauwatosa, 47271 T3
Wauzeka, 768 P5
Wayside, 275 L11
Webb Lake, 40 F3
Webster, 653 F2
Wentworth, 70 D3
Werley, 40 Q5
W. Allis, 61254 Q11
W. Bend, 28152 N11
W. Bloomfield, 100 L9
Westboro, 200 H6
Westby, 2045 N5
Westfield, 1217 M8
W. Milwaukee, 4201 U4
Weston, 12079 J8
Weston, 30 J3
W. Salem, 4540 M5
Weyauwega, 1806 L9
Weyerhaeuser, 353 G4
Wheeler, 317 J3
White Creek, 150 M7
Whitefish Bay, 14163 P11
Whitefish Bay, 50 J13
Whitehall, 1651 L4
White Lake, 329 H9
Whitelaw, 730 L11
Whitewater, 13437 Q10
Whiting, 1760 K8
Whittlesey, 125 H6
Wild Rose, 765 L8
Willard, 100 J5
Williams Bay, 2415 R10
Wilson, 176 J2
Wilton, 519 M6
Winchester, 100 E7
Wind Lake, 5202 Q11
Wind Pt., 1853 Q12
Windsor, 2533 P8
Winnebago, 1500 A6
Winneconne, 2401 M10
Winter, 344 F5
Wiota, 80 R7
Wisconsin Dells, 2418 N7
Wisconsin Rapids, 18435 L7
Withee, 508 J6
Wittenberg, 1177 J9
Wonewoc, 834 N6
Woodboro, 325 G8
Woodford, 150 R7
Woodman, 96 P5
Woodruff, 1300 F7
Woodville, 1104 J2
Wrightstown, 1934 L11
Wyalusing, 20 Q4
Wyeville, 146 M6
Wyocena, 668 N8
Yellow Lake, 90 F2
Yuba, 92 N6

WYOMING PG. 176

CAPITAL
Cheyenne
NICKNAME
Equality State
POPULATION
493,782, rank 50
AREA
97,809 sq mi, rank 9

Counties

Albany, 32014 F11
Big Horn, 11461 B8
Campbell, 33698 B11
Carbon, 15639 G9
Converse, 12052 D11
Crook, 5887 A12
Fremont, 35804 E8
Goshen, 12538 E12
Hot Sprs., 4882 C7
Johnson, 7075 B10
Laramie, 81607 G12
Lincoln, 14573 F4
Natrona, 66533 D9
Niobrara, 2407 D12
Park, 25786 B6
Platte, 8807 F12
Sheridan, 26560 A10
Sublette, 5920 E5
Sweetwater, 37613 F7
Teton, 18251 C5
Uinta, 19742 H4
Washakie, 8289 C8
Weston, 6644 C12

Cities and Towns

Acme, 20 A9
Afton, 1818 E4
Aladdin, 10 A13
Albany, 80 H10
Albin, 120 G13
Alcova, 20 E9
Almy, 125 G4
Alpine, 550 D4
Alta, 400 C4
Alva, 10 A12
Arapahoe, 1766 D7
Arlington, 10 G10
Arvada, 33 A10
Atlantic City, 39 E7
Auburn, 276 E4
Baggs, 348 H8
Bairoil, 97 F8
Banner, 30 B9
Barnum, 10 C9
Bar Nunn, 936 E10
Basin, 1238 B8
Beckton, 80 A9
Bedford, 169 D4
Bentonite Spur, 10 A13
Beulah, 40 B13
Big Horn, 198 A9
Big Piney, 408 E5
Big Sandy, 10 E6
Big Trails, 10 C9
Bill, 10 D11
Bitter Creek, 125 G7
Bondurant, 155 D5
Bonneville, 30 D8
Boulder, 30 E6
Boxelder, 10 E11
Buffalo, 3900 B9
Buford, 10 H11
Burgess Jct., 20 A8
Burlington, 250 B7
Burns, 285 H13
Burntfork, 30 H5
Burris, 10 D6
Byron, 557 A7
Calpet, 7 F5
Carlile, 60 B12
Carpenter, 80 H13
Carter, 8 G5
Casper, 49644 E10
Centennial, 191 G10
Cheyenne, 53011 H12
Chugwater, 244 G12
Clark, 30 A6
Clay Spur, 90 C12
Clearmont, 115 A10
Cody, 8835 B6
Cokeville, 506 F4
Colony, 10 A13
Cora, 76 D5
Cowley, 560 A7
Crowheart, 163 D6
Daniel, 89 E5
Dayton, 678 A9
Deaver, 177 A7
Devils Tower, 10 B12
Diamondville, 716 F4
Dixon, 79 H8
Douglas, 5288 E11
Dubois, 962 C6
E. Thermopolis, 274 C8
Eden, 388 F6
Edgerton, 169 D10
Egbert, 20 H13
Elk Basin, 10 A7
Elk Mtn., 192 G10
Elkol, 10 G4
Emblem, 20 B7
Encampment, 443 H9
Esterbrook, 32 E11
Ethete, 1455 D7
Etna, 123 D4
Evanston, 11507 G4
Evansville, 2255 E10
Fairview, 277 E4
Farson, 242 F6
Federal, 10 G12
Fontenelle, 19 F5
Ft. Bridger, 400 G5
Ft. Laramie, 243 F12
Ft. Steele, 30 G9
Ft. Washakie, 1477 D7
Four Corners, 10 B13
Foxpark, 50 H10
Frannie, 209 A7
Freedom, 100 D4
Frontier, 50 F4
Garland, 95 A7
Gillette, 19646 B11
Glendo, 229 E12
Glenrock, 2231 E11
Granger, 146 G5
Grass Creek, 20 C7
Green River, 11808 G6
Greybull, 1815 B8
Grover, 137 E4
Guernsey, 1147 F12
Hamilton Dome, 10 C7
Hampshire, 10 C12
Hanna, 873 F10
Harriman, 20 H11
Hartville, 76 F12
Hat Creek, 10 D12
Hawk Sprs., 69 F13
Hillsdale, 80 G12
Hoback Jct., 40 D4
Horse Creek, 10 G11
Horton, 10 B13
Hudson, 407 E7
Hulett, 408 A12
Huntley, 21 F13
Hyattville, 73 B8
Iron Mtn., 10 G11
Jackson, 8647 C4
James Town, 552 G6
Jay Em, 10 E12
Jeffrey City, 106 E8
Jenny Lake, 20 C4
Kane, 10 A8
Kaycee, 249 C10
Kelly, 125 C4
Kemmerer, 2651 F4
Kinnear, 125 D7
Kirby, 57 C8
La Barge, 431 F5
LaGrange, 332 G13
Lance Creek, 51 D12
Lander, 6867 E7
Laramie, 27204 G11
Lightning Flat, 10 A11
Linch, 100 C10
Lingle, 510 F12
Little America, 56 G5
Lonetree, 61 H5
Lost Cabin, 20 D8
Lost Sprs., 1 E12
Lovell, 2281 A7
Lucerne, 525 C8
Lusk, 1447 E12
Lyman, 1938 G5
Lysite, 20 D8
Madison, 20 A4
Mammoth Hot Sprs., 275 A4
Manderson, 104 B8
Manville, 101 E12
Marbleton, 720 E5
Mayoworth, 10 C9
McFadden, 10 G10
McKinnon, 49 H5
Meadowdale, 10 E12
Medicine Bow, 274 F10
Meeteetse, 351 B7
Meriden, 20 G13
Merna, 30 D5
Midvale, 30 D7
Midwest, 408 D10
Milford, 30 E7
Mills, 2591 J4
Moorcroft, 807 B12
Moose, 80 C4
Morton, 20 D7
Mtn. View, 1153 G5
Mtn. View, 103 J4
Muddy Gap, 20 F8
Newcastle, 3065 C13
New Haven, 10 A12
Norris, 20 A4
Old Faithful, 30 B4
Opal, 102 F5
Orchard Valley, 550 K2
Orin, 30 E11
Orpha, 10 E11
Osage, 215 C12
Otto, 40 B7
Parkerton, 10 E10
Parkman, 137 A9
Pavillion, 165 D7
Piedmont, 10 G4
Pine Bluffs, 1153 H13
Pinedale, 1412 E5
Pine Haven, 222 B12
Pitchfork, 40 B6
Pt. of Rocks, 3 G7
Powder River, 51 D9
Powell, 5373 A7
Quealy, 80 G6
Ralston, 233 A7
Ranchester, 701 A9
Rawlins, 8538 G9
Recluse, 10 A11
Redbird, 20 D13
Red Desert, 30 G8
Reliance, 665 G6
Riner, 10 G8
Riverside, 59 H9
Riverton, 9310 D7
Riverview, 10 D13
Robertson, 59 H5
Rock River, 235 G10
Rock Sprs., 18708 G6
Rockypoint, 10 A11
Rolling Hills, 449 E11
Rozet, 90 B11
Ryan Park, 10 G10
Saddlestring, 40 B9
Sage, 10 F4
St. Stephens, 70 D7
Sand Draw, 10 E8
Saratoga, 1726 G9
Savery, 20 H8
Seminoe Dam, 10 F9
Shell, 70 B8
Sheridan, 15804 A9
Shoshoni, 635 D8
Sinclair, 423 F9
Slater, 82 F12
Smoot, 182 E4
S. Torrington, 550 F13
Spotted Horse, 20 A10
Story, 887 B9
Sundance, 1161 B12
Sunrise, 10 F12
Sunshine, 20 C6
Superior, 244 G6
Sussex, 70 C10
Sweetwater Sta., 20 E8
Table Rock, 82 G7
Ten Sleep, 304 C8
Teton Vil., 175 C4
Thayne, 341 D4
Thermopolis, 3172 C7
Tie Siding, 10 H11
Torrington, 5776 F13
Tower Jct., 20 A5
Turnerville, 155 E4
Ucross, 10 B10
Ulm, 10 A10
Upton, 872 B12
Valley, 30 B6
Van Tassell, 18 E13
Veteran, 28 F12
Walcott, 30 G9
Wamsutter, 261 G8
Wapiti, 20 B6
W. Thumb, 20 B5
Wheatland, 3548 F12
Willwood, 100 A7
Wilson, 1294 C4
Winchester, 60 C8
Wolf, 40 A9
Woods Landing, 100 H10
Worland, 5250 C8
Wright, 1347 C11
Wyodak, 125 B11
Yoder, 169 F13

Canada

ALBERTA PG. 179

CAPITAL
Edmonton
POPULATION
2,696,826, rank 4
AREA
255,286 sq mi, rank 6

Cities and Towns

Abee, 25 E17
Acadia Valley, 118 J19
Acme, 600 J16
Airdrie, 15946 J16
Alberta Beach, 640 F16
Alcomdale, 55 F16
Alder Flats, 115 G15
Aldersyde, 47 K16
Alix, 765 H17
Alliance, 220 H18
Altario, 26 H19
Amisk, 214 G19
Andrew, 484 F17
Ardmore, 234 E19
Armena, 50 G17
Arrowwood, 163 K17
Ashmont, 202 E18
Athabasca, 2313 E16
Atikameg, 22 C14
Atmore, 30 D17
Balzac, 5 J16
Banff, 6098 J15
Barons, 285 L17
Barrhead, 4239 E15
Bashaw, 774 G17
Bassano, 1272 K17
Bawlf, 351 G17
Bear Canyon, 56 C11
Beaumont, 5810 F16
Beauvallon, 7 F18
Beaver Crossing, 18 E19
Beaverdam, 15 E19
Beaverlodge, 1997 D11
Beaver Mines, 54 M16
Beiseker, 708 J16
Bellevue, 1046 M16
Bellis, 88 E17
Benalto, 88 H16
Bentley, 987 H16
Berwyn, 606 C13
Bezanson, 68 D12
Big Valley, 308 H17
Bindloss, 14 K19
Bittern Lake, 193 G17
Black Diamond, 1811 K16
Blackfalds, 2001 H16
Blackfoot, 183 F19
Blackie, 301 K16
Blairmore, 2118 L16
Blue Ridge, 232 E15
Bluesky, 192 C12
Bluffton, 129 G16
Bodo, 26 H19
Bon Accord, 1493 F16
Bondiss, 86 E17
Bonnyville, 5100 E19
Botha, 194 H17
Bowden, 1014 H16
Bowen Island E18
Bow Island, 1688 L19
Boyle, 802 E17
Bragg Creek, 591 K15
Brant, 46 K17
Breton, 521 G15
Breynat, 22 D17
Brooks, 10093 K18
Brownfield, 27 H18
Brownvale, 122 C12
Bruce, 61 G18
Bruderheim, 1198 F17
Brûlé, 161 G13
Buck Creek, 100 G15
Buck Lake, 63 G15
Burdett, 286 L18
Busby, 68 F16
Byemoor, 39 H17
Cadogan, 100 H19
Cadomin, 86 G13
Cadotte Lake, 275 B14
Calgary, 768082 K16
Calmar, 1797 G16
Camrose, 13728 G17
Canmore, 8354 K15
Canyon Creek, 242 D15
Carbon, 450 J17
Carcajou, 17 A13
Cardston, 3417 M17
Carmangay, 258 L17
Caroline, 472 H15
Carseland, 578 K17
Carstairs, 1887 J16
Carway, 5 M17
Caslan, 23 E17
Castor, 970 H18
Cayley, 334 K16
Cereal, 211 J19
Cessford, 31 J18
Champion, 362 L17
Chauvin, 400 G19
Cherhill, 80 F15
Cherry Grove, 113 E19
Chestermere, 1911 K16
Chinook, 38 J19
Chisholm, 28 D16
Clairmont, 496 D12
Clandonald, 135 F19
Claresholm, 3427 L16
Cleardale, 51 C11
Clive, 517 H16
Clyde, 410 E16
Coaldale, 5731 L17
Cochrane, 7424 J16
Cold Lake, 4089 E19
Colinton, 195 E16
Compeer, 21 H20
Condor, 99 H15
Conklin, 191 C18
Consort, 794 H19
Coronation, 1166 H18
Coutts, 386 M18
Cowley, 273 M16
Craigmyle, 81 J18
Cremona, 380 J16
Crossfield, 1899 J16
Crowsnest Pass, 2118 L16
Cynthia, 71 G15
Czar, 199 G19
Dalemead, 32 K16
Dapp, 26 E16
Daysland, 679 G17
Deadwood, 22 B13
DeBolt, 103 D12
Delburne, 641 H17
Delia, 208 J17
Derwent, 110 F18
Desmarais, 218 C16
Devon, 4496 F16
Dewberry, 185 F19
Dickson, 65 H16
Didsbury, 3553 J16
Dixonville, 89 B13
Donalda, 235 G17
Donnelly, 375 C13
Drayton Valley, 5883 G15
Drumheller, 6587 J17
Duchess, 693 K18
Dunmore, 200 L19
Duvernay, 26 F18
Eaglesham, 159 C12
E. Coulee, 175 J17
Eckville, 901 H16
Edberg, 137 G17
Edgerton, 372 G19
Edmonton, 616306 F16
Edson, 7399 F14
Egremont, 62 E17
Elk Pt., 1403 E19
Ellscott, 6 E17
Elmworth, 4 D11
Elnora, 247 H17
Empress, 186 J20
Enchant, 103 L18
Endiang, 29 H18
Enilda, 156 D14
Ensign, 17 K17
Entwistle, 453 F15
Erskine, 318 H17
Esther, 8 H19
Etzikom, 54 L19
Evansburg, 740 F15
Fabyan, 98 G19
Fairview, 3316 C12
Falher, 1149 C13
Falun, 25 G16
Faust, 352 D14
Fawcett, 122 E16
Ferintosh, 130 G17
Flatbush, 33 E16
Fleet, 28 H18
Foremost, 556 M19
Forestburg, 930 G18
Ft. Kent, 163 E19
Ft. Macleod, 3034 L17
Ft. McMurray, 33078 F4
Ft. Saskatchewan, 12408 F17
Ft. Vermilion, 782 F4
Fox Creek, 2321 E13
Gadsby, 40 H17
Galahad, 175 G18
Gem, 24 K18
Gibbons, 2748 F16
Gift Lake, 314 C14
Girouxville, 332 C13
Gleichen, 335 K17
Glendon, 418 E18
Glenwood, 295 M17
Goodfare, 11 D11
Gordondale, 78 C11
Grande Cache, 4441 F11
Grande Prairie, 31140 D12
Granum, 337 L17
Grassy Lake, 327 L18
Green Court, 72 F15
Grimshaw, 2661 C13
Gunn, 121 F16
Guy, 57 D13
Gwynne, 124 G17
Hairy Hill, 46 F18
Halkirk, 131 H18
Hanna, 3001 J18
Hardisty, 808 G18
Hay Lakes, 352 G17
Hays, 91 L18
Hayter, 80 G19
Heath, 14 G19
Heinsburg, 60 F19
Heisler, 195 G18
High Level, 3093 E3
High Prairie, 2907 D14
High River, 7359 K16
Hilda, 43 K20
Hill Spr., 220 M16
Hines Creek, 437 C12
Hinton, 9961 F13
Hoadley, 9 G16
Hobbema, 30 G16
Holden, 397 F17
Huallen, 28 D11
Hughenden, 258 G19
Hussar, 157 J17
Huxley, 78 H17
Hylo, 22 E17
Hythe, 712 D11
Iddesleigh, 14 K18
Imperial Mills, 19 D18
Innisfail, 6116 H16
Innisfree, 238 F18
Irma, 472 G18
Iron River, 7 E18
Iron Sprs., 86 L17
Irricana, 823 J16
Irvine, 330 L20
Island Lake, 187 D16
Island Lake South, 76 D16
Islay, 205 F19
Jarvie, 98 E16
Jasper, 3815 G12
Jean Côté, 65 C13
Jenner, 141 K19
Joussard, 256 D14
Kananaskis, 117 K15
Kathyrn, 29 J16
Keg River, 135 A13
Kelsey, 26 G17
Keoma, 40 J16
Kikino, 183 E17
Killam, 1048 G18
Kingman, 79 G17
Kinsella, 50 G18
Kinuso, 258 D15
Kirkcaldy, 24 K17
Kirriemuir, 28 H19
Kitscoty, 643 F19
Lac La Biche, 2611 D18
Lacombe, 8018 H16
La Corey, 40 E19
Lafond, 35 F18
La Glace, 176 D11
Lake Louise, 500 J14
Lamont, 1581 F17
Langdon, 279 K16
Larkspur, 11 E16
Lavoy, 122 F18
Leavitt, 10 M17
Leduc, 14305 G16
Legal, 1095 F16
Leslieville, 137 H15
Lethbridge, 63053 L17
Lindale, 26 G15
Lindbergh, 50 F19
Linden, 565 J16
Little Buffalo, 185 B14
Little Smoky, 28 E13
Lloydminster, 11317 F19
Lodgepole, 206 G15
Lomond, 170 K17
Longview, 303 K16
Loon Lake, 167 B15
Lougheed, 253 G18
Lousana, 47 H17
MacKay, 18 F14
Madden, 36 J16
Magrath, 1867 M17
Mallaig, 189 E18
Manning, 1295 B13
Mannville, 758 F18
Manola, 29 E15
Manyberries, 96 M19
Markerville, 55 H16
Marlboro, 186 F13
Marten Beach, 38 D15
Marwayne, 449 F19
Mayerthorpe, 1669 F15
McLaughlin, 41 G19
McLennan, 867 C13
Medicine Hat, 46783 L19
Meeting Creek, 21 G17
Metiskow, 65 G19
Michichi, 42 J17
Milk River, 929 M18
Millet, 1894 G16
Millicent, 12 K18
Milo, 117 K17
Minburn, 95 F18
Mirror, 487 H17
Monarch, 217 L17
Monitor, 60 H19
Morinville, 6226 F16
Morningside, 68 G16
Morrin, 275 J17
Mtn. View, 100 M17
Mulhurst, 301 G16
Mundare, 578 F17
Musidora, 13 F18
Myrnam, 294 F18
Nacmine, 447 J17
Nampa, 427 C13
Nanton, 1665 K16
Neerlandia, 101 E15
Nestow, 15 E16
Nevis, 31 H17
New Brigden, 24 H19
Newbrook, 99 E17
New Dayton, 47 M18
New Fish Creek D13
New Norway, 270 G17
New Sarepta, 359 F17
Nisku, 40 F16
Niton Jct., 79 F14
Nobleford, 558 L17
N. Star, 49 B13
Notikewin, 17 B13
Okotoks, 8510 K16
Olds, 5815 J16
Onoway, 788 F16
Orion, 11 M19
Oyen, 1009 J19
Paradise Valley, 141 G19
Parkland, 50 L16
Patricia, 84 K18
Peace River, 6536 C13
Peers, 113 F14
Penhold, 1625 H16
Peoria, 13 C12
Perryvale, 11 E16
Pibroch, 88 E16
Pickardville, 176 E16
Picture Butte, 1669 L17
Pincher Creek, 3659 M16
Pocahontas, 10 G12
Pollockville, 2 J18
Ponoka, 6149 G16
Provost, 1904 H19
Purple Sprs., 26 L18
Queenstown, 15 K17
Radway, 176 E17
Rainbow Lake, 1138 E3
Rainier, 29 K18
Ralston, 413 K19
Ranfurly, 78 F18
Raven, 12 H16
Raymond, 3056 M17
Redcliff, 4104 L19
Red Deer, 60075 H16
Redwater, 2053 F17
Red Willow, 29 H17
Reno, 23 C13
Ribstone, 48 G19
Richdale, 14 J18
Rimbey, 2106 G16
Robb, 196 G13
Rochester, 92 E16
Rochon Sands, 86 H17
Rockyford, 346 J17
Rocky Mtn. House, 5805 H15
Rocky Rapids, 50 G15
Rolling Hills, 164 L18
Rosalind, 195 G17
Rosebud, 72 J17
Rosedale, 305 J17
Rosemary, 332 K18
Round Hill, 102 G17
Rowley, 11 H17
Rycroft, 667 C12
Ryley, 465 F17
St. Albert, 46888 F16
St. Francis, 15 G16
St. Isidore, 180 C13
St. Lina, 24 E18
St. Michael, 39 F17
St. Paul, 4861 E18
St. Vincent, 43 E18
Sandy Beach, 171 F16
Sangudo, 398 F15
Scandia, 115 K18
Schuler, 88 K20
Scotfield, 9 J18
Seba Beach, 124 F15
Sedalia, 15 H19
Sedgewick, 937 G18
Seven Persons, 107 L19
Sexsmith, 1481 D12
Shaughnessy, 321 L17
Sheerness, 5 J18
Sibbald, 33 J19
Skiff, 10 M18
Slave Lake, 6553 D15
Smith, 258 D16
Smoky Lake, 1087 E17
S. Baptiste, 66 E16
Spedden, 56 E18
Spirit River, 1112 C12
Spring Coulee, 66 M17
Spruce Grove, 14271 F16
Standard, 366 J17
Stand Off, 682 M17
Stavely, 453 L16
Stettler, 5220 H17
Stirling, 874 M17
Stony Plain, 8274 F16
Strathmore, 5282 K17
Streamstown, 15 F19
Strome, 269 G18
Sturgeon Hts., 62 D13
Suffield, 182 L19
Sundre, 2028 J15
Sunnybrook, 51 G16
Sunnynook, 13 J18
Sunset House, 106 D13
Swalwell, 68 J17
Swan Hills, 2030 E15
Sylvan Lake, 5178 H16
Taber, 7214 L18
Tangent, 39 C13
Tawatinaw, 9 E16
Teepee Creek, 6 D12
Therien, 52 E18
Thorhild, 486 E17
Thorsby, 725 G16
Three Hills, 3022 J17
Tilley, 368 K18
Tofield, 1726 F17
Tomahawk, 97 F15
Torrington, 177 H16
Trochu, 958 H17
Tulliby Lake, 18 F19
Turin, 91 L17
Turner Valley, 1527 K16
Twin Butte, 6 M16
Two Hills, 1040 F18
Valhalla Ctr., 42 D11
Valleyview, 1906 D13
Vauxhall, 1011 L18
Vega, 30 E15
Vegreville, 5337 F18
Vermilion, 3744 F19
Veteran, 317 H19
Viking, 1081 G18
Vilna, 274 E18
Vimy, 196 E16
Vulcan, 1537 K17
Wabamun, 645 F15
Wainwright, 5079 G19
Waiparous, 47 J15
Walsh, 69 L20
Wandering River, 63 D17
Wanham, 167 C12
Warburg, 549 G16
Wardlow, 28 K18
Warner, 421 M18
Warspite, 79 E17
Warwick, 28 F18
Waskatenau, 237 E17
Waterton Park, 135 M16
Water Valley, 105 J15
Watino, 22 C13
Wayne, 43 J17
Welling, 53 M17

Wembley, 1441 D11
Westlock, 4317 E16
Wetaskiwin, 10959 G16
Whitecourt, 7783 E14
Whitelaw, 146 C12
Widewater, 237 D15
Wild Horse M20
Willingdon, 309 F17
Wimborne, 59 H16
Winfield, 198 G16
Woking, 91 D12
Worsley, 30 B11
Wrentham, 58 M18
Youngstown, 239 J18

BRITISH COLUMBIA PG. 178

CAPITAL
Victoria

POPULATION
3,724,500, rank 3

AREA
365,946 sq mi, rank 5

Cities and Towns

100 Mile House, 1850 J9
150 Mile House, 899 H9
70 Mile House, 179 J9
Abbotsford, 105403 M8
Adams Lake, 110 K11
Ahousat, 17 M5
Alert Bay, 612 K4
Alexis Creek, 243 H8
Alkali Lake J8
Altona, 154 B10
Anahim Lake, 260 G6
Applegrove L12
Argenta, 132 L13
Armstrong, 3906 K11
Arrow Park L12
Ashcroft, 1858 K9
Aspen Grove, 26 L10

Famous Wall Drug, South Dakota

Athalmer K14
Avola, 160 J11
Baldonnel, 86 C10
Balfour L13
Bamfield, 256 M6
Barkerville G9
Barrière, 1653 J10
Bear Lake, 270 E8
Beaton, 7 K13
Beaverdell, 280 M11
Bella Bella, 121 H3
Bella Coola G4
Big Bar Creek J8
Big Bay, 14 K6
Big Creek, 69 J8
Big Lake Ranch, 127 H9
Birch Island, 221 J11
Birken, 109 K8
Black Creek, 1950 L6
Blind Bay, 454 K11
Blind Channel K5
Blubber Bay, 34 L6
Blue River, 283 H11
Boat Basin L4
Boston Bar, 391 L9
Boswell, 139 M14
Bouchie Lake G8
Bowen Island, 1791 L7
Brackendale L7
Bralorne, 78 K8
Bridge Lake, 16 J10
Brisco, 138 K14
Buffalo Creek, 36 J9
Buick, 113 B9
Burnaby, 179209 M8
Burns Lake, 1793 E6
Burton, 220 L13
Cache Creek, 1115 K9
Campbell River, 23851 L6
Canal Flats, 685 L14
Canim Lake, 64 J10
Canyon Hot Sprs. J13
Castlegar, 7027 M13
Cawston, 843 M11
Cedar, 3178 M7
Cedarvale, 36 D3
Chase, 2460 K11
Chasm, 77 J9
Cherryville, 500 L12
Chetwynd, 2980 C9
Chilanko Forks, 123 H7
Chilliwack, 60186 M9
Christina Lake, 26 M12
Clearwater, 244 J10
Clinton, 729 K9
Coal Hbr., 206 K3
Coalmont, 83 M10
Cobble Hill, 1527 N7
Coldstream, 8975 L11
Colwood, 13848 M1
Comox, 11069 L6
Coombs, 840 M6
Copper Creek, 7 K10
Coquitlam, 101820 M8
Courtenay, 17335 L6
Craigellachie, 71 K12
Cranbrook, 18131 M14
Crawford Bay, 295 L14
Creston, 4816 M14
Cumberland, 2548 L6
D'Arcy, 60 K8
Darfield, 101 J10
Dawson Creek, 11125 C10
Dawsons Landing, 13 H4
Delta, 95411 M7
Denman Island, 866 L6
Dome Creek, 51 F10
Douglas Lake, 62 L10
Duncan, 4583 N7
Dunster, 27 G11
Edgewater, 518 K14
Edgewood, 128 L12
Elkford, 2729 L15
Elko, 165 M15
Endako, 102 E6
Erickson, 516 M14
Esquimalt, 16151 N1
Fairmont Hot Sprs., 249 L14
Falkland, 361 K11
Fanny Bay, 538 M6
Fauquier, 154 L12
Fernie, 4877 M15
Field, 237 J14
Forest Grove, 276 J9
Ft. Fraser, 370 E7
Ft. Nelson, 4401 E3
Ft. St. James, 2046 E7
Ft. St. John, 15021 C10
Ft. Steele, 99 M15
François Lake, 69 E6
Fraser Lake, 1344 E6
Galena Bay, 16 K13
Galloway, 63 M15
Ganges, 1457 N7
Germansen Landing, 44 C7
Gibsons, 3732 M7
Gillies Bay, 502 L6
Gold Bridge, 68 K8
Golden, 3968 J13
Gold River, 2041 L5
Goodlow, 23 B11
Grand Forks, 3994 M12
Granisle, 446 D5
Granite Bay, 37 K6
Grasmere, 147 M15
Gray Creek, 202 M14
Greenwood, 734 M12
Grindrod, 421 K11
Groundbirch, 15 C10
Hagensborg, 606 G5
Halfmoon Bay, 260 M7
Hanceville, 68 H8
Harrogate, 37 K14
Harrop, 172 M13
Hazelton, 347 D4
Hedley, 402 M10
Hendrix Lake, 3 H10
Heriot Bay, 308 L6
Hixon, 191 F8
Honeymoon Bay, 436 N6
Hope, 6247 M9
Hornby Island, 894 M6
Horsefly, 131 H9
Hosmer, 271 M15
Houston, 3934 E5
Howser, 38 L13
Hudson's Hope, 1122 C9
Invermere, 2687 K14
Jaffray, 375 M15
Jesmond, 8 J9
Johnsons Landing, 43 L13
Jordan River, 44 N7
Kaleden, 1118 M11
Kamloops, 76394 K10
Kaslo, 1063 L13
Kelowna, 89442 L11
Kemano, 367 F4
Kent, 4844 M9
Keremeos, 1167 M11
Kersley, 283 G8
Kildonan, 15 M6
Kimberley, 6738 L14
Kimsquit, 4 G4
Kingsgate, 75 M14
Kitamaat Vil. E3
Kitimat, 11136 E3
Kitwanga, 30 D4
Kleena Kleene, 92 H6
Kootenay Bay, 40 L13
Kootenay Crossing, 2 K14
Kyuquot, 97 L4
Lac la Hache, 420 H9
Lac Le Jeune, 39 K10
Ladysmith, 6456 M7
Lake Country, 9007 L11
Lake Cowichan, 2856 N7
Lakelse Lake, 248 E3
Langford, 17484 N7
Langley, 22523 M8
Lantzville, 408 M7
Lazo, 1201 L6
Likely, 268 G9
Lillooet, 1988 K9
Lions Bay, 1347 M7
Little Fort, 175 J10
Logan Lake, 2492 K10
Lone Butte, 71 J9
Lone Prairie, 125 D9
Longworth, 8 F9
Loos, 8 F10
Lower Nicola, 780 L10
Lumby, 1689 L12
Lytton, 322 L9
Mackenzie, 5997 D8
Madeira Park, 669 L7
Mahood Falls H10
Malakwa, 357 K12
Manson Creek, 32 C7
Maple Ridge, 56173 M8
Masset, 1293 F1
McBride, 740 G10
McLeod Lake, 51 D8
McLure, 273 K10
Meadow Creek, 133 L13
Merritt, 7631 L10
Merville, 865 L6
Mica Creek, 13 H12
Midway, 686 M12
Mirror Lake, 1 L13
Mission, 30519 M8
Moberly Lake, 242 C9
Monte Creek, 65 K11
Monte Lake, 68 K11
Montney, 21 B10
Mt. Currie, 59 K8
Moyie, 94 M14
Nakusp, 1736 L13
Nanaimo, 70130 M7
Naramata, 1069 M11
Nelson, 9585 M13
Nemiah Valley, 35 J7
New Denver, 579 L13
Newgate, 50 M15
New Westminster, 49350 C5
Nimpo Lake, 164 H6
Noralee, 22 E5
N. Bend, 314 L9
N. Vancouver, 41475 A2
N. Vancouver (DM), 30418 A4
Oak Bay, 17865 N7
Ocean Falls, 29 G4
Okanagan Ctr., 360 L11
Okanagan Falls, 1874 M11
Oliver, 4285 M11
Oona River, 35 E2
Ootsa Lake, 32 F5
Osoyoos, 4021 M11
Parksville, 9472 M6
Parson, 84 K14
Pavilion, 22 K9
Peachland, 4524 L11
Pemberton, 855 L8
Penny, 10 F9
Penticton, 30987 M11
Pink Mtn., 19 B8
Port Alberni, 18468 M6
Port Alice, 1331 K4
Port Edward, 700 E2
Port Hardy, 5283 K4
Port McNeill, 2925 K4
Port Moody, 20847 A6
Port Neville, 6 K5
Port Renfrew, 158 N6
Pouce Coupe, 894 C11
Powell River, 13131 L6
Prespatou, 421 B10
Prince George, 75150 F8
Prince Rupert, 16714 E2
Princeton, 2826 M10
Procter, 233 M13
Qualicum Beach, 6728 M6
Quathiaski Cove, 221 L6
Quatsino, 91 K3
Quesnel, 8468 G8
Quilchena, 24 L10
Radium Hot Sprs., 530 K14
Red Rock, 121 F8
Refuge Cove, 17 L6
Revelstoke, 8047 K12
Richmond, 148867 M7
Riondel, 315 L13
Riske Creek, 181 H8
Rivers Inlet, 7 H4
Robson, 299 M13
Rock Creek, 51 M12
Rolla, 113 C11
Roosville, 40 M15
Rossland, 3802 M13
Rosswood, 181 D3
Royston, 1219 L6
Saanich, 101388 N7
Salmo, 1202 M13
Salmon Arm, 14664 K11
Sanca, 25 M14
Savona, 541 K10
Sayward, 440 K5
Sechelt, 7343 M7
Seton Portage, 96 K8
Shearwater, 48 H3
Shelley, 68 F8
Sicamous, 2827 K12
Sidney, 10701 N7
Silverton, 241 L13
Sinclair Mills, 47 F9
Sirdar, 34 M14
Slocan Park, 372 M13
Smithers, 5624 D4
Sointula, 672 K4
Sooke, 4733 N7
Sorrento, 662 K11
Southbank, 126 E5
S. Hazelton, 654 D4
S. Pender Island, 133 N7
S. Slocan, 438 M13
Spallumcheen, 5322 L11
Sparwood, 3982 L15
Spences Bridge, 165 K9
Spillimacheen, 77 K14
Springhouse, 143 H8
Sproat Lake, 777 M6
Spuzzum, 33 L9
Stewardson Inlet M4
Stewart, 858 E2
Stoner, 65 F8
Stuart Island, 2 K6
Sullivan Bay, 7 K4
Summerland, 10584 M11
Summit Lake, 50 E8
Surrey, 304477 M8
Taghum, 456 M13
Tahsis, 940 L4
Takysie Lake, 35 F5
Ta Ta Creek, 114 L14
Tatla Lake, 52 H6
Taylor, 1031 C10
Tchesinkut Lake, 106 E6
Telkwa, 1194 D4
Terrace, 12779 D3
Tête Jaune Cache, 143 G11
Three Valley, 20 K12
Tofino, 1170 M5
Tomslake, 23 D11
Topley, 176 E5
Trail, 7696 M13
Trout Lake, 41 K13
Tulameen, 164 M10
Tumbler Ridge, 3775 D10
Tupper, 33 D11
Ucluelet, 1658 M5
Union Bay, 615 L6
Upper Fraser, 132 E9
Usk, 147 D3
Valemount, 1303 G11
Van Anda, 348 L6
Vancouver, 514008 M7
Vanderhoof, 4401 E7
Vavenby, 396 J11
Vernon, 31817 L11
Victoria, 73504 N7
View Royal, 6441 M1
Walhachin, 63 K9
Wardner, 195 M15
Wasa, 23 L15
Wells, 240 G9
Westbank, 577 L11
Westbridge, 63 M12
W. Vancouver, 40882 A3
Westwold, 369 K11
Whistler, 7172 L8
Williams Lake, 10472 H8
Willow River, 313 E8
Windermere, 821 K14
Winlaw, 521 M13
Winter Hbr., 54 K3
Wonowon, 84 B9
Woss, 354 K4
Wycliffe, 622 M14
Wynndel, 871 M14
Yahk, 173 M14
Yale, 169 M9
Ymir, 227 M13
Youbou, 797 M6
Zeballos, 232 L4

MANITOBA PG. 181

CAPITAL
Winnipeg

POPULATION
1,113,898, rank 5

AREA
250,946 sq mi, rank 7

Cities and Towns

Alexander, 274 M13
Alonsa, 103 K14
Altamont, 62 M15
Altona, 3286 N16
Amaranth, 152 K14
Angusville, 123 K12
Arborg, 1012 K16
Arden, 57 L14
Argyle, 39 L16
Ashern, 692 J15
Ashville, 17 J13
Austin, 439 L14
Bacon Ridge, 8 K14
Baden, 54 G12
Bakers Narrows, 150 C11
Baldur, 341 M14
Balmoral, 169 L16
Barrows, 139 G11
Beausejour, 2712 L17
Bellsite, 37 G12
Belmont, 257 M14
Benito, 460 H11
Beresford, 30 M13
Beulah, 35 L12
Bield, 13 J12
Binscarth, 463 K12
Birch River, 419 G12
Birnie, 50 L14
Birtle, 720 L12
Blumenfeld, 167 N15
Boissevain, 1544 N13
Bowsman, 358 H12
Brandon, 39175 M13
Broad Valley, 33 K16
Brookdale, 92 L14
Brunkild, 89 M16
Bruxelles, 41 M14
Camperville, 579 H13
Carberry, 1493 M14
Cardale, 24 L13
Carman, 2704 M15
Carrick, 17 N18
Carroll, 33 M13
Cartwright, 345 N14
Chatfield, 22 K16
Churchill, 1073 F6
Clandeboye, 163 L16
Clanwilliam, 75 L13
Clearwater, 91 N14
Cowan, 68 H12
Cranberry Portage, 800 D12
Crandall, 32 L12
Crane River, 226 J14
Cromer, 27 M12
Crystal City, 433 N14
Cypress River, 239 M14
Dallas, 12 J16
Darlingford, 157 N15
Dauphin, 8266 J13
Dauphin River, 10 H15
Decker, 16 L12
Deepdale, 4 J11
Deerhorn, 8 K15
Deleau, 4 M12
Deloraine, 1041 N12
Dominion City, 356 N16
Douglas, 147 M13
Duck Bay, 427 H13
Dunrea, 105 M13
Durban, 31 H11
E. Braintree, 143 M18
E. Selkirk, 599 L17
Eddystone, 251 K14
Eden, 81 L14
Edrans, 15 L14
Elgin, 116 M13
Elie, 485 L16
Elkhorn, 514 L12
Elma, 80 L18
Elm Creek, 328 M15
Elphinstone, 155 K13
Emerson, 737 N16
Erickson, 507 L13
Eriksdale, 313 K15
Ethelbert, 315 J13
Fairfax, 22 M13
Fairford, 30 J14
Falcon Lake, 156 M18
Fisher Branch, 432 J16
Flin Flon, 6572 C11
Fork River, 72 J13
Forrest, 69 L13
Foxwarren, 129 K12
Fraserwood, 76 K16
Gardenton, 56 N17
Garland, 28 J13
Gilbert Plains, 748 J12
Gillam, 1158 G6
Gimli, 1574 K16
Gladstone, 927 L14
Glenboro, 663 M14
Glenella, 130 K14
Glenora, 43 N14
Goodlands, 73 N12
Grahamdale, 19 J15
Grande-Clairière, 12 M12
Grande Pt.e, 451 G19
Grandview, 856 J12
Great Falls, 90 K18
Gretna, 538 N16
Griswold, 36 M12
Grosse Isle, 221 L16
Grunthal, 733 M17
Gunton, 160 L16
Gypsumville, 130 H15
Hamiota, 847 L12
Harding, 18 L12
Hargrave, 12 L12
Hartney, 462 M12
Harwill, 5 J16
Haywood, 151 M15
High Bluff, 130 L15
Hilbre, 23 J15
Hillside Beach, 119 K17
Hnausa, 46 K16
Hochfeld, 261 N15
Hodgson, 98 J16
Holland, 405 M14
Inglis, 187 K12
Inwood, 144 K16
Kane, 14 M16
Kelwood, 123 K14
Kemnay, 77 M13
Kenton, 162 L12
Kenville, 108 H12
Killarney, 2208 N13
Kirkella, 13 L11
Kleefeld, 349 M17
Kola, 61 M11
Komarno, 83 K16
La Broquerie, 472 M17
Lac du Bonnet, 1070 L17
Ladywood, 39 L17
Lake Francis, 17 L16
Landmark, 783 M17
Langruth, 145 L15
La Rivière, 210 N15
La Salle, 600 M16
Lauder, 17 M12
Laurier, 184 K13
Lavenham, 18 M14
Lena, 13 N13
Lenore, 36 L12
Letellier, 185 N16
Lorette, 1474 M17
Lowe Farm, 313 M16
Lundar, 523 K15
Lynn Lake, 501 F5
Macdonald, 74 L15
MacGregor, 898 L14
Mafeking, 214 G12
Makaroff, 8 J11
Makinak, 19 K13
Mallard, 128 H13
Manigotagan, 197 J17
Manitou, 781 N15
Manson, 9 L11
Marchand, 186 M17
Mariapolis, 103 M14
Marquette, 43 L16
Matheson Island, 122 H16
Matlock, 98 L16
McAuley, 120 L11
McCreary, 537 K14
McMunn, 42 M18
Meadow Portage, 99 J13
Medora, 67 N12
Meleb, 11 K16
Melita, 1152 N12
Menzie, 13 K12
Miami, 377 M15
Miniota, 217 L12
Minitonas, 598 H12
Minnedosa, 2443 L13
Minto, 104 M13
Mitchell, 811 M17
Molson, 75 L17
Moore Park, 18 L13
Moosehorn, 241 J15
Moose Lake, 556 E13
Morden, 5689 N15
Morris, 1645 M16
Mulvihill, 23 K15
Myrtle, 28 M16
Napinka, 95 N12
Narcisse, 10 K16
Neelin, 11 N14
Neepawa, 3301 L14
Nesbitt, 23 M13
New Bothwell, 301 M17
Newdale, 182 L13
Ninette, 243 M13
Ninga, 108 N13
Niverville, 1615 M16
Novra, 23 G12
Oak Bluff, 126 G17
Oakburn, 187 K12
Oak Lake, 369 M12
Oakland, 45 L15
Oakner, 19 L12
Oak Pt., 162 K15
Oak River, 142 L13
Oakville, 421 L15
Ochre River, 210 K13
Onanole, 404 K13
Overflowing River, 14 F12
Pelican Rapids, 151 G12
Petersfield, 143 L16
Pierson, 220 N12
Pilot Mound, 716 N14
Pinawa, 1669 L18
Pine Dock, 113 H17
Pine Falls, 794 K17
Pine River, 218 H12
Piney, 74 N18
Pipestone, 153 M12
Plumas, 253 L14
Plum Coulee, 729 N16
Pointe du Bois, 129 L18
Poplarfield, 62 K16
Poplar Pt., 210 L15
Portage la Prairie, 13077 L15
Powerview, 759 K17
Prawda, 114 M18
Princess Hbr., 12 H16
Rapid City, 408 L13
Rathwell, 132 M15
Red Deer Lake, 49 F11
Regent, 3 N13
Reinfeld, 314 N15
Reinland, 256 N15
Rennie, 121 M18
Renwer, 14 H12
Reston, 620 M12
Richer, 434 M17
Riding Mtn., 132 K14
Rivers, 1117 L13
Riverton, 566 K16
Roblin, 1885 J12
Roland, 325 M15
Rorketon, 165 J14
Rosa, 28 N17
Roseisle, 69 M15
Rosenfeld, 276 N16
Rosenort, 358 M16
Ross, 153 M17
Rossburn, 580 K12
Rossendale, 42 M15
Rounthwaite, 7 M13
Russell, 1605 K12
St. Alphonse, 12 M14
St. Ambroise, 229 L15
St. Claude, 609 M15
Ste. Agathe, 477 M16
Ste. Anne, 1511 M17
Ste-Geneviève, 101 M17
Ste. Rita, 68 L17
Ste. Rose du Lac, 1047 K14
St. Eustache, 282 L16
St. François Xavier, 367 L16
St-Georges, 265 K17
St. Jean Baptiste, 515 N16
St. Labre, 65 M18
St-Lazare, 289 L12
St. Leon, 141 M15
St. Malo, 846 M17
St. Martin Jct., 13 H14
St-Pierre-Jolys, 925 M16
San Clara, 89 J11
Sandilands, 78 M17
Sandy Hook, 157 K16
Sandy Lake, 291 L13
Sanford, 484 M16
Selkirk, 9881 L17
Seven Sisters Falls, 152 L18
Shoal Lake, 801 L12
Shortdale, 11 J12
Sidney, 128 M14
Sifton, 182 J13
Silver, 70 K16
Silverton, 15 K12
Sinclair, 40 M12
Skownan, 80 H13
Snowflake, 21 N15
Somerset, 471 M15
Souris, 1613 M13
Southport, 688 L15
Spearhill, 9 J15
Sprague, 179 N18
Springstein, 138 M16
Sprucewoods, 242 M13
Starbuck, 249 M16
Steep Rock, 54 J14
Steinbach, 8478 M17
Stockton, 30 M14
Stonewall, 3689 L16
Stony Mtn., 1744 L16
Strathclair, 377 L13
Stuartburn, 57 N17
Sundown, 54 N17
Swan Lake, 327 M14
Swan River, 3986 H12
Tenby, 7 L14
Teulon, 1055 L16
Thalberg, 10 L17
The Pas, 5945 E12
Thompson, 14385 G6
Tilston, 14 M12
Tolstoi, 8 N17
Toutes Aides, 13 J14
Traverse Bay, 118 K17
Treesbank, 23 M13
Treherne, 675 M14
Valley River, 19 J13
Vassar, 16 N18
Venlaw, 7 J12
Victoria Beach, 196 K17
Virden, 2956 M12
Vista, 3 K12
Vita, 36 N17
Vivian, 50 L17
Vogar, 6 K15
Wanless, 152 D12
Warren, 510 L16
Wasagaming, 166 K13
Waskada, 288 N12
Waterhen, 9 H14
Wawanesa, 485 M13
Wellwood, 62 L14
Westbourne, 65 L15
Westgate, 6 G11
Wheatland, 30 L13
Whitemouth, 316 L18
Whitewater, 2 N13
Winkler, 7241 N15
Winnipeg, 618477 M16
Winnipeg Beach, 746 K16
Winnipegosis, 730 J13
Woodlands, 200 L16
Woodnorth, 11 M12
Woodridge, 160 M17
Zhoda, 24 N17

NEW BRUNSWICK PG. 186

CAPITAL
Fredericton

POPULATION
738,133, rank 8

AREA
28,355 sq mi, rank 11

Cities and Towns

Acadieville, 266 F7
Acton, 275 H5
Allardville, 675 E7
Alma, 312 J8
Anagance, 165 H7
Anse-Bleue, 522 D8
Apohaqui, 376 H7
Aroostook, 397 F4
Arthurette, 217 F4
Astle, 218 G5
Atholville, 1376 C5
Aulac, 64 H9
Back Bay, 559 K5
Baie-Ste-Anne, 1941 E8
Baie Verte, 150 H9
Baker Brook, 629 E2
Balmoral, 1975 D6
Barachois, 783 G9
Barnaby River, 299 F7
Bartibog Bridge, 151 E7
Bas-Caraquet, 1775 D8
Bass River, 250 G8
Bath, 629 G4
Bathurst, 13815 D7
Bay du Vin, 64 E7
Bayfield, 125 H9
Beechwood, 307 F4
Belledune, 2060 D7
Benton, 158 H4
Beresford, 4720 D7
Bertrand, 1379 D8
Berwick, 158 H7
Black River, 166 J6
Black River, 55 F7
Blacks Hbr., 1148 K5
Blackville, 957 F6
Bloomfield, 43 J6
Boiestown, 348 G6
Bonny River, 176 J5
Bouctouche, 2459 G8
Bristol, 707 G4
Burnsville, 160 D8
Burnt Church, 88 E7
Burtts Corner, 910 H5
Cambridge-Narrows, 634 H6
Campbellton, 8404 C5
Canaan Forks, 34 H7
Canterbury, 415 H4
Cap-des-Caissie, 209 G8
Cape Enrage, 12 J8
Cape Tormentine, 89 H10
Cap-Pele, 2242 G9
Caraquet, 4653 D8
Central Blissville, 116 J5
Centreville, 559 G4
Chance Hbr., 179 K5
Charlo, 1610 C6
Chipman, 1518 G6
Clair, 905 E2
Cloverdale, 123 G4
Coal Branch, 69 G7
Codys, 146 H6
Coldstream, 232 G4
Coles Island, 188 H6
Collette, 306 F7
Connors, 85 E2
Cormierville, 399 G8
Cornhill, 127 H7
Cross Creek, 137 G5
Cumberland Bay, 239 H6
Currie, 103 F4
Dalhousie, 4500 C6
Dawsonville, 130 C5
Debec, 237 G4
Dieppe, 12497 H8
Doaktown, 986 G6
Dorchester, 1179 H8
Douglas Hbr., 100 H6
Drummond, 983 E4
Edmundston, 11033 E3
Eel River Crossing, 1446 C6
Elgin, 251 H7
Escuminac, 237 E8
Evandale, 85 J6
Everett, 16 E4
Flatlands, 185 C5
Florenceville, 707 G4
Fosterville, 72 H3
Four Falls, 198 F4
Fredericton, 43507 H5
Fredericton Jct., 736 J5
Gagetown, 660 H6
Gaspereau Forks, 58 G6
Geary, 1084 H5
Glassville, 172 G4
Gondola Pt., 4324 J6
Grafton, 433 G4
Grand Bay-Westfield, 3713 J6
Grande-Anse, 965 D8
Grand Falls, 6133 E4
Grand Manan, 2577 L5
Hammondvale, 137 J7
Hampstead, 89 J6
Hampton, 4081 J6
Hanford Brook, 39 J7
Harcourt, 130 G7
Hardwood Ridge, 191 G6
Hartland, 892 G4
Harvey, 383 H5
Hatfield Pt., 237 J6
Havelock, 351 H7
Hillsborough, 1272 H8
Hopewell Cape, 456 H8
Hoyt, 618 J5
Inkerman, 55 D8
Irishtown, 181 G8
Janeville, 212 D7
Jemseg, 201 H6
Juniper, 438 F4
Kedgwick, 122 D4
Kedgwick River, 11 D4
Kent Jct., 89 F7
Keswick Ridge, 581 H5
Kilburn, 197 F4
Kingston, 689 J6
Kouchibouguac, 257 F8
Lac Baker, 226 E2
Lakeville, 246 G4
Lamèque, 1671 D8
Lavillette, 541 E7
Lepreau, 170 K5
Letete, 165 K5
Lindsay, 177 G4
Little Ridge J4
Longs Creek, 76 H5
Lords Cove, 155 K5
Lorne, 856 D6
Losier Settlement, 329 D8
Lower Hainesville, 243 G4
Lower Jemseg, 79 H6
Ludlow, 152 G6
Maces Bay, 241 K5
Maisonnette, 675 D8
Maltais, 405 D5
Mann Mtn. Settlement, 86 C5
McAdam, 1570 J4
McLean Settlement, 48 G8
Meadow Brook, 120 H8
Mechanic Settlement, 17 H7
Meductic, 236 H4
Melrose, 63 H9
Memramcook, 4904 H8
Menneval, 86 D4
Millerton, 216 F7
Millville, 321 G4
Minto, 3056 H6
Miramichi, 19241 E7
Miscou Ctr., 519 C8
Moncton, 59313 H8
Moores Mills, 176 J4
Nackawic, 1167 H4
Napadogan, 74 G5
Nash Creek, 219 D6
Nashwaak Bridge, 336 G5
Nashwaak Vil., 425 G5
Nauwigewauk, 195 J6
Neguac, 1735 E8
New Bandon, 99 D7
New Canaan, 67 H7
New Maryland, 4284 H5
New Mills, 167 C6
Newtown, 122 H7
Nictau, 26 E4
Nigadoo, 961 D7
N. Esk Boom, 39 F7
Norton, 1390 J7
Notre-Dame, 787 G8
Oak Pt., 102 J6
Oromocto, 9194 H5
Paquetville, 731 D8
Parker Ridge, 97 G5
Parkindale, 49 H8
Penobsquis, 465 H7
Perth-Andover, 1861 F4
Petitcodiac, 1425 H7
Petit Rocher, 2078 D7
Petit Shippagan, 130 D8
Pigeon Hill, 674 D8
Pine Ridge, 13 G8
Plaster Rock, 1220 F4
Pointe-Verte, 1122 D7
Pokeshaw, 114 D7
Pokiok, 91 H4
Pomeroy, 9 J5
Pont-Lafrance, 852 E8
Port Elgin, 445 H9
Price Settlement, 57 E8
Prince of Wales, 116 J6
Quarryville, 218 F7
Quispamsis, 8839 J6
Red Bank, 246 F6
Renous, 600 F6
Rexton, 908 F8
Richibucto, 1414 F8
Riley Brook, 147 E4
River de Chute, 32 F3
Riverside-Albert, 415 H8
Riverview, 16653 H8
Riviere-du-Portage, 789 E8
Rivière-Verte, 929 E3
Robertville, 1251 D7
Robinsonville, 153 D5
Rogersville, 1336 F7
Rosaireville, 85 F7
Rothesay, 1695 J6
Rowena, 83 F4
Sackville, 5393 H9
St. André, 433 E4
St. Andrews, 1752 K4
St-Antoine, 1463 G8
St-Arthur, 877 D5
St-Basile, 3321 E3
St-Charles, 500 F8
St. Croix, 60 J4
Ste-Anne-de-Kent, 495 G8
Ste-Anne-de-Madawaska, 1273 E3
Ste-Marie-de-Kent, 550 G8
St-François-de-Madawaska, 631 E2
St. George, 1414 K5
St. Hilaire E3
St-Ignace, 467 F8
St-Isidore, 912 D8
St-Jacques, 2767 D3
St-Jean-Baptiste-de-Restigouche, 291 D4
Saint John, 72494 J6
St. Leonard, 1450 E3
St-Léonard-Parent, 219 E3
St-Louis de Kent, 1015 F8
St. Margarets, 35 F7
St. Martins, 386 J7
St-Paul, 356 G8
St-Quentin, 2424 D4
St. Stephen, 4961 J4
Salisbury, 1878 H8
Scotch Ridge, 88 J4
Sevogle, 192 E6
Shediac, 4664 G8
Shediac Ridge, 169 F7
Shemogue, 355 G9
Shippagan, 2862 D8
Siegas, 273 E3
Smiths Corner, 28 G7
Somerville, 382 G4
S. Tetagouche, 224 D6
Springfield, 150 H6
Stanley, 426 G5
Stickney, 180 G4
Sunny Corner, 705 F6
Sussex, 4293 H7
Sussex Corner, 1337 H7
Tabusintac, 370 E8
Tay Creek, 84 G5
Taymouth, 321 G5
Thomaston Corner, 45 H4
Three Brooks, 40 F4
Tide Head, 1170 C5
Tracadie-Sheila, 4773 D8
Tracy, 605 H5
Turtle Creek, 103 H8
Tweedside, 158 J5
Upper Blackville, 78 F6
Upper Brockway, 70 J4
Upper Cape, 85 H9
Upper Gagetown, 257 H6
Upper Hainesville, 260 G4
Upper Kent, 295 F4
Upper Woodstock, 244 G4
Waterside, 65 J8
Welsford, 277 J5
W. Quaco, 124 J7
Whites Brook, 103 D4
Wickham, 97 J6
Williamsburg, 277 G5
Wilsons Beach, 525 K5
Windsor, 34 G4
Wishart Pt., 46 E8
Woodstock, 5092 G4
York Mills, 89 H4
Youngs Cove, 111 H6
Zealand, 602 H5

NEWFOUNDLAND PG. 187

CAPITAL
St. John's

POPULATION
551,792, rank 9

AREA
156,649 sq mi, rank 10

Cities and Towns

Admiral's Beach, 255 F19
Argentia, 121 E19
Arnold's Cove, 1115 E19
Badger, 997 D17
Baie Verte, 1708 C17
Bartletts Hbr., 180 B17
Bay de Verde, 594 D20
Bay L'Argent, 377 E18
Bay Roberts, 5472 E19
Bellburns, 114 B16
Belleoram, 564 E18
Big Brook, 29 A17
Birchy Bay, 735 C18
Bishop's Falls, 4048 D18
Bloomfield, 650 D19
Bonavista, 4526 D19
Botwood, 3613 D18
Branch, 351 F19
Brig Bay, 199 B17
Britannia, 85 D19
Buchans, 1056 D17
Buchans Jct., 166 D17
Burgeo, 2098 E16
Burin, 2682 F18
Burnside, 68 D19
Campbellton, 642 C18
Cape Anguille, 107 E15
Carbonear, 5168 E20
Carmanville, 913 C19
Cartwright, 628 E12
Catalina, 1155 D20
Centreville-Wareham-Trinity, 1328 D19
Change Islands, 460 C18
Channel-Port aux Basques, 5243 E15
Churchill Falls, 797 F11
Clarenville, 5335 D19
Coal Brook, 136 E15
Colinet, 208 E19
Come By Chance, 300 E19
Conception Bay South, 19265 E20
Conche, 345 B17
Cook's Hbr., 260 A17
Cottrell's Cove, 93 C18
Corner Brook, 21893 D16
Cow Head, 665 C16
Cox's Cove, 898 C16
Croque, 155 E17
Curzon Vil., 94 C16
Daniel's Hbr., 430 E16
Deadman's Bay, 244 C19
Deer Lake, 5222 D16
Doyles, 92 E15
Eastport, 557 D19
Eddies Cove West, 92 B17
Elliston, 461 D19
Embree, 819 C18
Englee, 827 B17
Ferryland, 667 F20
Flat Bay, 214 D16
Fleur de Lys, 375 C17
Flower's Cove, 354 A17
Fogo, 832 C19
Forteau, 505 A17
Fortune, 1969 F18
Fortune Hbr., 118 C18
Fox Cove-Mortier, 442 F18
Fox Island River, 98 D16
François, 186 E17
Frenchman's Cove, 220 F18
Gambo, 2339 D19
Gander, 10364 D18
Garnish, 691 E18
Glenwood, 893 D18
Glovertown, 2292 D19
Goobies, 99 E19
Goose Cove East, 315 A17
Grand Bank, 3328 F18
Grand Bruit, 65 E15
Grand Falls-Windsor, 14160 D18
Grates Cove, 270 D20
Great Brehat, 138 A18
Great Codroy, 128 E15
Great Hbr. Deep, 196 B17
Grey River, 181 E17
Hampden, 651 C17
Hants Hbr., 519 E19
Happy Valley-Goose Bay, 8655 11
Harbour Breton, 2290 E18
Harbour Grace, 3740 E19
Harbour Mille, 219 E18
Hare Bay, 1224 D19
Harrys Hbr., 188 C17
Hawke's Bay, 514 B17
Heart's Content, 538 E19
Hermitage-Sandyville, 687 E18
Highlands, 131 E15
Holyrood, 2090 E20
Hopedale, 591 E11
Howley, 336 D17
Humber Arm South, 1991 D16
Isle aux Morts, 988 E16
Jackson's Arm, 470 C17
Joe Batt's Arm-Barr'd Islands-Shoal Bay, 1028 C19
King's Cove, 175 D19
Labrador City, 8455 F11
Lamaline, 440 F18
L'Anse aux Meadows, 61 A18
Lark Hbr., 381 D16
La Scie, 1254 C18
Lawn, 95 F18
Lewisporte, 3709 C18
Little Bay Islands, 244 C18
Lourdes, 58 D15
Main Brook, 424 A17
Mainland, 507 D15
Marystown, 6742 F18
Millertown, 134 D17
Monroe, [illegible] D19
Mt. Moriah, 748 D16
Mt. Pearl, 25519 E20
Musgrave Hbr., 1386 C19
Musgravetown, 687 D19
Nain, 96 E11
Nameless Cove, 88 A17
New Ferolle, 119 B17
New-Wes-Valley, 3061 C19
Nippers Hbr., 226 C17
Norris Pt., 50 B16
Northern Bay, 302 E20
Old Perlican, 747 D20
Paradise, 60 E20
Parsons Pond, 530 C16
Pasadena, 445 D16
Peterview, 62 D18
Petit Forte, 114 E18
Pilley's Island, 432 C18
Pinware, 114 A17
Placentia, 013 E19
Pt. Leamington, 783 C18
Port Albert, 122 C18
Port au Choix, 1146 B16
Port Blandford, 603 D19
Portland Creek, 114 C16
Port Rexton, 439 D19
Port Saunders, 876 B16
Portugal Cove-St. Philip's, 5773 F17
Port Union, 542 D19
Pouch Cove, 1885 E20
Rattling Brook, 159 C17
Red Bay, 235 A17
Renews-Cappahayden, 503 F20
River of Ponds, 308 B16
Robert's Arm, 963 C18
Rocky Hbr., 1066 C16
Roddickton, 1103 B17
Rose Blanche-Harbour Le Cou, 814 E16
Round Hbr., 23 C18
St. Alban's, 1563 E18
St. Andrew's, 229 E15
St. Anthony, 2996 A18
St. Barbe, 1[illegible]1 A17
St. Bernard's-Jacques Fontaine, 751 E18
St. Bride's, 42 F19
St. Catherine's E19
St. George's, 1536 D16
St. John's, 101936 E20
St. Julien's, 105 B17
St. Lawrence, 1697 F18
St. Mary's, 617 F19
St. Pauls, 384 C16
St. Shotts, 209 F19
St. Teresa, 127 D16
St. Vincent's-St. Stephen's-Peter's River, 589 F19
Sally's Cove, 53 C16
Seal Cove, 560 C17
Seldom-Little Seldom, 533 C19
Ship Cove, 218 A17
Shoe Cove, 300 C18
Sop's Arm, 327 C17
Southport, 134 E19
Spaniard's Bay, 2771 E19
Springdale, 3381 C18
Stag Hbr., 280 C19
Stephenville, 7764 D16
Stephenville Crossing, 2283 D16
Summerville, 278 D19
Terra Nova, 28 D19
Terrenceville, 737 E18
Torbay, 5230 E20
Traytown, 333 D19
Trepassey, 1084 F19
Trinity East, 190 D19
Trout River, 688 C16
Wabana, 3136 E20
Wabush, 2018 F11
Whitbourne, 988 E19
Windsor Hts., 378 G17
Witless Bay, 1118 E20

NORTHWEST TERRITORIES PG. 177

CAPITAL
Yellowknife

POPULATION
39,672, rank 11

AREA
520,850 sq mi (est.), rank 3

Cities and Towns

Aklavik, 727 B3
Déline, 616 D3
Ft. Good Hope, 644 C3
Ft. Liard, 512 E3
Ft. McPherson, 878 C3
Ft. Providence, 748 E4
Ft. Resolution, 536 E4
Ft. Simpson, 1257 D3
Ft. Smith, 2441 E4
Hay River, 3611 E4
Inuvik, 3296 B3
Norman Wells, 798 C3
Rae-Edzo, 1662 D4
Sachs Hbr., 135 B4
Tsiigehtchic, 162 C3
Tuktoyaktuk, 943 B3
Tulita, 450 D3
Wrigley, 167 D3
Yellowknife, 17275 E4

NOVA SCOTIA PG. 186-187

CAPITAL
Halifax

POPULATION
909,282, rank 7

AREA
21,425 sq mi, rank 12

Cities and Towns

Advocate Hbr., 196 J8
Albany Cross, 12 L8
Aldersville, 112 K8
Allendale, 113 N7
Alma, 370 J11
Alton, 216 K10
Amherst, 9669 H9
Annapolis Royal, 583 L7
Antigonish, 4860 J13
Apple River, 78 J8
Arcadia, 770 N6
Arichat, 886 J14
Arisaig, 103 H12
Aspen, 123 J13
Athol, 68 J9
Aylesford, 1121 K8
Baddeck, 1064 H14
Ballantynes Cove, 30 H13
Bangs Falls, 45 M8
Barrington, 175 N7
Barronsfield, 25 H9
Bass River, 112 J10
Bay St. Lawrence, 154 F15
Bear Cove, 47 M6
Bear River, 881 L7
Beaver River, 286 M6
Bedford, 13638 L10
Belle Côte, 184 G14
Belle-Marche, 290 F14
Ben Eoin, 143 H15
Berwick, 2195 K8
Big Bras d'Or, 314 G15
Big Hbr., 54 G15
Big Pond, 133 H15
Birchtown, 221 N7
Blockhouse, 700 L8
Blue Mtn., 148 J12
Boisdale, 138 H15
Boylston, 167 J13
Brenton, 202 M6
Breton Cove, 49 G15
Bridgetown, 994 K7
Bridgewater, 7351 L8
Brighton, 270 L6
Broad Cove, 186 M8
Brookfield, 917 J10
Brooklyn, 1253 M8
Brooklyn, 610 K9
Brule, 70 H11
Caledonia, 312 L8
Caledonia, 66 J12
Cambridge, 178 K9
Canning, 908 K9
Canso, 1127 J14
Cape George, 153 H13
Capstick, 28 F15
Carleton, 351 M6
Catalone, 312 H16
Central Argyle, 139 N6
Central Grove, 96 L6
Centreville, 286 N7
Centreville, 206 L6
Centreville, 1086 K8
Charleston, 206 M8
Charlesville, 116 N6
Chebogue Pt., 87 N6
Chelsea, 369 L8
Cherry Hill, 166 M8
Chester Basin, 695 L9
Chéticamp, 979 F14
Cheverie, 196 K9
Church Pt., 487 L6
Clam Hbr., 78 L11
Clark's Hbr., 980 N7
Clementsport, 385 L7
Clementsvale, 281 L7
Cleveland, 110 J14
Clyde River, 271 N7
Cole Hbr., 20 J14
Colpton, 89 L8
Comeau's Hill, 107 N6
Comeauville, 300 M6
Conquerall Mills, 548 M8
Corberrie, 96 M6
Craigmore, 60 H13
Creignish, 178 H13
Crescent Beach, 77 M8
Cross Roads Country Hbr., 236 J13
Crowell, 38 N7
Culloden, 119 L6
Dalhousie Road, 66 L8
Darlings Lake, 114 M6
Dartmouth, 65629 L10
Delaps Cove, 65 K7
Denmark, 90 H11
D'Escousse, 232 J14
Digby, 2199 L6
Diligent River, 175 J8
Dingwall, 263 F15
Drum Head, 85 K13
Dundee, 116 H14
Dunvegan, 140 G14
Earltown, 72 J11
E. Bay, 254 H15
E. Dalhousie, 74 L8
E. Earltown, 20 J11
E. Ferry, 98 L6
E. Lake Ainslie, 150 H14
E. Quoddy, 17 K12
E. River St. Marys, 87 J12
Eastville, 32 J11
Economy, 141 J9
Ecum Secum, 182 K12
Elderbank, 206 K11
Elmsdale, 1112 K10
Elmsvale, 170 K11
Enfield, 2588 K10
Englishtown, 139 G15
Erinville, 67 J13
Eskasoni, 2076 H15
Falkland Ridge, 84 L8
Five Islands, 264 J9
Folly Lake, 32 J10
Forties, 333 L8
Fourchu, 6 H15
Fox Pt., 441 L9
Framboise, 44 H15
Frasers Mills, 106 J13
Fraserville, 33 J8
Freeport, 397 L5
Gabarus, 110 H15
Garden of Eden, 59 J12
Georgeville, 52 H12
Glace Bay, 23038 G16
Glencoe, 67 J12
Glenelg, 100 J12
Glenholme, 209 J10
Glenville, 44 G14
Goldboro, 95 K13
Goldenville, 22 K13
Gore, 118 K10
Goshen, 175 J13
Grand Étang, 384 G14
Grand Narrows, 25 H14
Grand River, 72 J15
Granville Ctr., 108 K7
Great Vil., 477 J10
Greenfield, 203 M8
Gunning Cove, 81 N7
Guysborough, 494 J13
Hacketts Cove, 413 L9
Halfway Cove, 85 J14
Halifax, 113910 L10
Hampton, 158 K7
Harbourville, 165 K8
Harmony, 196 J11
Havre Boucher, 481 J13
Hazel Hill, 228 J14
Hebron, 716 M6
Hectanooga, 97 M6
Hemford, 245 L8
Herring Cove, 1923 L10
Hopewell, 487 J11
Indian Brook, 62 G15
Indian Gardens M8
Ingomar, 113 N7
Ingonish, 607 F15
Ingonish Ferry, 47 F15
Inverness, 1785 G14
Iona, 131 H14
Irish Cove, 16 H15
Isaacs Hbr., 114 K13
Italy Cross, 237 M8
Joggins, 491 J8
Johnstown, 29 H15
Jordan Falls, 264 N7
Judique, 444 H13
Kelleys Cove, 115 N6
Kempt, 97 L7
Kemptown, 160 J11
Kemptville, 67 M6
Kennetcook, 372 K10
Kentville, 5551 K8
Ketch Hbr., 252 L10
Kingsport, 270 K9
Kingston, 7806 K8
Kingsville, 27 H14
Kolbec, 109 H9
Lake Charlotte, 225 L11
L'Ardoise, 284 J15
Larrys River, 205 J14
Linden, 83 H9
Liscomb, 104 K13
Lismore, 97 H12
Little Narrows, 128 H14
Little River, 190 L6
Little River Hbr., 150 N6
Liverpool, 3048 M8
Livingstone Cove, 63 H13
Lochaber, 246 J13
Loch Lomond, 41 H15
Lockeport, 692 N7
Londonderry Sta., 129 J10
Lorne, 190 J11
Lorneville, 124 H9
Louisbourg, 1152 H16
Lower E. Pubnico, 181 N6
Lower Economy, 62 J9
Lower Eel Brook, 228 N6
Lower W. Pubnico, 854 N6
Lower Woods Hbr., 494 N6
Lundy, 47 J13
Lunenburg, 2599 L9
Mabou, 412 H13
Mabou Mines, 39 H13
Maccan, 448 H9
Mahone Bay, 1017 L9
Main-à-Dieu, 375 H16
Maitland, 250 J10
Malay Falls, 73 K12
Malignant Cove, 113 H12
Mapleton, 99 J9
Maplewood, 105 L8
Marble Mtn., 53 H14
Margaree Forks, 269 G14
Margaree Hbr., 81 G14
Margaree Valley, 299 G14
Margaretsville, 176 K7
Marie Joseph, 88 K12
Marion Bridge, 315 H15
Mavillette, 288 M6
Meaghers Grant, 208 K11
Meat Cove, 34 F15
Medway, 107 M8
Melford, 44 H14
Melrose, 24 J12
Meteghan, 984 M6
Meteghan River, 553 M6
Meteghan Sta., 280 M6
Middle Clyde River, 2 N7
Middlefield, 81 M8
Middle Musquodoboit, 721 K11
Middle Ohio, 84 M7
Middle River, 114 G14
Middleton, 1800 K7
Militia Pt., 3 H14
Milton, 1770 M8
Minudie, 25 H9
Monastery, 424 J13
Mooseland, 65 K11
Moose River Gold Mines, 19 K11
Morden, 181 K8
Morristown, 264 K8
Morristown, 55 H13
Moser River, 284 K12
Mt. Uniacke, 1359 K9
Mulgrave, 896 J13
Mushaboom, 216 K12
Musquodoboit Hbr., 886 L11
Nappan, 223 H9
Neils Hbr., 248 F15
New Albany, 191 K8
New Edinburgh, 207 L6
New Germany, 892 L8
New Glasgow, 9812 J12
New Hbr., 258 K13
Newport Corner, 437 K9
New Ross, 336 L8
New Salem, 72 J8
Newton Mills, 54 K11
New Tusket, 122 M6
New Waterford, 10713 G16
Nine Mile River, 329 K10
Noel, 84 J10
N. E. Margaree, 164 G14
Northfield, 36 L7
N. Grant, 301 J12
Northport, 117 H9
N. Shore, 38 G15
Ogden, 25 J13
Ohio, [illegible] L6
Ohio, [illegible] J12
Old Barns, 130 J10
Orangedale, 129 H14
Oxford, 1352 H9
Paradise, 318 K7
Parkdale, 79 L8
Parkers Cove, 417 K7
Parrsboro, 1617 J9
Peggys Cove, 120 L9
Pembroke, 74 K9
Petit-de-Grat, 454 J14
Petit Étang, 394 F14
Pictou, 4022 J11
Pinehurst, 222 L8
Pleasant Bay, 334 F14
Pleasant River, 141 L8
Plympton, 208 L6
Pt. Cross, 232 G14
Pt. Michaud, 43 J15
Pomquet, 512 J13
Popes Hbr., 97 K12
Port Bickerton, 282 K13
Port Clyde, 170 N7
Port Dufferin, 7 K12
Port Greville, 98 J8
Port Hastings, 362 J13
Port Hawkesbury, 3809 J14
Port Hood, 835 H13
Port Howe, 99 H10
Port Joli, 92 M8
Port La Tour, 181 N7
Port l'Hébert, 32 N8
Port Maitland, 503 M6
Port Medway, 285 M8
Port Morien, 578 G16
Port Mouton, 290 M8
Port Philip, 38 H10
Port Shoreham, 32 J13
Portuguese Cove, 385 L10
Pubnico, 255 N6
Pugwash, 755 H10
Queensport, 103 J14
Queensville, 53 H14
Quinan, 106 M6
Richfield, 31 M6
River Denys, 107 H14
River Hebert, 773 J9
River John, 411 H11
River Philip, 141 J9
Riverport, 301 M9
Roman Valley, 9 J13
Rossway, 137 L6
Sable River, 102 N7
St. Bernard, 305 L6
St. Pauls, 17 12
St. Peter's, 731 14
Salmon River, 327 M6
Sambro, 405 10
Sandford, 274 M6
Sand Pt., 55 14
Sandy Cove, 129 L6
Sandy Pt., 772 N7
Scots Bay, 177 J9
Scotsburn, 303 J11
Scotsville, 122 G14
Seafoam, 34 H11
Seaforth, 207 L10
Shag Hbr., 227 N6
Sheet Hbr., 828 K12
Shelburne, 2132 N7
Sherbrooke, 397 K13
Ship Hbr., 111 K11
Shubenacadie, 1192 K10
Shunacadie, 44 H15
Skir Dhu, 26 G15
Soldiers Cove, 95 H15
Sonora, 16 K13
Southampton, 244 J9
S. Brookfield, 201 L8
S. Harbour, 291 F15
S. Lake Ainslie, 21 H14
S. Maitland, 166 J10
S. Milford, 36 L7
S. W. Margaree, 188 G14
S. W. Port Mouton, 232 M8
Spanish Ship Bay, 102 K12
Springfield, 194 L8
Springhill, 4193 J9
Spry Hbr., 177 K12
Stellarton, 4968 J12
Stewiacke, 1405 K10
Stewiacke Cross Roads, 65 K11
Stillwater, 79 K13
Stormont, 50 K13
Strathlorne, 170 G14
Streets Ridge, 62 H10
Sunny Brae, 183 J12
Sydney, 34871 G15
Sydney Mines, 17294 G15
Tangier, 111 K11
Tatamagouche, 726 H11
Terence Bay, 906 L10
The Lookoff, 41 K8
Three Mile Plains, 1295 K9
Tiverton, 26 L5
Toney River, 112 H11
Trafalgar, 2 J12
Trenton, 2952 J12
Truro, 11938 J10
Tusket, 395 M6
Upper Musquodoboit, 434 K11
Upper Ohio, 10 M7
Upper Rawdon, 323 K10
Upper Stewiacke, 137 K11
Victoria Bridge, 22 H15
Victoria Hbr., 112 K8
Wallace, 248 H10
Walton, 228 K9
Watt Section, 209 K12
Waverley, 1925 L10
Wedgeport, 239 N6
Welsford, 161 H11
W. Bay, 132 H14
W. Brook, 28 J9
Westchester Sta., 199 J10
W. Dalhousie, 200 L7
W. Dover, 275 L9
Western Head, 236 M8
Western Shore, 1017 L9
W. Jeddore, 55 L11
W. LaHave, 257 M8
W. Mabou Hbr., 74 H13
Westport, 32 M5
Westville, 3976 J11
Weymouth, 330 L6
Whitehead, [illegible] J14
White Pt., 192 M8
Whites Lake, 980 L10
Whycocomagh, 349 H14
Wilmot, 640 K8
Windsor, 3725 K9
Windsor Forks, 309 K9
Windsor Road, 418 L9
Wine Hbr., 16 K13
Wolfville, 3833 K9
Wreck Cove, 2 G15
Yarmouth, 7568 N6

NUNAVUT PG. 186-187

CAPITAL
Iqaluit

POPULATION
24,730, rank 13

AREA
800,775 sq mi (est.), rank

Cities and Towns

Arctic Bay, 639 B7
Arviat, 1559 E6
Baker Lake, 1385 D6
Cambridge Bay, 1351 C5
Cape Dorset, 1113 D8
Chesterfield Inlet, 337 E7
Gjoa Haven, 879 C6
Igloolik, 1174 C8
Iqaluit, 4220 D9
Kugluktuk, 1201 C4
Pangnirtung, 1243 C9
Pond Inlet, 1154 B8
Rankin Inlet, 2058 E7
Repulse Bay, 559 D7
Resolute, 98 B6
Sanikiluaq, 631 F9
Taloyoak, 648 C6

ONTARIO PG. 182-183

CAPITAL
Toronto

POPULATION
10,753,573, rank 1

AREA
412,573 sq mi, rank 4

Cities and Towns

Actinolite, 119 F15
Acton, 7632 J9
Addison, 104 F18
Ailsa Craig, 1044 K6
Ajax, 64430 H12
Alexandria, 3531 D20
Alfred, 1228 C19
Algoma Mills, 198 B4
Algonquin, 158 F18
Allan Park, 69 G8
Allenford, 345 F7
Alliston, 8225 H10
Almonte, 4611 D17
Alton, 955 H9
Alvinston, 1037 L6
Amherstburg, 10245 N3
Angus, 9723 G10
Appin, 244 L6
Apple Hill, 256 D20
Appleton, 205 E17
Apsley, 331 F13
Arden, 239 F16
Argyle, 92 G12
Ariss, 125 J9
Arkell, 126 J9
Arkona, 560 K6
Arnprior, 7113 D17
Aroland, 271 A16
Arthur, 2139 H8
Astorville, 350 B11
Athens, 997 F17
Atikokan, 3900 B13
Atwood, 877 J7
Auburn, 244 H6
Aurora, 34857 H11
Avening, 70 G9
Avonmore, 585 D19
Aylmer, 7018 L8
Ayr, 3151 K9
Ayton, 606 H8
Baden, 62 K8
Bailieboro, 294 H13
Bala, 490 E10
Balderson, 63 E17
Baldwin, 400 G11
Ballinafad, 320 J9
Baltimore, 26 H13
Bancroft, 2554 E14
Bannockburn, 34 F14
Barrie, 79191 G10
Barrow Bay, 86 E7
Barry's Bay, 1186 D14
Batawa, 274 G14
Bath, 1389 G16
Battersea, 309 G17
Baxter, 320 G10
Bayfield, 833 J6
Bayside, 56 H14
Baysville, 315 E11
Beachburg, 902 C16
Beamsville, 7689 K11
Beardmore, 440 A15
Beaverton, 3009 G11
Beeton, 2886 H10
Belgrave, 437 H7
Belle River, 4531 M4
Belleville, 37083 G15
Belmore, 126 H7
Belwood, 304 J9
Bent River, 87 E10
Berkeley, 158 G8
Bervie, 95 H7
Bethany, 603 G12
Bewdley, 825 H13
Big Chute, 116 F10
Birch Island, 10 B6
Birds Creek, 468 E14
Bishops Mills, 82 E18
Blacks Corners, 117 E17
Blackwater, 79 G11
Blenheim, 4873 M5
Blind River, 3152 B4
Bloomfield, 687 H15
Bluevale, 174 H7
Blyth, 991 J7
Blytheswood, 8 N4
Bobcaygeon, 2753 F12
Bognor, 118 F8
Bolsover, 71 F11
Bolton, 10569 H10
Booth's Hbr., 11 L9
Bothwell, 990 M6
Bourget, 970 D19
Bowmanville, 27594 H12
Bracebridge, 13223 E11
Bradford, 14865 H10
Braeside, 715 D16
Brampton, 268251 J10
Brantford, 84764 K9
Bridgenorth, 1671 G13
Bright, 323 K8
Brighton, 4584 H14
Brinston, 151 E19
Brisbane, 240 J9
Britt, 19 C8
Brockville, 21752 F18
Brodhagen, 136 J7
Brooke, 991 F8
Brooklin, 2063 H12
Brucefield, 212 J6
Bruce Mines, 653 B2
Brudenell, 61 D15
Brunner, 202 J8
Brussels, 1131 J7
Buckhorn, 69 F13
Burgessville, 483 L8
Burk's Falls, 946 D11
Burleigh Falls, 38 F13
Burlington, 136976 K10
Burnstown, 83 D16
Burritts Rapids, 82 E18
Byng Inlet, 10 C8
Cache Bay, 64 B9
Calabogie, 180 D16
Caledonia, 7033 K10
Caledon Vil., 1265 H9
Cambridge, 101429 K9
Camilla, 110 H9
Camlachie, 208 K5
Campbellford, 3647 G14
Canfield, 160 L10
Cannington, 2018 G12
Capreol, 3410 A8
Caramat, 168 A16
Cardiff, 542 E13
Cardinal, 1777 F18
Cargill, 146 G7
Carleton Place, 3450 E17
Carnarvon, 126 E12
Carp, 443 D17
Carrying Place, 76 H14
Cartier, 472 A7
Casselman, 2877 D19
Castleton, 356 H14
Cataract, 111 H9
Cayuga, 1015 L10
Cedar Acres, 16 D18
Cedar Sprs., 34 N5
Centreville, 195 G16
Chalk River, 974 B14
Chapleau, 2934 C18
Charing Cross, 481 M5
Charlton, 297 B20
Chatham, 43409 M5
Chatsworth, 522 G8
Cheney, 106 D19
Chepstow, 219 G7
Cherry Valley, 342 H15
Chesley, 1904 G7
Chesterville, 1497 E19
Clarence Creek, 442 D19
Clarksburg, 769 F9
Clifford, 775 H8
Clinton, 3216 J6
Cloyne, 78 F15
Cobalt, 1401 C20
Cobden, 1020 C16
Coboconk, 423 F12
Cobourg, 16027 H13
Cochrane, 4443 A19
Coe Hill, 56 F14
Colborne, 2054 H14
Colchester, 1960 N4
Cold Sprs., 189 H13
Coldwater, 1254 F10
Collingwood, 15596 G9
Comber, 1480 N4
Combermere, 236 E14
Commanda, 60 C10
Conestogo, 692 J8
Conn, 125 H8
Consecon, 353 H14
Cookstown, 1466 G10
Corbeil, 309 B11
Corbett, 55 K6
Corbetton, 91 H9
Cordova Mines, 1 1 F14
Corinth, 203 L8
Cornwall, 47403 E20
Cottam, 723 M4
Courtland, 917 L8
Courtright, 1046 L5
Craighurst, 90 F10
Creemore, 1285 G9
Creighton, 140 A7
Crow Lake, 81 F16
Crysler, 555 D19
Crystal Beach, 6321 L12
Crystal Falls, 136 A10
Curran, 261 D19
Curries, 55 K8
Dacre, 52 D15
Dalkeith, 69 D20
Dalrymple, 53 F11
Damascus, 118 H8
Dashwood, 171 K6
Deacon, 110 D15
Dealtown, 282 N5
Deep River, 4491 B14
Delhi, 4155 L8
Delmer, 132 L8
Deloro, 183 F14
Delta, 55 F17
Denbigh, 151 E15
Denfield, 111 K7
Desbarats, 298 B2
Desboro, 85 G8
Deseronto, 1811 G15
Devlin, 678 B12
Dicksons Corners, 58 K8
Dobbinton, 53 G7
Domville, 258 F18
Dorset, 261 E12
Douglas, 273 D15
Dover Ctr., 69 M5
Dowling, 1979 A7
Drayton, 1427 J8
Dresden, 2589 M5
Driftwood, 44 A19
Drumbo, 531 K8
Dryden, 6711 A12
Duart, 121 M6
Dublin, 255 J7
Dunbar, 77 E19
Dunchurch, 427 D10
Dundalk, 1776 G9
Dunedin, 76 G9
Dungannon, 239 H6
Dunnville, 12471 L10
Dunsford, 201 G12
Dunvegan, 117 D19
Durham, 2641 G8
Dutton, 1315 L6
Dyer Bay, 49 E7
Eagle, 56 M6
Eagle Lake, 246 E12
Earlton, 911 C20
E. Linton, 135 F8
Echo Bay, 793 A2
Edgar, 102 G10
Edgewater Beach, 120 M3
Eganville, 1319 D15
Elizabethville, 95 H13
Elliot Lake, 13588 A4
Elmira, 7497 J8
Elmvale, 860 F10
Elmwood, 364 G7
Elora, 3346 J8
Elphin, 57 E16
Embro, 338 K8
Embrun, 3946 D19
Emsdale, 202 D11
Englehart, 1703 B20
Enniskillen, 168 H12
Ennismore, 366 G13
Enterprise, 371 G16
Erieau, 499 N5
Erie Beach, 251 N5
Erin, 2633 J9
Erinsville, 98 G15
Escott, 68 G17
Espanola, 5454 B6
Essex, 6785 N4
Estaire, 117 B8
Ethel, 216 J7
Etobicoke, 328718 J10
Eugenia, 168 G8
Evansville, 81 C5
Exeter, 4472 K7
Fairground, 149 M8
Fenelon Falls, 2040 F12
Fergus, 8884 J9
Ferndale, 57 E7
Feversham, 138 G9
Field, 145 A9
Finch, 456 E19
Fishers Glen, 54 L9
Fisherville, 288 L10
Flesherton, 625 G8
Flinton, 216 F15
Florence, 184 M5
Foleyet, 381 B18
Fordwich, 510 H7
Forest, 3020 K6
Foresters Falls, 169 C16
Formosa, 443 H7
Ft. Erie, 27183 L12
Ft. Frances, 8790 B12
Ft. Irwin, 143 E13
Foxboro, 1150 G15
Foymount, 114 D15
Frankford, 2096 G14
Fraserville, 225 G13
French River B8
Gananoque, 5219 G17
Gelert, 90 E12
Georgetown, 26193 J10
Geraldton, 2627 A16
Gilmour, 121 F14
Glammis, 92 G7
Glen Allen, 123 J8
Glencairn, 152 G9
Glencoe, 2178 L6
Glen Orchard, 122 E10
Glen Robertson, 494 D20
Glen Tay, 178 E17
Gloucester, 104022 D18
Goderich, 7553 J6
Gogama, 596 C19
Golden Lake, 197 D15
Golden Valley, 100 C10
Gooderham, 503 E13
Gore Bay, 907 C5
Gorrie, 446 H7
Gowanstown, 224 J8
Gowganda, 103 C19
Grafton, 134 H14
Grand Bend, 1027 K6
Grande Pointe, 186 M5
Grand Valley, 1611 H9
Granton, 328 K7
Gravenhurst, 10030 E11
Greenbank, 105 H12
Green Lane, 133 C20
Greens Corner, 177 L9
Green Valley, 479 D20
Griffith, 131 D15
Grimsby, 9585 K10
Gros Cap, 516 A1
Guelph, 95821 J9
Guthrie, 131 G10
Hagar, 86 A9
Hagersville, 2364 L9
Haley Sta., 92 D16
Haliburton, 1434 E12
Hallville, 149 E18
Hamilton, 467799 K10
Hampton, 745 H12
Hanover, 6844 H7
Harcourt, 32 E13
Hardwood Lake, 50 E15
Harrington, 117 K7
Harriston, 2008 H8
Harrow, 2806 N4
Harrowsmith, 696 G16
Harwood, 139 H13
Hastings, 1140 G14
Havelock, 1352 G14
Hawkesbury, 10162 C20
Hawkestone, 188 G11
Hearst, 6049 A17
Heathcote, 117 G8
Hensall, 1187 J7
Hepworth, 470 F7
Heyden, 204 A1
Hickson, 246 K8
Highgate, 446 M6
Highland Grove, 173 E13
Hillsburgh, 1164 H9
Hillsdale, 523 F10
Hilton, 158 F14
Hilton Beach, 213 B2
Holland Ctr., 256 G8
Holmesville, 84 J6
Holstein, 272 H8
Honeywood, 162 G9
Hope Bay, 126 E7
Hopetown, 39 E16
Hornepayne, 1458 A17
Horning's Mills, 287 H9
Horseshoe Lake, 136 D10
Hotham, 59 B10
Houghton Ctr., 53 M8
Hudson, 450 A13
Huntingford, 93 K8
Huntsville, 15918 D11
Hurkett, 145 B15
Huron Park, 969 K7
Hyde Park, 164 L7
Hyndford, 60 D15
Ilderton, 681 K7
Ingersoll, 9849 L8
Ingleside, 1894 E19
Inglewood, 309 H10
Ingoldsby, 140 E12
Innisville, 71 E17
Inverary, 590 G16
Inverhuron, 451 G6
Inwood, 215 L6
Iona Sta., 76 L7
Iron Bridge, 777 B3
Irondale, 75 F12
Iroquois, 1278 E19
Iroquois Falls, 5714 B19
Ivanhoe, 30 G15
Jaffray Melick, 4244 A12
Janetville, 566 G12
Jarvis, 1710 L9
Jasper, 209 E17
Jeannettes Creek, 244 M5
Jellicoe, 125 A15
Johnstown, 862 F18
Kaladar, 224 F15
Kanata, 56247 D17
Kapuskasing, 10036 A18
Kars, 1575 E18
Kashabowie, 26 B14
Katrine, 98 D11
Kearney, 837 D11
Keewatin, 2058 A11
Kelvin, 119 L8
Kemble, 73 F8
Kemptville, 3272 E18
Kenilworth, 101 H8
Kenora, 10063 A11
Kent Bridge, 76 M5
Kentvale, 9 B2
Keswick, 17068 G11
Killaloe, 669 D15
Kilsyth, 183 G7
Kimberley, 144 G8
Kincardine, 6620 G6
Kingston, 55947 G16
Kingsville, 5991 N4
Kinlough, 57 H7
Kinmount, 197 F12
Kintore, 136 K7
Kippen, 66 J6
Kirkfield, 101 F12
Kirkland Lake, 9905 B20
Kirkton, 226 K7
Kitchener, 178420 J8
Kitigan, 106 A18
Komoka, 1060 L7
Kurtzville, 101 H8
Lafontaine, 207 F9
Lakefield, 2444 G13
Lake Park, 95 E17
Lake St. Peter, 281 E13
L'Amable, 315 E14
Lanark, 865 E17
Lancaster, 825 D20
Langton, 437 L8
Lansdowne, 426 G17
La Passe, 97 C16
La Salle, 20566 N3
Latchford, 338 C20
Leamington, 16188 N4
Lefaivre, 334 C19
Leith, 137 F8
Limoges, 1236 D19
Lindsay, 17638 G12
Linwood, 695 J8
Lion's Head, 580 E7
Lisle, 413 G9
Listowel, 5467 J8
Little Britain, 402 G12
Little Current, 1575 C6
Lively, 6890 A7
Lombardy, 51 F17
Londesborough, 186 J7
London, 325646 L7
Long Beach, 121 L11
Longlac, 2074 A16
Long Pt., 360 M9
Long Sault, 1509 E19
Loretto, 781 H10
L'Orignal, 1959 C20
Loring, 318 C9
Lorneville, 32 G12
Louisville, 99 M5
Lucan, 1958 K7
Lucknow, 1215 H6
Luton, 90 L8
Lyn, 57 F18
Lyndale, 113 L7
Lyndhurst, 215 F17
Lyons, 87 L8
Maberly, 7 F16
MacTier, 614 E10
Madawaska, 308 D14
Madoc, 1464 F15
Magnetawan, 241 C10
Maidstone, 864 N4
Maitland, 465 F18
Mallorytown, 510 F18
Manilla, 443 G12
Manitouwadge, 3395 B16
Manitowaning, 442 C6
Mar, [illegible] F7
Marathon, 4791 B16
Markdale, 1354 G8
Markham, 173383 H11
Markstay, 440 A8
Marlbank, 133 G15
Marmora, 1483 G14
Marsville, 1 3 H9
Marten River A10
Martintown, 531 E20
Marysville, 124 G15
Massey, 1171 B6
Matachewan, 453 B19
Matheson, 984 B19
Mattawa, 2281 B12
Maxville, 885 D19
Maynard, 205 F18
Maynooth, 135 E14
McArthurs Mills, 91 E14
McDonalds Corners, 98 E16
McGregor, 312 N3
M'Chigeeng, 34 C5
McKellar, 73 D10
McKerrow, 269 B6
Meaford, 4681 F8
Melbourne, 433 L6
Meldrum Bay, 43 C4
Merlin, 723 N5
Merrickville, 1027 E18
Metcalfe, 1536 D18
Micksburg, 54 C15
Middlemiss, 64 L6
Middleport, 65 K9
Middleville, 67 E16
Midland, 15035 F10
Mildmay, 1110 H7
Milford, 178 H15
Milford Bay, 226 E11
Millbrook, 1312 G13
Miller Lake, 189 E7
Millhaven, 223 G16
Milton, 2104 J10
Milverton, 1618 J8
Minaki, 128 A11
Mindemoya, 392 C5
Minden, 1111 E12
Mine Ctr., 103 B12
Minesing, 336 G10
Mississauga, 544382 J10
Mitchell, 3670 J7
Mitchell's Bay, 223 M5
Molesworth, 95 J7
Monetville, 19 B9
Monkland, 59 E19
Monkton, 541 J7
Mono Mills, 696 H9
Montreal River Hbr., 53 E17
Moorefield, 296 J8
Moose Creek, 494 E19
Moosonee, 1939 H9
Morewood, 254 E19
Morpeth, 269 M6
Morrisburg, 2588 E19
Morriston, 267 J9
Mountain, 132 E18
Mtn. Grove, 114 F16
Mt. Albert, 2158 H11
Mt. Brydges, 2229 L7
Mt. Elgin, 246 L8
Mt. Forest, 4530 H8
Mt. Pleasant, 676 L9
Mt. Pleasant, 235 G13
Mt. Salem, 340 L8
Muskoka Falls, 137 E11
Nairn, 33 K6
Nakina, 654 A16
Nanticoke, 23485 L9
Napanee, 5450 G16
Nellies Corners, 71 L10
Neustadt, 568 H7
Newboro, 291 F17
Newburgh, 729 G16
Newbury, 430 M6
New Dundee, 1082 K8
New Hamburg, 6494 K8
Newholm, 30 E11
New Liskeard, 5112 C20
New Lowell, 448 G9
Newmarket, 57125 H11
Newry, 81 J7
Niagara Falls, 78917 K11
Niagara-on-the-Lake, 13238 K11
Nile, 107 H6
Nipigon, 2110 B15
Nixon, 103 L9
Nobel, 462 D8
Nobleton, 1177 H10
Noelville, 572 B8
Norham, 116 G14
Norland, 310 F12
N. Augusta, 218 F18
N. Bay, 54332 B11
Northbrook, 329 F15
N. Buxton, 10 M5
N. Lancaster, 140 D20
N. York, 589653 H11
Norwich, 2 60 L8
Norwood, 1369 G14
Nottawa, 512 G9
Novar, 300 D11
Oakdale, 6 L5
Oakville, 128405 J10
Oakwood, 35 G12
Odessa, 1102 G16
Oil City, 26 L5
Oil Sprs., 733 L5
Oliphant, 3 0 F7
Omemee, 1171 G12
Ompah, 12 E16
Onaping, 2 02 A7
Opasatika, 352 A18
Ophir, 15 A2
Orangeville, 21498 H9
Orillia, 27846 F11
Ormond, 19 E18
Orono, 165 H12
Orr Sta., 14 G10
Orr Lake, 92 F10
Orrville, 139 D10
Oshawa, 139364 H12
Ottawa, 721136 D18
Otterville, 853 L8
Owen Sound, 21390 F8
Oxford Mills, 166 E18
Oxtongue Lake, 169 D12
Pain Court, 398 M5
Paisley, 1103 G7
Pakenham, 406 D17
Palmer Rapids, 284 D14
Palmerston, 2468 H8
Parham, 17 F16
Paris, 8987 K9

PRINCE EDWARD ISLAND
PG. 186-187

CAPITAL
Charlottetown

POPULATION
134,557, rank 10

AREA
2,185 sq mi, rank 13

Cities and Towns

QUEBEC
PG. 184-186

CAPITAL
Québec

POPULATION
7,138,795, rank 2

AREA
594,857 sq mi, rank 2

Cities and Towns

Crazy Horse Memorial, South Dakota

SASKATCHEWAN
PG. 180-181

CAPITAL
Regina

POPULATION
990,237, rank 6

AREA
251,865 sq mi, rank 7

Cities and Towns

YUKON TERRITORY
PG. 177

CAPITAL
Whitehorse

POPULATION
30,766, rank 12

AREA
186,660 sq mi, rank 9

Cities and Towns

Mexico

MEXICO
PG. 188-189

CAPITAL
México

POPULATION
95,772,462

AREA
756,066 sq mi

Cities and Towns

Puerto Rico

PUERTO RICO PG. 190

CAPITAL
San Juan

POPULATION
3,808,610

AREA
3,435 sq mi

Cities and Towns

Points of Interest

Salt Lake City, Utah

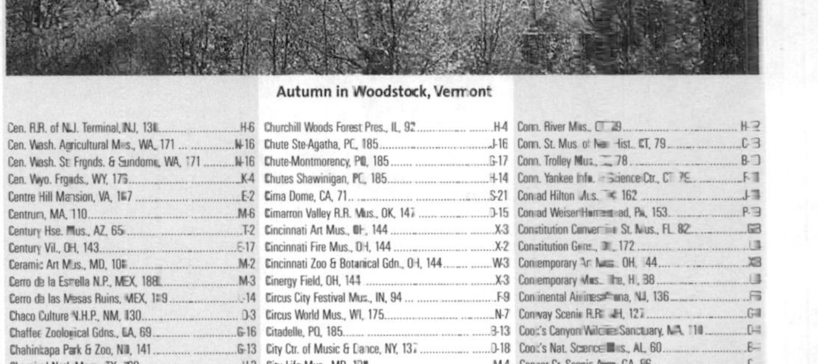

Autumn in Woodstock, Vermont

Marby Mill, Virginia

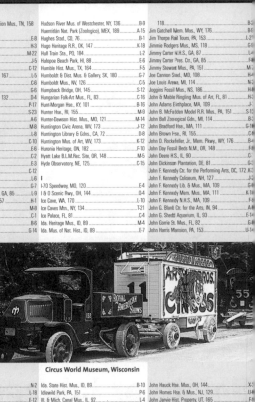

Circus World Museum, Wisconsin

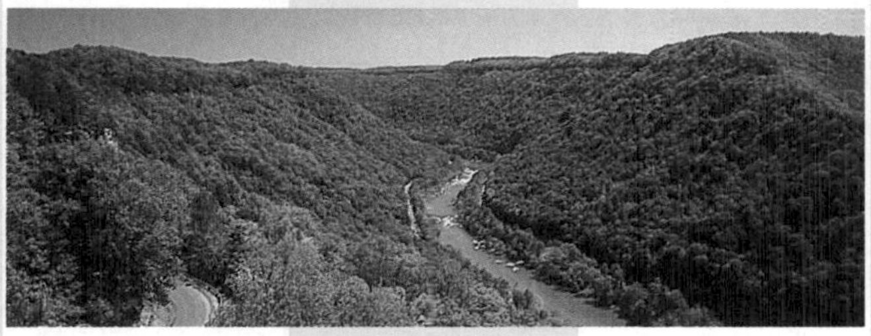

New River Gorge, West Virginia

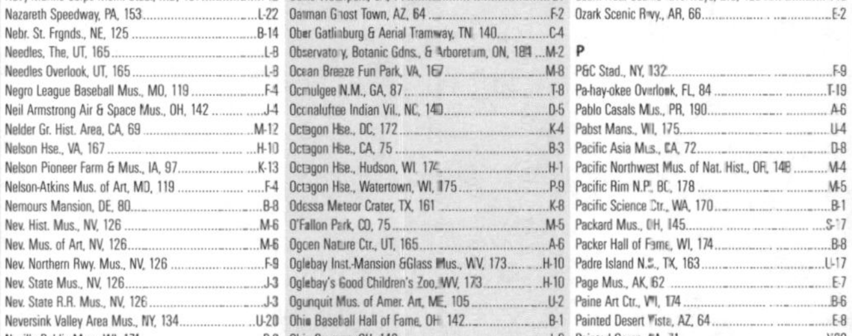

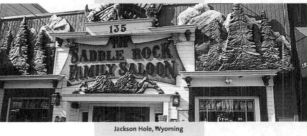

Jackson Hole, Wyoming

Mayan Ruins at Chichen Itza, Yucatan, Mexico

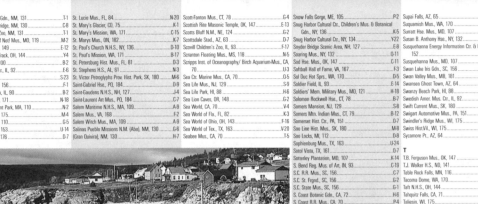

Cape Breton Island, Nova Scotia, Canada

Hanauma Bay, Oahu, Hawaii

Photo Credits:

Cover:
Stone/Getty Images: Tom Bean (top left); **Reader's Digest** (bottom left); **The Stock Market** Paul Endress (Back cover & spine), John Feingersh (bottom right).

A. B. Sheldon Nature Photography: 227 (center); **Bob Peak Photography:** 227 (top); **©Corbis:** 33 (bottom top left); Tony Arruza: 35 (top left); Craig Aurness: 200 (bottom center), 217 (center); Tom Bean: 208 (bottom), 219 (top); Gary Braasch: 224 (top); Jan Butchofsky-Houser: 34 (left); Leslie & Mark Degner: 194 (bottom); Ric Ergenbright: 217 (bottom), 218 (top), 223 (bottom); Kevin Fleming: 10 (top left), 35 (bottom top); Todd Gipstein: 45 (top right); Philip Gould: 26 (top left); Farrell Grehan: 46 (top left); Dan Guravich: 219 (center); Dave G. Houser: 11 (top right center), 22 (top right), 224 (bottom); Liz Hymans: 206 (bottom center); Michael S. Lewis: 206 (top center), 227 (bottom); Charles Mauzy: 210 (bottom); Buddy Mays: 26 (right center), 202 (bottom center), 217 (top); Kevin R. Morris: 22 (top left), 23 (top left & top center); David Muench: 19 (top center), 22 (bottom), 26 (left center), 35 (top center), 198 (top), 204 (top), 210 (top), 220 (top); Pat O'Hara: 11 (top center), 226 (top); Douglas Peebles: 10 (top right); Carl & Ann Purcell: 27 (top center); James Randklev: 220 (center); Jim Richardson: 220 (bottom); David Sailors: 34 (center); Scott T. Smith: 196 (bottom); Joseph Sohm/ChromoSohm Inc.: 226 (bottom); Paul A. Souders: 204 (bottom center); Tim Thompson: 53 (top center); Craig Tuttle: 224 (center); Kennan Ward: 10 (top center); Tim Wright: 218 (center); **Victor Englebert:** 52 (bottom right); **FOLIO, Inc.:** 194 (top center); Linda Bartlett: 47 (top left); Walter Bibikow: 21 (bottom), 23 (top right), 43 (bottom top); 47 (bottom), 54 (right), 229 (top); Skip Brown: 33 (top left); Walter P. Calahan: 30 (top left); John Coletti: 250; Richard Cummins: 13 (bottom), 16 (center), 17 (center), 18, 31 (bottom center & bottom right), 44 (top left), 243 (bottom); Cameron Davidson: 41 (bottom left); Claudia Dhimitri: 35 (top right), 236 (top); Steve Dunwell: 45 (bottom & bottom top), 242 (bottom); David Falconer: 12 (bottom left), 21 (top center), 32 (top left), 198 (bottom), 228 (bottom), 247; David R. Frazier Photolibrary: 12 (top left), 228 (top); Mark E. Gibson: 10 (bottom), 15 (left), 37 (left); Alan Goldstein: 43 (top center); Jeff Greenberg: 11 (top), 21 (top right), 43 (top), 240 (top); Brigitta L. House: 200 (bottom); Everett C. Johnson: 29 (top left center), 229 (bottom), 240 (bottom); James LeMass: 30 (center); Fredde Lieberman: 28 (bottom left); Robert Madden: 19 (top right); Fred Maroon: 19 (top left), 246 (top); Jerry Mesmer: 37 (right); Al Messerschmidt: (bottom); Richard T. Nowitz: 239 (top), 253 (top); John Skowronski: 40 (bottom top), 241 (top); Pete Souza: 41 (top & top center); Catherine Ursillo: 47 (top right), 238 (top); Michael Ventura: 33 (top), 202 (top); **Scott Humphries/Digitally Correct:** 51 (left center & right center); **ImageState, Inc.:** John Gnass: 13 (top right); **International Stock:** 56, 221 (bottom), 223 (top); **James P. Rowan Photography:** 12 (top right & bottom right), 14 (top & center), 16 (top), 20 (top center), 21 (top left), 23 (right center), 24, 25 (top right center, top right & left center), 26 (top right), 28 (top left & bottom right), 29 (top left & top right), 32 (bottom), 38 (left), 39 (bottom right), 40 (top), 41 (bottom right), 42 (bottom right), 218 (bottom), 222 (top & bottom), 234 (bottom), 238 (bottom), 239 (bottom), 242 (top), 244 (top), 245 (bottom), 246 (bottom), 252 (top); **Jerry L. Whaley Photography, Inc.:** 225 (center); **Calvin Larsen/Affordable Photo Stock:** 226 (center); **Robert Holmes Photography:** 2-3, 13 (top center), 14 (bottom), 15 (right), 17 (right) 25 (top left center), 26 (bottom center), 30 (top right), 36 (top left), 46 (top right & bottom), 47 (top center & bottom top), 48 (right), 49 (top right center & center), 50 (center), 51 (bottom top right), 52 (bottom left center), 53 (right center), 54 (top & left), 55 (top), 194 (top & bottom center), 202 (top center), 204 (bottom), 208 (top), 219 (bottom), 221 (center), 222 (center), 225 (top), 234 (top), 235 (bottom), 237, 241 (bottom), 243 (top), 244 (bottom), 245 (top), 251 (bottom), 254; Ben Davidson: 52 (bottom left), 232 (top); Dewitt Jones: 20 (top left), 200 (top center), 206 (top), 251 (top); Brian McGilloway: 16 (bottom), 20 (bottom), 52 (bottom right center), 53 (top left), 210 (top center), 233 (top), 253 (bottom); **Scott T. Smith:** 225 (bottom); **Michael C. Snell/Shade of the Cottonwood:** 26 (top center); **SuperStock:** 4, 19 (center), 25 (top left), 31 (top left), 39 (top right), 55 (bottom), 198 (top center), 216 (bottom), 223 (center); Gene Ahrens: 44 (center); Tom Algire: 5; Ping Amranand: 39 (bottom top right); Alan Briere: 36 (top right); David Forbert: 38 (right), 39 (top left); Gala: 39 (bottom left), 48 (left); Anne Gransden: 198 (bottom center); George Hunter: 51 (bottom); Tim Hursley: 31 (top center), 33 (bottom left); Dale Jorgensen: 11 (bottom right center); Hubertus Kanus: 37 (center); Ann B. Keiser: 50 (top left); Henry Lehn: 202 (bottom); Herb Levart: 42 (top center); D. C. Lowe: 13 (top left); Malak: 50 (top right); Ernest Manewal: 196 (top), 216 (center); Joanna McCarthy: 206 (bottom); Larry Prosor: 221 (top); Mick Roessler: 53 (top left center); Yoshio Tomii: 22 (top right); Steve Vidler: 49 (bottom); **Tom Till Photography:** 8-9, 12 (center), 17 (left), 20 (top right), 23 (left center), 25 (right center), 27 (top left), 28 (top right), 31 (top right & bottom left), 32 (top right), 33 (top right & bottom right), 34 (right), 35 (bottom center), 36 (top center & bottom), 39 (top center), 40 (top center), 42 (top left), 44 (top right), 45 (top left), 49 (top), 192-193, 196 (top center & bottom center), 200 (top), 204 (top center), 208 (top center & bottom center), 210 (bottom center), 214-215, 216 (top), 232 (bottom), 233 (bottom), 235 (top), 236 (bottom), 249, 252 (bottom); **David Yanko/VIRTUALSK.COM:** 51 (top left).

READER'S DIGEST HOME AND HEALTH PUBLISHING
Editor-in-Chief: Neil Wertheimer
Art Director: Michele Laseau
Marketing Director: Dawn Nelson
Vice President and General Manager: Keira Krausz

Reader's Digest is a registered trademark of The Reader's Digest Association, Inc.

Library of Congress Cataloging in Publication Data: Has been applied for

ISBN: 0-7621-0430-9

Address any comments about The Money Savers Travel Atlas to:
The Reader's Digest Association, Inc.
Editor-in-Chief,
Home and Health Publishing
Reader's Digest Road
Pleasantville, NY 10570-7000

rd.com
For more Reader's Digest products and information, visit our website at RD.com

FOR MOBIL TRAVEL GUIDE
Research Editor: Brenda McLean
Research Editor: Nancy Swope
Publishing Coordinator: Shawn Viane
Vice President: Jeff Harris

FOR PUBLICATIONS INTERNATIONAL, LTD.
Senior Art Director: John Hansen
Production Editor: Holli Phend
Electronic Publishing Specialist: Michael Anderson
Publications Coordinator: Julie Greene
Director, Database Development: Pat Hagle

This edition published by The Reader's Digest Association by arrangement with Mobil Travel Guide and Publications International, Ltd.

FOR READER'S DIGEST
Senior Editor: Nancy Shuker
Senior Design Director: Elizabeth Tunnicliffe

Printed in China

1 3 5 7 9 10 8 6 4 2

STATE PARK NAME	LOCATION	TELEPHONE	SEASON	HOURS	Strollers	Wheelchairs	Handicapped Access	Picnic Area	Food service	Kiddie Area/Rides	Live Entertainment	Adult One-Day Ticket*
Alaska												
Pioneer Park	Airport Way & Peger Rd., Fairbanks	907/459-1087	Mem. Day-Labor Day	11 am-9 pm		X	X	X	X	X	X	¢
Arizona												
Old Tuscon Studios	201 S. Kinney Rd., Tucson	520/883-0100	All Year	10 am-6 pm	X	X	X	X	X	X	X	$$
California												
Disneyland	1313 Harbor Blvd., Anaheim	714/781-4565	All Year	8 am-varies (S) 10am-varies (W)	X	X	X		X	X	X	$$$$
Knott's Berry Farm	8039 Beach Blvd., Buena Park	714/220-5200	All Year	9am-midnight (S) 10am-varies (W)	X	X	X		X	X	X	$$$$
Marine World Africa USA	2001 Marineworld Pkwy., Vallejo	707/643-ORCA, 644-4000	March 27-Nov. 1	10 am-varies	X	X	X		X	X	X	$$$$
Paramount's Great America	4701 Great America Pkwy., Santa Clara	408/988-1776	Mid-March-Mid-Oct.	10 am-varies	X	X	X		X	X	X	$$$$
SeaWorld San Diego	Sea World Dr. & I-5, San Diego	800/SEA-WRLD (exc. CA) 619/226-3901	All Year	10 am-varies	X	X	X		X	X	X	$$$$
Six Flags Magic Mountain/Hurricane Harbor	26101 Magic Mtn. Pkwy. & I-5, Valencia	805/255-4100	Mar.-Oct. Nov.-Feb.	10 am-varies Wknds. & Holidays	X	X	X		X	X	X	$$$$
Universal Studios	100 Universal City Plaza, Universal City	818/508-9600	All Year	8 am-10 pm (S) 10 am-7 pm (W)	X	X	X		X	X	X	$$$$
Colorado												
Elitch Gardens	2000 Elitch Circle, Denver	303/595-4386	May-Sept.	Varies	X	X	X		X	X	X	$$$$
Florida												
Busch Gardens Tampa Bay/Adventure Island	Busch Blvd. & 40th St., Tampa	813/987-5171, 978-5082	All Year	Varies	X	X	X		X	X	X	$$$$
Cypress Gardens	2641 S. Lake Summit Dr. (SW of Winter Haven)	800/282-2123, 863/324-2111	All Year	9:30 am-5:30 pm	X	X	X		X	X	X	$$$$
Marineland of Florida	9600 Ocean Shore Blvd., Marineland	888/279-9194	All Year	9:30 am-4:30 pm			X		X		X	$$
Miami Seaquarium	4400 Rickenbacker Causeway, Miami	305/361-5705	All Year	9:30 am-6 pm	X	X	X		X		X	$$$
SeaWorld Orlando	Central Florida Pkwy., off I-4 Exit 28, Orlando	800/327-2424	All Year	9 am-varies	X	X	X		X	X	X	$$$$
Silver Springs/Wild Waters	5656 E. Silver Springs Blvd., Silver Springs	800/234-7458, 353/236-2121	All Year	10 am-5 pm	X	X	X		X		X	$$$$
Universal Studios Florida	1000 Universal Studios Plaza, Orlando	407/363-8000	All Year	9 am-varies	X	X	X		X	X	X	$$$$
Walt Disney World Resort	I-4 w, Exit 26 B, Lake Buena Vista	407/824-4321	All Year	Varies	X	X	X		X	X	X	$$$$
Weeki Wachee Springs/Buccaneer Bay	FL 50 at Jct. US 19, Spring Hill	877/GO WEEKI	All Year	10 am-4 pm	X	X	X		X	X	X	(T)$$
Georgia												
Georgia's Stone Mountain Park	US 78, Stone Mountain (16 mi. E of Atlanta)	800/317-2006	All Year	6 am-midnight	X	X	X	X	X	X	X	$$$
Six Flags Over Georgia	275 Riverside Pkwy., Austell (12 mi. W of Atlanta)	770/948-9290	Mar.-Oct.	10 am-varies	X	X	X		X	X	X	$$$$
Idaho												
Silverwood Theme Park	26225 N. Hwy. 95 (I-95), Athol	208/683-3400	Mem. Day-Labor Day	11 am-varies	X	X	X		X	X	X	$$$
Illinois												
Six Flags Great America	542 N. Route 21	847/249-4636	Late Apr.-Nov.	10 am-varies	X	X	X		X	X	X	$$$$
Indiana												
Holiday World & Splashin' Safari	452 E. Christmas Blvd., Santa Claus	877/463-2645	Mid-May-Early Oct.	10 am-varies	X	X	X		X	X	X	$$$
Iowa												
Adventureland Park	Jct. I-80 & US 65 (NE of Des Moines)	800/532-1286	May-Sept.	10 am-varies	X	X	X		X	X	X	$$$
Kentucky												
Kentucky Kingdom/Hurricane Bay	937 Phillips Lane, Louisville	800/SCREAMS	Mid-May-Oct.	10 am-varies	X	X	X		X	X		$$$
Massachusetts												
Six Flags New England	RT 159, 1623 Main St., Agawam (5 mi. W of Springfield)	413/786-9300	Apr.-Oct.	10 am-varies	X	X	X		X	X	X	$$$$
Michigan												
Michigan's Adventure Amusement Park	4750 Whitehall Rd., Muskegon	231/766-3377	Mid-May-Early Sept.	11 am-varies	X	X	X		X	X		$$$
Minnesota												
Valleyfair	One Valleyfair Dr.(MN 101), Shakopee	800/FUN RIDE, 952/445-7600	May-Sept.	10 am-varies	X	X	X		X	X	X	$$$$
Missouri												
Silver Dollar City	399 Indian Point Rd., Branson	800/475-9370, 417/338-2611	Early Apr.-Dec.	9:30 am-6 pm (S) 1-10 pm (W)	X	X	X		X	X	X	$$$$
Six Flags St. Louis	30 mi. SW via I-44, Exit 261 in Eureka	314/938-4800	Apr.-Oct.	10 am-varies	X	X	X		X	X	X	$$$$
Worlds of Fun/Oceans of Fun (T)$$$$	4545 Worlds of Fun Ave. (I-435, Exit 54), Kansas City	816/454-4545	Apr.-Oct.	10 am-varies	X	X	X		X	X	X	
Nevada												
Ponderosa Ranch, Home of "Bonanaza"	100 Ponderosa Ranch Rd. (NV 28), Incline Village	775/831-0691	Apr.-Oct.	9:30 am-5 pm	X	X	X		X		X	¢
New Hampshire												
Canobie Lake Park	I mi. E of I-93, Exit 2, Salem	603/893-3506	Apr.-Labor Day	Varies	X	X	X		X	X	X	$$
New Jersey												
Mountain Creek Resort	200 NJ 94, Vernon	973/827-2000	Mid-June-Labor Day	11 am-varies			X		X	X	X	$$$
Six Flags Great Adventure	I-195, Exit 16, near Jackson	732/928-1821	Late Mar.-Early Nov.	10 am-varies	X	X	X		X	X	X	$$$$
New York												
Six Flags Darien Lake	9993 Allegheny Rd., Darien Center	585/599-4641	Late May-Sept.	10 am-10 pm	X	X	X		X	X	X	$$$$
Great Escape & Splashwater Kingdom	US 9, S of Lake George	518/792-3500	Mem. Day-Labor Day	10 am-varies	X	X	X	X	X	X	X	$$$$
North carolina												
Ghost Town in the Sky	U.S. 19, Maggie Valley	804/926-1140, 800/446-7886	May-Nov. 1	Varies			X	X	X	X	X	$$$
Paramount's Carowinds	Off I-77, Exit 90 (10 mi. S of Charlotte)	800/888-4FUN, 704/588-2600	Mid-Mar.-Mid-Oct.	10 am-varies	X	X	X		X	X	X	$$$$
Ohio												
LeSourdsville Lake Amusement Park	5757 Middletown-Hamilton Rd. (OH 4), Middletown	513/539-2193	Apr.-Sept.	11 am-varies	X	X	X	X	X	X	X	$$
Cedar Point	Causeway Dr., off U.S. 6, Sandusky	419/627-2350	Mid-May-Early Oct.	10 am-varies	X	X	X		X	X	X	$$$$
Six Flags World of Adventure	1060 Aurora Rd. (OH 43), Aurora	330/562-8303	May-Oct.	10 am-varies	X	X	X		X	X	X	$$$
Paramount's Kings Island	5688 Kings Island Dr., Kings Island (N of Cincinnati)	513-754-5901, 800/832-1133	Mid-Apr.-Mid-Oct.	10 am-varies	X	X	X		X	X	X	$$$$
Oklahoma												
Frontier City	11501 NE Expy. (off I-35N), Oklahoma City	405/478-2412	Easter-Oct.	Varies	X	X	X		X	X	X	$$$
Pennsylvania												
Dorney Park & Wildwater Kingdom	3830 Dorney Park Rd., Allentown	610/395-3724	Mid-May-Early Oct.	10 am-varies	X	X	X		X	X	X	$$$$
Hersheypark	100 W. Hersheypark Dr., Hershey	800/HERSHEY	May-Sept.	10 am-varies	X	X	X		X	X	X	$$$
Kennywood	4800 Kennywood Blvd., West Mifflin (SE of Pittsburgh)	412/461-0500	Mid-Apr.-Labor Day	11 am-varies	X		X	X	X	X	X	$$$
Sesame Place	100 Sesame Rd., Langhorne (20 mi. NE of Philadelphia)	215/752-7070	Mid-May-End Oct.	Varies	X	X	X	X	X	X	X	$$$$
Tennessee												
Dollywood	1020 Dollywood Lane, Pigeon Forge	865/428-9488	Apr.-Dec.	10 am-varies	X	X	X		X	X	X	$$$$
Texas												
SeaWorld San Antonio	Ellison Dr. & Westover Hills Blvd., San Antonio	210/523-3611	Mar.-Oct.	10 am-varies	X	X	X		X	X	X	$$$$
Six Flags AstroWorld	9001 Kirby Dr., Houston	713/799-8404	Mar.-Oct.	10 am-varies	X	X	X		X	X	X	$$$$
Six Flags Fiesta Texas	1700 I-10W at jct. Loop 1604, Exit 555 at LaCantera, San Antonio	210/697-5050	Mar.-Early Nov.	10 am-varies	X	X	X		X	X	X	$$$$
Six Flags Over Texas	I-30 at TX 360, Arlington	817-530-6000	Mar.-Jan. 1	10 am-varies	X	X	X		X	X	X	$$$$
Utah												
Lagoon Amusement Park	I-15 in Farmington	801/451-8000	Mid-Apr.-Oct.	Varies	X	X	X	X	X	X	X	$$$$
Virginia												
Busch Gardens Williamsburg/Water Country USA	One Busch Gardens Blvd., Williamsburg	800/343-7946	Mar.-Oct.	10 am-varies	X	X	X		X	X	X	$$$$
Paramount's Kings Dominion/Hurricane Reed	I-95 & VA 30, Doswell (N of Richmond)	800/528-1234	Apr.-Early Oct.	10 am-varies	X	X	X		X	X	X	$$$$

*All-inclusive ticket: $ ◗ under $5, $$ ◗ $15–$20 $$$ ◗ $20-$30 $$$$ ◗ over $30 ¢ ◗ Admission under $10 or free; pay as you go
(T) theme park only (S) summer (W) winter Hours and days subject to change. Phone first.